The Mississippi

The Mississippi

A VISUAL BIOGRAPHY

Quinta Scott

University of Missouri Press   Columbia and London

University of Missouri Press
Columbia and London

University of Missouri Press, Columbia, Missouri 65201
Printed and bound in China

5 4 3 2 1 14 13 12 11 10

Library of Congress Cataloging-in-Publication Data

Scott, Quinta, 1941-
The Mississippi : a visual biography / Quinta Scott.
p. cm.
Includes bibliographical references and index.
Summary: "A photographic documentation of the Mississippi River, illustrating the geographical and botanical features of the river and its wetlands. Using 200 color photographs and accompanying vignettes, Scott explains how we have changed each site depicted, how we try to manage and restore it, and the wildlife that occupies it"—Provided by publisher.
ISBN 978-0-8262-1840-7 (alk. paper)
1. Mississippi River—Pictorial works. 2. Mississippi River Valley—History. 3. Physical geography—Mississippi River Watershed. 4. Natural history—Mississippi River Valley. 5. Nature conservation—Mississippi River Valley. 6. Mississippi River Valley—Description and travel. I. Title.
F351.S35 2009
917.7'02—dc22

2009000919

This paper meets the requirements of the American National Standard for Permanence of Paper for Printed Library Materials, Z39.48, 1984.

Designer and compositor: Kristie Lee
Printer and binder: Four Colour Imports, Ltd.
Typeface: Vendetta

The University of Missouri Press offers its grateful acknowledgment for a generous contribution from The Bay and Paul Foundations in support of the publication of this volume.

In Memory of Ruth Ferris, Jeannette Shaklee, and Mary Gieselmann

Contents

Photographs

Acknowledgments

Ruth Ferris was a remarkable teacher with a passion for the Mississippi River and for steamboats. She transferred that love to at least two generations of fifth graders. I was one of those fifth graders. For years I looked for a river project. Not until I made a photograph of an old oxbow in Mississippi did I find my project: document the Mississippi and its wetlands from Lake Itasca to the Gulf of Mexico.

Such an effort never would have happened without the funding from the Bay and Paul Foundations and their director, Fred Bay, who stayed solidly behind this effort for fifteen years. A word of thanks goes to Dave Eustis, executive director of the Southwestern Illinois Resource Conservation and Development, Inc.; Suzi Wilkins Berl, former executive director of the Mississippi River Basin Alliance; and John Shewmaker and Melanie Johnson of the Taproots School of the Arts, all of whom sponsored the project, making it possible for me to receive the grant from the foundations.

First, there are the librarians at the St. Louis Public Library; Joe Winkler in the map room and Bill Olbrich and Kevin Roach in government documents supplied me with the U.S. Geological Survey maps that allowed me to locate and name the places I photographed. The staff of the interlibrary loan department tracked down any and all geological texts I requested.

Geologists are very generous people. As I learned the geological history of the Mississippi River and its wetlands, geologists helped me understand what I was learning and read parts of the text for me. Robert E. Criss at Washington University in St. Louis read and corrected the introductory text. H. E. Wright Jr. at the University of Minnesota read the section on the formation of the headwaters. Richard C. Anderson at Augustana College in Rock Island, Illinois, read over the section on the Port Byron and Andalusia Gorges. E. A. Bettis III at the University of Iowa helped me understand the Des Moines Rapids. Edwin J. Hajic, a geologist in private practice, put the opening of Thebes Gap and the formation of Sny Island into perspective and gave me copies of his work on the American Bottom. Other geologists sent me tear sheets of their published papers: Margaret Guccione, University of Arkansas; Michael D. Blum, Louisiana State University; and Torbjörn E. Törnqvist, Tulane University. Finally, starting with help in understanding the chronology of the formation of the meander belts on the Lower Mississippi valley, Whitney Autin, at the College at Brockport, State University of New York, responded to my queries every time I asked on a variety of subjects.

There are others who helped me understand a variety of issues along the Mississippi and Louisiana coast: Claude Strausser, a potomologist with the St. Louis District of the Corps of Engineers, spent a morning helping me understand the intricacies of the Flood of 1993. Steve Cobb at the Vicksburg District gave me a copy of Roger Saucier's 1994 *Geomorphology and Quaternary Geologic History of the Lower Mississippi Valley.* Dick Steinbach, manager of the Mark Twain National Wildlife Refuge, affirmed that I was on the right track, tying the geological history of the Mississippi to the modern river, and he read and commented on an early draft on the Upper Mississippi. Eugene S. Schweig III at the U.S. Geological Survey, CERI, University of Memphis, read the text on the New Madrid earthquakes. Hans M. Williams at the Arthur Temple College of Forestry, Stephen F. Austin University, sent me articles on his work on the

Lake George Reforestation project in the Yazoo Basin. Robert A. Morton of the U.S. Geological Survey in St. Petersburg, Florida, advised me on the Madison Bay wetland-loss hot spot in the Terrebonne Basin. Delbert Wittenaur, Monroe County, Illinois, commissioner, confirmed that the Columbia, Illinois, levee that broke in 1993 leaked, but the new levee held in 2008.

There are the people who showed me their landscapes: Sidney Montgomery of Jackson, Mississippi, toured the batture lands north of Vicksburg with me and explained the restoration work being done at Tara Wildlife at Eagle Lake, Mississippi. Sidney also introduced me to other private landowners who were restoring their properties. Lester Goodin spend a morning showing me the tree screen he and Jerry Rapp, a hydraulic engineer with the St. Louis District, planted on Missouri Sister Island to keep the Mississippi from cutting a new channel across the narrow point bar. Diane Bordon-Billiot with the Sabine NWR hiked with me the boardwalk along the freshwater impoundment at the refuge while she explained the damage Hurricane Rita had done to the refuge.

Then there are the people with boats: One does not photograph and write about wetlands without getting out into the wetlands in a boat. John Shewmaker and I canoed Horseshoe Lake near St. Louis to see if the big-view camera would work from a canoe. It did. Suzi Wilkins Berl arranged for me to join the board of the Mississippi River Basin Alliance to cross the Barataria Basin between Lafitte, Louisiana, and the Naomi Siphon along the Mississippi River. They were more than willing to stop while I made photographs. Mike Davis, with the Minnesota DNR at Lake City, took me Up-in-the-Islands, where I was able to photograph the interior of Island 42 in Pool 5 of the Upper Mississippi. Charles F. Fryling Jr., associate professor of landscape architecture at LSU, imparted his love of the Atchafalaya River swamp and took me canoeing on Upper Flat Lake. Rodney Linker of Luhr Brothers, Columbia, Illinois, arranged for a tour of the Barataria Basin Landbridge Shoreline Protection project along Bayou Rigolettes with George Michael. There, Luhr Brothers was erecting concrete sheetpile walls to halt shoreline erosion. Mr. Michael also gave me a look at Bayou Dupont and the Pen. Jack Bohannan, manager of the Southeast Louisiana National Wildlife Refuge, arranged for Max Latham to introduce me to crevasses in the Delta National Wildlife Refuge. Captain Wendy Wilson Billiot and I spent a day in the fresh marshes of the Western Terrebonne Basin. Jessica Kastler, the Louisiana coordinator at the Gulf Coast Research Laboratory of the University of Southern Mississippi at Ocean Springs, when she was on the faculty at the Louisiana Universities Marine Consortium, arranged for Carl Sevin to take me out to Timbalier Island. When the seas became too rough, we repaired to Bayou Petit Caillou and Lake Boudreaux, work that would not have been done otherwise. Without Carl I never would have understood the Louisiana year. When the seas calmed, Jerome Zeringue, lately executive director of the Terrebonne Parish Levee and Conservation District, now director of Louisiana's Coastal Protection and Restoration Authority, borrowed a boat from Steve Smith of T. Baker Smith in Houma, Louisiana, and accompanied me to Timbalier Island. He fished; I made photographs. Andrew Barron of the Barataria-Terrebonne National Estuary Program ferried me out to Little Lake at the foot of the Barataria Landbridge.

Bev Jarrett, retired director and editor-in-chief of the University of Missouri Press, put her faith in half a book and, with great good humor, hung in there for three years while I got my act together. Dwight Browne, the production manager and interim director, was ever patient with panic attacks and misfired emails. Sara Davis, assistant managing editor, shepherded me through the editing process.

Finally, Barrie Scott canoed the headwaters, took the white-knuckle trip to the Delta Refuge, hiked the Benson Wildlife Area and the White River National Wildlife Refuge in Arkansas, and almost fell down laughing when a snake drove me out of an Arkansas swamp. The support of this good man is essential to everything I do. He does for me what I will not do for myself.

The Mississippi

Assembling the Mississippi Basin

It took a million years to assemble its basin; sixty thousand years to shape it into the master river of the North American continent; nine thousand years to construct its modern floodplain; three hundred years to mold it to our needs, damaging it, in some cases, beyond repair. In the last years of the twentieth century we began to make efforts to restore its damaged ecosystems.

When French missionaries and fur traders first ventured along the Mississippi River three hundred years ago, they found a dynamic landscape that had been shaped by glacial melt over the last million years. From the tamarack and sedge swamps at the headwaters to the salt marshes of the Gulf of Mexico, the Mississippi River was an integrated system of river and wetlands, governed by natural processes, which moved water and sediment downstream.

Assembling Its Basin: A Glacial History

Midwesterners are resigned to them—those great loops of cold that swing down from the Arctic, bringing clear, freezing days in January and cool, sunny days in August. A loop can reach as far south as New Orleans. As it pushes out warm, moist air from the Gulf of Mexico, it creates thunderstorms in summer and snow and ice storms in winter. As the loop slides off to the east, warm, moist air again rises up from the Gulf and fills the void, bringing hot, hazy summer days and cool, gray winter days.

Cycles of chilling and warming have gone on for eons. As the earth cooled down in Pleistocene times, the snow in the extreme north did not all melt one summer. Fresh snow fell the following winter and did not all melt. Winter after winter, snow built up and compacted into ice. It took ten feet of snow to build one foot of ice and millennia to build a sheet of ice almost two miles thick. Warm, humid air from the Gulf of Mexico nourished the great mass of ice. Sea level dropped. As the load of ice grew heavier, its weight pressed down the earth's crust. The flow of the ice scoured the land and plucked out fragments of rock as it slid south into the Mississippi Basin. Several times this cycle of cooling and warming drew ice sheets into the center of the North American continent. Each time the glacier pushed south, it rearranged the landscape it crossed. As each glacier melted it rearranged the rivers, including the Mississippi, the southward-flowing master river.

The successive ice sheets erased all evidence of the preglacial Mississippi River. Geologists know that the ancient Mississippi met the ancient River Teays, which flowed northwest out of the Appalachians, in central Illinois. Together the rivers streamed south down what are now the Illinois and Mississippi Rivers to the Mississippi Embayment, which extends from southeastern Missouri and southern Illinois south to the Gulf of Mexico. How it got to its confluence with the Teays is a matter of speculation.

The river may have eroded its valley between St. Paul and Rock Island before the advance of the first ice sheet. Or it may have flowed along the modern Wisconsin River to the Baraboo range, then along the Yahara River through the now-buried Paw Paw valley to the Rock River, where it connected to the River Teays. Or it may have flowed through central Iowa through a valley that ran from the northwest to the southeast.

The Mississippi Embayment opened up during Cretaceous times when the Ouachita Mountains on the west split from the Appalachians on the east. The Gulf of Mexico poured in, filling the gap. By the beginning of the glacial era the embayment had filled with sediment carried by rivers pouring out of the Ouachitas, the Appalachians, and the Nashville Dome, as well as from the Mississippi on the north. The rivers built alluvial fans, which overlapped and spread to the center of the embayment and pushed the shoreline of the gulf southward.

The preglacial Lower Mississippi shared a narrow valley—the Western Lowlands—along the western edge of the embayment with better-established rivers from the Ozark Plateau—the St. Francis, the Current, the Black, and the White. On the eastern edge—the Eastern Lowlands—the lower Ohio and Tennessee Rivers occupied a topographic low between the alluvial fan and the upland that would be named Crowley's Ridge. This ridge divided the Ohio-Tennessee and the Mississippi-Ozark systems and extended from the head of the embayment to a point south of Helena, Arkansas, where the two systems met to form a somewhat larger river.

Of the three rivers that flowed out of the northern tableland in preglacial times, the southward flowing Mississippi was the least impressive. Its basin included neither the Missouri, which rose in the Rockies and drained east across the northern Great Plains and then north into Hudson Bay, nor the upper Ohio, which drained into the Atlantic via the St. Lawrence. The glaciers rearranged it all and turned the postglacial Mississippi into the master river of the continent.

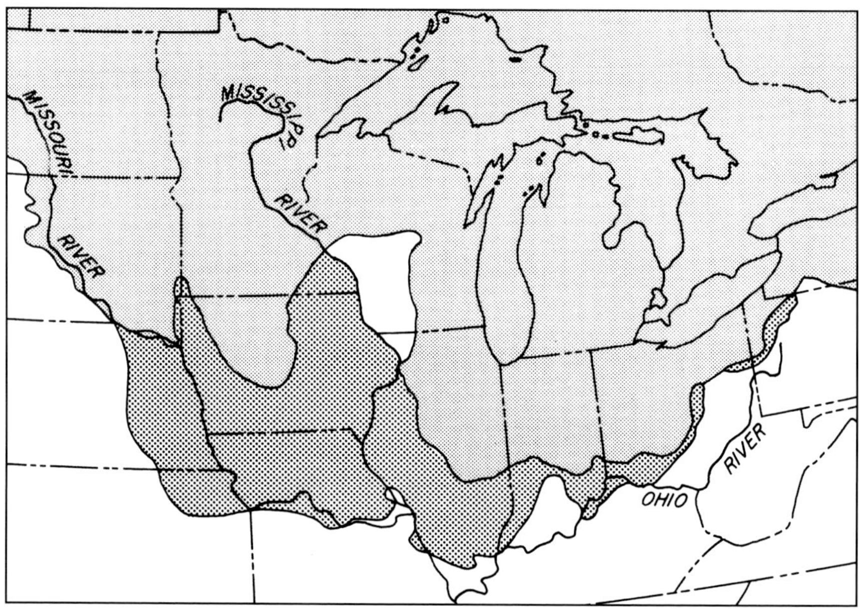

The extent of glaciation between the Missouri and Ohio Rivers. The dark gray area represents the southern extent of the early glacial ages. The light gray represents the southern limit of the Wisconsin ice sheet 20,000 years ago. The white areas represent areas never covered by ice. From H. E. Wright Jr., *Geological History of Minnesota Rivers*, 1990. By permission of the Minnesota Geological Survey.

Rearranging the Landscape—Early Pleistocene Times

As long as 790,000 years ago, an ice sheet plowed into Minnesota from the northwest, cleared the forests and stripped the soil from a landscape marked by plateaus of Paleozoic rocks, and ground to a halt against the slightly higher Wisconsin arch in southwest Wisconsin. As the glacier waned, a stream of meltwater ran along the eastern edge of the ice and cut a gorge through the layers of Paleozoic rock—wide through soft sandstone or softer shale, narrow through harder limestone—creating the bluffs of the Mississippi downstream from St. Paul. Though the gorge filled with till during later glacial advances, this marginal stream established the location of the modern Mississippi between St. Paul and Rock Island, Illinois.

At the gorge south of Rock Island, the Mississippi turned east through the Princeton Bedrock Valley to join the Teays to form the Illinois. Twice ice advancing from the north and northeast repeatedly blocked the river's southward flow during the later Illinoian stage of glaciation. The river pooled behind the ice, at Hennepin and Cordova, Illinois, and formed large glacial lakes. Sediment in the lakes settled to the bottoms. The lakes, filled with low-sediment water, spilled through their outlets in torrents, which carried great erosive power, and cut, first, the Andalusia Gorge between Andalusia, Illinois, and Muscatine,

Iowa, and, second, the Port Byron Gorge between Cordova and Andalusia. The Illinoian glacier retreated and filled the new gorges with drift. The Mississippi shifted back to its ancient course.

This process repeated itself twenty thousand years ago with the advance of the Lake Michigan lobe of the last or Wisconsinan glacial stage. As it pushed west across the Princeton Bedrock Valley, Glacial Lake Milan pooled behind the ice lobe. The lake drained away, meltwater reexcavated the Port Byron and Andalusia Gorges and connected the Mississippi to its present channel south of Muscatine, Iowa. The advance and retreat of Michigan lobe filled the Princeton Valley with glacial drift. The Mississippi never returned to its ancient channel.

South of Muscatine, Iowa, the ancient Iowa-Cedar flowed through the modern Mississippi valley to the mouth of the ancient Mississippi-Illinois at Grafton, Illinois, and on south to its confluence with the Missouri.

Before the ice sheets pushed south, the Missouri River headed in the Rockies and flowed into Hudson Bay via the Nelson River. A pre-Illinoian ice sheet pushed into the upper Missouri River valley from the northeast and blocked its natural drainage to the northeast. The Missouri cut a new channel along the margin of the glacier. Twice the Missouri cut parallel channels through North Dakota. As the ice sheet withdrew, meltwater fixed the new channel as far south as Kansas City, where the Missouri emerged from the glaciated region. It picked up the preglacial channel of the Kansas River and flowed east to the Mississippi.

Before the first glaciers pushed down from the north, the preglacial upper Ohio flowed north to an eastward-draining master stream and thence to the Atlantic. A much shorter lower Ohio emptied into the Mississippi Embayment. The ancient River Teays carried waters from the Appalachians to its confluence with the preglacial Mississippi in central Illinois. Illinoian ice pushed down into Ohio, Indiana, and Illinois and filled the downstream portion of the Teays Valley with drift, obliterating it. The remnant of the ancient Teays ponded against the ice in Ohio, spilled over, flowed along the glacial margin, and connected the preglacial upper Ohio with the lower Ohio River.

The last glacier, the Wisconsinan, advanced into North America about 110,000 years ago, introduced the first humans to the North American continent, and set the course of the whole of the Mississippi. The Laurentian ice sheet covered all of Canada to the eastern Rocky Mountains, covered most of Minnesota and Wisconsin, and reached south into Iowa and Illinois. During this period, Asians who lived in the cold, treeless environment of Siberia crossed a land bridge between Siberia and Alaska, an unglaciated corridor that remained free of ice, possibly 27,000 years ago. The Paleoindians, the earliest Ice Age hunters, drifted south and developed a distinctive culture (the Clovis) in parts of Canada, the United States, and Mexico. They hunted mammoths, mastodons, and other megafauna. Within 13,500 years the migrants had evolved into the ancestors of modern American Indians.

The waxing and wasting of the Wisconsinan ice sheet shaped the headwaters between Lake Itasca and the Falls of St. Anthony at Minneapolis, fixed the course between the falls and Mississippi Embayment, and diverted the river from the western side of the embayment through Thebes Gap to its eastern side.

Shaping the Master River—The Wisconsinan Glacier

When a glacier pushes across a landscape, it knocks down trees, scrapes up soil, grinds down rock. Granite resists; sandstone and limestone do not. They are easily pulverized into gravel, sand, and rock flour—silt. Boulders and cobbles roll against one another, crushing one another, creating till—a chaotic arrangement of sediment that is carried along, under, and in the ice while working its way up over the snout of the ice lobe to the very top. As the ice pushes southward, the climate cools ahead of it. Northern plants and animals escape southward. A carpet of sedges dotted with spruce take up residence in a broad band across the front of the ice and even between the lobes of ice.

When the climate warms and the ice sheet stops, the surface melts and deposits an end moraine, a jumble of materials carried in the ice—chunks of ice, rock, sand, and gravel mixed in a sandy, clayey matrix. Should the ice stall against the moraine for a very long time, a drainage system forms. Fast-moving streams erode tunnel valleys in, on, and under the body of ice. As the ice retreats from the moraine, sheets of meltwater, laden with sand and gravel, wash from the moraine or the glacial margin and form an outwash plain. As ice draws back, stopping and starting, advancing and withdrawing, it lays down recessional moraines, conglomerations of rock and chunks of ice covered with drift. Blocks of ice, buried in a moraine or an outwash plain, melt and form kettle lakes. Finally, a moraine or a lobe of ice can act like a dam and catch the flow of meltwater. A glacial lake pools behind the dam. Glacial sediment in the water settles to the bottom of the lake. When the ice dam melts away or the lake fills and spills over the moraine, it carries the power to shape a river.

As the ice retreats, the sedges and spruce follow it north, taking root even on the sediment-covered snout of the ice. A coniferous forest—white and black spruce, balsam fir, tamarack, white and red and jack pines, birch and aspen—spreads across the landscape. This is the intricate process that shaped the headwaters of the Mississippi.

Shaping the Headwaters

The Mississippi headwaters did not come together in a tidy geographic timeline north to south. Nor did they come together in a tidy, well-defined channel. Rather they emerged in bits and pieces from the watery landscape, as the wasting of the lobes of the Wisconsinan ice sheet shifted back and forth across the Minnesota landscape north of Minneapolis.

Somewhere between fourteen thousand and twenty thousand years ago the Wadena lobe came to a standstill in north-central Minnesota, where it remained for a very long time, possibly hundreds of years. Huge amounts of till and outwash built up across the ice front and formed the hilly terrain of the Itasca Moraine, which runs east and west across Clearwater, Hubbard, and Beltrami Counties. Fast-moving streams, running under immense pressure from the weight of the ice, reamed a web of tunnels into the stalled ice. The streams had the power to carry along any sand or rocks that dropped from the tunnel walls and to bore tunnel valleys into the drift under the ice. When the lobe retreated, the streams lost their erosive power. The roofs and walls of the tunnels collapsed into the valleys, burying huge lumps of ice under gla-

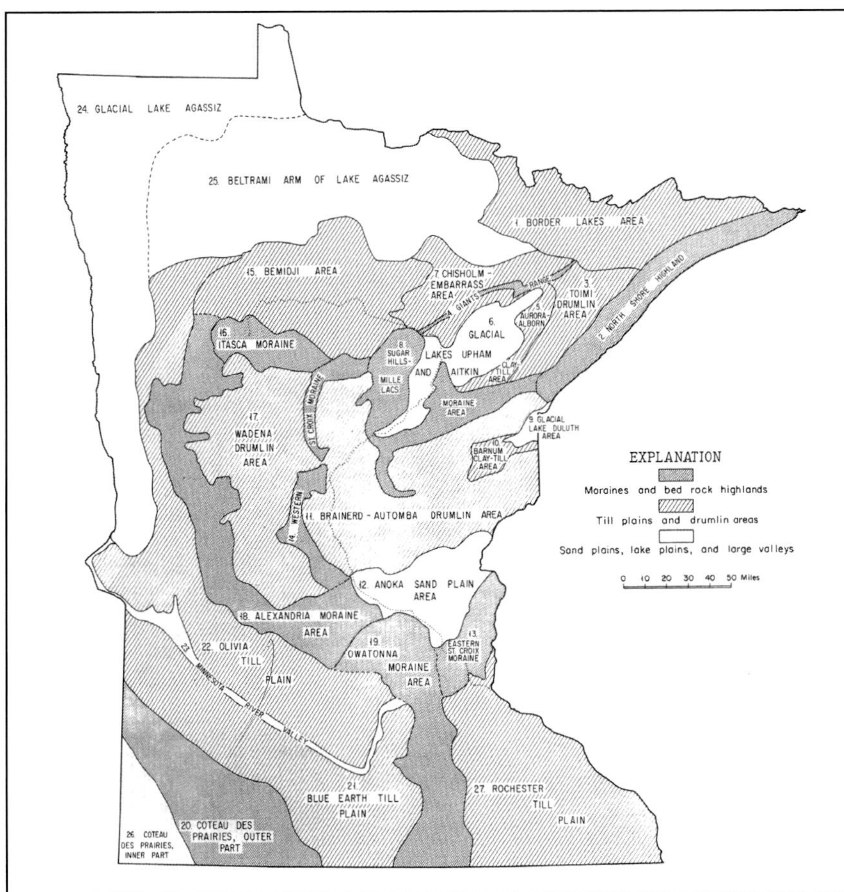

The glacial landforms that shaped the headwaters of the Mississippi in Minnesota. The dotted line represents the Mississippi. From P. K. Sims and G. B. Morey, eds., *Geology of Minnesota: A Centennial Volume,* 1972. By permission of the Minnesota Geological Survey.

cial debris. When the ice rocks melted, the debris fell into the resulting pits, which filled with water, forming kettle lakes. In the Itasca Moraine, strings of kettle lakes, connected by swampy creeks, mark the courses of these subglacial streams. The eastern and western arms of Lake Itasca and their accompanying strings of smaller lakes, Elk Lake to the southwest and Mary Lake to the southeast, occupied two such tunnel valleys. The Mississippi River broke out of the northern arm of Lake Itasca.

North of the Itasca Moraine the movement of the Wadena lobe shifted, no longer going from north to south but from northwest to southeast in the form of the Koochiching lobe. When the Wadena and Koochiching lobes retreated behind a complex of outwash plains and moraines into the Red River lowland, two things happened. First, massive blocks of ice broke off the thinning ice sheet and were buried under a veneer of drift in an outwash plain across which the Mississippi would flow between Bagley and Grand Rapids. When the ice melted, kettle lakes formed and filled to overflowing. The Mississippi spilled eastward from lake to lake across the outwash plain: Bemidji to Andrusia to Cass to Winnebigoshish.

Like the Wadena lobe at the Itasca Moraine, the Superior lobe settled in the bedrock lowland north of Minneapolis for a very long time and deposited St. Croix Moraine. Shaped like a boomerang, it attached itself to the Itasca Moraine at Walker, Minnesota, swung down and framed the bedrock lowland north of Minneapolis, and veered northeast into Wisconsin. Meltwater streamed between the moraine and the wasting ice sheet and coalesced into the Mississippi between Brainerd and Little Falls. Floods of meltwater, filled with sand and gravel, drilled a horsetail of tunnel valleys under the ice and through the southern St. Croix Moraine.

The lobe advanced and retreated several times. With each advance, the tunnel valleys funneled sandy outwash through the moraine and deposited it in Dakota County to the south. With each retreat, the flood of outwash stopped and glacial meltwater settled in the catch basin rimmed by the St. Croix Moraine.

The Superior lobe readvanced. Outwash streaming from the lobe flowed down the St. Croix into the Mississippi Gorge south of St. Paul and deposited an alluvial fan, which blocked drainage from the bedrock lowland to the St. Croix River. Meltwater, streaming off the lobe, pooled into Glacial Lake Anoka. Low-sediment meltwater from the lake broke through the southern segment of the St. Croix Moraine and established the course of the Mississippi between Minneapolis and Fort Snelling to the south.

Finally, twelve thousand years ago, the St. Louis sublobe of the Koochiching lobe slipped through a narrow neck between moraines near Grand Rapids,

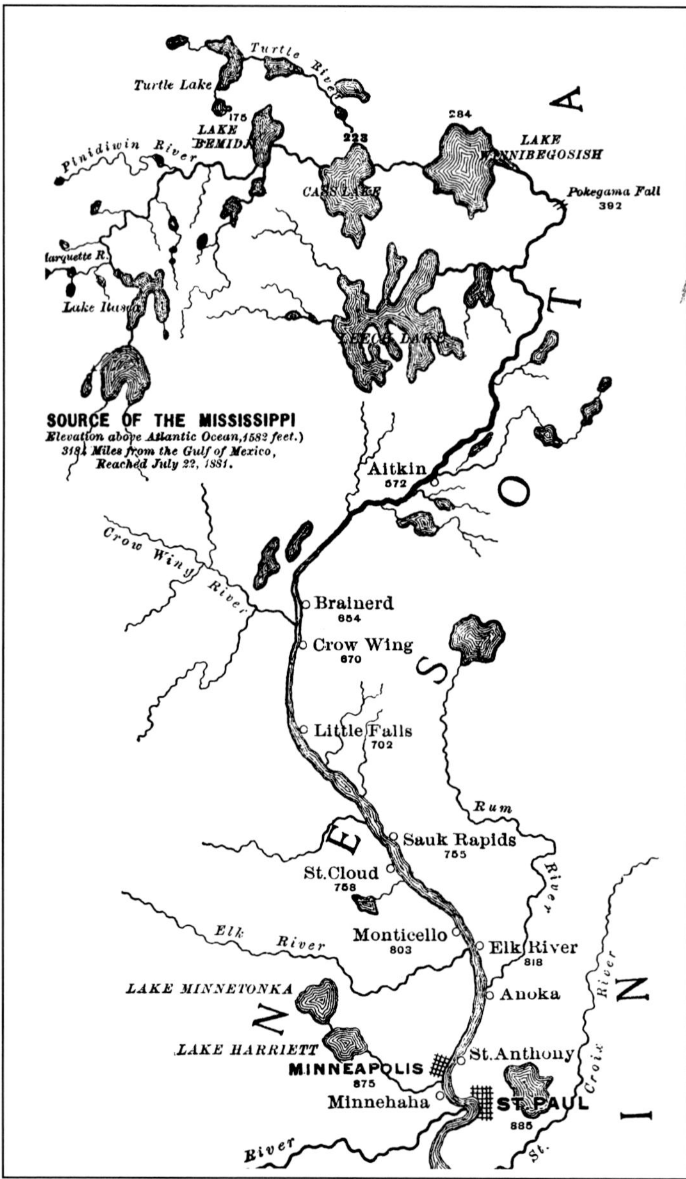

The headwaters of the Mississippi.
From William Glazier, *Down the Great River*, 1887.

blossomed to the northeast and north, and halted against the Mesabi Range. The lobe wasted from its center, forming Lake Aitken-Upham, which was dammed by the debris-laden margins of the ice. The lake broke in two—Upham to the north, Aitken to the south. Lake Aitken pooled against a moraine to the south, laid down by the retreating Superior lobe. Sediment settled onto its lake bed, creating low-sediment waters, which breached the moraine, cut a channel south, and drained away. It left behind a flat, clay-lined bed, across which the Mississippi formed a sinuous channel, connecting its northern inlet near Grand Rapids to its southern outlet. The breaching of Glacial Lake Aitken was the final piece that connected the source of the Mississippi in the Itasca Moraine with the headwaters that formed south of Little Falls.

Floods of Glacial Outwash—Mississippi Valley Train—Upper River

In a process that began twenty thousand years ago and continued for over ten thousand years, the Wisconsinan ice sheet withdrew from Minnesota, Wisconsin, and Iowa and sent pulses of outwash or meltwater down the Mississippi and its tributaries to the Gulf of Mexico. Floods of outwash, filled with debris—clay, sand, or gravel, oozing from the southern margins of the retreating ice sheet or from an ice-filled end moraine—formed an outwash plain. An outwash plain that fills a river gorge is called a valley train. Sometimes the meltwater carried sediment rich in clay; other times it was laden with sand and gravel; still other times it carried only a light load of sand. In each case, the wasting glacier pushed out more sediment than the river could handle. The river deposited its load of debris as a valley train. With each pulse of outwash, the river incised the valley train of the previous flood, creating terraces, each one lying several feet below its predecessor. Taken in sequence, these layers of history tell the story of the formation of the Mississippi floodplain, south of St. Paul, Minnesota.

As the Superior and Des Moines lobes of the Wisconsinan glaciation wasted, tributary streams, particularly the St. Croix, carried meltwater laden with glacial debris to the Mississippi Gorge and laid down a valley train of glacial outwash that extended from Minnesota clear to the Gulf of Mexico.

At St. Paul the outwash filled the gorge to a point 125 feet above the present floodplain. The valley train dammed the mouths of the tributaries, causing sediment-filled backwater lakes to form. Over the course of more than six hundred miles the valley train narrowed to a height of fifteen feet at the Big Muddy River in southern Illinois. Geologists named it the Savanna terrace after a remnant near Savanna, Illinois. Not long after its release from the headwaters region, outwash flowed into the Lower Mississippi valley and through the Bell City–Oran Gap in Crowley's Ridge, the upland between the Western and Eastern Lowlands, and continued south clear to the Gulf of Mexico.

As the ice sheet retreated and the streams of sediment-laden meltwater ceased, little streams eroded gullies in the valley train, drying out silt that lay on its surface, turning it to rock flour. The winds picked up, creating huge dust storms that lifted the rock flour out of the river valley and carried it to the adjacent uplands. There it came to rest in thick layers of silt, called loess, near the river, thinning as it blew farther from the river. Layer upon layer of loess built up, thicker on the eastern uplands than on the western, because the prevailing winds blew from the west. There it lay, stored on the uplands, waiting to be returned to the Mississippi by its tributaries when the river built its modern floodplain.

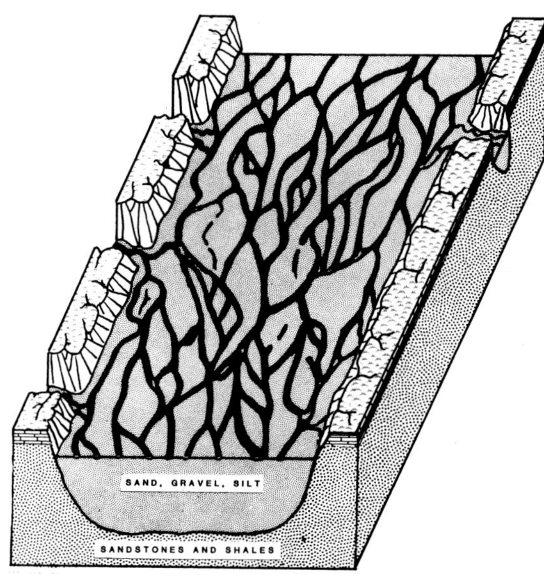

Glacial outwash filled the Mississippi Gorge in the form of a valley train. From Calvin R. Fremling, *Immortal River,* 2005. By permission of the University of Wisconsin Press.

The Work of River Warren and Other Great Floods

A little more than sixteen thousand years ago, the lobes of the Wisconsinan sheet began to withdraw north of the divides that separate drainage to the Arctic and to the Atlantic from that to the Gulf of Mexico. Debris-laden meltwater pooled between the divides and the retreating ice sheet, forming glacial lakes. Most of the debris settled to the bottom. Low-sediment water accumulated behind the divides and spilled over in massive floods, turning the rivers into sluiceways. The floods washed away most of the valley train, leaving terraces clinging to the sides of the gorges.

The glacial ancestors to the Great Lakes—Duluth, Nipissing, Chicago, Maumee—formed behind the divides that separated drainage to the Gulf from that to the Atlantic. Lake Duluth in the Superior Basin drained along the Brule River to the St. Croix; Lake Nipissing covered the Great Lakes region and drained through the Rock, the Illinois, and the Wabash; Lake Maumee along the Wabash to the Ohio; Lake Chicago along the Des Plaines to the Illinois and the Mississippi.

Lake Agassiz ponded behind the complex of outwash plains and moraines laid down by the retreat of the Wadena, Koochiching, and Rainey lobes, the divide that separated drainage to the Arctic from that to the Gulf of Mexico. The lake formed in two parts, separated by a wall of ice. When the ice wall melted, one lake drained into another, forming Lake Agassiz.

Lake Agassiz covered the Red River lowland, reaching north out of Minnesota into Manitoba and Saskatchewan. River Warren broke out of Lake Agassiz in a torrent that poured over the Big Stone Moraine at Browns Valley, Minnesota, and scoured the Minnesota River Gorge to bedrock. When the glacial flood entered the buried channel at St. Paul, River Warren Falls developed and retreated upstream, gnawing away at the soft sandstone that lay under the limestone cap. The caprock collapsed, creating the Mississippi Gorge between St. Paul and Fort Snelling. At Fort Snelling, River Warren Falls eroded past the entrance to the Mississippi and created the Falls of St. Anthony, a tributary waterfall, which eroded the gorge, filled with fallen blocks of limestone, between Fort Snelling and Minneapolis.

South of St. Paul, River Warren scoured the Upper Mississippi, creating the Savanna terrace. It fixed the westward diversion of the river from central Illinois through the Andalusia and Port Byron Gorges between Rock Island, Illinois, and Muscatine, Iowa. South of Muscatine, River Warren joined the Iowa, the Des Moines, and the Missouri and widened the gorge; two to four miles wide south of the Des Moines grew to five to eleven miles wide south of the Missouri River to Thebes Gap. It was a greatly enlarged river that thundered into the lower valley, washed away much of the valley train, and left ridges of outwash that rose slightly above the surrounding landscape. Finally, River Warren spread a classic alluvial fan at the foot of Thebes Gap.

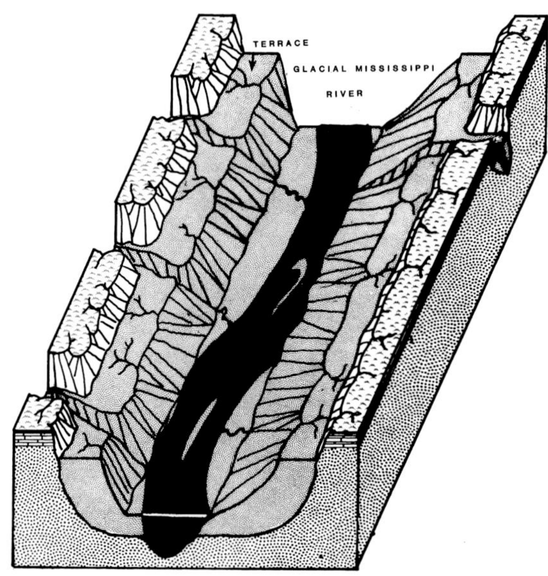

Glacial floods downcut through the valley train, leaving flat terraces clinging to the side of the gorge. From Calvin R. Fremling, *Immortal River,* 2005. By permission of the University of Wisconsin Press.

When River Warren expired, it deposited its own valley train in the upper river gorge, below the elevation of the earlier Savanna valley train it had carved into ridges and terraces. When the Mississippi established its modern floodplain, it eroded the River Warren valley train into the Kingston terrace, named after a remnant near Kingston, Iowa.

Until very recently geologists speculated that the ice sheet readvanced and once again closed off drainage to the east, restored drainage of Lake Agassiz down the Mississippi, laid down new valley trains in the Bell City–Oran Gap and the Eastern Lowlands, and fixed the diversion of the river through Thebes Gap. In the mid-1990s a new generation of geologists speculated that Lake Agassiz never again spilled into the Mississippi. Several years later, geologists working in the Gulf of Mexico found no evidence of large discharges of meltwater into the Gulf after the diversion of Lake Agassiz to the Atlantic. But there was evidence of smaller discharges beginning about 9,700 years ago, possibly from other glacial lakes, particularly Lake Duluth in the Superior Basin, which continued to send debris-laden floods down the Mississippi. South of Muscatine these floods wove a braided pattern across the Kingston terrace, and deposited a terrace below it south of the Missouri River. The floods spilled through Thebes Gap into the Eastern Lowlands, and caused the final and permanent diversion of the river through the gap about 9,100 years ago.

With that the glacial age in the Mississippi Basin came to an end and the Holocene began. The Mississippi began building its floodplain where, in the lower valley, an oak-hickory forest had replaced the spruce and pine of the glacial era, and in the upper valley, a mixed hardwood forest had stabilized the uplands to the east and the north. On the west, grasslands pushed east across the Mississippi between the mouth of the Wisconsin River and the mouth of the Missouri River to a line that extends south from the tip of Lake Michigan.

As the ice sheet retreated north 13,500 years ago, humans advanced onto habitable land created in its wake. The Clovis culture gave way to the Dalton. Surveys of archeological sites throughout the Mississippi valley reveal that the Dalton people settled in Iowa between 9,000 and 12,000 years ago and along

Bayou Meto in Arkansas, possibly 12,000 years ago. Everywhere they hunted the mammoth and the wooly mastodon. The hunting may have led to the extinction of megafauna in the North America.

As the temperatures continued to warm and the climate dried and prairie grasses spread across the Upper Mississippi valley, the Archaic period began about 9,000 years ago. Nomadic hunters gravitated to the river valleys. For the most part they returned to the same sites year after year, sites where game was plentiful. Toward the end of the Archaic period, 4,500 and 2,500 years ago, the hunters adopted a semisedentary lifestyle and developed a communal culture. They continued to hunt, but they also fished the rivers and gathered nuts and berries from the forests. And, they built burial mounds.

Building the Floodplain—The Upper Mississippi River

When a fast-moving tributary reaches its confluence with a slow-moving river or a still body of water, it almost slows to a halt. The tributary drops its load of sediment in the slow-moving river, which is incapable of shifting it downstream. It builds an alluvial fan—a delta—which fills the slow-moving stream with sediment. This was the case when the fast-moving Chippewa flowed into the Mississippi, dropped its sandy load, and built a fan that dammed the Mississippi. Lake Pepin backed up behind it. Similarly, the Mississippi flowed into the Gulf of Mexico, dropped its load of sediment, and built a delta. In each case the river built a floodplain.

When the Wisconsinan floods petered out 9,100 years ago, the Mississippi slowed to a trickle, running along the bottom of a wide, flat-bottomed bedrock canyon between St. Paul and Thebes Gap. Geologists call a stream that is incapable of moving the sediment delivered to it by its tributaries "underfit." The tributaries dropped their loads of fine sediment—much of it glacial debris stored in the tributaries and loess from the surrounding uplands—in the Mississippi, building alluvial fans at their mouths, filling the gorge with layer upon layer of alluvium up to one hundred feet deep, forcing the main channel to the opposite side of the gorge. Silt and sand backed up into the mouths of the tributaries, sometimes damming them and forming lakes.

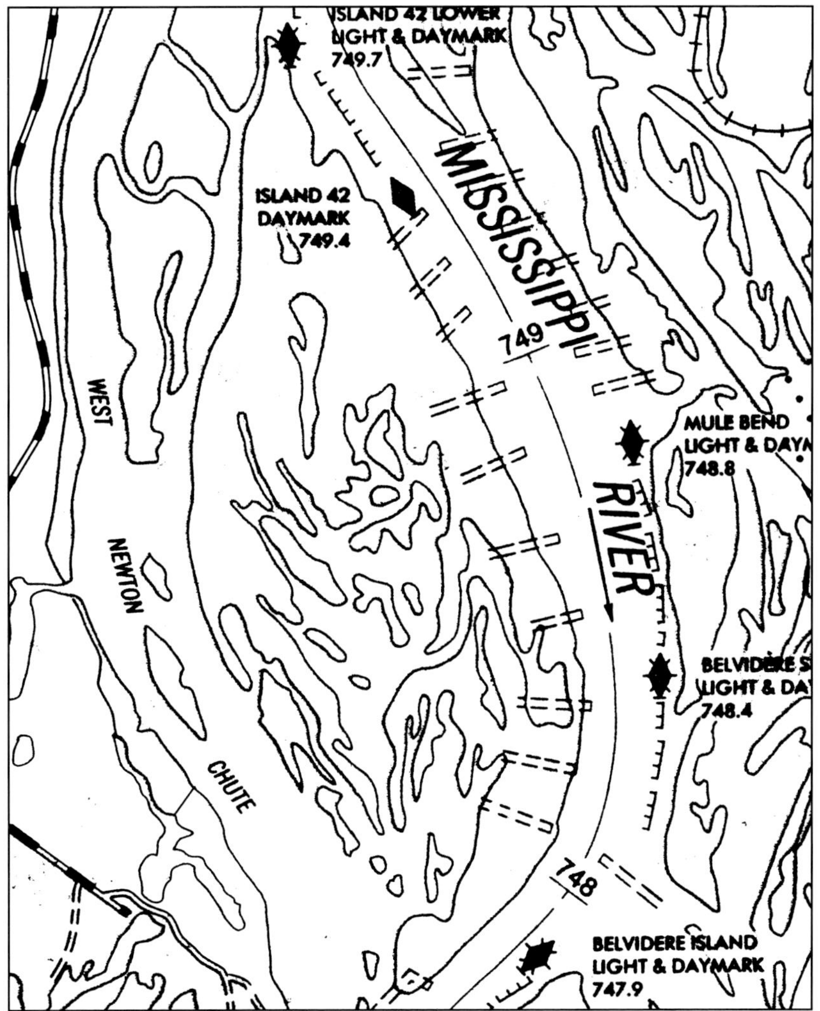

A classic V-shaped island. From U.S. Army Corps of Engineers, *Upper Mississippi River Navigation Charts,* 1989.

Downstream from the tributaries, V-shaped or horseshoe-shaped islands formed, each with the point of the "V" facing upstream. Protected bays and lowlands formed within the islands. The islands moved downstream as they eroded on the upstream side and caught the eroded sediments on the downstream side. Channels, bounded by natural levees built of fine sediment, braided between the islands as they also slid downstream. Abandoned channels turned into sloughs or deep backwater lakes. This process accelerated during seasonal flooding. When the river was down, vegetation took root on the islands and prevented their erosion.

An island starts out as a sandbar, where cottonwood takes root. If it is not washed away in a flood, mud settles on it. Black willows take root, protect the island from being washed away in the next flood, and catch more sediment and debris. The island grows and becomes capable of supporting larger trees. In succeeding floods, it catches still more sediment and debris and grows. It becomes a timber island. So it goes until the island reaches the level of the floodplain and can support a hardwood forest. In the shallow, protected bays and lowlands water-tolerant marsh plants—sedges, plantains, and lilies—take root.

Where the alluvial fans of the tributaries blocked the main channel of the Mississippi, riverine lakes such as Lake Pepin and possibly others formed upstream. Lake Pepin originally extended from Wabasha, Minnesota, at the mouth of the Chippewa, sixty miles north to St. Paul. The Mississippi itself built a delta at the head of Lake Pepin, filling in the floodplain between St. Paul and Red Wing, Minnesota, at the head of the lake today.

South of Rock Island to Muscatine, Iowa, where the slope of the riverbed is very steep and the Mississippi flows over bedrock through the Port Byron and the Andalusia Gorges, the floodplain narrowed. The tributaries built lozenge-shaped islands and sandbars that divided the main channel. South of Muscatine, where the rivers from the west—the Iowa, the Skunk, the Des Moines, and the Missouri—and the Illinois from the northeast meet the Mississippi, the valley broadened, cut away by repeated glacial flooding. Again, tributaries deposited their sediment at their confluences with the slow-moving Mississippi and built a floodplain through which the big river meandered. South of the Missouri River, the tributaries—Indian Creek, Wood River, and Cahokia Creek—flowed out of the uplands, cut through the Savanna terrace, and deposited their alluvial fans on the Kingston terrace, flowed across the American Bottom, and deposited small amounts of sediment in the Mississippi, forming small islands at their mouths.

Geologists, examining meander belts on the American Bottom, south of the Missouri River, and on the Mississippi Bottom, north of Thebes Gap, have found evidence that the river flowed in a braided regime for about 500 years after the cessation of glacial floods. Then, about 9,500 years ago, it started to meander in large sinuous loops and continued to do so for 7,000 years. About 2,500 years ago the Mississippi began meandering in tighter loops, which it maintained until the river adopted its modern channel about 1,100 years ago.

Building the Floodplain—Lower Mississippi River

As the last glacier retreated, both the Upper Mississippi and Ohio Rivers carried glacial outwash to the lower river. As the ice sheet wasted north of the three-way divide in Minnesota, the huge volumes of outwash ceased. The catastrophic floods began; and sea level began to rise, which they continued to do while Lake Agassiz drained to the east or to the north. South of Thebes Gap, the Lower Mississippi flowed in a braided pattern and started to bury much of the coarse-grained valley train with fine sediment delivered to it from its upper basin. It did so rapidly over the first five thousand years. Over time its regime switched from a braided channel running down a steep slope and over coarse outwash to a meandering channel running down a gentle slope and through fine sediment.

That change in the Mississippi probably started at the southern end of the valley and progressed northward. In its southern reaches at least, the Mississippi as we know it—with its wide meander belt, its broad natural levees, its deep channel, and its well-drained backswamp—did not exist. Rather it splayed out into an anastomosing regime, into multichanneled streams that delivered a continuous stream of fine sediment to the lower valley, filling shallow lakes in the valley train to form a muddy, poorly drained backswamp. As each lake filled, the streams would crevasse and splay out into fingerlike rivulets, creating more small multichanneled streams, which would fill other depressions and extend the backswamp. The process created a gulfward-thickening wedge of mud as sea level rose.

Five thousand years ago as the rise in sea level slowed, the climate warmed, and prairie grasses spread across Iowa into southern Wisconsin and northern Illinois, the lower river received less sediment from its upper basin. It shifted to a meandering regime, first in divided channels, flowing in simple meander belts. As sea level stopped rising, and the upper river delivered even less sediment to the lower, it occupied a single channel, flowing in a complex meander belt. Both simple and complex meander belts contributed sediment to the floodplain but only when the river washed over its bank and dropped the heaviest sands and silts closest to its channel. Flood by flood, the river built a levee—to an average height of fifteen feet in a complex meander belt, less in a simple meander belt—above the adjacent floodplain. Relieved of the heavy sand, the floodwaters washed a carpet of fine silts across the deposits of both the valley train and the multichanneled stream to create a well-drained backswamp on which cypress-tupelo forests replaced the oak-hickory forests of an earlier era. As it did so, the slope of the river flattened and the river twisted and turned between its natural levees.

Note: A river rolling downstream runs crooked, looping back and forth in sharp bends between its natural levees. As the river flows, it shaves sand and silt from the bank on the inside, or concave side, of a bend, widening the channel at that point. It deposits the sand and silt on the outside, or convex side, of the bend. In this way the bends slither downstream in much the same way the V-shaped islands in the Upper Mississippi Gorge slide downstream. In time the neck of a point of land—called the point bar—between two bends narrows. In a flood the river can cut a new channel across the narrow neck. The ends of the old bend fill with a silt-and-clay plug, and the bend becomes an oxbow lake. Vegetation takes root in the still, shallow ends of the lake; it grows and dies and decays, filling first the ends of the lake with a marshy wetland forest. Gradually, the whole lake fills and matures into a floodplain forest. A single-channeled, complex meander belt makes more and larger cut-offs than a divided-channel, simple meander belt.

Also note: When a meandering river becomes too long and its slope too flat, it searches for a shorter, steeper route to the sea. The river works its way to

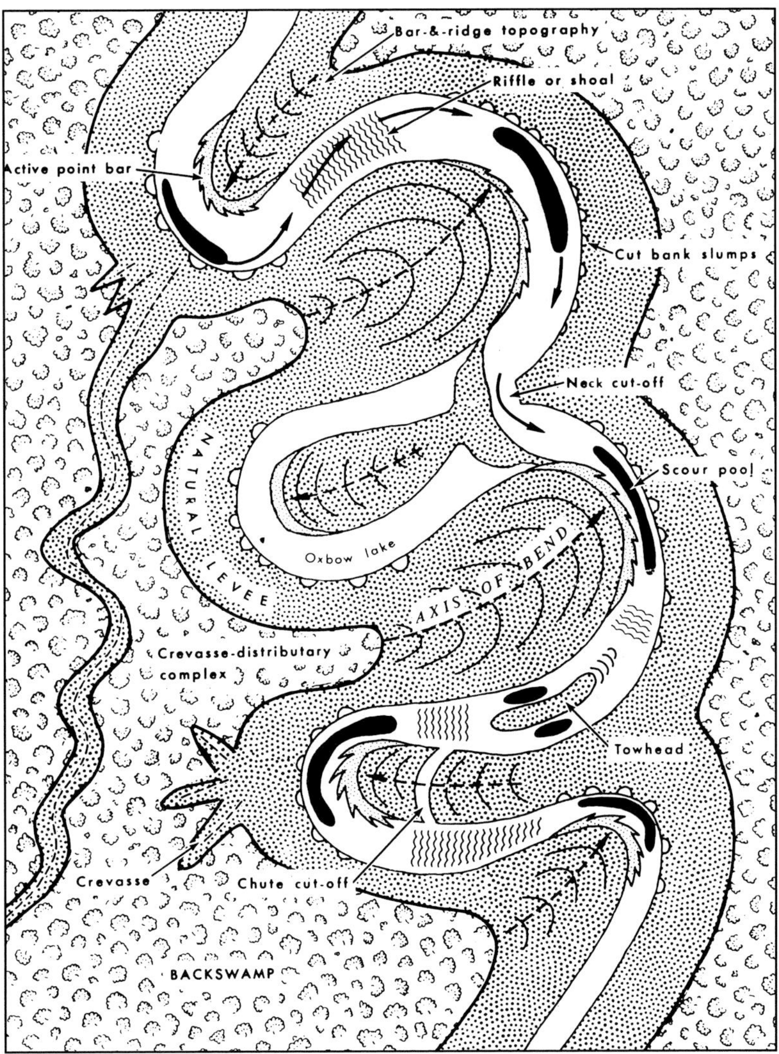

The typical features of the Mississippi meander belt. Active point bar receives deposits. River shaves sediment from concave-cut bank. A neck cutoff. A chute cutoff. From Roger Saucier, *Geomorphology and Quarternary Geologic History of the Lower Mississippi Valley,* 1994 (adapted from Gagliano and van Beek, 1970).

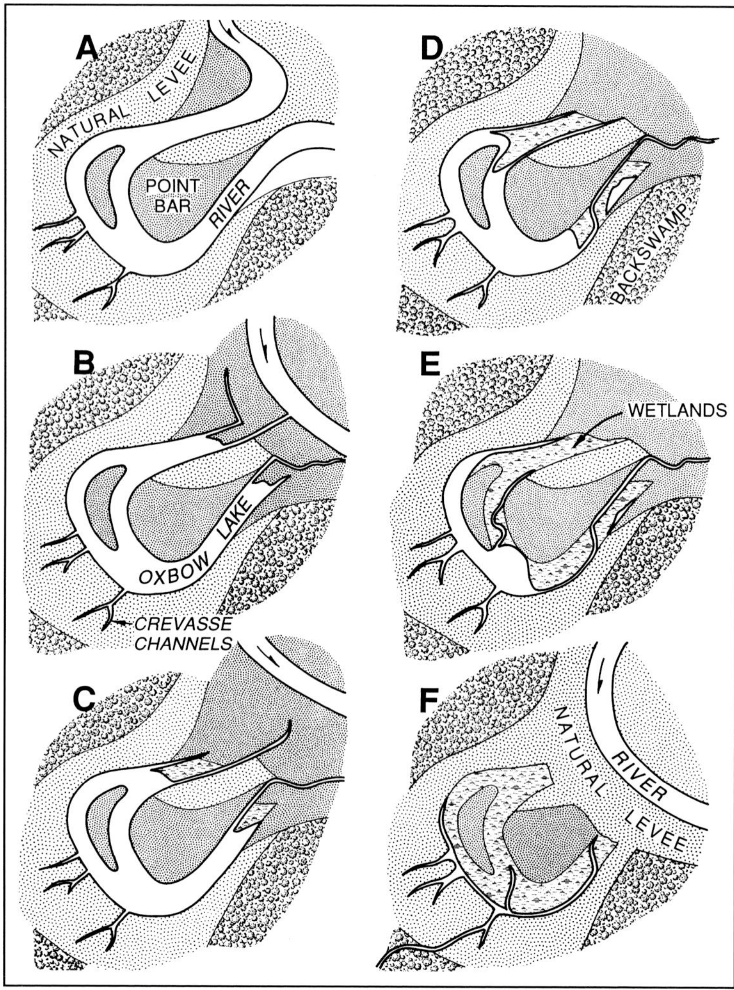

The life cycle of a typical neck cutoff becoming an oxbow lake. **A.** Point bar. **B.** River cuts across neck of point bar, forming oxbow lake with batture channels still connected to the river. **C** and **D.** Batture channels deliver sediment to the oxbow when the river floods. **E.** Wetlands form in the deltas of the oxbow. **F.** Oxbow evolves into a swamp forest. From Roger Saucier, *Geomorphology and Quarternary Geologic History of the Lower Mississippi Valley,* 1994.

the very edge of its meander belt, blows out a crevasse in its natural levee, and splays out into deltalike finger-channels, one of which picks up a small backswamp stream. Over time the stream deepens and widens. It builds a natural levee and starts meandering within its own belt. The old channel begins to fill with silt and clay at the point of diversion, making it impossible for it to recapture the full flow of the river. When the new channel captures 60 percent of the flow of the old, diversion is inevitable, and the channel builds and widens its own meander belt, building up a levee, and laying down a backswamp.

In the 9,100 years since glacial age ended in the Mississippi valley, the Mississippi has flowed in five, possibly six, different regimes. For the first 4,500 years an anastomosing river filled the floodplain with mud. In the last 5,000 years a meandering river has washed a well-drained backswamp between four meander belts, two simple meander belts that flowed in divided channels and two complex meander belts that flowed in a single channel.

Geologists are not sure when, in the last 5,000 years, the Mississippi started to meander between Thebes Gap and Memphis. The oldest dated oxbow in the region formed about 2,400 years ago, 400 years after the modern meander belt formed. Between Memphis and Vicksburg, the Mississippi ranged across its lower valley along as many as six different courses, at first through the Yazoo Basin, occupying the Yazoo, Coldwater, Sunflower Rivers and others; then through the St. Francis Basin, occupying the St. Francis River and Big Creek. Between Vicksburg and the head of the Delta it meandered in the Tensas Basin, occupying Walnut Bayou and the Tensas and Black Rivers.

In the 8,000 years it took the Mississippi to adopt its modern meander belt, the Archaic culture evolved into the Woodland culture. From 2,500 to 1,100 years ago the Woodland people, though still hunter-gatherers, became increasingly sedentary, created fired-clay pottery, and cultivated squash and sunflowers. They continued to build mounds and developed religious rituals centered on them.

About 1,400 years ago the Mississippian culture emerged in the Mississippi valley between St. Louis and New Orleans. The Mississippians were an agricultural people who created a civilization based on farming—the cultivation of corn, squash, and beans. They settled on the high banks of rivers and

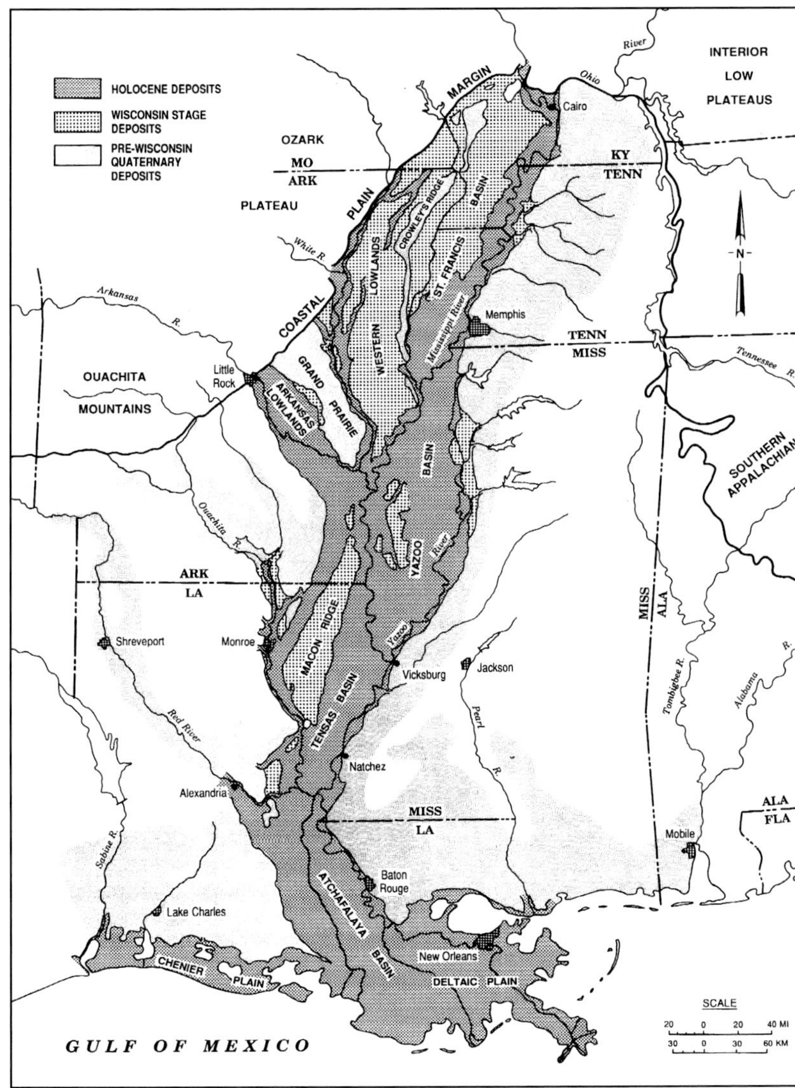

The Mississippi alluvial valley, deltaic plain, and Chenier Plain: the distribution of glacial and postglacial deposits in basins of the Lower Mississippi valley. From Roger Saucier, *Geomorphology and Quarternary Geologic History of the Lower Mississippi Valley*, 1994.

sloughs throughout the floodplain of the Mississippi. Small family groups located near larger communities of a dozen or more families. At the hub of each was a small, flat-topped mound, the site of their religious and civic life. The center of Mississippian culture was at Cahokia, a population center of 30,000 people in the thirteenth century, where Monks Mound covered fourteen acres and measured a hundred feet high and was surrounded by numerous smaller mounds.

During this period, the American Indian tribes—the Ioway, Oto, Winnebago, Sauk, and Fox that the French encountered in the Upper Mississippi valley—developed. They lived in villages in southern Wisconsin, in northern Illinois, and in Iowa along the west bank of the Mississippi as far south as Keokuk.

Building the Deltaic Plain

With the wasting of the Wisconsinan glacier, the water sucked up by the ice sheet returned to the Gulf of Mexico along the Mississippi, carrying with it a huge load of glacial debris and other sediment. The early Wisconsinan valley train extended clear to the Gulf of Mexico. With the bursting of Lake Agassiz, sea level rose so quickly that, at first, the river could not form a delta. Twelve thousand years ago, the Gulf of Mexico washed well inland, almost to the latitude of Baton Rouge. When the river delivered finer sediments to the Gulf, they were carried offshore. When it deposited the coarser materials, they formed sand sheets close to shore.

Ten thousand years ago, as River Warren tapered off along the Mississippi and Lake Agassiz drained to the St. Lawrence and Hudson Bay, the river began depositing sediment into the Gulf of Mexico, building its deltaic plain at temporary halts in the rise of sea level. The ice sheet continued to melt; sea level continued to rise over the next four thousand years. In its search for the shortest, steepest route to the sea, the Mississippi formed a new distributary channel every few thousand years. As soon as the old one became too long and too flat, the river scoured a crevasse in the natural levee of the old channel, formed a new channel or splay of channels, and built a new delta complex. In this way the river constructed a series of overlapping delta complexes, which formed its estuary, the Gulf Coast of Louisiana.

It began its work on the western side of the valley. The earliest named delta, the Maringouin complex, which formed between 7,200 and 6,100 years ago, has been completely buried by later deposits. When the Teche complex formed between 6,000 and 3,500 years ago, it laid its deposits inland from the Maringouin. The deposits of later deltas buried most of it. As the rise in sea level slowed 4,500 years ago, the Mississippi initiated the St. Bernard complex in the eastern deltaic plain. The river continued building the St. Bernard complex as sea level became constant 3,500 years ago. The Mississippi formed the Lafourche complex fifteen hundred years ago, and the present delta, thirteen hundred years ago.

Note: The distributary channel of a river functions much like its trunk channel: it builds a natural levee, adding to it with each flood; it washes freshwater, fine silts, and clays over its natural levee into a poorly drained marsh; and it can split into a splay of branching channels—each one pushing into the Gulf, each one forming a natural levee, each one washing freshwater, fine silts, and clays into a poorly drained marsh. Together they form an estuary, a delta lobe laced together by a network of natural levees.

Basins, which form between the branching channels, fill with marshes—saline marshes closest to the delta front, freshwater inland swamps farthest away. In between, the marshes progress from freshwater to brackish to saline as the lobe pushes out into the Gulf of Mexico. As each delta lobe deteriorates, first an erosional headland composed of an interdistributary marsh is formed, from which waves and currents winnow coarse sand and mold it into beaches and a flanking barrier arc. At the Gulf edge of the headland the beach migrates slowly inland. The barrier arc migrates inland and sideways, driven by waves washing onto the beach at an angle and sliding back into the sea along the steepest slope, ninety degrees to the shoreline. Storms create tidal inlets, which enlarge over time and break the arc into distinct barrier islands. After the headland breaks from the mainland, the interdistributary marsh ceases to form the core of the new island. The islands continue to migrate inland and sideways. Storms erode ever-larger tidal channels through the islands until

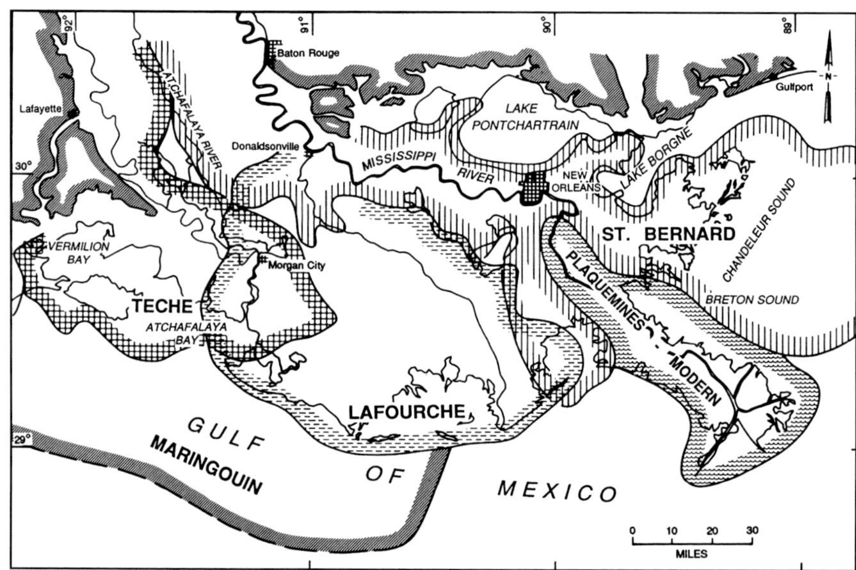

The Mississippi delta lobes that formed from the Louisiana Coast. From Roger Saucier, *Geomorphology and Quarternary Geologic History of the Lower Mississippi Valley*, 1994 (adapted from Frazier, 1967).

they are completely destroyed, leaving only sandy, submerged shoals as with Ship Shoal and Trinity Shoal.

There it is: the river Europeans found more than four hundred years ago, It was a free-flowing river governed by alternating periods of flood and drought. Floods created a system of sloughs, islands, oxbows, and backwaters. Drought consolidated muddy flats and allowed wetland vegetation to sprout and grow. Floods could wash away a floodplain forest but create a new sandbar; drought would allow vegetation to take root and hold the sandbar in place in the next flood. Spring floods contributed freshwater, sediment, and nutrients to the coastal wetlands and flushed saltwater from them. The riverine landscape was forever changing yet always in balance.

When, in 1541, Hernando de Soto and his party ventured out of a cypress swamp in Tunica County, Mississippi, south of Memphis, they found a river a mile and a half wide and in full flood, its churning, muddy waters carrying trees stripped from its banks. When, in 1673, Marquette and Joliet slipped down the Wisconsin into the Upper Mississippi, they found a gentle, slow-moving river, embraced by towering bluffs, weaving its way between islands wooded in willow, silver maple, cottonwood, hackberry, pecan, and elm. When, in 1832, Henry Rowe Schoolcraft crossed the boggy landscape between the Schoolcraft River and Lake Itasca, he found a cool, transparent stream, no more than ten feet wide and a foot deep and overhung by black spruce, flowing from the northern arm of Lake Itasca. It was the head of Mississippi. It was a working river.

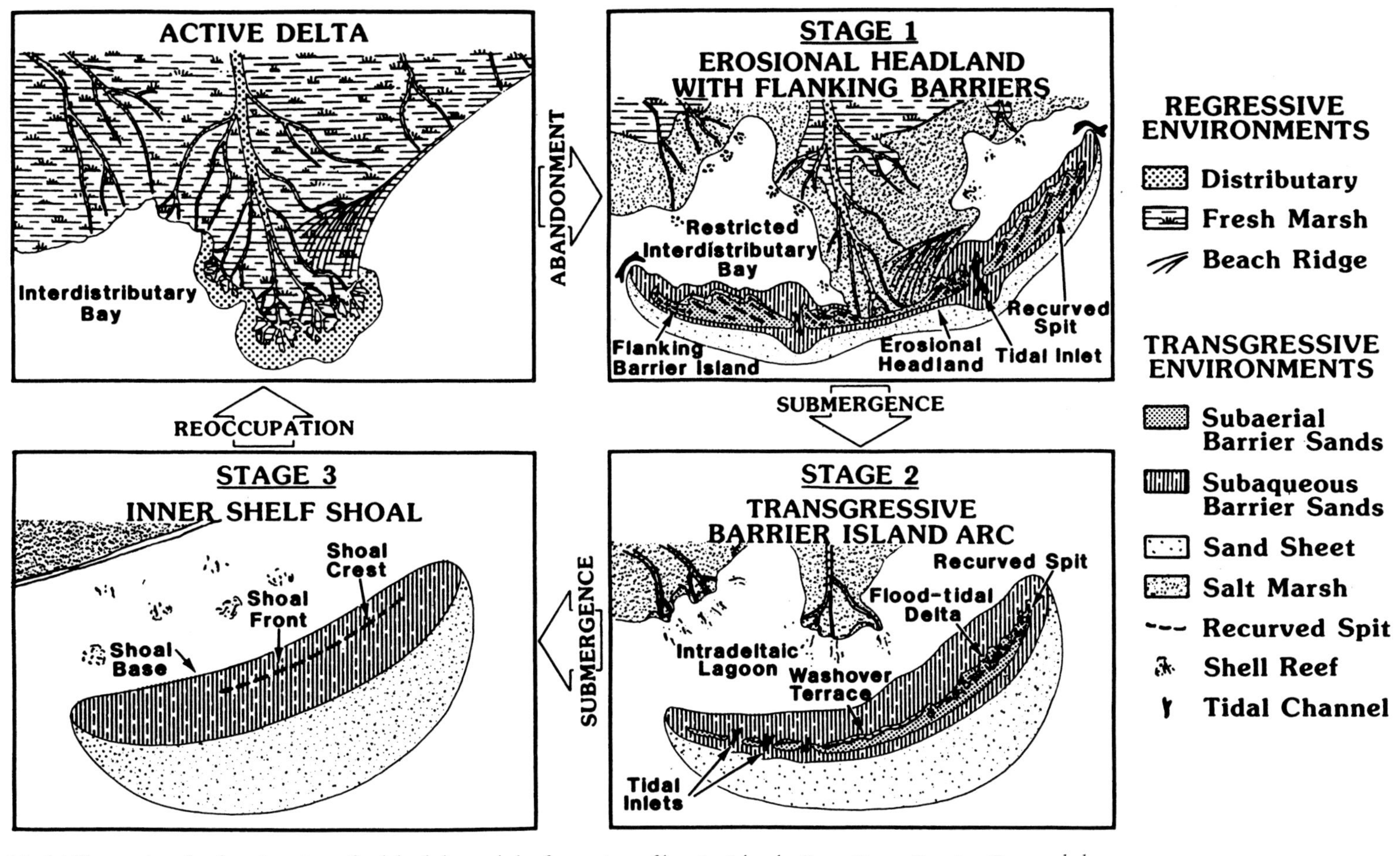

Model illustrating the deterioration of a delta lobe and the formation of barrier islands. From Roger Saucier, *Geomorphology and Quarternary Geologic History of the Lower Mississippi Valley,* 1994 (adapted from Penland and Boyd, 1981).

European Exploration and Political Control of the Mississippi

Hernando De Soto encountered remnants of the Mississippians as he crossed the southeast to the Mississippi, but he found a culture that was in decline and had abandoned Cahokia in about 1500. By the time Marquette and Joliet arrived at the mouth of the Wisconsin River in 1673 Mississippian culture had vanished from the Mississippi valley, wiped out by exotic diseases brought by the Spanish and the scattering of its population. Only among the Natchez in Mississippi did the culture continue in agricultural villages centered on ceremonial mounds.

When de Soto arrived at the east bank of the Mississippi and crossed into Arkansas, he visited in towns of Quizquiz, tribes that spoke a Tunican dialect (the language of the Tunica and Koroa tribes) and occupied lands on both sides of the Mississippi in Mississippi, Arkansas, and Louisiana. Archeologists also believe de Soto encountered the Natchez, who rejected his claim that he was the "son of the sun."

The French in Canada knew the Illiniwek, a confederation of Algonquian tribes—Cahokia, Kaskaskia, Michigamea, Moingwena, Peoria, and Tamaroa—who lived in Wisconsin, northern Illinois, and parts of Iowa and Missouri. When Marquette and Joliet ventured down the Mississippi to its confluence with the Arkansas in 1673, they came upon a group of Quawpaw villages. In 1682 LaSalle followed them to the confluence of the two rivers and claimed ownership of the lands drained by the Mississippi for France in a ceremony at the Quawpaw village of Kappa. He named the territory Louisiana in honor of Louis XIV. Three years later Nicolas Perrot established a trading post among the Ioway at Prairie du Chien, just north of the Wisconsin River. In 1689 Perrot negotiated a treaty that gave the French possession of lands drained by the Upper Mississippi. Missionary priests from the Seminary of Foreign Missions in Quebec, Canada, settled among the Tamaroa in at Cahokia in 1699 and established a village on Cahokia Creek; Jesuits led the Kaskaskia from the Illinois River to the peninsula between the Kaskaskia and Mississippi Rivers where they established a village in 1703. These were the first permanent European settlements along the Mississippi.

The Founding of New Orleans

Louis XIV understood that whoever controlled the Mississippi controlled access from the Gulf of Mexico to French Canada and the lucrative fur trade in the Mississippi basin. In 1684 he dispatched La Salle to the Gulf of Mexico to establish a colony at the mouth of the river, a buffer against Spanish and English encroachment. LaSalle sailed right on past the Mississippi, concealed by sandbars deposited at its mouth, and wound up on Matagorda Bay near Victoria, Texas, where he built Fort St. Louis. With his three ships lost—the first taken by pirates, the second sunk, the third run aground—he set off on foot in search of the Mississippi. His soldiers mutinied and murdered him in 1687.

Ten years later Louis XIV dispatched Pierre Le Moyne d'Iberville to the Gulf of Mexico with instructions to establish a colony on the Mississippi at the Gulf of Mexico. Two years later, on March 2, 1699, d'Iberville stumbled upon North Pass, the easternmost pass from the Mississippi. Over the next two years he established Fort Boulaye on the east bank of the Mississippi about fifty-four miles above North Pass, explored the Mississippi as far north as Natchez, made side trips through Lakes Maurepas and Pontchartrain, and discovered Bayou St. John, a small stream that flowed into the western rim of Lake Pontchartrain. He followed the bayou to its end, the natural levee, high ground, on a bend of the Mississippi. He died in 1706, before he could finish his task. It was left to his brother, Jean Le Moyne, Sieur de Bienville, to establish the French port on the bend in the Mississippi, where Bayou St. John gave easy access to Lake Pontchartrain and the Gulf of Mexico and the French access to the Great Lakes from the Gulf. It was February 1718.

New Orleans grew as a port and became the capital of Louisiana. Cypress swamps surrounded the village on all sides, cypress the French cut and shipped to France. Farmers in Illinois Country, where French priests had established Cahokia in 1699 and Kaskaskia in 1703, produced vast quantities of grain, which they shipped down the river to New Orleans. After the English took Illinois Country in 1762 at the end of the French and Indian War and the Spanish took Louisiana in 1763 at the end of the Seven Years War, Americans between the Appalachians and the Mississippi shipped their goods down the Ohio and Mississippi to New Orleans and the Gulf of Mexico.

Like Louis XIV, Thomas Jefferson understood that whoever controlled New Orleans controlled the Mississippi. In 1801 Spain ceded Louisiana back to Napoleon's France. Fearing that French possession of New Orleans would force the United States into an alliance with the British to defeat France, Jefferson sent Robert Livingston to Napoleon with an offer to buy New Orleans for ten million dollars. That Napoleon might be willing to sell all of Louisiana was never a consideration. But he was, and he did, for fifteen million dollars. The United States controlled the Mississippi and its drainage between the Appalachians and the Rockies. Americans now owned the Mississippi, and we would begin to control the river and mold it to our needs.

Managing the Mississippi for Flood Control and Navigation to 1860

We just can't leave it alone. We have dammed it, leveed it, jettied it, snagged it, shortened it, dredged it, and channelized it. In our endless effort to control its natural processes we have changed the way the Mississippi flows across its floodplain. We have logged and drained the uplands, eliminating their natural capacity to store water, thus sending more water and sediment into the river. We have logged and drained the bottomlands, eliminating their natural capacity to store water, sending still more water and sediment into the river. We have leveed its banks, cutting the river from its floodplain and reducing its ability to carry the ever-increasing amounts of water we have delivered to it.

Since Americans took control the Mississippi River two centuries ago, we have demanded that it carry more and more water while restricting its capacity to do so. And, while we have been controlling its floods, we have also been controlling—sometimes intentionally, sometimes inadvertently—the amount and character of the sediment it delivers to its floodplain and to the Gulf of Mexico. At the end of the twentieth century we started to think about trying to restore the river while continuing to insist that we maintain the dams, the levees, and the jetties we use to control it.

Since 1819, when Congress charged the U.S. Army Corps of Engineers with surveying and improving the Mississippi for navigation, the Corps has been our instrument of change on the river itself. Whatever task Congress demanded of the Corps, the engineers performed. For the first 150 years, the Corps managed the river for navigation and flood control.

Then, in 1969, Congress passed the National Environmental Policy Act and demanded that the Corps state the impact on the environment of each of its projects. In 1972 Congress passed the Clean Water Act, put the Corps in charge of regulating the dredging and filling of the nation's wetlands, and gave the U.S. Fish and Wildlife Service the authority to review and comment on each Corps project. In 1986 Congress put the Corps and the Fish and Wildlife Service in charge of initiating the environmental and habitat restoration on the Upper Mississippi; in 1990 it added the restoration of the Louisiana coast. At the same time Congress ordered the Corps to either prove that each of its water resource projects would have "no adverse effect" on habitat for fish and wildlife or produce a plan to mitigate the adverse effects of each project. In doing so Congress put the Corps at cross-purposes with its traditional constituents, the navigation and agricultural industries.

During the last quarter of the twentieth century, the Corps of Engineers was in constant hot water over control of the river with its new constituents, the environmental and river conservation movements. The Corps had essentially completed the task that Congress had assigned it in 1819, that of reengineering the Mississippi for navigation and flood control. What was left was tinkering around the edges, maintaining infrastructure, expanding locks, building pumps, channelizing rivers for flood control (and doing it again when the channels silted in). It was the tinkering that attracted the attention of the young environmental movement concerned about the decline of the river's ecosystem. It was the tinkering that caused a series of brouhahas during the first decade of the twenty-first century. The story begins in New Orleans, where Jean-Baptiste Le Moyne, Sieur de Bienville, laid out his port city on the natural levee of the Mississippi.

The Founding of New Orleans and the First Artificial Levees

Over the objections of engineers Le Blond de la Tout and Adrien de Pauger, Bienville laid out the town on the east bank of the Mississippi at the point where the river swings nearest to Bayou St. John and Lake Pontchartrain to the north. Residents built their houses on high ground, on the natural levee. Within months, a great flood inundated the new town site. Six years after its founding, the City of New Orleans passed an ordinance requiring its residents to add three feet to the natural levees in order to protect property. Because there were no levees on the west bank, when the river flooded, it spread west. By 1728 people in New Orleans had completed the three-foot levee. Seven years later a massive flood worked its way around the levee and swamped the city. Citizens responded by lengthening the existing levees and adding others on the opposite bank where people had begun to settle. Within twenty years of settlement, French plantation owners in Louisiana had added forty-two miles of three-foot levees to both sides of the river.

A year after Bienville established New Orleans the French built a military outpost at the site of Baton Rouge on the east bank of the river. By 1812 the levees extended to Baton Rouge and to Old River, two hundred miles upstream of New Orleans, on the west bank. Neither levee was continuous. Each protected productive plantation land. By 1828 the levees were continuous in southern Louisiana, but two of the distributaries of the Mississippi—bayous that carried floodwater away from the big river, Bayous Plaquemine and Lafourche to the west—continued to carry floodwater to the developing backswamp regions. There, settlers had laid out villages along the natural levees of those distributaries.

As Louisianans extended the levees north and south of New Orleans, they developed levee districts to spread the cost among the people who deforested, drained, farmed, and lived on the marshy backswamps as well as those who lived and farmed on the natural levees. As the artificial levees grew higher on both sides of the river, they pinned the river between them. The river deposited its sediment on its bed instead of on its backswamp at floodtime. Flood levels grew higher. So did the levees. It was an endless cycle. By the middle of the nineteenth century Louisiana's levees measured six feet. Upriver Mississippians and Arkansans were engaged in the same process.

Further upriver and along the Ohio—in Ohio, Indiana, Illinois, Missouri, Iowa, Wisconsin, and Minnesota—American Indians were ceding their lands to the United States and to the steady stream of settlers heading west. Settlers came down the Ohio from places where they had already begun to strip the forests and drain the wet prairies, thus increasing the runoff of both water and sediment to the rivers. They worked their way up the Mississippi to Illinois, and then to Missouri, where farmers cleared the lands nearest the rivers. In 1826, with the completion of the Erie Canal, New Englanders traveled across the Great Lakes to northern Illinois and on to Iowa, Wisconsin, and Minnesota, where they stripped the forests and drained the wet prairies. All this activity increased the runoff to the rivers, bringing ever-larger floods and ever-higher levees to the Lower Mississippi.

Managing the Lower River for Navigation

American Indians used the river for navigation. They floated downriver on logs strapped together. They paddled upriver in dugouts, canoes, and pirogues. They ferried one another across the river in bullboats, hide-covered tubs woven from saplings. Europeans adopted the canoe and the pirogue, but when they needed to move freight, they used the flatboat, the keelboat, and the barge. They floated their wares downriver in the raftlike flatboat. They poled and rowed their freight upriver in round-bottomed keelboats. Barges were merely larger keelboats capable of carrying a hundred tons.

Our efforts to control the river for navigation came at the beginning of the nineteenth century. In 1801, when Zadok Cramer published *The Navigator,* his first book of navigation charts of the Lower Mississippi, we started looking at navigation—for human-powered boats. While his charts were crude, his text was helpful to flatboat captains. He ignored the names of islands in the river—some had several, confusing flatboat navigators—and numbered them, starting with number 1 south of the Ohio River. In addition, he described the conditions of the channels that flowed around islands. *The Navigator* was so successful that Cramer followed it with a dozen later editions.

The War of 1812 against the British introduced the U.S. Army Corps of Engineers to the Mississippi. Like Louis XIV and Thomas Jefferson, the British understood that New Orleans was the key to controlling the Mississippi and the American West. They attacked New Orleans two weeks after the Treaty of Ghent had been signed in Belgium and the war officially ended; General Andrew Jackson defeated them on January 8, 1815. The U.S. Army sent its Corps of Engineers to New Orleans to build fortifications around the city to discourage the British from ever attacking the city again.

In February 1819 Congress gave the Corps of Engineers possession of the Lower Mississippi with instructions to survey and improve the river for navigation. Navigation, and only navigation, would be the engineers' focus until 1850. Steamboats had been plying the lower river for more than three years. Indeed, Henry Miller Shreve's steamboat *Enterprise* had been instrumental in winning the Battle of New Orleans in the War of 1812.

Robert Fulton tested his first steamboat, the *Clermont,* on the Hudson River. He powered the deep-hulled oceangoing ship with a small steam engine, which turned paddle wheels mounted on either side of the ship. He and his partner, Robert Livingston, reserved the exclusive rights to operate their steamboats on New York rivers and on the Lower Mississippi, where the need for something more efficient than a human-powered keelboat was critical. In October of 1811 their deep-hulled steamboat *New Orleans* headed down the Ohio and then the Mississippi to New Orleans. The trip took three months, as the deep-hulled boat maneuvered the sandbars of the Ohio and Mississippi. On the return trip, the boat bucked the strong Mississippi current as far as Natchez and quit. In the two years before it sank, the *New Orleans* ran between New Orleans and Natchez. Fulton and Livingston gave up their dream of navigating the western rivers.

Henry Miller Shreve understood shallow rivers. He grew up in western Pennsylvania, where the Allegheny and the Monongahela Rivers unite to form the Ohio. After his father's death in 1802, Shreve worked a flatboat. Five years later, barely twenty-two, he purchased his own keelboat and became a successful merchant-navigator on the western rivers. He watched as the *New Orleans* floundered on the shoals of the Mississippi and set about improving on Fulton's design, using his experience on flatboats. He set a steam engine and its boiler above the deck of a shallow-draft, flat-bottomed boat that would draw as little as a foot of water and could navigate a river choked with sandbars. In 1817 when Fulton and Livingston gave up their monopoly on river trade on the Mississippi, Shreve was ready with the *Enterprise.*

In the first dozen years steamboats plied the Mississippi, many were lost to snags in the river: "planters" were logs that stood straight up in the river, firmly anchored to the bottom by tons of silt; "sawyers" were also anchored to the bottom, but at an angle. They bobbed up and down with the current, above and below the waterline, threatening to rip holes in the hulls of oncoming steamboats. Of the one thousand boats lost between 1811 and 1851, snags took out 55 percent.

Lightweight and shallow-drafted, steamboats skimmed the surface of the river. Their boilers demanded huge amounts of fuel, wood harvested from the riverbank. Small boats burned between twelve and twenty cords of wood a day; large boats fifty to seventy-five cords a day. To keep the boats light and therefore profitable, few carried more than a day's worth of fuel on board. Hence, the boats had to stop and take on wood once or twice daily. In the early years the crews went ashore to cut and gather firewood from the bank. If they couldn't find good wood on the bank, they used driftwood. As river traffic increased, farmers and backwoodsmen harvested the floodplain timber, seasoned it, and sold it from woodyards located every few miles along the bank.

By 1822 when army engineers Simon Bernard and Joseph G. Totten made the first official survey of the Mississippi River with an eye to improving navigation, they noted that planters and sawyers had ceased to be a problem south of Baton Rouge because the forests adjacent to the river had been stripped to power steamboats. Once the floodplain was cleared north of Baton Rouge, planters and sawyers would cease to obstruct navigation on the Lower Mississippi. In the meanwhile, they recommended the removal of planters and sawyers and the construction of wing dams to increase the Mississippi's current and direct it to the center of the river. There, it would scour through sandbars and create a deeper, more reliable channel for navigation.

In 1824 Congress set snag removal between New Orleans and the Missouri River as its first priority. Once again Henry Shreve was ready. He had been at work on a snag boat for three years: a double-hulled steamboat with a derrick, capable of lifting huge trees out of the river, mounted on its deck. Shreve started work in 1825. In 1829 the Corps put him in charge of the lower river.

And, Shreve created the first cutoff. In 1831 Shreve mounted a dredge on his multihulled snag boat and created his first cutoff, excavating a new channel across the neck of the bend that housed both the head of the Atchafalaya, a distributary of the Mississippi, and the mouth of the Red, a tributary. By doing so he cut eighteen miles from the length of the river and accelerated the process by which the Atchafalaya would be ready to capture the Mississippi and carry it to the Gulf of Mexico. In 1837 the Corps of Engineers turned its attention to improving the birdfoot delta for navigation.

Sandbars in the passes in the Mississippi birdfoot delta had plagued navigators since LaSalle approached the mouth of the Mississippi from the Gulf in 1684 and lost it among the sandbars. In 1832 the State of Louisiana proposed dredging a canal to connect the river at Fort St. Philip to Breton Sound, north of the Head of Passes. Congress ordered a survey of the proposal and found the ten million dollar price tag too high. Hence, starting in 1837 and continuing for eighteen years, the Corps dragged harrows through the sandbars to stir them up. Then they dredged. The sandbars reformed. In 1856 Congress authorized $300,000 to hire a contractor to try jetties. Two years later the Corps found a few piles of willows scattered among the sandbars. The Corps tried a propeller dredge. It stuck in the mud. They tried a scraper dredge. In 1860 they went back to harrows. It would be another fifteen years before James Buchanan Eads solved the problem of sandbars at the mouth of the river.

Managing the Lower River for Flood Control

By the middle of the nineteenth century the cost of maintaining levees in Louisiana had grown beyond the ability of most levee districts to pay. Following an 1849 flood that swamped the Lower Mississippi valley, Congress wrote the Swamp and Overflow Land Act, deeding swampland to the State of Louisiana. A year later Congress extended the act to states bordering the Lower Mississippi as well as Missouri, Illinois, Iowa, and Wisconsin, adding Minnesota in 1860. The states sold swampland to pay for levees. In 1852 the Louisiana legislature divided the state into drainage districts. Each taxed landowners in order to build levees. The districts built their levees too close to the river, leaving no floodplain to absorb floods and the levees increasingly vulnerable to attack by the river. Complicating their efforts was a fight among the engineers about how to improve and control the river centering on which was the best means of controlling floods—adding levees or expanding outlets (distributaries that would carry floodwater away from the big river).

In 1850 Congress authorized a study of the river in order to learn the principles that govern its behavior and dictate its functions. Until now the army engineers had attended only to navigation, in spite of an 1822 suggestion by engineers Bernard and Totten that levees be extended clear to the Missouri River. Andrew Atkinson Humphreys, an army engineer trained at West Point, wanted to do the survey. So did Charles Ellet Jr., a civilian engineer trained in France. Congress authorized $50,000 for the survey and divided it between the two engineers.

Ellet concluded that floods threatened to create higher and higher levees, creating a false sense of security. He proposed preserving and enlarging natural outlets such as Bayou Lafourche and Bayou Plaquemine, adding artificial outlets that carried floodwater away from the river, and building reservoirs on the tributaries to withhold floodwater from the flooded Mississippi until it could accept it. He published his report as a book in October 1851 at a moment when Humphreys lay in a hospital bed, exhausted by the competition, his survey incomplete. The army shelved the project until 1857 when Humphreys revived it and turned the work over to his assistant Lt. Henry Abbot. They issued their *Report on the Physics and Hydraulics of the Mississippi River* on the eve of the Civil War.

Humphreys and Abbot tested every existing theory about controlling the river and found them all wanting. Levees-only proponents argued that a river hemmed between levees would become a self-dredging machine, its current would speed up, and it would scour its own bottom, making it deeper and more capable of carrying ever-larger amounts of floodwater and sediment and more capable of carrying ships requiring deep drafts. Humphreys concluded that a fast-moving river between levees would not always carry more sediment than a slow-moving river. He observed that it would scour its banks rather than its bed. He warned against closing natural outlets and averred that artificial outlets might help lower flood stages. His conclusions confirmed Ellet's theories formed ten years earlier. However, Humphreys could not accept ideas other than his own. Instead, he attacked Ellet's conclusions. Ellet wanted outlets; Humphreys now opposed them: they might create new distributaries; they were costly. Ellet wanted reservoirs; Humphreys rejected them. Humphreys settled on levees and levees only to protect the alluvial plain south of Cape Girardeau, Missouri, from flooding. They were cheap, they were easy, and they would speed up the current and force the river to scour and deepen its own channel and become a self-dredging machine. Humphreys and Abbot shelved their report for the duration of the Civil War, when all work on the river came to a halt.

The Founding of St. Louis

In August 1763 the last French governor of Louisiana granted trading rights with the Osage and other tribes of Upper Louisiana to Maxent, Laclede and Company, traders in New Orleans. Their monopoly covered the Missouri River and its tributaries and the territory west of the Mississippi and clear north to the Minnesota River. Pierre Laclede Liguest left New Orleans in search of a site for a trading post close to the confluence of the Mississippi and Missouri. Liguest knew that the British had taken possession of Illinois Country a year earlier, at the end of the French and Indian War, and that he had no choice but to locate his trading post on the west bank of the river. He also knew that France had ceded Louisiana to the Spanish at the end of the Seven Years War and his post would come under Spanish rule.

Nevertheless, he journeyed north in search of a site. He rejected Ste. Genevieve, founded in 1732; it was too close to the river. In December, Laclede and his fourteen-year-old assistant, August Chouteau, selected a site on a bluff, out of reach of the river's floods, and south of the Missouri River. When navigation opened up the following February, Chouteau began clearing the site of St. Louis and building its first structures.

Geography dictated its location, ten miles south of the confluence of the Mississippi and Missouri. To the north and east were glaciated prairies of northern Missouri and all of Illinois. To the southwest were the mineral-rich Ozark hills. From its beginnings it was the primary upriver trading partner of New Orleans, and during the first half of the nineteenth century, the city would become the commercial center of the upper Midwest. As long as river transportation dominated trade, fur harvested in the Louisiana backcountry, timber harvested from the uplands, grain produced on the rich alluvial soils of the floodplains and on the glaciated prairies, and minerals taken from the Ozark hills went downriver from St. Louis to New Orleans and then to the eastern cities of the United States, Europe, or the Caribbean. Beginning with the Louisiana Purchase, Americans heading west outfitted themselves in St. Louis, making the city the point of embarkation for western settlement. In 1817 the *Zebulon Pike* docked on the St. Louis levee, bringing steamboat travel to St. Louis.

Navigation on the Upper Mississippi

Early nineteenth-century steamboat travel on the upper river between St. Louis and St. Paul was a bumpy ride and could be a dangerous one. Bedrock ledges and jagged boulders lay just beneath the surface. Beginning in 1817 and continuing for six years, Maj. Stephen H. Long of the Corps of Engineers surveyed the Upper Mississippi for improvements and recommended building canals around the rapids. In the spring of 1823, a dozen years after steamboats arrived on the lower river and six years after the *Zebulon Pike* arrived in St. Louis, the steamboat *Virginia* negotiated the Des Moines rapids north of Keokuk and the Rock Island rapids at Rock Island, wove its way through the braided islands to Fort Snelling, and initiated steamboat travel on the Upper Mississippi.

In 1835 the Corps of Engineers sent Lt. Robert E. Lee to survey the Rock Island rapids and to remove a tree-covered sandbar from the St. Louis harbor, where the navigation channel was migrating toward the east bank. He demonstrated the effectiveness of wing dams by directing the current of the river against the sandbar with a single wing dam. He dredged some of the larger rocks from the Rock Island rapids, but a canal was not built around the upper rapids until 1907.

Finally, while Henry Shreve's snag boat *Helipolis* finished the monumental job of removing snags from the river between New Orleans and St. Louis in 1830, six years after it began, snagging did not even begin on the upper river until after the Civil War. Deadly planters and sawyers remained in the river.

In spite of planters and sawyers, rocky ledges and boulders, and sandbars, more steamboats plied the upper river in the 1820s, 1830s, and 1840s than the lower river. They were smaller than those on the lower river and carried less tonnage in order to negotiate the bumpy ride before them. Improvements would come to the Upper Mississippi, albeit later than those on the lower river and only after the Civil War.

Stripping the Land of Timber

During the Pleistocene era, the glacial ice sheets pushed down into the Upper Mississippi Basin, rearranging the landscape and setting the courses of the Mississippi and its midwestern tributaries. In the northern reaches of Minnesota and Wisconsin a coniferous forest of white, red, and jack pines, white and black spruce, balsam fir, and tamarack followed the retreat of the ice sheets. The Jesuit priests, who settled Illinois Country beginning in 1703, described the deep, dense forest that lined the banks of the Mississippi between the Illinois River and the Ohio. In 1750 Jesuit Father Vivier described how deep: a half league to four leagues, that is, between two and fifteen miles deep. Captain Amos Stoddard found the forests to be a mile deep in 1812. In his 1831 *Guide for Emigrants,* John Mason Peck detailed the rich diversity of a forest a half mile to two miles deep: black walnut, ash, hackberry, elm, sugar maple, honey locust, buckeye, catalpa, sycamore, cottonwood, pecan, hickory, mulberry, and oak. And, he noted that steamboat crews cut the cottonwoods closest to the river for fuel.

The boats' insatiable appetite for wood decimated the floodplain forests between St. Louis and the Ohio. With the trees gone the river chewed away on the banks, making a wider and shallower river. The old French villages that occupied the floodplain lost the protection the bottomland forests had afforded them. Cahokia found the river lapping at its doorstep. Half of Ste. Genevieve vanished into the river. All of Kaskaskia disappeared as the Mississippi cut across its narrow peninsula and took over the channel of the Kaskaskia River, leaving what remained of the town on the Missouri side of the river.

If the steamboats operating out of St. Louis had a voracious appetite for wood, so did the city itself. Half the timber harvested in the Upper Mississippi valley went to St. Louis for its houses and shops. The rest went to the new cities on the prairies of Iowa, Minnesota, Nebraska, Kansas, and the Dakotas, where few trees grew.

The timber industry discovered the pine lands of the northern half of Wisconsin in the 1830s, cut the wood, and sent it down the St. Croix, the Chippewa, the Black, and the Wisconsin Rivers to the Mississippi. White pine is an exceptional wood. It is strong. It is buoyant. And, it was abundant. Loggers stripped the pineries of northern Michigan, Wisconsin, and Minnesota. They skidded logs out of the forest along ice-covered roads on horse-drawn sleighs, which carried the timber to river landings where workers piled logs on the bank to await the spring. As the snowpack melted in the spring and sent floods down the river, loggers cut the timber loose, and the river pigs guided the logs downstream to the mills. In the 1850s the mills along the St. Croix began assembling rafts of sawn wood, five hundred feet long and covering two acres. Soon, loggers found they could lash raw lumber into rafts and float the rafts downriver. Logging railroads pushed farther back into the pineries and brought cut timber to the landings. So it went, until the beginning of the twentieth century, when they stripped the pinewoods bare, increasing the runoff of water and sediment into the rivers.

Draining the Uplands for Agriculture

When the ice sheets withdrew, they stopped and started, stopped and started, leaving behind recessional moraines, hills of glacial drift. Between the moraines the prairie landscape was flat and wet. How wet varied from season to season, year to year, depending on the amount of snowmelt, the intensity and duration of spring rains. Some years the wet prairies dried out; others they stayed wet all year.

In the early nineteenth century, America was a nation of farmers. The unreliable wet prairies with their tall grasses and dense sod were unsuited to row crops but good for raising cattle. Wet soil made for poor farming; farmers were only marginally successful at draining the land. Drainage ditches worked only on narrow strips of land. Ditches lined with stones and backfill worked until they silted in. Mole draining, four- to six-inch holes drilled three to four feet into the ground, worked as long as the sides of the holes remained hard and smooth, as long as the holes were not broken up by tree roots, or burrowed into by real moles, or damaged by the freeze/thaw cycle of the Midwest winter. At mid-century American farmers turned to drain tiles.

In 1835 John Johnston, a Scottish farmer near Geneva, New York, laid the first drainage tiles on his three hundred-acre farm. Johnston imported a U-shaped drain tile from Scotland, set up a tile-molding machine, and produced a set of tiles that he installed in a network of ditches nearly three feet deep in one of his fields. His productivity rose considerably. Other farmers noticed. Drain tile factories began to appear across the Lake Plains and the upper Midwest.

Farmers laid two- to four-inch clay tile tubes end to end and at least four feet down and forty to one hundred feet apart depending on the character of the soil: closer for clay, farther apart for loam. Water entered at the joint on the lower side, while the upper side of the joint was carefully sealed. The rows of tile followed the natural drainage of the fields and carried the water to a ditch and ultimately to a stream in the Upper Mississippi basin. Indiana farmers laid their first tiles in 1850, Illinois farmers in 1858; by 1890 hundreds of thousands of miles of tile had been laid in both states. The practice spread to Iowa and Minnesota in the 1880s. Farmers continued to drain the wet prairies throughout the twentieth century, sped by the invention of efficient ditch-digging machines.

The practice was effective. It aerated the soil so organic matter decomposed more quickly. Tile draining lowered the water table so roots could penetrate down in the spring rather than spread out laterally. Hence, they would be closer to the water table in September when it was low.

In 1850 Illinois, Iowa, Wisconsin, and Minnesota produced twelve million bushels of wheat and over sixty-three million bushels of corn. Within ten years, wheat production more than tripled and corn production doubled. Steamboats began pushing barges, sometimes as many as five, each capable of holding ten thousand pounds of grain sewed up in sacks. Their destinations were St. Louis or New Orleans or railheads along the river's edge. Even as grain production soared, the dominance of the steamboat was waning.

Ever since the first train reached the east bank of the Mississippi 1854, the railroad has competed with the river, first for passenger traffic, then for commodities. As the river lost traffic to the railroad, river interests demanded improvements to navigation. This has been the case from the close of the Civil War to the present day.

In 1854 the Chicago and Rock Island Railroad established a railhead at Rock Island, where it crossed the river on the first bridge in 1856. By the eve of the Civil War, railroads terminated at Galena, Quincy, East St. Louis, and Cairo, Illinois, and Prairie du Chien and La Crosse, Wisconsin. At first steamboats carried passengers between railheads. Then, after the railroads laid their tracks along the riverbanks, ferries did a brisk business carrying passengers across the river.

The river continued to carry commodities. Midwestern farmers shipped their grain on steamboats, which began pushing barges to accommodate the demand. Lumber companies continued to float timber down the river. But the Civil War and a drought almost closed down the Upper Mississippi. In 1864 the river was so low that few steamboats could negotiate the sandbars between St. Louis and St. Paul, leaving the railroads to capture the shipment of essential goods. Steamboats would have to wait until the war ended before navigation improvements came to the Upper Mississippi.

Improving the River for Navigation after the Civil War

The Civil War halted efforts to improve the Mississippi. At the end of the war, the nation faced pressing problems all along the river. Sandbars still clogged the mouth of the Mississippi; southern levees lay in ruins; drought on the Upper Mississippi made navigation on the Upper Mississippi all but impossible. Pioneers were streaming across the Mississippi into the Great Plains, increasing demands on the river and the southern forests in its floodplain.

In 1866 the army made Gen. Andrew Atkinson Humphreys chief of engineers of the Corps of Engineers. Humphreys had no opposition. Charles Ellet, Jr. had died during the war and thus offered no alternative. By the 1870 Humphreys's rule of the Corps of Engineers was complete. He acknowledged no ideas other than his own; he accepted no criticism; he tolerated no rivals. Enter James Buchanan Eads. Eads had his own notions of how to govern the river for flood control and navigation and how to scour a channel through the sandbars at the mouth of the river.

Opening the Mouth of the River

Sandbars still discouraged the growth of navigation at the mouth of the river. They retarded the growth of New Orleans, which had already lost its domination of western trade to the railroads. Nevertheless, both southerners and westerners demanded that the mouth of the river be opened. In 1868 Humphreys set a massive dredge, the *Essayons,* to work on the sandbars. The *Essayons* tried and periodically did open a channel, only to have it close, and the dredge broke down repeatedly. Finally, Humphreys and the Corps revived the idea of excavating an eighteen-foot-deep canal, first proposed in 1832, to connect the river at Fort St. Philip to the Gulf of Mexico through Breton Sound to the east. Eads had another idea.

Eads knew the river intimately. A self-taught engineer, he had invented a diving bell and walked the river's bottom, salvaging the cargo of sunken steamboats. He knew its currents; he knew its scouring power. He had strong opinions on how to manage and improve the Mississippi. He opposed the levees-only policy. He advocated cutoffs to shorten the river and speed floods downriver. More important to the future of navigation along the river, he proposed building jetties at the mouth of the river to open a shipping channel to the Gulf of Mexico.

In 1874, Eads proposed building parallel piers extending far out into the Gulf of Mexico. Jetties would narrow the river and increase and concentrate its current and cut a channel through the sandbars. He promised a channel 350 feet wide and 28 feet deep, wide enough and deep enough to accommodate two oceangoing vessels sailing in opposite directions. And he proposed building the jetties at his own risk. The government would not pay him a dime until he achieved a twenty-foot channel; thereafter, it would pay for each two-foot increment gained until the channel reached 28 feet. The battle royal that followed over river policy—Eads's jetties or Humphreys's canal—ended when Congress authorized Eads to build jetties in South Pass, the smallest and the shallowest in the Birdfoot Delta. South Pass was silting in, becoming land. Only eight feet of water covered its sandbar. Reeds and an occasional stand of willow anchored its banks.

Build he did in South Pass, extending his jetties two and one-third miles into the Gulf. By October 4, 1876, Eads had achieved a twenty-foot channel, which oceangoing vessels had already begun using. It took another two and a half years to produce a channel thirty feet deep, two feet deeper than the channel Eads had promised five years earlier.

The Levees: Navigation or Flood Control

The war ripped great holes in the southern levees. Levees provided less protection to the alluvial plain in 1869 than they had in 1854. The backswamps, which had been drained as a result of the 1850 Swamp Act, reverted to swamps. After the war Humphreys inspected the levees and recommended that the federal government spend several million dollars to rebuild them. Congress refused to appropriate the funds for levees for flood control—aid to private landowners was unconstitutional—leaving it to southerners to form levee districts to do the job. Humphreys continued to recommend levees and levees only to deepen the Mississippi and speed floods downstream. Once again he bumped up against Eads.

With the mouth of the river open to traffic, Eads and Humphreys went head to head in the press on the future of control of the river. Eads wanted a civilian agency, independent of the Corps of Engineers, to govern the Mississippi. Humphreys attacked the results at South Pass. Eads attacked the Humphreys/Abbot report that advocated levees only; the scouring action of those set as much as a mile back from the river would only be effective come floodtime. Eads wanted jetties in the river, like those in South Pass, to scour a deeper channel in high water and low, for both flood control and navigation; Humphreys rejected jetties. Eads wanted cutoffs to speed floods downstream; Humphreys rejected cutoffs.

In 1879, just as the army certified the thirty-foot depth of the South Pass channel, Congress created the Mississippi River Commission, a bureaucracy made up of both civilian and army engineers with an army engineer at its head. It would control the Lower Mississippi. Humphreys resigned as chief of engineers and retired from the army; Eads was appointed to the commission. States bordering the Lower Mississippi formed additional levee districts whose members would work with the new commission on the matter of levees for flood control and would request funds for levees for flood control directly from the commission rather than going to Congress.

Two years later at the 1881 Mississippi River Improvement Convention, Quincy Adams Gillmore, lieutenant colonel of engineers, brevet major general, and president of the Mississippi River Commission conflated levees for flood control with improvements for navigation. Congress, persuaded that levees aided navigation, appropriated the funds between 1881 and 1890. It was a fiction. Congress understood that some funds would go to levees for flood control, but such levees were never tall enough or strong enough to restrain destructive floods. Nor did they scour a deep, reliable navigation channel. Congress would continue to maintain the fiction until it lifted the restriction on funding levees for flood control after the Flood of 1890. In 1917 Congress passed the first act dedicated solely to flood control.

In 1882, the commission adopted Humphreys's levees-only policy. The commission refused to consider artificial outlets to siphon off floodwater—Gillmore had noted in his 1881 speech that they would deplete the river of its floodwaters and injure navigation; the commission rejected cutoffs to shorten and speed a flooded river downstream; and it ignored reservoirs to store floodwater. Eads resigned in protest.

The commission did not reject training structures—wing dams made of rock set perpendicular from the bank to accelerate the current, direct it to the center of the river, and scour a deeper channel for navigation. In his 1881 speech in St. Louis, Gillmore did observe that the commission should design a plan for channel improvement and address the sandbars and shoals that impede navigation, noting, "Bad navigation is produced by a wide river, and good navigation by a narrow one." Where the Mississippi was three thousand feet wide or less at low water, navigation was unobstructed by sandbars year-round. More than three thousand feet meant trouble. To create an eight-foot channel between New Orleans and Cairo the engineers first ran wing dams out from the shore to direct the river's current to its center, scour a narrower channel, and eliminate sandbars. Then they armored the inside bends with revetments to keep the banks from caving. Without revetments the increased speed of the current boosted the river's natural desire to meander and scour the opposite bank. Finally, they closed side channels to keep the river from taking one of them as its main channel. The approach would shift navigation policy from the piecemeal removal of planters and sawyers.

It was not easy. For the next fifteen years the Corps set wing dams along one side of the shoreline and revetments along the opposite side. But, by 1896, when Congress authorized a navigation channel 9 feet deep and 250 feet wide at low water, the Corps of Engineers had to accept that the wing dams had not scoured a reliable channel and had to concentrate its attention on revetments. The Mississippi River Commission estimated that armoring the banks between Cairo and Vicksburg would cost $63 million and take forty years.

Changing the Nature of the Upper Mississippi

In the years following the Civil War, two things—sandbars and railroads—hindered success of the Upper Mississippi as a commercial navigation corridor. Other than the Des Moines and Rock Island rapids, sandbars were the greatest obstruction to steamboats and timber rafts. From one day to the next, steamboat captains could not be assured just where the navigation channel would be. With each rise the river erased the existing channel and formed new sandbars. With each fall the river scoured a new channel across the sandbars.

Ever since the first train reached the east bank of the Mississippi in 1854, the railroad has competed with the river, first for passenger traffic, then for commodities. As the river lost traffic to the railroad, river interests demanded improvements to navigation. This has been the case ever since the close of the Civil War.

At the war's end, Chief of Engineers Humphreys dispatched his protégé, Maj. Gouverneur Kemble Warren, to St. Paul to survey the Upper Mississippi between the Falls of St. Anthony and the Rock Island rapids with an eye to constructing a four-foot navigation channel. Warren, a topographical engineer, knew both the Upper and Lower Mississippi. In 1853 Maj. Stephen A. Long had sent him to the Upper River to survey the Des Moines and Rock Island rapids. Later in that decade he had spent two years studying the Lower Mississippi for Humphreys's report.

Warren studied the efforts of steamboat companies and timber rafters to open navigation channels through sandbars. From them he learned about closing dams set across the heads of side channels and wing dams set in the main channel. Warren concluded that creating a four-foot navigation channel at low water with the closing dams and wing dams would destroy the natural character of the Upper Mississippi. He understood he needed to use the river's propensity to scour a channel through its sandbars; however, that was slow and unpredictable. He recognized that constricting the river by closing off side channels and directing current against sandbars through the use of wing dams put the river's scouring power to work more efficiently. Placing wing dams in the most difficult reaches might open a channel within each reach, but it would also carry sand through the reach and deposit it downstream, creating more problems. To be successful, wing dams and closing dams would have to be installed the full length of the river, forever changing its character. Warren did snag planters and sawyers and cut down trees that leaned over the navigation channel. By the mid-1870s passage along the Upper Mississippi was easier but still difficult in low-water years.

Finally, when he made his report to Congress in 1869, Warren suggested building a system of forty-one reservoirs on the headwaters of the Mississippi, the St. Croix, the Chippewa, and the Wisconsin Rivers. Retaining water in the uplands for release into the Upper Mississippi at low water would facilitate navigation in the four-foot channel.

In 1872 Congress ordered the Corps to create a deeper channel between Alton, Illinois, and the Meramec River, a forty-mile stretch that included the St. Louis harbor. For the first time engineers built closing dams across side channels. They extended perpendicular wing dams—made of rock cut from the bluffs and willows cut from the islands—from the bank to accelerate the current and direct it to the center of the river. The engineers reinforced the bank opposite the wing dams with revetments—riprap rock piled on the bank.

A year later Capt. J. Throckmorton of the Corps in Minnesota opened the door to channel constriction north of Alton. Five miles below St. Paul, Pig's Eye Island, surrounded by sandbars, divided the river into two channels. At low water sand stretched from bank to bank. The Corps closed the east channel with a brush dam laid between the east bank and the head of the island.

In 1874 the chief of engineers directed Col. J. N. Macomb, commander of the Rock Island District, to survey the Upper Mississippi between the Falls of St. Anthony and the Illinois River at Grafton with an eye to creating a four-and-a-half- to six-foot channel. Macomb hired Montgomery Meigs, a Harvard-trained engineer who had experience with the channel improvements on European rivers, which had sandy bottoms similar to that of the Mississippi. Meigs understood that the river created new sandbars with each rise and then scoured through them with each fall. Like Warren before him he wanted to use the river's natural scouring action to create a channel. Unlike Warren he was willing to change the river's character by closing side channels and building wing dams. He understood that as the river scoured a deeper channel, it would also build land along the bank by pushing sediment between the wing dams. In due time the captured sediment would support a floodplain forest. All this Meigs put in his report to Congress in 1875, his survey of the river completed only between St. Paul and La Crosse, Wisconsin.

By 1878 midwestern farmers, beaten down by the exorbitant rates charged by the railroads, were demanding a four-and-a-half-to-six-foot navigation channel capable of accommodating barges carrying 100,000 bushels of grain. On June 18, 1878, Congress ordered the Corps of Engineers to put Meigs's report into action and scour a permanent four-and-a-half-foot low-water channel between St. Paul and Alton by constricting the river. The chief of engineers put Capt. Alexander Mackenzie, the new commander of the Rock Island District, in charge of the task. Like those before it, the project was not easy. Only as it neared completion in 1906 did engineers develop a formula for scouring a four-and-a-half-foot channel eight hundred feet wide.

Building Reservoirs on the Headwaters

Beginning in 1880, Congress returned to Gouverneur Kemble Warren's 1869 report that urged a system of reservoirs on the headwaters of the Mississippi and authorized the construction of five retention dams and reservoirs. Doing so would improve navigation on the channel, ease floods, and regulate the flow of water for power. The Corps had completed dams at Lake Winnibigoshish, Leech Lake, Pokegama Falls, Grand Rapids, and Pine Creek by 1884. By releasing water from the reservoirs the Corps could raise the Mississippi twelve to eighteen inches at Minneapolis, a foot at Hastings (twenty-seven miles downstream), and six inches at Red Wing (fifteen miles beyond Hastings). However, releases had little effect south of Red Wing. In flood times, the reservoirs were successful in retaining floodwater in the headwaters region until the river below St. Paul could absorb it. The system of locks and dams built on the Upper Mississippi after 1935 made them obsolete.

Work on the river continued through the last decades of the nineteenth century and into the early decades of the twentieth. During the 1880s, the Corps continued the work started in 1872 south of Alton to the Ohio in order to encourage the river to scour an eight-foot channel. In 1888, the Corps once again tackled the Rock Island rapids, dredging enough rock from the rapids to create a channel six feet deep and four hundred feet wide. In 1896 they deepened the channel between St. Louis and the Ohio to nine feet, first with dredging only, then they added wing dams to a program of regular dredging.

River traffic continued to decline. Ferries did move people and goods across the river. But packetboats were disappearing by 1882; long-distance passengers took the train. Even with the training structures, the river could not be depended on to stay within its defined navigation channel. Railroad rates might be outrageous, but the tracks, once laid, stayed put. By 1892 timber rafting had disappeared. Nothing replaced it. River towns declined. The river carried only local freight. Midwesterners pushed for a six-foot channel to recapture freight from the railroads and restore prosperity.

The river that Montgomery Meigs and Alexander Mackenzie created realized all of Gouverneur Kemble Warren's fears. The four-and-a-half-foot channel required nineteen hundred wing and closing dams along the river's banks over the course of 336 miles. Opposite the wing dams the Corps laid 197 miles of revetments. The Corps stripped the banks of willow saplings and leaning trees, over ninety thousand for the four-and-a-half-foot channel. The six-foot channel created more of the same: higher wing dams, more and higher closing dams, more miles of riprap, and fewer trees. Side channels silted up behind the closing dams. The six-foot channel required continual dredging, and the engineers deposited the dredge behind closing dams, blocking side channels permanently. The old river was gone.

The old river had been a maze of shallow channels, bound by natural levees, weaving around wooded V-shaped islands, which protected the still, interior pools where fish and waterfowl bred and fed. The new river wanted to be a single deep channel, its banks closer together. The islands in the old river eroded with every flood and re-formed when the river was down. In the new river the Corps scoured away the islands that interfered with navigation and armored the heads of the others with riprap to prevent erosion. Wing dams caught the scoured sediment, filling the space between them. The bank crept to the center of the river. Pioneer trees, willows and cottonwoods, took root, followed by oaks and hickories. By 1930 a mature floodplain forest occupied the spaces between the wing dams and sometimes the dams themselves. Farmers turned silt-filled side channels to farmland.

In 1902 navigation boosters from the struggling river towns along the Upper Mississippi formed the Upper Mississippi River Improvement Association with the intent of modernizing that section of the Mississippi and increasing its navigation channel to six feet. Steamboat operators, who were building bigger boats to carry heavier loads in a failing effort to compete with the railroads, needed the deeper channel. River cities needed the commerce. Even though farmers took no interest in the project, nor did cities away from the river, Congress responded to the boosters' demands in 1907 and authorized the Corps to dredge and maintain a six-foot channel between St. Louis and Minneapolis. At the same time the engineers constructed a canal around the upper end of the Rock Island rapids at Le Claire, Wisconsin. In 1913 at Keokuk, Iowa, a hydroelectric dam that incorporated a navigation lock into its design harnessed the power of the Des Moines rapids.

With the six-foot channel complete, steamboats evolved into barges, and the barges grew until the six-foot channel was too shallow. Commercial navigation became unprofitable. In 1930 Congress decided a nine-foot channel in the stretch of the Mississippi between the Missouri River and St. Paul would solve these problems.

Logging and Draining the Floodplain

After the Civil War, pioneers streamed across the Mississippi, leaving behind the fertile lands of the upper Midwest for the treeless Great Plains. Their demand for lumber for houses and barns was unprecedented. In the South the war had destroyed the towns and plantations and crippled the agricultural economy but had left the great swamp forests—with their vast stands of bald cypress, tupelo, and other hardwoods—intact.

Southerners looked to the trees as the foundation for a revived economy. Northerners, having stripped the piney woods around the Great Lakes, looked to the South as a new source of timber. Congress passed the 1876 Timber Act, which promoted the sale of public forest land—5.7 million acres in the South had sold by 1888—and provided tax breaks to those who developed the forests for logging. Southerners pushed the act; northerners took advantage of it and bought up huge tracts of land in a region where 333 billion cubic feet of timber stood ready to be harvested, if they could figure out how to cut the giant trees—some ten feet in diameter—and then, how to get them out of the swamps.

Cajun swampers and lumberjacks learned how to cut the cypress: They cut slits in the trees—five to ten feet above the water line—drove planks into the slits, and built scaffolds so they could reach the point where the trunks tapered enough to cut. Some trees took days to bring down. Horace Butters, a Michigan logger, took his experience with an aerial cable skidder—cables supported by tower trees and powered by a steam engine—and adapted it to removing cypress logs from swamps. It worked, but the skidder had to be dismantled and reassembled as the logging operation moved from place to place. William Baptist of New Orleans revolutionized cypress logging with his pullboat, a steam-operated winch mounted on a barge. A five thousand-foot cable pulled each cut cypress, which had been streamlined with nose cones to prevent snagging, to a location where the felled trees could be floated to the mills. A pullboat, anchored to a piling, a tree, or a stump, could clear a forest within a five thousand-foot radius of the anchor, tearing up the forest floor, making it impossible for new trees to germinate. When the loggers finished, they had cut 1.6 million acres of forest in Louisiana alone.

Draining the Floodplain

The loggers who stripped the forest swamps in the lower valley sold the naked land to small farmers and entrepreneurs—cheap. But the land was too wet for farming, and farmers along the streams in the alluvial valley could not be sure that their land, once drained, would stay drained. In 1917 Congress authorized the Mississippi River Commission to build levees for flood control as well as navigation. The levees would, in theory, enable the river to scour a deeper channel and would, again, in theory, protect adjacent farmlands from flooding. Farmers and entrepreneurs formed drainage districts to share the costs of draining the land and building levees. In addition, the Corps of Engineers provided public drains and large outlets. Between the flood of 1882 and that of 1916, the Corps spent $30 million on levees to protect drained land; the drainage districts spent $90 million. In Mississippi and Arkansas, drainage districts competed for the highest levee on opposite banks of the river.

Whoever had the highest levee had the best chance of staying dry come floodtime. Levees burst with each flood between 1882 and 1927, inundating former swamps in which bottomland hardwoods quickly took root, returning the land to swamp.

In southeastern Missouri, at the head of the alluvial valley, the loggers who had stripped the Eastern Lowlands of its ancient oak, hickory, tupelo, and cypress forest in the last years of the nineteenth century found themselves paying taxes on a million acres of flooded land at the beginning of the twentieth. Between 1910 and 1928 they organized the Little River Drainage District, harnessed the Little River between 304.4 miles of levees, and dug 957.8 miles of ditches, the ditches spaced approximately a mile apart—all designed to drain the region and render it arable. The plan was to deliver the water to the Missouri state line and let the State of Arkansas worry about how to get it to the St. Francis and then to the Mississippi. Instead, engineers extended the Little River levees—the river rises in the Eastern Lowlands—to the valley wall to carry runoff directly from the uplands to the Mississippi.

Along the floodplains of the Upper Mississippi and Illinois Rivers, farmers organized themselves into drainage districts to raise the funds to build levees, to dig ditches to lower the water table, and to pump out the excess water in order to drain the land for row crops. In 1886 the Sny Island Drainage District convinced Congress to authorize the Corps of Engineers to use funds for navigation to enhance the fifty-mile Sny Island Levee, which protected 110,000 acres of floodplain. The Corps objected: levees had nothing to do with navigation. Nevertheless, the engineers riprapped the river side of the levee and directed the river's current away from it with wing dams. In 1895 Congress authorized the funding of the thirty-five-mile Flint Creek levee south of the Iowa River to Burlington and the fifty-mile Warsaw-to-Quincy levee on the opposite bank.

While Congress authorized the funding of no more levees until the Flood Control Act of 1917, farmers, aided by the U.S. Department of Agriculture, continued to build them. In 1911 the Department of Agriculture provided complete instructions for such work in a manual written by S. M. Woodward. In 1914 the Mississippi River Commission, which was in charge of levees along the Lower Mississippi, counted fifty-two levee and drainage districts between Rock Island and Cape Girardeau, Missouri. Look at the Corps of Engineers navigation maps for the Upper Mississippi: from Muscatine, Iowa, to Thebes Gap the floodplain is broken into drainage districts. Explore the bottomlands in southern Iowa, central and southern Illinois, and parts of Missouri, you will find ditch witches at work clearing out drainage ditches, which inevitably fill with sediment. Patrol the levees, and you will find pumping stations at the points where the ditches meet the levees, pumping excess water over or through the levees. By 1910 there were six such pumping stations between Muscatine, Iowa, and Hannibal, Missouri, draining 150,000 acres.

In the early years, farmers ran steam engines almost continuously during the spring and early summer to rid their lands of water that seeped in as the rivers rose outside the levees and the water table rose inside. After 1910 the nascent electric-power industry discovered a market that would increase the demand for electricity and diversify its load. Hence, the utilities encouraged the continued drainage of floodplains with the use of electric pumps. In 1913 the Mississippi Power Company completed a hydroelectric dam that spanned the Mississippi between Keokuk, Iowa, and Hamilton, Illinois, thus assuring that the drainage districts had a dependable source of power, accelerating the drainage of the floodplain south of Muscatine, and sending more and more water and sediment into the river.

If the logging and draining of the wet prairies in the uplands and the logging and draining of the swamps in the bottomland were effective for agriculture, they were devastating for wildlife. Waterfowl lost their breeding places on the prairies. Sandhill cranes had disappeared from Iowa by 1894. The Ivory-billed Woodpecker and the panther lost habitat with the fragmentation of the southern swamp forests. In the last decades of the nineteenth century, Americans began to count the cost.

The Beginnings of the Restoration Movement

Even though the decline of America's fisheries was noted in the last years of the eighteenth century and Congress addressed the issue with a law in 1871, the conservation movement built slowly as American conservationists created organizations that inventoried America's natural landscape and its inhabitants and worked to restore and enhance animal habitat and Congress created agencies to address the declining fisheries and disappearing birds. The movement began with ladies' hats and the founding of the Audubon Society in 1896.

In the late nineteenth century, fashionable American ladies' hats were laden with feathers—white feathers from egrets, gray-blue feathers from herons, pink feathers from flamingos, gull feathers, tern feathers—or sometimes all or parts of stuffed birds: sparrows, bluebirds, warblers, hummingbirds, and the heads of owls, along with fruit, flowers, furs, and frogs. It was quite a load to carry. And it was threatening the very existence of egrets and herons in the nation's wetlands.

Americans finally responded in disgust and formed Audubon Societies in state after state and waged the first conservation effort to halt the killing of birds to gussy up ladies' hats. Mrs. Harriet Hemenway and her cousin Miss Minna Hall, both of Boston, founded the Audubon Society in 1896 when they invited Boston's society ladies to a series of teas and persuaded them to boycott feathered hats. The cousins created a movement, which spread to other cities and states. In most cases women formed the clubs and invited the men, civic leaders and scientists, to join them. Theodore Roosevelt joined the board of the New York Society, William Brewster, a Harvard ornithologist, the Massachusetts club. In 1901 the state clubs joined together to form the National Association of Audubon Societies for the Protection of Wild Birds and Animals, shortened to the National Audubon Society in 1940.

In 1900 four years after Hemenway and Hall formed the Boston Audubon Club, Congress passed the Lacey Act, forbidding the interstate shipment of wildlife killed in violation of state laws. As the nation's first conservation act, it authorized the secretary of the interior to restore game and other birds to habitats where they had become scarce or were threatened by extinction, and to regulate the introduction of American or foreign birds or animals into alien habitats. The act directed the secretary to collect information about the breeding habits of game birds and their preservation. The Lacey Act would later be amended many times, and by the beginning of the twenty-first century, it would govern the regulation of invasive species.

Europeans immigrating to America found rivers, lakes, and coastal waters teeming with fish: Atlantic salmon on the East Coast; lake trout in the upper Great Lakes; catfish, sturgeon, and bass on the inland waterways. In the late eighteenth century, anglers noticed there were fewer fish swimming in the rivers and streams. By the end of the nineteenth century, fish were disappearing from the nation's waters at a disturbing rate as we dumped sewage and industrial pollution in our rivers, stripped the forests and tilled the soil in ways that eroded the land and washed it into our waterways, and caught fish faster than they could reproduce.

Alarmed by the decline of food fishes, Congress created the U.S. Commission on Fish and Fisheries in 1871, which became the Bureau of Fisheries in

1903. States followed with their own commissions. Conservation became an issue on the Upper Mississippi in 1876 when the Iowa Fish Commission began rescuing fish stranded in the flooded backwaters along the Iowa shoreline. It was a chore that had to be done before the river fell, leaving the fish stranded in pools that would ultimately dry out. The practice spread to six other states along the Upper Mississippi. By the 1920s folks were rescuing 150 million fish a year from the river's backwaters. The conservation practices of the day—closed seasons and stocking fish from hatcheries—could not reverse the decline, which continued until the middle of the twentieth century.

In 1885 Congress established the Division of Economic Ornithology and Mammalogy within the Department of Agriculture. The new agency's first task was to document the geographic distribution of plants and animals throughout the nation and to study the role of birds in controlling agricultural pests. The office became the Division of Biological Survey in 1905. In 1939 the Bureau of Fisheries and the Bureau of Biological Survey moved out of the Agricultural Department and into the Department of the Interior. Congress merged the two a year later to create the U.S. Fish and Wildlife Service.

While people were rescuing fish from the Upper Mississippi's backwaters every year, the backwaters themselves became an issue. Farmers wanted to drain them for agriculture; cities wanted to use them as sewage dumps. As the argument continued, ever more silt washed down from the uplands, filling them. On April 10, 1891, the secretary of the interior withdrew the islands on the Mississippi north of the Ohio River from federal sale to individuals. Presumably, this protected the islands between St. Paul and Cairo, Illinois, from private ownership and from logging and draining for agriculture. The islands remained relatively undisturbed, their forests intact. They could, however, be altered for navigation and were as the Corps of Engineers scoured the six-foot navigation channel.

In the early twentieth century, President Theodore Roosevelt launched the Progressive Era in conservation and put the U.S. in the business of creating and managing national fish and wildlife refuges. In 1903, using his power of executive order, Roosevelt set aside Pelican Island, Florida, as a refuge for the brown pelican, which commercial hunters had been slaughtering for its feathers. The following year Roosevelt urged Congress to set aside forest reserves and public lands for the preservation of "bison, wapiti, and other large beasts once so abundant in our woods and mountains and on our great plains, and now tending toward extinction." By the time he left office Roosevelt had designated fifty-two areas refuges.

In 1907 Roosevelt established the Inland Waterways Commission to address the decline in navigation on the nation's waterways. A year later the commission recommended a multipurpose approach to America's rivers to be directed by one agency in the executive branch. For the first time Americans would address navigation, flood control, waterpower, and conservation in planning control of its rivers. But, even before the commission made its report, Congress set aside comprehensive planning on the Upper Mississippi and authorized construction of the six-foot channel in the Rivers and Harbors Act of 1907.

In 1919 Iowans founded the American School of Wildlife at McGregor, Iowa, and invited University of Iowa faculty to lecture on the issues of pollution and fish and wildlife on the Upper Mississippi. Three years later, in January 1922, Will H. Dilg and fifty-three others in Chicago formed the Izaak Walton League, named after the seventeenth-century author of *The Compleat Angler.* As president of the newly formed conservation organization, Dilg traveled thousands of miles, promoting the league, signing up new members among midwestern sportsmen, and working for passage of state conservation measures. He worked the cities along the Upper Mississippi during the summer of 1923, attended a conference at the School of Wildlife, and devised a plan for a wildlife refuge along the Upper Mississippi.

A proposal to drain the Winneshiek Bottoms—thirty thousand acres of backwater that stretched for thirty miles north of Lansing, Iowa—provided Dilg with the opening to push for his refuge. Dilg decried the proposed drainage project in the Izaak Walton League's magazine, *Outdoor America,* and suggested that the United States purchase all the bottomlands between Rock Island and the foot of Lake Pepin at Wabasha, Minnesota. Congress approved $1.5 million for the purchase of the land for the new refuge in June 1924. In 1930, when the Corps of Engineers began design of the nine-foot navigation channel on the Upper Mississippi, the league forced engineers to consider the needs of fish that breed in the backwaters in the design of the dams.

While the Lacey Act became an excellent tool for enforcing wildlife protective laws, it was ineffective in its early years because there were too few enforcement officers. Hence, Congress added the Weeks-McLean Act as a rider to a 1913 appropriation bill for the Department of Agriculture. Congress hoped the new act would stop commercial market hunting of "all wild geese, wild swans, wild ducks, plover, woodcock, rail, wild pigeons, and all other migratory game and insectivorous birds which in their northern and southern migrations pass through or do not remain permanently the entire year within the borders of any State or Territory."

In 1918 the U.S. signed the Migratory Bird Treaty Act with Great Britain (for Canada), which protected all migratory birds, their parts, their eggs, their nests, and their feathers. The U.S. has since signed migratory bird treaties with Mexico, Russia, and Japan. The Duck Stamp Act, passed in 1934, required duck hunters to purchased a stamp in order to hunt waterfowl. Over the years funds from the stamp have gone to the acquisition of 4.5 million acres of waterfowl habitat. In 1947 the U.S. Fish and Wildlife Service defined the four flyways in North America in its effort to improve the management of migratory birds.

While Congress addressed migratory birds, market hunting, and the possible extinction of whole species, conservationists were beginning to address the birds' loss of habitat. A group of preservationists, people interested in preserving natural areas, and scientists specializing in ecology, the study of how living creatures interact with their environments, formed the Ecological Society of America in 1915. The society started with a mixed agenda. On one hand, some founders wanted to support ecologists and publish their research; on the other, some founders wanted to promote the preservation of natural areas. The preservationists split off from the ecologists in 1917 and formed the Committee for the Preservation of Natural Conditions. In 1923 Barrington Moore, then-secretary and past president of the society, testified before the House Agricultural Committee against the draining of the Winneshiek Bottoms on the Upper Mississippi. In 1926 the committee cataloged all the known patches of wilderness left in North and Central America and published *The Naturalist's Guide to the Americas,* the result of a decade of research. Over the next twenty-five years the two groups would evolve into the Nature Conservancy and create tools for preserving and restoring the American landscape.

The Flood of 1927

We gauge the danger of a flood by the height of its crest and the speed at which a volume of water is moving downriver. Those are measured by multiplying the speed of the current by the width of the river at any given point by its depth at that point, its cross-section. The slower the current, the higher the crest, because a slow-moving river needs a bigger cross-section. Conversely, the faster the current, the lower the crest, because a fast-moving river can make do with a smaller cross-section.

The velocity of the current is dependent on the slope of the river to the sea. The steeper the slope, the faster the current moves. When a river flows in a straight line, the current accelerates. When a river flows around curves, it slows, just as it does when it bumps into the riverbank, when it bumps over rocks in the riverbed, when the wind blows upstream. The amount of sediment it carries slows it down. Friction slows it down. Pour a surge of water from a tributary into a low river, and the surge will speed up and skid across the top of the river. Pour a surge of water into a high river, and the high river will act like a dam, forcing water to slow down, pile up, and back up, causing lakelike conditions in the tributary until the high river can accommodate the flood.

A flood with a single crest speeds down the river and is done with—not terribly dangerous. More dangerous are floods with multiple crests: the first fills the storage capacity of the river—increased on the Mississippi by levees two, three, even four stories tall—causing later crests to rise even higher.

Three great floods on the Mississippi during the twentieth century and one at the beginning of the twenty-first focused our attention on how we have altered the river since the French settled New Orleans in 1718. In 1927 the haphazard system of levees constructed by the Corps of Engineers, plantation owners, and others collapsed during a massive flood that soaked the broad alluvial valley almost wall to wall. In 1973 a dam set across the head of the Atchafalaya almost collapsed in a major flood along the Lower Mississippi, a forewarning of what many feel is the inevitable diversion of the Mississippi to the Atchafalaya. In 1993 the haphazard system of levees built by the Corps of Engineers and farmers along the Upper Mississippi and Lower Missouri collapsed during a massive flood, fixing our attention on our uses of the floodplain south of Rock Island, Illinois. In 2005 the almost total collapse of the incomplete and aging hurricane-protection levees in southeastern Louisiana led to the flooding of New Orleans, bringing into focus the destruction of the coastal swamps and marshes that fringed the Gulf of Mexico and protected the city from hurricanes.

After each flood we reexamined, sometimes successfully, sometimes not, our relationship with the river and how we would manage it for navigation, flood control, and, in the years following World War II, for fish and wildlife. While our efforts to restore the river started before the Flood of 1993, the flood shone a light on the need to restore the river and its floodplain. The drowning of New Orleans highlighted the need to restore the Louisiana coastal marshes.

The Flood of 1927

In 1881 Gen. Quincy Adams Gillmore, president of the Mississippi River Commission, described the reasoning behind the levees-only policy: "There is little doubt that levees do exert some direct action in enlarging the bed of the river during those periods of flood, when, by preventing the overflow of adjacent lands, they actually cause the water to rise to a higher level within the river-bed than it would attain if not thus restrained; for the simple reason that, other things being equal, the deeper the water in the bed of a stream the greater will be the velocity and the greater its scouring power."

The Corps of Engineers and the Mississippi River Commission held to the levees-only policy from 1879 until 1927, when a disastrous flood on the Lower Mississippi put the lie to the assumption that levees would protect the floodplain by scouring a deeper channel that would speed floods downstream.

In 1940 Gen. Harley B. Ferguson, president of the Mississippi River Commission who had a hand in developing the Mississippi River and Tributaries Project that supplanted the levees-only policy, wrote *History of the Improvement of the Lower Mississippi River for Flood Control and Navigation, 1932–1939* and described the natural course of a Lower Mississippi flood before the construction of artificial levees. When the Mississippi in flood broke through its natural levees and filled the rim swamps along the eastern wall between Cairo and Memphis and between Vicksburg and Baton Rouge, the water eventually returned to the river. When the river broke through its eastern natural levee south of Baton Rouge, it flowed east and south to the Gulf of Mexico, never to return to the river. When the river broke through its natural levees in the center of the alluvial valley between Memphis and Vicksburg, the water sometimes returned to the river. At other times the flood crossed over and broke through the west bank, filling the Tensas and Boeuf Basins, and streamed to the Gulf via the Tensas, Boeuf, and Atchafalaya Rivers, never to return to the Mississippi. If its western tributaries, north of the Arkansas, were not in flood when the Mississippi broke through its natural levee on the west, floodwater returned to the river via the mouths of the tributaries. However, if the tributaries were in flood, water backed up into the tributaries—sometimes for several hundred miles—overtopped their natural levees, and streamed to the Gulf along the Tensas, Boeuf, and Atchafalaya Rivers. The construction of the artificial levees on the Mississippi and its tributaries forced all the water that might have drained down the Atchafalaya into the Mississippi.

It started raining in August 1926, the midst of the dry season in a normal year, and did not stop for a year. The rain began in a line that stretched from the Great Plains east to Ohio and Kentucky and soaked the central Mississippi Basin. On September 1 rivers flooded from western Iowa to central Illinois. The flooding continued—in Nebraska, Kansas, Oklahoma, and Indiana—through September and October. The water levels along the Missouri, Ohio, and Mississippi rose. The Upper Mississippi flooded north of Cairo in October, and then the Lower Mississippi flooded at Memphis. The rain stopped in late October, only to start again as snow in the upper basin and rain in the lower. Christmas brought the beginning of flooding along rivers in the lower basin.

January 23, 1927, found the head of the Ohio River at the confluence of the Monongahela and Allegheny at Pittsburgh flooding. Downtown Cincinnati was flooded five days later. On February 26, twenty-nine days after it had crested at Pittsburgh, the flood streamed past New Orleans. On March 1, yet another flood crested at Pittsburgh and took thirty-eight days, nine days longer than the first, to reach New Orleans. The river was filling up.

February opened with a deluge in the Lower Mississippi valley; the river continued to fill. Rain continued through March. High winds roughed up the surface of the river and created waves that slammed against the levees, stripping away pieces of their crowns. Rain and snow continued in the west. At St. Louis, the river rose six feet in twenty-four hours. At Point Pleasant, West Virginia, at the mouth of the Kanawha River, the Ohio was rising two feet a day. In late March, four separate crests surged past Cairo, each one higher than the last, putting tremendous pressure on the levees to the south. By early April the Upper Mississippi was in full flood south of Iowa; the Ohio, west of the Green River; the Missouri, east of Kansas City. All the rivers in the alluvial valley were reaching record flood levels. So was the Mississippi south of the Arkansas.

By 1927 federal levees were precisely engineered earthen dams. A thirty-foot levee was 188 feet wide at its base; its flat crown was 8 feet wide; and its sides were each 90 feet wide, giving the levee a three-to-one slope. Earth for the levees came from borrow bits—300 feet wide and 14 feet deep—on the river side of the levee. On a newly constructed levee, the borrow pit acted like a dry moat, which the flooded river would fill. Dense, thickly rooted Bermuda grass planted on the slopes of the levee prevented erosion and allowed for close visual inspection of the levee for weak spots. No other planting was allowed. On the land side of the levee a banquette buttressed the levee on the inside against the pressure of a flooded river on the outside.

As massive as they are, levees are fragile come floodtime. Leave a stick in the levee during construction, when it rots, it creates a cavity, weakening the levee. Let a small animal or crawdad burrow into the levee, it creates a cavity, weakening the levee. Let it rain for days and weeks and months, water will saturate the levee's soil, weakening the levee. Build the levee of light, sandy soil, it is vulnerable to wave wash from wind or barge traffic. A flooded river roaring downstream might scour the levee's base.

The weight of the flood is the greatest danger to the levee. Two, three, four stories of water press against the levee, seek out its vulnerabilities, and saturate it, burrowing underneath it and erupting as sand boils—geysers of river water—on the inside. If the spout is muddy, the river is eroding the core of the levee. The taller the levee is, the more massive the crevasse, the greater the damage to the land when it breaks.

After each flood the Corps of Engineers, which has set standards for Mississippi levees since 1879, raised the levees three feet above the flow-line of the flood. This policy prevailed into the twenty-first century, but not all levees along the Lower Mississippi were federal levees in 1927. The mainline was a haphazard collection of federal levees, levees that met federal standards, and old levees that had been built immediately after the Civil War.

In 1927 the levees started breaking in March, first on the Mississippi at Laconia Circle, Arkansas, on March 29, then along the Arkansas, and then again on the Mississippi, a federal levee failed at Dorena, Missouri, on April 16. Water from the Dorena break inundated New Madrid to the south, where the flood in the streets was eighteen inches higher than the flood in the river.

Throughout the month of April, levees collapsed. The devastating break came on April 21 at Mounds Landing, Mississippi, where the river ran straight and fast before slowing down for a right turn. The levee at Mounds Landing—eighteen miles north of Greenville—had been constructed by the local levee district in 1867. On April 19 the river washed over the sandbags at Mounds Landing; two days later it burst through the levee, creating a break three-quarters of a mile wide and scouring a channel a half-mile wide, a hundred feet deep, and a mile inland.

For ten days the river flowed through the crevasse at the rate of 468,204 cubic feet per second. Water covered a million acres of Mississippi Delta land in the southern Yazoo Basin to a depth of ten feet. For months floodwater sluiced through the crevasse, inundating the region clear to the eastern valley wall, sixty miles away. South it flowed to Greenville at the pace of fourteen miles a day and ripped through the eight-foot protection levee around the city. Two weeks later, on May 3, the flood slammed into the valley wall where it curves toward the river just north of Vicksburg, thundered back to the river, burst through the levee at Cabin Teele Plantation on the opposite bank, and spread west to Monroe City, Louisiana, at the western wall. It drained south along the Tensas, the Boeuf, the Ouachita, the Red, and the Atchafalaya Rivers, all in full flood, all carrying water from breaks along the Arkansas to the north.

South of the Red River in the northern reaches of the Atchafalaya Basin, Bayou des Glaises snakes east and west across the landscape to its confluence with the Atchafalaya. In 1927 its natural levees were barriers to floods streaming south from the Red. Its haphazard levees and those of the Atchafalaya had long protected the Atchafalaya Basin and the lands of the deltaic plain to the south. After May 3, a twenty-four-foot flood, impounded between the valley wall on the west and the mainline levee along the Mississippi on the east, cascaded south toward Bayou des Glaises. On May 9 waves broke over the Bayou des Glaises levee. It rained eleven inches. On May 12 the levees along the bayou crumbled, first at Cottonport, then at Kleinwood, Bordelonville, Willard Station, Moreauville, Hamburg. The crest of the flood had left the Mississippi and was rolling south along the Atchafalaya River. Early on the morning of May 17, the flood ripped a 2,000-foot hole in the high, strong levee on the west bank of the Atchafalaya River at Melville, Louisiana. It spread out into three currents: one tore west, one north, the third south. A week later a second break came on the east bank at McCrea, Louisiana. A wall of water forty feet high roared through the crevasse at thirty miles an hour and pooled into an inland sea thirty-two feet deep. Water flowing at 950,000 cubic feet per second scoured the Atchafalaya, deepened it, widened it, made it ever more eager to capture the Mississippi.

One would think with the crest of the flood swamping the Atchafalaya Basin west of the Mississippi that the pressure would be relieved from the levees at New Orleans. It was, but not from the minds of the people of New Orleans. They demanded that a levee be blown and an artificial spillway be created south of the city so the floodwaters could drain away. At noon on April 29 the city of New Orleans dynamited the levee at Caernarvon, thirteen miles south of Canal Street. The levee, made of hard blue clay, held. For ten days the city picked away at the levee with dynamite until it finally blew open a break that allowed the flood to flow through at 250,000 cubic feet per second. Ironically, on April 30, the Glasscock levee on the west bank north of New Orleans had given way, and more floodwater had poured into the Atchafalaya Basin, taking more pressure off the levees at New Orleans.

The flood eased up in late May, only to reassert itself in June as northern snowmelt in the Rockies poured down the Missouri. When the last of the floodwater drained away to the Gulf of Mexico in August, the rivers of the alluvial valley had destroyed 120 levees, inundated 165 million acres, and given lie to the Mississippi River Commission's promise that its levees-only policy could scour a deeper Mississippi and protect all the land on the Lower Mississippi floodplain.

Reengineering the Lower and Upper Mississippi

Less than a year after the floodwaters drained away, Congress passed the Flood Control Act of 1928, putting the governance of the Mississippi firmly in the hands of the federal government and the U.S. Army Corps of Engineers. The act authorized the Corps to design a comprehensive plan for control of the Lower Mississippi River and its tributaries. The collapse of the levees-only policy taught the Corps' engineers that they had to give land back to the river to protect the rest of the alluvial valley from disasters like the 1927 flood.

Politicians from every drainage basin in the larger Mississippi Basin wanted their rivers considered: Arkansas had suffered from flooding along the Arkansas, the White, and the St. Francis and wanted those included in the plan; New Mexico wanted the Canadian; Oklahoma, the Arkansas, Cimarron, and Canadian; North Dakota, the Missouri; Kansas, the Kansas and Missouri; Pennsylvania and Ohio, the Ohio. The cost, to Calvin Coolidge's cost-conscious administration, was getting out of hand. Gen. Edgar Jadwin, chief engineer of the Corps, who had stated in 1926 that the levees would contain any flood the Mississippi could produce, proposed a plan that incorporated only the alluvial valley, including the Arkansas, the White, and the St. Francis Rivers. It would take thirteen years and several chief engineers to fully formulate the plan, which would be called the Mississippi River and Tributaries Project.

Jadwin based his design on a project flood that would stream past the mouth of the Arkansas River at the rate of 3,000,000 cubic feet per second. First, he raised and thickened the existing levees and built new ones, leading to the familiar quarrel between those who lived on the west bank and those who lived on the east bank over who would get the highest levees. Jadwin incorporated Charles Ellet's floodways in his plan and returned portions of the floodplain to the river, but refused to consider cutoffs, first proposed by James Buchanan Eads in 1874. Nor were Ellet's reservoirs on the tributaries in his plan. They had been considered and rejected as being too expensive. A final decision was left to his successor, Gen. Lytle Brown, who took over after Jadwin's retirement in 1929.

Jadwin designed the New Madrid Floodway to protect towns along the Mississippi and Ohio Rivers north of Bird's Point, Missouri. Between Bird's Point and New Madrid he would return land to the river by setting a levee five miles back from the mainstem levee. He united the two levees with a fuse plug—a low, weak levee—that would blow in a flood or, failing that, be dynamited, diverting a flow of 550,000 cubic feet per second from the flooded Mississippi. The water would then be returned to the river just north of New Madrid. The Corps has opened this safety valve once, in the Flood of 1937.

Jadwin reversed a 1927 plan to close the Atchafalaya at its head and established two floodways that fed into the Atchafalaya, the first at Old River, the head of the Atchafalaya and the mouth of the Red River, and the second twenty miles south at Morganza. The two would relieve the flooded Mississippi of 1.5 million of the 3 million cubic feet of water per second and send it down the Atchafalaya via the West Atchafalaya and the Morganza Floodways along with the whole of the Red River. A network of levees would guide floodwater to the Atchafalaya where more levees, set seventeen miles apart, would protect towns on the east and west sides of the basin. To release the water from the Atchafalaya, the Corps constructed an artificial outlet to the Gulf of Mexico from Wax

Lake. The plan called for the Corps to open the Morganza Floodway before the West Atchafalaya, and it has done so once, in 1937.

Finally, the plan included a spillway thirty miles north of New Orleans, at Bonnet Carre, which would carry off another 250,000 cubic feet per second and send it overland seven miles to Lake Pontchartrain, leaving no more than 1,250,000 cubic feet per second of floodwater to stream past New Orleans. The Corps opened the Bonnet Carre Floodway in 1945, 1950, 1973, 1975, 1979, 1983, 1997, and 2008.

Jadwin planned a fifth, huge floodway that would run from the mouth of the Arkansas 155 miles south through southern Arkansas and northern Louisiana. The Boeuf Floodway would carry floodwater to the Gulf through the Boeuf Basin and the Atchafalaya. It would duplicate flooding that had escaped the Mississippi regularly along Cypress Creek before the Corps closed the mouth of the Creek, located fifteen miles south of the Arkansas. But the folks in Arkansas and Louisiana who had demanded that Cypress Creek be closed in 1921 insisted that it stay closed in 1928. In 1936 Congress authorized the Eudora Floodway, which would deliver floodwater to the Gulf through the Tensas Basin and the Atchafalaya, but that was also nixed. Congress abandoned both floodways with the Flood Control Act of 1941, which pulled all the elements of the Mississippi River and Tributary Project together.

In 1929, the new chief of engineers, Gen. Lytle Brown, turned to James Buchanan Eads's proposal for cutoffs. Col. Harley B. Ferguson recommended the cutoffs as a substitute for the rejected Boeuf Floodway; they would increase the flood-carrying capacity of the Mississippi between the Arkansas and Red Rivers. The Corps built a hydraulics laboratory at Vicksburg to test Eads's theory that shortening and straightening the river with cutoffs would speed a flood downstream. It worked. The engineers dredged sixteen cutoffs across point bars in the 1930s and 1940s, mostly south of the Arkansas.

However, while cutoffs might have increased the Mississippi's carrying capacity below the Arkansas, without reservoirs on the Arkansas and the White Rivers, a floodway would still be needed in the Tensas Basin. The inlet for the Eudora Floodway would be near Arkansas City and, like the Boeuf Floodway, it would carry floodwater to the Red River backwater region and the Atchafalaya. Not until the Corps of Engineers incorporated reservoirs on the Arkansas and White Rivers into the plan in 1935 were the Boeuf and Eudora Floodways finally dropped from the plan. In addition, the Corps dammed upland tributaries and retained floodwater in the resulting lakes: Wappapello Lake on the St. Francis in the St. Francis Basin; and Lake Arkabutia on the Coldwater, Sardis Lake on the Tallahatchie, Enid Lake on the Yocona, and Grenada Lake on the Yalobusha—all in the Yazoo Basin.

In addition to the floodways and the reservoirs, Jadwin, and Ferguson after him, designated the lower portions of the St. Francis, the White, the Yazoo, and the Red River Basins as flood-storage areas, where the flooded Mississippi could back up behind the levees and flood these regions. While the backwater storage areas lowered flood stages on the Mississippi, they created resentment among people who each year lost lands to flood storage. Hence, the Corps added levee protection for 1,930 square miles of the lower St. Francis Basin and along the west bank of the Yazoo River in the Yazoo Basin to protect valuable farmland from backwater flooding. In adding levee protection the Corps of Engineers acknowledged that it would turn both basins into bowls that interior streams and drainage canals would fill with their own floods. Gates in the levees or pumps would be needed to dry the bowls out. With the abandonment of the Boeuf and Eudora Floodways in the Flood Control Act of 1941 came the promise to those living in the St. Francis, Yazoo, and Red River backwaters that pumps would be installed to eliminate interior flooding.

The 1928 plan had also provided for channel improvements for navigation. Gone was the theory that levees turned the river into a self-dredging machine that would scour a deep navigation channel and speed floodwater downstream. On the contrary, deprive a flooded river of its ability to deposit sediment on its natural levee and in its backswamp, and it will deposit it in its bed, raising the bed, making it necessary to raise the levees and dredge the channel constantly. Dredging to enlarge the primary channel and to remove obstructions and constrictions to the channel was one piece of the 1928 navigation plan, as was widening the cross-section in areas to accommodate larger floods. Cutoffs across point bars corrected the alignment of the channel as well as hastened floods downriver, but the faster current encouraged the river's urge to meander. Hence, the engineers found it necessary to control erosion on the inside curves of horseshoe bends—the cutbank—with revetments made of riprap, asphalt paving, old cars, or sandbags. Failing that, the engineers used corrective dredging "to direct and control natural forces." Dikes, jetties set perpendicular to the bank, encouraged the river to scour a deeper channel, to deposit sediment in side channels, and to erode banks where the river was too narrow, thus widening the cross-section.

The final plan as it was formulated in 1941 had weaknesses. The reservoirs came to serve two functions—flood control and recreation—which operated at cross-purposes. To use them for flood control, the Corps had to keep their water levels low, so there would be room in the pools when the rains came. To use them for recreation, the Corps had to keep the pools full, leaving no room for when the rains came. The levees, on the whole, were more uniform, but some fell short of the height dictated by the flow-line of the 1927 flood. Of the 1,608 miles of levees, 304 miles were a foot or two too short. Levees that had been adequate in 1930 were not in 1950, because sediment deposited by the river had raised its bed. Those levees that had been raised in 1950 were too low by 1973. Between Greenville and Vicksburg some were six feet too short. And, the levees south of Baton Rouge prevented the river and its annual inputs of freshwater and sediment from reaching its coastal wetlands. The Barataria and Terrebonne Basins shifted from river-dominated systems to tidal-dominated systems. No longer did the river's spring floods flush out winter's salt water intrusion. The promised pump for the Yazoo Backwater area would cause a great hue and cry at the beginning of the twenty-first century before it was finally cancelled. The cutoffs straightened the river in sixteen places and sped up the current, but they increased the river's urge to meander. In the sixty years after the cuts were made, the river reclaimed some of its length through meandering. The engineers countered with more and more revetments. Examine the Corps' Lower Mississippi navigation maps, and you will see that each revetment is named and dated.

After a series of devastating floods across the nation and in the Ohio valley, Congress had passed the Flood Control Act of 1936, which declared flood control nationwide a proper function of the federal government and put it in the hands of the Corps of Engineers. The United States would build dams and levees wherever the engineers deemed necessary. Congress required local interests to provide the land, the easements, and the rights-of-way for construction of levees and dams, to agree to maintain the levees, and to hold the government harmless in case of damages caused by the dams and levees. The Corps responded with hundreds of projects that permanently altered wetlands throughout the nation by changing the way water flowed through them.

Finally, in the 1950s, 1960s, and 1970s, the Corps of Engineers expanded the scope of the Mississippi River and Tributary Project to include flood control on the tributaries, pump stations on backwater storage areas, and lock and dam projects to make shallow tributaries like the Arkansas River navigable.

Reengineering the River for Navigation—Dams on the Upper Mississippi

When, in 1927, Congress authorized a survey of the Upper Mississippi between the Missouri River and Minneapolis with an eye to creating a nine-foot navigation channel, it was once again an effort to make commercial navigation north of St. Louis profitable. The six-foot channel authorized in 1907 had failed to return commerce to the river; it required continual dredging; and it could not accommodate the large, heavy tows that plied the Lower Mississippi. In 1917, in an effort to demonstrate that the six-foot channel could carry "coarse freight cheaper than the railroads," the Corps allowed private firms to ship iron ore between St. Paul and St. Louis, coal between St. Louis and St. Paul, and John Deere plows between Moline and Minneapolis on barges owned by the federal government. At the end of the experiment the Corps concluded that, with proper towboats and barges, efficient terminals, and good management, the river could carry freight 40 percent cheaper than the railroad; nevertheless, the following year no freight passed between St. Paul and St. Louis. All traffic was local.

The decline of shipping on the river concerned midwesterners, who perceived the completion of the Panama Canal as a threat to commerce, both rail and barge. It was cheaper to ship goods from the East Coast to the West Coast via the canal than it was to ship them from the Midwest to either coast by rail. The folks who depended on cheap transportation to get their goods to market looked to a nine-foot channel and increased barge traffic as a means of bringing their shipping costs in line with those through the Panama Canal.

A nine-foot channel at low water would require dams to raise the water level on the river and dredges to maintain the channel. However, with the proposed construction of navigation dams came concerns about water pollution and wildlife conservation. It was a conflict that had been brewing for decades on the Upper River.

Pollution in the Upper Mississippi had become an issue with the logging, tiling, and draining of the uplands and the growth of the cities in the valley. Loggers, who stripped the white pine forests of the Upper Midwest, sent the logs down the Mississippi, St. Croix, Black, Wisconsin, and Chippewa Rivers to sawmills, which processed the logs into lumber and dumped the sawdust into the rivers, which carried it to the Mississippi. At the end of the nineteenth century, the Mississippi was no more capable of carrying away sawdust than it had been of carrying away silt nine thousand years earlier. The sawdust built up in the river, obstructing navigation.

After deforestation and with increased tiling and draining of the uplands, the tributaries deposited ever more silt in the river, burying the mussel population under layers of mud. During the last decades of the nineteenth century, large cities and small constructed sewer systems that emptied directly into the river, again obstructing navigation. Mix the sewage with the silt, and the polluted Mississippi would spread the foul blend farther downriver than would the clear river. When the mixture hit an obstruction, it settled to the bottom, decayed slowly, depleted the oxygen supply, and damaged the health of the river.

Under pressure from the Corps of Engineers, Congress passed the Rivers and Harbors Act of 1890, which included provisions that could have ended the dumping of sawdust and sewage into the river, had it been enforced. It was not until the 1899 Rivers and Harbors Act that Congress authorized the Corps to issue permits to regulate any dredging, filling, dumping, and construction and otherwise prohibited any such activities that might impede navigation. However, neither Congress nor the Corps of Engineers addressed water quality or wildlife conservation with the 1899 act.

Congress did authorize the Upper Mississippi National Wildlife Refuge in 1924, but the river flowing through the new refuge was the main sewer for towns and villages along its banks. And in 1927 Congress authorized the Corps of Engineers to study the feasibility of a nine-foot navigation channel that would require the construction of dams to achieve, thus flooding the refuge and assuring that the pool behind each dam would turn into a catch basin for sewage.

Maj. Charles L. Hall, chief engineer of the Rock Island District and manager of the 1927 survey, raised questions about the economic viability of the nine-foot channel in his 1928 report and again a year later. Hall, one member of a special board of engineers established by the Corps to complete the survey, was directed to assess the effect of the dams on fish and wildlife. What he found gave him new reasons to oppose the dams: The dams would magnify the river's pollution problems and destroy its fish and wildlife. He stated as much at the American School of Wildlife at McGregor, Iowa, in 1928 and 1929. As a result, he lost his voice on the board that did the survey and made the final report.

In 1929 the Corps issued a preliminary report that declared the nine-foot channel feasible. A constituency was building that wanted to see all the uses of the river considered in planning the dams: navigation, flood control, soil conservation, water supply, hydroelectric power, pollution, recreation, and fish and wildlife habitat. The most powerful voices belonged to the navigation boosters represented by the Mississippi Valley Association, formed by a group of several hundred businessmen and shippers in 1925. The association, in turn, formed the Upper Mississippi Valley Barge Line Company. The company raised $670,000, built a fleet of barges, and leased it to the government-owned Inland Waterways Corporation, which began operating between St. Louis and Minneapolis. This accomplished, the barge line company continued as a lobbying organization, testifying before Congress and the courts in support of the nine-foot channel. Cities along the river invested in upgraded barge terminals whose potential payoff depended on the nine-foot channel being approved. Two years before the report on the adverse effects of the dams was completed, lobbyists for the cities and the barge industry persuaded Congress to authorize the channel and the dams. When the report came out, it outlined the effects of the channel on water quality and related activities, including the harvesting of ice, boating, swimming, and fishing, as well as the effects on wildlife.

There was plenty of evidence for the adverse effects of the dams lying behind the existing dams at Keokuk, completed in 1911; at Minneapolis–St. Paul, completed in 1917; at Hastings, Minnesota, thirty-seven miles south of St.

Paul, completed in 1930; and behind the natural dam at the foot of Lake Pepin. The rotting mixture of silt and sewage backing up behind the dams at Keokuk and Lake Pepin depleted the oxygen and created a habitat for fauna that thrive in low-oxygen conditions. Closing dams across backwater sloughs directed the current to the main channel and silt into the sloughs, leading to a scarcity of plankton, food for young fish. The pool behind the dam at Minneapolis–St. Paul collected sewage from all the sewers in Minneapolis and eleven of those in St. Paul. The one at Hastings collected the rest, backed sewage up the St. Croix, and created a stench at Prescott, Wisconsin. The pools behind the dams were on the verge of becoming giant septic tanks. Valuable fish, spoonbill and sturgeon, were losing out to domestic and industrial pollution and to overfishing. The constant water level behind the dams made it impossible for fish to breed in the flooded backwaters. Pleasure boating was no longer a pleasure. Swimming was unthinkable.

The Corps of Engineers, as an institution, was focused on navigation not pollution. Cities along the river wanted the nine-foot channel but demanded that the federal government build sewage-treatment plants if the Corps built the dams. Other than oil dumped from vessels floating on the river, the Corps believed the waste from city sewers to be a state and local problem and did not take water pollution into account in designing the dams.

The Bureau of Fisheries and the Bureau of Biological Survey, along with the Izaak Walton League and other conservationists, forced the Corps to modify its original design for the dams. The final specification called for stable, shallow levels in the backwaters where fish breed; and the government purchased much of the newly flooded land along the edges of the pools behind the dams for fish and wildlife refuges. The Corps sold much of this land to the U.S. Fish and Wildlife Service in 1958 for the creation of the Mark Twain National Wildlife Refuge between Rock Island and the mouth of the Ohio River.

In spite of the Corps' attention to wildlife when it constructed the nine-foot channel, ever since the dams were completed, the Corps has been engaged in constant struggles both with conservationists over the actual operations of the locks and the levels of the pools and with the Fish and Wildlife Service over management of the refuges and Corps-owned lands for wildlife. During World War II, the Corps drew down the pools considerably to aid navigation on the Lower Mississippi, increasing the possibility of winter fish-kill. In 1943 twenty-two fisheries biologists from Illinois, Iowa, Missouri, Wisconsin, Minnesota, and U.S. Fish and Wildlife formed the Upper Mississippi River Conservation Committee (UMRCC) with an eye to ending the drawdowns and to promoting the preservation of natural and recreational resources on the Upper River. While the Corps ended the policy of winter drawdown after the war, the UMRCC wanted a permanent policy. In 1948 Congress passed a measure proposed by August Anderson of Minnesota that instituted a policy of stable pool levels year-round. That was changing by the end of the twentieth century. In 1994 the St. Louis district of the Corps of Engineers began drawing down the water level

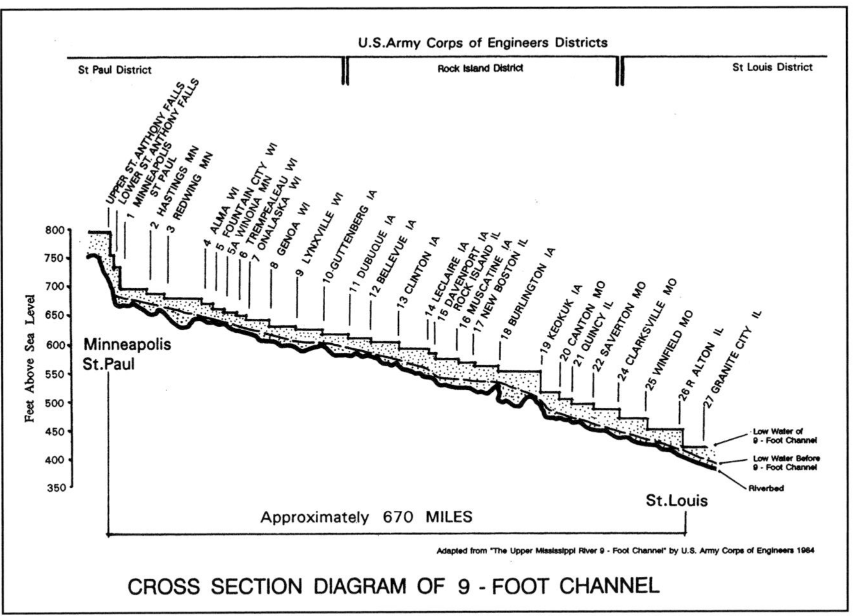

In section, the Upper Mississippi River nine-foot channel resembles a water "stairway." Each lock and dam is situated higher than the one below it. Instead of the river channel becoming more shallow as one moves upriver, a nine-foot depth is maintained from lock to lock, enabling fully loaded commercial barges and tows to use the river without having to transfer cargo to smaller and smaller barges as they proceed upriver. Drawing by Catherine Colby, National Park Service.

behind the dams in its region between May and August in order to allow seeds to germinate on flooded islands in the river.

The dams forced cities along the river to build sewage-treatment plants. The State of Minnesota approved the creation of a sanitary district for Minneapolis–St. Paul in 1933, and the district completed its first sewage plant in 1938 with 30 percent of its funding coming from the federal Public Works Administration, a New Deal agency. The availability of federal funds for sewage treatment stimulated the construction of other treatment plants up and down the river. St. Louis, located on a wider, deeper, free-flowing Mississippi twenty-five miles below the last dam and nineteen miles south of the river's confluence with the Missouri, continued to dump its sewage in the river until 1968, when its first treatment plant went on line. The city did so with the blessing of the Corps, which saw no obstruction to navigation from the city's sewage. Not until the passage of the Clean Water Act of 1972 were all cities, towns, and industrial plants required to stop dumping sewage and other pollutants into the nation's waterways.

From Minneapolis to Alton, the river drops 327 feet in elevation. Along that stretch of the Upper Mississippi, the locks and dams and the nine-foot channel formed a river staircase of twenty-six shallow lakes or pools. The locks lifted or dropped shipping from one pool to the next. The dams created three distinct habitats within each pool: In the tailwater, downstream from the dam, the river remained almost unchanged, a maze of deep sloughs and wooded islands, a home to diving ducks, especially scaup. Here, transitory islands that might have washed away in the next flood became permanent islands. In the midsection of each pool, there were large areas of shallow, open water where the dams flooded hay meadows and floodplain forests. These areas turned into broad marshlands—Weaver Bottoms, Spring Lake, and others—where wildlife such as fish and puddle-ducks like mallards thrived. Look on the Upper Mississippi navigation maps, and you will see ghosts of meadows and wooded islands marked with red dots. They were the new marshlands, but they are also stump fields, dangerous to navigation. Directly behind each dam the lakes were wide open, also the home of diving ducks. The best of the new habitats were to be found north of the Wisconsin River behind dams seven through four. The tailwaters of pools fifteen through ten most closely resembled old river conditions. In 1939, with the last of the pools filling up, the channelized Upper Mississippi was the best it would ever be. Indeed, it would be thirty years before the adverse effects of the dams on the river would become evident.

The nine-foot channel was a commercial success. Grain returned to the river, slowly at first, but by 1964 corn and soybeans represented 30 percent of the commodities shipped on the river, climbing to 52 percent by 1995. Coal and petroleum products were the next most important commodities, followed by nonmetallic minerals and then industrial and agricultural chemicals. According to navigation boosters, the increase in shipping outstripped the ability of the 600-foot locks to handle it, leading to a brouhaha over lock expansion at the beginning of the twenty-first century.

The Beginnings of the Environmental Movement

Even as the Corps of Engineers reengineered the Mississippi River landscape with the construction of levees and dams along the river, Congress took its first stab at changing the way the Corps handled wetlands. In 1934 the legislators became concerned that Corps construction projects were draining too many wetlands and passed the Fish and Wildlife Coordination Act. The act suggested, but did not require, that the engineers consult with federal and state fish and wildlife agencies when designing dams and levees. The engineers never took the act seriously. Two years later, congressional passage of the Flood Control Act of 1936 led to accelerated filling of wetlands for the construction of dams and levees over the next thirty years. In 1946 Congress amended the Fish and Wildlife Coordination Act to allow the U.S. Fish and Wildlife Service to establish the River Basins Study Program so that the agency could monitor Corps projects with the goal of minimizing, or better yet, preventing damage to fish and wildlife from the construction of levees, dams, or dikes along the nation's rivers. Little changed. However, in the fifty years after the passage of the 1934 act, culminating with the passage of the 1986 Water Resources Development Act, Americans began to recognize the urgent need to reverse the decline of natural habitats. Individuals acting on their own would restore prairies and wetlands. Groups would form organizations that would find ways to preserve and protect the landscape and urge Congress to do the same.

Congress considered restoration of landscapes in 1937 and passed the Pittman-Robertson Act. Formally known as the Federal Aid in Wildlife Restoration Act, it funded the selection and restoration of wildlife habitat, the improvement of wildlife management, and the distribution of information about wildlife. Funds for restoration came from an 11 percent tax on guns, ammunition, and archery equipment, and a 10 percent tax on handguns. The Department of the Interior distributed the money to the states according to the number of licensed hunters in each state and the size of the state, reimbursing the states for 75 percent of the cost of each restoration project.

In 1950 Congress modeled the Federal Aid in Sport Fish Restoration Act (Dingell-Johnson Act) on the Pittman-Robertson Act, creating a program and designating funds for the management, conservation, and restoration of the nation's fisheries. Taxes on the sale of fishing equipment funded the program, with the federal government again paying 75 percent of the cost; tax money was distributed based on the number of anglers in each state and the size of its land/water area.

As the U.S. ventured into habitat restoration for the first time, individuals and groups were beginning their own efforts at landscape restoration. In 1935 Aldo Leopold purchased a farm outside Madison, Wisconsin, and began the painstaking process of restoring it to the prairie it had once been. He and his colleagues at the University of Wisconsin established the university's arboretum in 1935, where they began learning by trial and error how to restore prairies to land that had been turned over to farm fields and pastures. They later moved on to restoring wetlands and forests. In his book *A Sand County Almanac*, Leopold outlined his "land ethic," which he based on four values: that land is a community of organisms that are integrated, stable, and beautiful.

Another group of conservationists, responding to the loss of wetlands on the Great Plains during the Dust Bowl of the 1930s, organized Ducks Unlimited

(DU). The group raised money with the intent of restoring wetlands in Canada, where most of North America's waterfowl breed. In 1938 the new organization took on its first project, the restoration of the Big Grass Marsh in Canada. By the beginning of the twenty-first century DU had developed an extensive toolbox for wetlands restoration. DU helped restore hydrology by mimicking the historic flow of water through bottomland forests in the Mississippi alluvial valley, where its volunteers planted fifteen million hardwood seedlings. DU acquired land, created conservation easements on private land, and offered financial incentives to private landowners to manage their lands for waterfowl and wildlife. Its scientists and biologists worked with farmers and ranchers to make their lands more wildlife-friendly. Working with the U.S. Fish and Wildlife Service and its corporate partners, DU financed and designed wetland restoration projects in critical regions throughout North America. Finally, it engaged private corporations such as Anheuser-Busch, GMC Truck, and Pennzoil, foundations and individuals, and federal, state, and local agencies in meeting the goals of the North American Waterfowl Management Plan.

In 1943 state biologists, concerned that navigation on the Upper Mississippi was squeezing out fish and wildlife and recreation, formed the Upper Mississippi River Conservation Committee (UMRCC) and launched the first long-term monitoring of fish and wildlife resources on the river. From its inception the UMRCC spoke for the river's ecosystem every time the Corps of Engineers proposed changes in the operation of the navigation system. The group lobbied successfully to stop the winter drawdowns of the navigation pools during World War II and saw the passage of the antidrawdown law in 1948 that required the Corps of Engineers to maintain stable pool levels year-round. In 1945, when navigation boosters proposed deepening the navigation channel on the Upper River to twelve feet, UMRCC biologists studied the consequences—higher dams, more dredging, and increased traffic—and saw to it that the notion was cancelled. In short, any proposal that might affect fish and wildlife on the Upper Mississippi had to make its way around the biologists first.

In 1946 a second group of scientists picked up the mantle of the old Ecological Society of America and formed the Ecologists Union with the resolution to take "direct action" to save natural areas. The group changed its name to the Nature Conservancy four years later. Direct action turned out to be the direct purchase of land for conservation, as its key protection method became land acquisition. In 1955 the Nature Conservancy purchased sixty acres for preservation along the Mianus River Gorge on the New York/Connecticut border. To fund future purchases the conservancy established its Land Preservation Fund, a revolving loan fund that remained its primary conservation tool into the twenty-first century.

Direct action turned out to be private/public partnerships in the preservation of landscapes. In the 1960s the Nature Conservancy formed its first private/public partnership with the Bureau of Reclamation to comanage an old-growth forest in California. It expanded this approach considerably in 1988 when the Conservancy teamed up with the Arkansas Natural Heritage Commission on the Big Woods project, an effort to preserve the forested lands in the White River basin, including wooded areas along the Cache, Bayou de View, the lower Arkansas, and the Mississippi Rivers. Three years later the partnership outlined a plan to connect the patches of bottomland forest through the purchase of land from timber companies, farmers, and hunters along the White, Cache, and Bayou de View Rivers. In 2005 the Nature Conservancy, the Cornell Lab of Ornithology, and other partners announced the rediscovery of the Ivory-billed Woodpecker along Bayou de View in the Big Woods.

Direct action turned out to be conservation easements. A private landowner donated to the conservancy a conservation easement on six acres of salt marsh in Connecticut in 1961. The easement allowed the owner to retain title to the land and the conservancy the right to enforce restrictions on the uses of the land.

The conservancy added a fourth device to its conservation toolbox when it purchased a tract of land in 1966 in Virginia, which it later sold to the federal government. The conservancy would continue to use this tool throughout the rest of the twentieth century. Should a tract of land come up for sale, the conservancy was in a position to purchase it and hold it until Congress could authorize the U.S. Fish and Wildlife Service to purchase the land for a wildlife refuge. Hence, in 1988 the conservancy purchased 11,255 acres, including 750 acres of old-growth bottomland forest, from the Fisher Lumber Company near Ferriday, Louisiana, and sold it to the U.S. Fish and Wildlife Service for the new Bayou Cocodrie National Wildlife Refuge.

Beginning at midcentury and continuing for more than twenty-five years, conservationists raised the alarm on a new threat to the health of birds: pesticides, specifically DDT. In 1945 *Audubon,* the society's monthly magazine, published the first article about the devastation DDT was wreaking on birds. The birds ingested DDT as it worked its way through the food chain. As it and other pesticides accumulated in their systems, they laid eggs with paper-thin shells that could not survive incubation. It was not until 1960 that the society began documenting the decline of bird species, particularly the Bald Eagle, from DDT. It was another two years before Rachel Carson's book, *Silent Spring,* was published, alerting the general public to the dangers of DDT. And it was another ten years before a campaign, led by the Environmental Defense Fund and the Audubon Society, persuaded Congress to ban DDT in the United States.

Richard M. Nixon signed the Endangered Species Act into law in 1973, protecting hundreds of threatened and endangered species, including the endangered American Bald Eagle. Congress put administration of the act in the hands of the U.S. Fish and Wildlife Service and the National Marine Fisheries Service, established three years earlier. It is a measure of the success of both the ban on DDT and the Endangered Species Act that in 1994 Fish and Wildlife downlisted the Bald Eagle to threatened and considered removing the bird from the list altogether in 2006.

Congress recognized the value of public/private partnerships in the restoration of landscapes, acknowledged that 73 percent of the nation's landscape is held privately and that the health of wildlife populations depends on habitat found on private lands, and established the Conservation Reserve Program (CRP) in 1985 and the Wetlands Reserve Program (WRP) in 1990. Administered by the Soil Conservation Service, now called the National Resources Conservation Service, both programs provide technical and financial help to landowners to encourage them to take erodible lands out of production for ten years, in the case of the CRP, and to remove wetlands from production and restore them for fish and wildlife, in the case of the WRP.

In 1987 Congress established the Partners for Fish and Wildlife within the U.S. Fish and Wildlife Service. The program enlists private landowners as well as state and federal agencies in restoring landscapes for wildlife habitat and provides assistance to landowners who want to restore habitat on their properties. In 2006 the program estimated that it would cost $300 per acre to restore water to a site, $150–$175 an acre to restore a marsh, and $3,000 per mile to stabilize an eroding streambank with a riparian buffer planted in trees and shrubs.

A New Role of the Corps of Engineers

In the years following World War II, lawyers joined what became known as the environmental movement. Old-line conservation organizations, such as the Sierra Club, formed in 1892, and the National Wildlife Federation, formed in 1937, sued both industrial polluters and the federal government. New organizations, such as the Environmental Defense Fund, formed in 1967, and the Natural Resources Defense Council, formed in 1971, operated on the concept that nature itself had legal standing before the courts. These organizations would press the Corps of Engineers to enforce the environmental laws Congress would pass in the 1970s, laws that would leave the engineers at cross-purposes with their traditional tasks on the Mississippi River, those of navigation and flood control.

Congress actually passed the first of the laws in 1969. The National Environmental Policy Act required the Corps (and every other federal agency) to issue a statement on the impact of each of its projects on the environment. In 1972 the Clean Water Act required the Corps to expand the focus of its activities beyond navigation and flood control: Congress reached back to the 1899 Rivers and Harbors Act, which authorized the Corps to regulate the dredging, filling, and dumping of solid waste into the nation's navigable waterways, to put the Corps in charge of regulating the dredging and filling of the nation's wetlands.

By 1972 the Corps had spent almost 150 years surveying, snagging, leveeing, dredging, and filling the Mississippi and its floodplain for navigation and flood control with no regard for the riparian landscape. Its longtime constituents were the shipping industry, real estate developers, and farmers. Now, Congress put the Corps in charge of the nation's wetlands, and the engineers acquired a new constituency: river conservationists and environmentalists. Under Section 404 of the act, Congress authorized the Corps of Engineers to issue permits for the dredging and filling of wetlands under guidelines developed by the newly formed Environmental Protection Agency (EPA). The EPA can, in effect, deny a permit or kill a Corps project if it finds there will be a "significant degradation of municipal water supplies, including surface or groundwater; or significant loss or damage to fisheries, shellfishing, wildlife habitat, or recreation areas." Finally, using the Fish and Wildlife Coordination Act of 1934, Congress gave the U.S. Fish and Wildlife Service the authority to review and comment on the effects activities proposed or permitted by the Corps would have on fish and wildlife.

The engineers balked. Most saw their role as providing infrastructure for economic development. Most engineers and their constituents in the development and dredging industries considered Section 404 a license to dump and dredge—in short, an exception to the EPA's authority over water quality. The EPA saw Section 404 as a way to put the Corps to work protecting water quality and wetlands from indiscriminate dumping, dredging, or filling. Two environmental groups—the Natural Resources Defense Council and the National Wildlife Federation—filed suit in federal court to force the Corps to work with the EPA and write rules that would protect all waters in the United States, including rivers and their adjacent wetlands.

In May 1975 the Corps responded and put before the public four proposed sets of regulations that included requirements that a rancher apply for a permit to enlarge a stock pond and that a farmer apply for a permit to plow a field or deepen an irrigation ditch. A press release warned of $25,000-per-day fines and yearlong imprisonment for violators of the new rules. Farmers, ranchers, and environmentalists were outraged. The Natural Resources Defense Council labeled the rules a scare campaign and demanded that the Corps rewrite them. So did Congress and the head of the EPA. The Corps cooled the furor with a second set of regulations in July 1975. The Corps of Engineers and environmentalists have been leery of one another ever since.

Reengineering the Atchafalaya

The lawyers for the new environmental organizations demonstrated their tenacity when they forced the Corps of Engineers to adhere to the National Environmental Policy Act and issue an environmental-impact statement on channelization of the Atchafalaya River. To understand the need for the statement, we have to understand the history of the Atchafalaya Basin.

Six hundred years ago the Atchafalaya Basin consisted of the meander belt of the Atchafalaya River, its backswamp, natural levees at the head of the basin, and a large lake or series of lakes that extended from just north of Lafayette, Louisiana, south to Morgan City. There the natural levee of Bayou Black protected the lake from salt water intrusion. South of Bayou Black freshwater marshes extended to the Gulf of Mexico. In the last six hundred years silt from the Atchafalaya River and other bayous that lace the basin have nearly filled the ancient lakes with silt.

What remain are Dauterive Lake, the northernmost lake, and Lake Fausse Pointe, which is connected to Grand Lake and Six Mile Lake to the south. They are shallow lakes—only nine or ten feet at their deepest points and as shallow as eighteen inches in regions of high sedimentation. Multichanneled streams, the Atchafalaya River and its distributary bayous that deliver the silt, have filled the lakes since 1917. The lakes are three-quarters of their former size. The process continues, accelerated by human intervention, intervention that started when Henry Shreve created a cutoff at Turnbull's Bend on the Mississippi.

Before Henry Shreve created his cutoff in 1831, the Red River flowed into the Mississippi at Turnbull's Bend. The bend also housed the head of the Atchafalaya. Shreve dredged a new channel across the neck of Turnbull's Bend and shortened the river. The upper part of Turnbull's Bend, renamed Upper Old River, silted in. The lower part of Turnbull's Bend, renamed Lower Old River, became the mouth of the Red River as well as the head of the Atchafalaya. The Atchafalaya sucked in debris from the Mississippi, which created a log dam across the head of the distributary. The State of Louisiana broke open the log dam in 1860, and the Atchafalaya immediately enlarged and deepened its channel and carried off more and more of the Mississippi. In 1872 the Red River joined itself to the head of the Atchafalaya. Water flowed back and forth between the Red-Atchafalaya and the Mississippi along Lower Old River, depending on the level of the Mississippi. The two rivers performed this two-step until 1945, when the Atchafalaya captured the Red completely.

Every flood after 1880 widened and deepened the Atchafalaya as each followed its natural course down the Mississippi to the Atchafalaya. The latter drew off more and more of the former and its load of silt and deposited the silt at the southern reaches of the basin.

In the wake of the Flood of 1927, Gen. Edgar Jadwin left the head Atchafalaya open as the only distributary carrying water from the main channel of the Mississippi. He turned the river and its swamps into a floodway, 1,400,000 acres of farmland and river swamp broken into three parts, hemmed between levees set seventeen miles apart. The Morganza and West Atchafalaya Floodways of today occupy pastureland and soybean fields separated by bayous lined with oak, pecan, and sweet gum. They feed into the Atchafalaya Basin Floodway, the largest river swamp in the world, freshwater lakes where clumps of young tupelo and cypress stand among the rotted stumps of trees that were logged and dragged from the swamp after the Civil War. Bayous lined with willows weave in and out of the lakes.

The biggest problem with Jadwin's plan was/is the Atchafalaya and its floodway. The Mississippi wants to divert to the Atchafalaya. Should it do so, the old channel of the Mississippi would narrow and silt in. New Orleans would lose its status as a deepwater port. So would Baton Rouge. By 1950 the distance along the Mississippi between Old River and the Gulf was 315 miles, along the Atchafalaya only 142 miles. The slope of the Atchafalaya was three times greater. With the Flood of 1950 it became clear that the Atchafalaya would capture the Mississippi by 1975 and the Corps of Engineers would be unable to stop it without extraordinary measures. In 1954, Congress authorized the Corps of Engineers to do so. The Corps responded with the Old River Control Structure.

The Corps of Engineers reconstructed Turnbull's Bend just north of Upper Old River by digging an overflow channel between the Mississippi and the Red Rivers and setting the Low Sill Structure—a dam across the channel—in the mainline levee. The dam was 556 feet long with eleven bays, each equipped with an independent gate. Curved wing-walls captured the Mississippi and directed it into the gates. The designers supported the structure with steel "H" beams, piles, driven at all different angles ninety feet into layers of fine sediment, sand, and gravel. They could not anchor the dam in bedrock; that was too far down. They drove sheets of steel into the muck below the dam to mitigate erosion and seepage.

The Low Sill Structure rationed the day-to-day flow of the Mississippi into the Atchafalaya. The Overbank Structure, 3,358 feet long with seventy-three gated bays, built north of the Low Sill Structure, rationed the flooded Mississippi into the West Atchafalaya Floodway. The Corps closed Lower Old River with an earthen dam and dug a narrow channel just to the south in which they installed a navigation lock to ease shipping between the Mississippi and the Atchafalaya. The Corps completed the Low Sill Structure and the Overbank Structure in 1959. They completed the navigation lock four years later. The Overbank Structure was made to operate in tandem with a similar structure located at Morganza twenty miles south of Old River. The Morganza Structure released floodwater into the Morganza Floodway, which funneled water

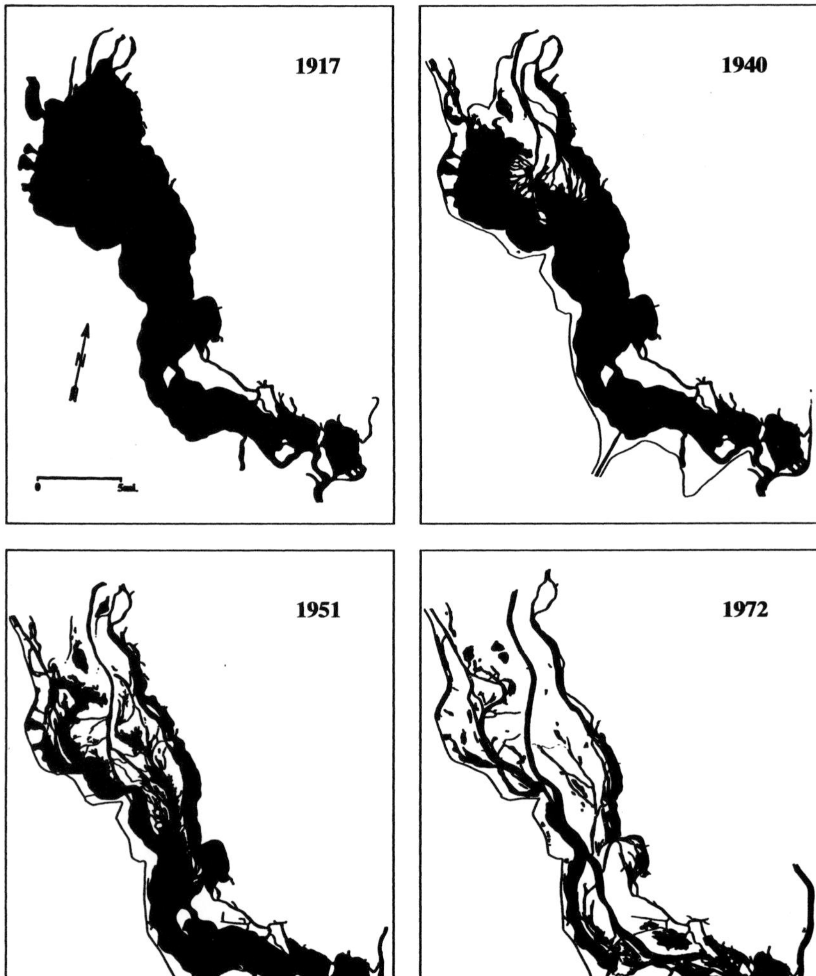

Illustration of the filling of Grand Lake and Six Mile Lake with sediment between 1917 and 1972. From Martin Reuss, "Designing the Bayous," Office of History, U.S. Army Corps of Engineers, 1998.

to the start of the east Atchafalaya levee near Pigeon Lake. The West Atchafalaya Floodway funneled floodwater between levees to the start of the west Atchafalaya levee near Breaux Bridge, Louisiana. Together, they could siphon off 1,500,000 cubic feet per second from a 3,000,000-cubic-foot flood on the Mississippi.

The Corps of Engineers speeded up the deposit of silt in the lakes when the agency hemmed the Atchafalaya between levees and turned in into a floodway. Instead of spreading its silt across the basin, the river deposited silt in the lakes between the levees and in the channel bed, necessitating higher levees, which sank of their own weight.

Beginning in 1963, as the Corps completed the Old River Control Structure, the engineers made plans to dredge and deepen the river to enable it to carry off floodwater more efficiently. The Corps blocked off side channels and dredged forty-one miles of the northern stretch of the river. The people who fished and hunted the Atchafalaya and its swamps feared channelization would dry out the swamp. The expense of the Vietnam War stopped the project in 1968. In 1971, when the Corps was ready to resume dredging, the National Wildlife Federation forced the agency to consider the environmental impact of channelization on the Atchafalaya Basin and propose alternatives. In its 1974 draft statement, the Corps refused to consider alternatives. It was still refusing in its second draft two years later. The struggle between environmentalists and the Corps continued for six more years. When the agency issued its third statement in 1982, the engineers got their channelized river below mile 90. The environmentalists got a 46,000-acre state wildlife management area and thirteen environmental management units in the lower third of the basin, projects that would mitigate some of channelization's effects on the basin.

The Flood of 1973

In 1973 in the midst of the struggle between those who love the Atchafalaya with its river swamp and the Corps of Engineers, the Mississippi flooded, almost destroyed the Old River Control Structure, and threatened to divert down the Atchafalaya to the Gulf of Mexico.

The last half of the twentieth century sent more and more water down the Mississippi. Drainage districts channelized streams to speed floodwater off agricultural lands. Little rivers like the Fabius in Marion County and the Cuivre in St. Charles County, Missouri, ran fast and straight across their floodplains, leaving behind their old meanders to silt in, oxbows stranded in cornfields. Yazoo streams like Cahokia Creek, once twenty-five miles long and running in multiple channels south across the American Bottom in Madison County, Illinois, ran straight as an arrow due west and between levees to the Mississippi at the northern end of the floodplain.

Air-conditioning turned the Deep South into a bearable place to live in the summer. The cities grew, requiring more houses with more roofs, more shopping centers with more parking lots, and more roads to get to them. All through the Mississippi Basin, developers turned wetlands into suburban subdivisions, reducing the natural storage places for water. All this water, cascading off all that pavement and all those rooftops, had nowhere to go but the Mississippi. As a result, floods grew bigger even though there was less rain.

By no means was the Flood of 1973 the equal of the Flood of 1927, but it did demonstrate the weaknesses in the Mississippi Rivers and Tributaries Project. The reservoirs worked and retained floodwaters until the river could accept them. Normal rainfall prevailed between the 1950s and 1973. The river adjusted to lower flows and silted up, raising its bed. With continued dependence on levees, the river continued to deposit silt in its channel, raising its bed more. Levees that had been adequate in 1950 were not in 1973. The floodways were problematical. For instance, the New Madrid Floodway ran through valuable farmland in New Madrid and Mississippi Counties, Missouri; farmers were reluctant to see their lands and their homes flooded. The Corps of Engineers used it only once, in 1937. The farmers in the West Atchafalaya Floodway, one section of the three-part Atchafalaya Floodway, felt the same way. It has never been used. Farms also occupied the Morganza Floodway but with no permanent buildings. The Corps of Engineers used the Bonnet Carre Floodway to funnel floodwater into Lake Pontchartrain in 1945 and 1950. On the eve of the Flood of 1973, the Low Sill Structure, designed to ration one-third of the Mississippi into the Atchafalaya at a rate of 350,000 cubic feet per second, had never been tested.

The rain started in the fall of 1972 and continued through the winter and into the spring of 1973. The Mississippi and its tributaries began to rise. The Mississippi crested several times. The river was filling up, guaranteeing higher crests. Still, rainfall in 1973 was a mere 20 percent above normal, but flood crests were four to six feet higher than expected. A flood flowing past Vicksburg at 1,800,000 cubic feet per second, which had produced a flood stage of 43.7 feet in 1950, produced a level of 50.6 feet in 1973.

In April 1973 the Mississippi tore through the open gates of the Low Sill Structure at 500,000 cubic feet per second; the structure almost ripped itself apart. The river crashed against the south wing-wall and scoured a hole in the inflow channel. Forty feet deep, the hole exposed the fins of sheet steel set there to prevent erosion and seepage under the structure. As the water poured through the open gates at five times the force of Niagara Falls, it also scoured a hole in the outflow channel 130 feet deep, deeper than the reach of the ninety-foot steel "H" piles that supported the structure. Had the two holes met, the 200,000-ton structure might have collapsed. Finally, on April 14 the south wing-wall did collapse. To relieve pressure on and save the Low Sill Structure, the Corps of Engineers opened the Overbank Structure and the Morganza Floodway.

When the floodwaters receded, the engineers began their repair work, pouring tons of cement and bentonite into the scour holes. They drilled more holes—the size of dinner plates—the length of the structure and filled them. They rebuilt the south wing-wall. All the while, for three and a half years, they left the gates open to relieve pressure on the compromised structure. For three and a half years the Atchafalaya deepened its channel and increased its advantage over the Mississippi. When they did close the gates, they reduced the head between the Mississippi and the Atchafalaya from thirty-seven feet to twenty-two feet to relieve pressure on the compromised structure. They also dug a new channel and built a second Old River Control Structure, an auxiliary structure, about a third of a mile south of the Low Sill Structure to spare the compromised structure. Seven tall towers rise above six gates, each sixty-two feet wide. The Corps started construction in 1981. By 1983, when the third-greatest flood of the twentieth century surged down the river, the new structure was no more than a concrete foundation sitting on dry ground. The Old River Control Structure held. The Corps completed the auxiliary structure in 1986, the same year the river's ceaseless pounding began to take its toll on the Low Sill Structure, damaging one of its eleven gates.

In 1986, after they repaired the Low Sill Structure and completed the new structure, the Corps' engineers were convinced they had management of the Atchafalaya right. The Mississippi would not divert. Geologists and hydrologists were not so sure. When the Atchafalaya takes over the Mississippi, it could happen with a hundred-year flood or a five-hundred-year flood that breaks through the mainline levee somewhere in the region. It will splay out into rivulets, any one of which could find the Atchafalaya. And, at the beginning of the twenty-first century, there were some who reasoned that maybe we should allow the Atchafalaya to capture the Mississippi, but with the engineering of the takeover under control.

The Water Resources Development Act, 1965–1986

A team of environmental lawyers, railroad lawyers, and a pair of reform-minded, some would say parsimonious, presidents ganged up on the Corps of Engineers and navigation boosters and forced the redesign of a major dam on the Upper Mississippi, the establishment of user fees for its construction, the declaration of the Upper Mississippi as a nationally significant ecosystem, the passage of the Upper Mississippi River Management Act, and the institution of cost sharing on most Corps of Engineers water projects in the 1986 Water Resources Development Act.

It started with the passage of the 1965 Water Resources Planning Act, an effort to coordinate and centralize water policy and the planning of water-resource projects financed by the federal government. To this end Congress established the Water Resources Council, a group similar to President Theodore Roosevelt's 1907 Inland Waterways Commission, that would coordinate water policies and publish "principles and standards" to guide the development of water projects. The law also set up river basin commissions, including the Upper Mississippi Basin Commission, to further coordinate water policy and prepare the Upper Mississippi River Comprehensive Basin Study that would address navigation, flood control, and conservation on the river. By 1973 the "Principles and Standards" for water projects required that federal agencies plan for national and regional development, environmental quality, and social effects in preparing water projects.

In 1968, at a time when the Corps was deepening the channel on the Lower Mississippi to twelve feet, Congress authorized a second study of the twelve-foot channel on the upper river. Barge lines wanted a uniform depth on inland waterways nationwide. Biologists with the Upper Mississippi River Conservation Committee, who were opposed to the project, concluded that deepening the channel to twelve feet would require more of everything: higher dams, deeper dredging, higher water levels, higher levees to protect farmland and cities. And the twelve-foot channel would accelerate the damage to fish and wildlife in backwaters caused by the nine-foot channel. These, finally, were the reasons the twelve-foot channel was rejected in 1972.

In 1974 Congress replaced the Flood Control Acts and the Rivers and Harbors Acts and passed the first Water Resources Development Act (WRDA), the omnibus bill that authorizes the Corps' water projects. For the first time, Congress directed all federal agencies to consider nonstructural measures when designing flood protection, authorized several flood-control projects that incorporated nonstructural measures in their designs, and required that 80 percent of their costs come from the federal treasury.

After 1986 the biannual WRDA became the means by which Congress authorized individual water projects and set policy. More important, it became the means by which Congress initiated restoration efforts on the Upper Mississippi and along the Gulf Coast. Congress made a start in this direction with the Water Resources Development Act of 1976, when it formalized the Great River Environmental Action Team—initiated two years earlier by the St. Paul District of the Corps, the U.S. Fish and Wildlife Service, and the Upper Mississippi River Basin Commission—and ordered the Corps to look at the multiple demands on the Upper Mississippi—navigation, fish and wildlife, hydropower, flood control—and make recommendations for its improved management.

To that end Congress authorized $9,100,000 for the development of a river-system-management plan for the Upper Mississippi River due in 1982. Finally, Congress ordered the Corps of Engineers to plan and establish wetlands as a part of any larger water project.

Then, Congress hit a stumbling block: Americans elected Jimmy Carter president in November 1976. When he took office the following January, he signaled his independence from traditional politics by submitting a list of eighteen previously authorized water projects for deletion and defunding. Congress disagreed. The two remained locked in a stalemate over water policy for the duration of Carter's term. The stalemate continued through Ronald Reagan's first term and into his second.

During those ten years, Congress and the two presidents struggled over how to pay for new water projects, including expensive, expansive navigation projects. President Carter wanted to avoid low-benefit, wasteful water projects; he wanted to promote water conservation; and he wanted the states to share the costs of water projects. In 1977 he issued executive orders that wedded floodplain management to wetlands protection in reducing damages from floods.

Carter's struggle with Congress came to a head over how to pay for the replacement of Lock and Dam 26 on the Mississippi at Alton, Illinois. That story started in 1968 when the St. Louis District of the Corps of Engineers proposed replacing the aging lock and dam at Alton with a new dam with two 1,200-foot locks to be built two miles downstream from the old dam. The Corps proceeded with its design, and the secretary of the army approved the dam under the authority of the 1909 Rivers and Harbors Act, which authorized him to order the maintenance and repair of existing navigation facilities. Congress appropriated construction funds in 1974. The Izaak Walton League and the Sierra Club objected. So did eighteen railroads.

In August 1974 environmentalists, again led by scientists with the Upper Mississippi River Conservation Commission, saw the dam as another effort to increase the depth of the navigation channel to twelve feet, to bring increased traffic to the river and, thus, increased damage to its ecosystem. The railroads saw increased traffic on the river as a threat to their business. The disparate organizations teamed up and filed suit to block construction of the dam. U.S. Judge Charles Richey issued a temporary restraining order, halting bidding on construction. His reasoning: The dam was not a repair job, but a new structure that Congress had never authorized. And, the Corps' environmental-impact statement failed to examine the impact of the dam systemwide and propose alternatives.

The St. Louis District held hearings, attended by the environmentalists and the railroads, and issued a draft statement that discussed the enviromental impact of the two-lock dam on the river and examined alternatives. The Board of Engineers for Rivers and Harbors, an independent panel that reviewed Corps projects, suggested a single 1,200-foot lock. The Corps accepted the recommendation and issued its final environmental statement in March 1976. The courts dismissed the lawsuit. In March 1977 the U.S. Department of Transportation issued a study that concluded that there was "no immediate economic need" for the dam and changes could be made in the operations of the old dam at half the cost of building a new dam. Congress ignored the report.

Then, there was the matter of paying for the dam. When the Ninety-fifth Congress (1977–1978) addressed authorization, Senator Pete Domenici of New Mexico introduced legislation establishing user fees, to be imposed on the barge companies and other users of the inland waterways, to help pay for the dam. Congress broke from the principle of total federal responsibility for inland-waterway-navigation projects and authorized the construction of the new dam at Alton, using the first waterways fuel tax to help pay for it.

Moreover, Congress ordered the Corps of Engineers to mitigate, acre for acre, terrestrial wildlife habitat inundated by water as a result of the construction of the new dam. In doing so the Corps purchased 862 acres on Cuivre Island where they planted nut-bearing trees on its ridges. Congress also directed the Corps to prepare a comprehensive master plan for the management of the Upper Mississippi River Basin System due in 1982, put it in the hands of the Upper Mississippi River Basin Commission, and prohibited the Corps from increasing the navigation capacity of the system until the plan was completed. Finally, Congress prohibited any federal agency from even studying the feasibility of deepening the navigation channels of the Mississippi without congressional authorization.

Reagan came into office in 1981 with a zeal to deregulate. He zeroed out funding for the Water Resources Council, established in 1965, along with the various river basin commissions, including the Upper Mississippi Basin Commission, also established in 1965. The Reagan administration substituted a loose set of "Principles and Guidelines" for the stricter 1972 "Principles and Standards" that the Water Resources Council used in the formulation and evaluation of federal water projects. When he did so, he zeroed out the possibility of comprehensive planning and made national economic development the sole aim of federal water projects.

The new principles and guidelines, issued in March 1983, required the Corps to develop projects that were cost-effective, politically feasible, and environmentally sound. Finally, Reagan refused to sign any spending bill for water projects that did not include user fees or other forms of cost sharing. The 1986 Water Resources Development Act did that and much more, but only after the matter of the second lock at Lock and Dam 26 was resolved.

The Water Resources Development Act of 1986

While the Corps agreed to a single 1,200-foot lock at the Alton dam, the second lock did not go away, even after Congress authorized construction of the dam. Included in the Comprehensive Master Plan for the Management of the Upper Mississippi was an examination of the impact of the second lock on increases in river traffic and increases in ecosystem damage. Development of the plan became a negotiation between the Corps of Engineers and scientists from the Upper Mississippi River Conservation Committee, who formed the planners' environmental work team. The engineers wanted the lock; the scientists wanted ecosystem restoration. The engineers got a lock, but only a six-hundred-footer; the scientists got the Environmental Management Program and recognition of the Upper Mississippi River as a nationally significant ecosystem. Congress included both and more when it passed the Water Resources Development Act of 1986.

With passage of the 1986 WRDA, Congress ordered the Corps of Engineers to produce a habitat-mitigation plan in the feasibility study for each water resource project—be it a dam, a canal, a levee, or a navigation or flood-control proposal—or prove that the project would have "no adverse effect" on habitat. In addition, Congress directed that habitat-mitigation costs be included in project costs. Once Congress approved a project, it ordered that construction and habitat mitigation happen simultaneously. The act provided that the federal government finance fish- and wildlife-enhancement costs when benefits had a national character. Where the benefits were not entirely national, Congress required that nonfederal interests contribute 50 percent of the costs for the feasibility study for any water project and 25 percent for the rehabilitation of any project and its operation and maintenance.

Environmentalists hoped that the cost-sharing requirements for nonfederal projects would mitigate the public's desire for wetland-destroying pork-barrel water projects. What it did was narrow the Corps' focus on any given water project to the desires of its local sponsors. Hence, if a local group wanted a section of a stream dredged and channelized for flood control, the Corps as well as the local sponsors and their congressional supporters too often failed to consider the basinwide consequences of such a project—for instance, that it might cause headward erosion upstream and siltation downstream or might harm fish and wildlife. Hence, Corps project proposals often ran afoul of the guidelines laid down by the EPA and the U.S. Fish and Wildlife Service for water projects.

In Section 1135 of the 1986 act, Congress also required the Corps to review existing water-resource projects for any modifications needed to improve the surrounding environment. For the first time Congress put the environmental benefits of a project, including measures for fish and wildlife enhancement, on an equal footing with the economic benefits of that project. Equally important, Congress set up a two-year demonstration program for modifications to existing projects. In addition Congress established an Office of Environmental Policy under the chief of engineers. The new office would be responsible for environmental policy related to the water-resources programs of the Corps of Engineers.

To balance the increasing demands of commercial navigation with environmental and recreational needs, Congress attached Section 1103, the Upper Mississippi River Management Act, to the 1986 Water Resources Development Act. The act recognized that the Upper River is both a valuable commercial navigation system and a nationally significant ecosystem that should be managed in light of the diversity of opportunities the river offers. Under this section the Departments of Natural Resources of the five states that border the Upper Mississippi, the U.S. Fish and Wildlife Service, and the U.S. Army Corps of Engineers initiated the Upper Mississippi River System Environmental Management Program, a demonstration program of habitat restoration and enhancement projects along the Upper Mississippi River, as well as the Minnesota, St. Croix, Black, Illinois, and Kaskaskia Rivers.

Finally, Congress set up a Long Term Resource Monitoring Program on the Upper Mississippi. The U.S. Geological Survey (USGS) administered the program, which provided decisionmakers with the information they needed to balance the Upper Mississippi's needs as an ecosystem with its needs as a navigation system. Within the USGS, the Upper Midwest Environmental Sciences Center and six field stations, operated by the states along the river, collected data on land cover and land use, water levels and water quality, sedimentation, fish, vegetation, and invertebrates and issued an annual report on the state of the river.

In the 1990 WRDA, Congress put the 1986 demonstration program on a continuing basis, made it apply to water projects constructed before 1986, and appropriated $15,000,000 for the work. That year Congress also set environmental protection as one of the primary missions of the Corps of Engineers in the planning, designing, construction, operation, and maintenance of water-resource projects. As a part of the Corps' water-resource program, Congress set an interim goal of "no net loss" of the nation's remaining wetland base, as defined by acreage and function, and directed the secretary of the army to use all appropriate authorities to restore and create wetlands in order to meet these goals. Congress also included the Coastal Wetlands Planning, Protection and Restoration Act, known as the Breaux Act, within the 1990 WRDA to fund plans for the restoration of deteriorating marshlands along the Gulf of Mexico and other coastal areas.

To standardize the identification and delineation of wetlands, the Corps wrote a wetlands-delineation manual in 1987. Two years later the agency collaborated with the EPA, the U.S. Fish and Wildlife Service, and the Soil Conservation Service to revise and strengthen the identification and delineation of wetlands in an interagency manual, only to have it rejected by those who feared it would lead to excessive regulation of lands that may or may not be wetlands. The Corps and the other agencies tried again in 1991, only to come up with a manual that was too weak in defining wetlands. Hence, the Corps, the EPA, and Fish and Wildlife continued to use the 1987 Corps manual.

Finally, in February 1997, Congress passed its Energy and Water Development Appropriations Act and directed the Corps of Engineers to reorganize and reduce the number of its divisions. In doing so the Corps placed responsibility for the entire length of the Mississippi in the hands of the new Mississippi Valley Division, based in Vicksburg. Each of the districts—the St. Paul, the Rock Island, the St. Louis, the Memphis, the Vicksburg, and the New Orleans—would report to the commander of the new division, who would also serve as the president of the Mississippi River Commission. The move, in essence, put the whole of the river under the jurisdiction of the commission, thus assuring continuation of the struggle between the U.S. Army Corps of Engineers and environmentalists and river conservationists into the twenty-first century. Environmentalists and river conservationists feared that the commission would fixate on its traditional constituents (the navigation industry, real estate developers, and farmers) and ignore ecosystem restoration.

Restoration Efforts on the Upper Mississippi

As the twentieth century drew to a close, Americans recognized that we could not stop the degradation of landscapes by simply preserving selected tracts of wetlands, bottomland forests, grasslands, and other ecosystems by "walling them off" in natural wildlife areas. We would have to restore landscapes while allowing people restricted use of wildlife areas in the form of hunting, fishing, hiking, birding, photography, and other nondestructive uses. We also realized that in draining the wetlands, logging the forests, and plowing up the grasslands, we had destroyed very natural systems we would have to engage in order to successfully restore wetlands, forests, and grasslands. In short, we had to learn how the landscapes we had destroyed worked, how to mimic the way they had functioned, and then how to restore and manage the new landscapes.

Before European settlement, the Mississippi landscape was an integrated system of river and wetlands that had taken many thousands of years to create. Three factors influence how wetlands work: their positions in the landscape, or their geomorphic setting; their water sources, or hydrology; and the flow and fluctuation of water through them, or their hydrodynamics or hydraulics. Alter any one of these functions, and the creation of new wetlands is difficult. However, some wetlands can be restored. To that end the Corps of Engineers developed new tools and applied them to small-scale restoration projects on the Upper Mississippi.

By the time Congress passed the 1986 WRDA, requiring that the Corps of Engineers balance habitat needs with navigation needs on the Mississippi, the river and its basin had ceased to be an integrated system of river and wetlands. The dams, the levees, and the dikes that drastically altered the landscape and dependent habitat were not going away. The only way to restore habitat was to try to mimic those natural processes that had been destroyed by the dikes, the dams, and the levees.

At the beginning of the twenty-first century, sediment, too much or too little, plagued the Mississippi from St. Paul to the Gulf of Mexico. Too much sediment, trapped behind the channel dams, plagued the Upper Mississippi between St. Paul, Minnesota, and Alton, Illinois, where the backwaters were filling with sediment and turning to land. Too much sediment, diverted from the main channel by wing dams and dikes, plagued the whole river between St. Paul and the Gulf of Mexico, where side channels were filling up and turning to land. Too much sediment, hemmed between levees and deposited on the riverbed, plagued the Lower Mississippi between Cairo, Illinois, and the Gulf of Mexico, where sediment that did remain in the water column was deposited in deep water near the continental shelf. Hence, too little sediment plagued the Delta, where the delta front subsided for want of new deposits.

The 1986 Upper Mississippi River Management Act—specifically, the Section 1135 demonstration program—allowed Departments of Natural Resources of the states bordering the Upper River to look at and address the problems that had been plaguing the river since the completion of the channel dams and the nine-foot channel in the 1930s. The agencies initiated dozens of projects to restore fish and wildlife habitat in the Upper Mississippi over the next fifteen years. The state agencies paid half the cost of developing each project and a quarter of the cost of implementing it. The Corps of Engineers paid the rest. Upon completion each project was handed over to either the state agency that had proposed the project or the U.S. Fish and Wildlife Service for maintenance.

Of all the problems that plagued the Upper Mississippi, the two that caused the most damage were the flooded conditions of the lower half of each of the navigation pools and the accumulation of sediment. The twenty-six navigation pools between St. Paul and Alton were filling up with sediment washed down from agricultural, residential, commercial, and highway development in the uplands. The Corps of Engineers had to dredge constantly to maintain the nine-foot channel. Dredge materials dumped on islands eroded back into the river. Tows dragged plumes of resuspended sediment behind them. As the wakes of large tows eroded islands lining the main channel, silt and sand washed into backwater sloughs. As the backchannels filled with sediment, wind fetch picked up in shallow waters, causing wave action, which stirred up loose sediment. Loose sediment made it impossible for aquatic plants to take root, causing low-oxygen conditions. Fish and turtles lost spawning grounds in which to breed and feed. As wetlands turned to land, waterfowl and furbearers also lost places to breed and feed.

The tools the Corps of Engineers and the natural resource agencies developed to solve sedimentation problems—dikes, dams, culverts, revetments, levees, and dredging—looked eerily similar to those that had caused them. In Pool 5, the agencies built culverts to direct the flow of water into the backwaters of Island 42, to decrease the amount of silt flowing in and increase the amount of dissolved oxygen. In Pools 5 through 10, they used rockfill—revetments—to stabilize banks in backwaters. In Pools 8 and 11, they constructed islands with dredge spoils and planted windbreaks to reduce turbidity in the water and create habitat for aquatic plants and animals. At Lansing Big Lake in Pool 9 and at Spring Lake in Pool 13, they constructed dikes and levees to keep silt-laden water out of prime backwaters and to control water levels so that aquatic vegetation could take root. At Ambrough Slough in Pool 10, they dredged backwaters and side channels to create deep-water habitat for fish. At Cuivre Slough in Pool 26, they modified the wing dams and closing dams that maintained the navigation channel to allow water to flow into side channels and set hardpoints, short rock-filled structures like wing dams, to scour deep-water habitat for fishes.

Throughout the navigation system, the steady water level maintained by the Corps of Engineers in the navigation pools discouraged the growth of wetland plants in places where, during normal summer low flows, vegetation would take root on exposed mud flats in backwater sloughs, providing food for fish and wildlife. In the late 1990s, the St. Paul District of the Corps experimented with temporary drawdowns, lowering the water level at selected sites along the Upper Mississippi. The district chose two sites, both small ponds along the bank of the river in the midsections of Pools 5 and 9. The engineers employed the same methods used by duck-hunting clubs along the river: they built temporary water-control structures at the outlets of Lizzy Pauls Pond, a fifty-two-acre lake in Pool 5, and Peck Lake, a fifteen-acre lake in Pool 9, and pumped out the water to dry out and consolidate bottom sediments. Dormant seeds responded; over two summers a healthy crop of arrowhead established itself at Peck Lake.

Just as the Environmental Management Program was getting started on the Upper Mississippi, the Flood of 1993 ripped across its floodplain and caused us to look, briefly, at how we manage its basin—its uplands and its bottomlands.

The Flood of 1993—Lessons Not Learned

Throughout the spring and summer of 1993, flooding along the Upper Mississippi destroyed many of the dikes, dams, and revetments that governed restoration projects. It devastated bottomland forests, cleared the floodplain of vegetation, eroded islands, and buried mussels and emergent and submergent plants under as much as two feet of sand. Those fish that find their food by sight suffered in the turbid water. Those mammals that migrated to higher ground along adjacent roads and railroad tracks became roadkill.

It was a familiar story: heavy snowmelt in the Rockies filled the western rivers in the Upper Mississippi Basin. Above-normal rain in the second quarter of 1993 saturated the soils and filled the reservoirs on the tributaries to the Missouri and Mississippi. By early June the upper basin was full. Then the real rains came.

A storm system stalled over the Midwest. The jet stream carries weather across the Midwest from west to east. Normally it slips north in the summer, but in 1993 it looped south over the western United States and turned to the northeast over the Midwest. High pressure in the southeast blocked storms moving east. Cold, dry Canadian air filled the trough over the western states. Moisture, drifting up from the Gulf, hit the cool northern air, and it rained and rained all summer long. On June 17 and 18, two to seven inches fell in southern Minnesota, northern Iowa, and southwestern Wisconsin; on July 4 and 5, two to four inches fell across Iowa; on July 8 and 9, two to eight inches fell on central Iowa; on July 15 and 16, four to seven inches fell across North Dakota and Minnesota, and seven and a half inches fell in Callaway, Missouri, halfway between St. Louis and Kansas City, near the Missouri River; on July 22 through July 24, two to thirteen inches fell in parts of Nebraska, Kansas, Missouri, Iowa, and Illinois. The total was 200 to 400 percent more rain than normal. All that rain had no place to go.

On June 23 the Corps had closed the St. Louis Port District. The Mississippi reached flood stage—thirty feet—at St. Louis three days later. On June 29 the Corps closed the Mississippi from Lock and Dam 24 at Clarksville, Missouri, clear to Minneapolis, leaving tows stranded on the flooded river. The rains in June flooded the Minnesota and Mississippi Rivers in Minnesota, and the Chippewa and the Black in Wisconsin, and pushed the flood stage at St. Louis to forty-three feet by July 12, equaling the 1973 flood. July's rains in Iowa rolled down the Skunk, the Iowa, and the Des Moines to the Mississippi, breached levees north of St. Louis, crested at St. Louis on July 20, and destroyed levees south of St. Louis over the next five days. The rains in the Great Plains brought record flooding to the Missouri from the James River in North and South Dakota, the Big Sioux in South Dakota, the Little Sioux in Iowa, the Platte in Nebraska, and the Kansas River in Kansas. The flood along the Missouri crested at 48.9 feet at Kansas City on July 27 and split the State of Missouri in two. When it spilled into the Mississippi, the flood crested at 49.47 feet at St. Louis on August 1. Levee breaks along the American Bottom, the great floodplain south of St. Louis, relieved pressure on the city, prevented the crest from going still higher, but angered farmers in Monroe County, Illinois, who saw their fields inundated.

All that rain falling on the plains and the prairie was stalled by high pressure in the southeast, and never reached the Ohio valley, which suffered through a drought in 1993. Hence, the Ohio River ran at low levels, and the Lower Mississippi absorbed its upper basin flood handily. However, the Flood of 1993 carried huge loads of agricultural runoff—nutrients in the form of phosphorous and nitrogen—to the Gulf of Mexico. Algae bloomed, died, and decayed along the Louisiana coast, soaking up the oxygen, exacerbating the low-oxygen Dead Zone in the Gulf.

Throughout the summer of 1993, it seemed as though the system of flood control on the Mississippi and Missouri Rivers was collapsing, day by day, image by image on the nation's television screens. Out of 1,576 levees—a haphazard collection of federal and local levees—in the Upper Mississippi Basin, 68.7 percent were damaged or destroyed by the flood. Of the fifteen heavy-duty federal levees constructed and maintained by the Corps, only 3 were breached; of the 214 constructed to the Corps specifications but maintained by local levee districts, 36 were damaged; of the 1,347 constructed and maintained by local levee districts, 1,082 were overtopped as the river reclaimed its floodplain. These last were agricultural levees that protected farmlands and were never intended to hold back floods like those of 1993. Tell that to the farmers, who suffered $8.454 billion losses in crop and livestock production in 1993. Ripple that through the midwestern economy by a multiple of 2.2, and the total agricultural loss came to $17.6 billion.

Evidence of damage to the floodplain forest became apparent in the summer of 1994 when trees, exposed to standing water for much of the summer of 1993, either failed to leaf out or dropped leaves after they did. While there was damage to the forest in pools north of Pool 17, the extreme damage became evident in 17, and progressed south to the mouth of the Ohio, where flood levels had been higher and the duration longer. Pool 4 lost only 1.1 percent of its canopy trees, while Pool 17 lost 18.1 percent, Pool 26, 37.2 percent, and Cuivre Island in Pool 26, 60 percent of its forest. The saplings, the future canopy trees, were almost wiped out with a loss of 70 to 80 percent. The spring of 1994 produced an abundance of first-year seedings, mostly silver maple and box elder. Patches of black willow, eastern cottonwood, and sycamore sprouted on mud flats where the flood had killed all vegetation and deposited new sediment.

The flood brought into focus many of the changes we have made in the Upper Mississippi Basin since the Louisiana Purchase. The Administration Floodplain Management Task Force, headed by the director of the White House Office of Environmental Policy, the associate director of the Office of Management and Budget, and the assistant secretary of agriculture for natural resources, directed the formation of the Interagency Floodplain Management Review Committee, made up of representatives of many federal, state, local, and tribal agencies, to evaluate the state of flood control and floodplain management in the Upper Mississippi Basin. The committee produced a clearheaded analysis of what did and did not cause the flood: all that rain caused the flood, fifty-four inches between September 1992 and August 1993 in Iowa alone. The rain saturated the soil and filled the reservoirs, both natural and otherwise. And it rained everywhere. Clouds hung over the landscape from November 1992 through August 1993, slowing the evaporation of all that water.

Navigation dams, for all the problems they have brought to the Upper Mississippi, did not cause the flood, though they did create slight increases in flood heights locally. Levees did not cause the flood, although levees, by constricting the floodplain, forced higher and higher flood levels. Indeed, destroy all the levees—other than those protecting the city—in the St. Louis region, and the peak crest at St. Louis would have been reduced by only 2.5 feet. When the river broke through two levees on the American Bottom, south of St. Louis, it reduced the peak stage at the city by 1.6 feet.

Ruptured levees did damage farmland. Water bursting through a levee can scour a "blew hole" twenty-five to fifty feet deep and hundreds of yards long and spread sand several yards deep across the landscape. Locate a levee in the wrong place—say, across the site of an old river channel or a natural cutoff—and damage from a rupture multiplies.

In groping for ways to lessen the destructiveness of floods in the Upper Mississippi Basin, the committee reviewed the changes we have made to the basin in the last two hundred years. The clearing of the floodplain for agriculture, the logging of the uplands, and draining of the wet prairies and the floodplain, the filling of prairie potholes, the filling of wetlands for subdivisions, strip malls, and parking lots: all conspired to restrict the river's storage capacity and send more water and sediment to the river.

Since the 1930s we have reduced the risk of living in floodplains—potential storage areas—with protection levees, federally subsidized insurance programs, and federal disaster loans and payments. Protection levees made the folks who lived, worked, and farmed behind them feel safe, safe enough to increase development of floodplains. Federally subsidized crop insurance protected farmers against losses from floods. Federally subsidized flood insurance provided cheap protection against losses in communities that adopted floodplain zoning, though not all participating communities were vigilant in their zoning regulations. Failing that, once governors and presidents declared an inundated floodplain a "disaster area," federal disaster loans and payments covered losses from flooding, obviating the need for flood or crop insurance. Build a hundred-year levee, design it to take care of a project flood—one that might occur once in a hundred years by the Corps of Engineers' definition—and flood insurance was no longer required for development, which could proceed as though the floodplain were on the uplands.

By 1993 building in a floodplain was a "no-lose" proposition. There were people living in floodplains in every state along the Mississippi, save Wisconsin, who had collected disaster and insurance payments every time the river flooded. Louisiana topped the list; Missouri came in fourth nationally. In St. Charles County, Missouri, the National Wildlife Federation identified 1,382 properties—the most in the country—that experienced repeated losses at a total cost to the taxpayer of $58,017,815.

The staggering cost of the 1993 flood to the taxpayer in disaster and crop-insurance payments to farmers and flood-insurance payments to homeowners in flood-prone regions caused governments at all levels—federal, state, and local—to rethink flood protection along the Mississippi and the Missouri Rivers. The interagency committee found the system of mapping floodplains for a project flood, the so-called hundred-year flood on which zoning regulations were based, underfunded and inaccurate. Local communities wrote zoning regulations for floodplains, sometimes according to the rules of the National Flood Insurance Program, sometimes not. And there was only a five-day waiting period before insurance became active.

The committee made its recommendations: Move people out of the floodplain. Buy their land at preflood, market value, and turn it into parks and wetlands. Put the risk back into living and farming in the floodplain, or at least make the cost commensurate with the risk. Require folks who stay in the floodplain to buy insurance to meet the cost of flood-related damage before the flood. Require a fifteen-day waiting period before the insurance kicks in. Require farmers to buy crop insurance. Persuade Congress to stop authorizing disaster loans and payments after floods to those who should have carried flood and crop insurance but did not.

While the committee noted that few of its recommendations would have prevented the devastation of 1993, they believed that most would be a big help in ameliorating the damage from smaller floods. Conservation tillage, terraces, crop rotations, field borders, sediment and debris basins, strip-cropping, and permanent vegetation would all help hold rain where it falls on upland agricultural lands, thus reducing soil erosion and runoff. These practices would have the added advantage of reducing the amount of nitrogen discharged into the Gulf of Mexico, thus reducing the size of the Dead Zone, which doubled as the 1993 flood poured into the Gulf.

Upland wetlands—particularly the prairie potholes in the wet prairies of north-central Iowa, east-central Illinois, Minnesota, eastern South Dakota, and North Dakota—hold rain where it falls, as do small headwater reservoirs along the tributaries. Potholes, with their ill-defined drainage network from pothole to pothole, retain more surface runoff in small, twenty-five-year floods than do floodplain wetlands with their open drainage network along streams. Restoration of upland wetlands would function much the same as small upland reservoirs. Large reservoirs, like those on the Missouri River and the Coralville Reservoir on the Iowa River, are effective in reducing downstream flooding in large floods like that of 1993. Without them the peak crest at St. Louis would have been five feet higher.

The interagency committee accepted levees as a legitimate form of flood control and outlined its vision for the use of structural means of flood control such as levees and reservoirs: Build high levees around cities and towns. Build upland reservoirs to store floodwater until the main stem river can handle it. Restore upland and floodplain wetlands. Set low agricultural levees back from the river to broaden the area of floodplain available for storage. Set gates in agricultural levees across sloughs to keep them wet throughout the year and maintain fish and wildlife habitat. Turn a portion of the floodplain outside the agricultural levees into wildlife refuges. Elevate major highways and railroads that run across floodplains. Split the cost of levees on main stem rivers among the state and federal governments and local levee districts. Finally, the committee recommended using nonstructural means of flood control wherever possible. Again, move people out, and turn the floodplain over to parks and wetlands.

Lastly, the interagency committee found that no single government entity—federal, state, local, or tribal—was in charge of the whole Upper Mississippi watershed, including the tributaries, the main stems of the Mississippi and Missouri, the floodplains, and runoff from the logged, tiled, and drained uplands. It found several agencies with complementary goals for the river but no coordination between them. It found separate government programs for land use, pollution, and wetlands but no effort to integrate the programs. It found no basinwide flood-control strategy, nor any basinwide ecosystem-management strategy. The Corps of Engineers took care of navigation and some levees; local districts took care of the rest of the levees. The U.S. Fish and Wildlife Service took care of the Upper Mississippi Fish and Wildlife Refuge and the Mark Twain National Wildlife Refuge Complex; state governments took care their wildlife refuges, mostly in the floodplain; local levee and drainage districts or local communities took care of the rest of the floodplain. The Environmental Protection Agency took care of pollution in the river. The Soil Conservation Service, now called the Natural Resources Conservation Service, took care of runoff from the uplands, and so on. It found numerous agencies working on mitigation—buyouts—but no coordination between them. Flooded-out folks who wanted to be bought out couldn't figure which government agency—federal, state, or local—was doing the buying. In short, no one talked to anyone else.

The interagency committee found numerous activities under way on the river: the Upper Mississippi–Illinois Waterway Navigation Study, the Upper Mississippi River Basin Floodplain Management Assessment, the Upper Mississippi River Environmental Management Program, and numerous Corps of Engineers studies of individual levee projects, but no coordination among the agencies conducting the studies. It found nothing like the Mississippi River and Tributaries Project that had been guiding flood control in the Lower Mississippi since the Flood of 1927. It found a haphazard collection of levees, similar to those that had lined the Lower Mississippi on the eve of the Flood of 1927. It found that local districts built levees to varying heights and standards. It found that both the Corps and local districts had built levees with little attention to river hydraulics or the riparian environment in front of or behind the levees—what the committee called the river's ecosystem.

The interagency committee proposed an institutional framework to coordinate all these activities. Under the aegis of the White House, federal agencies—the U.S. Fish and Wildlife Service (within the Department of the Interior), the Federal Emergency Management Agency, the Soil Conservation Service and the Forest Service (within the Department of Agriculture), the Environmental Protection Agency, and the Corps of Engineers under the Department of the Army—and a revived Water Resources Council (set aside by deregulation in the 1980s) would coordinate basinwide projects and planning and provide technical expertise. A revived Upper Mississippi Basin Commission and a revived Missouri River Basin Commission (also set aside by deregulation in the 1980s) with federal, state, local, and tribal membership would set goals for the basin and focus on water resources in the basin. The Mississippi River Commission—which had been established in 1879 to govern the whole river but had focused solely on the Lower River and the Mississippi River and Tributaries Project since the Flood of 1927—would expand its duties to oversee the Upper Mississippi and the Missouri Rivers. It would also develop an Upper Mississippi River and Tributaries project with input from an advisory board that included representatives from the above agencies and state and local governments.

The goal of these coordinated efforts was to give those agencies concerned with ecosystem management on the Upper Mississippi an equal voice with those in charge of flood control and navigation. Environmentalists' and river conservationists' major concern with the proposed framework was that the Mississippi River Commission—with its domination by the Corps of Engineers and its historical concentration on navigation, levees, and agriculture at the expense of ecosystems and multiple-use interests—would be put in charge of the whole river. In 1997, it was.

The committee issued its report, *Sharing the Challenge: Floodplain Management into the Twenty-first Century,* in June 1994. Developers and property-rights groups objected to proposals that local governments adopt stricter zoning and building codes in floodplains. The Corps of Engineers objected to the suggestion that it give greater weight to the environmental impact of dams and levees on the river as a whole. Other federal agencies objected to the revival of the Water Resources Council to coordinate basinwide projects.

In January 1994 river conservationists complained that the interagency report had disappeared into a "black hole." Senator Christopher "Kit" Bond (R-Missouri), chair of the Environment and Public Works Committee, who objected to efforts to prevent the Corps of Engineers from rebuilding some of the destroyed levees, blocked legislation that would have made the recommendations in *Sharing the Challenge* law and, with it, the opportunity to develop a national flood-control policy. As a result, many of the levees along the Mississippi and Missouri in the St. Louis region were rebuilt and new levees added within the next dozen years, handing over 18,000 acres to actual or proposed development on floodplains protected by one hundred- to five hundred-year levees.

On the floodplain peninsula between the Mississippi and Missouri, the two rivers flow side by side for ten miles, the Missouri at a higher elevation than the Mississippi. In the Floods of 1973, 1986, and 1993, the Missouri broke through its artificial levee and took a hike across the peninsula to the Mississippi. In 1993 the peninsula did store 260 billion gallons of water directly upstream from St. Louis, where the flood came within eighteen inches of topping the city's floodwalls. *Sharing the Challenge* recommended leaving places like this peninsula as flood-storage areas, places where agriculture and wildlife could flourish.

The Great Rivers Habitat Alliance calls this peninsula the Confluence Floodway, and many groups want to get their hands on it. Developers looked at that flat, open space and saw houses, office buildings, and factories. The developers of New Town safely located their houses in the five hundred-year floodplain, wrapped a levee around it, and sold houses to buyers who did not have to buy flood insurance. The City of St. Peters built a $22.5 million four-mile-long levee and wanted to put an office/industrial park behind it, if it could persuade FEMA to remove its 1,600 acres from the floodway insurance maps. If it couldn't, the project was toast. St. Charles County wanted to expand its Smartt Airport. Four huge resting lakes, managed for ducks, surround it. Ducks and airplanes don't mix. The FAA recommends that sites of runways for piston-powered planes be at least five thousand feet from wetlands or standing water, ten thousand feet for turbine-powered planes, and five miles for approach or departure airspace.

Adolphus A. Busch IV, a member of the family that brewed Budweiser and a landowner on the Confluence Floodway, and others (American Rivers, The Mule Deer Foundation, Missouri Coalition for the Environment, Missouri Department of Conservation, National Rifle Association, Missouri Waterfowl Association, Conservation Federation of Missouri, Missouri Stream Team, Rocky Mountain Elk Foundation, Delta Waterfowl, Missouri Department of Natural Resources, National Wild Turkey Federation, Quail Forever, U.S. Fish and Wildlife Service, Ducks Unlimited) saw the need to preserve the floodway for agriculture and wildlife. These are the people who formed the Great River Habitat Alliance in June 2000 to protect up to half of the 100,000-acre natural floodplain between the Missouri and Mississippi with conservation easements and outright purchase from people willing to sell their land; better yet, people could donate it. It was a loose partnership of public agencies and private organizations that hoped to create its own patchwork quilt of intensely managed private and public tracts, farms, and conservation easements. FEMA approved the St. Peters levee on June 26, 2008, and the Great Rivers Habitat Alliance sued to have the ruling reversed on December 29, 2008.

Some things did change: James Lee Witt, director of the Federal Emergency Management Agency, educated Americans on the hazards of flooding and encouraged those who lived in flood-prone regions to buy insurance. State and local governments did review their flood-management policies and write tighter controls. Federal and state governments did move over twelve thousand families out of the Midwest floodplains and acquire interest in over 250,000 acres of flood-prone land. Congress did reform flood-insurance law and require lenders to urge at-risk homeowners to buy flood insurance and buy it at least thirty days before the flood as opposed to five. Congress did allow homeowners to use their flood-insurance payments to elevate their houses above a one hundred-year flood or move out of the floodplain altogether. Congress did make similar requirements for crop insurance.

In its 1995 report on the flood, the Corps of Engineers acknowledged the risks of occupying floodplains. The agency allowed that structural flood-control measures had their limitations and that floodplains were best managed with a combination of structural and nonstructural controls. With the 1996 Water Resources Development Act, Congress added floodplain management to the Corps of Engineers' duties, and authorized the engineers to use nonstructural as well as structural means of flood control.

The flood opened new opportunities for fish and wildlife in the navigation pools directly north of Alton, Illinois, and in the side channels of the open river south of St. Louis. In the following years, farmers, who had drained and cultivated the most flood-prone land immediately adjacent to the river, became willing sellers. They offered the U.S. Fish and Wildlife Service and the Corps of Engineers opportunities to purchase their lands and reconnect them to the rivers. Congress provided the means under Public Law 103–75, passed on August 12, 1993, to help farmers whose lands were damaged by the flood. The law authorized the U.S. Fish and Wildlife Service to expand the Mark Twain National Wildlife Refuge Complex with the purchase of up to 11,400 acres. Fish and Wildlife added the Harlow, Meissner, and Wilkinson Island Divisions to the refuge.

Finally, Congress ordered the Corps of Engineers to prepare a comprehensive plan for the Upper Mississippi River in the Water Resources Development Act of 1999. The St. Louis District published the draft of the plan in 2006, which addressed water and land resources in the "interest of systemic flood reduction." The plan did not cover the whole of the Upper Mississippi watershed and limited its scope to the floodplains of the Mississippi and Illinois Rivers. It emphasized flood control in concert with environmental sustainability, restoration, and habitat management; navigation and its infrastructure; sediment and nutrient reduction; and recreational opportunities.

Middle Mississippi Restoration

Moist-Soil Management and Side-Channel Restoration in the St. Louis District

> Catahoola Lake lies west of this place & communicates with the Red river during the time of the great annual inundation; but all other parts of its superficies during the dry season from July to November & often latter, are completely drained & become clothed in the most luxuriant herbage: the bid of the Lake then becomes the residence of immense herds of Deer, of Turkeys, Geese, Ducks, Cranes &c&cc feeding on the grass and grain.
>
> —William Dunbar, 1804

William Dunbar documented at the beginning of the nineteenth century what we in the twenty-first call moist-soil management at Catahoula Lake in Louisiana. During the dry season, Catahoula Lake went dry, the mudflats consolidated, and the grasses took root, creating food for wildlife in the fall and winter.

The 1993 flood did not change the fact that the Environmental Management Program was a separate authorization from navigation. Nor did it change the fact that the Corps' primary focus on the Upper Mississippi was navigation. In 2002, when the St. Paul engineers published their draft of plans for the pools in their district, they considered the possibility of instituting summer drawdowns in every pool, an action that could affect navigation. The St. Louis District already had begun such a program, with great success.

In the summer of 1994, Ken Dalrymple, a biologist with the Missouri Department of Conservation, visited David Busse, the lock master at Lock and Dam 26 at Alton, Illinois. He had a proposal: draw down Pool 26 and let the grasses grow. Busse did just that and initiated the St. Louis District's ambitious drawdown program. Every May Day the lock masters dropped the water levels of Pools 26, 25, and 24 a mere six inches for thirty days, allowing islands directly north of each dam to dry out and seeds on them to germinate. After thirty days they raised the levels slowly, slowly enough for plants—smartweed, wild millet, chufa, yellow foxtail, pigweed, rice cutgrass, and panicum—to keep their growing tips above water. Over the next several years, the Corps of Engineers and the biologists with the Missouri Department of Conservation lowered the water levels in the three pools and produced over two thousand acres of new moist vegetation—food and protective covering for ducks and filters for nitrogen flowing off corn and soybean fields. American Rivers, the national river conservation organization, recognized the success of the program and gave the St. Louis District an award.

The concept of managing water levels for moist plant production had been around since the 1940s when Frank Bellrose, a research biologist with Illinois Natural History Survey with a passion for wood ducks, observed that plants germinated on exposed mudflats during summer lows and that ducks flocked to these sites during their fall migration. He noted that moist soils are those that are too wet for the consistent production of row crops and too dry for the growth of submergent and emergent aquatic plants. The U.S. Fish and Wildlife Service developed the techniques for designing and constructing moist-soil impoundments at the Mingo National Wildlife Refuge in the Western Lowlands of southeastern Missouri between 1968 and 1982.

In 1999 the Corps of Engineers' Ecosystem Management and Restoration Research Program published its technical report on moist-soil impoundments that described the design and construction of such impoundments and their management. The report outlined ways to enhance the production of naturally occurring wetland plants by choosing the location of impoundments carefully, with particular attention to topography, soils, and water sources. The report detailed methods of mimicking the natural hydrology of wetlands through the control of water in and out of leveed impoundments and listed the succession of plants most likely to attract wildlife. Finally, the report outlined the management of leveed impoundments, including the timing and duration of drawdowns and flooding, the ways to control undesirable vegetation and to develop seed banks.

South of Lock and Dam 26 at Alton, Illinois, the Mississippi runs unencumbered by dams, but harnessed between tall federal levees, divorced from its floodplain, and armored against bank erosion, its scouring power directed to its navigation channel by very tall wing dams. South to the Ohio River we called it the Middle Mississippi.

The wing dams, which were so successful in maintaining a viable navigation channel, directed the river's sediment to open side channels, filling them, welding their islands to the mainland. At the end of the twentieth century only twenty-three side channels remained on the Middle Mississippi, kept free of sediment by closing dams at their heads. Most lost bathymetric (depth) diversity; they tended to be shallow with few deep scour holes. Some dried out when the river ran low. Fish lost critical habitat for breeding, feeding, and resting.

The Flood of 1993 made acute the need to restore habitat for fish and wildlife to side channels and their adjacent lands. In 1994 engineers from the Applied Engineering Center of the St. Louis District of the Corps of Engineers, who understood the physics of moving water and sediment, and biologists with the U.S. Fish and Wildlife Service, the Illinois Department of Natural Resources, and the Missouri Department of Conservation, who understood the needs of fish living in the side channels, collaborated in developing new tools to save the remaining side channels for fish habitat.

Since the Flood of 1927 the Corps had used large-scale hydraulic models to test changes they planned in the river. In 1929 Gen. Harley B. Ferguson built a very large model of the Lower River to test Eads's theory that cutoffs would speed floods downstream. But large models like the one at Vicksburg were expensive to build. The collaborators devised a tabletop model on which they could test ways to move water and sediment around and create habitat for fish in the remaining Middle River side channels. The small scale allowed them to model each side channel individually. They could try out various schemes: modify existing river wing dams, notch or remove closing dams across the heads of side channels, install chevron dikes or traditional dikes or hard points in them, or dredge excess sediment from them.

Notches in closing dams allowed water to flow through and scour sediment from side channels. Removing them altogether was better. Hard points, mini–wing dams constructed of rock or wood and set in side channels, forced water to scour side channels without a significant buildup of sediment between points. At the same time hard points scoured deep holes, habitat for fish, particularly catfish, under the points. Small chevron dikes, "C"-shaped dikes, allowed water to flow around them and open up side channels, while producing scour holes on the insides of the dikes for fish habitat. Once the collaborators understood the dynamics of creating habitat in each channel, it was an easy step to move on to constructing the improvements.

At the end of the 1990s the collaborators went on to develop the Mississippi River Side Channel Rehabilitation and Conservation Project with the aim of restoring the twenty-three remaining side channels on the Middle River and ten of those that had closed completely. They carried their plan beyond restoring the channels themselves to acquiring land adjacent to the channels. Given the additional land they could reforest the banks of the channels, some of which were farmed clear up to their edges; reestablish the ridge and swale bottomland topography, where water flowing through the channels eroded or deposited sediment on the banks; regain cut bank habitat, places where fish could rest and nest; and provide the public with access to the side channels for recreation and education. They noted that in some cases it would make more sense for private individuals, industry, or organizations such as the Nature Conservancy and the American Land Conservancy to acquire the lands bordering the channels.

In 2000 the U.S. Fish and Wildlife Service established the Middle Mississippi National Wildlife Refuge, within the Mark Twain Complex, between St. Louis and Cairo, to manage lands purchased in the wake of the 1993 flood and those lands the service hoped to bring into the refuge in a region where few lands were publicly owned.

In 1997 the Fish and Wildlife Service gave the Mark Twain Complex approval to study the possibility of expanding the refuge by 60,000 acres. Resource managers put together a wish list of nearly 56,000 acres and ranked them in four tiers: 27,659 acres in the top tier, 14,084 in the second tier, 8,537 in the third, and 5,393 in the fourth. The service assigned 14,758 acres in the top tier to the Middle Mississippi Refuge, where most of the land was in private hands. By 2005 the service had purchased 4,300 acres on four islands: Harlow, Wilkinson, Meissner, and Beaver. The service planned to reconnect the islands to the river, and manage them as a forest corridor for nesting and migrating birds and as an aquatic habitat for big river fish.

From 1993 to 2008 the American Land Conservancy (ALC) worked to identify and retire as much flood-prone farmland in the batture lands, outside the levees, of the Middle Mississippi as it could purchase and then restore wetlands on islands, open up side channels to fish, and reforest floodplains. Harriet Burgess and Martin Litton founded the ALC in 1990 with an interest in taking on small, complex projects that other conservation organizations avoided. The ALC's Middle Mississippi venture was just such a project.

In July 2002 all the people—state, federal, and not-for-profit agencies—with a stake in restoration, conservation, navigation, and flood control on the main stem of the Middle River joined to form the Middle Mississippi River Partnership. In September 2005 the partnership issued its plan for developing a "network of diverse and sustainable natural resources on public and private lands in the Middle Mississippi River corridor between the Missouri and Ohio Rivers that adequately supports fish and wildlife habitat and provides conservation benefits consistent with a variety of other uses." The collaborators listed the resources they would address: forests, wetlands, wildlife habitat, aquatic habitat, nonnative invasive species, water quality, recreational opportunities, floodplain management, and the importance of sustainable natural resources to the economic viability of the region. The group outlined strategies that would allow individual participants to work in unison to achieve the goals of the plan, including a program of education and outreach.

Together the agencies could do what single agencies could not do alone: The U.S. Fish and Wildlife Service could make plans to restore side channels that flow through the Middle Mississippi River National Wildlife Refuge, plans that could be implemented by the U.S. Corps of Engineers. The American Land Conservancy could purchase land in the batture lands and donate it to the new Middle Mississippi River National Wildlife Refuge. Ducks Unlimited could restore land on Rockwood Island and donate it to the growing refuge. The model the partners devised was similar to the one followed by the Lower Mississippi River Conservation Committee along the main stem of the Lower River.

Restoration Efforts on the Lower Mississippi

Whereas work started on the Upper Mississippi only after the passage of the 1986 Water Resources Development Act and work on the Middle Mississippi after the 1993 flood, restoration work along the Lower River itself started in 1981 when the Corps of Engineers initiated, as a part of the Mississippi River and Tributaries Channel Improvement and the Mississippi River Levees and Channel project, the Lower Mississippi River Environmental Program. For the first time, the Corps looked at the ecological resources on and the ecological damage done to the main stem of the Lower Mississippi and to the active floodplain between the levees and the river. Over the next twenty years the engineers at the Vicksburg District attempted to devise ecologically sound ways to maintain the navigation channel and build levees.

They developed a River and Environmental Geospacial Information System that documented land cover, terrestrial habitat, aquatic habitat, soils, engineering works, hydrography/topography, survey control, and infrastructure and put all this information in one database. Using this system, the engineers rewrote the design manuals for levee borrow pits, revetments, and dikes. New specifications for levees required smaller borrow pits and pits with irregular bottoms that left trees standing on small islands. And, engineers became experts on the breeding and feeding habits of the Interior Least Tern, an endangered bird.

Least Terns like their privacy, and they don't like trees. They are colonial and territorial. They will attack any predator, be it two-footed, four-footed, or winged. They make their summer homes on isolated sand- or gravel bars in the Mississippi, Arkansas, and Missouri Rivers, nesting on open, sparsely vegetated sandbars in the middle of streams where they can see predators approach. They feed on small fish they pluck from shallow sloughs.

The Corps of Engineers has been at war against sandbars ever since 1835, when Lt. Robert E. Lee demonstrated the effectiveness of dikes by using one to direct the current of the river against a sandbar and remove it from the St. Louis harbor. After the flood of 1927, as a part of the Mississippi River and Tributaries Project, the Corps of Engineers increased its use of dikes to remove isolated sandbars from the navigation channel. What they couldn't remove with dikes, they dredged. The terns lost their habitat. In 1985 the U.S. Fish and Wildlife Service declared the Interior Least Tern endangered and sought help from the Corps of Engineers in its recovery.

The Vicksburg and Memphis Districts on the Lower River and the St. Louis District on the Middle River, working with the U.S. Fish and Wildlife Service and the various state natural resource agencies, implemented plans to help the terns recover. They constructed islands and sandbars from dredge material, which they kept free of vegetation. They notched existing dikes to allow water to scour channels through dike fields—the accumulation of sand scoured from the main channel lying between dikes—and create small sandbars.

They provided habitat for fish—tern food. They placed chevron dikes—"C"-shaped—on the shallow side of the river to accomplish the same end and to produce a scour hole on the inside of the dike for fish. When they built a closing dam across a chute, they included a three hundred-foot notch in the top to allow water to continue to flow through the deepest part of the chute, saving spawning and feeding habitat for fish. They roughed up the finish on revetments to increase the population of microinvertebrates—caddisfly and midge larvae—fish food. They set some notched revetments offshore and parallel to the bankline to create slow-moving side channels for fish. The terns reappeared along the Lower Mississippi.

In 1990 the Corps of Engineers joined the U.S. Fish and Wildlife Service, the U.S. Geological Survey, the U.S. Environmental Agency, the USDA Natural Resources Conservation Service, and the water quality and fish and wildlife agencies of the states bordering the Lower Mississippi to form the Lower Mississippi River Conservation Committee, a nonprofit organization dedicated to "renewing and effectively managing the natural resources" of the main stem of the river, the region between the levees. Funding for the committee came from private contributors and foundations, including the TARA Foundation, the Little River Foundation, and the Ohrstrom Foundation. The committee assembled a geographic information system that detailed the Lower Mississippi ecosystem, its hydrology, the location of its dikes, revetments, and levees, the boundaries of its public lands, land cover and use, satellite imagery, and the topography of its riverbed—its bathymetry.

In the early years of the new century the U.S. Fish and Wildlife Service turned its attention to the floodplain between the river and the valley walls. During the twentieth century the systematic logging and draining of the floodplain and its conversion to agriculture rendered the Lower Mississippi alluvial valley one of the most endangered ecosystems in the United States. Americans, who settled the valley beginning in the early eighteenth century, found twenty-five million acres of forested wetlands. Over the next three centuries they reduced the bottomland forest to four million acres, fragmented across a landscape dominated by well-drained fields of soybeans and cotton. The wetlands served as the primary wintering grounds for waterfowl, shorebirds, and wading birds, the forest the primary breeding ground for the largest and smallest of its residents—the Louisiana black bear, the Ivory-billed Woodpecker, and neotropical songbirds who returned each spring from Central and South America.

In September 2002 the U.S. Fish and Wildlife Service laid out five goals for the lower valley in its final draft of its Lower Mississippi River Ecosystem Plan: "Conserve, enhance, protect and monitor migratory bird populations and their habitats; protect, restore, and manage its wetlands; protect and/or restore imperiled habitats and viable populations of all endangered, threatened, and candidate species and species of concern; protect, restore and manage its fisheries and other aquatic resources; restore, manage, and protect National Wildlife Refuges and National Fish Hatcheries."

To accomplish its goals, the Fish and Wildlife Service would do the following: Assure that migrating birds can find suitable habitat for feeding, nesting, and resting by encouraging the seasonable flooding of croplands by private owners and by providing moist-soil habitats for waterfowl on federal and state refuges. Restore wetlands and prairies in the floodplain. Restore bottomland hardwood forests on the wildlife refuges through its Carbon Sequestration Initiative. Encourage private landowners to restore wetlands through the Wetland Reserve and the Conservation Reserve Programs. Restore habitat in the rivers for the pallid sturgeon and in the forests for the Louisiana black bear. Improve water quality in the rivers and bayous for mussels, particularly Louisiana pearlshell and fat pocketbook mussels. Increase wetlands and habitat for aquatic species in the floodplain lying between the river and the levees. Improve water management in the Atchafalaya Basin. Support the restoration work being done along the Louisiana marshes in the Gulf of Mexico.

Restoring bottomland forests was the highest priority of the Fish and Wildlife Service in the Lower Mississippi Valley. Working with private landowners and the Department of Agriculture, Fish and Wildlife would restore forests on private lands to hasten the recovery of the Louisiana black bear. A group of public and private conservation groups, the Lower Mississippi River Joint Venture, would work to restore lands for migratory songbirds and to identify sites for future conservation efforts. The long-term goal of all these groups was to provide "forest islands," ranging from 10,000 to 100,000 acres, as forest bird conservation zones.

Reforested land in the Lower Mississippi Valley has the potential to become a major sink for the sequestration of carbon. In 1992 the U.S. Fish and Wildlife Service began working with corporate partners to reforest 65,000 acres of publicly and privately held land in the Southeast. The program appealed to electric power companies, which emit 40 percent of the nation's carbon dioxide. Beginning in 1999, in partnership with the Entergy Corporation, Dynegy,

Inc., Texaco, Future Forest, and the Trust for Public Land, the service planted bottomland hardwoods (oaks—Nuttall, Shumard, water, willow, overcup, and cherrybark; pecans—sweet and bitter; green ash, sweet gum, cypress, persimmon, red maple, red mulberry, and American sycamore) on four thousand acres of cleared land in the Tensas National Wildlife Refuge in Louisiana. In 2000 the service formed a partnership with Environmental Synergy, Inc., and a second one with the Conservation Fund and American Electric Power in the Catahoula National Wildlife Refuge with the intention of reforesting 10,000 acres for carbon credits.

A 2008 McKnight Foundation grant of $800,000 to the Nature Conservancy for its work in restoring the whole of the Mississippi could go a long way to encouraging private owners of marginal farmland in the Lower Valley to restore their acres to bottomland hardwoods. The conservancy would use part of the grant to set the value of "ecosystem services" that bottomland forests provide people: the storage of floodwater, the sequestration of carbon, and the capture of sediment and pollutants. The goal is to restore between one and two million acres of forest in the Lower Valley by demonstrating the profitability of restoring bottomland forests. Income would come from the sustainable harvesting of timber, the leasing of forested wetlands for recreation, and the selling of carbon credits, once the market and science for doing so are established. Setting the value of ecosystem services would set the market. Finally, the grant would allow the Nature Conservancy to hire a scientist to work with the Corps of Engineers on restoring the Lower River to a more natural condition.

Managing the Delta for Oil, Gas, and Navigation

Changing the Delta: Subsidence

When a fast-moving, sediment-laden stream meets a slow-moving or still body of water, it drops its load of sediment and forms a delta. As long as a distributary continues to deliver sediment to a delta front, and as long as flood deposits feed the basins between the separate channels, mudflats form in the basins and are quickly colonized by freshwater marsh vegetation. Once the distributary ceases to deliver sediment to the delta front, once flood deposits no longer feed the basins between separate channels, and once the cycle of growth and decay in the marsh can no longer sustain the marsh, seawater seeps in and begins to eat away at the marsh, replacing it with shallow lakes or bays.

At the beginning of the twenty-first century, Louisiana was disappearing, subsiding, at the rate of one acre every twenty-four minutes. Project that rate over a year, and Louisiana was losing 20,000 to 25,000 acres, or 25 to 35 square miles, per year. From 1920 to 2000, Louisiana lost 600,000 acres of vegetated wetlands. If the loss continued at this rate, the Louisiana shoreline would creep inland some thirty-three miles along some stretches of the coast before 2050. The process started with the first levee built at New Orleans in 1723. Every change in the natural functions of the river since that date has decreased the amount of sediment delivered to the Gulf of Mexico for the construction of coastal marshes.

It was a familiar story: Artificial levees, extending clear to the Gulf of Mexico, may have protected landowners from flooding, but they also prevented the river from refreshing wetlands with sediment. Revetments may have stabilized the channel, but they reduced erosion of the banks, a primary source of sediment in the marshes. James Buchanan Eads's jetties may have allowed the river to cut a thirty-foot navigation channel through the sandbar blocking the South Pass, but they delivered sediment carried by the river to very deep water at the continental shelf. Closure of the old distributaries—Bayou Manchac in 1814, Bayou Plaquemine in 1868, Bayou Lafourche in 1904—may have prevented flooding in the backcountry of Louisiana, but it cut the flow of Mississippi sediment to the coastal marshes. Channel dams may have improved navigation on the Upper Mississippi, but they retained its sediment north of Alton, Illinois. Dams—built for a potpourri of reasons: hydroelectric, flood control, navigation, irrigation, recreation—on the Missouri that once supplied the Mississippi with 60 percent of its sediment did the same. In short, at the beginning of the twenty-first century, the coastal marshes received 80 percent less sediment than they had at the beginning of the twentieth. Louisiana was disappearing as its coastal marshes receded, a process that was aggravated by other changes in the Delta.

Changing the Delta: Drilling for Oil in Louisiana

Take a square mile of marsh: It has four miles of edge habitat, the place where the water meets land. Oysters settle in the shallow water and form beds. Small marine animals, grass shrimp or mud crabs, gather in the rough surface of the bed. Fish and reptiles congregate in search of the crabs and shrimp. Wading birds and waterfowl flock to the shallows in search of the fish and reptiles.

Dredge a canal through the marsh: it creates two more miles of places for critters to flourish. Dredge another canal in the opposite direction: It creates more edge, which attracts more critters, but it leaves less marsh to hold it all together. Erosion sets in, and the marsh breaks into ponds. The marsh continues to erode; the ponds enlarge, join, and turn to open water. Edges disappear; habitat disappears; the shrimp, crabs, red drum, speckled trout disappear. So do waders and waterfowl. Anchovies, bluefish, ladyfish, and mackerel—species that thrive in open water—appear. This is what happened to the Louisiana coast after Louisianans discovered oil in their marshes.

Louisianans noticed oil seeping out of the ground as early as 1812, but it did not start flowing until 1901 when the Heywood brothers struck oil near Jennings. That well quickly sanded up, but the following year the brothers drilled a working well at Anse le Butte near Breaux Bridge in the Atchafalaya Basin. By the end of the year five wells were producing almost 600,000 barrels of oil. Commercial production began in 1906 and moved oil out of the state by rail. Standard Oil of New Jersey built the first Louisiana refinery at Baton Rouge in 1909.

Louisianans got their first whiff of natural gas when a geologist noticed an island burning, also in 1812. In 1870 a night watchman at an ice plant in Shreveport struck a match and discovered natural gas leaking from an artesian well. The owner of the plant piped the gas to his plant to light it. In 1908 Louisianans laid their first pipeline between a field in Caddo and Shreveport, where the gas was sold for domestic and industrial use. As they drilled more and more wells, Louisianans learned they were floating on a sea of oil and gas: 1913, they opened Bull Bayou Field in northwest Louisiana; 1916, the Monroe Gas Field on the western edge of the alluvial valley; 1921, the Haynesville Gas Field in northwest Louisiana; 1940, Olla Field in LaSalle Parish at the western edge of the alluvial valley; 1947, the first field in the Gulf of Mexico; 1948, a field at the Main Pass of the Mississippi; 1949, in Vermilion Bay in delicate coastal marshes; 1950, a field at the South Pass of the Mississippi.

To access their derricks the oil companies dredged long, straight navigation and exploration canals—an urban grid laid over the sinuous bayous that meandered through the coastal marshes. They dropped their dredge material—spoil banks—along the edges of their canals and changed the hydrology of the marshes. Dredge a canal trending east and west, and its spoil bank stops the sheetflow of water south. Dredge it trending north and south, and it conveys salt water into fresh and brackish marshes.

And extensive oil extraction after 1965 may have activated the South Louisiana Growth faults, creating subsidence "hotspots" in the Terrebonne Basin. In the first years of the twenty-first century, geologists began looking at growth faults as the primary cause of subsidence along the Louisiana coast. They run east and west through the bedrock that lies deep under the coastal marshes. The very weight of that inverted mountain of sediment may cause them to slip. When they do, it's quiet, hardly noticeable. No rivers run backward, no church bells ring in Boston as they did when the New Madrid fault cut loose on the Mississippi in 1811 and 1812. No, fault-bound blocks sink and tilt, pull the coastal wetlands down with them, and the Gulf of Mexico flows in. They are in constant motion; they are uncontrollable.

Changing the Delta: Mississippi River Gulf Outlet and Other Navigation Canals

In 1718 Jean Baptiste LeMoyne, sieur de Bienville, laid out the site of New Orleans on the natural levee of the Mississippi just south of Lake Pontchartrain. Bayou St. John ran north from the edge of town through the backswamp and gave New Orleans access to the Gulf of Mexico through the lake. From its beginnings New Orleans looked for a better way to connect the Gulf to the river, which at normal flow, ran ten feet higher than Lake Pontchartrain. Not until July 1914 did Louisiana's legislature authorize the New Orleans port authority to build the Inner Harbor Navigation Canal, a deepwater connection between the lake and the river, known locally as the Industrial Canal. Not until May 1923 did engineers overcome soft, mucky soils and the ten-foot disparity between the river and the lake and excavate a canal thirty feet deep at low water, with a bottom width of 150 feet and a channel width of 300 feet, and construct a lock 74 feet wide and 640 feet long that could ease shipping between the river and the lake.

As Louisianans increased their knowledge of the Louisiana coast throughout the nineteenth century, they began looking for a more efficient way to get to Berwick Bay at the mouth of the Atchafalaya River. They had an inefficient route up the Mississippi from New Orleans to Bayou Plaquemine, which gave them access to the Atchafalaya River and, ultimately, to Berwick Bay. In 1829 the State of Louisiana authorized R. R. Barrow to create an inland waterway from the west bank of the Mississippi across the Barataria Basin to Houma, where his channel picked up Bayou Black, which carried boats to Berwick Bay via Bayou Chene and Boeuf Bayou. That waterway ceased operation around 1860 and Barrow's Canal silted in. After 1880 the Corps of Engineers reexamined this route several times, but nothing happened until 1919, when Congress authorized the Gulf Intracoastal Waterway (GIWW), which ultimately ran parallel to Barrow's Canal and a little to the south.

Not until 1942 did the Corps of Engineers complete dredging a channel nine feet deep and one hundred feet wide between Apalachee Bay, Florida, and Port Isabel, Texas, at the Mexican border. The Corps increased the canal's depth to 12 feet and its width to 125 feet in 1949. In southwestern Louisiana the GIWW runs just south of the uplands and the Atchafalaya Basin. As it approaches the deltaic plain, it cuts across the natural levees of the bayous that form the Lafourche Delta, through the marshes of Barataria Bay, and into New Orleans, where it connects first with the Mississippi River, then the Industrial Canal, and finally with the last few miles of the Mississippi River Gulf Outlet.

With the completion of the Industrial Canal in 1923, the port authority intended to ask Congress to authorize the Mississippi River Gulf Outlet (MRGO), connect it to the new canal, and run it through Breton Sound to the Gulf of Mexico. The project was stuck in limbo until Congress authorized it in 1956. Design started a year later and construction a year after that. It was to be 650 feet wide and 36 feet deep with a bottom width of 500 feet. It extended from the "T" intersection of the Industrial Canal and the GIWW, in the heart of New Orleans, seventy-six miles out through the degrading St. Bernard subdelta into Breton Sound. It was built with the hope of bringing industrial development to St. Bernard Parish.

The Corps excavated the new channel through forty-five miles of cypress swamp and brackish-to-saline marshes in Orleans and St. Bernard Parishes and dredged another thirty miles through submerged aquatic vegetation that anchored the floor of the shallow bays of Breton Sound. When completed in 1965, it cut thirty-seven miles off the trip between New Orleans and the Gulf of Mexico. By 2005 erosion from wave wash had widened the canal to 2,200 feet. The Corps of Engineers spent $22 million a year dredging it to 40 feet, but container ships had outgrown MRGO's 44-foot-deep navigation channel and were using the Mississippi to reach the Port of New Orleans. MRGO was obsolete. Two ships a day used it.

In the years after its completion, MRGO channeled salt water into the freshwater marshes and swamps southeast of New Orleans, destroyed 1,500 acres of cypress swamp, converted more than 11,000 acres of fresh/intermediate marsh and cypress swamp to brackish marsh and more than 19,000 acres of brackish marsh to saline marsh, and destroyed 4,000 acres of saline marsh. Oyster production moved inland with the salt water; white shrimp disappeared to be replaced by brown; 650,000 fur-bearing animals lost habitat. So did waterfowl. Finally, even though the Corps bound MRGO with levees designed to hold back a 17.5-foot storm surge, New Orleans, its surrounding parishes, and the Mississippi Gulf Coast lost the buffer, the marshes and cypress forests, that would absorb the surges generated by hurricanes roaring in from the Gulf of Mexico.

Changing the Delta: The Dead Zone

With the Clean Water Act of 1972, Congress charged the newly created Environmental Protection Agency with eliminating all pollutant discharges from identifiable points—sewers and factories—into the nation's waters by 1985. The law did nothing to limit runoff from agricultural lands where the nation's farmers were using increasing amounts of nitrogen fertilizer, nitrates, to nourish their crops.

All plants need nitrogen but cannot absorb nitrogen gas, which makes up 78 percent of the earth's atmosphere. Hence, farmers spread ammonium nitrate or nitrate nitrogen, which are soluble in water, across their fields. If they spread more than their wheat, corn, or soybeans can absorb, the remainder seeps into the groundwater and from there into the nation's waterways. The Mississippi Basin, which holds five-sixths of the nation's farmland, flushes its excess nitrates into the river and, ultimately, into the Gulf of Mexico. Other sources of nitrogen in the Mississippi come from livestock farms and poorly treated human waste.

Nitrate-rich, freshwater from the Mississippi, lighter than salt water, floats on the surface of the Gulf off the shore of the coastal wetlands. Normally, wind stirs the mix into the salt water, but in summer, when the weather is warm and the Gulf calm, the layers of fresh and salt remain stratified. Algae bloom in the nitrogen-rich layer of freshwater, die, sink into the saltier layer and decompose, soaking up the available oxygen, creating a hypoxic zone, the Dead Zone. Fish and shrimp flee the oxygen-depleted waters. Plants, plankton, and oysters, which cannot escape, just die. Young fish and shrimp, which breed in the Gulf's coastal wetlands, cannot cross the barrier that is the Dead Zone on their migration from their nurseries to the Gulf itself. Hypoxia is a natural phenomenon in the Gulf, but as levels of dissolved nitrogen in the Mississippi River increased decade by decade after 1900 and jumped dramatically after the 1950s, when farmers began applying more and more nitrogen to their crops, the size of the hypoxic zone also increased. By 1996 it covered an area the size of New Jersey. In June 2008, with midwestern farms planting nutrient-hungry corn to fuel the boom in ethanol, heavy rains washed the crop and the nutrients from the fields, and with the Mississippi in full flood, scientists at Louisiana State University predicted that the Dead Zone would grow to 10,000 square miles, up 1,600 square miles from its 2002 high.

Restoring the Louisiana Coast

The U.S. Geological Survey breaks the Louisiana Gulf Coast into nine basins, seven of which have been fed by distributaries of the Mississippi River over the last five thousand years. The two exceptions are the westernmost basins, the Calcasieu/Sabine and the Mermentau. Rather, long shore currents, westerly currents carrying sediment from the various Mississippi distributaries, built ridges of sand and mud along the shoreline west of Vermilion Bay. In the remaining seven, only Atchafalaya Bay in the Terrebonne Basin was gaining new land at the beginning of the twenty-first century, funneling sediment from the Red River, the Mississippi, and the Atchafalaya through the lower Atchafalaya and the Wax Lake Outlet into the bay.

The compacted sediments of the Teche/Vermilion Basin, the remnant of the Teche subdelta abandoned by the river 3,200 years ago, were relatively stable at the turn of the century. The basin lost only 9 percent of its landmass after 1932. After 2000 the basin continued to lose land at the projected rate of 600 to 900 acres a year, or 3 percent of Louisiana's total land loss.

The Pontchartrain Basin, which encompasses Lakes Maurepas, Pontchartrain, and Borgne, as well as Chandeleur Sound and was a part of the St. Bernard subdelta, lost 8 percent of its landmass, mostly from the land bridges between Pontchartrain and Maurepas and Pontchartrain and Borgne. The remaining three were losing land at a tremendous rate, 600,000 acres of vegetated wetlands in the eighty years before 2000. The loss was catastrophic.

The Breton Sound Basin holds the remnant of the St. Bernard subdelta that formed 3,200 years ago along Bayou Terre des Boeufs, Bayou a Loutre, and Bayou Sauvage. It lies east of the modern Mississippi. It lost 17 percent of its wetlands to open water before 2000. The Barataria Basin, west of the modern Mississippi, holds the remnant of the St. Bernard subdelta that formed along Bayou des Famillies. It too lost 17 percent of its landmass. Both basins received deposits from the Plaquemine subdelta, which formed just south of New Orleans along the modern Mississippi. The Barataria Basin also received deposits from the eastern distributaries of the Lafourche subdelta. The Terrebonne Basin holds the remnant of the Lafourche subdelta that formed along Bayou Lafourche and other distributaries in the delta fifteen hundred years ago. It lost 20 percent of its wetlands. The Mississippi River Delta Basin formed along the Balize subdelta of the modern Mississippi 1,300 years ago. It lost 70 percent of its wetlands. In short, the younger the subdelta is, the greater the loss of landmass was, partly because the sediments had less time to compact and therefore eroded more easily. However, human events caused most of the loss.

Until 1904 Bayou Lafourche carried 12 percent of the Mississippi's water and sediment to the Gulf of Mexico. In 1903 local interests built a temporary closing dam at its head at Donaldsonville. The dam prevented flooding along the old distributary, but it also cut the stream of freshwater and sediment to its headland. Until the early 1900s the modern Mississippi River refreshed the marshes in the Breton Sound, the Barataria Basin, Terrebonne Basin, and the Mississippi River Delta Basin with freshwater and new sediment every time it flooded. After the Flood of 1927 the Corps of Engineers, as a part of the Mississippi River and Tributaries Project, raised the artificial levees south of New Orleans, armored the banks with rock, and cut off the supply of water and sediment to the basins. The Terrebonne and Barataria Basins and Breton Sound, which depended the most on Mississippi water and sediment, shifted from river-dominated to tidal-dominated systems. No longer could the river overtop its banks or blow a crevasse in its natural levee and feed the marshes. Most of the sediment the river did deliver to the Gulf of Mexico—436,000 tons a day in 2000, down from 1,576,000 tons a day in 1951—slipped over the continental shelf to the ocean floor hundreds of feet down. Loose sediment that was deposited in the modern delta compacted almost as soon as it was deposited or was swamped as sea level rose.

The Mississippi River–Gulf Outlet in the Breton Sound Basin; the GIWW, the Barataria Waterway, and the Empire-Gulf Waterway in the Barataria Basin; the Houma Navigation Canal in the Terrebonne Basin: these and innumerable oil-exploration canals crisscrossed the coastal marshes. The waterways cut across natural levees, dredged up wetlands, and created spoil banks, levees of dredge material that disrupted the natural flow of water across the wetlands. Marshes above the spoil banks drowned as water backed up against them; marshes below starved for want of water. Their destruction created open lakes. Each vessel passing through the canal dragged a wake behind it, which eroded the bank, creating still more open water. Finally, the canals broke down the zone between freshwater and salt water, allowing salt to bleed into freshwater marshes, killing native plants, forcing wildlife to adapt or go elsewhere.

It took almost thirty years for the Corps of Engineers to address the problem after the U.S. Fish and Wildlife Service made its first inventory of Louisiana coastal wetlands in 1953 and reported the early losses. A year later Congress asked the Corps of Engineers to look at the problem and recommend modifications to the Mississippi River and Tributaries Project that would address the loss of wetlands. In 1958 Fish and Wildlife sent a report to the New Orleans District recommending that the Corps find a way to introduce freshwater into coastal wetlands to stop the intrusion of salt water. In 1962 the Corps submitted a review of the Mississippi River and Tributaries Project to Congress that included the Fish and Wildlife report. Three years later Congress passed the Flood Control Act of 1965, authorizing the Corps to find a way to introduce floods of freshwater into marshes to the right and the left of the natural levee of the Mississippi near New Orleans. Congress reiterated the need to save the marshes with the Water Resources Development Act of 1974 and again in 1986.

Not until 1982 did the Corps of Engineers begin to study the feasibility of diverting freshwater and sediment from the leveed and armored trunk channel of the Mississippi to the Breton Sound to the east of the river and the Barataria Basin to the west. It was. Four years later, working with the Louisiana Department of Natural Resources, the Corps started construction on the Caernarvon Freshwater Diversion Structure, gated culverts set in the mainline levee at Caernarvon, fifteen miles below New Orleans. The structure was designed to divert freshwater from the Mississippi east into the head of Breton Sound. In 1991, almost forty years after the first report, the engineers opened the gates December through February to divert as much as eight thousand cubic feet of water per second into Breton Sound. The engineers released lesser amounts the rest of the year to supplement rainfall and maintain the desired ratio of fresh- to salt water.

In 1990 Congress passed an act specifically aimed at restoring the coastal wetlands. The 1990 WRDA included the Coastal Wetlands Planning, Protection and Restoration Act, known as the Breaux Act, which funded plans to restore deteriorating marshlands along the Gulf of Mexico. It was comparable to the Upper Mississippi River Management Act, which funded restoration projects on the Upper River.

For nine years after the passage of the Breaux Act, restoration work across the Louisiana coast proceeded bit by bit. A variety of agencies did work here and there, diverting water and sediment from the trunk channel of the Mississippi and using dredge materials to reclaim headlands and barrier islands. The Corps and the Louisiana DNR reinforced the west bank of Bayou Lafourche, south of Leeville, and restored the West Belle Headland, using dredge scooped up from the bayou to maintain its twenty-seven-foot navigation channel. The EPA, the National Marine Fisheries Service, and the Louisiana DNR restored East Timbalier Island and the Isles Dernieres with dredge material from Timbalier Bay, which they anchored in place with dune grasses and sand fencing. The Louisiana DNR, which owned the Pass a Loutre Wildlife Management Area, and the U.S. Fish and Wildlife Service, which owned the Delta National Wildlife Refuge, blew crevasses in the natural levees of the Mississippi Delta to tap water and sediment coming down the Mississippi and restore wetlands in their respective refuges. The Superior and Mobile Oil Company and the U.S. Army Corps of Engineers did similar work in Main Pass. In all, the various agencies initiated ninety-three projects in seven basins, but the work lacked focus, even though Congress poured forty million dollars a year into coastal restoration between 1991 and 1998.

Coast 2050

Like the Corps of Engineers, the U.S. Fish and Wildlife Service, and the state resource agencies working to restore the Upper Mississippi, the people working to restore the Louisiana coast could mimic the natural processes that built the marshes, but they had to live with the changes made to the whole of the Mississippi Basin. The dams on the Upper Mississippi and Upper Missouri would remain in place and continue to retain in the upper part of the basin sediment needed for marsh building in the gulf. The levees along the main stem of the river would remain in place and deprive the marshes of water and sediment from spring flooding. The navigation channel through the Birdfoot Delta would continue to deliver freshwater and sediment to very deep water near the continental shelf at the mouth of the river. In 1998 the Louisiana DNR, the Corps of Engineers, the U.S. Fish and Wildlife Service, the EPA, the National Oceanic and Atmospheric Administration, the Louisiana Department of Wildlife and Fisheries, Louisiana State University, the University of New Orleans, and state and local agencies formed Coast 2050 to manage the Breaux Act funds more efficiently. The participants in Coast 2050 recognized the necessity of breaking away from the piecemeal restoration of the Louisiana coast.

They set three goals for coastal restoration: Restore the ecosystem to self-sustainability so that it is able to maintain itself against the natural forces, subsidence and erosion, which cause the loss of marshes. Introduce enough freshwater through diversions from the Mississippi at the head of each basin to maintain diverse habitats by restoring the natural flow of water through each basin—fresh to intermediate to brackish to saline. Stabilize the flow of water across landforms—natural levees and backswamps—and restore pathways across various habitats, such as the overflow of fresh water, sediment, and nutrients into marshes or the migration of saltwater organisms to freshwater in order to breed.

Next, they detailed the means of achieving their goals: Use dredge materials from maintenance operations on waterways to create, restore, and protect wetlands. Use dredge materials where natural marsh-building processes do not or cannot occur. Control the population of nutrias—rodents with prodigious appetites for wetland plants—which are capable of turning marshlands into open water. Stabilize the width and depth of the major navigational canals that criss-crossed the region, using bank reinforcement. Stabilize the shores of the Gulf, the bays, and the lakes in the coastal plain, using vegetation where possible, bank reinforcement where not. Pump through pipelines freshwater and sediment directly into wetlands. Stabilize banks and reestablish wetlands with vegetative planting. Restore, protect, and maintain the natural levees created by distributaries of the Mississippi. Build terraces to improve nursery habitat, reduce wind fetch, and trap sediment. Explore new ways of using offshore and riverine sand and sediment to restore wetlands and beaches. Reduce the loss of sediment at the mouth of the Mississippi. Divert freshwater, nutrients, and sediment from the Mississippi into adjacent basins. Deliver diverted water and sediment to marshes and swamps rather than to waterways.

Louisianans had used many of these strategies in the seven years after the passage of the Breaux Act in 1990. But, the work done by various agencies was expected to reverse only 22 percent of the land loss anticipated by 2050. Louisianans decided to focus their attention on individual basins. They started with Barataria Basin, which lies between the modern Mississippi and the Lafourche subdelta.

On February 18, 2000, the New Orleans District of the Corps of Engineers and the Louisiana Department of Natural Resources signed the Coast 2050 Feasibility Cost Share Agreement to split the cost of two feasibility studies of wetlands restoration and barrier-island restoration in Barataria Basin. The partners quickly rolled the studies into one. The agencies laid out their ambitions for the proposed work in the basin in the Louisiana-Ecosystem Restoration Study, completed in October 2003.

If successful, the study would lay the foundation for the agencies to tap funding sources other than those coming from the Breaux Act, 10 percent of the estimated cost of $14 billion over thirty years. Other sources of funding might come from future Water Resources Development Acts or the Conservation and Reinvestment Act. The latter, if ever passed into law, would channel Outer Continental Shelf oil and gas revenues into the Land and Water Conservation Fund, set up in 1964, and other conservation programs, which the Corps and the Louisiana DNR could then tap for coastal restoration.

The Louisiana Coastal Area Ecosystem Restoration Study

The New Orleans District of the Corps of Engineers completed the draft comprehensive study for implementing the Coast 2050 project in October 2003. President George W. Bush's Office of Management and Budget balked at the $14 billion price tag. The OMB asked Louisiana to come up with a simpler, and possibly cheaper, plan that would identify the most pressing needs, and propose a program of cost-effective projects that would begin to address them within ten years. The OMB also requested that the Coast 2050 collaborators design a science and technology program to identify the gaps in our knowledge of how wetlands were formed, what caused their loss, what engineering and hydrologic tools would restore them effectively, what habitat shifts would come with restoration, and how restoration would affect the people and businesses—stakeholders. That done, the collaborators would come up with demonstration projects and studies that would address these uncertainties and create cost-effective prescriptions for coastal restoration that would work over fifty years. In November 2004 the Corps of Engineers and the Louisiana Department of Natural Resources issued the Louisiana Coastal Area Study (LCA Study).

The study proposed five pressing projects: Restore the Mississippi River Gulf Outlet (MRGO); divert freshwater along Hope Canal into the Maurepas wetlands in the Lake Pontchartrain Basin east of the river; restore the Barataria barrier shoreline; reintroduce freshwater to Bayou Lafourche to nourish wetlands in the Barataria and Terrebonne Basins; divert water and sediment from the Mississippi south of New Orleans at Myrtle Grove into the Barataria Basin. The cost would come to $864,065,000. In addition to the five projects, the study included developing the Science and Technology Program, the Demonstration Program, and the Beneficial Use of Dredge Program—each at a cost of $100 million, and the Investigations of Modifications to Existing Structures Program at a cost of $10 million.

The 2004 document also included large-scale and long-term concepts in need of study: the Acadiana Bays Estuarine Restoration Study, the Upper Atchafalaya Basin Study, the Chenier Plain Freshwater and Sediment Management and Allocation Reassessment Study, the Mississippi River Delta Management Study, the Mississippi River Hydrodynamic Study, and the Third Delta Study. Taken together, the cost of these studies came to $60 million.

Finally, the study recommended ten other near-term projects, which would address critical needs, including some in the Terrebonne Basin: a lock on the Houma Navigation Channel that would halt the intrusion of salt water into the basin, inputs of freshwater from the Atchafalaya that would counter the intrusion of salt water in the wetlands in the northern part of the basin, restoration of the barrier shoreline, and shoring up of the landbridge between Caillou Lake and the Gulf of Mexico. The study also recommended modification of various diversions in other parts of the coast, including the Caernarvon and Davis Pond Diversion projects. The total cost of the study came to $1,995,981,000, a far cry from the $14 billion over thirty years the Coast 2050 project was estimated to cost.

As the Corps and the DNR were finishing the LCA Study, the office of the Louisiana governor asked the national academies—private, nonprofit entities that provide science, technology, and health-policy advice to the federal government—to review it for its effectiveness for comprehensive restoration over the long term. The ocean studies board of the National Research Council brought together a group of scientists, engineers, and interested parties—all of whom had worked on the problems of land loss and many of whom had proposed solutions—to make presentations on various aspects of coastal restoration and review the study.

"Timid," the board concluded in its analysis of the study. While the five projects, plus the demonstration projects, plus the other aspects of the study might yield near-term success, the study avoided big ideas. The board congratulated the authors of the study for looking at the possibilities of the Third Delta Conveyance Channel, a proposal to dredge a channel parallel to Bayou Lafourche, tap the Mississippi for freshwater and sediment and deliver it to lower reaches of the Barataria and Terrebonne Basins, where the deposit of new sediment might build not one but two new deltas. But it berated the authors of the study for not addressing other big ideas that would deliver large amounts of sediment over a longer time. For example: If the Birdfoot Delta were to be abandoned and the river's sediment to be delivered to shallow waters in Barataria Basin to the west and Breton Sound to the east instead of very deep waters at the outer edge of the continental shelf, new land could be built where it was desperately needed. The board also criticized the study for not addressing the difficult issues attached to stakeholders who might lose property and businesses to ecosystem restoration and who needed to be included in the planning process. Finally, the council noted that neither the study nor the state had drawn up a map of what coastal Louisiana would look like. What would be the desired distribution of habitats that guided restoration in the future?

Louisiana Coastal Impact Assistance Plan

At the beginning of the twenty-first century, oil companies were paying the federal government $5 billion a year to drill along the Louisiana coast, but the State of Louisiana saw little of it. In 2003 Senator Mary Landrieu (D-Louisiana) added a provision to the pending energy bill that would funnel some of that money back to states for coastal reconstruction. When passed and signed in August 2005, the energy bill returned $250 million annually between 2007 and 2010 to be divided among the six eligible states: Alaska, Alabama, California, Louisiana, Mississippi, and Texas. Louisiana began taking proposals for use of the funds and in February 2007 issued the draft of its Louisiana Coastal Impact Assistance Plan, the blueprint for spending the $523 million the state would receive between 2007 and 2010. The plan, if approved by the U.S. Minerals Management Service, would enhance management of Mississippi River water and sediment, protect and restore critical land bridges, protect and restore barrier islands' shorelines, protect interior shorelines, and conserve Louisiana's coastal forests in its swamps and along its natural levees.

The National Research Council titled its critique of the LCA Study *Drawing Louisiana's New Map.* On Monday, August 29, 2005, Hurricane Katrina redrew the map of Breton Sound and flooded New Orleans. A month later Hurricane Rita redrew the map of the Chenier Plain on the western edge of the Louisiana coast.

At 5:30 in the morning Hurricane Katrina struck and wiped out 118 square miles of coastal marshlands. On September 25, Hurricane Rita added to the toll as it ripped up marshlands in southwestern Louisiana and washed salt water as far as twenty miles inland. Together the two hurricanes destroyed 217 square miles of wetlands and brought home to Louisianans, if not all Americans, the necessity of restoring their marshlands. Katrina's winds yanked strips of marsh up by their roots and rolled them up like carpets; rent tears in the marsh that allowed small lakes to form; pushed marshes into accordion folds; scoured the marsh, flipped it, and, finally, balled it into sofa-sized clumps that blew across the landscape like tumbleweed. In the face of such a loss, the LCA Study—a proposal that included restoring the Mississippi River Gulf Outlet, a navigation channel Louisianans wished gone—looked grossly inadequate. So did the far more extensive Coast 2050 proposals.

The Flood of 2005—The Law of Unintended Consequences

On Friday, August 26, 2005, Hurricane Katrina ripped across the Gulf of Mexico toward the coasts of Louisiana, Mississippi, and Alabama. It was a Category Five hurricane, packing winds of 175 miles per hour, and it was headed straight for New Orleans. Sunday night the winds slowed, and the hurricane shifted its course to the east. It was a Category Three hurricane pushing a Category Five storm surge that crossed the Mississippi about seventy-five miles south of New Orleans, continued straight north through the tattered marshes of Breton Sound and Lake Borgne, and hit the Mississippi/Alabama coast, wiping out the lovely string of towns that lay between New Orleans and Mobile: Bay St. Louis, Pass Christian, Gulfport, Biloxi. The western edge of Katrina howled through New Orleans Monday morning at wind speeds of sixty miles an hour. As soon as she passed, the citizens of New Orleans expressed relief that the city had been spared a direct hit by the hurricane, though it had sustained a considerable amount of wind and water damage. They were slow to realize that the levees were breaking and the city was flooding, and had been since early morning.

Katrina made landfall at the town of Buras several miles north of the Head of Passes on the Mississippi. Buras lies in a trough between the hurricane levee that fronts the Barataria Basin and protects the tiny towns of Plaquemines Parish along the western bank of the Mississippi from storm surges and the main stem levee that protects the towns from flooding along the Mississippi. The great swell of water breached the storm levee, tripped over the river levees, leaving them intact and inundating Plaquemines Parish, and continued into Breton Sound to the east. It was 7:00 A.M.

To the north at New Orleans water levels began to rise within the Mississippi River Gulf Outlet (MRGO), Gulf Intracoastal Waterway (GWII), and the Inner Harbor Navigation Canal (Industrial Canal). After the first small breach in the city occurred at about 5:00 A.M., water levels in the canals dropped. If that had been the sole break in the city's storm-protection system, Katrina would have been a nuisance not a catastrophe.

As the storm surge passed through Breton Sound, the counterclockwise swirl of the winds drove a wall of water up to 18 feet high west into Lake Borgne and against the Mississippi River Gulf Outlet (MRGO) hurricane levees that fronted on the lake. These levees, designed to withstand a 17.5-foot surge, were incomplete, two to four feet too low, built of very wet dredge spoils of highly erodible shell-rich sand from MRGO, and laid on swampy soils. These are the levees that protected St. Bernard Parish and the Lower Ninth Ward. They had been built in stages over the course of forty years to allow the levee soils to dry out and the soils underneath to compact under the levees' increasing weight. And they had been built to specifications set in 1965 and never updated, even though the facts on the ground had changed. Sea level had risen; the ground had sunk. When Katrina's storm surge washed them away between 6:00 and 7:00 A.M., the Corps of Engineers was awaiting congressional approval of funds to complete the final stage of construction.

The surge rolled over and through MRGO's frontage levees and ripped across seven to ten miles of open swamp, which should have absorbed the surge had it not been eroded by salt water intrusion from MRGO. Finally, it overtopped the secondary levees, constructed of erosion-resistant clay, which surrounded the populated sections of St. Bernard Parish. The surge crested at seven and half to ten feet above sea level, pushed houses out of its way, flipped cars, and delivered shrimp boats deep into residential neighborhoods. Water filled the protected basin of St. Bernard Parish to an elevation of twelve feet above sea level, so that even neighborhoods located above sea level were swamped. The destruction was ruinous.

The same surge that eroded MRGO's levees pushed west through the marshlands, breached a levee made of light, sandy soil and lightweight shell-sand fill dredged from the GIWW, and spilled into the populated area of New Orleans East. And it poured through a V-shaped funnel into the shared GIWW/MRGO channel that separates St. Bernard Parish from New Orleans East. It hit the "T" intersection of the waterway and the Industrial Canal, which connects Lake Pontchartrain to the Mississippi. The surge split and flowed both north and south along the canal. It breached the levee surrounding New Orleans East to the north. And it breached the levee surrounding the Lower Ninth Ward to the south, washing houses off their foundations, carrying a barge into the streets, and reaching a flood level of fourteen feet above sea level in a part of the city that was four feet below sea level. It was 7:45 A.M.

Finally, the Lake Borgne surge breached the west wall of the Industrial Canal at the eastern edge of New Orleans, allowing limited amounts of water into downtown. When the surge subsided, the flow of water stopped, a pause in the flooding of New Orleans.

As the eye of Katrina passed to the east of New Orleans, its counterclockwise winds whipped up a storm surge in Lake Pontchartrain, which lashed the southern shore of the lake. The lake rose, but not quite to the tops of its levees, except at the west end of New Orleans East, where there was moderate overtopping of a floodwall that was lower than adjacent earthen levees. Even as the surge at the eastern edge subsided, more water poured into New Orleans East.

That was serious, but more serious was water surging into the Seventeenth Street Canal, the Orleans Canal, and the London Avenue Canal, which extended from the northern end of downtown to the lake. Three breaches occurred: the first at the south end of the London Avenue Canal between 7:00 and 8:00 A.M., the second on the north end of the London Avenue Canal between 7:30 and 8:30 A.M., and the third at the north end of the Seventeenth Street Canal at about 9:00 A.M. In each case water scoured the levees to depths well below sea level, and water poured into the city. It was 9:30 A.M.

By Monday evening 80 percent of New Orleans was underwater. Water flowed into the city until the flood in the streets reached the level of the lake, drowning the pumps that were designed to siphon out every drop of rain that falls on New Orleans.

In the following weeks it became a cliché to say that New Orleans had been a disaster waiting to happen. Some say it had been since the day Bienville platted the city on the natural levee of the left bank of the river just to the south of Lake Pontchartrain. The natural levee was the last spit of semidry land before the landscape gave way to the coastal marshes that would slow incoming hurricanes. And, semidry is the operative adjective: A dense cypress forest bordered by a marsh separated the town site from the lake. Bayou St. John gave access to the lake and then to the Gulf through Lake Borgne and a series of passes through the marshes. To the east, south, and west of New Orleans the same cypress forest gave way to freshwater marshes and then saltwater marshes that protected New Orleans from hurricanes like Katrina.

Until the early twentieth century, the City of New Orleans stayed within the bounds of the Mississippi's natural levee, keeping the cypress swamps and marshes as a buffer between the city and the lake. In the 1920s New Orleans cut the cypress swamp, drained the marshes, reclaimed land from the lake, and erected a stepped seawall that rose 9.6 feet above sea level to keep the lake out of the neighborhoods that followed. The city engulfed Bayou St. John, turning its banks into a park. An intricate drainage system pumped every drop of water that fell on New Orleans out of the city. An equally intricate system of levees and floodwalls kept water from the Mississippi and Lake Pontchartrain out of the city but created a bowl into which the city settled as the drained land under its neighborhoods compacted.

First, the drainage system: Getting water and sewage out of New Orleans was always a problem. Nor did the people of New Orleans separate the draining of water from their streets from the disposal of sewage from their homes until the mid-1890s. The canals that carried water and sewage to the Mississippi or to Lake Pontchartrain were one and the same. Bienville's engineer, Pierre Le

Blond de la Tour, and his assistant, Adrien de Pauger, platted a grid, fourteen blocks wide, six blocks deep, on the natural levee of the Mississippi. A ditch surrounded each block. Two larger ditches delivered water and sewage to a canal that wrapped around the city. The canal deposited the mix in the swamp that bordered Lake Pontchartrain. With each heavy rain the ditches flooded, turning each block into an island. Throughout the eighteenth and nineteenth centuries New Orleans continued to drain its water and sewage through canals to Lake Pontchartrain. Not until 1895 did New Orleans develop an adequate drainage system to remove storm water from the city and separate it from the city's sewage.

The 1895 drainage plan lifted New Orleans's sewage up over the levees and into the Mississippi and pumped its storm water into Lake Pontchartrain and to Lake Borgne through existing and new canals with pumps located at low points on the northern edge of the city. In the years before August 2005 the city enlarged the system as it drained the marshes and people settled the neighborhoods between the river and Lake Pontchartrain. The swampy ground under the new suburbs compacted and sank. The city surrounded the pumps on the Seventeenth Street, London Avenue, and Orleans Canals, located two to three miles inland from the lake. By August 2005 the bottom of the bowl lay lower in the landscape than the bottom of Lake Pontchartrain.

On August 29, 2005, two hundred miles of canals led to twenty-two pumping stations located at low points in the bowl. The pumps, some in use for almost a century, were capable of pumping thirty-five billion gallons of water per day out of the city into Lake Pontchartrain and Lake Borgne. The city's storm system was designed to carry rainwater to large box culverts that were connected to pumping stations, which spanned the outfall canals. The pumps sucked water out of the culverts and spewed it into the canals, which carried the water to the lakes. Locks at the end of the canals allowed water to flow to the lake and kept the lake from backing into the canals. The city could open the locks to release water when the lake fell below the level in the canals. Originally, the canals were ditches bounded by levees.

As the threat from storm surges on Lake Pontchartrain increased, the Corps of Engineers built segmented I-walls that were two feet wide at the base, a foot wide at the top, and ten to fourteen feet high, anchored into the crown of the levees with steel plates. The Corps of Engineers chose the I-wall because its slim profile could be shoehorned into the surrounding neighborhoods. These were the walls that failed on August 29, 2005, when Katrina's storm surge swept across Lake Pontchartrain and into the canals.

In the weeks following the hurricane, engineers sorted out just what had happened along the Seventeenth Street and London Avenue Canals. New discoveries came to light weekly. In the early weeks the Corps of Engineers and scientists at Louisiana State University debated whether the walls had been overtopped by the storm surge and the levees on which they sat undermined, leading to their collapse. In addition the National Science Foundation and the American Society of Civil Engineers sponsored an investigation of the levee failure led by engineers from the University of California at Berkeley. The team issued its initial findings at the beginning of October: The walls of the Seventeenth Street and London Avenue Canals had not been overtopped. The team turned its focus to the soil supporting the walls at the breaches, some of which had washed into backyards thirty-five feet from the canals. When the team examined the soil borings and design and construction documents for the floodwalls, they determined that spongy peat extending fifteen to twenty-one feet below sea level lay under the walls at the breaches. To compensate, construction contractors had driven steel sheet piling through the peat to a depth of seventeen feet below sea level. At the end of October, investigating engineers speculated that Katrina's flood in the canals had bored through the weak soil under the canal walls and shoved it, the steel pilings, and the concrete walls out of its way and into the streets of New Orleans. The detailed report on the investigation was published on July 31, 2006.

Now the levees: After the Flood of 1927 the focus of flood control on the Mississippi south of the Arkansas River has been to reduce the level of a major flood streaming past New Orleans. To do so the Corps of Engineers designed the Atchafalaya and Bonnet Carre Floodways to siphon floodwater from the Mississippi before it arrived at New Orleans. The last time the Mississippi had breached the New Orleans levees was in 1890. Since then the major threat of flooding has been from Lake Pontchartrain. The first time the Corps opened the Bonnet Carre Floodway, in 1937, water spilled over the Lake Pontchartrain levees into Jefferson Parish.

The levee and floodwall system that collapsed on August 29, 2005, had been designed in the 1960s in response to Hurricane Betsy, which tore across the Louisiana coast in 1965 with winds of 160 miles an hour and struck the city with winds reaching 100 miles an hour. A tidal surge breached the west levee of the Industrial Canal and poured up to eight feet of water into low-lying neighborhoods. Waves washed over the lakefront seawall, but a secondary levee kept water out of adjacent neighborhoods. In response to Betsy, Congress passed the Flood Control Act of 1965 and authorized the Corps of Engineers to build the Lake Pontchartrain and Vicinity Hurricane Protection Project in St. Bernard, Orleans, Jefferson, and St. Charles Parishes to protect against "the most severe meteorological conditions considered reasonably characteristic for that region."

The hurricane levee would ring the city and attach to the Mississippi levees, which measured twenty-five feet above sea level. It would enclose New Orleans on both the east and west banks, forming a bowl, several bowls actually: Orleans East Bank, New Orleans East, the Ninth Ward in St. Bernard Parish, St. Bernard Parish, two in Plaquemines Parish along the Mississippi south of New Orleans, and others on the west bank of the Mississippi and west of Orleans East Bank. The system was designed to protect each enclosed area from storm surges up to the standard project hurricane (SPH), a Category Three hurricane. By August 2005 the hurricane levee system was old, incomplete, neglected, underfinanced, and sinking. Within the Orleans East Bank bowl, the city itself, save the original site—the natural levee on which Bienville set his town—had sunk below sea level. Neighborhoods closest to the lake had sunk as much as ten feet below sea level. Only the French Quarter, built on the natural levee, sat above sea level, but only by one foot.

Several different criteria applied to the Lake Pontchartrain levees and allowed them to vary in height and still withstand the waves generated by an 11.5-foot storm surge. On August 29, 2005, the storm surge across Lake Pontchartrain was less than eleven feet above sea level. The levees along the lake held. Earthen levees protected by wetlands held.

The only earthen levees that failed were those along the Mississippi River Gulf Outlet, constructed of highly erodible sandy soils dredged from the shipping channel and set on swampy soils. In 2004 the Louisiana State Legislature passed a resolution, sponsored by representatives and senators from St. Bernard Parish, asking their congressional representatives to close MRGO permanently. While MRGO was not the hurricane expressway some thought it to be, Hurricane Katrina's storm surge rode into the heart of New Orleans on the section of the channel that MRGO shares with the GIWW and collided with the Industrial Canal at the "T" intersection. Miles of levees in Breton Sound failed, up to 90 percent, swamping 95 percent of St. Bernard Parish, home to 65,500 people who lived on 465 square miles of land, encompassed by 1,794 square miles of water, marsh, and land, the ragged fringe of the Gulf of Mexico. When the storm surge passed, 30,000 houses in St. Bernard Parish and 10,000 in the Lower Ninth Ward of New Orleans adjacent to the Industrial Canal had been lost. On September 13, 2005, the same group of legislators pleaded with Congress to close permanently the Mississippi River Gulf Outlet. They succeded. The Corps closed MRGO in July 2009.

Sorting Out What Happened

It is a second cliché to say that Hurricane Katrina was a perfect storm. Its aftermath was. What happened to New Orleans was the culmination of everything we have done to change the Mississippi River since 1718. In the wake of the Flood of 1993 the White House created the Interagency Floodplain Management Review Committee, headed by Dr. Gerald Galloway. Made up of representatives of federal, state, local, and tribal agencies, the committee evaluated the state of flood control and floodplain management in the Upper Mississippi Basin and issued *Sharing the Challenge: Floodplain Management into the Twenty-first Century*, published in June 1994, less than a year after the floodwaters receded. It was hoped that after Katrina a similar group would issue a document that would cause us to rethink how we protect New Orleans from the most dangerous hurricane we can imagine, a Category Five; how we control the Mississippi south of New Orleans; whether we rebuild the Lower Ninth Ward or the New Orleans suburbs in St. Bernard Parish or leave them to return to marsh; and how we rebuild the marshes that absorb incoming hurricanes. And it was hoped that such a document would not be sucked into the political black hole into which the 1994 document disappeared.

As of March 3, 2009, when the New Orleans District of the Corps of Engineers forwarded its plan for a Category Five hurricane to the National Academy of Sciences for peer review, such a comprehensive document had not happened. Granted, the task of sorting out the recovery of New Orleans and the towns in St. Bernard and Plaquemines Parishes, the reconstruction of the destroyed levees, and the restoration of the Louisiana coast was a task far more daunting than sorting out flood control on the Upper Mississippi. On the other hand, what needed to be done in terms of rebuilding the levees and reconstructing the coast was known and had been known for years and years. What did happen was scattershot and in the first instance counterproductive.

On September 22, Senators Mary Landrieu and David Vitter introduced the Louisiana Katrina Reconstruction Act in the Senate. Its price tag, a demand of $250 billion from the federal treasury for every project conceivable in Louisiana and some that were not, was over and above the $63 billion Congress had already appropriated for emergency relief in Louisiana. It was, in the cliché politicians apply to unrealistic bills, "dead on arrival." And it conjured up images of the corruption that seemed to be endemic to Louisiana politics.

In the weeks following Katrina, the New Orleans District of the Corps of Engineers established two task forces to address hurricane protection for New Orleans. The first, Task Force Guardian, was charged with meeting the immediate need of repairing and restoring New Orleans's hurricane levees to pre-Katrina levels. The engineers had accomplished the work by the beginning of the 2006 hurricane season and had moved on to raising the levees high enough to provide hundred-year protection by 2011.

The Interagency Performance Evaluation Team (IPET), one of a series of engineering studies in the first year that sorted out what had happened, was a $20 million internal investigation of the Corps' role in the disaster.

When Lt. Gen. Carl Strock, the chief of engineers, appeared before the Senate Appropriations Subcommittee on April 5, 2006, two months before the release of the report, he acknowledged that the design of the I-walls on the Seventeenth Street Canal was flawed and the walls could not withstand the force of the water surging into the canal from Lake Pontchartrain. The Corps issued a final draft of the six thousand-page report on June 1, 2006, and its final draft in June 2008. It was comprehensive but incomprehensible to the lay reader, but it too acknowledged that had the design of MRGO's levees and the I-walls along the stormwater canals not been faulty, Katrina's devastation would have been much less severe.

The National Academy of Engineering and the National Research Council were both hired to review the Corps' investigation. Their review came in five parts released over several years. The academies concluded in their first report that the draft of the IPET first report was weak in its analysis of hydrology, hydraulics, and hurricane surge and waves. In writing its final report the Corps needed to help the public understand the failure of the levees and floodwalls. The Corps needed to be clear in its explanation of the geologic setting and the foundations on which individual levees and floodwalls sat, of the structural design of floodwalls, of the physical changes to the levee system over time, and of the hydraulic loading against the levees, that is, the force of the storm surge against the floodwalls or levees. While the Corps seemed to have amassed the necessary data—base maps, climate, design criteria, geology, hydrology, etc.—the academies noted that the Corps needed to analyze it in a timely manner and to collect it in "a clear definitive, and system-wide approach" from the outset of the study. Finally, because most people would only read the executive summary, the Corps needed to make that summary technically correct and less opaque to the broad spectrum of readers: elected officials, journalists, and citizens.

The University of California at Berkeley assembled the Independent Levee Investigation Team, a group of thirty-seven volunteer engineers, working on a $350,000 budget funded by the National Science Foundation. The engineers studied the levees and why they failed. The Berkeley team issued its report, which drew on the technical information in the Corps' IPET report, on July 31, 2006. Robert Bea, one of the Berkeley engineers, described the history of the development of the concept of the "standard project hurricane" (SPH) and the levees it required for *Fortune* magazine: In the 1950s, at the request of Congress, the National Weather Service and the Corps of Engineers developed the standard project hurricane as a unit of measure that could be used to define the level of threat from any given hurricane in any given region. After Hurricane

Betsy swept through New Orleans in 1965, the Corps of Engineers measured its plans for hurricane protection in New Orleans by the SPH. But this could be confusing, because the SPH was invented before the Saffir-Simpson system of categorizing hurricanes. And, while the New Orleans levees were built to withstand a Category Three hurricane, the SPH for New Orleans could vary between a Category Two and a Category Four storm. Moreover, the Category Three levees had been designed after Hurricane Betsy, when there were healthy marshes stretching out in front of them. By the time Katrina rolled through, the marshes had been decimated, particularly those in Breton Sound and Lake Borgne, where MRGO had destroyed the acres and acres of marsh and swamp that protected the levees that fronted on the navigation channel and those that fronted on New Orleans's Lower Ninth Ward and St. Bernard Parish. Finally, the team found that in 1985 the Corps had tested a two hundred-foot section of sheet pile/floodwall in the Atchafalaya Basin south of Morgan City in soils similar to the I-walls along the canals in New Orleans. When tested against a ten-foot wave, the wall failed when the wave reached eight feet. The Corps had known for twenty years that the canals' walls could fail.

Team Louisiana, led by Dr. Ivor van Heerden and his colleagues from the Louisiana State University Hurricane Research Center, launched a deeply motivated study of what happened and why on behalf of the State of Louisiana. Team Louisiana's report answered some of the questions the academies asked. The team declared that the Corps of Engineers managed the hurricane levees in Greater New Orleans "like a circa 1964 flood control museum" and continued to use design criteria set in 1965 even though much had changed in the intervening forty years. By 1972 the wind speed of a standard project hurricane had risen from 107 miles per hour to 129, and then to 140 by 1979, but the earliest figure remained the design criteria. Increase the wind speed by 20 percent, and the elevation of a storm surge could increase by 40 percent. The SHOSH model for storm surges, devised by the National Hurricane Center in 1979, showed the Greater New Orleans levees could be overtopped by a Category Three storm. The Corps of Engineers used local mean sea level interchangeably with National Geodetic Vertical Datum of 1929 (NGVD29), regional sea level. In 1965 NGVD29 was 1.3 to 1.6 feet below local mean sea level. Using these figures the Corps built the levees too short. Nor did the Corps take into account the rate of subsidence (three to four feet per century) in the New Orleans area. The Corps ignored the fact that local sea level had risen 0.4 feet in the intervening forty years and New Orleans had sunk 1.5 feet. Add them together, and the engineers were designing and maintaining levees for a city that was lying two feet lower in the landscape, relative to sea level, than it had in 1965. Hence, the crowns of levees were as much as six feet too short, leading to prolonged overtopping during Katrina.

Nor did the Corps follow existing engineering practices in the design of the levees. Soft clays under the Seventeenth Street Canal levees led to their failure. Erosion-prone shell-rich sand in the MRGO levees led to their failure. The Corps failed to armor levee slopes against erosion on the New Orleans East and Chalmette clay back levees, noting that the short duration of hurricane floods made armor unnecessary. The Corps consistently underestimated the ability of MRGO and the GIWW to funnel surges out of Lake Borgne into the heart of New Orleans. The Corps opted for a levees-only plan along the south shore of Lake Pontchartrain and rejected a proposal for barriers across passes from Lake Borgne into Lake Pontchartrain which could have reduced storm surges into the latter by as much as five feet. Finally, the levees could not be replaced or rehabbed after forty years, as would normally be the case, because they had never been completed.

Congressional and State Action

In the months following Katrina, Congress ordered the New Orleans District of the Corps of Engineers to do three tasks simultaneously: Restore destroyed levees to pre-Katrina levels. Raise all levees to a hundred-year level (one that had a 1-in-100 chance of occurring in any given year) by 2011. Design a comprehensive hurricane-protection system that protected the Louisiana coast from a Category Five hurricane. Congress directed the Corps, in close cooperation with the State of Louisiana and its agencies, to develop the Louisiana Coastal Protection and Restoration Study (LACPR) in November 2005 with the Energy and Water Development Appropriations Act of 2006 and in

December with the Department of Defense, Emergency Supplemental Appropriations to Address Hurricanes in the Gulf of Mexico, and Pandemic Influenza Act of 2006. Congress ordered a concrete, flexible plan that Congress could approve, sidestepping the traditional, time-consuming approval process, and the Corps could build. The study would analyze and design comprehensive hurricane protection that included flood control, coastal restoration, and hurricane-risk reduction, and the Corps would submit a preliminary technical report for a Category Five or a thousand-year hurricane by July 2006 and a final report by December 2007.

Congress did direct the Corps to come up with the plan to close MRGO, but it allowed the Corps to rebuild the MRGO levees by lining its banks with riprap, piles of stones sinking into soft soil. While the Corps protected Louisiana's cypress forests from unsustainable logging under the Clean Water Act, the Corps emphasized flood protection and rural levee building over wetlands restoration in the November 2004 Louisiana Coastal Area Study (LCA Study). The environmental groups urged Congress to commit to coastal restoration, back its commitment with funds from the drilling revenues on the Outer Continental Shelf, and order the Corps of Engineers to trash the LCA Study and start over with the input of scientists and engineers from outside the agency.

Congress did include the LCA Study in the 2005 Water Resources Development Act, but passage of the bill had been held up for five years by wrangling over Corps reform. Congress finally passed the Water Resources Development Act in September 2007 despite a threatened a presidential veto. The act was vetoed, and Congress overrode it.

What the State Did

Beginning in October 2005, Governor Kathleen Babineaux Blanco initiated Louisiana's process of renewal and established the agencies that would work with the Corps of Engineers on the LACPR Study. On October 15, she established the Louisiana Recovery Authority to plan for the state's recovery and rebuilding in light of Katrina and Rita. The authority, which could fill the role of the interagency committee after the Flood of 1993, would work with local, state, and federal agencies to address both short- and long-term planning for recovery. The governor would appoint the thirty-three members of the board of directors, and the state senate would approve them. The LRA broke down recovery needs into task forces and recovery teams that covered all aspects of life in Louisiana. It also formed committees to deal with the federal, state, and local legislatures, and it appointed a subcommittee to audit the huge amounts of federal money spent on recovery.

On January 18, 2006, Governor Blanco created a second authority to start the process of coastal reconstruction, the twenty-one-member Coastal Protection and Restoration Authority (CPRA), and charged its members with shaping the first comprehensive coastal-protection plan. It could also fill the role the interagency committee had in 1994.

In welcoming the members to the commission the governor noted that the most important part of the plan would be to integrate coastal restoration with hurricane protection. Levees were essential, but so were marshlands to absorb and reduce the force of a hurricane's storm surge attacking the levees. She envisioned the commission as the single agency that would coordinate the work of the federal, state, and local agencies that were responsible for protecting Louisiana's coast. She asked the commission to work aggressively with the Corps of Engineers to design a strong levee system, to set standards for the levee districts, which would operate and maintain the levees, and remove all opportunities for political patronage in the staffing, financing, and operations of local levee districts. She charged the commission with identifying and pursuing funding, particularly Louisiana's fair share of the outer continental shelf federal revenues from oil and gas leases, which would go directly into coastal protection and restoration. Finally, she asked the board to "recommend formal state policy regarding the Mississippi River Gulf Outlet."

The State of Louisiana rolled its Wetland Conservation and Restoration Authority into the Coastal Protection and Restoration Authority and called for a comprehensive coastal protection master plan that incorporated immediate protection from hurricane surges and long-term coastal ecosystem sustainability with an eye to social and economic recovery. For the first time the state would coordinate coastal restoration with hurricane protection. The authority would work with the Corps on its LACPR Study and with state, parish, and local interests, as well as nongovernmental organizations. The authority published *Louisiana's Comprehensive Master Plan for a Sustainable Coast* in May 2007. The state authorized $200 million in budget surplus money to start work on implementing the plan immediately and continue over a three-year period.

At the same time the state created the Louisiana Coastal Protection and Restoration Financing Corporation, which would sell bonds to be paid off with oil and gas revenues. Money raised from the bonds would fund projects over a ten-year period and free the state from having to wait on the federal government to provide a steady stream of revenue for coastal reconstruction. On the second anniversary of Katrina, the state and the nation were still waiting for Congress to pass the 2006 Water Resources Development Act, which had become the 2007 act, which would authorize the Morganza-to-the-Gulf of Mexico Hurricane and Storm Protection System, the New Orleans–to-Venice Levee System, and the five critical projects outlined in the LCA Study.

Ongoing Programs after Katrina

Meanwhile the Coastal Wetlands Planning, Protection, and Restoration Act—the Breaux Act—was still targeting funds to small-scale, short-term projects. In the seventeen years after passage of the Breaux Act in 1990, the Louisiana Department of Natural Resources had approved 138 projects, of which 67 had been constructed, affecting over 52,000 acres of marsh. After 1998 the strategies developed for the Coast 2050 effort were used to evaluate projects developed under the Breaux Act. The 2004 LCA Study, the Louisiana Coastal Area Ecosystem Restoration plan, had yet to be implemented or funded. The new master plan would coordinate with and build on all previous plans. And the plan would coordinate with the Hurricane Protection for New Orleans Metropolitan Area and the communities surrounding Lake Pontchartrain, the yet-to-be-authorized Donaldsonville-to-Gulf hurricane-protection plan for the New Orleans West Bank, Lafourche Parish, and communities in the Barataria Basin; the yet-to-be-authorized Morganza-to-the-Gulf hurricane-protection plan for the communities along the distributaries in Terrebonne and Lafourche Parishes; and the hurricane-protection plan for the Atchafalaya River Delta, Arcadiana, and the Chenier Plain. All involved construction of hurricane levees, nine to fifteen feet high, some of which cut across wetlands to get from one natural ridge to another.

There were other programs in Louisiana geared to coastal restoration. The Environmental Protection Agency developed the National Estuary Program in 1989, of which the Barataria-Terrebonne National Estuary Program is a part. Working with government, private, commercial, conservation, and civic interests, the program developed a Comprehensive Coastal Management Plan for the Barataria and Terrebonne Basins that included the restoration of barrier islands, the long-distance pumping of sediment to create marshes, and shoreline stabilization. Similarly, the Lake Pontchartrain Basin Foundation published its Comprehensive Management Plan in January 2006 that addressed hurricane protection and coastal restoration of the north-shore riverine habitats, in the cypress swamps around Lake Maurepas, of the marshes along the southern shore, of the Breton Sound and Lake Borgne estuaries, of the East Orleans Landbridge and MRGO–Lake Borgne Landbridge, and of the Chandeleur barrier islands.

Other Ideas for Restoration

Aside from the governmental agencies, there were plenty of people out there with plenty of new ideas for coastal restoration. Some were quirky: The lieutenant governor of Illinois offered to ship sediment dredged from the Illinois River downstream to Louisiana for marsh building. Some were very dramatic: Richard Sparks proposed building a new New Orleans, a port city on the developing lobe of the Atchafalaya, saving old New Orleans for its historical and cultural character, letting the Mississippi divert to the Atchafalaya, and tapping the sediment building up behind the reservoir dams on the Missouri River. Sherwood Gagliano proposed excavating a new distributary that would flow parallel to Bayou Lafourche, split into two distributaries, and deliver freshwater and sediment to the Terrebonne estuary on the west and the Barataria estuary on the east.

Others tried to push the debate beyond old solutions: Ivor van Heerden proposed stretching a hurricane levee from the Pearl River on the Louisiana/Mississippi border west to Morgan City and beyond—that would roughly parallel the GIWW. He would divert freshwater and sediment from the Mississippi and Atchafalaya through numerous floodgates in the levee. In addition he would abandon the Birdfoot Delta, let it be reworked into barrier islands, and divert massive amounts of freshwater and sediment from the Mississippi to Barataria Bay to the east and Breton Sound to the west from a point thirty-two miles upstream of the Head of Passes. Finally, he would rebuild barrier islands in Terrebonne Bay, Barataria Bay, Breton Sound, and Chandeleur Sound, using sediment excavated from the Ship Shoal and other underwater sources of sand in the Gulf of Mexico.

In January 2006, the Working Group for Post-Hurricane Planning for the Louisiana Coast—an independent group of scientists and engineers that included familiar names like Gerald E. Galloway, who headed the Interagency Floodplain Management Review Committee that examined the 1993 flood—published a study that insisted that planning for hurricane protection, navigation, and coastal restoration must be done in concert rather than isolation as had been the case up until Katrina. Protecting New Orleans must include a combination of levees and a sustainable coastal landscape. The group postulated that a sustainable Louisiana coast could be established with an efficient use of the Mississippi's resources. The scientists recommended reexamining the Louisiana Coastal Area Study for economically and environmentally sustainable approaches to ecosystem restoration and storm-damage reduction. The group scrutinized each of the five near-term critical projects—Bayou Lafourche reintroduction, MRGO restoration, diversion at Hope Canal, Barataria Basin shoreline restoration, and the diversion at Myrtle Grove—in light of their integrated plan and found them all wanting for hurricane protection as well as ecosystem restoration. Only the environmental restoration of MRGO addressed navigation.

The report concluded that Congress and the State of Louisiana should: Engage professionals—scientists, economists, and engineers—and local governments and stakeholders in developing a vision for the future of the Louisiana coast. Acknowledge that there were four ways to reduce storm damage: build effective hurricane levees around large population centers; create self-sustaining wetlands that reduce storm surges and wind fetch; limit storm surges along artificial channels like MRGO; and maintain barrier islands. Mitigate the disruption of coastal landscape caused by navigation channels like MRGO and the Houma Navigation Channel. Separate authorization and financing of hurricane protection, restoration, and navigation from the Water Resources Development Act process. Engage stakeholders and responsible agencies in planning and innovative decision-making. Establish the Coastal Louisiana Authority, a new federal-state management and fiscal framework for guiding Louisiana's hurricane-protection and coastal-restoration program.

The group also designed a new framework for funding Louisiana's needs for coastal restoration, hurricane protection, and navigation. Congress and the administration would authorize and then appropriate $200 million per year for ten years to support the new Coastal Louisiana Authority, which would guide the organization and financing of the integrated program, using information derived from the new Coastal Assessment Group, which would examine each proposed project to assure that it incorporated the needs of ecosystem restoration, hurricane protection, and navigation; and identify the social, economic, and environmental objectives served by each project. Finally, the group suggested that the state create the Louisiana Coastal Investment Corporation, which would issue fifty-year bonds to fund ecosystem restoration, storm protection, and navigation.

In August 2007, a group of coastal scientists and engineers chaired by John Lopez issued their report, funded by the McKnight Foundation and titled *Comprehensive Recommendations Supporting the Use of the Multiple Lines of Defense Strategy to Sustain Coastal Louisiana.* The report responded to and added to the state's *Comprehensive Master Plan for a Sustainable Coast,* published in May 2007, and to the Corps of Engineers' Louisiana Coastal Protection and Restoration plan, both of which adopted the multiple lines of defense strategy, proposed by Lopez for the Lake Pontchartrain Basin Foundation in 2006. The strategy was a planning tool that set priorities and coordinated restoration methods and coastal-habitat and flood-protection projects. Unlike other restoration proposals, it acknowledged the importance of flood protection, both engineered and coastal habitat restoration, but with an emphasis on wetlands as flood protection. For example: most levees are adjacent to freshwater environments. Therefore, to protect the levees from wind and water, cypress forests should be planted out front of the levees.

The plan organized the Louisiana coast into the four basins laid out in the Coast 2050 plan. It used natural and manmade features in the landscape, lines of defense that impede storm surges and reduce store damage. Working inland from the Gulf of Mexico, the lines of defense were the continental shelf, the barrier islands, the bays, the sounds, marsh landbridges, natural ridges, manmade ridges, floodgates, flood levees, pump stations, home and building elevations, and evacuation routes. Hence, if you understand that the natural levee of an abandoned distributary is a hydrological barrier, as the Bayou Lafourche ridge is the barrier between Barataria Bay and the eastern Terrebonne Basin, and that the ridges are corridors of economic activity, then it follows that hurricane levees protect commercial and residential development, restored cypress forests protect the levees, marsh landbridges impede salt water intrusion and protect the forests, barrier islands protect the marshes.

The paper established the goals for the distribution of various wetland habitats and their salinity regimes in each basin—fresh swamp, fresh marsh, intermediate marsh, brackish marsh, and salt marsh. The distribution of habitats should be mapped—something that had never been done but that had been recommended by the National Research Council in its 2006 review of the LCA Study. Future restoration projects should address the agreed distribution of habitat in their design.

The Post-Katrina Reports and Studies

In 2006 the New Orleans District of the Corps of Engineers and the Louisiana Department of Natural Resources began issuing the reports ordered by Congress and Governor Blanco. In July the Corps published the preliminary technical reports of the LACPR Study. It was a six-month effort to identify and describe the array of flood-control, hurricane-protection, and coastal-restoration actions that would be included in the final report, due out in December 2007. The final report would incorporate the work of the Louisiana Recovery Authority and the *Comprehensive Master Plan for a Sustainable Coast,* which the Louisiana Department of Natural Resources published in May 2007.

The framework for the comprehensive plan would break down the coast into the four geographic planning units described in the Coast 2050 restoration proposal of 1998; would describe the resources, both ecological and built, at risk in each of the units; would characterize the hurricane threat to each unit and quantify the probability of yearly occurrences; would develop structural, nonstructural, and coastal restoration measures for each unit and evaluate them; would integrate the various measures into alternative plans for each unit; would estimate the cost of each alternative, and would recommend further investigation of the most promising plans to further reduce the risk from hurricanes.

In February 2000, when the Corps of Engineers and the Louisiana DNR signed their agreement to initiate a feasibility study for the restoration of wetlands and barrier islands in Barataria Basin, everybody—engineers, politicians, and environmentalists—cheered. Secretary of the Interior Bruce Babbitt declared the Louisiana coast the equal of the Florida Everglades. Congressman Billy Tauzin (R-Louisiana) declared it the "beginning of a comprehensive, aggressive plan to save Louisiana's coastline." Senator John Breaux (D-Louisiana), author of the Breaux Act, declared it a step forward that would "maintain Louisiana's wetlands for our children and grandchildren."

When the state published *Louisiana's Comprehensive Master Plan for a Sustainable Coast,* nobody cheered. Scientists and engineers, who had been working on coastal restoration for decades, objected to the massive hurricane levees, Morganza-to-the-Gulf hurricane-protection plan that had been on the books for years and was ready for congressional authorization in 2003. When completed, the levee would stretch across the northern reaches of the Barataria Basin, run south to Larose, loop across the distributaries of the Terrebonne Basin to Houma. While it would follow existing hydrological barriers, some natural and some artificial, it would, in essence, cut the northern half of each basin from its southern half, completely altering its hydrology. To allow for the exchange of fish and wildlife, to allow for freshwater to trickle down into the southern regions of each basin, the Corps would poke holes in the levees, creating leaky levees, for which, the scientists objected, there was no scientific basis. Come a hurricane, floodgates on the holes could be closed, creating an impenetrable defense to a storm surge. Who knew if leaky levees would work?

"The operation of the environmental structures needs definition," noted the Working Group. "The science suggests that it wouldn't work," warned John Day, a professor of oceanography and coastal science at LSU. "I'm doing it to let the people of Louisiana know that the Morganza leaky levee proposal is, in our opinion, pure pork," threatened environmentalist Luke Fontana when he announced his plans to file a lawsuit to demand that the Corps follow environmental laws in the construction of the hurricane levee. "Its primary difficulties are in its assumptions, its science, and its failure to provide for the management of the landscape as a whole," commented Oliver Houck, professor of law at Tulane University and longtime environmentalist, in a letter to the governor's office. "A dusted off version of the Corps's old plans," grumbled Ivor van Heerden in *The Storm.* "Over-reliance on structures," criticized Leslie March of the Sierra Club–Delta Chapter. "In sum, we believe that the current federal and state plans contain several positive elements but, at bottom, rely on an engineering approach that carries high economic, structural and environmental risk, and threatens the sustainability of the very ecosystem we are all trying to save," wrote a group of sixteen coastal engineers and scientists to Governor Kathleen Blanco on March 13, 2007.

In April 2008 the Louisiana Coastal Protection and Restoration Authority appointed a panel of eight scientists to review the Morganza-to-the-Gulf levee in light of lessons learned from Katrina and Rita. It did so at the request of Terrebonne Parish officials, who wanted to put to rest questions about the efficacy of the levee. The scientists were to review all the information presented by the Terrebonne Levee and Conservation District, the Corps of Engineers, and the state and make their recommendations in August 2008.

The Task Force Guardian published its Hurricane Storm Damage and Risk Reduction System, the hundred-year levee, for New Orleans in June 2007. To define the hundred-year storm protection the engineers looked at the tracks of 152 hurricanes, recorded the speed at which each crossed the landscape and the amount of rainfall, the size of each storm surge, and the height of the waves that each generated. They also considered the expected rise in sea level, possible increases in storm severity, and the subsidence and the settlement of levees and floodwalls. From the data gleaned they developed a hurricane-protection system—a combination of levees, floodwalls, and floodgates—that would provide a hundred-year level of protection. The cost to bring the levees to a hundred-year level: $14.8 billion.

When the Corps published its hundred-year hurricane-protection system, it had yet to complete its Engineering and Operational Risk and Reliability Analysis, volume 8 of the IPET report. In reviewing volume 8, the National Academy of Engineering and the National Research Council noted in its fourth report that the hundred-year hurricane-protection system and the LACPR Study were dependent on the analysis in volume 8.

When the Corps began releasing its interim final IPET report in March 2007, it broke it down into a series of eight volumes. Volume 8 contained information essential to understanding the risk of future flooding and the resulting loss of life and property from hurricanes in New Orleans. The Corps did not release its draft of volume 8 until October 2007, which the National Academy of Sciences reviewed and found incomplete and urged the Corps to get on with the report for the sake of the people of New Orleans. When the national academies released its review of volume 8 in April 2008, its fourth of the IPET, the Corps had yet to issue the final draft of the volume. Nor was it available in March 2009.

In July 2007 the Corps revealed that it had changed the design standard in the LACPR Study for worst-case hurricane, a Category Five or thousand-year storm authorized by Congress, to a four hundred-year storm in its planning for protecting New Orleans. It did so in a briefing with a National Research Council committee that was reviewing the work. The engineers reasoned that damage from a thousand-year storm would not be that much greater than damage from a four hundred-year storm, but the cost would be greater.

On March 3, 2009, the New Orleans District sent the final technical report of the LACPR Study, due in December 2007, to the National Academy of Sciences for review and released it to the public two days later. The 4,000-page study used the multiple lines of defense strategy to cover all bases, but recommended no plan of action. It divided the Louisiana coast into five sections and recommended five or six sets of alternative plans for flood control (raising buildings or buyouts and relocations) measures, for hurricane-protection (levees, floodwalls, and floodgates) measures, and for coastal-restoration (wetland restoration) measures within each section. The cost of one combination of options came to $102.2 billion to build, allowing for cost overruns of 50 percent. "We took over a million different possibilities and we used a risk-informed decision-making framework to get to a reasonable number: 111 alternatives," explained Col. Al Lee, commander of the New Orleans district, to the *New Orleans Times-Picayune.* Alternatives included hurricane protection from hundred-year storms, four hundred-year storms, and thousand-year storms.

Louisianans were outraged. "The lack of specific recommendations violates the law in at least two places, " said Garret Graves, director of the state's Office of Coastal Protection and Restoration. He went on to say that the cooperation between the Corps and the Louisiana Department of Natural Resources, which Congress mandated when it authorized the LACPR Study in 2005, broke down after President Bush ordered the Corps to abandon specific recommendations, also mandated by Congress, in October 2006, three months after the preliminary technical report was issued.

The study did note the importance of the use of Mississippi water and sediment to coastal restoration and recommended that Congress amend the Flood Control Act of 1928, the Mississippi River and Tributaries Project, to allow the Corps to pursue environmental and coastal restoration projects in its management of the river as well as flood-control and navigation projects.

The Corps sent the study to the National Academy of Sciences for peer review, a process that should be completed by June 2009. Then, state and federal agencies and the public will review it before the Corps will produce a supplement that will document further action. Then the study will go to the chief of engineers, who will send it to the assistant secretary of the army for civil works. After final review, the secretary will send it to Congress. Should Congress agree to pay for additional study, the engineers will sort projects that can be done under authorized levee and coastal-restoration programs from those requiring new authorization.

In 2007 Congress added a provision to the study that all projects recommended before 2010 would be approved in just forty-five days, possibly en masse. If the Corps' recommended plan didn't get to Congress before 2010, it could get bogged down in federal politics. Louisianans were outraged.

Restoring the Louisiana coast was economically and environmentally necessary, although that necessity was little understood outside Louisiana. Its complex ecology sustains 30 percent of the nation's commercial seafood, 20 to 25 percent of the nation's oil and natural gas supply, 70 percent of the habitat used by the nation's migratory birds. Four hundred million tons of goods move through the Port of New Orleans yearly. Without this understanding, it was way too easy to overlook the failure of the Corps-designed levees and to blame the flooding of New Orleans on New Orleans and the deterioration of Louisiana's wetlands on Louisiana.

It was hoped at the end of 2005 that Katrina had changed everything, that Congress and the Corps of Engineers would understand the urgency of repairing New Orleans' levees and Louisiana's wetlands. The levees did get repaired by the beginning of the 2006 hurricane season and the Corps started the work of raising them to the hundred-year level of protection. The Corps did publish the preliminary technical report of the LACPR Study by July 2006. The state did publish its comprehensive restoration plan for flood control, hurricane protection, and coastal restoration by May 2007, and the Corps of Engineers did incorporate it into the LACPR Study. Everything after that came with excruciating slowness.

In the first week of March 2009, Louisiana's scientists, who had known since January that the LACPR Study would yield no definitive plan on publication, met in New Orleans for a symposium on Mississippi and Atchafalaya River diversions, their pluses and minuses. The New Orleans district, prompted by an array of environmental organizations who sensed that opportunities for coastal restoration were slipping away (the Environmental Defense Fund, the National Wildlife Federation, the National Audubon Society, the Nature Conservancy, the Coalition to Restore Coastal Louisiana, and the Lake Pontchartrain Basin Foundation), sponsored the symposium. Representatives and technical advisors from the various state and federal agencies involved in restoration (EPA, NOAA, NRCS, USFWS, USGS, the governor's Office of Coastal Activities, and the Louisiana Applied Coastal and Engineering and Science Division) attended the conference. The participants acknowledged that the future of the Louisiana coast is tied to the whole river, its geomorphology and its sediment and nutrient loads. Louisiana and its coast were also tied to the Corps of Engineers, because the engineers owned management of the river.

The scientists and state coastal restoration officials demanded that the Corps speed up efforts to design large-scale Mississippi and Atchafalaya diversions to rebuild Louisiana's wetlands, which Congress had mandated in 2005. Others noted that diversions could harm commercial and recreational fisheries should freshwater drive out saltwater species. And diversions must be designed to avoid the build-up of sediment in navigation channels at the mouth of the river that could disrupt shipping.

In 2009 it was clear that the Corps and Louisiana needed to speed up coastal restoration and truly incorporate it into hurricane protection, and into navigation, added the Working Group. Ivor van Heerden put Louisiana's dilemma very succinctly on the National Public Radio program *Living on Earth* on June 2, 2006. "Barrier islands protect the wetlands. The wetlands protect the levees. The levees protect the home." He also noted in *The Storm* that the United States could learn from the Netherlands, which protects its cities that are at or below sea level from a one-in-ten-thousand-years storm. And, Louisiana has one great advantage over the Netherlands: Louisiana still has wetlands.

Restoration Efforts—the Managed River

With the completion of the Upper Mississippi locks and dams, the Lower Mississippi mainline levees and reservoirs on its tributaries, the Old River Control Structure at the head of the Atchafalaya, and the dams on the Missouri the big job of engineering the Mississippi River for our navigation and flood control needs was, for the most part, done. What was left was managing the river. To do that the Corps of Engineers adapted and learned new skills.

In response to the Flood of 1927, the Corps of Engineers established the Waterways Experiment Station at Vicksburg, Mississippi, headquarters of the Mississippi River Commission. Its role was to help the commission develop and implement a flood-control plan for the Lower Mississippi valley. Out of this effort came the Mississippi River and Tributaries Project, which the engineers tested on a model of the Mississippi dug into a hillside outside of Vicksburg. After Congress added stewardship of the nation's wetlands with Section 404 of the 1972 Clear Water Act, the Waterways Experiment Station increased the scope of its research, adding a Coastal and Hydraulics Laboratory, a Geotechnical Laboratory, a Structures Laboratory, an Environmental Laboratory, and an Information Technology Laboratory to its complex. Over twelve hundred scientists and engineers—civil engineers, hydrologists, geologists, geomorphologists, biologists, or economists—studied the river and its floodplain and how they interact. Most were civilians; some were military personnel.

In 1940, Gen. Harley B. Ferguson, the president of the Mississippi River Commission, writing in his *History of the Improvement of the Lower Mississippi River for Flood Control and Navigation, 1932–1939,* outlined the Mississippi River and Tributaries Project and described the natural course of a Mississippi flood before the construction of levees. In 1944 the Mississippi River Commission published Harold Fisk's *Geological Investigation of the Alluvial Valley of the Lower Mississippi River* in which he documented how the Lower Mississippi had ranged across its alluvial valley over thousands of years before settling on its modern course. Roger T. Saucier, a geologist with the Waterways Experiment Station, updated Fisk's work fifty years later when the Mississippi River Commission published *Geomorphology and Quarternary Geologic History of the Lower Mississippi Valley* in 1994. Saucier thoroughly documented how the Lower Mississippi was formed by glacial melt and how it interacted with its floodplain. While younger geologists have modified Saucier's work in the years since its publication, it is still the basic text on how the river and its floodplain, unfettered by dikes and levees, worked together. And, it became a basis on which other federal agencies, the EPA and the U.S. Fish and Wildlife Service, evaluated Corps projects in the lower valley.

There was no "master work" on the Upper Mississippi or the headwaters that detailed how the river worked above Thebes Gap as did Saucier's work on the Lower Mississippi. The Rock Island and St. Paul Districts, however, commissioned similar work on the Upper River and the headwaters from research geologists from various universities in states along the river. Jeffrey D. Anderson, E. Arthur Bettis III, and James S. Oliver studied the landforms between the bluffs of the Upper Mississippi and the processes that shaped them. The group published *Landform Sediment Assemblage Units in the Upper Mississippi River Valley* in 1996. Their report documented valley trains—terraces and the floodplain in the Rock Island District between Guttenberg, Iowa, and Cap au

Gris, Missouri. A second group of geologists published a similar report on the landforms between Minneapolis and Guttenberg in the St. Paul District in 2001, and a third group, on the landforms in various regions in the headwaters. While all of these reports were geared to aiding archeologists in their search for potential ancient Native American sites, they also helped to define how the river worked.

Within the Waterways Experiment Station, the Environmental Laboratory supported the Wetlands Research Program for the study of the hydraulics, hydrology, sedimentation, erosion, water quality, and soils processes that affect wetlands. Scientists in the program developed techniques for the delineation and evaluation of wetlands, the restoration and establishment of wetlands, and the stewardship and management of wetlands. While the program was designed to support the Corps' regulatory responsibilities under Section 404 of the Clean Water Act, the results of its research applied to all aspects of wetlands management. In 1987 the Corps published its *Wetlands Delineation Manual,* to standardize the identification and delineation of wetlands and to set wetland boundaries.

In 1993 the Waterways Experiment Station published *A Hydrogeomorphic Classification for Wetlands,* followed two years later by *A Guidebook for the Application of Hydrogeomorphic Assessments to Riverine Wetlands,* which detailed all the variables that make riverine wetlands, like those along the Upper and Lower Mississippi, work. In 1997 the Corps collaborated with the Federal Highway Administration, the Natural Resources Conservation Service, the EPA, and the U.S. Fish and Wildlife Service on a "National Action Plan to Implement the Hydrogeomorphic Approach to Wetland Functions." The agencies based this approach to assessing wetland functions on three factors that influence how wetlands work: first, their positions in the landscape, or their geomorphic setting; second, their water sources, or their hydrology; third, the flow and fluctuation of water through various wetlands, or their hydrodynamics or hydraulics. Using this process, the agencies began to develop guidebooks that described the physical, biological, and chemical characteristics of regional wetlands, including *A Regional Guidebook for Applying the Hydrogeomorphic Approach to Assessing Wetland Functions of Selected Regional Wetland Subclasses, Yazoo Basin, Lower Mississippi River Alluvial Valley* in 2002, and a similar publication on the rivers in Arkansas in 2004. In November 2002 the St. Louis District of the Corps of Engineers teamed up with a host of state and federal agencies to produce the East St. Louis and Vicinity Interior Flood Control and Ecosystem Restoration Project. The agencies developed a hydrogeomorphic approach to solving the flooding problems along the creeks that flowed through the American Bottom in the vicinity of East St. Louis, Illinois.

For all their attempts to define wetlands in the Yazoo Basin, for all their restoration efforts on the Upper River and on the Louisiana coast, and for all their struggles to create islands and sandbars for Least Terns south of St. Louis, the Corps and Engineers, U.S. Fish and Wildlife Service, and the state natural resources agencies had to live with the changes made to the Mississippi River. They had to live with the levees along the Lower Mississippi, which made human settlement possible in the alluvial valley but which severed the floodplain and its wetlands from the river. They had to live with those same levees in the deltaic plain, which prevented the river from delivering freshwater and sediment to the coastal marshes. They had to live with the wing dams that scoured the nine-foot channel but filled the backwaters with sediment south of St. Paul. They had to live with the navigation dams on the Upper Mississippi, which changed the way the river flowed across its floodplain. At the turn of the twenty-first century the Corps, the U.S. Fish and Wildlife Service, and the state natural resource agencies drew up plans to do just that. The plans grew out of a controversy about whether or not to expand the locks on five of those dams and out of the 1999 Water Resources Development Act, which reauthorized the Upper Mississippi Environmental Management Program in perpetuity.

In 1988, at the urging of the barge and grain export industries—led by Con Agra, Cargill, and Archer Daniels Midland Corporations, Congress authorized the Corps of Engineers to begin a navigation study of the system of locks and dams on the Upper Mississippi and Illinois Rivers with an eye to relieving congestion at the 600-foot locks. Modern tow captains faced the daily hassle of moving their 1,200-foot tows through 600-foot locks on the Upper Mississippi. Their solution at the end of the twentieth century was to break them in two and move one 600-foot section through at a time. Traffic backed up.

It was a familiar story: the barge industry—one of the Corps' major constituents along with farmers, grain companies, and the construction industry—proposed that the locks at five of the dams of the Upper Mississippi and two on the Illinois be lengthened to twelve hundred feet. Lobbyists for the industry insisted that farmers in the Midwest, who exported their grain from ports in Louisiana, needed the improvements to the system of locks and dams to hasten their grain downriver. Their competition were growers in South America, where Brazil—the breadbasket of the tropics—had doubled its soybean acreage; where farmers in Argentina could produce corn at half of what it cost farmers in Iowa; where the Amazon River was unobstructed by dams; and where the Brazilian government and soybean farmers had built floating ports to rise and fall with the Amazon, which was 40 feet deep in the dry season and 120 feet deep the rest of the year.

The Corps was eager to meet the needs of farmers, the grain companies, and the barge industry, but the Flood Control Act of 1936 required that the Corps run a cost-benefit analysis of any new water project. Congress could fund a project only if its economic benefits exceeded its costs. The Corps initiated a $50 million study of the proposal in 1993 and assigned Donald Sweeney at the St. Louis District as its chief economist.

By April 1998 Sweeney and other economists had concluded that the Corps' old economic models had failed to acknowledge that a rise in barge costs would lead to a fall in usage. The Corps had traditionally compared the cost of shipping grain by barge to the cost of shipping it by railroad. It had failed to compare the cost of barge transportation to other alternatives: trucking it to markets closer to home, including places that would process it into pig feed, ethanol, corn sweeteners, or flour. Hence, the Corps had consistently overestimated the amount of traffic on the Upper River.

Much to the displeasure of his military bosses, Sweeney developed an economic model that forced the Corps to look at the realities of barge traffic. He concluded that fixing the old locks, providing temporary mooring facilities for waiting barges, and encouraging tow captains to help one another through the 600-foot locks would solve the problem for at least fifty years.

Presented with these findings, Corps leaders—Maj. Gen. Russell L. Fuhrman, director of the Civil Works Program; Gen. Phillip Anderson, Mississippi Valley Division commander; and Col. James Mudd, Rock Island District commander—relieved Sweeney of his duties as chief economist on navigation study, transferred the project to Mudd's Rock Island District, and extended the study past its original deadline of December 1999.

In early May 1999, Chris Brescia, the barge industry lobbyist with the Midwest Area River Coalition, and representatives from Con Agra, Cargill, and American Commercial Barge Lines met with Major General Anderson, Colonel Mudd, and other Corps officials to discuss the economics of the project. The industrial representatives impressed upon the Corps the importance to the industry's future of extending the locks. The general, in turn, impressed upon the economists working on the study the importance of justifying the lock expansion. The economists, in turn, found that, to satisfy the general, they had to alter the "n" in Sweeney's formula, Q=t*[(a-w)/(a-e)n], twice, downward from 2 to 1.5 and to 1.2 before extension of the locks became economically feasible. The "n" represented the alternatives to barge transportation.

At the end of June, Sweeney objected, suggesting, with the support of other economists, that the Corps was "cooking the books." He claimed that the Corps had altered a second study that had found that the present locks would not need renovations until 2033. The alteration allowed the Corps to state that immediate extension of the locks would save the cost of renovating them in 2015. In July 1999 the Corps disbanded the economics panel and pronounced the locks extension economically justified. On February 2, 2000, Donald Sweeney blew the whistle.

Sweeney filed a request for an investigation by the Office of Special Counsel, an independent federal agency. In his sworn affidavit he contended that Corps officials had made faulty forecasts about the value of reducing barge congestion on the five dams, had made arbitrary reductions in the cost of constructing the new locks, had inflated estimates of savings to be had from rebuilding the locks rather than fixing them, and had rejected economists' calculations that the whole problem of congestion could be handled by one tow helping another through the locks.

On February 15, 2000, the Pentagon promised an independent review of the project and an inquiry into alleged misconduct by top Corps officials. There were two: a report by the army's inspector general and a report by the National Academy of Sciences.

Before either government report was issued, three independent economists working with the Northeast-Midwest Institute—a think tank that concentrated on economic and environmental issues in the Northeast and Midwest—affirmed Sweeney's allegations that the Corps of Engineers had manipulated its figures to justify lock expansion in the study released in July 1999. On May 18, 2000, the institute released its report, written by Steven Berry of Yale University, Geoffrey Hewings of the University of Illinois, and Charles Leven of Washington University in St. Louis. The economists used information from the study and information garnered from a workshop organized to hear from farm groups, the navigation industry, environmentalists, and the Corps itself, all of whom had a stake in the future of navigation on the Upper Mississippi. The three men concluded that the Corps of Engineers had ignored evidence that grain exports had remained level since 1979 as well as outside experts' projections of demand for grain exports when it made its own projections. Therefore, any increase in congestion at the locks in question could not be substantiated. They noted that the Corps compared the cost of barge transportation only to that of rail transportation. Indeed, Corps economists ignored what farmers might do if the cost of exporting their grain topped the value of finding other markets. The Corps ignored the possibility of changing their management of the current system and privatizing it or charging congestion pricing or tolls. Finally, the Corps ignored the environmental cost of the project.

On December 6, 2000, the army inspector general, Lt. Gen. Michael Ackerman, vindicated Sweeney and found that three top Corps officials—Fuhrman, Anderson, and Mudd—had manipulated the economic study to justify lock enlargement. His report questioned the Corps' handling of all studies' projects it wanted to build, because its leadership put immense institutional pressure on its divisions to make positive recommendations for dam improvements, navigation projects, flood control projects, and others.

On February 28, 2001, the Corps temporarily suspended the navigation study after release of the National Academy of Sciences' report, detailing flaws in the agency's economic and environmental analyses. The academy based its report on the July 2000 draft of the economic feasibility study, on a draft of the environmental study, and on numerous other studies and reports on the navigation study. The academy congratulated the Corps of Engineers for developing Sweeney's formula, which it characterized as "the first comprehensive model of grain use and exports from the area surrounding the river system," but it castigated the engineers for using flawed data and assumptions when applying the formula to the growth of grain exports, and therefore of barge traffic, on the Upper Mississippi. The academy also congratulated the Corps for attempting to build a model of the environmental effects of extending the locks and increasing barge traffic, but again, it castigated the engineers for failing to acknowledge that large-scale structures on the Upper Mississippi have had and would continue to have long-term environmental effects on the river. The academy concluded that systemwide research was needed on the "cumulative effects of the existing navigation system on river ecology, on the environmental effects of recent navigation improvements, on the cumulative effects of increased towboat passage, and on site-specific effects of future construction activities on the Upper Mississippi."

The academy noted that environmental concerns had become central to operating the inland waterways and had to be treated as a "resource on par with waterway infrastructure" as opposed to an impediment to planning any improvements to the navigation system. The academy encouraged the Corps of Engineers to take an adaptive management approach to the lock extensions. Because the Corps could not precisely gauge either the damage that lock construction might do or that additional barge traffic might cause to the river's ecosystem, it could not know how to mitigate it. By maintaining flexible management policies the Corps could "recognize the limits of the river's resources" and avoid irreversible decisions that might impact the river's ecosystem.

The academy admonished the Corps and the barge industry to improve the management of the current navigation system. It encouraged them to distribute barge traffic more evenly through nonstructural alternatives: better scheduling, tradable lock permits, and congestion fees. It noted that "the benefits and costs of lock extensions should not be calculated until nonstructural measures for waterway traffic management have been carefully assessed." Finally, the academy concluded that the Corps' navigation study was too complex and too important to go without a second opinion from an "independent, expert, and interdisciplinary body from outside the Corps of Engineers and the Department of Defense."

At the same time the Corps of Engineers was treating the nation to a scandal over the navigation study, the Upper Mississippi River Conservation Committee, which had been championing the river's ecosystem since 1943, was developing a "strategy to restore and maintain the Upper Mississippi River System." The report detailed the importance of the river's natural resources, described how we have changed the river's physical processes, explained how we could use the processes to manage its ecosystem, itemized the components of a strategy for restoring the river's ecosystem, and laid out the means of implementing that strategy. The group published *A River That Works and a Working River* in January 2000.

Concurrently, an interagency group of resource managers from the Corps, the U.S. Fish and Wildlife Service, and states' natural resource agencies were itemizing the existing ecological conditions on the Upper River mile by mile. When Congress reauthorized the Environmental Management Program in the 1999 Water Resources Development Act, it required that the resource managers, those people most intimate with the loss of habitat along the river, perform a habitat-needs assessment of the Upper Mississippi to direct future restoration efforts of the river.

The interagency group delivered its technical report in October 2001. It covered the state of sedimentation in the river and its backwaters, the quality of aquatic and terrestrial vegetation in its backwaters and on its islands, the status of the fish and wildlife that inhabit its backwaters, its floodplain, and its islands, and the desired future conditions of its backwaters and its islands. Once the resources managers detailed the "desired future conditions" of the river, they developed individual pool plans. The first, plans for Pools 1 through 10 in the St. Paul District, became available in August 2002. The plans documented the state of the Upper Mississippi at the turn of the century and then set out the steps that would be necessary to stop the degradation of the river's ecosystem while living with the dams.

Against the backdrop of the assessment and with the reports of the National Academy of Sciences and the Northeast-Midwest Institute in hand, the Corps of Engineers resumed the navigation study in the spring of 2002. In response to the need to address the long-term environmental damage to the Upper Mississippi and put ecological needs on par with navigation, the Corps collaborated with other agencies—the U.S. Fish and Wildlife Service, the Environmental Protection Agency, the Maritime Administration—and the Department of Agriculture and the natural resources departments of the states bordering the river, and an array of conservation and environmental organizations. Many were the same people who developed the habitat-needs assessment and the environmental pool plans. The federal partners, as they were called, scheduled meetings with all people—including folks who used the river for recreation—interested in the Upper Mississippi in St. Louis; Bloomington, Minnesota; La Crosse, Wisconsin; and Peoria, Illinois. The Corps and its partners issued their interim report on the study in October 2002. In the executive summary, the partners noted that the report provided the framework for managing the Upper Mississippi as a "nationally significant ecosystem and a nationally significant commercial navigation system."

In the body of the report the Corps of Engineers noted that Congress had authorized the nine-foot channel solely for navigation. In the early twenty-first century, funds appropriated for the operation and maintenance of the nine-foot channel, including those for the locks and dams, could not be used for environmental restoration. The only funds that could be used for restoration were those for small-scale projects authorized under the Environmental Management Program of the Upper Mississippi Management Act of 1986. While Congress reauthorized the Environmental Management Program in 1999 for all time, the limited restoration the funds afforded to the program were not enough "to halt the ecological degradation of the system." Therefore, the Corps of Engineers and its federal partners stated the need for dual-purpose authorization from Congress that would allow the Corps to pursue environmental restoration and perform its maintenance chores on the nine-foot channel in the effort to sustain the delicate ecology of the river while providing a safe, dependable navigation system. With dual-purpose authorization the Corps of Engineers could manage the sediment that had been plaguing the Upper Mississippi since the construction of the dams. The Corps and its partners intended to request dual-purpose authorization when they submitted the final navigation study in 2004.

In January 2004, eight months before it issued its final report, the Corps of Engineers announced that barge traffic on the Upper Mississippi did not justify lock expansion, though the agency felt the conclusion was risky. Rather, Sweeny's suggestions—mooring cells, helper boats, and barge scheduling—should be implemented immediately. The engineers handed the issue to Congress. Environmentalists concurred; navigation interests did not. Nor did Senator Christopher "Kit" Bond (R-Missouri), who sat on two key committees, the Transportation and Infrastructure Subcommittee of the Environment and Public Works Committee, which would authorize the project, and the Transportation Appropriation Committee, which would fund it. While Congress considered the issue, the Corps would continue working on the report and would include a request for $5.3 billion over fifty years for ecosystem restoration in the final report as well as a request for $2.3 billion for lock expansion.

The Corps did ask for dual-purpose authorization when it published the final report on the feasibility of enlarging the locks on the Upper Mississippi and Illinois Rivers in September 2004. The recommended approach, titled "The Dual Purpose Integrated Plan," tied ecosystem restoration to the expansion of the locks at dams 20, 21, 22, 24, and 25. The recommendations also included a fifteen-year implementation schedule, an adaptive management plan as recommended by the national academy three years earlier, to address all the needs of the river and the response of the ecosystem to the extensions of the locks and any increase in barge traffic that might follow. The feasibility study also included a timetable for work in the Rock Island District, lock expansion at dams 14 through 18 and improving navigation efficiency with switchboats that would speed tows through locks 11 through 13. Congress authorized the report just as it was written when it passed the 2007 Water Resources Development Act and overrode President Bush's veto of the bill in December.

A final note: When the chief of engineers endorsed the recommended plan for lock expansion and ecosystem restoration and sent it to the assistant secretary of the army for civil works in December 2004, the secretary requested a reevaluation of the navigation component of the plan in light of "updated forecasting and transportation models." The reevaluation found that the lock expansion was necessary in light of the congestion on America's railroads and highways and the excess capacity on America's waterways. The report noted that in terms of fuel burned, barges are 7.5 times more efficient and therefore more ecologically friendly than trucks. It also looked at methods for measuring the economic value of ecological goods and service. As of April 2008 the Rock Island District was engaging in planning and design on both lock expansion and ecosystem restoration, expanding on the Upper Mississippi River Conservation Committee's *Working River* of 2000, the Upper Midwest Environmental Sciences Center's habitat-needs assessment of 2001, and the St. Paul District's pool plans of 2002.

On the open river south of St. Louis there was no Upper Mississippi Management Act that recognized the Upper River as a valuable ecosystem and allowed for small-scale restoration projects. While the St. Louis District cooperated with the Memphis and Vicksburg Districts on building islands and sandbars for Least Terns, the governing authority on the Mississippi open river was the Nine-Foot Navigation Channel Project. Engineers, working on the nine-foot channel, might note numerous potential projects that would benefit plants or wildlife, but without clear-cut authority from Congress, such projects could not happen. The St. Louis District, however, did produce a master plan for the 104 miles of open river south of St. Louis that outlined what the engineers would do if they could.

Even if the agencies had dual-authorization to carry out their plans, they still had to live with the dams on the Upper River and the channel-training devices south of St. Louis. They could mimic the flow of the river before construction of the dams by opening or closing dams on secondary channels, restoring flows through side channels, and reconnecting the river to its floodplain. They could establish connecting channels around dams to allow for fish migration. They could encourage the management of individual watersheds in hopes of retaining sediment in the uplands. They could hope to purchase farmland from willing sellers and return the floodplain to its natural habitat. They could draw down the pools every summer to consolidate sediments and let dormant seeds sprout. They could use their dredge to reconstruct eroded islands and natural levees in the lower pools and then anchor them with vegetation. They could do all of this and more, but they had to live with the dams.

No great scandal sparked the management plan that would coordinate restoration efforts on the Lower Mississippi River. In 2000 the Lower Mississippi River Conservation Committee published an Aquatic Resource Management Plan, a ten-year plan to address the declining aquatic habitat on the Lower River. Part of the plan was to work with the Corps of Engineers to develop a habitat-needs assessment for the active floodplain between the river and the main line levee that would identify critical habitat in need of restoration in the side channels and on the floodplain. Congress authorized the Lower Mississippi River Resource Assessment in the 2000 Water Resources Development Act to replace the scattered approach to identifying and restoring resources on the Lower River that had been taken by federal, state, local, and private agencies. Involved in the assessment would be the governors of the states bordering the river, the Corps, the EPA, the Fish and Wildlife Service, Ducks Unlimited, the Nature Conservancy, the Audubon Club, and state and regional resource managers. In January 2008 the Memphis District received $500,000 to assess habitat needs, recreational access to the river, and gaps in our knowledge of how people use the river.

Starting in the fall of 2001, members of the conservation committee met with resource managers from federal and state agencies, representatives of nongovernmental organizations like Ducks Unlimited and the Nature Conservancy, landowners, and people interested in recreation on the river. They convened a public meeting in each state and developed the Lower Mississippi River Conservation Initiative, a document roughly akin to the pool plans published by the St. Paul District for Pools 1 through 10 on the Upper Mississippi River. Resource managers examined the river mile by mile and noted where side channels needed to be opened, where sandbars needed to be isolated for Least Terns, where floodplain lakes needed to be restored, where backwaters needed to be dredged, where depth diversity in side channels needed to be restored, where boat ramps for anglers needed to be installed: 239 sites in all between the Ohio River and Gulf of Mexico. And, like the pool plans, the inventory was more wish list than reality, what restorers would do if they could and the funds were available.

Congress and the Corps

> The Corps works for Congress and when the boss says design for a Category 3 storm, culturally the Corps is not going to go back and say this is wrong.
>
> —William F. Marcuson III, former director of the Waterways Experimental Station, Vicksburg, *New York Times,* September 21, 2005

No matter what American Rivers said about expansion of the locks on the Upper Mississippi, no matter that the Corps of Engineers concluded that expansion was unnecessary, Senator Christopher "Kit" Bond (R-Missouri) intended to make sure it went through. And it did in the 2007 Water Resources Development Act. No matter how much work the Nature Conservancy did to restore the Big Woods in Arkansas or what other conservation groups had to say about the Grand Prairie irrigation project, the Arkansas congressional delegation could overrule them. And it did. No matter how often American Rivers declared the Big Sunflower one of the ten most endangered rivers in the nation because the Corps of Engineers wanted to dredge it for flood control, Senators Trent Lott and Thad Cochran of Mississippi would see to it that the Corps got its way. And they did, and they also saw to it that beneficiaries of the project were forgiven their part of the cost.

Dr. Gerald E. Galloway—retired brigadier general, former commander of the Vicksburg District of the Corps of Engineers, former member of the Mississippi River Commission, former head of the interagency committee that looked into the causes of the Flood of 1993—called American water policy and, by extension, water policy on the Mississippi floodplain and Louisiana coast "management by earmark." In July 2007, Galloway testified before the House Committee on Transportation and Infrastructure that the United States has no national water policy. Each water project authorized by Congress is funded for a single purpose only. The National Research Council reiterated this fact in its 2004 report to Congress on Corps planning, *U.S. Army Corps of Engineers Water Resources Planning: A New Opportunity for Service.*

It's a litany: Congress authorizes the Corps to do a project; the Corps does the project. And Congress loves big projects and the federal dollars they bring into local economies. Congress passes a Water Resources Development Act, authorizing Corps planning and construction activities, setting Corps policies and practices, and defining American water policy. It does so roughly every two years. Once Congress authorizes a Corps project, it never goes away, unless and until Congress deauthorizes it. However, once a project is authorized, Congress must appropriate funds for its planning and construction. This is done yearly through appropriation acts. In 2004 when the National Research Council looked into planning for Corps projects, its panel found a backlog of $50 billion worth of unfunded projects.

In March 2007 the *New Orleans Times-Picayune* created a flowchart of the approval process for coastal restoration projects or, actually, for any large restoration project in any state. The chart illustrated the bureaucratic roadblocks to ecosystem restoration.

A state, a county, or, in Louisiana, a parish identifies a project and asks its congressional representatives to initiate a Corps of Engineer feasibility study. Congress authorizes the study through a Water Resources Development Act or a separate bill, which must be passed by both houses and signed by the president. The money for the study can come from a Corps district office budget. Failing that it must come from the annual Energy and Water Development Appropriations Act, which must be passed by both houses and signed by the president. That can take a year or two.

Then the Corps begins three studies: A reconnaissance study—Is it worth doing? A feasibility study—Is it possible? An environmental impact study—What effect will it have on the environment? Sometimes the feasibility study and the environmental impact study are rolled together. After all, if the project is going to devastate the environment, it's not feasible. The studies go to the chief of engineers, who decides whether to recommend further action. If the chief does not recommend the action, the studies go to one of three offices—the secretary of the army, the White House Office of Management and Budget, or the Council on Environmental Quality—which can trash the results or order additional study. That can take two or three years.

If the chief does recommend the project, it goes to Congress for authorization in the Water Resources Development Act, which must be passed by both houses and signed by the president. That can take two or more years (seven in the case of the 2007 WRDA).

Then the Corps begins engineering and design. That can take a year or two.

Then construction begins.

And construction can take years because money for construction is doled out year by year in appropriation bills, which must be passed by both houses and approved by the president.

That can take years.

It's no wonder the Louisiana coastal marshes disintegrate and the Upper Mississippi deteriorates as proposals to save them wend their way through the bureaucratic process.

The 1986 Water Resources Development Act requires that the federal government pay the full cost of construction on the Inland waterways with 50 percent of the cost coming from fuel taxes paid into the Inland Waterways Trust Fund. The federal government pays 65 percent of the construction costs of structural flood-control projects, the local sponsor, 35 percent. For nonstructural flood-control or environmental-improvement projects, local sponsors can contribute their 35 percent in in-kind contributions—land, easements, rights of way, relocations, and disposal areas.

Environmentalists had hoped that the cost-sharing requirements would mitigate the public's desire for wetland-destroying, pork-barrel water projects. To some extent they did. The Corps shelved many projects when local sponsors found they could not or would not afford their share of the costs, but when local sponsors did come up with their share of the costs, it narrowed the Corps' focus on any given project from the project's basinwide consequences to the interests of the sponsors and their congressional supporters. Should a local group want a section of a stream dredged and channelized for flood control, that the project might cause headward erosion upstream, siltation downstream, and the degradation of backwaters was not important to its local sponsors or, in many cases, to their congressional supporters. In many cases Corps planners overlooked such issues in order to please sponsors. Hence, Corps project proposals often ran afoul of the guidelines laid down by the EPA and the U.S. Fish and Wildlife Service for water projects.

In short, the cost-sharing formula set in the 1986 Water Resources Development Act turned the local sponsor and the congressional backer of every water project into a Corps "client." And, like any good engineering firm, the Corps catered to its clients, thus bringing the agency into conflict with its role as the objective broker of the nation's water projects and its responsibility, as a good engineering firm, to tell its client what will and what will not work. Inevitably, such a narrow focus got the Corps' planners in trouble with the EPA and the U.S. Fish and Wildlife Service, which had oversight of the environmental impact of its projects.

The National Research Council pointed out this conflict in its 1999 report on the Corps' planning procedures, *New Directions in Water Resources Planning for the U.S. Army Corps of Engineers.* The army inspector general repeatedly emphasized this conflict in a December 2000 report on the Upper Mississippi River

Navigation Study. The conflict between the Corps as a "good engineering firm" and the Corps as "honest broker of water projects" was also evident in the controversy surrounding several other Corps project that made environmentalists and river conservationists crazy in the early years of the twenty-first century.

The new century found the U.S. Army Corps of Engineers drawing fire from environmentalists, river conservationists, the U.S. Fish and Wildlife Service, and the EPA over a series of projects the Vicksburg, Memphis, and Little Rock Districts were pursuing in the Lower Mississippi valley. The Big Sunflower Channelization Project was an effort at flood control, one that would speed water downstream, where it would back up behind the levee that protected the lower third of the Yazoo Basin from backwater flooding from the Mississippi. In fact, all the rivers that once flowed to the Yazoo backed up behind the levee. The Yazoo Pump project would pump excess water over the levee.

The White River Navigation project would dredge a nine-foot navigation channel along the White to river mile 254 at Newport, Arkansas. The Grand Prairie Demonstration project would allow rice farmers on Grand Prairie to irrigate their farms with water drawn from the White River. The St. Johns Bayou–New Madrid Floodway project would close the lower end of the New Madrid Floodway, turning it into a catch basin for rainwater that would require a pump to dry it out.

Each of these projects had a local client who would paid 35 percent of the cost of the project and a congressional sponsor who would shepherd funding for the project through the legislative process. However, congressional sponsors had the power to relieve the local client of its share of the cost of the project. They also had the power to raise projects from the dead. Authorized in 1941 and never deauthorized, the Yazoo Pump lay buried in the Corps' files for fifty-five years before Senators Trent Lott (R-Mississippi) and Thad Cochran (R-Mississippi) resurrected it in 1996—Lott from his powerful position as Senate majority leader and Cochran from his position on the Senate Subcommittee on Energy and Water Development of the Appropriations Committee. The Big Sunflower Channelization Project languished because local beneficiaries could not or would not pay their 35 percent of the cost. Then, Lott and Cochran persuaded the Corps to declare the dredging of 104.8 miles of the river "maintenance" of the clearing and snagging project of the 1940s, '50s, and '60s, thus relieving the sponsors of their share of the cost. When challenged about federal spending in the state of Mississippi in March 2001, Senator Lott stated, "Pork is in the eye of the beholder. As you well know, where I come from that's federal programs that go north of Memphis." This is what Gerald Galloway meant when he spoke of water policy by "earmark."

In 1988, Congress, in a rare move, deauthorized the White River Navigation Study. In 1996 Senator Dale Bumpers (D-Arkansas) saw to it that Congress reauthorized the study. Bumpers also pushed Congress to authorize the diversion of the White River to the Grand Prairie Demonstration Project. The Memphis District of the Corps of Engineers had terminated the project in 1991. Congress reauthorized it a year later. After Bumpers retired in 1998, Senator Tim Hutchinson (R-Arkansas) took on sponsorship of the project and announced the authorization of $17.8 million for the Grand Prairie Demonstration Project in a September 2000 press release. The Corps of Engineers started construction.

Senators also had the power to kill the efforts of President Bill Clinton's administration to reform the Corps of Engineers. One month after Donald Sweeney blew the whistle on the Upper Mississippi Navigation Study, Army Secretary Louis Caldera announced plans to restore civilian control of the Corps of Engineers and put responsibility for decisions about the Corps' civil works program firmly in the hands of the civilian assistant secretary of the army for civil works. Theoretically, this was unnecessary. Theoretically, the generals who administered the civil works program had been responsible to the assistant secretary since the 1980s, but over time the relationship had deteriorated.

In an attempt to rein in the Corps, Caldera wanted to put Corps of Engineers civilians, not Corps military officials, in charge of contacts with members of Congress. In short, Caldera wanted to bar the generals from lobbying Congress on their own. Finally, Caldera wanted to put the job of evaluating the final review of projects in the hands of civilian employees rather than those of military brass.

The three senators who oversaw the agency objected. In a letter addressed to Defense Secretary William S. Cohen, who supported the changes, Appropriations chair Ted Stevens (R-Alaska), Armed Services chair John W. Warner (R-Virginia), and Environment and Public Works chair Robert C. Smith (R-New

Hampshire) wrote that "the changes could politicize the Corps and 'threaten the interests of Congress.'" Warner asked Caldera to drop the reforms, stating that the senators were determined to maintain their traditional contact with the chief of engineers, always a member of the military and required by law to advise Congress on the technical aspect of proposed projects. Caldera backed down one week after his initial announcement. A month later, Stevens and Senator Pete V. Domenici (R-New Mexico) tacked on to a farm bill a rider that blocked all future efforts to reform the Corps of Engineers, its functions and activities, and assured that the agency's relationship with Congress would never, ever change.

The new Corps commander, Lt. Gen. Robert B. Flowers, defended his agency on March 15, 2001, before the Senate Subcommittee on the Environment and Public Works, chaired by Senator Bond (R-Missouri). Flowers told the panel that he would set up an independent review panel made up of senior Corps officials and outside experts to review all large and controversial studies, including the Upper Mississippi Navigation Study. Bond, an advocate for the barge industry and a champion of the Corps, vowed that the lock extension of five dams on the Upper Mississippi would go forward no matter what the Corps study concluded. The study, scheduled for completion in July 2001, was not concluded until 2004.

In light of the controversy swirling around Corps projects, particularly the Upper Mississippi Navigation Study, other members of Congress promoted reform of the Corps of Engineers. On March 29, 2001, Representative Ron Kind (D-Wisconsin) and Senator Russ Feingold (D-Wisconsin) introduced companion pieces of legislation in the House and the Senate that would reform the Corps' planning process, particularly its project review and authorization procedures. If passed, the Army Corps of Engineers Reform Act of 2001 would have required public involvement in the development of new or modified projects by directing the secretary of the army to establish a "stakeholder advisory committee to assist with the development of project feasibility studies, general reevaluation studies, and environmental impact studies." The bill would have opened the door to people other than the local sponsors of individual projects having a say in the draft of feasibility studies and environmental impact statements. That done, the bill would have required an independent review by a panel of experts of any project with an estimated cost of more than $25 million; of any project that might have an adverse impact on fish and wildlife; of any project that might adversely impact the local environmental, cultural, or other resources; of any project that might prove to be controversial. The bill would have established an Office of Independent Review for project reviews. The bill would have prohibited "the authorization or modification of any project that did not minimize its adverse impacts on natural hydrologic patterns, value, or diversity of aquatic ecosystems." The bill would have amended the 1986 Water Resources Development Act "to require the full and concurrent mitigation of authorized projects." The bill would have required the secretary of the army to establish "a record keeping system to track wetland and other habitat types impacted by authorized projects" and to make that information available to the public.

In short, the Wisconsin Democrats' reform would have invited public involvement—beyond the wants and needs of local sponsors—in the planning of Corps projects at the beginning of the process rather than at the end when the Corps puts the draft feasibility study and environmental impact statement for a project out for public comment. It would have ensured that controversial projects like the Yazoo Pump, the Big Sunflower Channelization Project, and the various schemes proposed for the White River would undergo independent review by people other than their local and congressional sponsors, the U.S. Fish and Wildlife Service, and the EPA. The bill went nowhere. The sponsors reintroduced their reforms yearly.

To complement the reform act, Senators Smith and Feingold along with Senator John McCain (R-Arizona) introduced the Corps of Engineers Modernization and Improvement Act of 2002, which, if passed, would have required the Corps to demonstrate that each project would yield $1.50 return on each dollar spent, would have required independent review of costly and controversial projects, and would have required the Corps to reevaluate projects that had been authorized for more than ten years but never built. The act, like the Kind/Feingold act, went nowhere. Again, the sponsors reintroduced their reforms yearly.

On February 28, 2001, President George W. Bush released the blueprint of his first budget. It included a 14 percent cut in the Corps of Engineers' civil works budget. Over the course of his first term, Bush would cut the Corps' budget by 50 percent. In addition, the Bush administration pledged to look into ongoing projects on rivers that carried little barge traffic to see if they were economically justified, environmentally sound, and held to established policies. The budget outline noted, "Serious questions have been raised about the quality, objectivity, and credibility of Corps' reports on the economic and environmental feasibility of proposed water projects." In a White House news release, the new administration announced it would target funds to the completion of ongoing projects, including environment-restoration work; it would reduce funding for new projects in light of the backlog of projects authorized but not funded; and it would provide a funding increase for the Corps' wetland-evaluation program. The administration noted that the army and the Corps of Engineers had taken steps to clarify the roles of the assistant secretary for civil works and the chief of engineers in light of strengthening the secretary's ability to oversee and review Corps projects. Finally, the White House noted that it would examine the need for independent review of controversial or costly projects proposed by the Corps and its congressional sponsors. The president's budget gave environmentalists and river conservationists hope that his administration would rein in the Corps. Bush's first budget director, Mitch Daniels, the administration's hawk on Corps reform, insisted that the Corps start no new projects until the agency focused on authorized, but unfinished projects. He zeroed out proposed projects like the Yazoo Pump and the Grand Prairie Demonstration Project that had environmentalists howling at the end of the twentieth century.

Bush reiterated his plans for the Corps of Engineers with every budget, but Congress, stymied over the matter of Corps reform, failed to pass a Water Resources Development Act during the first six years of his administration. The House included Corps reform in its version of the 2004 act, but the Senate left it out. In 2005 the House passed a bill that included a provision for review of all large Corps projects by an independent expert, but Senator Bond, chairman of the Senate Transportation and Infrastructure Subcommittee of the Environment and Public Works Committee, refused to include such a provision in the Senate version of the bill. Added in the Senate version of the bill were two amendments rejected by the House. The first would restrict the Corps regulatory responsibilities to navigable waters. The second would take away its authority to regulate activity or structures on private property that posed no safety threat to maritime traffic.

It has become a cliché to state, condescendingly, that many talented people staff the Corps of Engineers, be they civil engineers, hydrologists, geologists, geomorphologists, biologists, or economists. It is true. The Corps is an agency peopled by talented, dedicated public servants who know and understand the Mississippi and its wetlands. It is an agency that has adapted to and is trapped between fulfilling its two congressional mandates: to protect the nation's wetlands and plan its ecosystem restoration and to provide efficient navigation and flood control to enhance national economic development goals. It is an agency trapped between fulfilling the interests of its local clients and their congressional sponsors on single-purpose projects and enhancing the delicate ecology of the Mississippi and its floodplain. It is an agency that is trapped by the political impossibility of removing the dams from the Upper Mississippi and the levees from the Lower Mississippi in order to reconnect the river to its floodplain, restore flow through its backwaters, and allow it to deposit its sediment along its coastal plain. Hence, the Corps is left with the job of mimicking the ways the river flowed across its floodplain, its hydrologic and geomorphic processes, before Marquette and Joliet discovered "this so Reknowned river" in 1673.

Finally, as the twentieth century drew to a close, the Corps made great progress in understanding "this so Reknowned river." In December 1995 the Corps' Wetlands Research Program published a *Guidebook for the Application of Hydrogeomorphic Assessments to Riverine Wetlands.* On page seven of the introduction, which defines riverine wetlands, the authors noted that riverine landscapes are highly integrated landforms that take thousands of years to develop. Once wetlands are destroyed by channelization, drainage, levees, and dams, their re-creation is almost impossible, but they can be restored. "Impediments to restoration, if they exist, may be due more to lack of commitment and creative approaches to restoration or the lack of data required to detect differences in functioning than to a scarcity of sites for restoration."

By the year 2000, the Corps of Engineers, the U.S. Fish and Wildlife Service, and the state natural resource agencies had amassed information on the habitat needs along the Upper Mississippi and published the Habitat Needs Assessment. The Louisiana Department of Natural Resources had done the same and published the Coast 2050 proposal.

When it became clear at the end of the twentieth century that the restoration work on the Upper Mississippi and the Louisiana coast was not going to stop the degradation of those ecosystems, the Corps of Engineers and the federal and state natural resource agencies recommitted themselves to their restoration through the Desired Future Conditions program on the Upper Mississippi and Coast 2050 on the Louisiana coast. After 2001 the Corps found its staff shrinking, the demands of its military responsibilities increasing with the wars in Iraq and Afghanistan, and its homeland security responsibilities increasing at home. Hence, the question in 2008 was whether the tight budgetary conditions imposed by Congress and the Bush administration would allow the financial commitment necessary to fulfilling the hopes of the restoration programs.

By September 2005, with parts of New Orleans under twenty feet of water, it became unmistakably clear that the priorities of Congress and the Bush administration were totally out of sync with hurricane protection, whether from effective levees or from ecosystem restoration, in Louisiana. The drowning of New Orleans on August 29, 2005, revealed that Louisiana had ten years, tops, to reverse coastal land loss before the cost went beyond the reach of state and federal governments. Katrina also revealed that the Bush administration had already reduced its requests for the funding of hurricane protection by 44.2 percent since taking office in 2001. It had reduced funding for the Southeastern Louisiana Flood Control Projects—designed to improve drainage in Jefferson, Orleans, and St. Tammany Parishes—by even more. And, it had reduced the $14 billion estimate of the cost of restoring the coast to $1.9 billion. While Congress had restored some of the cuts in the two hurricane-protection projects, it had also appropriated $22 million for the dredging of the Mississippi River Gulf Outlet, $12 million for the Yazoo Pump, and $500,000 for the Grand Prairie Demonstration Project in 2005. By October, with Congress still tied in knots over Corps Reform, Senator Bond expressed concern that Hurricane Katrina had washed away the 2005 Water Resources Development Act.

It had. When floodwaters were finally pumped out of New Orleans, independent experts examined the destroyed levees and concluded that design flaws had caused their destruction. When the Corps issued its report in December 2006 on the destruction of the levees, the knots that had tied up Congress over Corps reform for five years began to come untied, and both the House and the Senate passed reform of the Corps of Engineers, but the two bodies could not reconcile their versions of reform until they went into conference in July 2007. They went into conference to resolve disputes over a $14 billion bill. They came out with a $23 billion bill. As Gerald Galloway complained: This was water policy by earmark.

There were plenty of people, inside and outside of government, who wanted Corps reform; who wanted independent review of Corps projects by an outside agency such as the National Academy of Sciences and the National Research Council; who wanted to update the Corps' quarter-century-old planning guidelines that would put environmental protection and restoration on equal footing with economic development; who wanted to raise the cost-benefit ratio that Corps projects would yield to $1.50 in benefits for every dollar spent; who wanted to flip the federal/local share of costs from 65 percent federal/35 percent local to 35 percent federal/65 percent local; who wanted "no net loss" of wetlands to mean "no net loss" of wetlands and require that the Corps replace wetlands destroyed acre for similar acre; who wanted the monitoring of mitigation; and who wanted the public to be able to scrutinize all Corps projects.

What they got was a director, appointed by the secretary of the army, of independent review within the Corps, who in turn would appoint a panel of experts to review all Corps projects costing more that $40 million. As for the other reforms: The Corps insisted it had transformed itself after the bruising it got in the 2000 whistle-blower scandal over the extension of the Upper Mississippi locks. Beginning in 2003 the agency issued a series of five circulars that detailed how it was considering the environmental benefits in planning each project, how it had initiated internal peer review, how it was working with other federal and state programs to develop projects, and how it had established an external peer-review process for very large projects, for projects that establish precedent-setting methods or models, or for projects that might change prevailing practices. Congress agreed and set the matter of Corps reform aside.

The passage of the 2007 water bill in September illustrated the disconnect between the politicians and the scientists on the matter of the Mississippi River and its floodplain. This was particularly evident in Louisiana, where the scientists, those people who have made it their lives' work to study the disintegration of its wetlands, have been ignored. Politicians see ecosystem restoration, navigation, and flood control in parallel universes; scientists see both coastal restoration and levees as flood protection. And they fully understand the detrimental effects navigation can have on marshes and swamps, and in the case of the MRGO funnel effect, on levees. In the wake of Katrina scientists expressed their clear doubts about the effectiveness of the Morganza-to-the-Gulf hurricane levee, a leaky levee that would cut across and impound swamps in Terrebonne Parish, yet Congress authorized it in the 2007 Water Resources Development Act. In the wake of Katrina the 2006 National Research Council report, *Drawing Louisiana's New Map,* looked at the proposal for the Louisiana Coastal Area Ecosystem Restoration and found it clearly inadequate, yet Congress authorized it in the 2007 Water Resources Development Act. The very passage of the new WRDA did nothing to stop the byzantine process that gets any project funded. Nor did it divorce coastal restoration from the WRDA.

The disconnect extended to the Upper Mississippi. The interagency group with Gerald Galloway at its head, which studied the causes of the Flood of 1993 and made a series of very sensible proposals, saw its work delivered into oblivion when Senator Bond refused to allow its recommendations to be put into law. Seven years after Donald Sweeney, the economist on the lock expansion project on the Upper Mississippi, blew the whistle on the Corps' math justifying the project, and three years after the Corps admitted that barge traffic on the Upper Mississippi did not justify the project, Congress authorized $2.2 billion for lock expansion in the new WRDA.

The first decade of the new century that opened with one of the Corps' own blowing the whistle on the Corps' manipulation of data and with a half dozen Corps projects that made environmentalists and river conservationists nuts closed with some notable successes. While Congress authorized lock expansion, it also authorized $1.72 billion ecosystem restoration in the 2007 WRDA, named the pairing the Navigation and Ecosystem Sustainability Program, and required that lock expansion and ecosystem restoration happen simultaneously. It was a very big start for the Upper Mississippi. Preconstruction design and engineering could proceed even though funds for construction had yet to be authorized. And they did.

Also big: Conservationists joined the navigation industry in lobbying Congress to fund the Navigation and Ecosystem Sustainability Program. In early 2008, the Nature Conservancy and the Audubon Society joined the Upper Mississippi River Basin Association, which represents the governors of the states bordering the river, and the Waterways Council, which represents the navigation industry, in lobbying Congress to begin funding the Navigation and Ecosystem Sustainability Program with an initial investment of $50 million for the fiscal year 2009. In February and March, the Nature Conservancy and its partners met with legislators and their staffs to built support for funding the program. At the same time the lobbying group urged Congress to continue funding the Environmental Management Program, which was authorized to receive $33.2 million per year.

The 2007 WRDA also authorized 75 percent of the funding necessary to conduct the White River Basin Comprehensive Study to sort out the demands put on the White River for navigation, irrigation, flood control, recreation, wildlife, and water supply.

In September 2007, Judge James Robertson of the Federal District Court of the District of Columbia ordered construction halted on the St. Johns Bayou–New Madrid pump project and the completed work dismantled, citing ecosystem damage. In January 2008 the deputy administrator of the EPA informed the Corps that his agency would review the Yazoo Pump, noting the damage it would do to the aquatic ecosystem in the bottom third of the Yazoo Basin, including damage to several national wildlife refuges and one national forest. In September the agency exercised its veto power over a Corps project and killed the pump.

Some things were left up in the air. In April 2008, the Louisiana Coastal Protection and Restoration Authority, at the request of Terrebonne Parish officials, appointed a panel of eight scientists to review the Morganza-to-the-Gulf levee in light of lessons learned from Katrina and Rita. In December the panel of scientists—chaired by Robert Twilley, director of wetland biochemistry at Louisiana State University—made its report and recommended that the proposed hurricane-protection system be built as designed along existing levees and roadbeds and that the lock on the Houma Navigation Canal proceed.

However, the panel also determined that the Corps, the Terrebonne Conservation and Levee District, and the state had failed to study the effects of the proposal on coastal restoration projects planned for Terrebonne and Lafourche Parishes and recommended a new study to determine if the project would be compatible with efforts to restore the basin's deteriorating wetlands. Finally, the panel recommended that the project be reviewed every five years to determine the changing risks to communities and wetlands in the basin.

The new study did not delay Terrebonne Parish's design and construction of its in-kind contributions to the project, $168 million worth of levees it authorized in September 2009 the wake of Hurricane Ike, which flooded the parish. The levees would be built along existing levees and parish roadbeds. The Corps of Engineers noted that the parish must build levees 28 feet high to meet the standards set in the wake of Katrina for protection against a hundred-year storm surge in order to qualify for federal reimbursement. Finally, the Corps noted that Congress would have to re-authorize the Morganza project because construction costs ($900 million), as approved by Congress, had ballooned to $10.7 billion in light of the post-Katrina standards for levees.

During the last third of the twentieth century the environmentalists wrung concessions out of the Corps that benefited the ecosystem. The engineers and scientists, those people who have been most intimately involved with the river over the centuries, relaxed the stranglehold they had on the hydrology and geomorphology of the whole of the river and learned to mimic the river's old ways in an effort to restore it. Its economists began to figure the economic benefits of ecosystem restoration along with those of navigation and flood control. If Congress will allow it, restoration should be the Corps' primary mission in the future and that bodes well for the next decades of the twenty-first century.

No amount of ecosystem restoration is going to return us to the river of de Soto or Marquette and Joliet or La Salle. We will never know that river. We can sense it from the explorers' written descriptions. But we are like John Madson, who knew and loved the Upper Mississippi and wrote in the 1980s, "Damn! I wish I could have seen that." We may have made radical changes to the river over the last three centuries, but it is still possible to enjoy all the experiences the modern Mississippi has to offer.

Wade across the source, where the Mississippi breaks out of Lake Itasca. Float the small stream that meanders through the wetland prairie in the headwaters. Hike to the edge of the bluff at Iowa's Pike's Peak State Park and gaze down at the island-braided river, running at the bottom of its underfit canyon. Understand that the Lower Mississippi is, to use a cliché, awesome and just a little bit scary; come floodtime, very scary. Fish the calm waters of its oxbows. Listen for the call of the Ivory-billed Woodpecker in the White River and Cache River National Wildlife Refuges. Go camping in the Delta National Forest; it retains the beauty of the Great Swamp that once covered more than 25,000,000 acres of the lower alluvial valley. Canoe the Great River Swamp of the Atchafalaya. Contrast the variety of vegetation in the fresh marshes of the western Terrebonne Basin with the uniformity of vegetation in the salt marshes of the central Terrebonne Basin. Meander through the tall stands of roseau cane that line the bayous of the Delta National Wildlife Refuge. On a calm day take a boat trip to a barrier island at the very edge of the Gulf of Mexico. The more people learn to know and love the Mississippi and the wetlands it created, the easier it will be to find the means to restore it.

The Headwaters

On February 12, 1889, the Minnesota Historical Society commissioned Jacob V. Brower, an archaeologist and naturalist, to make a detailed survey of Lake Itasca and its basin. At the completion of the survey, Brower published *The Mississippi River and Its Source,* in which he detailed early explorers' obsession with finding the source of the Mississippi. Each gave Itasca a different name. The Ojibwa called it Omoskos Sogiagon because it is shaped like an elk's head. The English and French translated that into Elk Lake and Lac la Biche, respectively.

The Ojibwa, who inhabited the headwaters, certainly knew Lake Itasca as the source of the Mississippi. European and American explorers, eager to discover the source of the river, depended on the Ojibwa to guide them through the watery landscape. In 1766, Jonathan Carver, an English explorer, set off to find the source but got no further north than the St. Francis River on the Anoka Sand Plain. David Thompson, an English astronomer with the Northwest Company, trekked across northern Minnesota from the Red River of the North to Turtle Lake (which empties into Cass Lake through Turtle Brook and Kitchi Creek) and concluded that it was the source. Starting in 1803, William Morrison made numerous trips to the Itasca Basin, where he may have recognized Lake Itasca as the source. Unfortunately, he lost the diaries of his 1803 trip when his canoe capsized. When Thomas Jefferson acquired Louisiana from the French in December of that year, early explorers of the Mississippi had not yet found its source.

Two years later, worried that that the Mississippi might head in British Canada, Jefferson dispatched Lt. Zebulon M. Pike to find the source. Pike and the members of his expedition poled a keelboat up the Mississippi from St. Louis, stopping at the settlements of Dubuque and Prairie du Chien. As winter set in at the end of October, Pike built a fort near Little Falls, Minnesota, and used it as his base of operations. In January he donned snowshoes and trudged to Leech Lake. This, he concluded, was the source of the Mississippi. Two weeks later he made his way to what became Cass Lake and declared it the upper source of the Mississippi.

Lewis Cass, governor of Michigan Territory, followed Pike in 1820. He set out from Detroit, crossed the Great Lakes, and traveled overland to Cass Lake. Ojibwa, who lived around the lake, informed him that the source of the Mississippi was at Lac la Biche, fifty miles "west-northwest" of Cass Lake, but would be too difficult to reach at low water. Young Henry Rowe Schoolcraft, who accompanied Cass, drew the expedition map, showing Lac la Biche north and west of Cass Lake.

On April 21, 1823, Italian exile Giacomo Constantino Beltrami boarded the *Virginia* at St. Louis and embarked on the first steamboat voyage up the Mississippi to Fort Snelling. From there he traveled up the Minnesota, down the Red River of the North, and across northern Minnesota to Red and Turtle Lakes and the Continental Divide that separates drainage to Hudson Bay from that to the Gulf of Mexico. He declared Lake Julia the northern source of the Mississippi. Lake Julia, however, lies north of the divide. When Beltrami's Ojibwa guide advised him of the existence of Lac la Biche, he put it on his map as the western source of the Mississippi and named it Doe Lake.

In 1832, Lewis Cass, now the secretary of war, dispatched Henry Schoolcraft, now the Indian agent at Sault Ste. Marie, to the region embraced by the Mississippi above the falls of St. Anthony. Cass charged him with learning about the Chippewa who lived in the region. Finding the source of the Mississippi was not the purpose of the expedition, but it was Schoolcraft's primary purpose in leading it.

Schoolcraft set out from Sault Ste. Marie, crossed Lake Superior, entered the St. Louis River, which took him to the East Savanna River. At its head he portaged six miles across the low divide, sometimes thigh-deep in muddy bogs, that separates drainage to Lake Superior from that to the Mississippi. He put in on the Savanna River, which carried him to Big Sandy Lake and the Mississippi River. He then paddled upriver to Cass Lake.

Oza Windib, an Ojibwa Chippewa, led Schoolcraft through one of the inlets to Cass Lake, up the Mississippi to Lake Bemidji, through Lake Irving to a fork in the river. The right fork carried the larger volume of water, making it a long and difficult ascent. The explorers took the left fork, later named Schoolcraft River in his honor, to its head at Ossawa Lake, and portaged to Lac la Biche. Schoolcraft and his crew remained only a few hours at Lac la Biche, long enough to survey its shores, collect a few botanical specimans, erect a flagstaff on an island in the lake, and name it Lake Itasca. When they departed, Oza Windib led them to the Mississippi, the northward-flowing outlet from the lake.

Joseph N. Nicollet, a French scientist and explorer, followed Schoolcraft to Lake Itasca in 1836. From Falls of St. Anthony, Nicollet, guided by his friend, Chagobay, a Chippewa, canoed up the Mississippi to the Crow Wing River. They worked their way up through the Crow Wing watershed to a portage that took them to Leech Lake. There, Chagobay handed Nicollet over to Keg-wed-zis-sag, the only Leech Lake Chippewa who knew the way to Lake Itasca from Leech Lake. Keg-wed-zis-sag led Nicollet to the mouth of the Kabekona River. They hacked their way upstream through fallen trees, groves of alders, and stands of high bush cranberries to a portage that led them to the Schoolcraft River. From there they followed Schoolcraft's route to Lake Itasca. Nicollet explored the shores of Lake Itasca, canoed and hiked up Nicollet Creek, and declared, with some justification, that the springs at its head were the source of the Mississippi.

In 1889, the State of Minnesota, with the intention of designating the Itasca Basin a state park, sent Jacob V. Brower to the Itasca region to survey and sort out the topography and hydrology of the Itasca Basin.

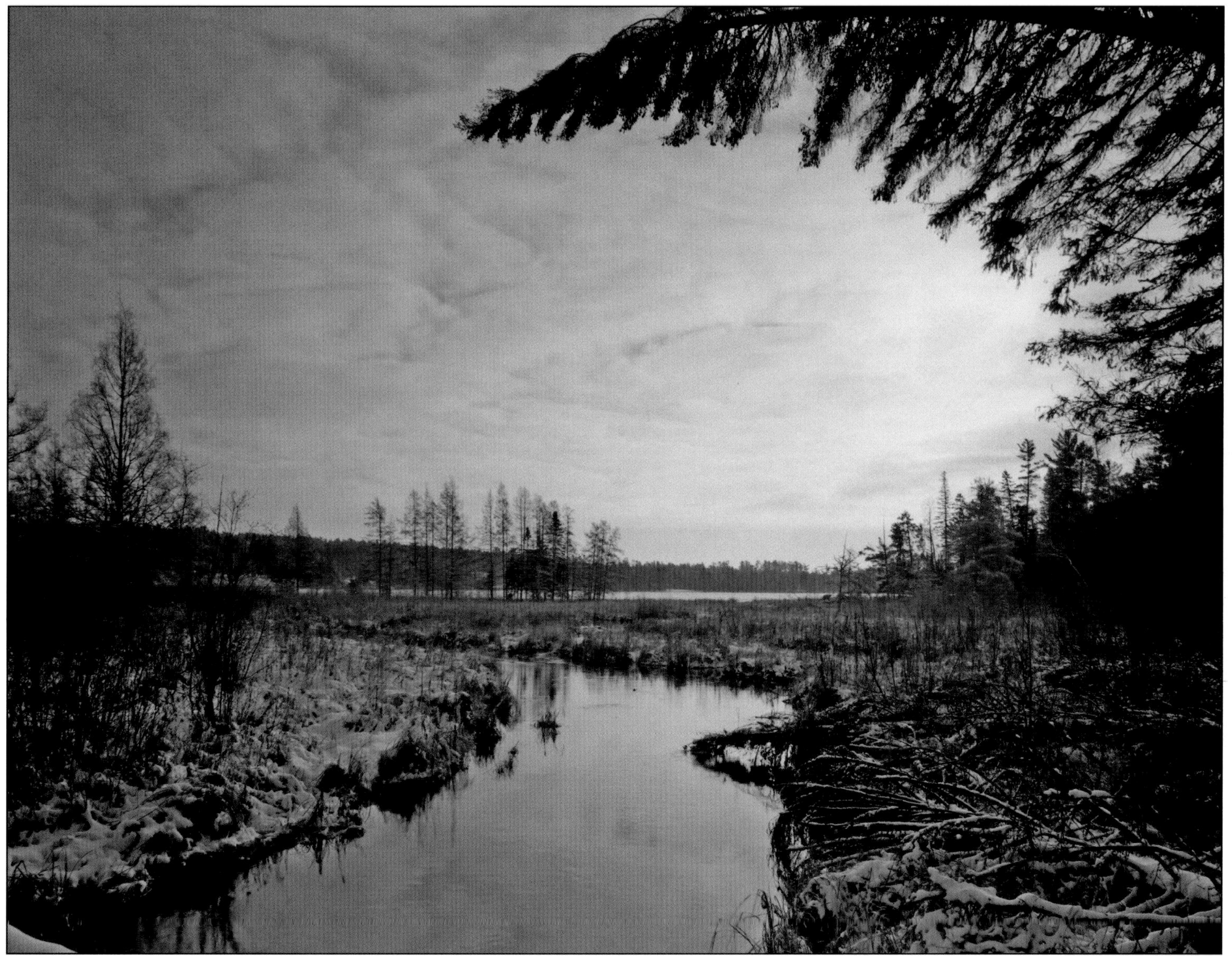

Itasca Moraine: The Source

Clearwater County, Minnesota

"The outlet of Itasca Lake, is perhaps ten to twelve feet broad, with an apparent depth of twelve to eighteen inches. The discharge of water appears to be copious, compared to its inlet."—Henry Rowe Schoolcraft, 1832

Lake Itasca collects water from various streams that rise in springs in the upper elevations of the Itasca Moraine and flow to it. The Mississippi breaks out of the northern arm of Lake Itasca through a swamp colonized by black spruce, tamarack, alder, and sedges. The shallow, narrow stream flows north through two tunnel valleys.

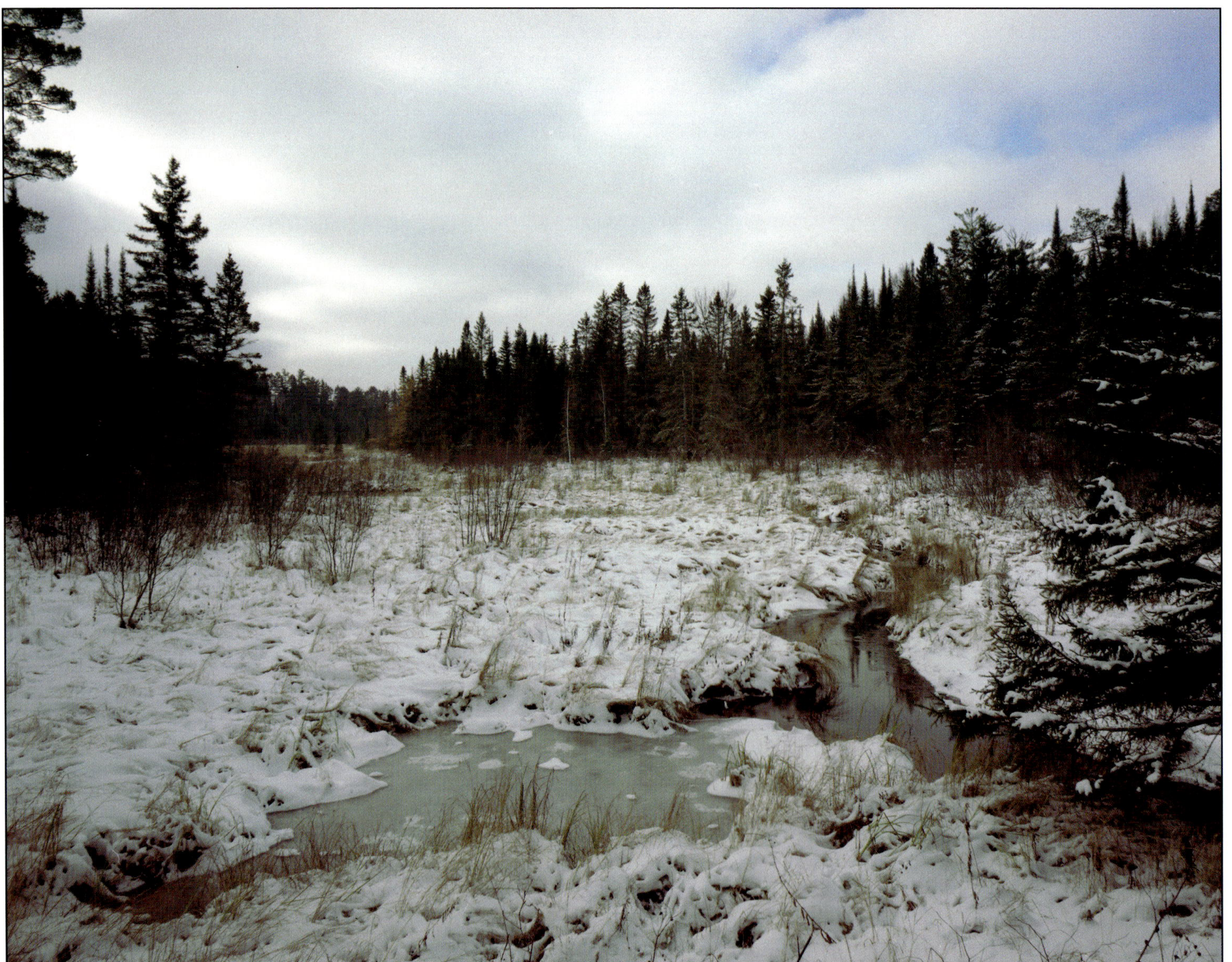

Itasca Moraine: Nicollet Creek

Clearwater County, Minnesota

In 1836, Keg-wed-zis-sag, an Ojibwa, led Joseph N. Nicollet to Lake Itasca. Nicollet surveyed the lake's shores and found that five creeks flowed to Itasca from the south, one into the eastern arm, four into the western arm. Only Nicollet Creek showed "signs of the capricious and encroaching propensities that characterize its power and course along its various stages of growth all the way down to the Gulf of Mexico." Nicollet Creek rises in springs—Mississippi and Nicollet Springs buried in glacial drift a hundred feet above Lake Itasca—and descends through a series of swampy lakes in Nicollet Valley to the west arm of the Itasca.

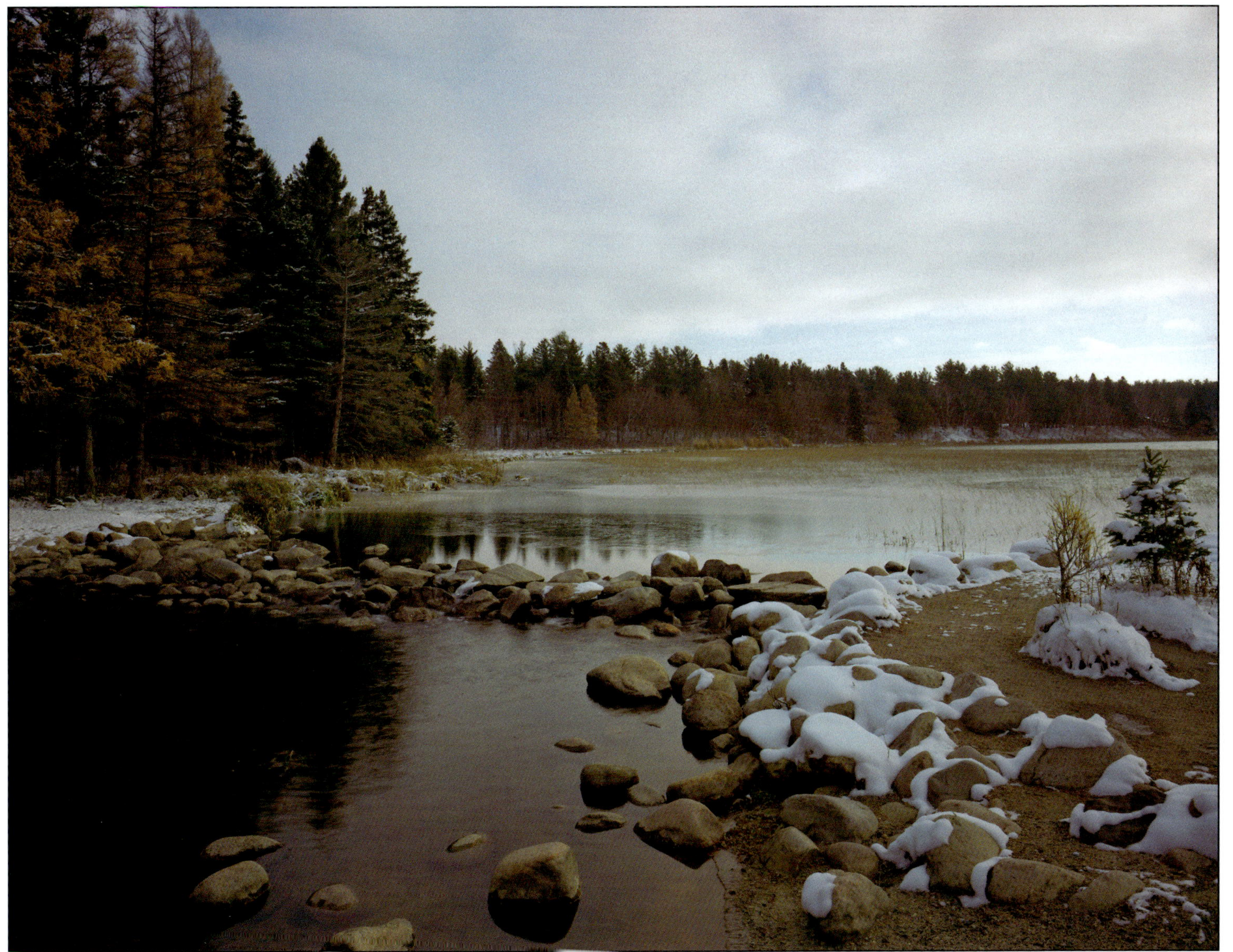

Itasca Moraine: Official Source
Clearwater County, Minnesota

Jacob Brower concluded that all the sources of the Mississippi had a common outlet through the northern arm of Lake Itasca, where the Mississippi trickles out of the lake over a small rapids today. The rapids are phony. In the 1930s, the State of Minnesota decided that wetland where the Mississippi truly heads was too swampy, too muddy, too ugly to be the source of the master river of the continent. The state had the Civilian Conservation Corps build a dam to stabilize the level of the lake and set the rocks that form the rapids on top. Workers hauled in sand and gravel to build an artificial channel that connects to the river 2,000 feet downstream.

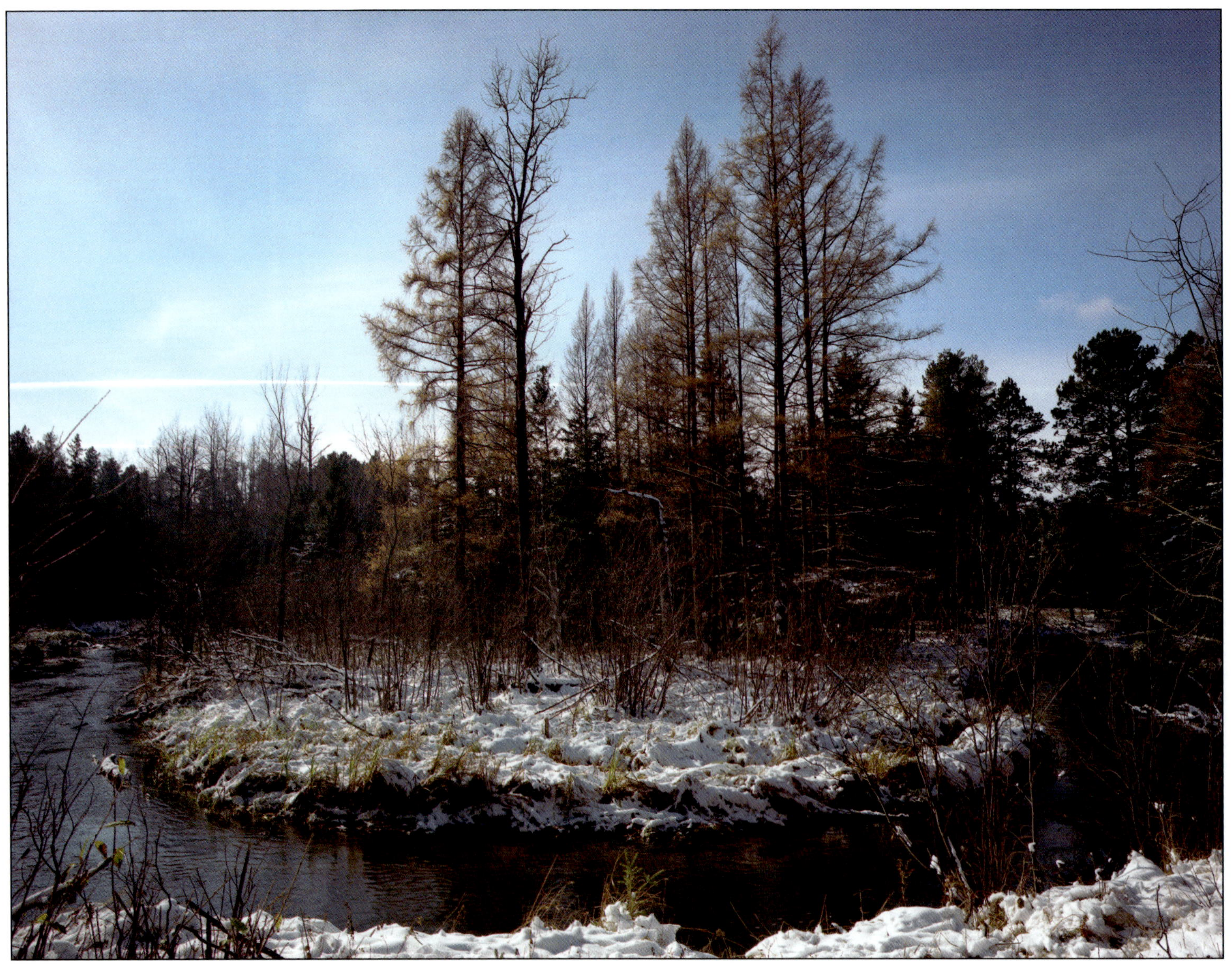

Itasca Moraine:
The Headwaters, Oxbow

Clearwater County, Minnesota

"We soon felt our motion accelerated by a current, and began to glide with velocity, down a clear stream with a sandy and pebbly bottom, strewed with shells and overhung by foliage."—Henry Rowe Schoolcraft, 1832

Once the Mississippi leaves Lake Itasca, the topography of the moraine directs the river's course through a tunnel valley, narrow at first between solid banks anchored by alder, tamarack, and white pine. Within the trough the river meanders, following fluvial processes that shape its course clear to the Gulf of Mexico.

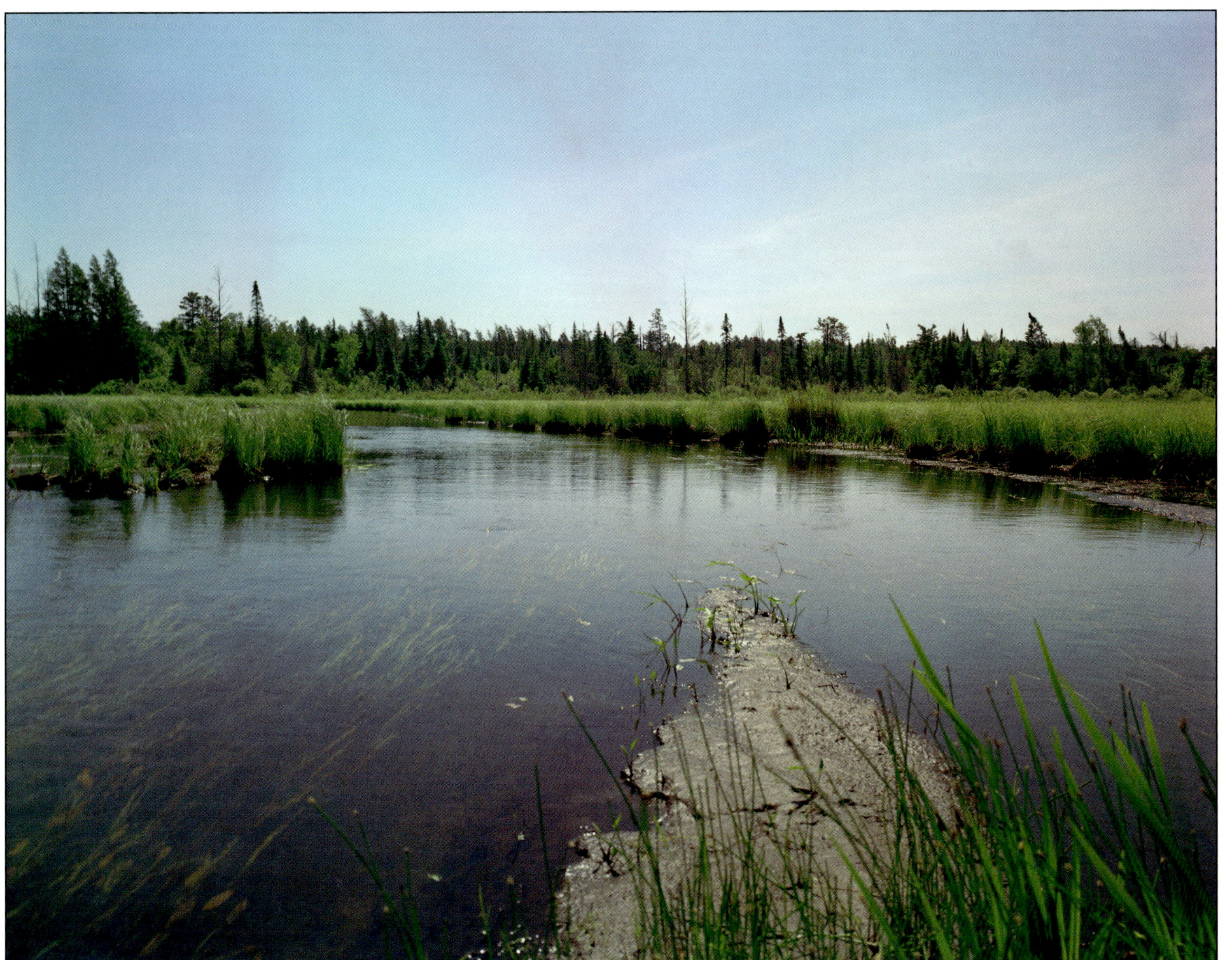

Headwaters: About Mile 1339

Clearwater County, Minnesota

"Soon the river escapes from the narrow valley and enters a large valley, opening to our view in the distance the wooded hills. The valley bottom is a flat, marshy prairie, broken up by clusters of shrubbery. The current is slower. The river is in a wandering mood."—Joseph N. Nicollet, 1836

Upon leaving Itasca State Park, the Mississippi meanders through a floating mat of sedges and bur weeds, and blue flag irises. Submerged aquatics—wild celery or grass-leaved arrowheads—anchor the riverbed, their leaves drifting north with the current. Water-tolerant alder, black spruce, tamarack mark the transition to the uplands.

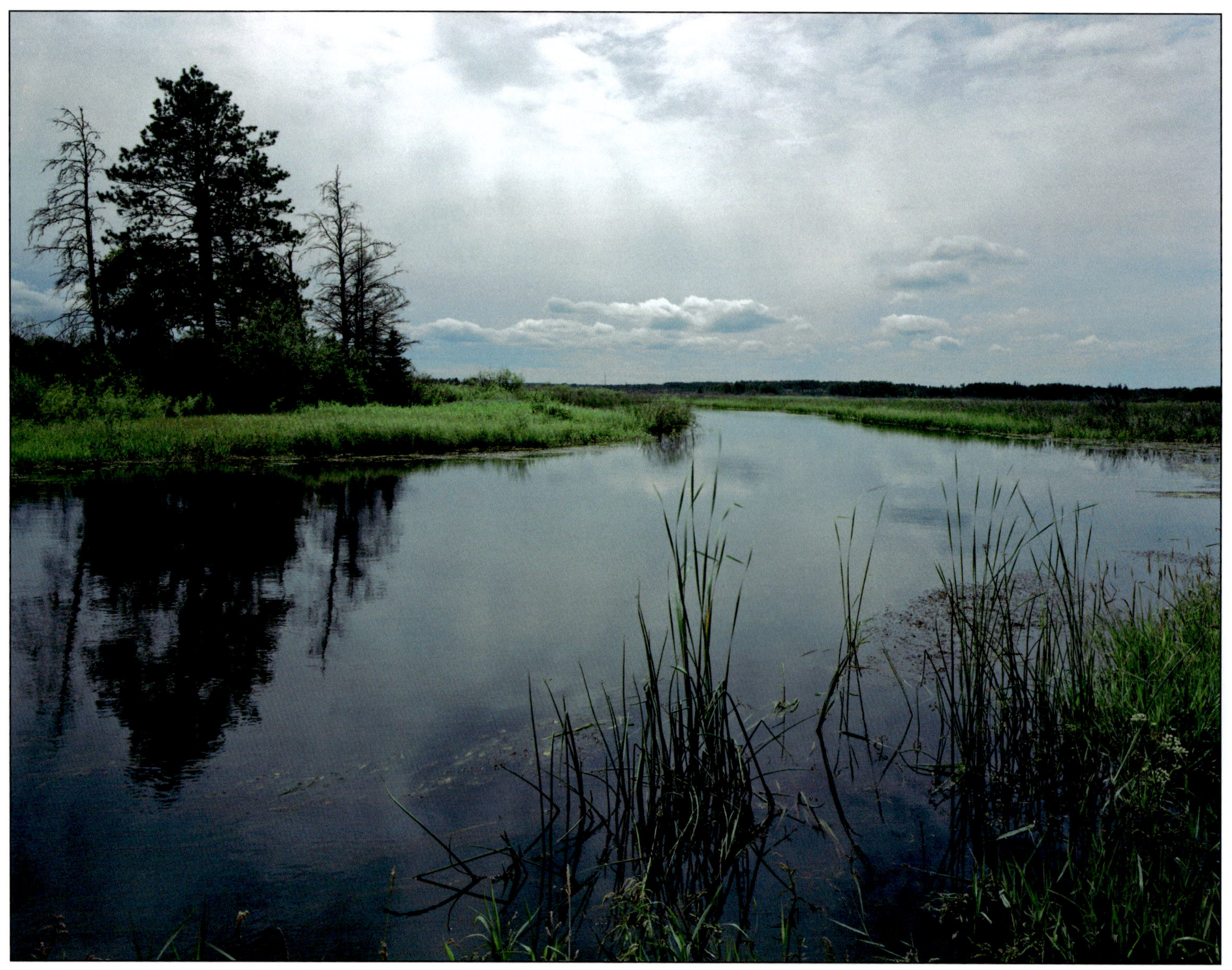

Headwaters: Alida
Hubbard County, Minnesota

"Several beautifully clear and cool springs were observed running from its base into the river."
—Henry Rowe Schoolcraft, 1832

At Vekins Dam the river slips into a narrow rocky tunnel valley, then out of it and into a wide trough filled with marshes near Alida. As the river approaches Bemidji, fresh springs, burbling out of the sand and gravel outwash of the Bemidji-Bagley aquifer, border the river and contribute two-thirds of the river's flow. Stands of spruce mark the places where springs bubble to the surface, places where the female brook trout builds her nest.

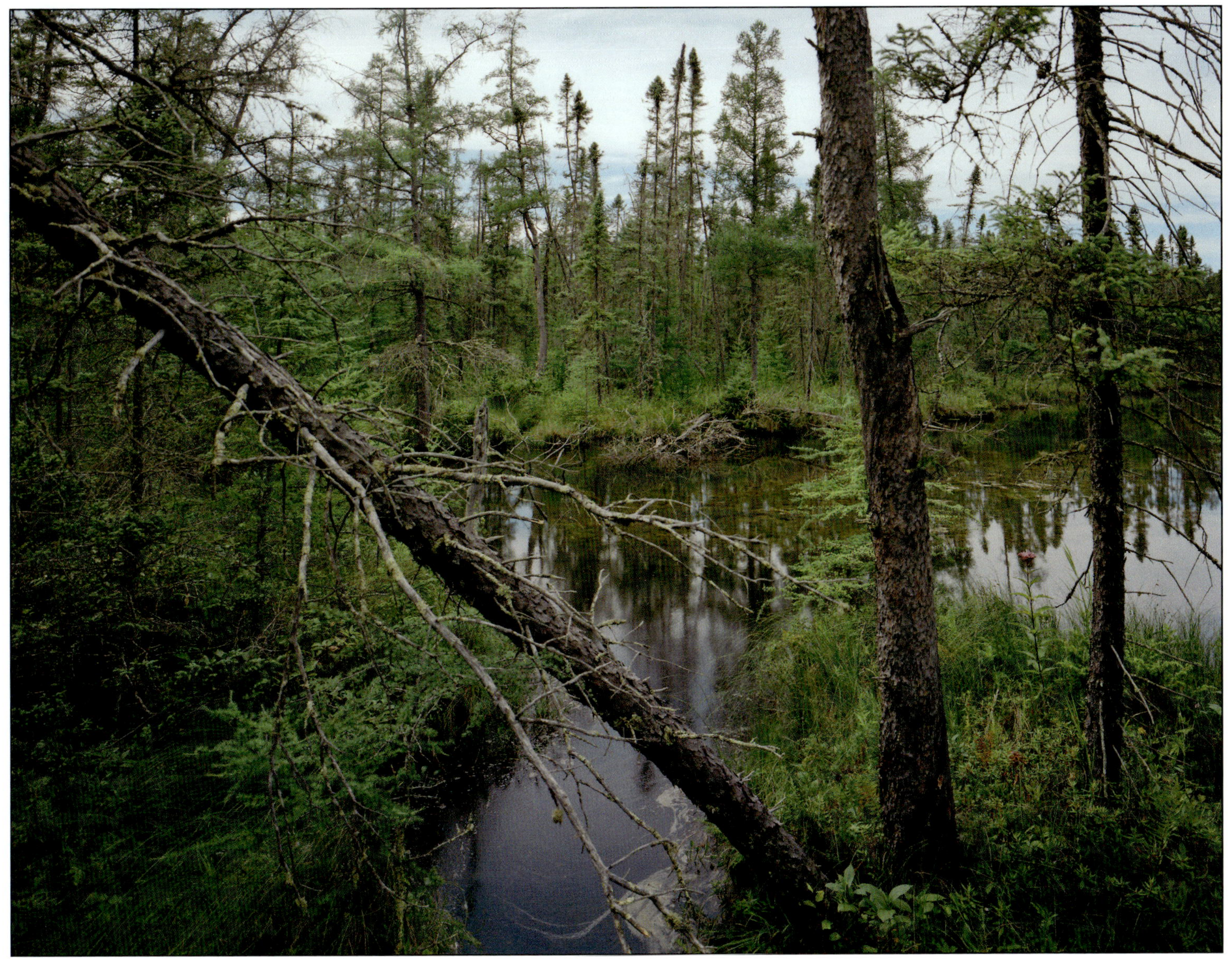

Headwaters: Bemidji Bog

Beltrami County, Minnesota

From the Itasca Moraine the Mississippi streams north to Lake Bemidji, turns east, and flows across an outwash plain dotted with kettle lakes. Nestled at the northern end of Lake Bemidji and slightly above is Bemidji Bog, once a bay to Bemidji, now a dying lake. Every lake dies. The process starts around the shallow edges where sedges and pond lilies grow and die. Plants migrate to the center as the lake grows smaller and shallower. In the cold, acidic waters of northern Minnesota where bacteria—decomposers—cannot thrive, plants do not decay. Peat—hostile to all but sphagnum moss, leather leaf, Labrador tee, and alders—accumulates. A bog forms.

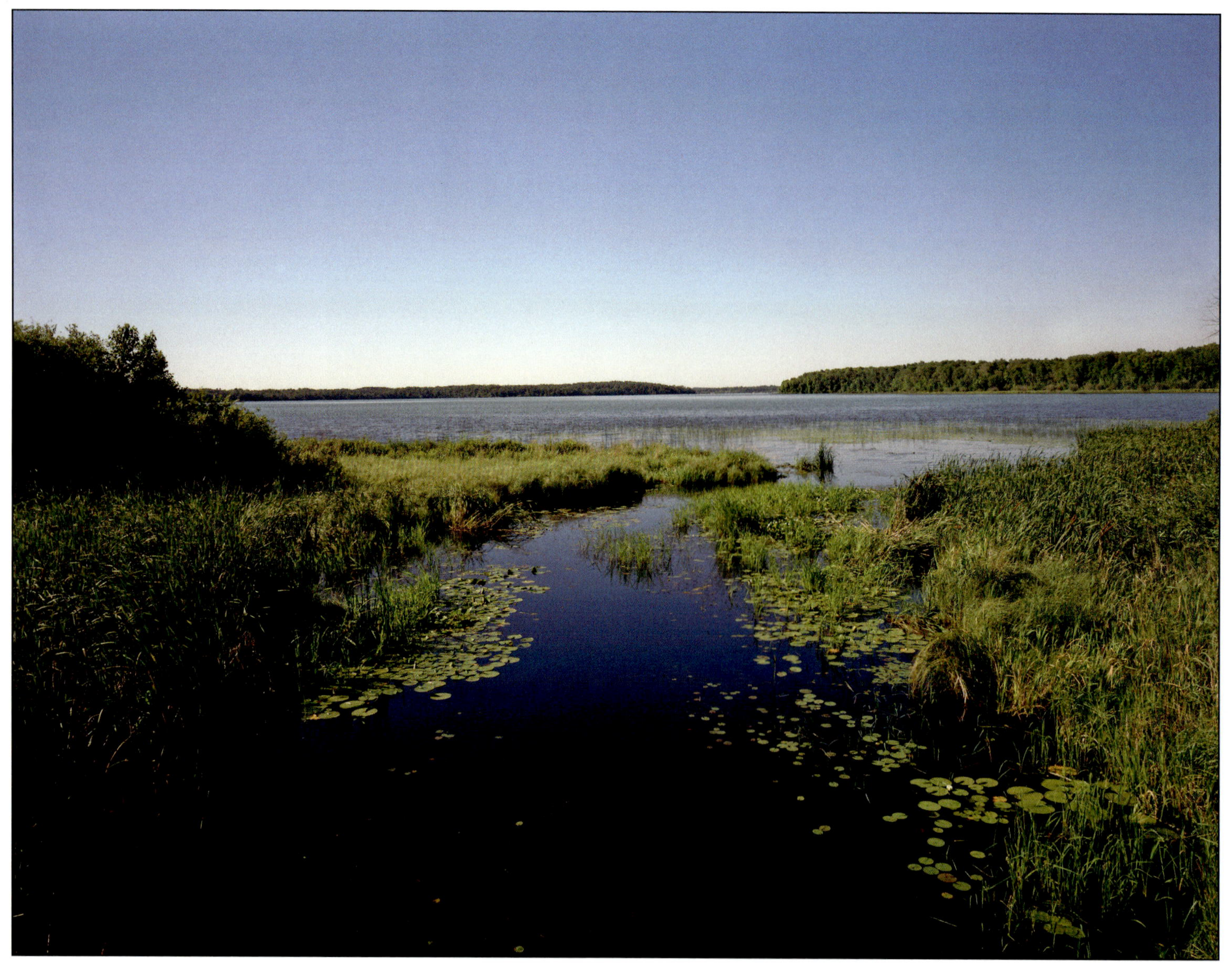

The Headwaters: Mississippi Meadows

Itasca County, Minnesota

Twelve dams harness the river between its source and the Falls of St. Anthony. Between Lakes Cass and Winnibigoshish the river meanders through a twelve-mile channel. The construction of the 1884 Winnibigoshish dam flooded its lower eight miles, raised the elevation of the lake nine feet, and drowned the tamarack and white cedar swamp along the shoreline. A sedge meadow edged with pond lilies replaced it, creating Mississippi Meadows. The river continues to flow through the marsh after the lakes have frozen and resumes its flow before the lakes thaw, thus providing refuge for ducks at all stages of their lives.

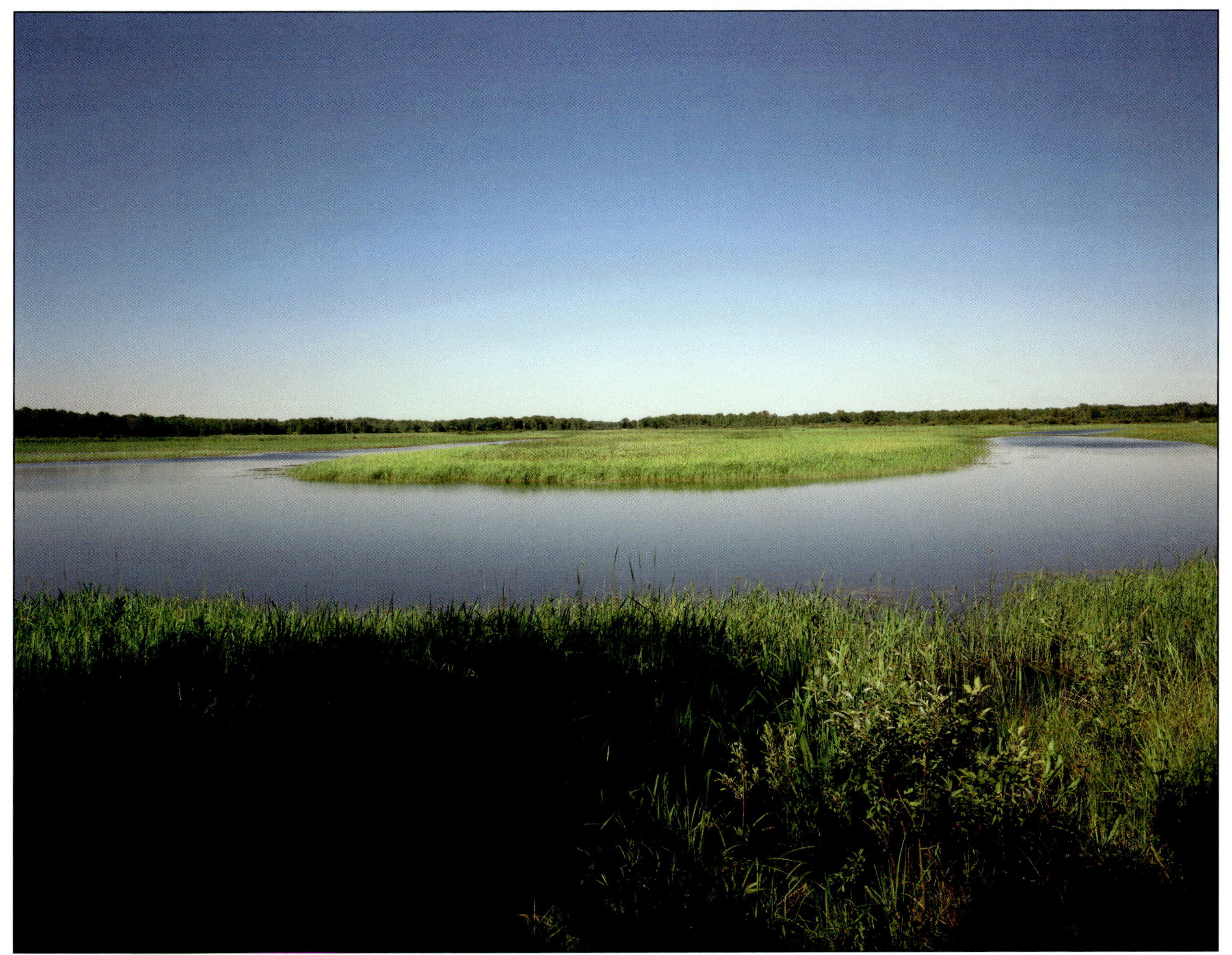

Headwaters: Cohasset
Itasca County, Minnesota

The dams turned the natural lakes into reservoirs. Steady water levels, five to ten feet above predam levels, damaged fisheries, wild rice fields, cranberry marshes, and hay meadows. Headwater dams, upstream at Lake Winnibigoshish and downstream at Pokegama Lake, forced the river to give up its meandering ways at Cohasset, where the river turned in an oxbow. Here, the river no longer follows the fluvial processes that shaped the bend, locking the oxbow, vegetated only by tall grasses anchored in outwash, in place. In February 2004 the St. Paul District offered the possibility of restoring the river's natural flow in some sections.

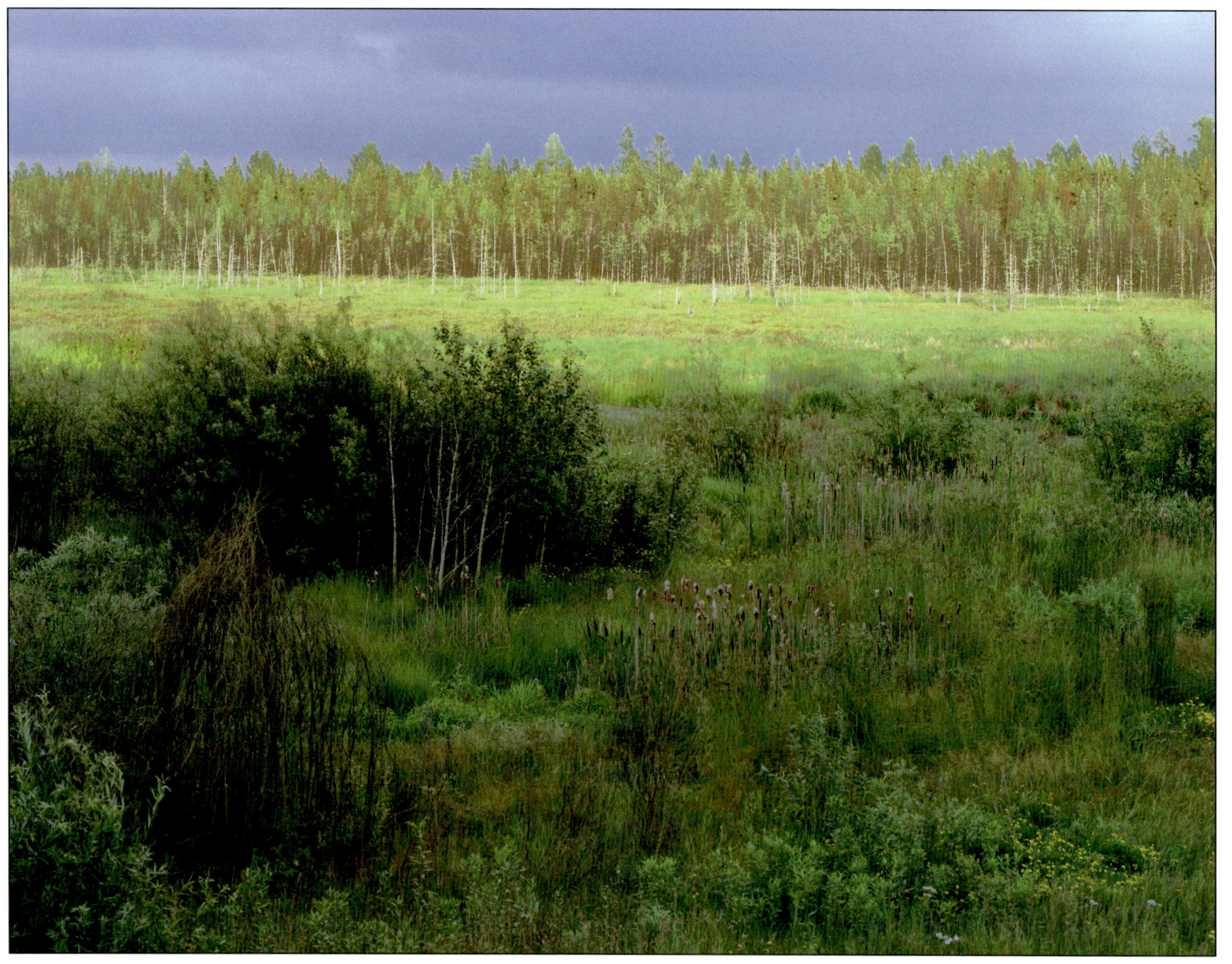

Glacial Lake Aitkin: Fleming Brook Savanna

Aitken County, Minnesota

When Glacial Lake Aitken drained away, it left behind a lake bed lined with clay, suitable for the development of bogs and shrub swamps. The Mississippi meanders across the lake bed in a sinuous channel, creating one oxbow after another and connecting the lake plain north of Grand Rapids with the stream that formed south of Little Falls. Wildlife roams the forest corridor along the river's edge. Flycatchers live in the open forest canopy, where they launch themselves from dead branches to snatch insects from the air. The cavities of dead and dying trees provide shelter for wood ducks, mergansers, owls, raccoons, and black bears.

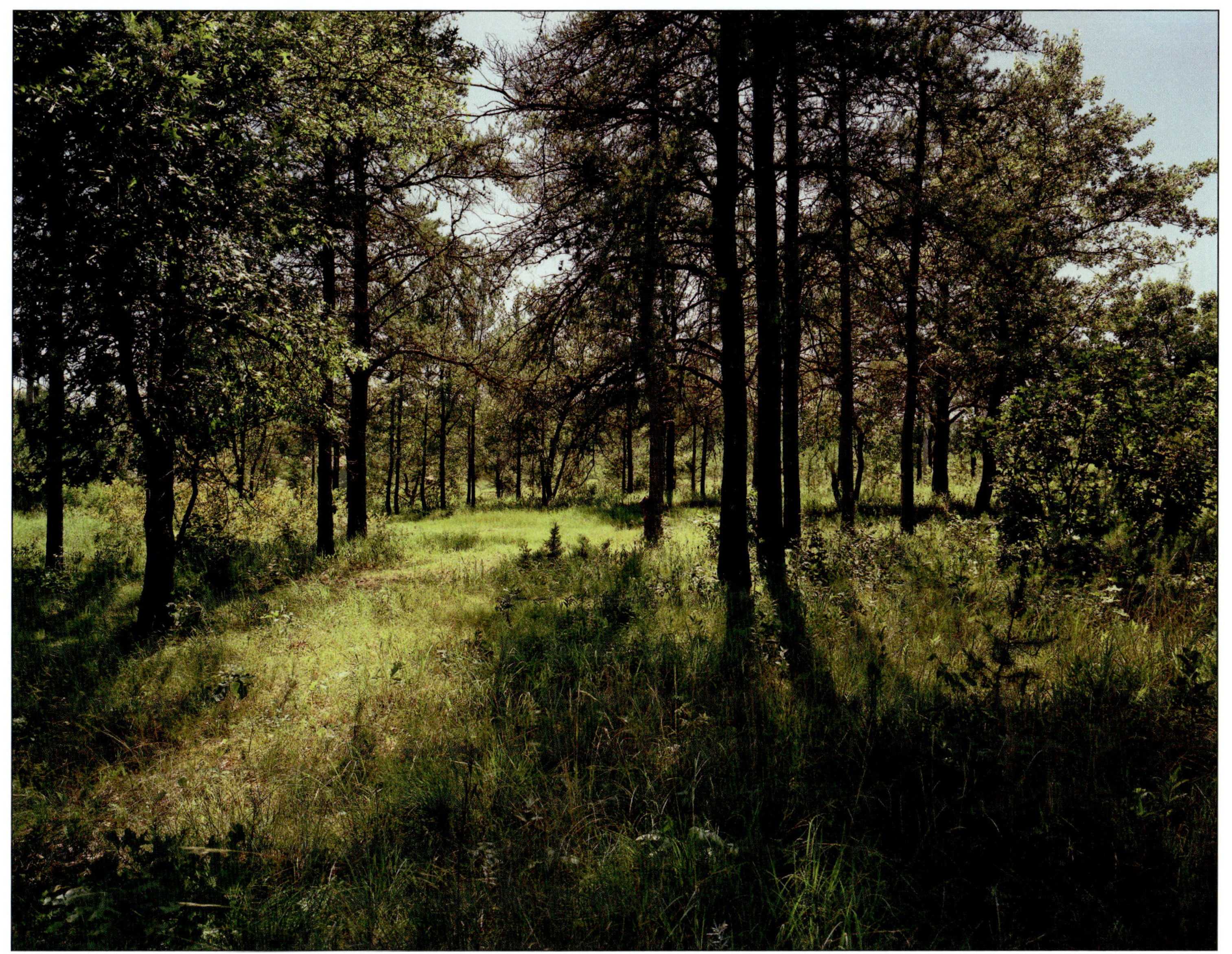

Headwaters, Brainerd: Jack Pine Savanna

Crow Wing County, Minnesota

The Nature Conservancy owns the Paul Bunyan Jack Pine Savanna—one of five jack pine savannas remaining in Minnesota—on 160 acres that somehow survived between a dump and a railroad. Jack pine depends on fire to regenerate and sun to thrive. Sticky resins keep its pinecones tightly sealed. Fire melts the resin, the cones pop open, the seeds fall out and germinate. Big bluestem, kalm's brome, muly-grass, and porcupine grass mixed with wildflowers—pink lady's slipper, blue-bead lily, and rattlesnake plantain—form the prairie under the canopy, Drought-tolerant forbs root in the sandy soil: silky prairie clover, blue-eyed grass, bird-foot violet, and gayfeather.

The Upper Mississippi

The Falls of St. Anthony were the geological and biological break between the headwaters and the Upper Mississippi. While navigating the rapids below the falls was often impossible, they provided an excellent spawning ground for fish and mussels. However, channel catfish, ubiquitous between St. Paul and Louisiana, never breached the falls to inhabit the headwaters, nor did lake sturgeon, white bass, or brook trout, which was introduced to the headwaters in the nineteenth century. Of the 123 species of fish that swim the Mississippi below the falls, 59 have never ventured above the falls.

It is a well-kept secret that the Upper Mississippi River, with its 2.7 million–acre floodplain and its towering bluffs, is a tourist mecca. In 1999 the Upper Mississippi River corridor, with fifty active Bald Eagle nests and eighteen active heron rookeries in its refuge, racked up eleven million recreational visits—more than Yellowstone Park. People came to hunt, fish, boat, bird- and eagle-watch, enjoy the fall colors, roam the old river towns, party at the festivals and fishing tournaments, and gamble on the riverboats. They spent $6.6 billion and provided jobs for 140,000, mostly in the hotel, restaurant, and retail industries.

The Upper Mississippi is the migratory flyway for 326 species of birds and 40 percent of all North American waterfowl—ducks, geese, swans, herons, and other wading birds. Along the river's 1,300 mile–corridor, 260 species of fish swim in its waters, 37 species of mussels live just off its muddy banks, 45 species of amphibians and reptiles inhabit its marshes, and 60 species of mammals prowl its floodplain in the Upper Mississippi Wildlife and Fish Refuge, the Mark Twain National Wildlife Refuge, and numerous state wildlife-management areas. Its watershed provides homes for thirty million people, who depend on its water for their municipal and industrial water supplies.

In 1999 Mississippi River towns pushed a total of 133.7 million tons of commodities worth $22.7 billion through the Upper River navigation system and employed 48,000 people to work the barges. Many of the problems plaguing the river can be attributed to the creation and maintenance of the nine-foot navigation channel.

Navigation improvements—locks, dams, dikes, and revetments—changed the way water flowed across the floodplain. Dams turned the river into a series of pools and made fish migration impossible. Agriculture, protected by levees, left the river below Rock Island disconnected from its floodplain. Water and wetlands dominated the floodplain north of Rock Island, leaving less than a quarter of the 2.7 million acres susceptible to the benefits of flooding, most of that north of Pool 13. Taken together the levees and the dams fragmented grasslands, forests, and marshes, leading to the loss of both habitat and diversity.

The early explorers of the Upper Mississippi found a floodplain forest of oak, shellbark hickory, northern pecan, and hackberry—hard-mast trees that produce nuts incased in hard shells—mixed with silver maple, cottonwood, willow, and green ash—trees that produce windblown seeds. Late-twentieth-century explorers of the Upper Mississippi found a forest dominated by silver maple and willow, mixed with some cottonwood and green ash. Loggers felled most of the oaks and hickories in the nineteenth century. Construction of the nine-foot navigation channel flooded out the rest.

Trees' locations in the floodplain determined whether they survived the steady water levels required by the nine-foot navigation channel. Willow, silver maple, cottonwood, and green ash all tolerate extensive flooding and grow on the lowest and wettest soils in the floodplain. Oak, hickory, pecan, and hackberry tolerate a little flooding but not the permanent flooding brought on by the nine-foot channel; those that survived the completion of the dams grew on drier soils on ridges that rose a foot or two above the floodplain. At the beginning of the twenty-first century, the U.S. Fish and Wildlife Service, the state departments of natural resources, and the Corps of Engineers all made concerted efforts to replace the nut-bearing trees on higher elevations in the floodplain.

With the beginnings of the Environmental Management Program in 1986, the Corps and the natural resources departments developed a variety of restoration techniques to mimic the presettlement state of the river. They dredged backwaters of sediment to restore fish habitat; they introduced well-oxygenated water into stagnant backwaters; they constructed islands with dredge, first to create windbreaks and reduce turbidity, then to create habitat; they stabilized banks, first with rock revetments, then with willow plantings; they opened closed side channels and notched wing dams to create side channels in dike fields.

Behind dams, sediment delivered to the Mississippi by its tributaries backed up, clouding and filling backwaters. In some cases toxins accompanied the sediment. Submerged vegetation, food for Canvasbacks, declined. The fingernail clam, food for scaups, the most numerous duck in North American, declined. In 1996, in an attempt to address sedimentation, Congress authorized the Small Watershed Program to provide technical and financial assistance to state and local governments to protect and restore watersheds damaged by erosion, flooding, and runoff. The watershed program provides money that enables farmers to adopt river-friendly practices: contour plowing, using chisel instead of moldboard plows to slow erosion; building livestock waste–settling basins; establishing buffer strips along streambanks and vegetating them in native warm-season grasses; erecting low-cost electric fences along the buffers to keep cows from trampling the grasses.

In the 1990s the Corps of Engineers instituted successful drawdowns of Pools 26, 13, and 8. Moist-soil plants took root on mudflats that had not been exposed since the 1930s; submergent and emergent plants took root in deeper waters. However, weather and politics could not guarantee a drawdown in every pool every summer.

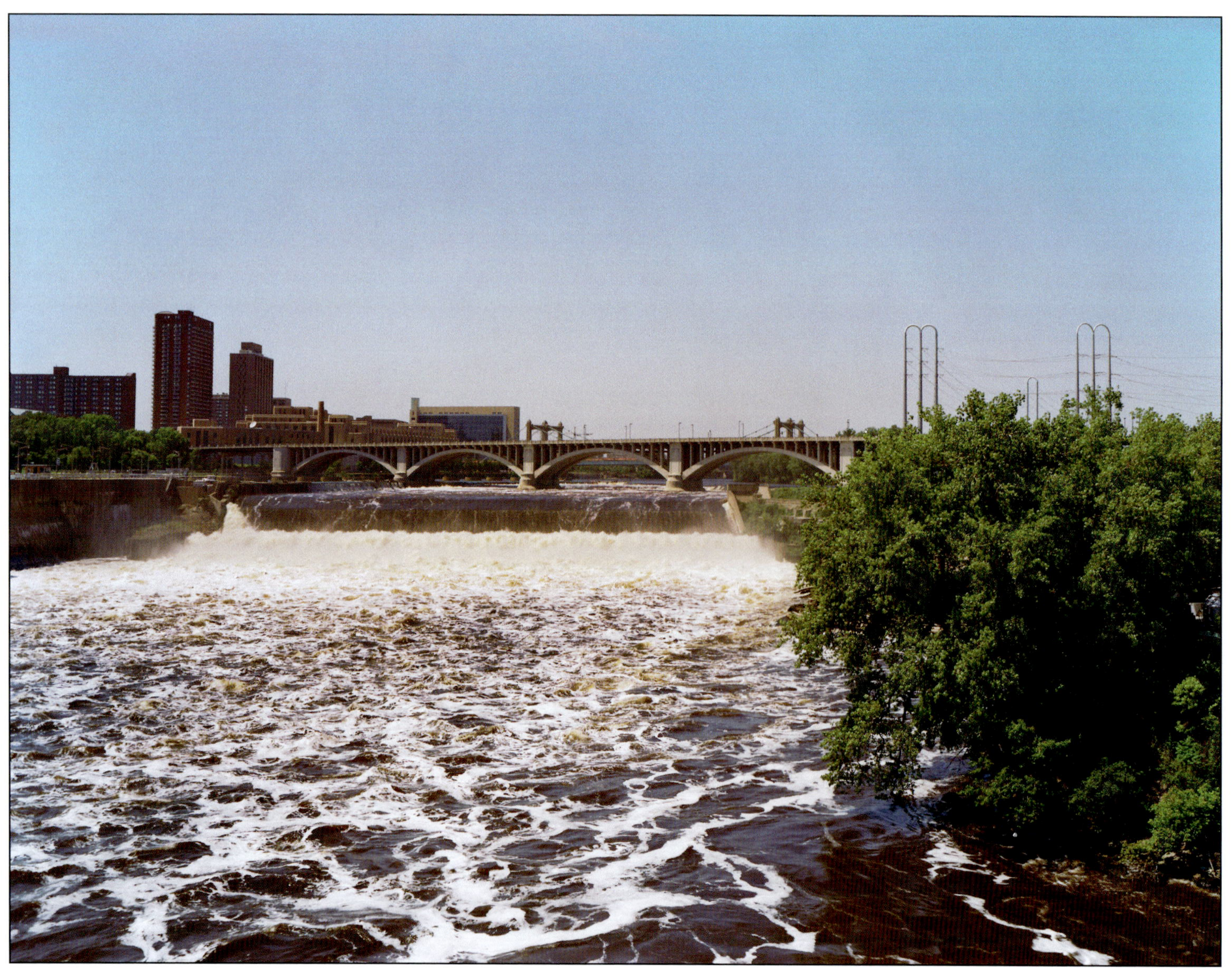

Mississippi Gorge: Falls of St. Anthony

Hennepin County, Minnesota

The falls no longer exist. Between 1848 and 1890, Minnesota industrialists altered them to produce power. In 1871 the milling industry built a stabilization dam above the falls to stop their retreat upstream. In 1917 the Ford Motor Company constructed a hydroelectric dam at the site of Lock and Dam 1 and submerged the rapids, which were then buried in sewage and sand trapped behind the dam. In 1963 the U.S. Army Corps of Engineers completed a pair of locks and dams to extend navigation four and a half miles above the falls. Today, what looks like a waterfall at the Falls of St. Anthony is water spilling over a dam.

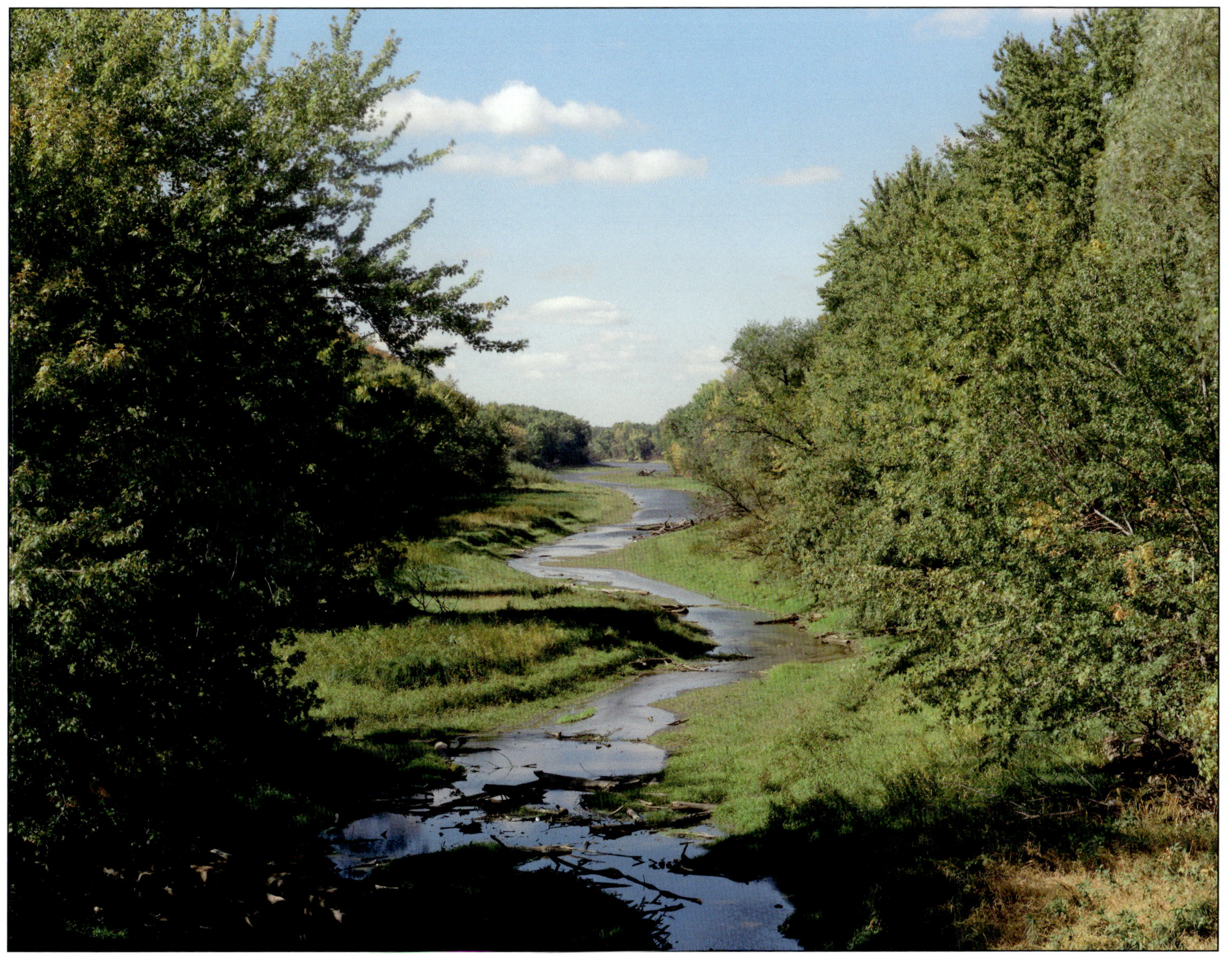

Vermilion Bottoms: Drainage to the Vermilion River

Dakota County, Minnesota

Vermilion Bottoms is remote. Bald eagles roost at the mouth of the Vermilion. It is a perfect breeding place for migrating: Red-shouldered Hawks, Gray Flycatchers, Great Blue Herons, Kingfishers, Yellow Prothonotary Warblers, and the rare Cerulean Warbler, which nests and feeds high in treetops. In all, 153 species of birds nest or migrate through the bottoms. But the floodplain forest on Vermilion Bottoms—made up of silver maple, cottonwood, willow, and green ash—is stressed and aging. Critical trees are missing—elm, green and black ash, hackberry, black willow, and swamp white oak. The birds are losing breeding habitat.

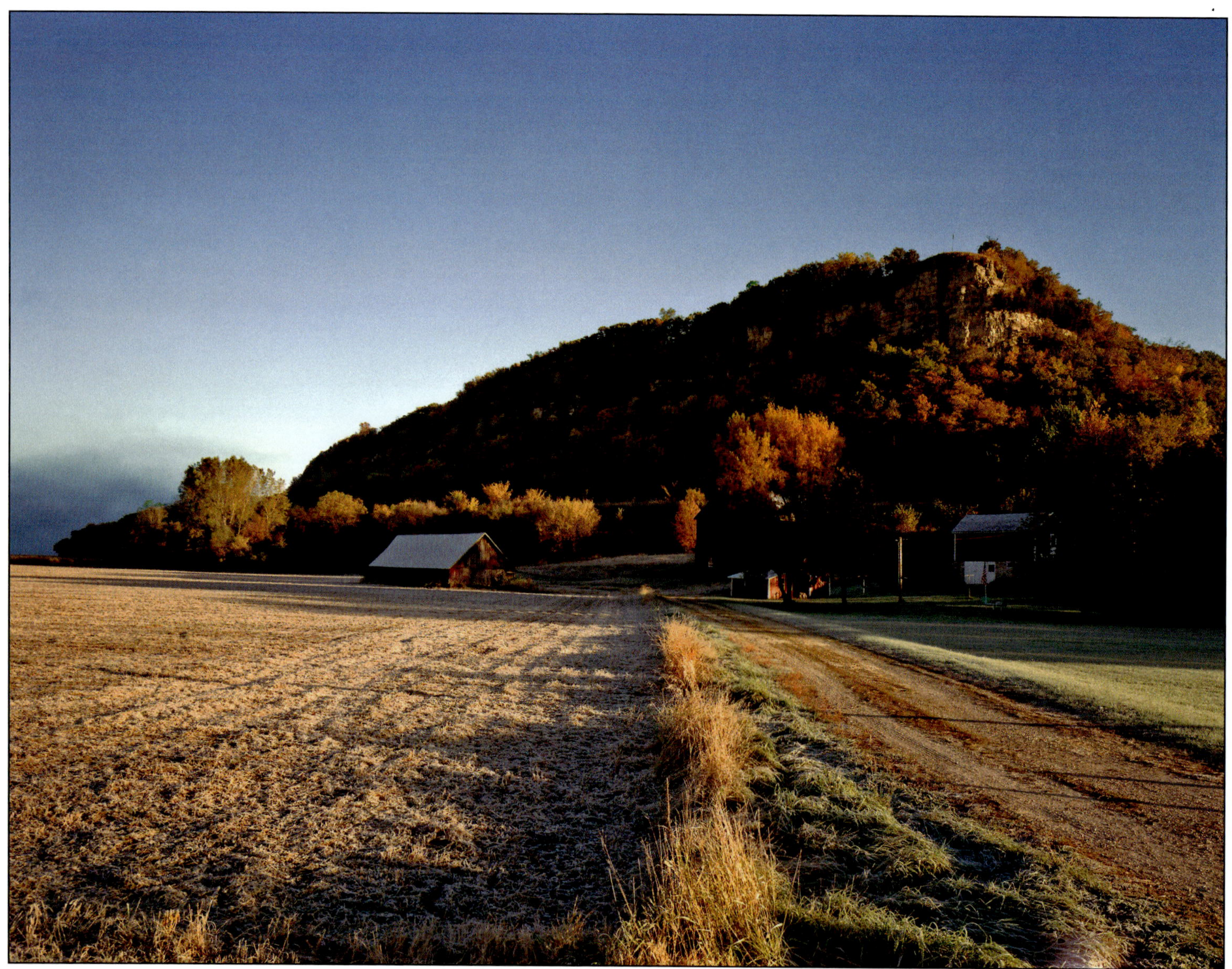

Trenton Terrace: Skidmore Bluff

Pierce County, Wisconsin

As the Wisconsin ice sheet withdrew from Minnesota, sediment-filled water deposited a valley train in the Mississippi gorge south of St. Paul. Glacial floods cut through it, leaving terraces clinging to the side of the gorge. A high terrace sits 271 feet below the crown of Skidmore Bluff, 29 feet above the floodplain of the Trimbelle River, and 49 feet above the normal level of Pool 3. When settlers from New England, New York, and Pennsylvania arrived in Pierce County after 1827, they found a flat plain occupied by oak savannas and woodland forests. They cleared it for farming.

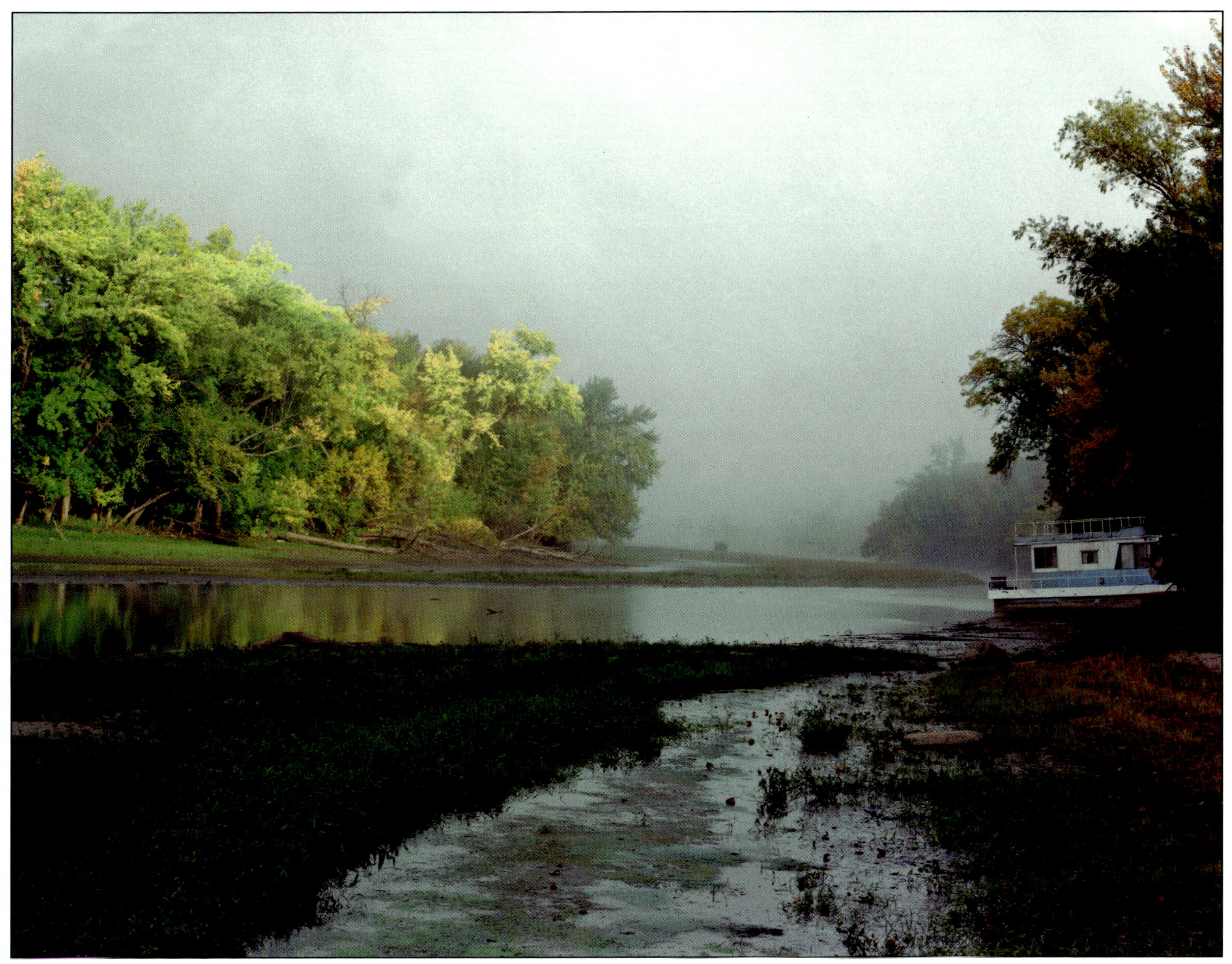

Trimbelle River: Trenton Slough

Pierce County, Wisconsin

Many trees on islands in the upper reaches of the navigation pools survived inundation after the construction of the dams. Many did not. Before the Corps closed the dams, trees in the lower reaches of each pool were cut. What was left: water-tolerant silver maple, which accepts long periods of flooding and its seedlings' submersion as long as the water is moving. It has been over seventy years since the completion of the dams, and the silver maples that colonize the Upper Mississippi are growing old and not regenerating. The Corps and various departments of natural resources are moving to replace them with nut-producing trees—oaks and hickories.

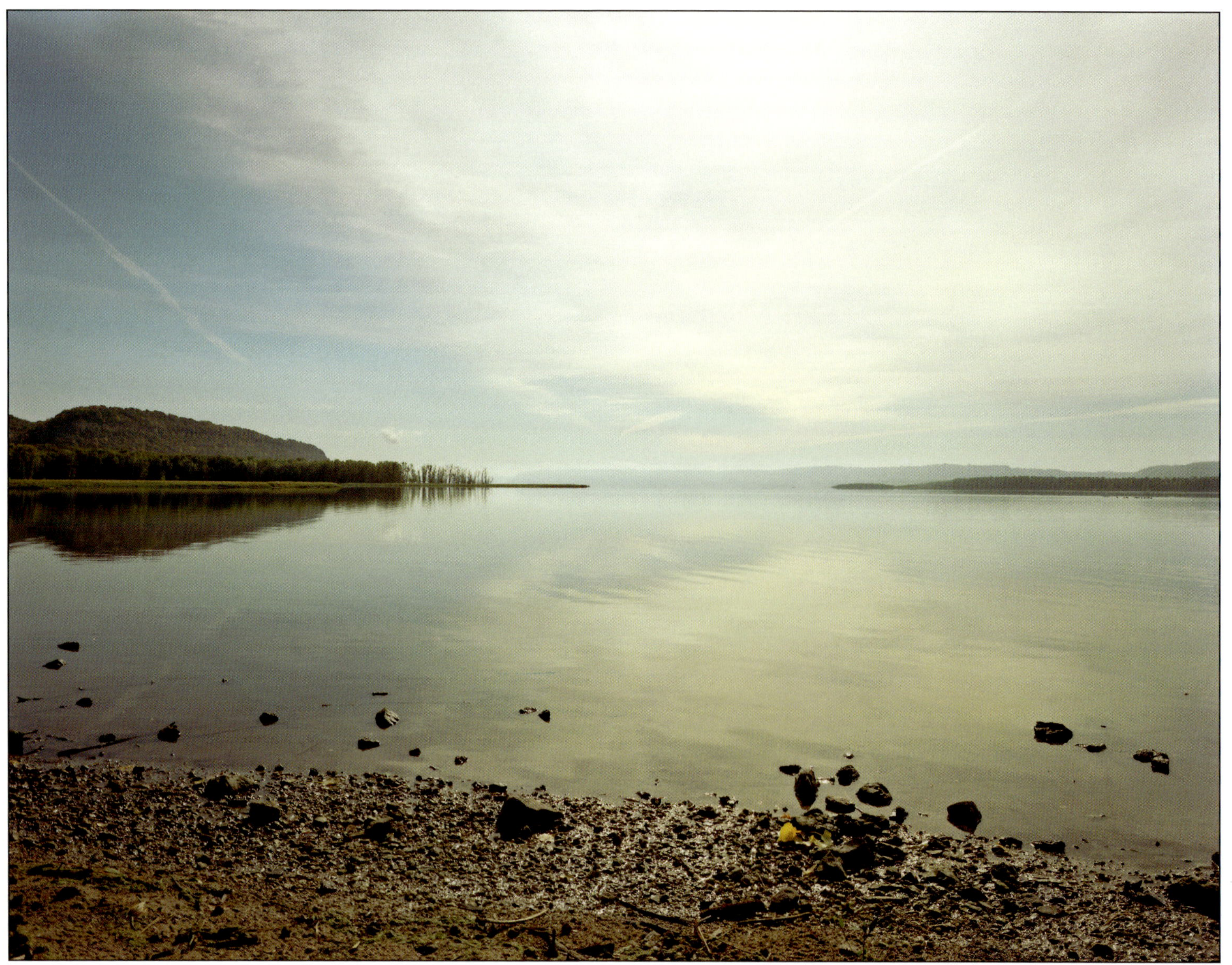

Lake Pepin: Catherine Pass

Pierce County, Wisconsin

"From the head of Lake Pepin to the Cannon river, the Mississippi is branched out into many channels, its bosom covered with numerous islands."—Zebulon Pike, 1805

At Red Wing the Mississippi breaks into two channels, each depositing sediment into Lake Pepin. Occasionally, a small basin will form between two distributaries and eventually become a shallow lake. Catherine Pass, a basin in the early stages of creation, formed at the head of Lake Pepin. The Pierce County Islands Wildlife Area, the only publicly managed waterfowl area in upper Lake Pepin, encompasses Catherine Pass. During duck season it is a "no-entry refuge," off-limits to hunters.

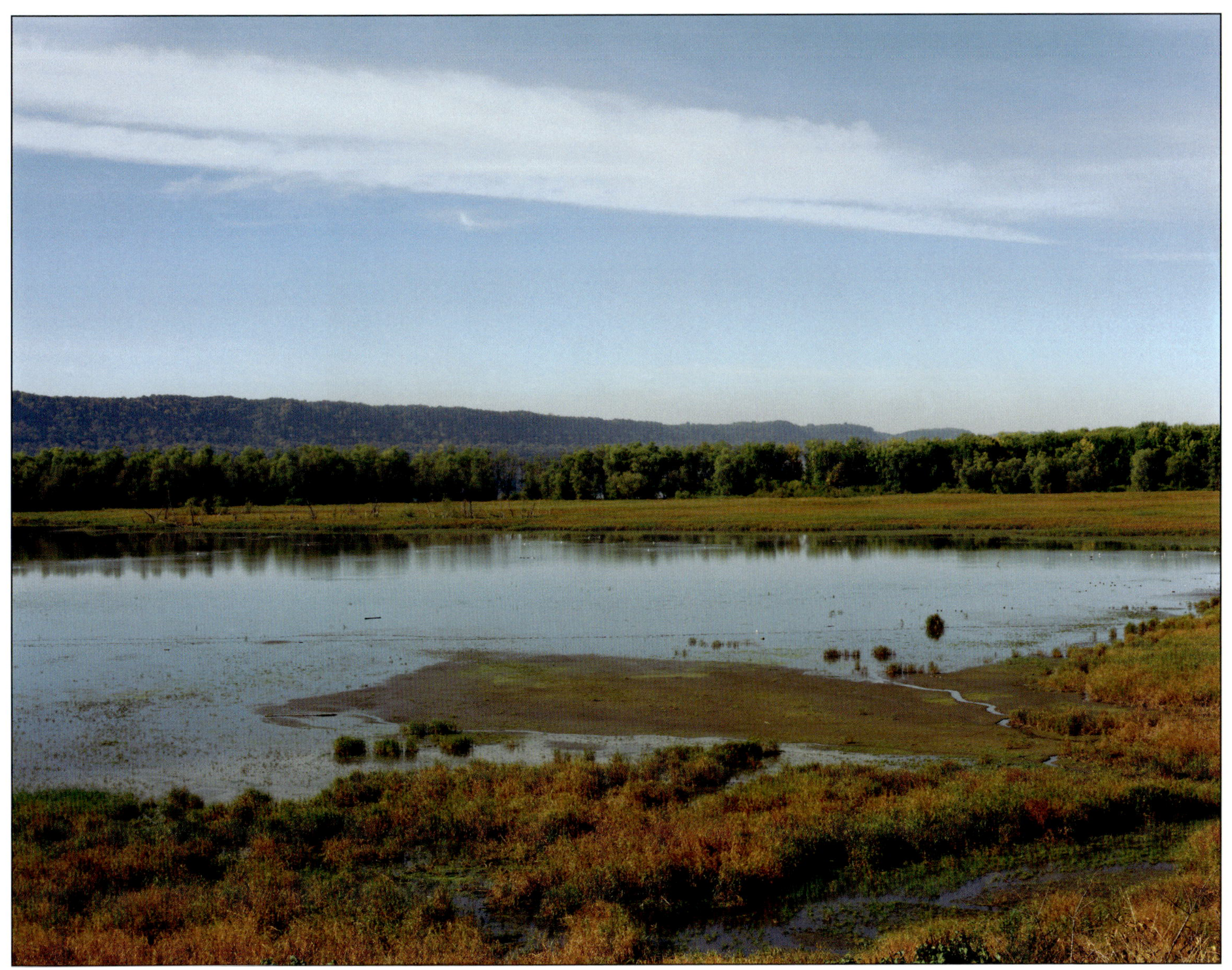

Lake Pepin: Rush River Delta

Pierce County, Wisconsin

The shores of Lake Pepin are the sheer bluffs of the Mississippi gorge, a few terraces, and the floodplain deltas of tributaries. The Rush River built its delta along the eastern shore of the lake. The isolated delta supports a floodplain forest of lowland hardwoods: silver maple, cottonwood, willow, and green ash. The forest supports warblers, flycatchers, vireos, the Red-shouldered Hawk, and the site of a Blue Heron rookery. Bulrush and smartweed, growing in the shallows, provide spawning places for northern pike and nurseries for ducks. Sandy spits, created by small drainages from the uplands, provide nesting places for turtles, terns, and shorebirds.

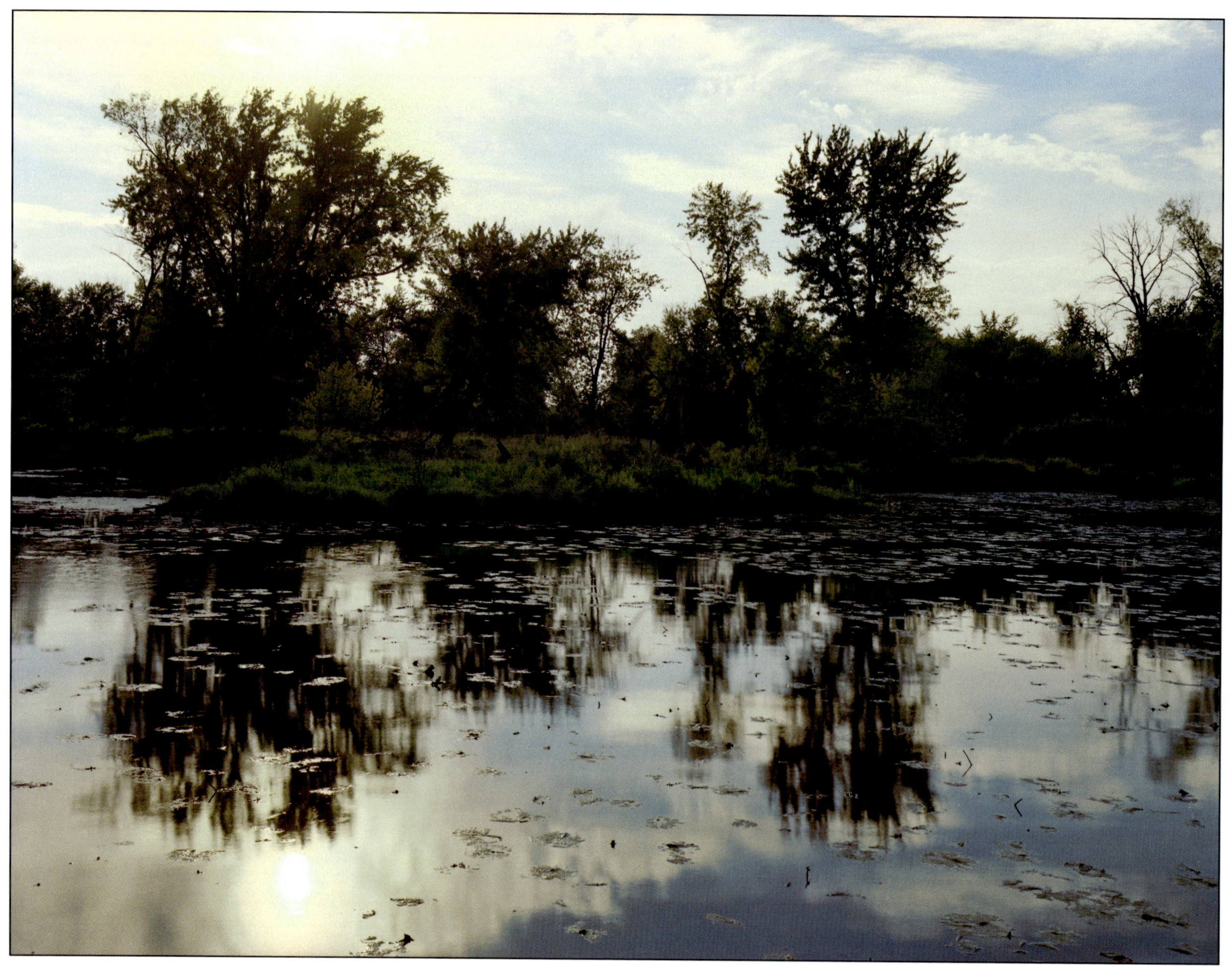

Pool 5: Island 42

Wabasha County, Minnesota

Island 42 is a classic V-shaped island that formed downstream from the mouth of a tributary. Its interior embraced a complex of forest, marsh, shallow lakes, and backwater sloughs. It provided roosting places for eagles, nesting sites for waterfowl, wintering and spawning grounds for fishes, and habitat for mussels with odd names: monkeyface, pistolgrip, round pigtoe, strange floater, wartyback, and washboard. Dam 5 held steady water levels in Pool 5. Levels of dissolved oxygen dropped in the island backwaters. To increase the level of oxygen the Corps built two culverts and a 900-foot-long channel to deliver fresher water to the stagnate backwaters.

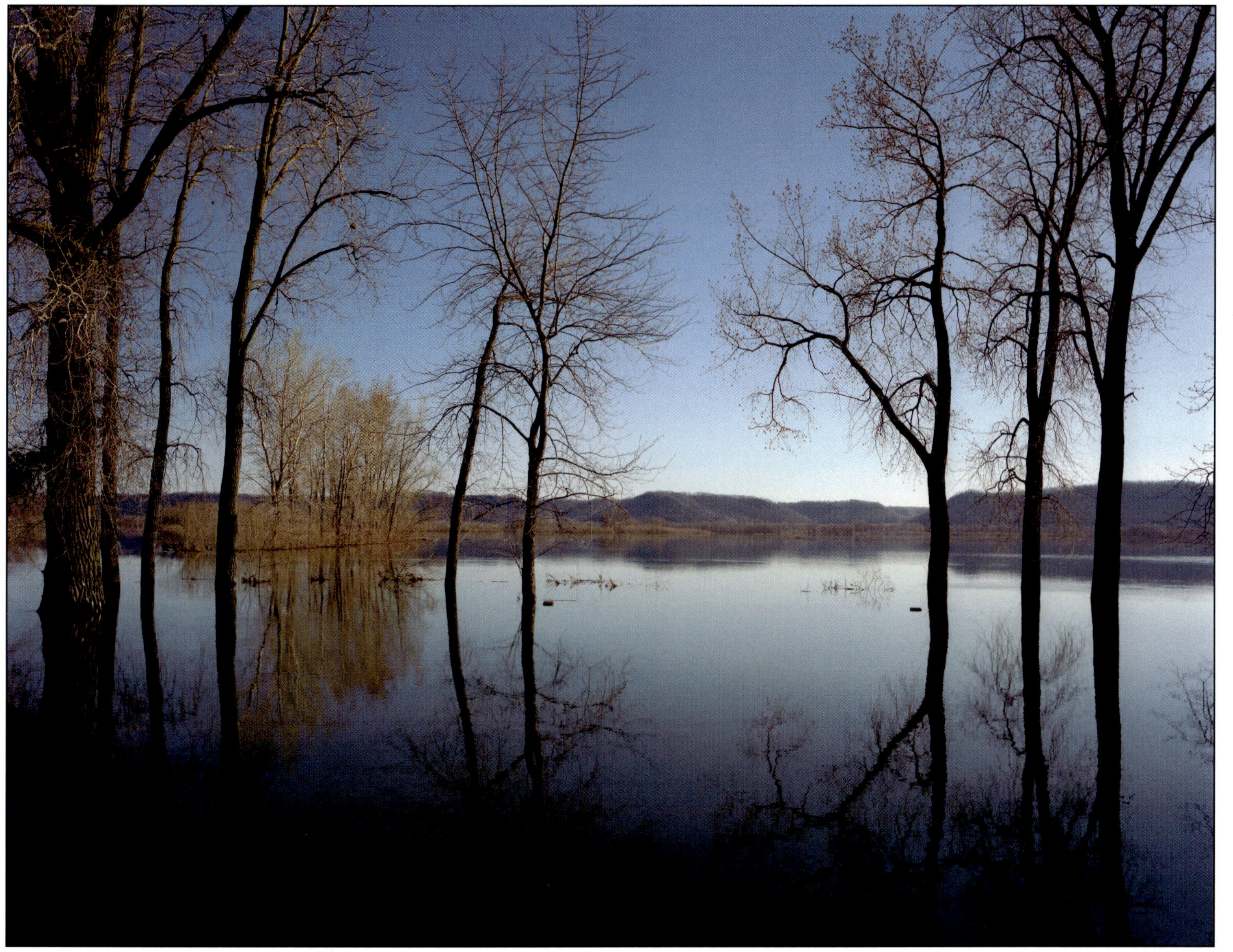

Polander Lake: Pap Slough

Winona County, Minnesota

In the years since Polander Lake pooled behind Dam 5a, sedimentation, wind fetch, and the flow of water through the lake have muddied its waters. To create deepwater habitat for fish, particularly paddlefish, the Corps dredged deep holes in parts of the lake. Paddlefish, older than dinosaurs, live in the slow, quiet waters of large rivers. They sweep their long, flat noses across the riverbed and pick up electrical currents generated by plankton, which they filter through their gills. They leave the river to breed in shallow streams with gravel beds. It's not easy; dams have impeded their migration to the streams where they lay their eggs.

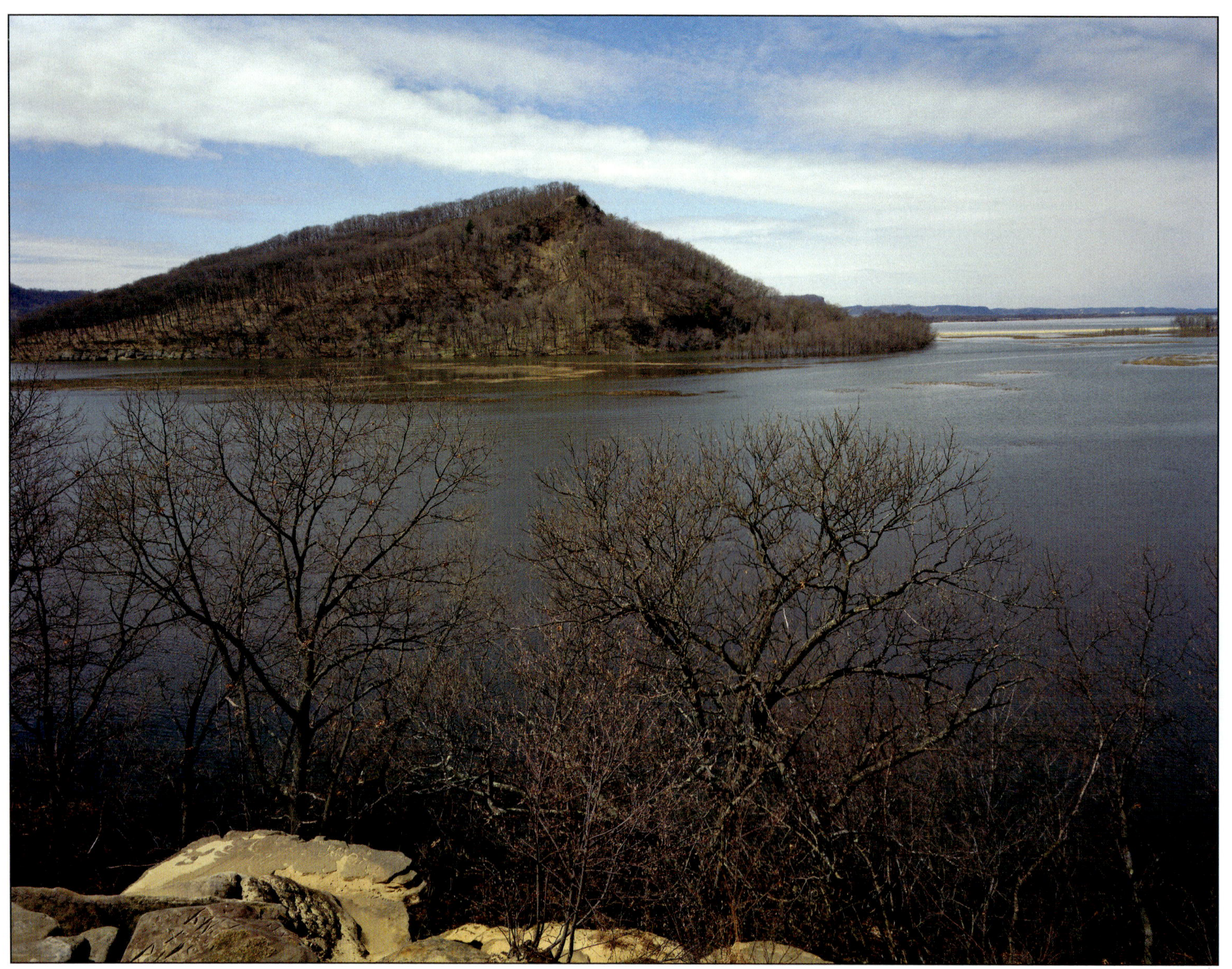

Trempealeau Mountain: From Perrot State Park

Trempealeau County, Wisconsin

"La Montaigne qui Trompe dans l'eau stands in the Mississippi near the east shore, about 50 miles below the Sauteaux (Chippewa) river, and is about two miles in circumference, with an elevation of two hundred feet, covered with timber. There is a small river which empties into the Mississippi, in the rear of the mountain, which, I conceive, once bounded the mountain on the lower side, and the Mississippi on the upper, when the mountain was joined to the main by a neck of prairie low ground, which in time was worn away by the spring freshes of the Mississippi; and thus formed an island of this celebrated mountain."—Lt. Zebulon Pike, 1805

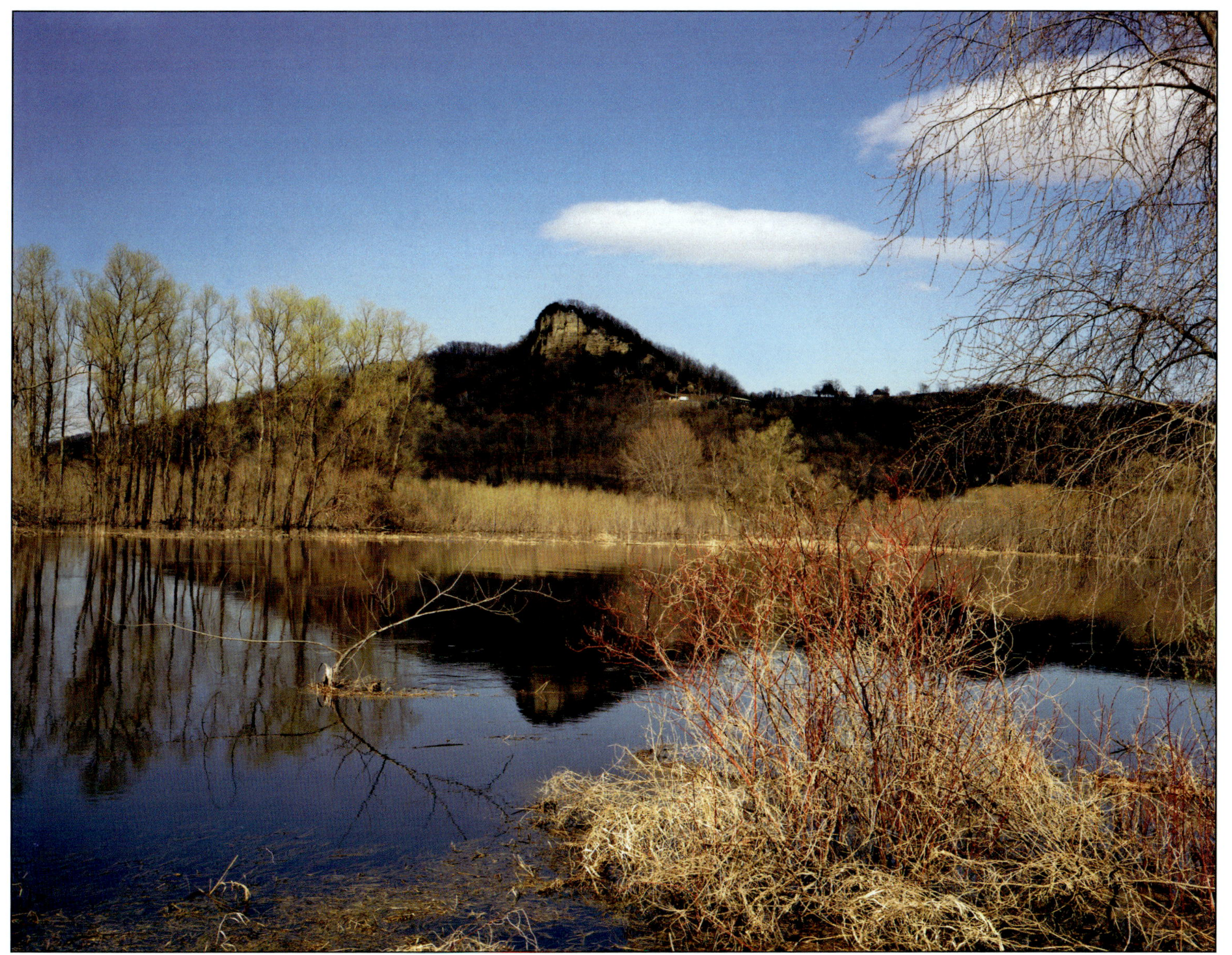

Goose Island: Running Slough
La Crosse County, Wisconsin

The U.S. Fish and Wildlife Service has closed Goose Island to hunting in all seasons. The service developed the system of closed areas in 1957–1958, assuring migrating waterfowl a network of feeding and resting places and dispersing waterfowl hunting throughout the Upper Mississippi refuge. With the steady decline of habitat on the Upper Mississippi, more and more birds were congregating in fewer and fewer places, leading to increased competition among hunters for places to hunt. Some have set up "firing lines" at the edges of closed areas, where they "skybust" birds, often out of range, as they leave closed areas, crippling more birds than they kill.

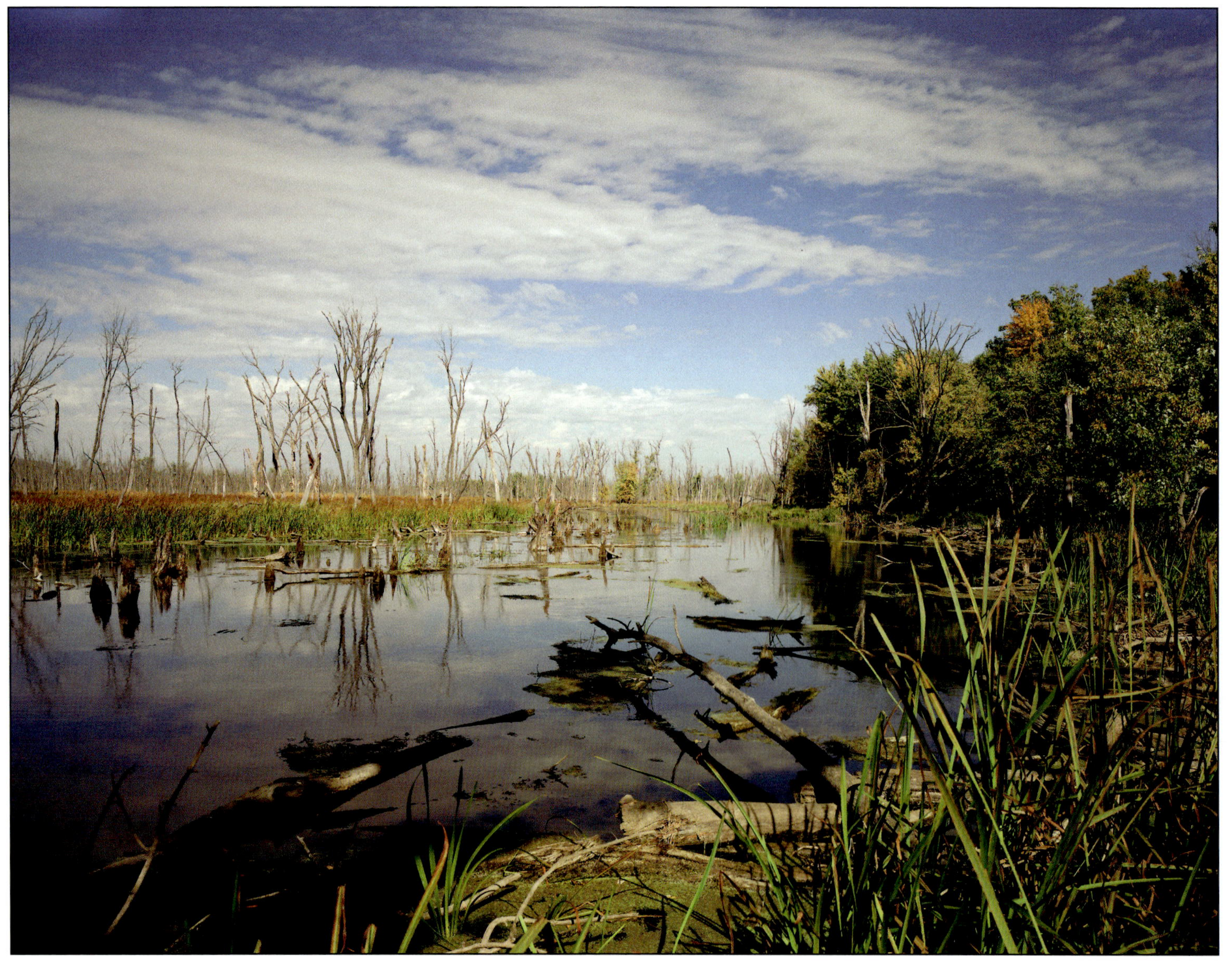

Reno Bottoms: Pig Pen Slough
Allamakee County, Iowa

"Immediately below most of the dams are incredible mazes of backwaters. The Reno Bottoms, on the Minnesota side across from Genoa, Wisconsin, has a reputation for being one of the most confusing labyrinths on the river. There are stories of people getting lost for days there. No map of the sluggish streams is much help. Many corridors end where a fallen tree blocks the way, or simply peter out in a patch of weeds. The current you were following to find your way might abruptly reverse direction. No, the Reno Bottoms, and backwaters like them, are no place for any boat that cannot be picked up and carried."—Reggie McLeod, 1994

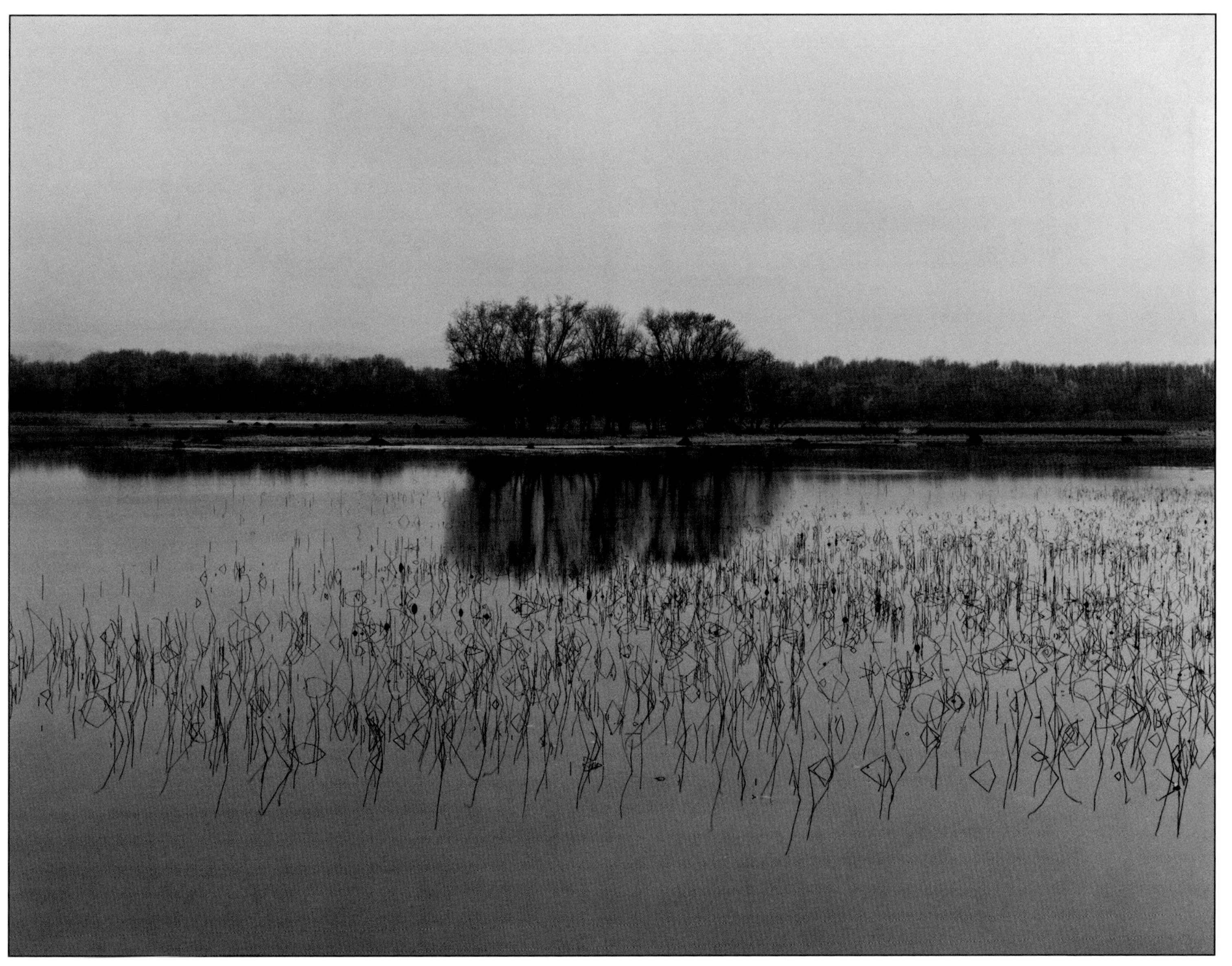

Winneshiek Bottoms: Henderson Slough

Allamakee County, Iowa

"To drain that area even though it were valuable for agriculture, which it is not, would be the same as destroying a library which contained manuscripts of which there were no other copies."—Barrington Moore, Ecological Society of America, testimony, House Agricultural Committee, 1923

In 1923 the Corps of Engineers wanted to drain 30,000 acres of Winneshiek Bottoms, a maze of sandy islands and shallow sloughs, and turn them over to agriculture. Moore's testimony and Will Dilg's work with the Izaak Walton League led to the creation of the Upper Mississippi National Wildlife and Fish Refuge in 1924.

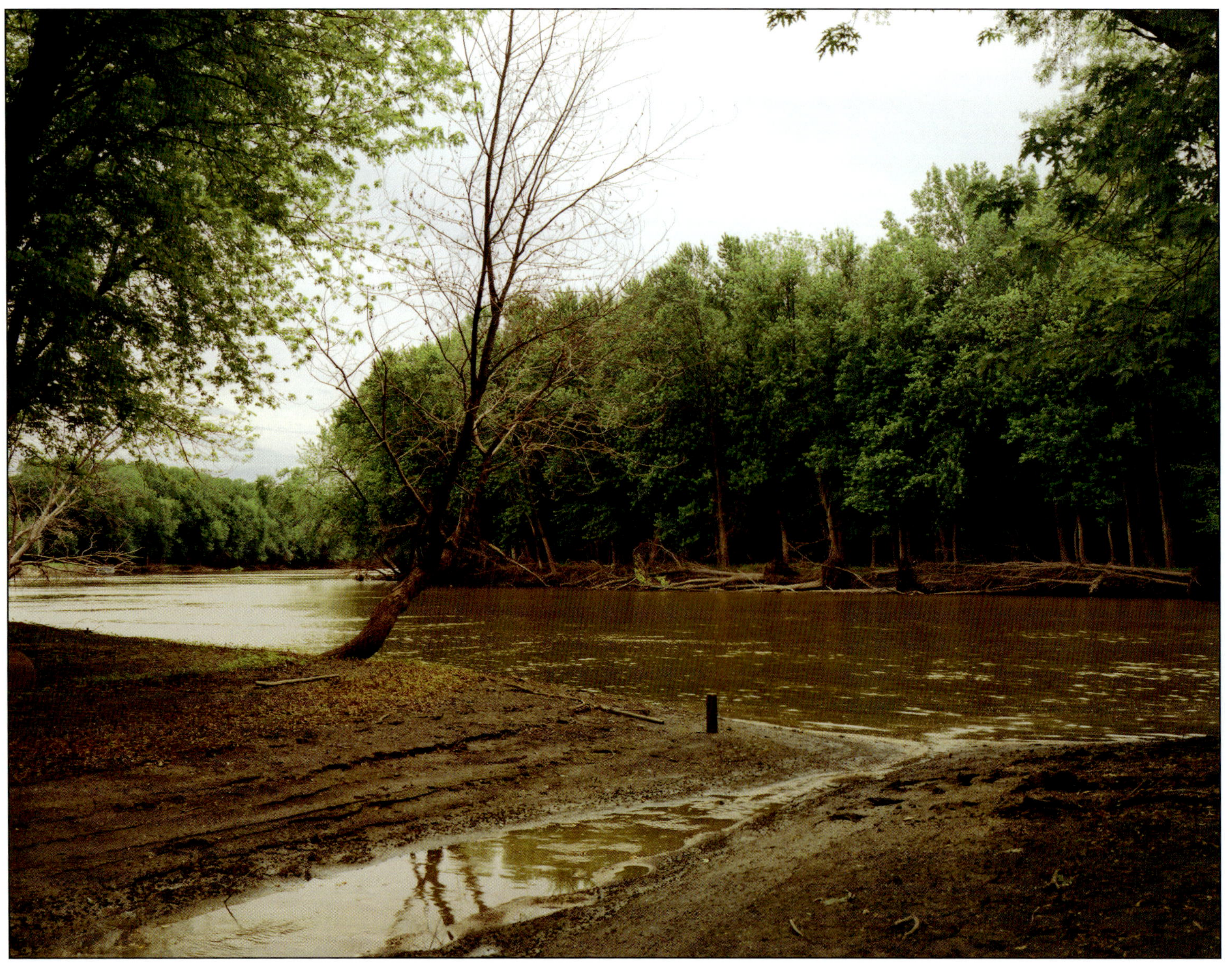

Harpers Slough: Delphey Island

Allamakee County, Iowa

At Harpers Slough the floodplain is a maze of wooded islands, an area closed to hunting that provides habitat for Tundra Swans, Canada Geese, dabbling and diving ducks, Black Terns, nesting eagles, bitterns, and cormorants. Its muddy bottom is home to a dense and diverse mussel population: the black sandshell, the butterfly, the hickorynut, the Higgins eye, the pearlymussel, the monkeyface, the mucket, the pistolgrip, the rock pocketbook, the round pigtoe, the spike, the strange floater, the wartyback, the washboard, the yellow sandshell, and the flat floater, a mussel that prefers very shallow backwaters. Zebra mussels and sedimentation threaten to bury them.

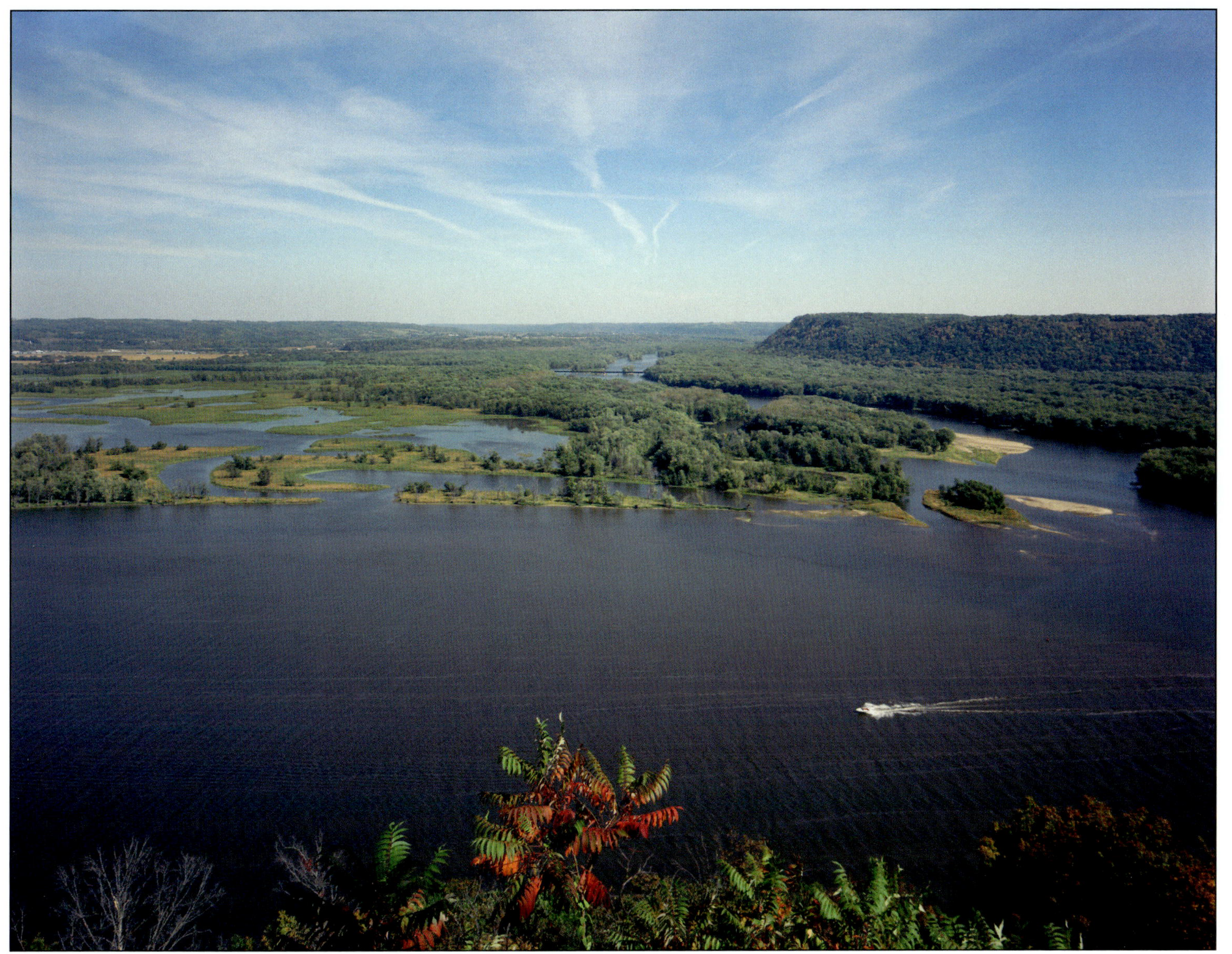

Wisconsin River Delta: Garnet Lake

Clayton County, Iowa

"Here we are, then, on this so renowned River, all of whose peculiar features I have endeavored to note carefully. The Mississippi River Takes its rise in various lakes in the country of the Northern Nations. It is narrow at the place where Miskous empties; its Current, which flows southward, is slow and gentle. To the right is a large Chain of very high Mountains, and to the left are beautiful lands; in various Places, the stream is Divided by Islands. On Sounding, we found ten brasses of Water. Its Width is very unequal; sometimes it is three quarters of a league, and sometimes it narrows to three arpents."—Father Jacques Marquette, 1673

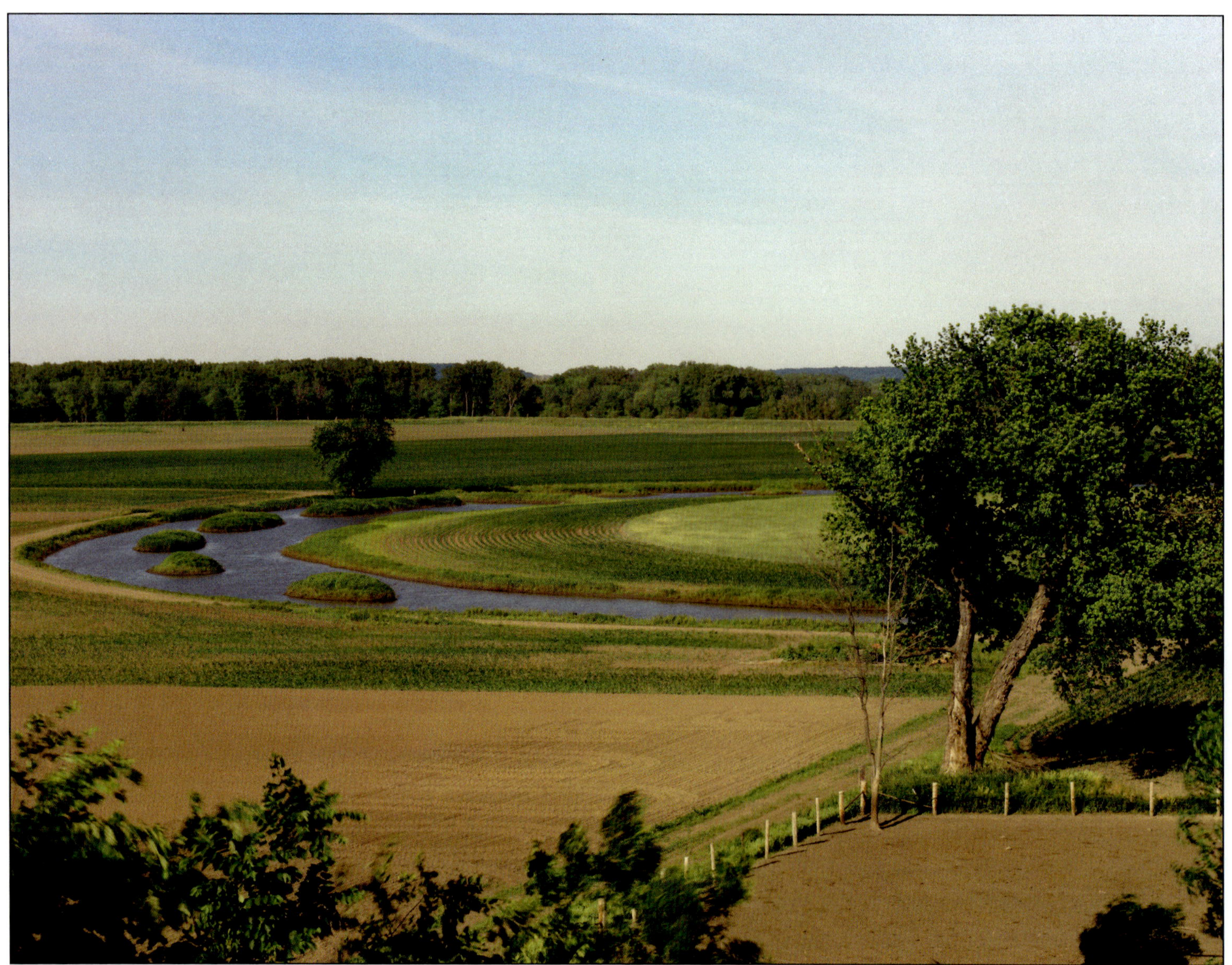

Oxbow: Maquoketa River

Jackson County, Iowa

The quiet oxbow lake on Roger Tarr's farm just north of the Maquoketa River was an ideal place to build a series of goose-nesting mounds. It was wide enough to isolate the mounds from the edge of the lake and deep enough to discourage predators that might raid the nests or livestock that might trample them. By building the mounds, Tarr increased the land/water fringe in the oxbow and the amount of wetland available to breeding waterfowl, an invitation to Mallards, Pintails, Gadwall, Shovellers, Blue-winged Teals, Redheads, Lesser Scaup, and Canada Geese to nest.

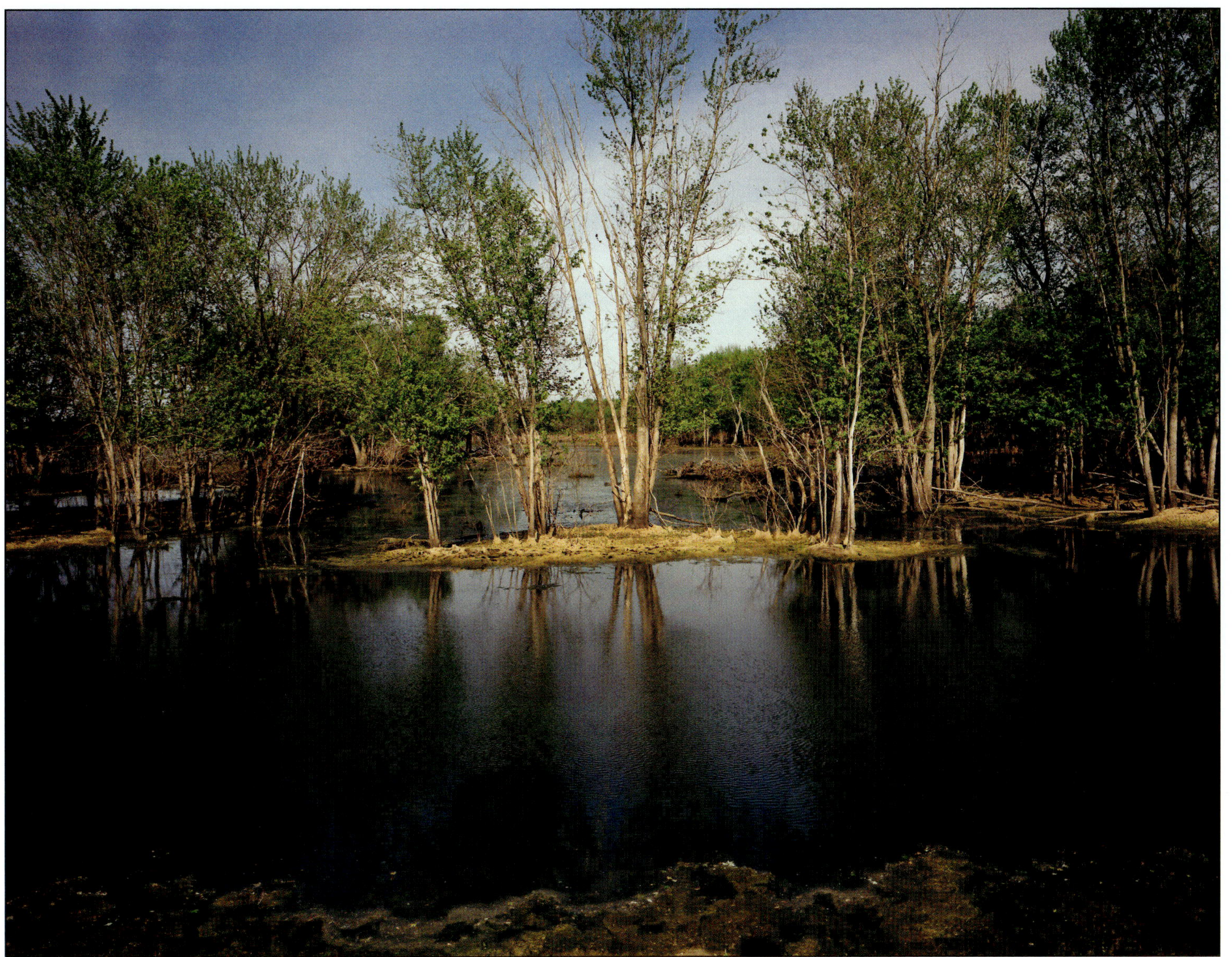

Green Island Wildlife Area: Fish Lake

Jackson County, Iowa

To maintain body weight during migration, ducks and geese must find good food every fifty to seventy miles along their route. Until they were flooded, the islands, mudflats, and backwaters along the river offered plenty of food. The Iowa DNR would like to set water-control structures, pumps and gates, into the levees that protect wildlife areas and provide waterfowl feeding places every fifty miles along the Iowa bank. This would allow wildlife managers to mimic the spring highs and summer lows on mudflats. They have built the necessary structures at the Green Island, Princeton, and Odessa Wildlife Areas, major stopping places for waterfowl.

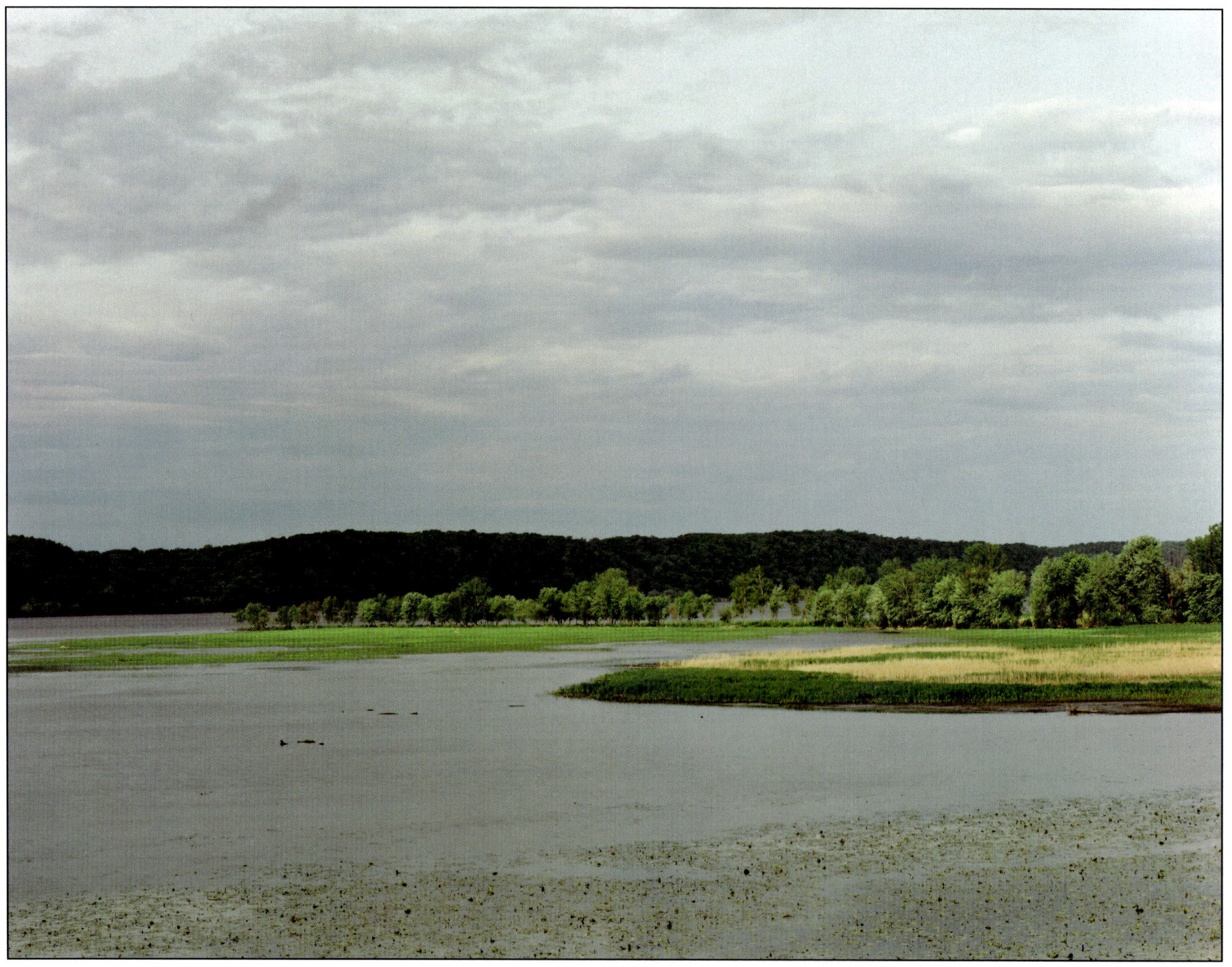

Spring Lake: Upper Mississippi Refuge
Carroll County, Illinois

Waterfowl, fish, and frogs prefer wetlands that are half water/half vegetation—a hemi-marsh. Cattail and bulrush along the margins provide nesting cover for waterfowl, their seeds food for ducks, and their stems and tubers food for muskrats and geese. In deeper water ducks browse on the seeds of water lilies, arrowheads, and spatterdock; beaver, muskrat, porcupine, and deer forage on the leaves, stems, and tubers. Muskrats cut stems for their lodges, create openings, and maintain the 50/50 balance. Failing that, wildlife managers at Spring Lake—separated from the river by a levee—flood, burn, mow, or disk unwanted woody plants to maintain the balance.

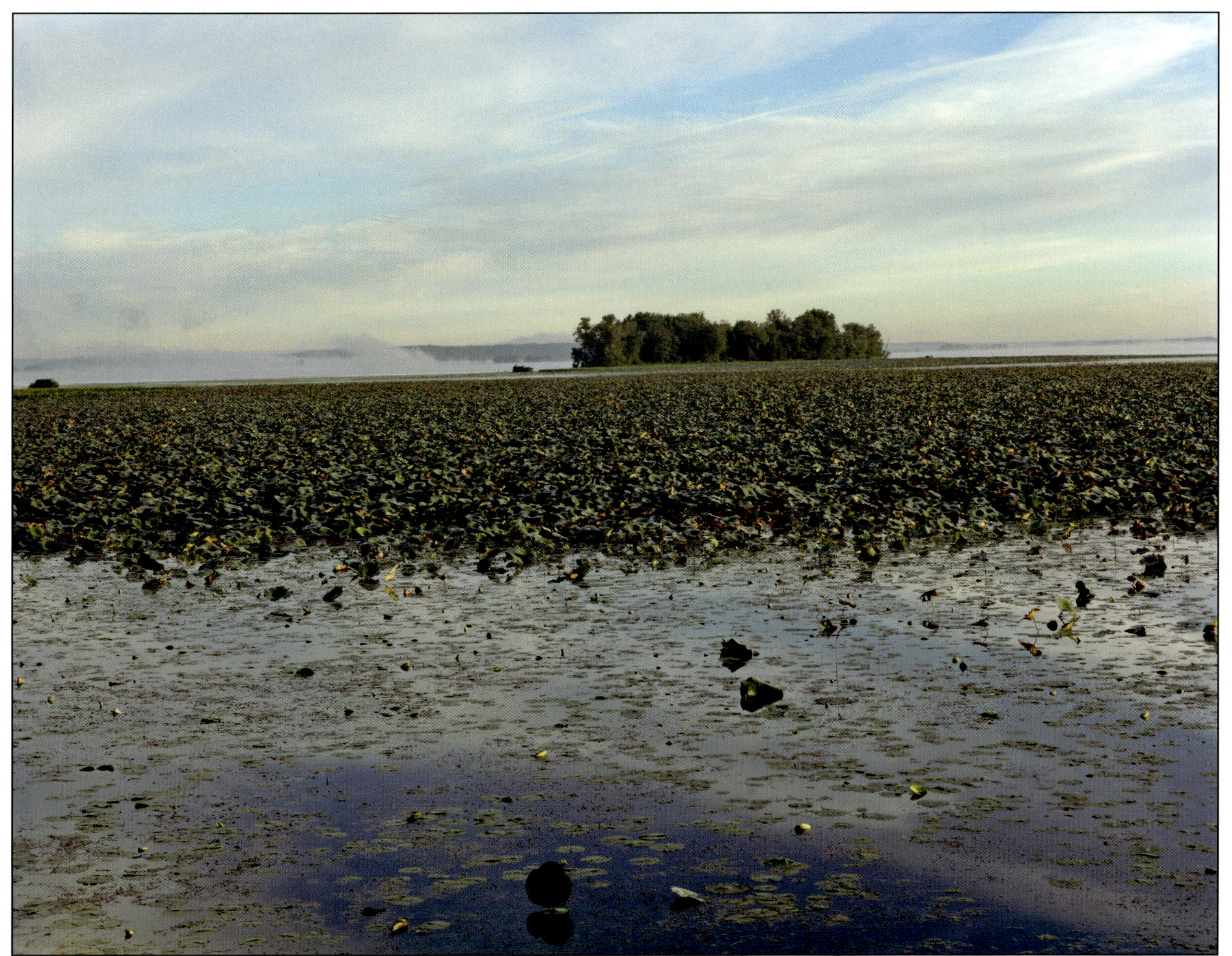

Lock and Dam 13: Potter's Marsh and Slough

Whiteside County, Illinois

Unlike at Spring Lake, no levees surround Potter's Marsh. After inundation, silt filled marsh and slough. Vegetation changed. Emergents replaced submergents in open water; terrestrials replaced emergents in marshy areas, clogging the slough. The Corps dredged to provide deepwater habitat for overwintering fish, built a sediment trap at its head to keep silt out, excavated potholes for waterfowl, and built resting and feeding habitat for migratory birds in a managed wetland. After those steps were completed in 1996, submergent vegetation returned to open water, emergent vegetation to terrestrial areas. Water lilies took root adjacent to Lock and Dam 13.

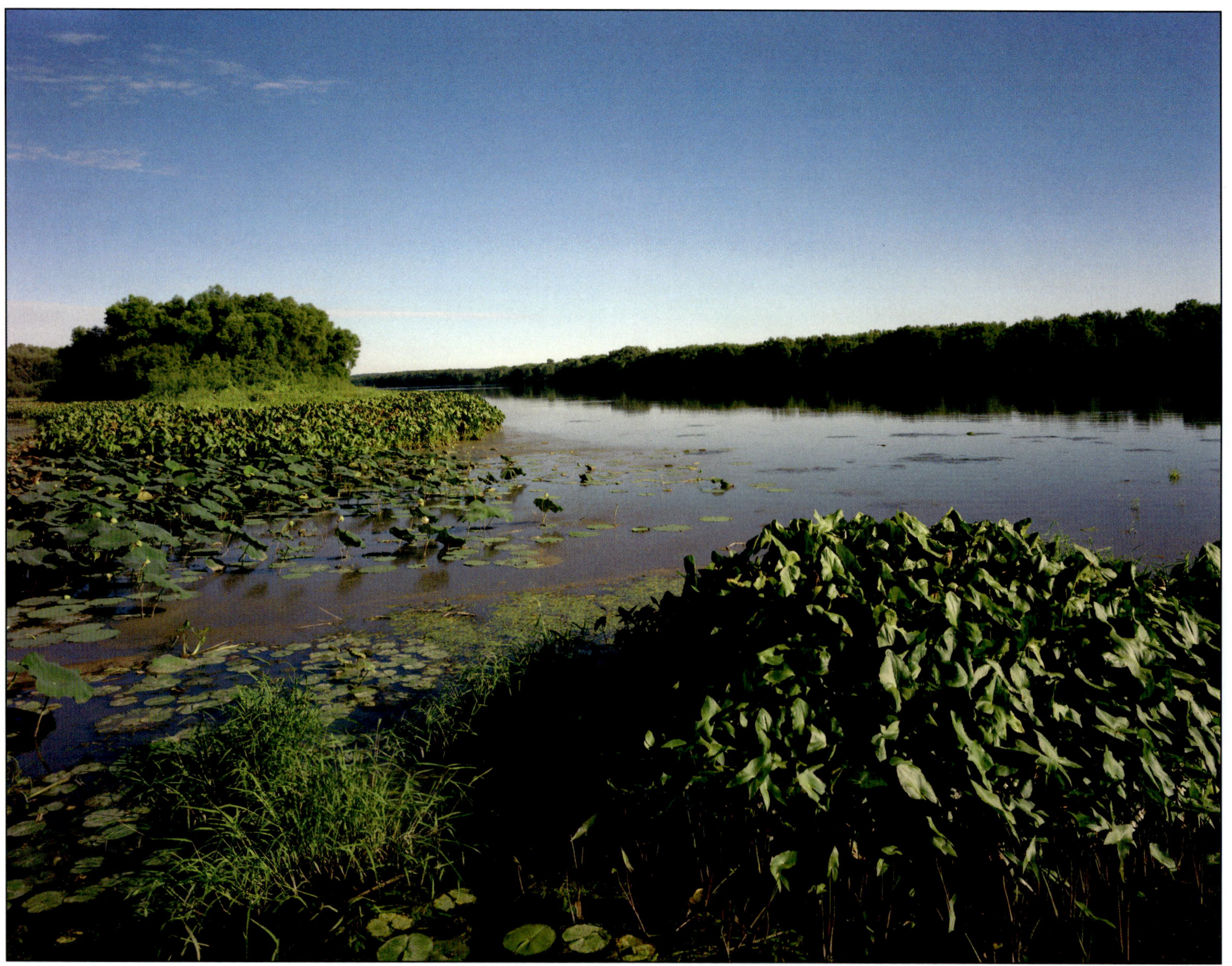

Andalusia Gorge: Geneva Island, Wyoming Slough

Scott County, Iowa

At the end of the twentieth century, Geneva Island, a collection of small islands and sloughs that separates Wyoming Slough along the west bank from the navigation channel on the east, typified many of the islands in the Upper Mississippi gorge. It was eroding at its head. Sediment chocked its interior sloughs and clogged Wyoming Slough. Sweetland Creek, which flows from the upland, added to the load of sediment in the slough where arrowhead bracket its mouth and American lotus and water lilies take root. That was bad news for anglers in Wyoming Slough who once found good fishing for channel catfish. Cats like their rivers running fast and deep and muddy.

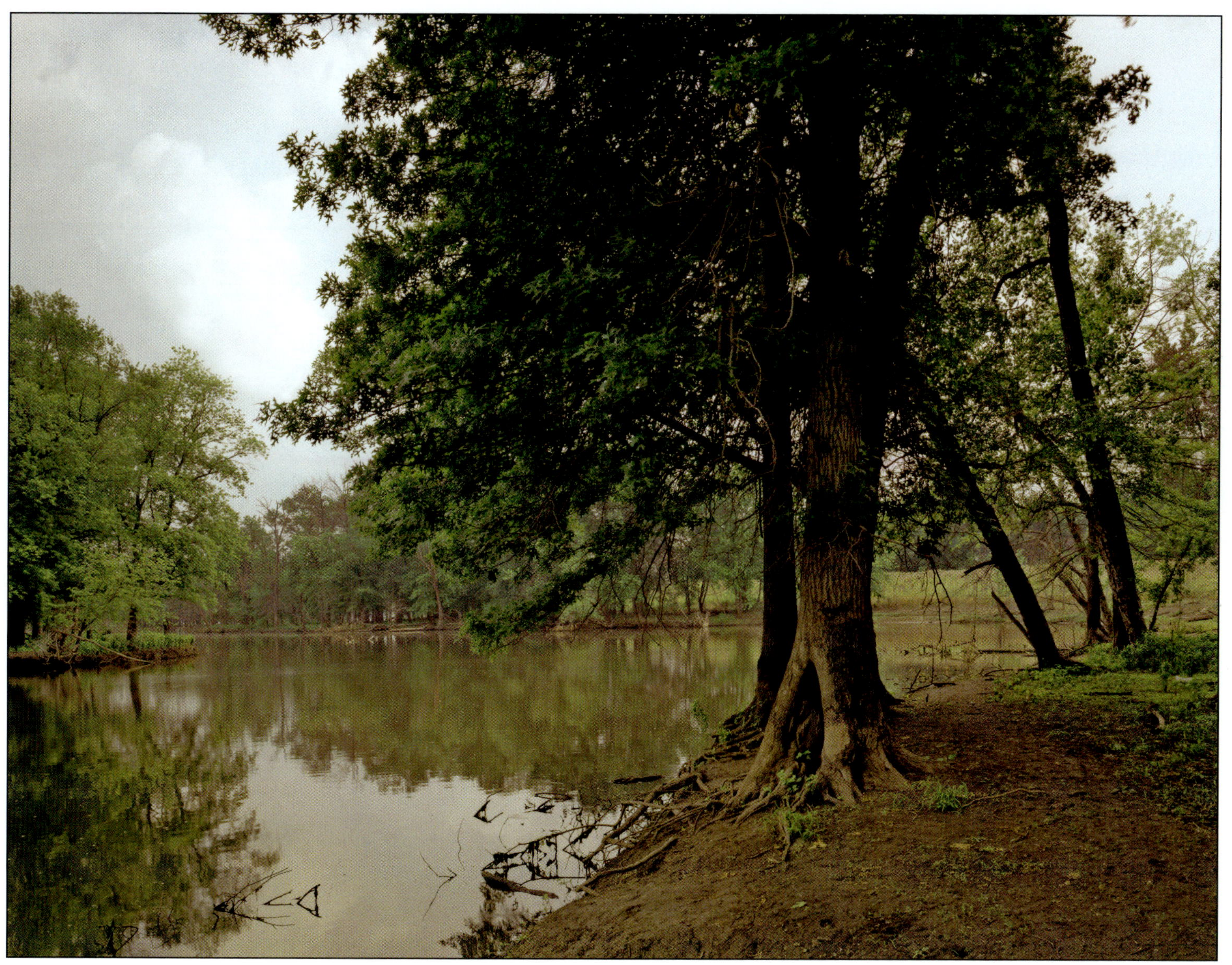

Port Louisa National Wildlife Refuge, Big Timber Division: Coolegar Slough

Louisa County, Iowa

Coolegar Slough runs through Big Timber, a 3,376-acre complex of backwater sloughs, potholes, and bottomland forests, dominated by pin and white oak, shagbark and shellbark hickory, silver maple, cottonwood, ash, and willow—habitat for eagles and osprey, migrating waterfowl and warblers, amphibians, and small fish. The slough is not protected by a levee, and silt is filling deepwater fish holes. During floods, fish migrate to refuge holes and sloughs. When the flood recedes, fish are stranded in backwaters unconnected to the river. Water stagnates; the fish die. The sloughs dry up; so do the fish. Should they survive the summer, they freeze in the winter.

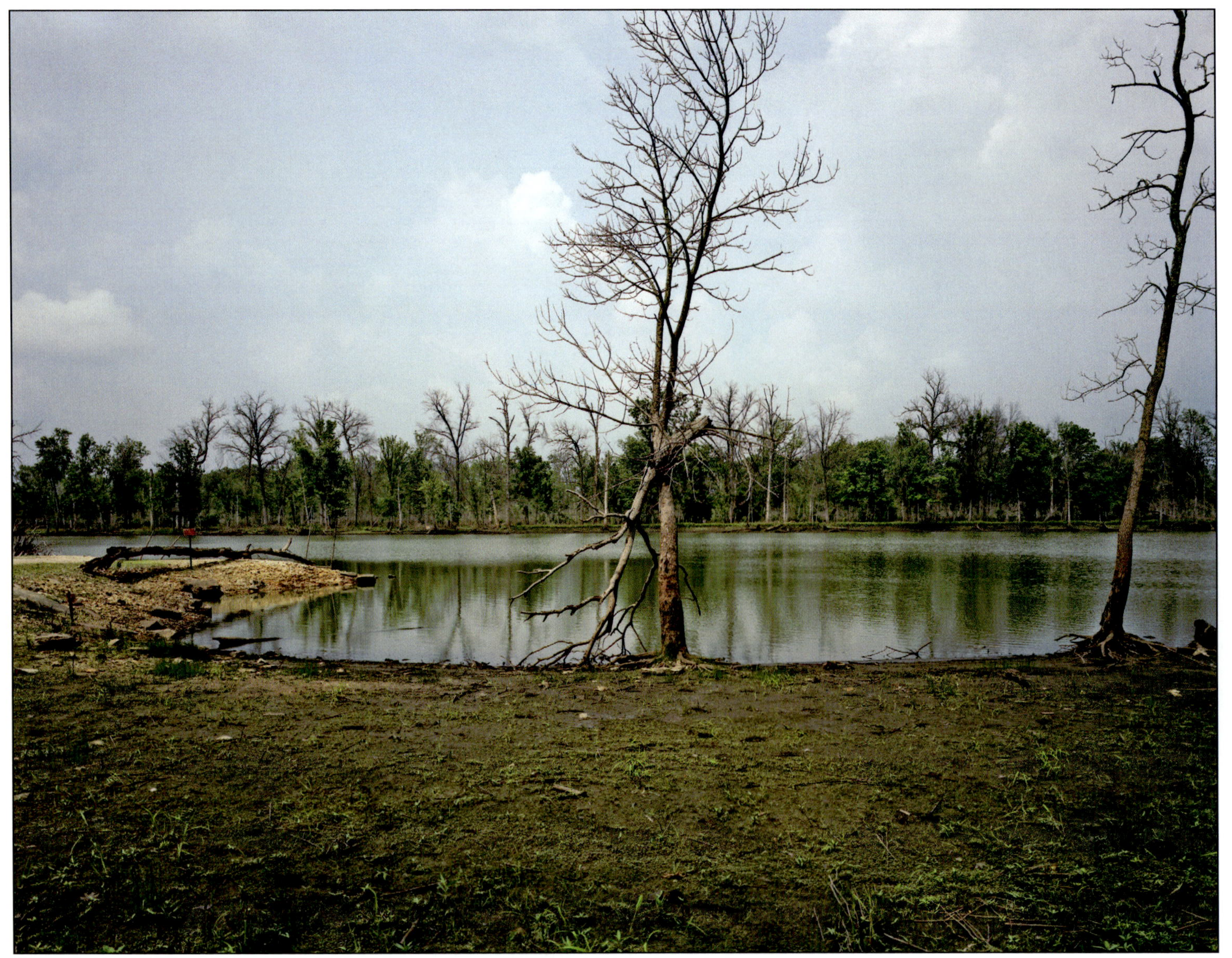

Lake Odessa: Sand Run

Louisa County, Iowa

In the summer of 1994, trees, exposed to standing water the previous summer, either did not leaf out or dropped leaves afterward. While there was damage to the floodplain forest north of Pool 17, the extreme damage came in 17 and progressed south to the Ohio, where flood levels were higher and the duration longer. The Port Louisa NWR and the Iowa DNR manage over 6,800 acres of backwater sloughs and forested islands in Pool 17. Here, the river breached the levee that protects the refuge, devastated its bottomland forests, and destroyed emergent plants. The refuge lost 18.1 percent of its canopy trees and up to 80 percent of its saplings, its future canopy.

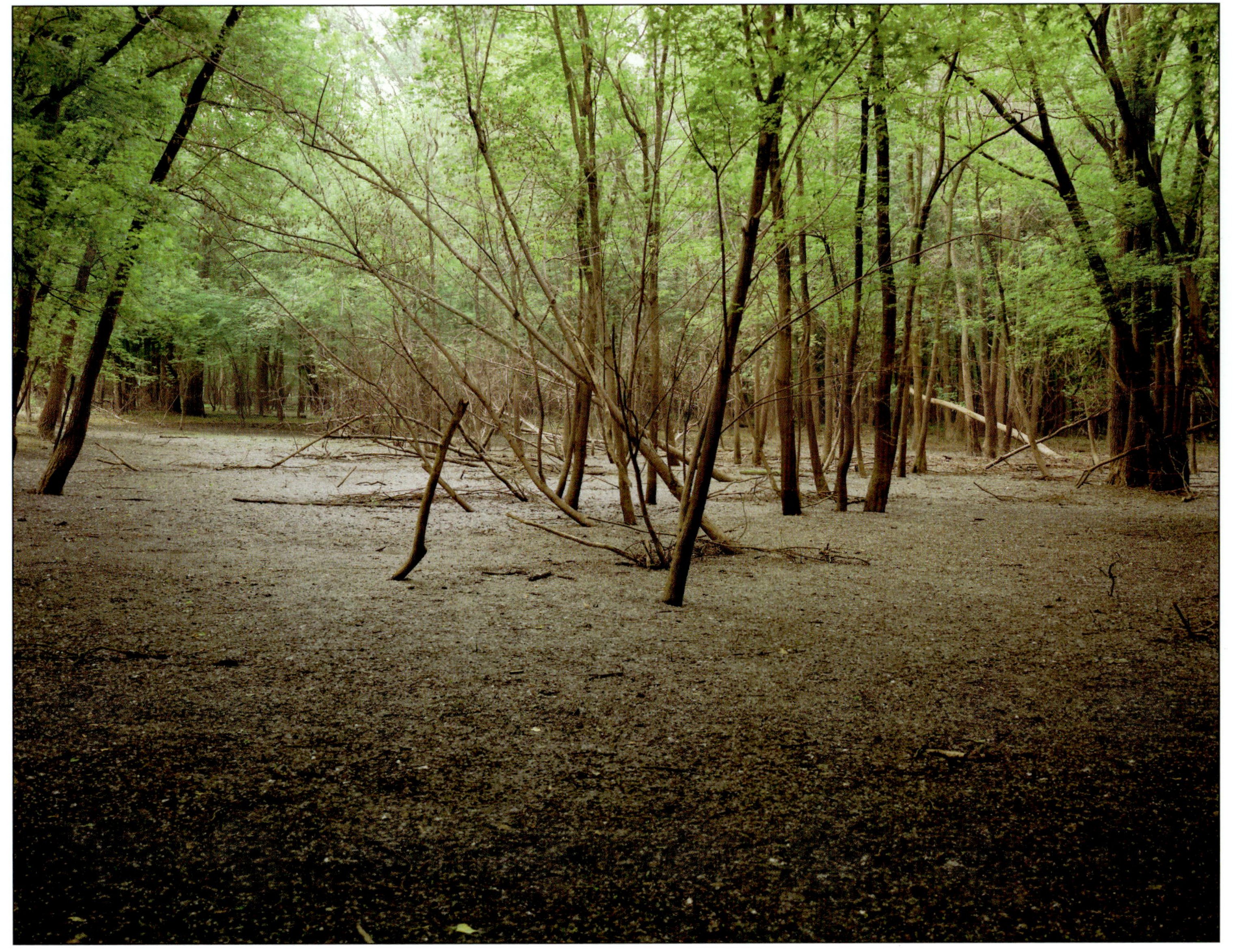

Henderson Creek: Oquawka State Wildlife Refuge
Henderson County, Illinois

The State of Illinois acquired 200 acres for the Oquawka Refuge in 1925 and added to it with a lease from the Corps of Engineers after the construction of Lock and Dam 18. By 1998 it had grown to 2,900 acres, supporting a mix of upland forest of red, white, and jack pine; bottomland forest; and marsh. The 430 acres of floodplain closest to the river were diverse and protected by a levee. The site was never drained, nor did the sloughs within the marsh ever fill with silt. The 1993 flood stripped the understory and damaged trees. The following spring the trees leafed out above the flood line, but not below, and were so stressed they dropped their leaves.

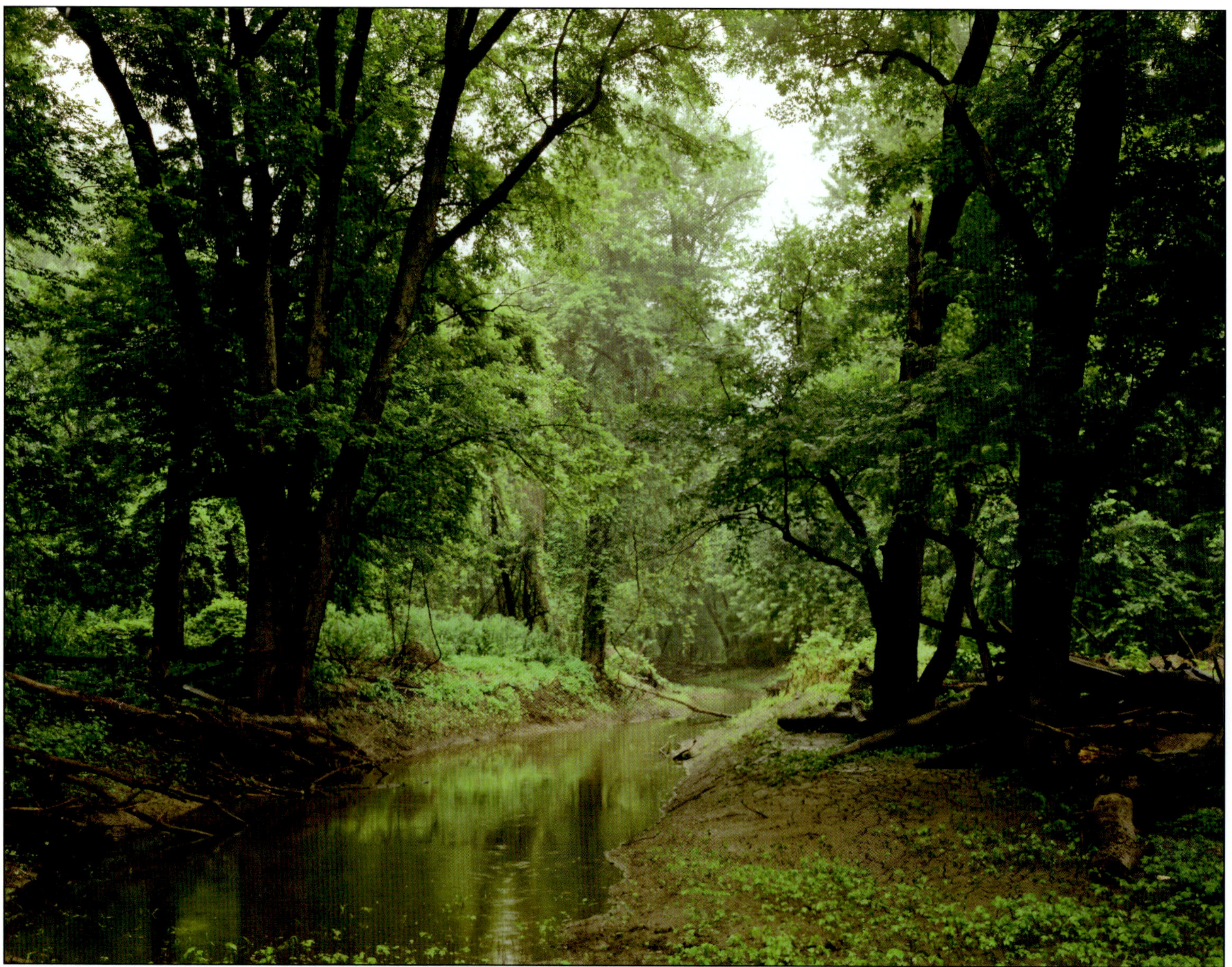

Canton Chute: Biggs Slough
Adams County, Illinois

Biggs Slough and Canton Chute run through the largest bottomland forest south of Rock Island. Most of the 4,670 acres lie on a complex of islands—Dillon Island, Barns Island, Long Island, Shandrew Island, and Flannigan Island—the rest, on the adjacent floodplain. The Corps of Engineers owns the islands; the Long Island Division of the Great Rivers Refuge manages them for wildlife and shares ownership of the floodplain with the Corps, where the engineers have two recreation areas. The region floods yearly. After the 1993 flood, refuge managers allowed land devoted to agriculture to revert to forest and planted nut-bearing hardwoods on the highest ground.

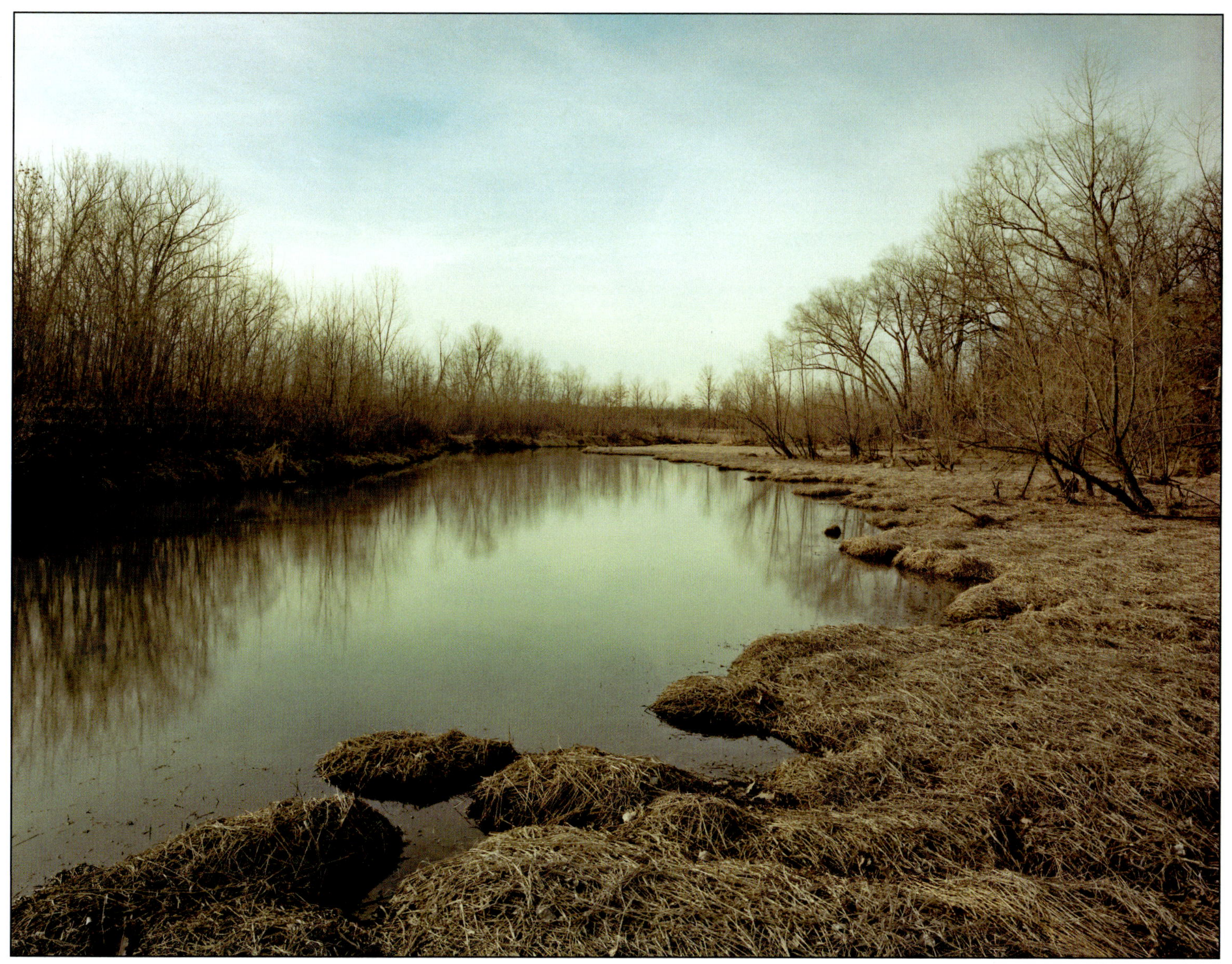

Sny Island: The Head of Sny, Oxbow

Adams County, Illinois

South of Ward Island the landscape drops twenty-one feet to Sny Island, where an oxbow of the Sny River butts up against a higher terrace. Here, River Warren flowed fifteen times wider than the modern river, cut away the Savanna terrace, and left a remnant rising above the Sny River. When the glacial flood expired, it left behind its riverbed as a large expanse of Kingston Terrace. The Sny is a yazoo stream, a branching channel of the Mississippi, and drains Sny Island. Farmers established the Sny Island Drainage District in 1880. Between 1892 and 1907, engineers shortened the Sny, straightened its kinks, cleared its trees, and dredged it.

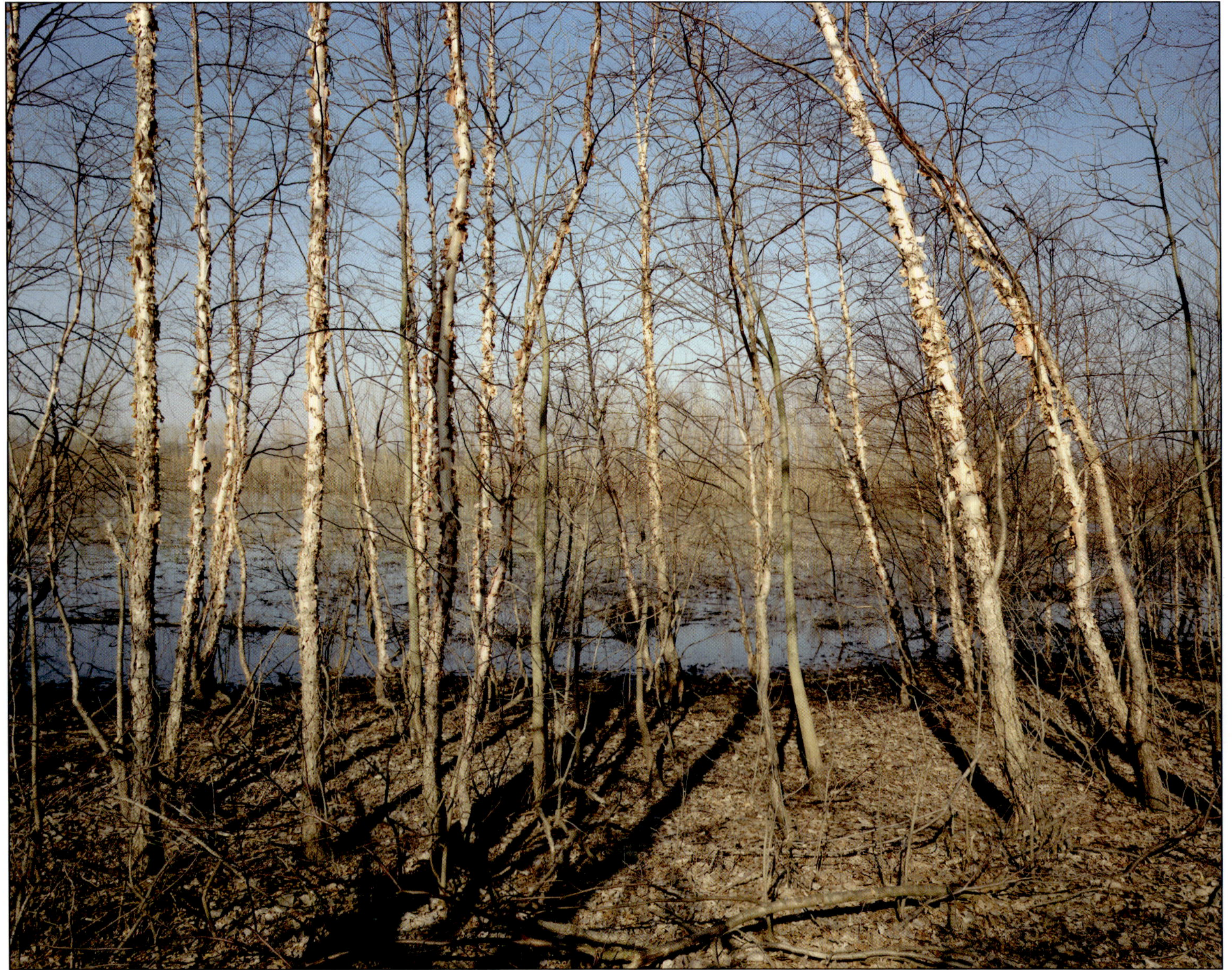

Sny Island: Cocklebur Slough

Pike County, Illinois

With the inundation of Pool 23, water backed up into the Sny. Rain that took four days to drain before the dams took four weeks after. Under the Emergency Flood Control Act of 1950 the Corps reconfigured the Sny drainage plan, channeled five creeks through three diversion channels that crossed the Sny on aquaducts and emptied into the Mississippi, built catch basins to retain silt in the uplands, strengthened the levee, dredged the Sny, and built three pumping stations. Seepage, traced to Pool 23, remained a problem. The Corps made a lump-sum payment that allowed farmers to tile-drain their fields. Cocklebur Slough, a small oxbow, survived as a wetland.

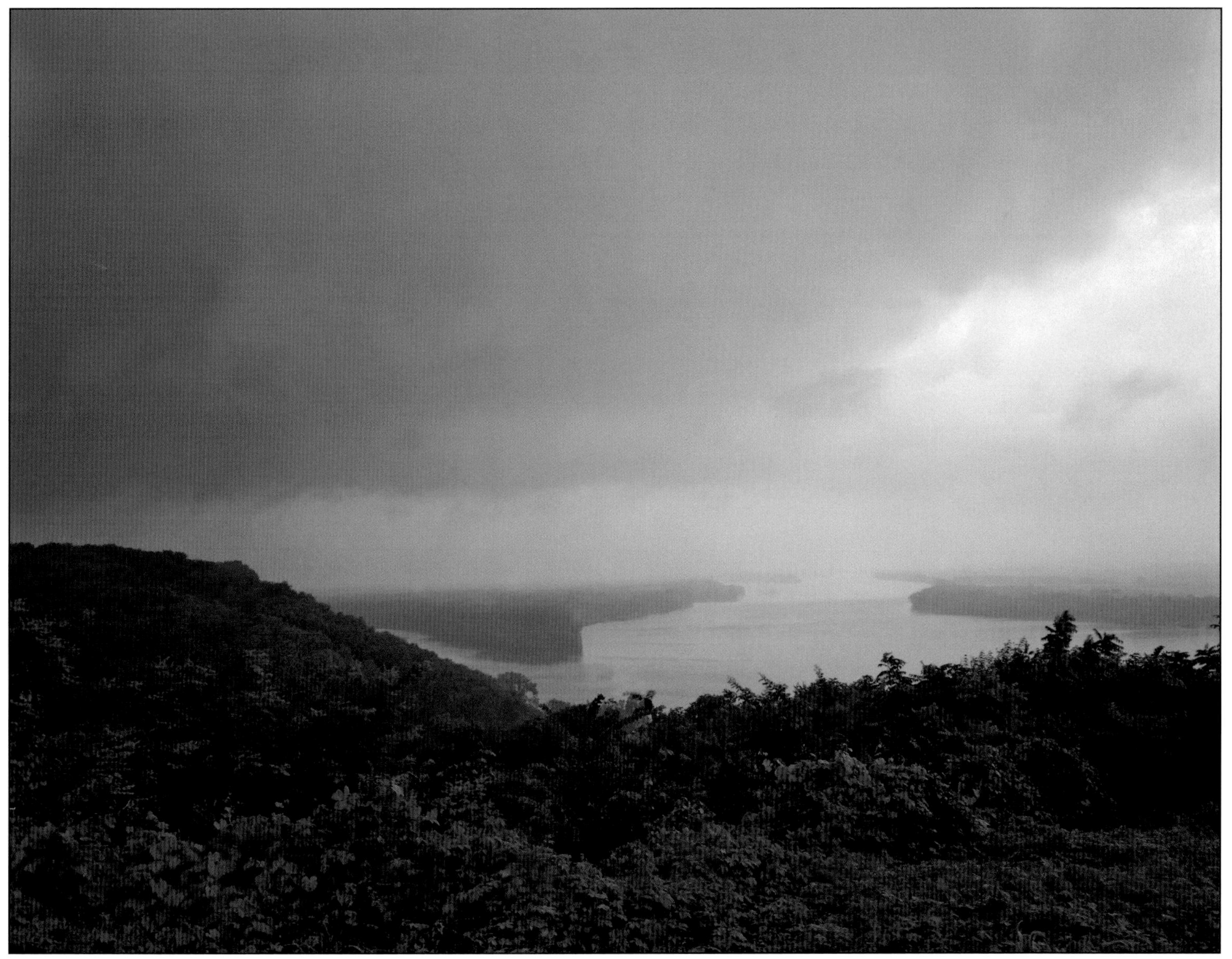

The Old Man: At the Mouth of the Salt River
Pike County, Missouri

The Salt River looped across its floodplain to its confluence with the Mississippi, leaving behind oxbows and sloughs. A bottomland forest of oak, ash, pecan, and sycamore took root close to the river. Migrating waterfowl flocked to the wetlands to feed on acorns and pecans and rest in the safety of its woods. The filling of Pool 24 in 1942 raised the water table under the forest seven feet, creating a permanent low-level flood. The forest deteriorated. In 1970 and 1971 the Missouri Department of Conservation, which managed Salt River lands for the Corps, purchased 6,636 acres of farmland and bottomland forest for the Ted Shanks Wildlife Management Area.

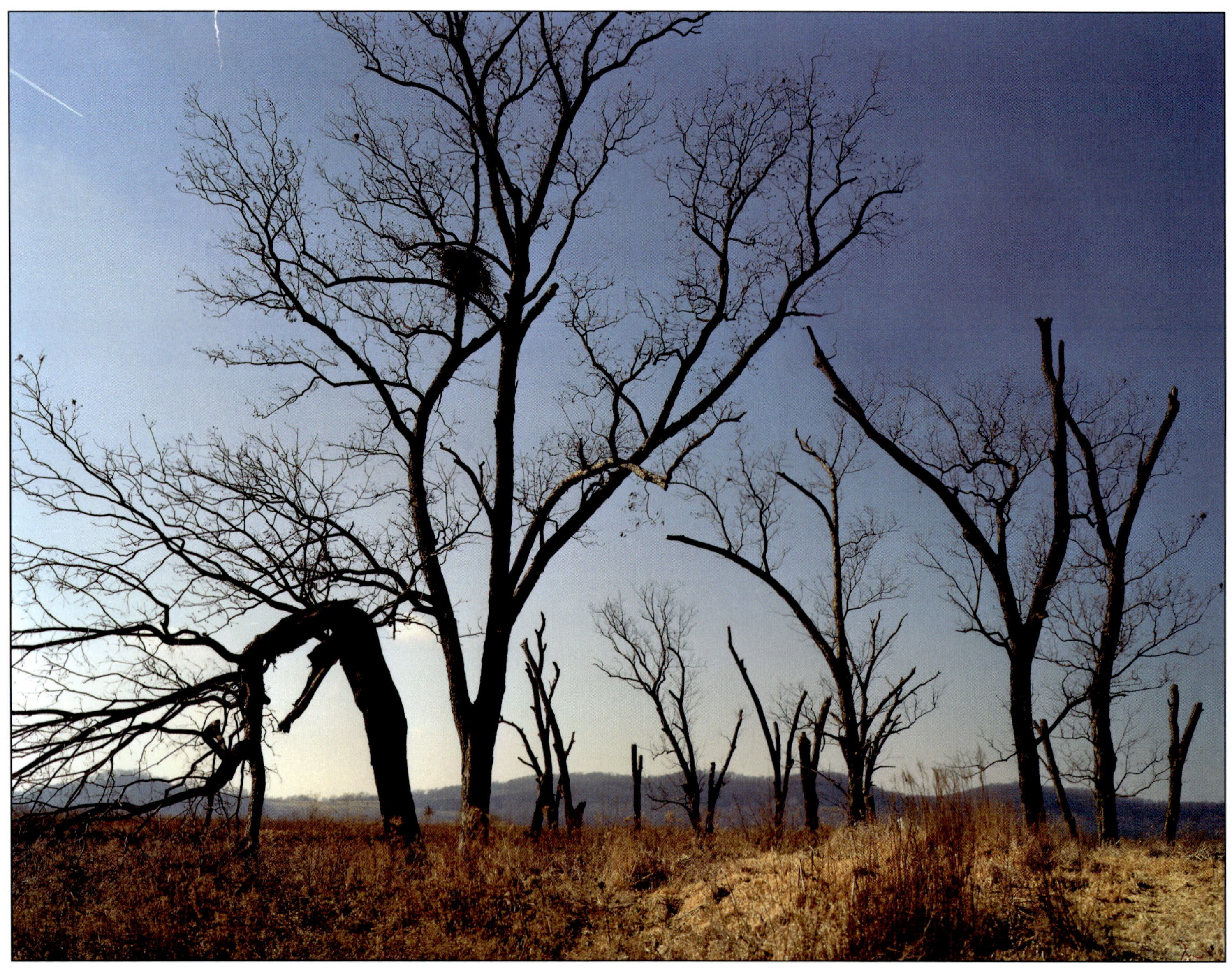

Ted Shanks Wildlife Management Area: Abandoned Eagle Nest

Pike County, Missouri

Managers broke the refuge into nineteen highly managed areas, where they governed water levels and followed a yearly schedule to manage it for waterfowl, shorebirds, frogs, reptiles, and mammals (muskrat and beaver). In early spring they draw down units to concentrate insects, crawfish, and amphibians in shallow water—food for early arrivals. In early summer they draw down moist-soil units for shorebirds that forage the edges. Bitterns, King Rails, Pied-billed Grebes, and American Coots nest in a semipermanent marsh and feed on amphibians and reptiles. Managers flood some moist-soil units in August for shorebirds and rails, others in the fall for ducks.

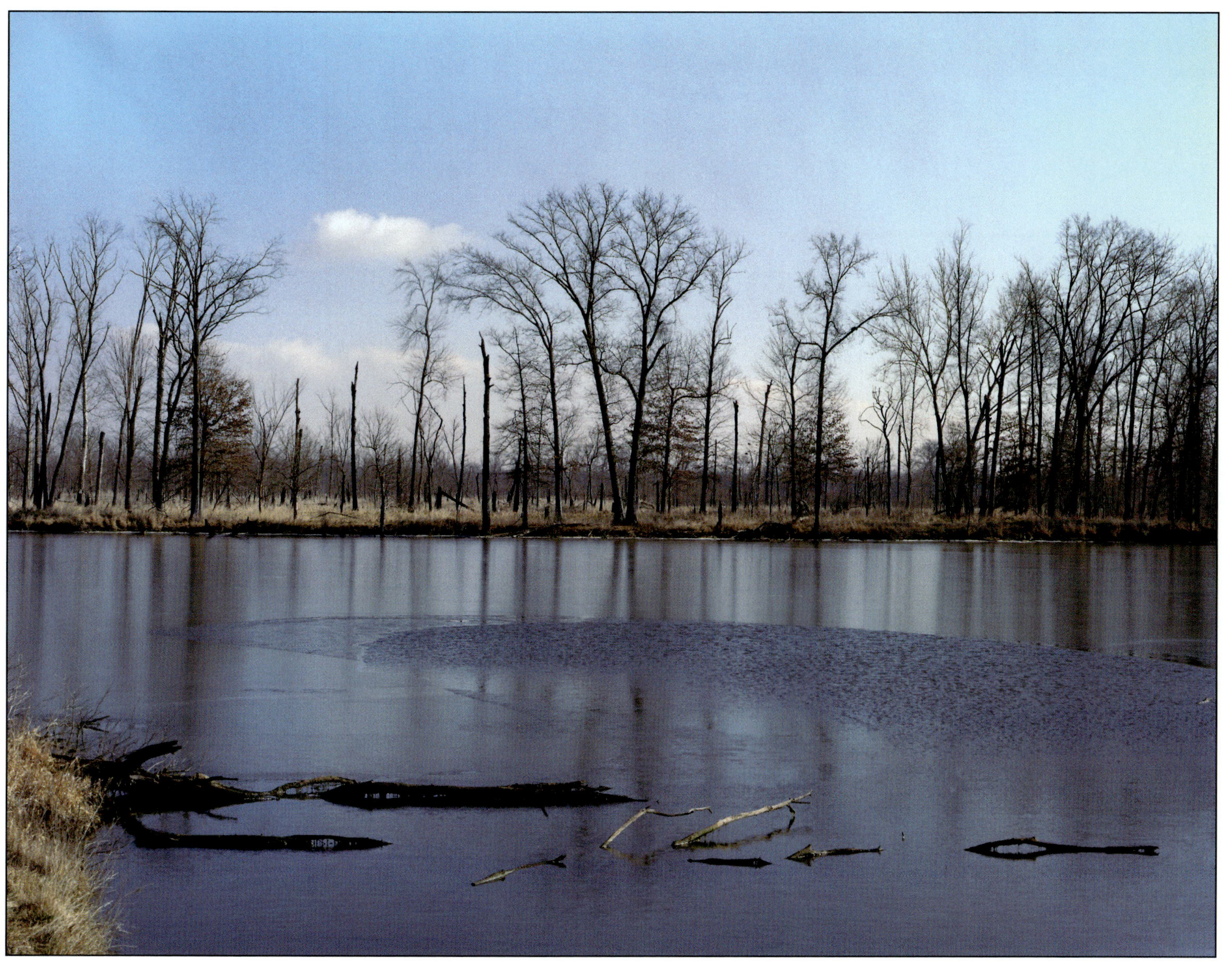

Ted Shanks Wildlife Management Area: Flag Lake
Pike County, Missouri

In June 1993 floodwater breached the levee protecting the refuge and washed in several feet of water that did not drain away until October. Thousands of trees, up to 90 percent in some areas, had died by the following fall. The loss made the low-lying portions of Ted Shanks even wetter, because a healthy forest can soak up as much as ten inches of water from the soil yearly and evaporate it through its leaves. Hence, the loss of 90 percent of the trees equaled nine extra inches of rain per year. When the refuge dried enough, foresters planted a new bottomland forest, 10,000 oak, sycamore, and pecan seedlings at the correct elevation above the water table.

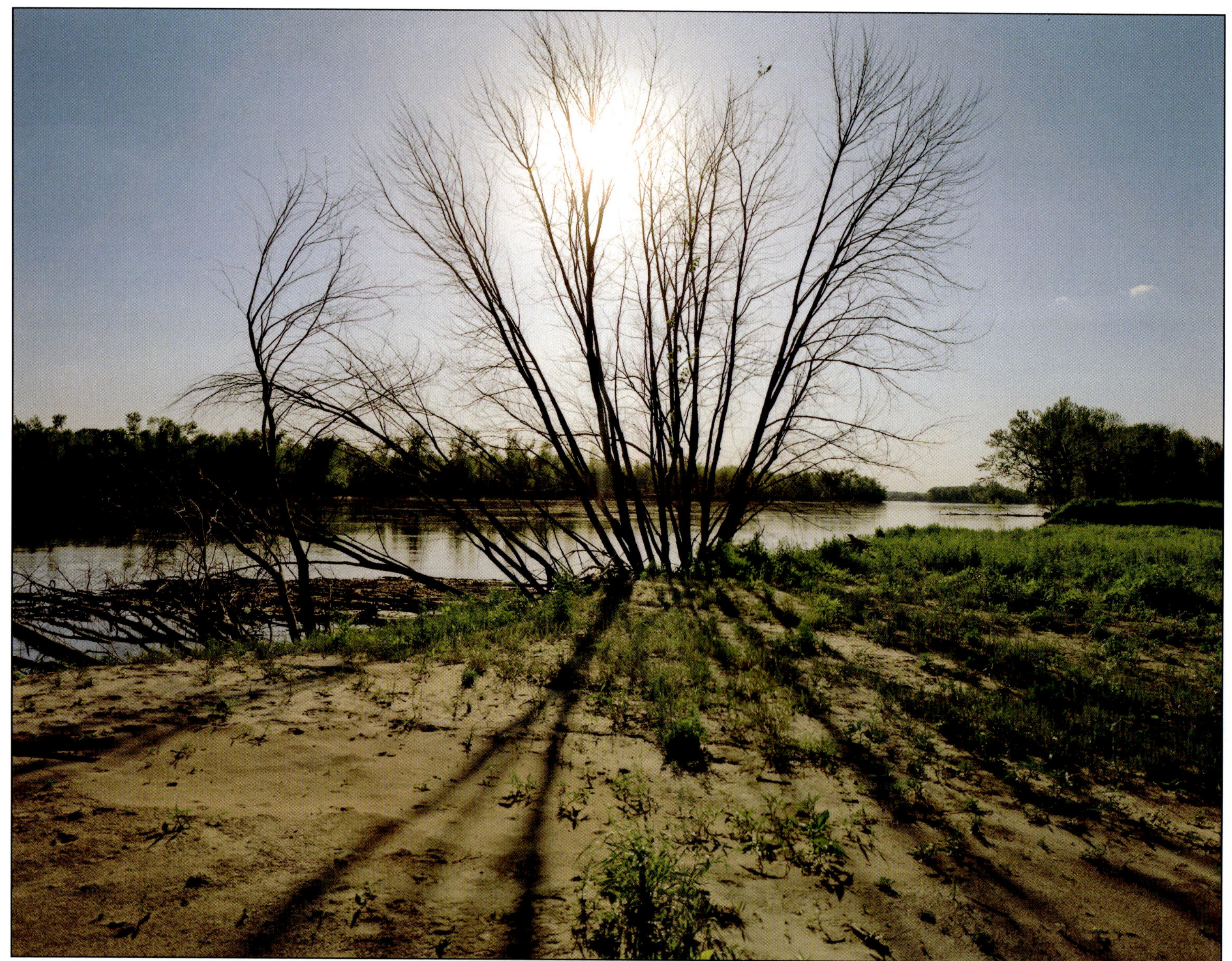

Clarksville Island: Clarksville Chute

Pike County, Illinois

Sport fish spawn in Clarksville Chute, making for high-quality fishing. The Corps' 2004 environmental impact statement for the extension of Lock 24 projected that lake sturgeon would lose ninety-five acres of forage habitat at the head of Clarksville Island. Channel catfish would lose habitat at the foot of the chute. Paddlefish would lose spawning but not foraging habitat. Walleye would find spawning habitat. Emerald shiners would lose habitat when the river flooded. New spawning and rearing habitat might be created for largemouth bass, but bass would lose habitat to sedimentation and to tow boats passing downstream of the new lock on the opposite bank.

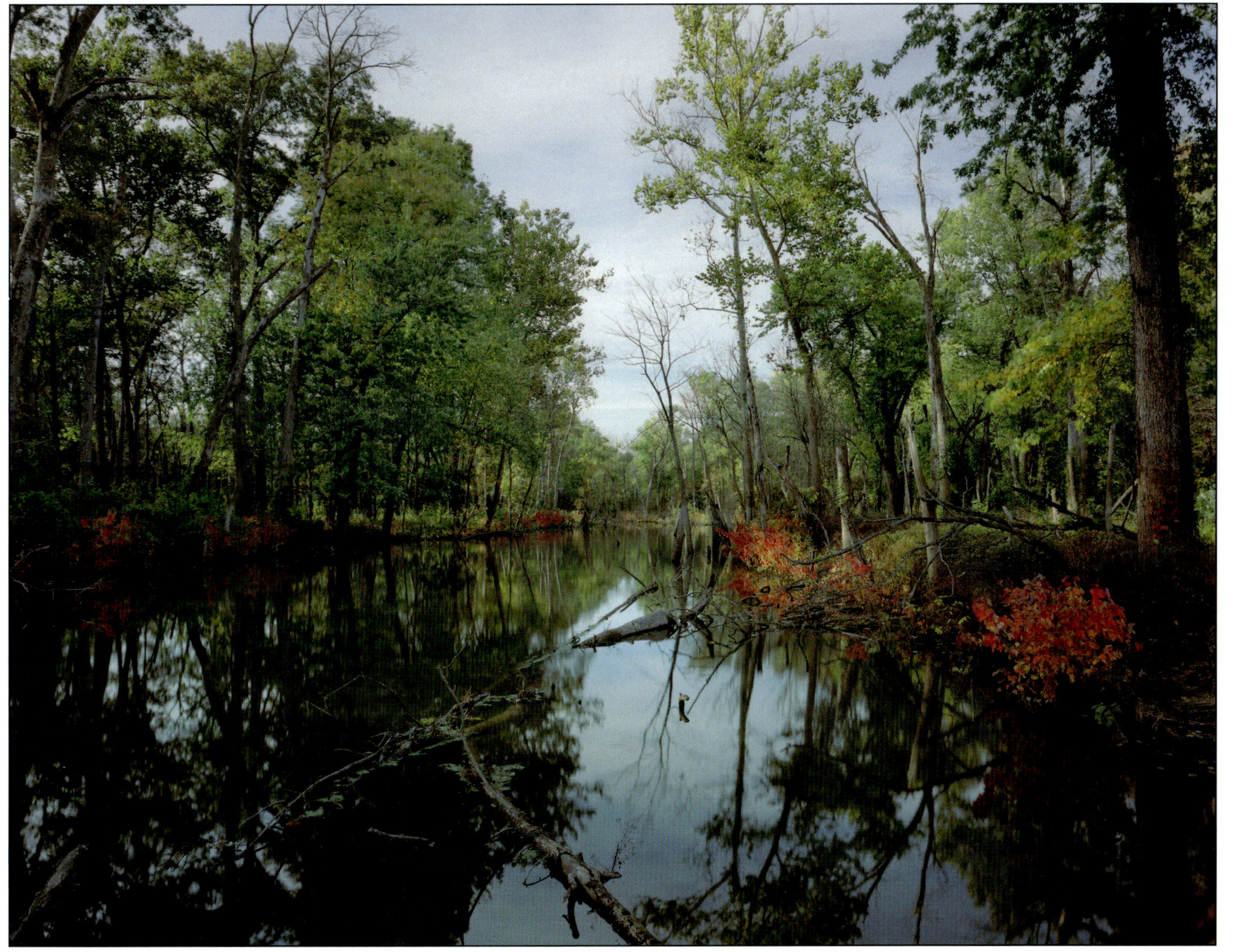

The Sny: Rip Rap Landing Wildlife Management Area

Pike County, Illinois

At the turn of the century, an expanding population of river otters, once a state endangered species, inhabited the forest and wetlands at Rip Rap Landing WMA, where it takes two to five miles of shoreline to support one otter. Between 1994 and 1997 the Illinois DNR instituted a program to restore otters to their former habitats and released 346 otters, trapped in Louisiana, into central and southern Illinois. Managers were helped in their efforts to bring back the otter by Illinois' record-setting number of beaver, who create excellent habitat for otters. Unable to burrow their own dens, otters move into abandoned beaver dens to raise their young.

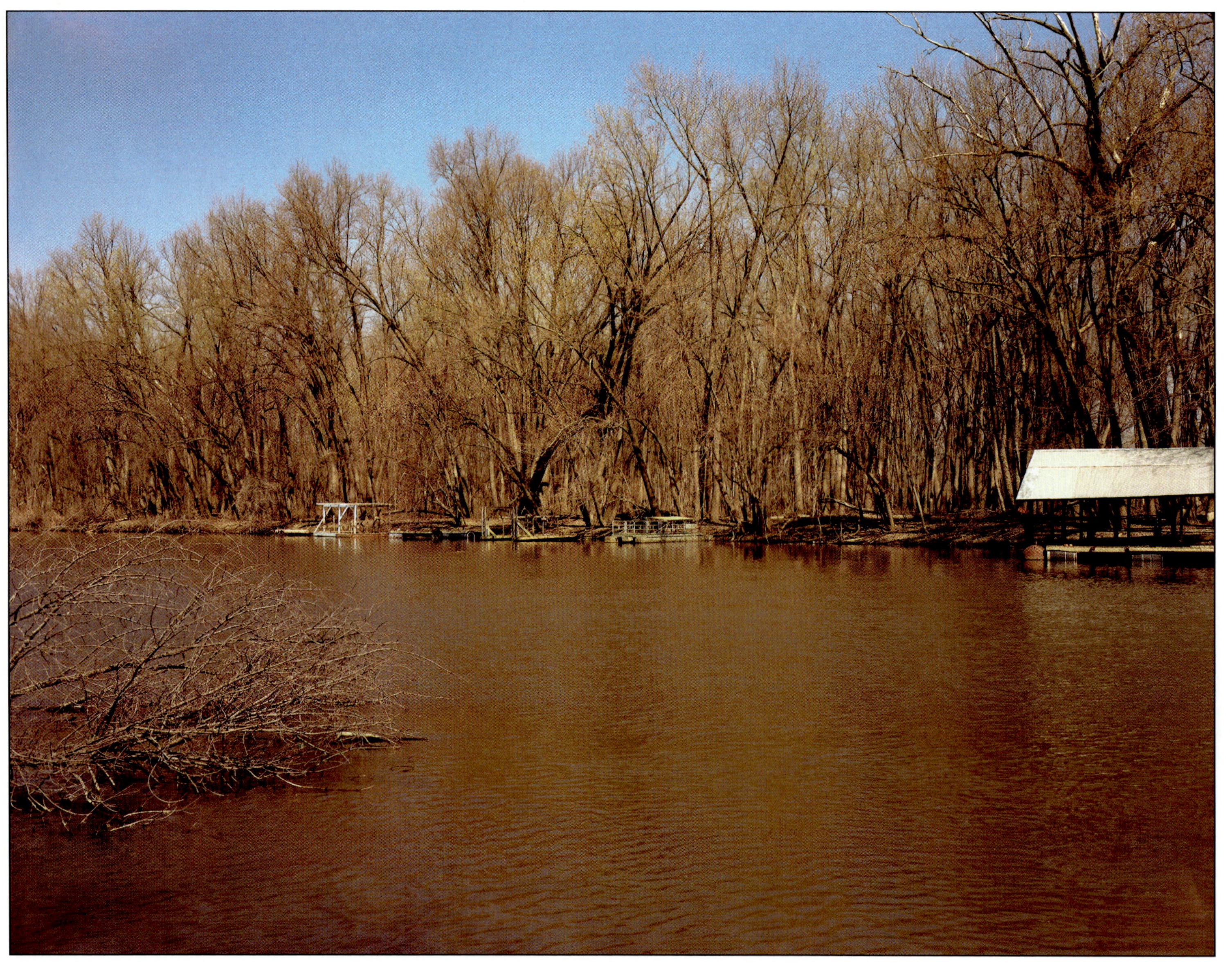

Westport Chute:
Westport Island
Lincoln County, Missouri

An old-growth forest, treed in silver maple, pecan, cottonwood, sycamore, and pin oak survives on the southern third of Westport Island. It offers an increasingly rare habitat in the Mississippi Valley, where the dams have made island formation impossible, where wind fetch and wave wash have eroded them. The island forests fared better during the 1993 flood than those on mainland refuges like Ted Shanks. Water rose as high, but it flowed through the forests, stripping ground cover and drowning trees but carrying more oxygen. Trees that died opened the canopy to new seedlings. Such disturbances contribute to the survival of old-growth bottomland forests.

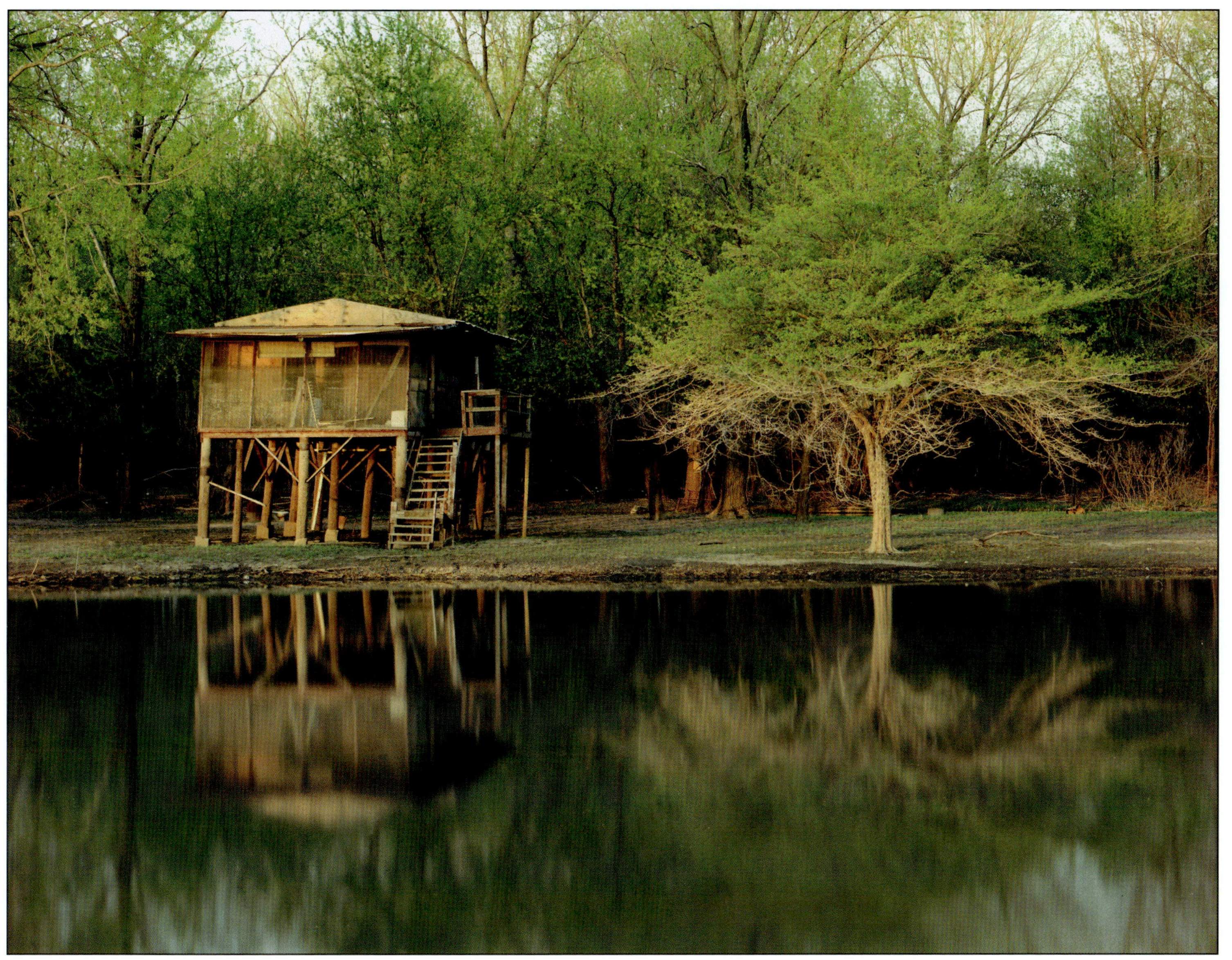

Norton Woods: Slough
Lincoln County, Missouri

The Norton Woods Conservation Area is a part of the Upper Mississippi Conservation Area, 14,906 acres of lands devoted to ducks and scattered in eighty-seven tracts on the floodplain and islands owned by the Corps and managed by the Missouri Department of Conservation. The area gives duck hunters controlled access to public lands between the Des Moines River and Lock and Dam 26 at Alton, Illinois. The passage of the 1944 Flood Control Act allowed the Corps to lease locations on Corps-owned land for recreational cottages. By 2000 there were 376 cottages dotting the shoreline, down from the 764 standing in 1988 when the Corps began phasing them out.

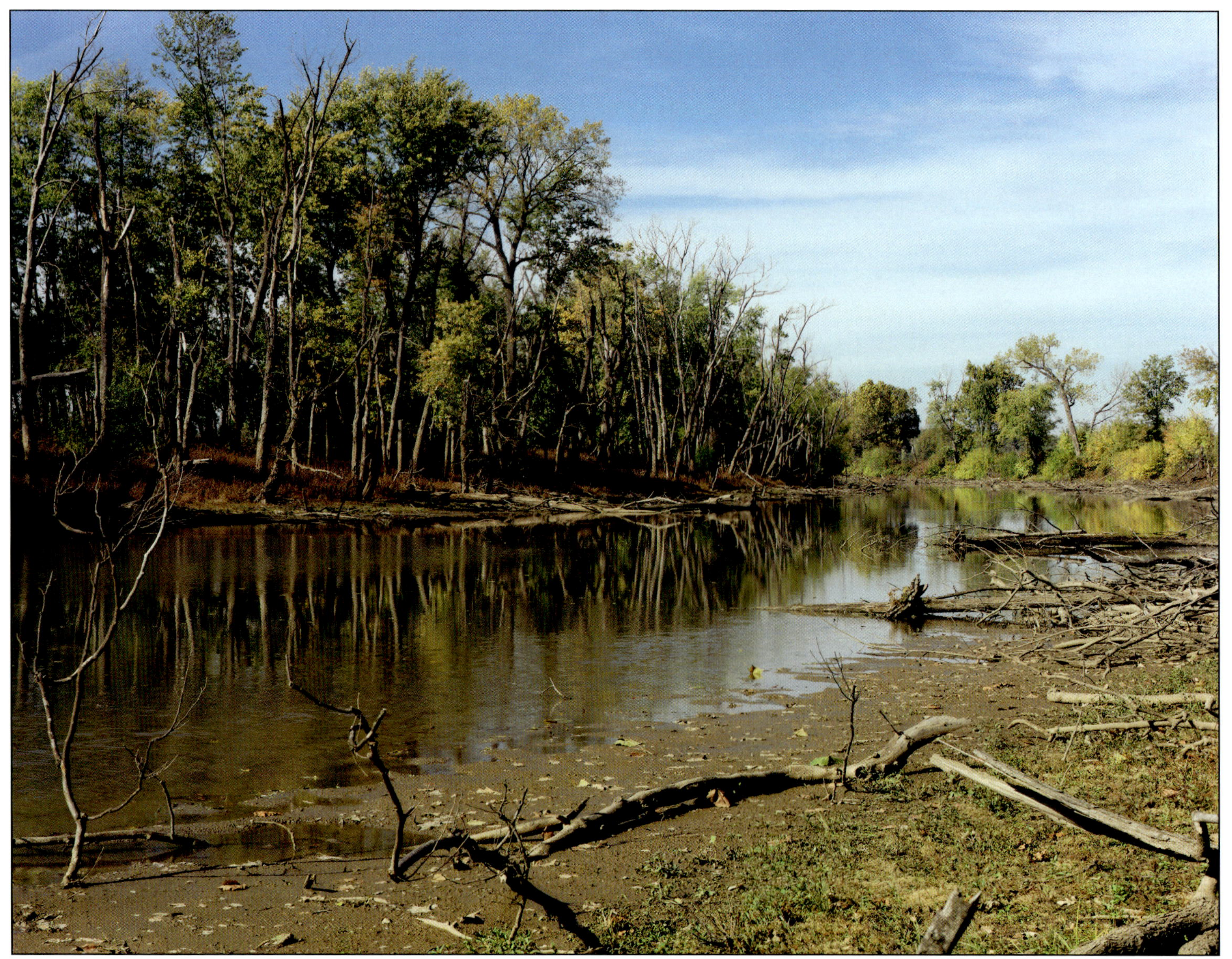

Cuivre River: Old Channel

Lincoln County, Missouri

The Cuivre River deposited sediment in the Mississippi and created Cuivre Island and Slough at its mouth. To hasten floodwater off farmland, engineers cut eight miles from the river, leaving its old channel to fill with decaying vegetation. The channelized river took a straight shot across the fields and deposited excessive amounts of sediment in Cuivre Slough, which runs between the mainland and the island. While a Mississippi flood could flush sediment from the slough, silt from the river clogged the slough at its head and threatened to weld the island to the mainland. Interior sloughs on the island filled with sediment and converted to bottomland forest.

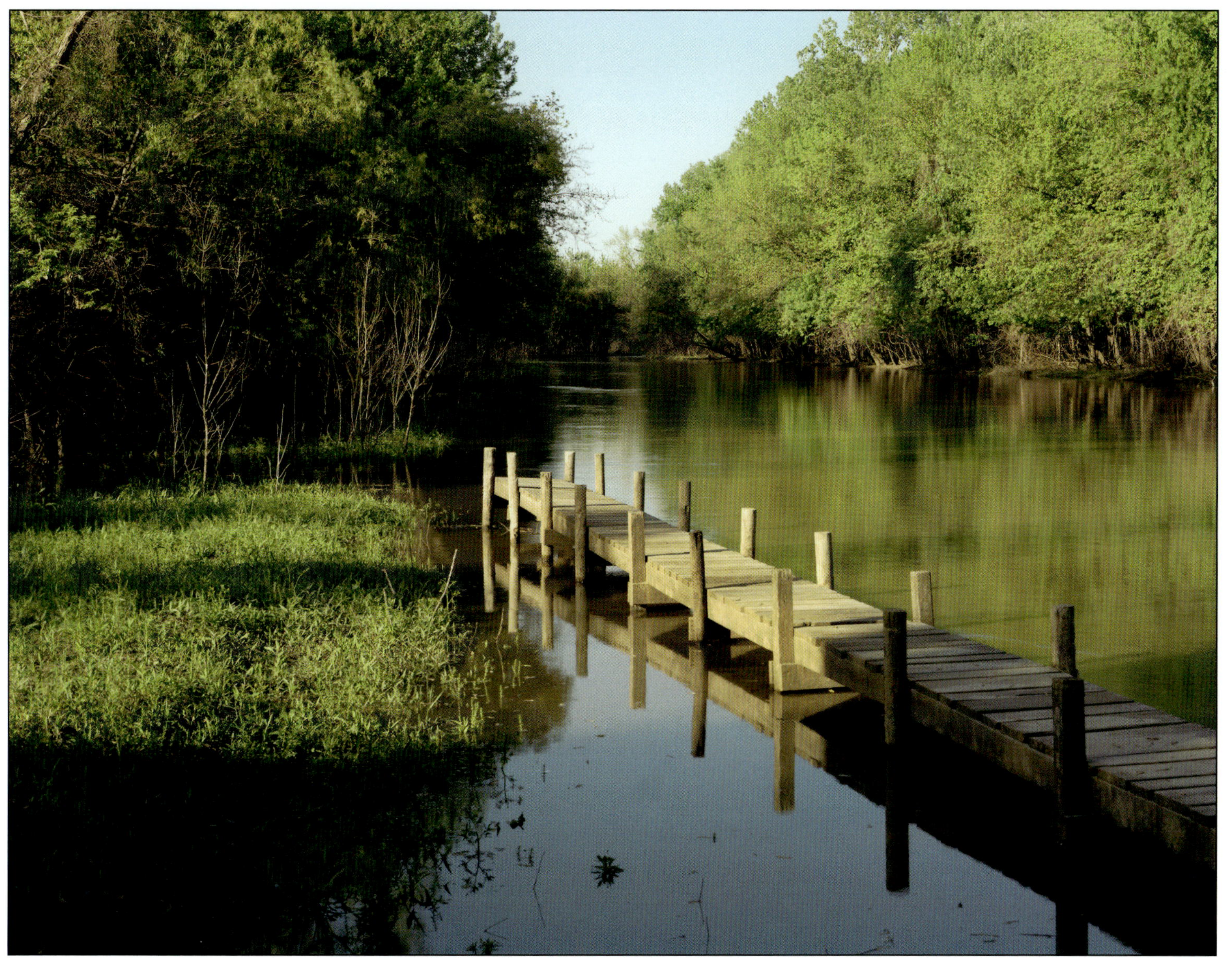

Cuivre Slough: Cuivre Island
St. Charles County, Missouri

In 1994 the Corps and the Missouri Department of Conservation started habitat rehabilitation on Cuivre Slough to arrest the accumulation of sediment. The project included Cuivre Island and a small tract of agricultural lands bordering on the slough. They used the tools they had developed for opening side channels: removed a closing dam to allow water to flow through the slough; constructed hard points in the slough to unclog it and scour deep holes for overwintering fish; expanded bottomland forests to stabilize its banks; planted fruit- and nut-producing trees on 120 acres of old fields and nut-bearing trees on ridges on Cuivre Island, food for wildlife.

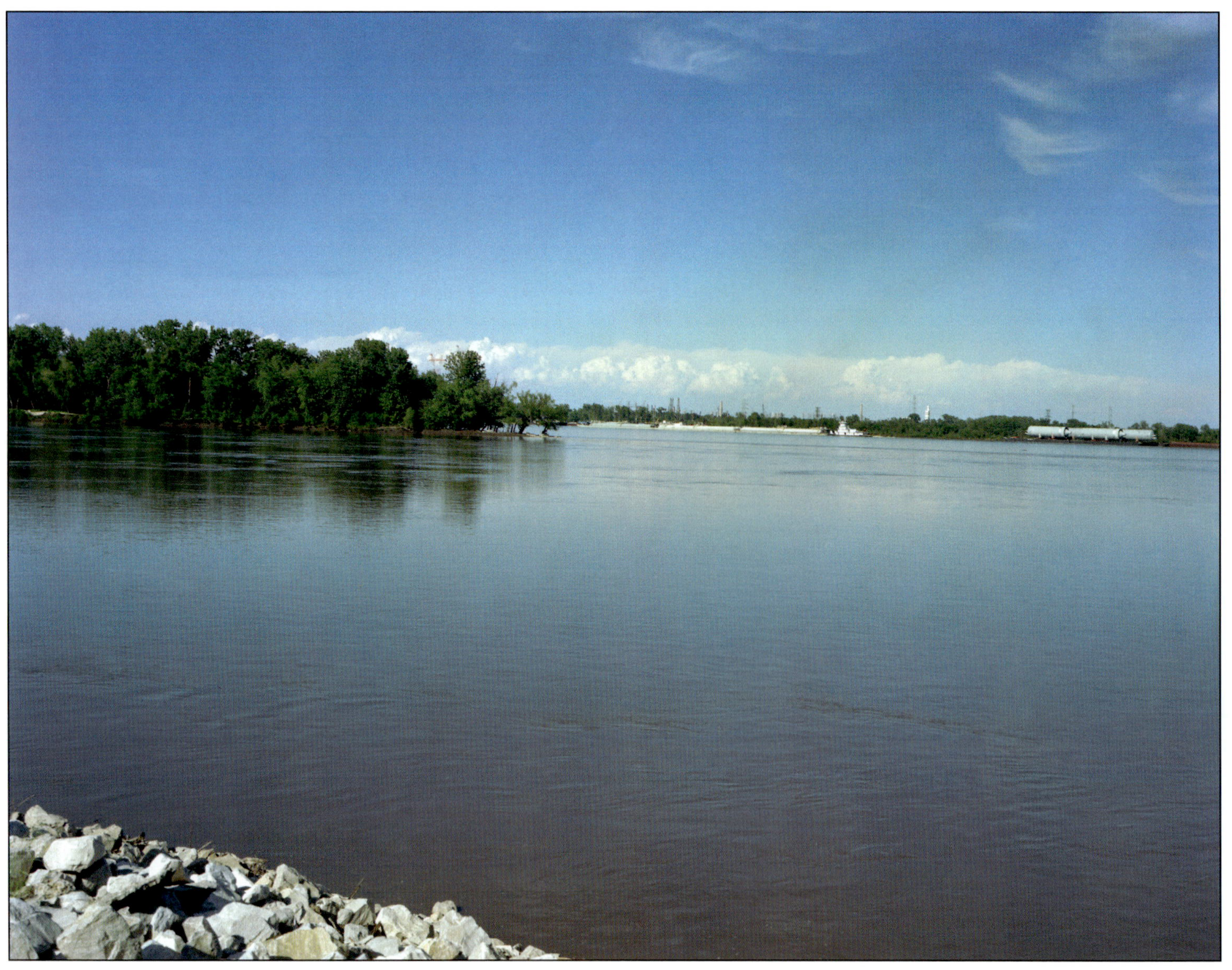

Confluence Missouri and Mississippi

St. Charles County, Missouri

Two refuges overlook the confluence. On the south bank of the Missouri the Missouri Department of Conservation purchased the 4,318-acre Columbia Bottoms in 1997, after the 1993 flood overtopped a levee and washed sand and debris over prime agricultural fields. Before the department opened the new conservation area in 2002, it re-created shallow marshes and bottomland forests and built a viewing stand on the bank. The State of Missouri acquired 1,121 acres for a park in 2001 on Mobile Island, built a short wheelchair-accessible walk to Confluence Point, and planned to restore the marshes and prairies of the natural floodplain behind it, using native trees and plants.

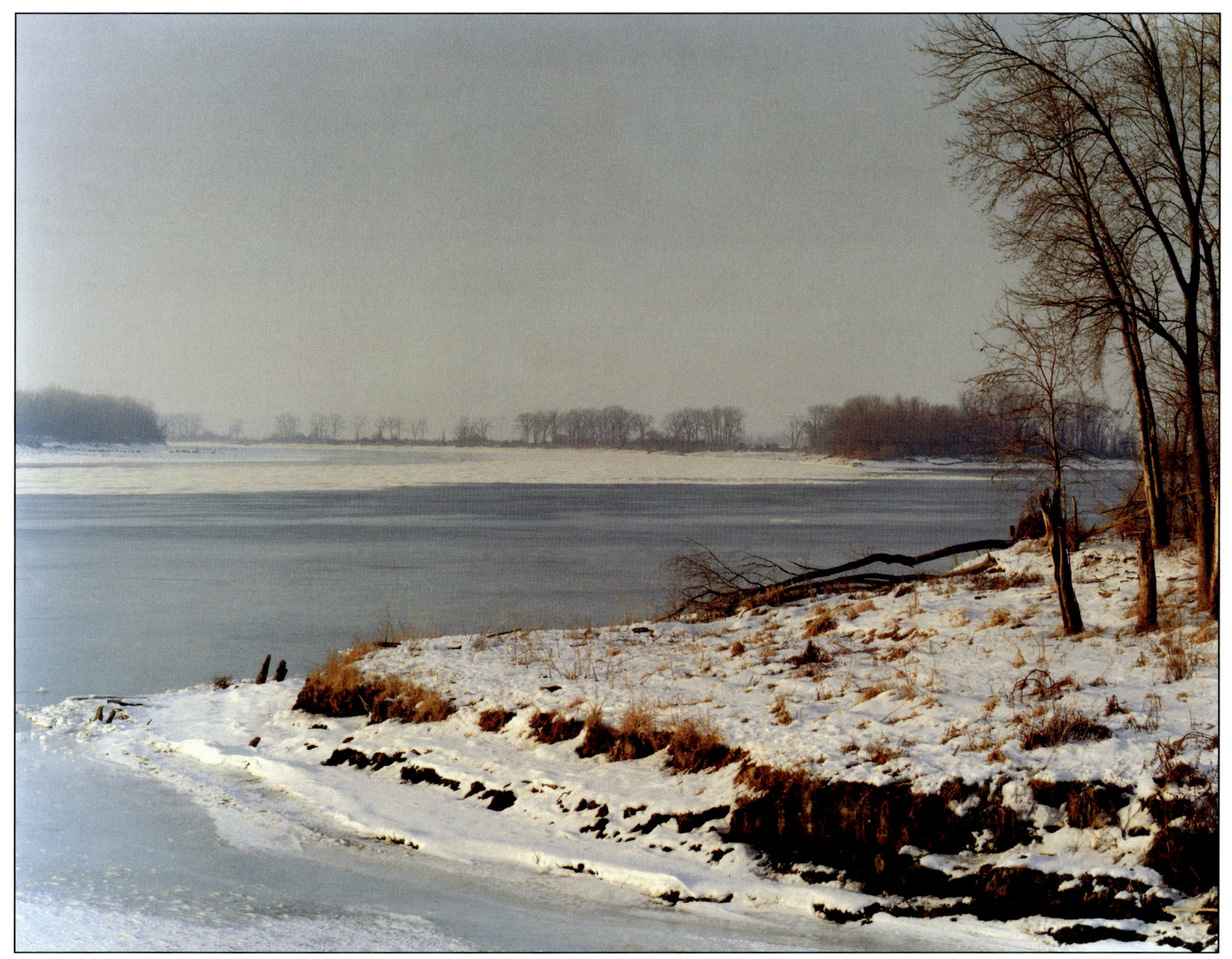

Confluence Missouri and Mississippi Rivers from the Cahokia Diversion Canal

Madison County, Illinois

"Sailing quietly in clear and calm Water, we heard the noise of a rapid, into which we were about to run. I have seen nothing more dreadful. An accumulation of large and entire trees, branches, and floating islands, was issuing from the mouth of the river Peketanoui."—Father Jacques Marquette, 1673

Look at any aerial photograph of the confluence. The Missouri spews a flume of silty water into the relatively clear Mississippi. They flow side by side downstream—the Missouri on the west, the Mississippi on the east. One can see this from the bank during cold winters when the Missouri spews ice into the ice-free Mississippi.

The American Bottom

> "The 'American Bottom' commences not far below Kaskaskia, and stretches along the eastern shore of the Mississippi eighty miles, terminating a little distance below the point which is opposite the mouth of the Missouri. It is from three to six miles wide, and divided into two belts. The first, bordering the Mississippi, is a heavily timbered bottom. The next, reaching to the foot of the perpendicular bluffs, is prairie of the richest quality, covered, in the season, with grass and flowers. Parts of this tract have been in cultivation with the exhausting crop of maise one hundred years, without apparently producing the slightest exhaustion of the soil. No description will convey an adequate idea of the power of vegetation, and the rank luxuriance with which it operates along this plain of exhaustless fertility."
>
> —Timothy Flint, 1833

The American Bottom, the first heavily urbanized floodplain south of St. Paul, extends for a hundred miles from Alton, Illinois, south to Chester near the mouth of the Kaskaskia River. Bluffs reaching up to two hundred feet define its eastern edge, the Mississippi its western edge. The bottom is eleven miles wide in its upper reaches where glacial floods, sluicing down the Mississippi, the Illinois, and the Missouri have shaved away the soft shales and coal of the valley wall. It narrows to three miles where the wall changes to hard limestone and dolomite.

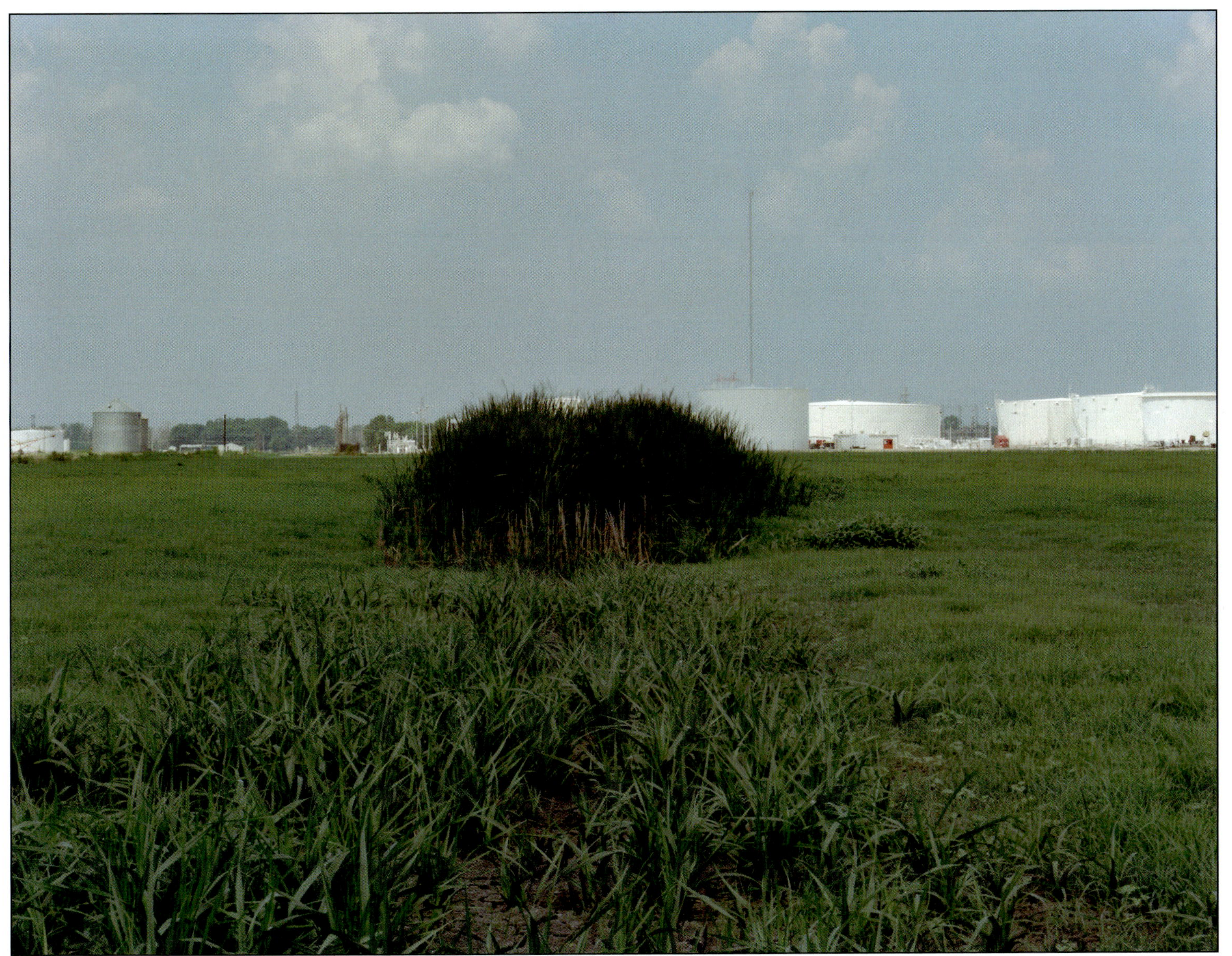

American Bottom: Grassy Lake
Madison County, Illinois

Americans, who settled in the American Bottom after 1785, found remnants of Grassy Lake in a vibrant landscape, made up of diverse floodplain communities—bottomland forests, prairies, wet prairies, shrub swamps, and marshes. Grassy Lake, 260 acres in 1800, lay at the center of a large marsh surrounded by prairie. Cattail, bulrushes, sedges, and reeds filled the marsh and attracted Red-winged Blackbirds, Yellow-headed Blackbirds, Marsh Wrens, rails, bitterns, waterfowl, and muskrats. Farmers drained the marsh. Grassy Lake filled with sediment and shrunk to a marsh in the midst of a wheat field, just south of the Clark and Shell Refineries at Wood River, Illinois.

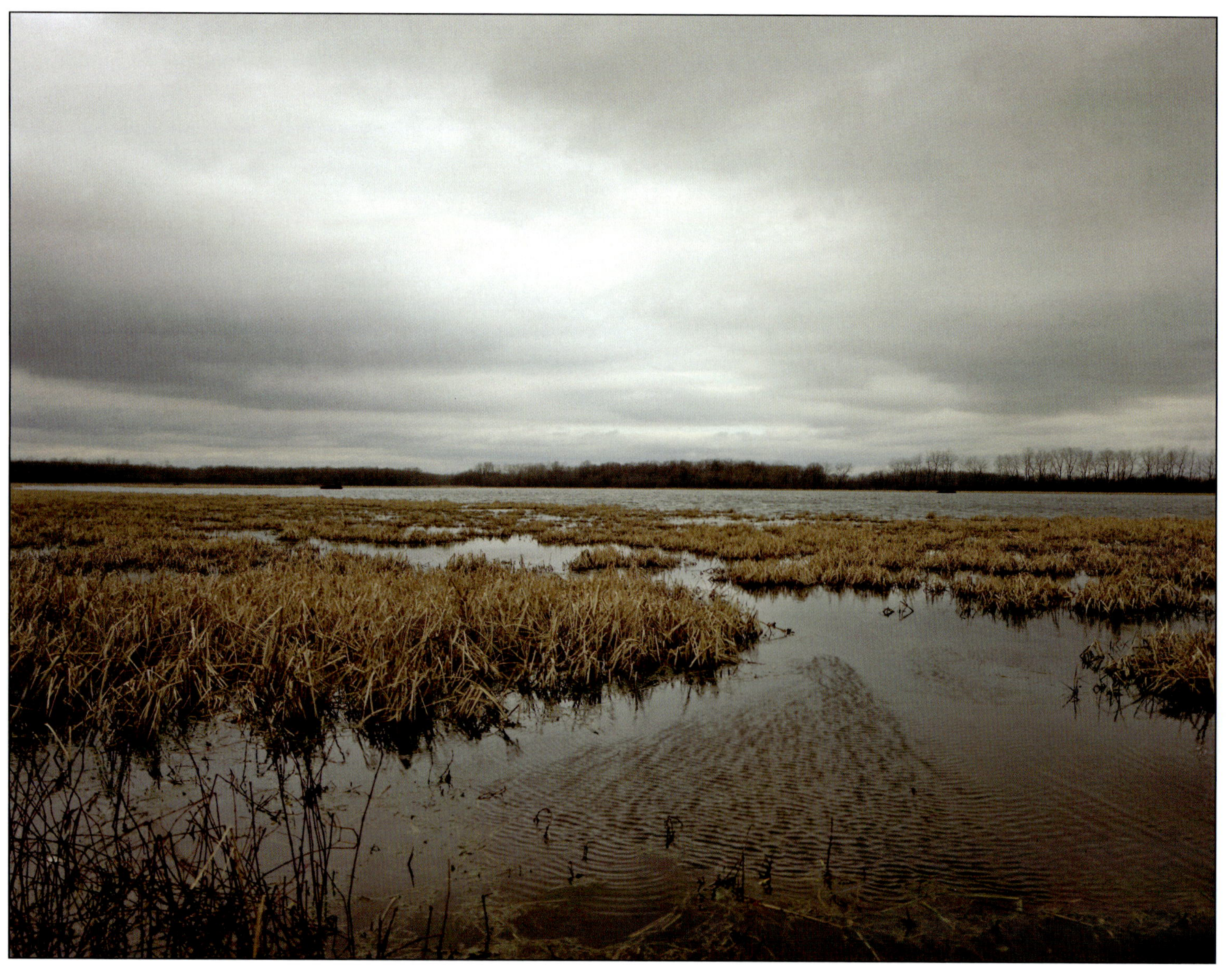

American Bottom:
Horseshoe Lake State Park

St. Clair County, Illinois

Horseshoe Lake—its closest neighbors, a steel mill, a NASCAR track, and an interstate highway—is an oasis. At 2,000 acres and two feet deep, Horseshoe Lake is large and shallow, made larger by the 6,000 acres of wetlands surrounding it. The Eurasian Tree Sparrow, which lives only in the St. Louis area, roosts in its trees. American Coots scuttle its surface before takeoff. Birders have sited the rare Marbled Godwit, a sandpiper. Shorebirds—plovers, stilts, herons, and avocets—visit regularly. So do gulls, terns, and cormorants. Thirty species of waterfowl stop by yearly, making it a link in the chain of habitats on the Mississippi Flyway.

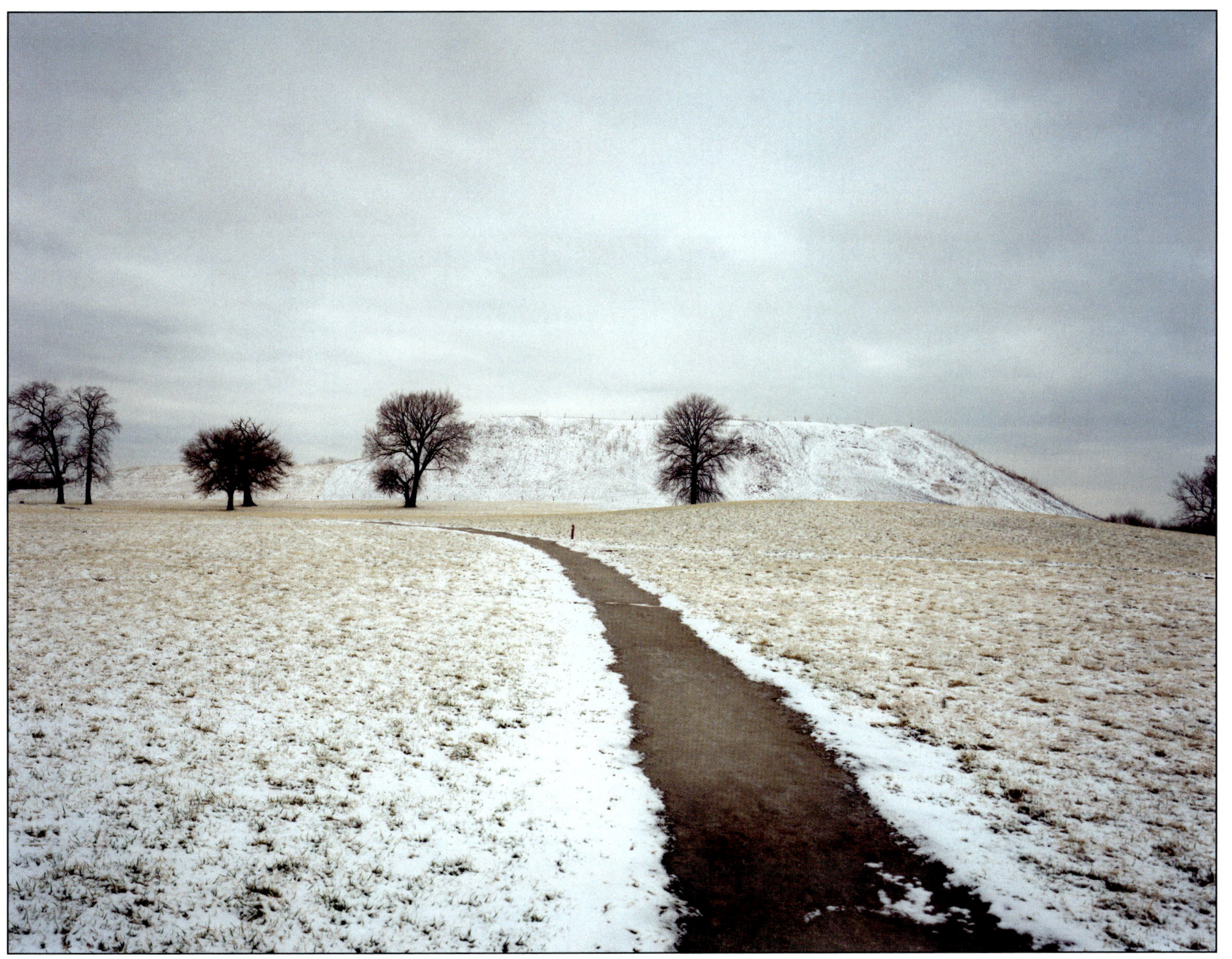

American Bottom: Monks Mound

St. Clair County, Illinois

"When I reached the foot of the largest mound, I was struck with a degree of astonishment, not unlike that which is experienced in contemplating the Egyptian pyramids. What a stupendous pile of earth! To heap up such a mass must have required years, and the labors of thousands."—Henry Marie Brackenridge, 1814

Humans have occupied the American Bottom for 8,000 years. The Mississippian mound builders spread out across the American Bottom about 700 A.D. They cleared trees, burned the prairies, and built their ceremonial mounds. Within two hundred years they had created a civilization based on farming.

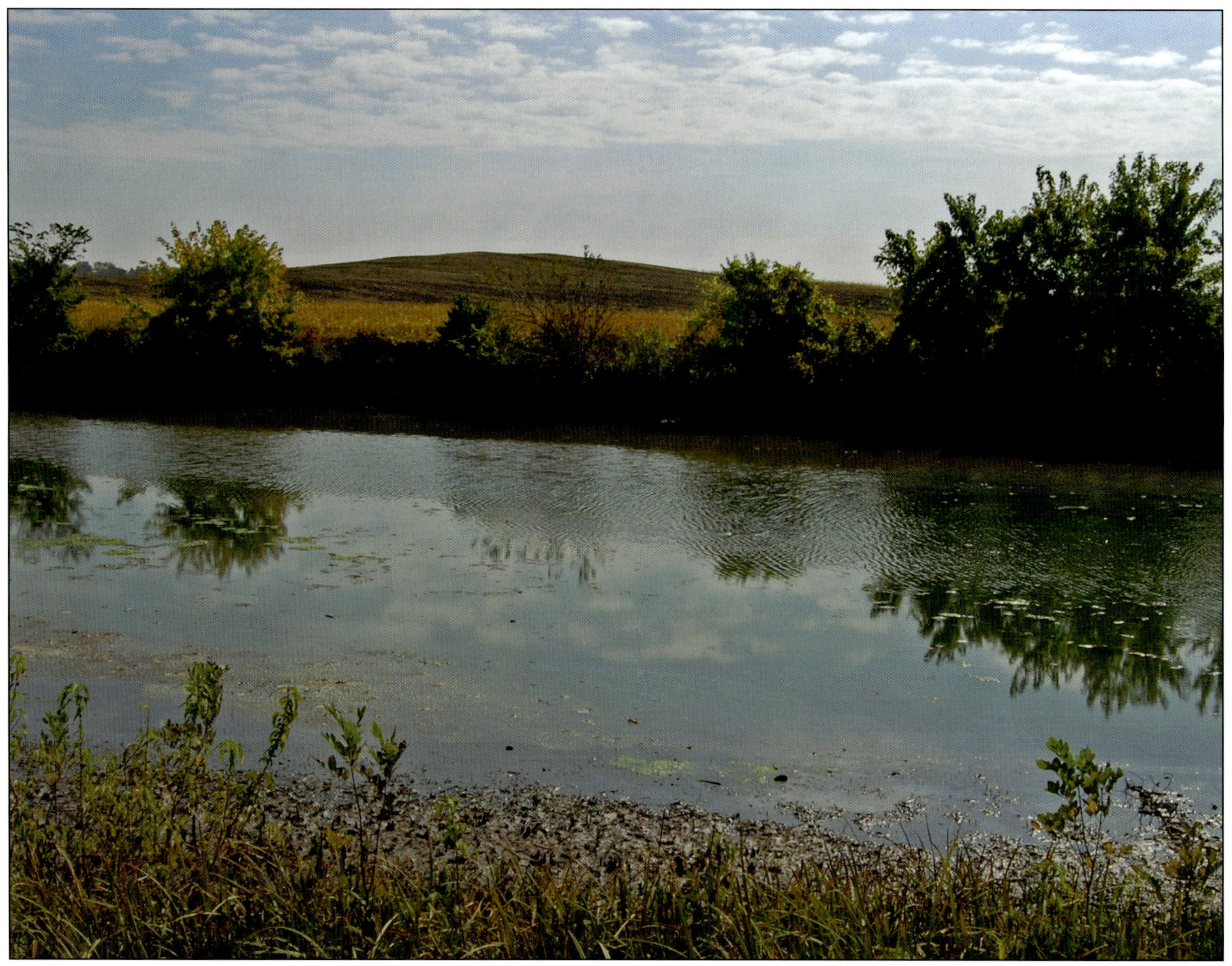

American Bottom: Fish Lake
Monroe County, Illinois

High ground lies on the north bank of Fish Lake, the site of a Late Woodland community 1,400 years ago and a Mississippian satellite village about 1,000 years ago. Residents of French Cahokia fled to it after a flood in 1760. The modern city of Dupo and its large railyards sit on it. Out in front of Fish Lake, productive wetlands, drained for agriculture in the nineteenth and twentieth centuries, stretched clear to the natural levee of the Mississippi and were a rich source of fish and waterfowl for those who settled near Fish Lake. The forest on its banks—walnut, hickory, pecan, oak, hackberry, and willow trees—supplied timber for their dwellings.

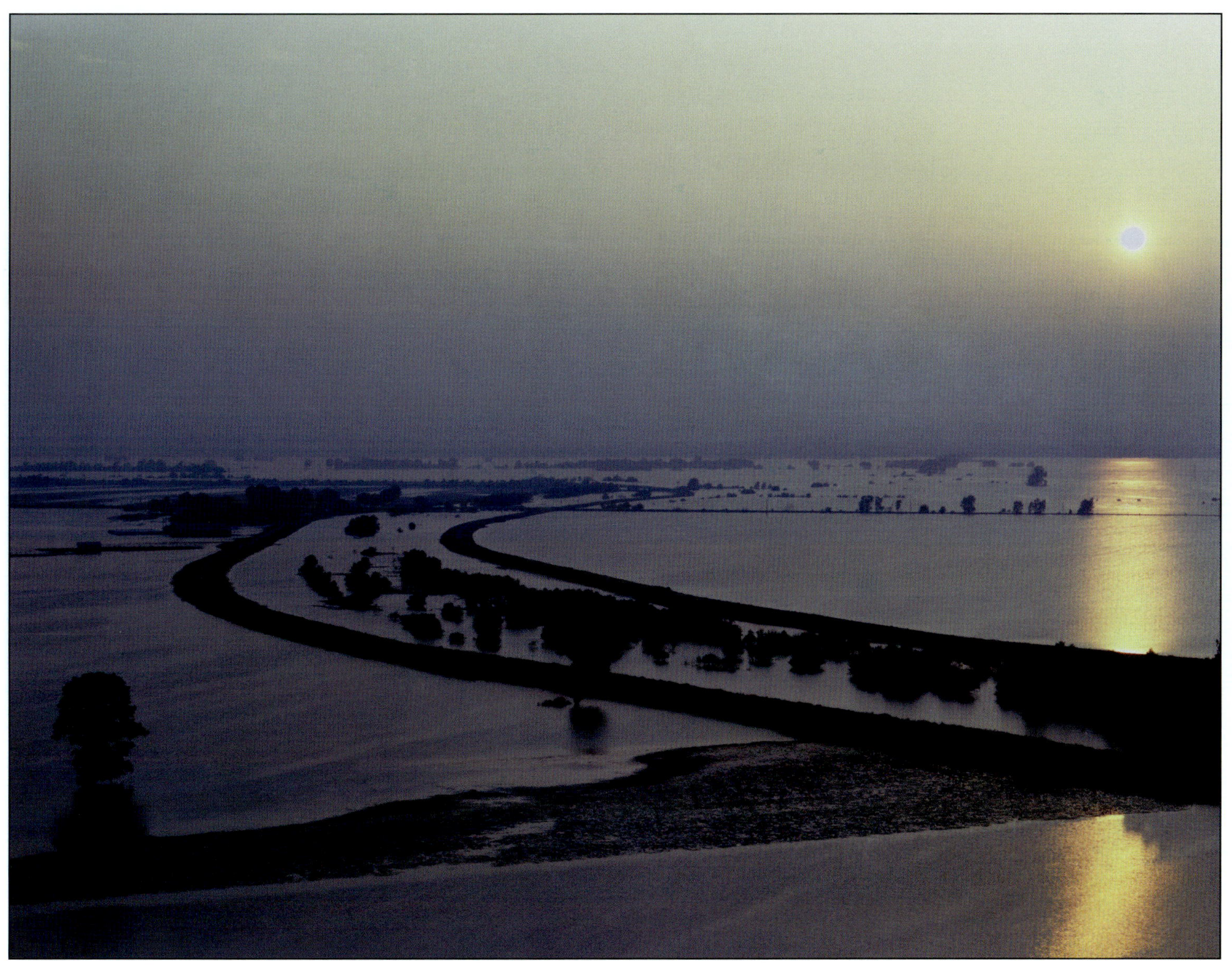

**American Bottom:
Fountain Creek, 1993**
Monroe County, Illinois

A C-shaped levee runs from bluff to bluff and protects Columbia Drainage and Levee District, forming a bowl. Floodwaters breached the northern section of the levee along the river, searched out Long Slash Creek, and tore south. The river, the floodplain, and the levee slope south. The Fountain Creek levee, while as tall as the levee at the break, sat two feet lower. The levee break at the northern end of the bowl filled it with water to the flood level of the river, higher than the elevation of the Fountain Creek levee. The levee broke in three places where Fountain Creek, Long Slash Creek, and the drained channel of Moredock Lake converge.

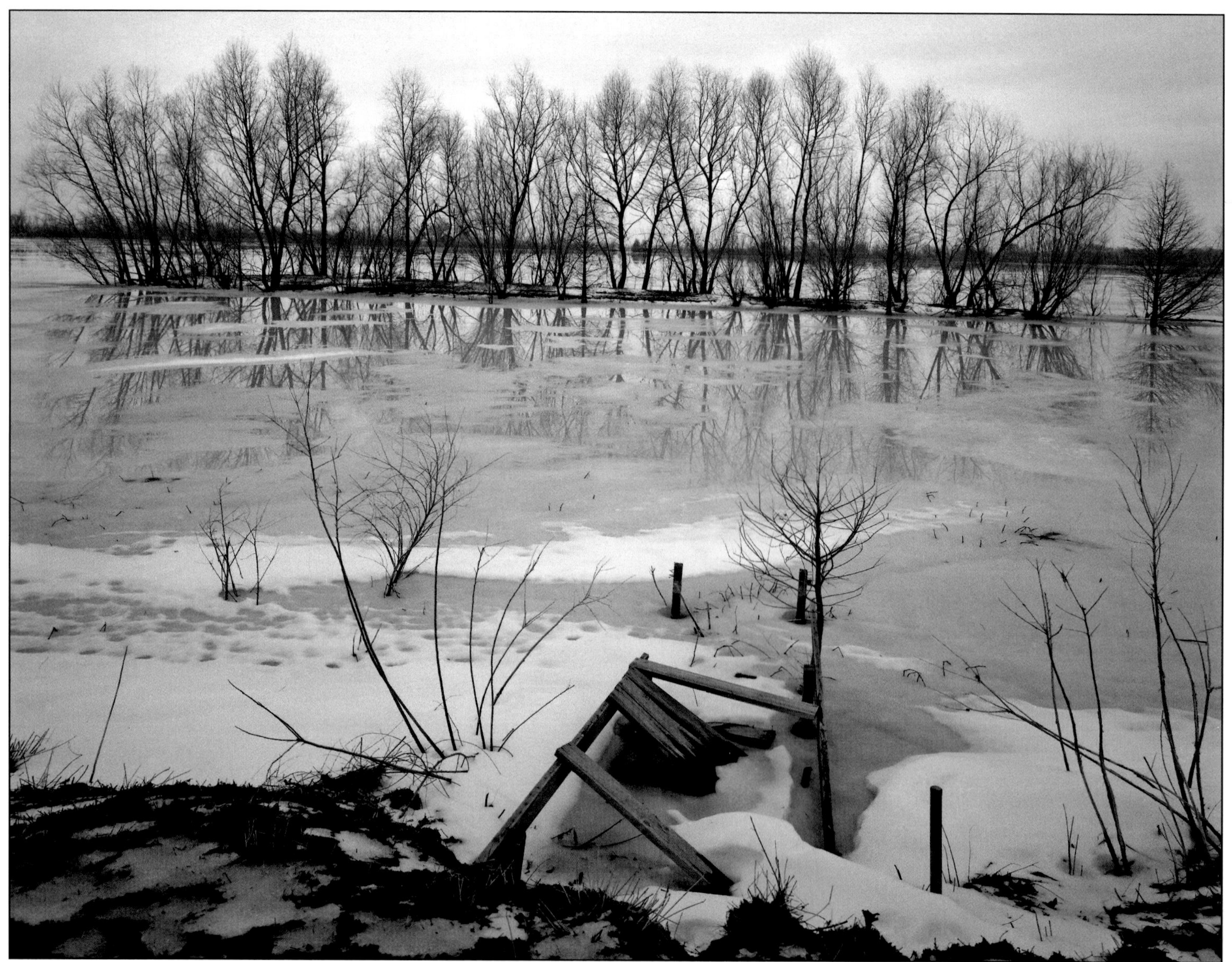

American Bottom: Moredock Lake

Monroe County, Illinois

Once Moredock Lake, an old oxbow, flowed against the bluff before turning west. At the end of the twentieth century, a flood-plain forest occupied its northern end, marshes fringed open water at its southern end, and a line of willows rooted in a sandbar. Farmers in the Columbia Drainage District drained most of the lake. Its channel remained as a low, sandy place in the landscape. The Fountain Creek levee broke where Long Slash Creek and the drained channel of Moredock Lake converge. Days of rain had saturated the sand in the ancient channels, compromising the ground under the levee. The levee sagged even lower. The flood breached it and roared south.

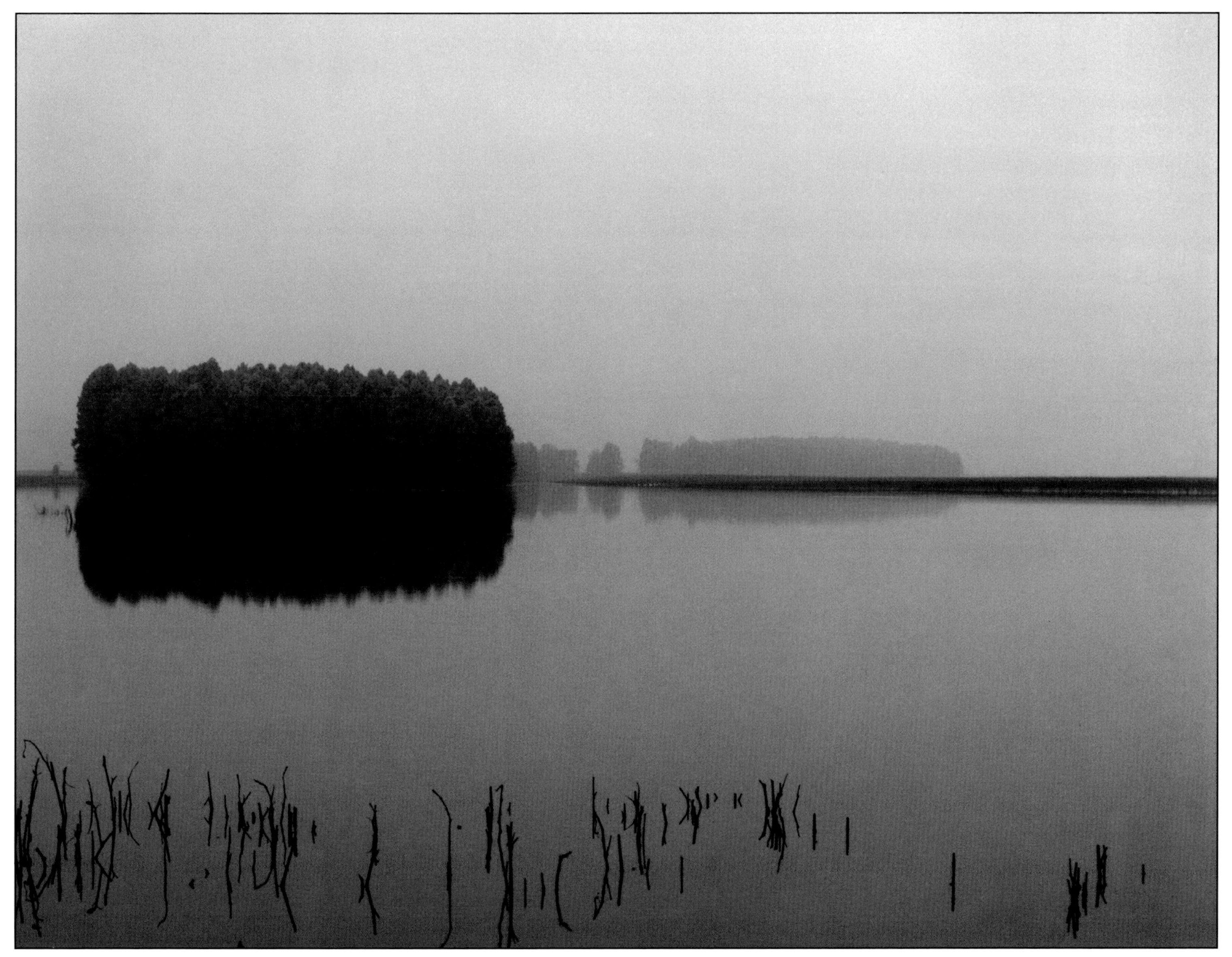

American Bottom: Mueller's Cypress
Monroe County, Illinois

The interagency committee that examined the 1993 flood and wrote *Sharing the Challenge* noted the danger of building levees across old river channels. The group suggested that levees that blew at old river channels not be rebuilt or be set back and the land returned to the river. Should such a levee be rebuilt, the group suggested that the sand be excavated from the old river channel and replaced with clay, giving the levee a clay core. In October 1993, the low place on Herbert Mueller's farm that wouldn't dry out and on which he planted a cypress grove, retained water long after the flood had drained back to the river.

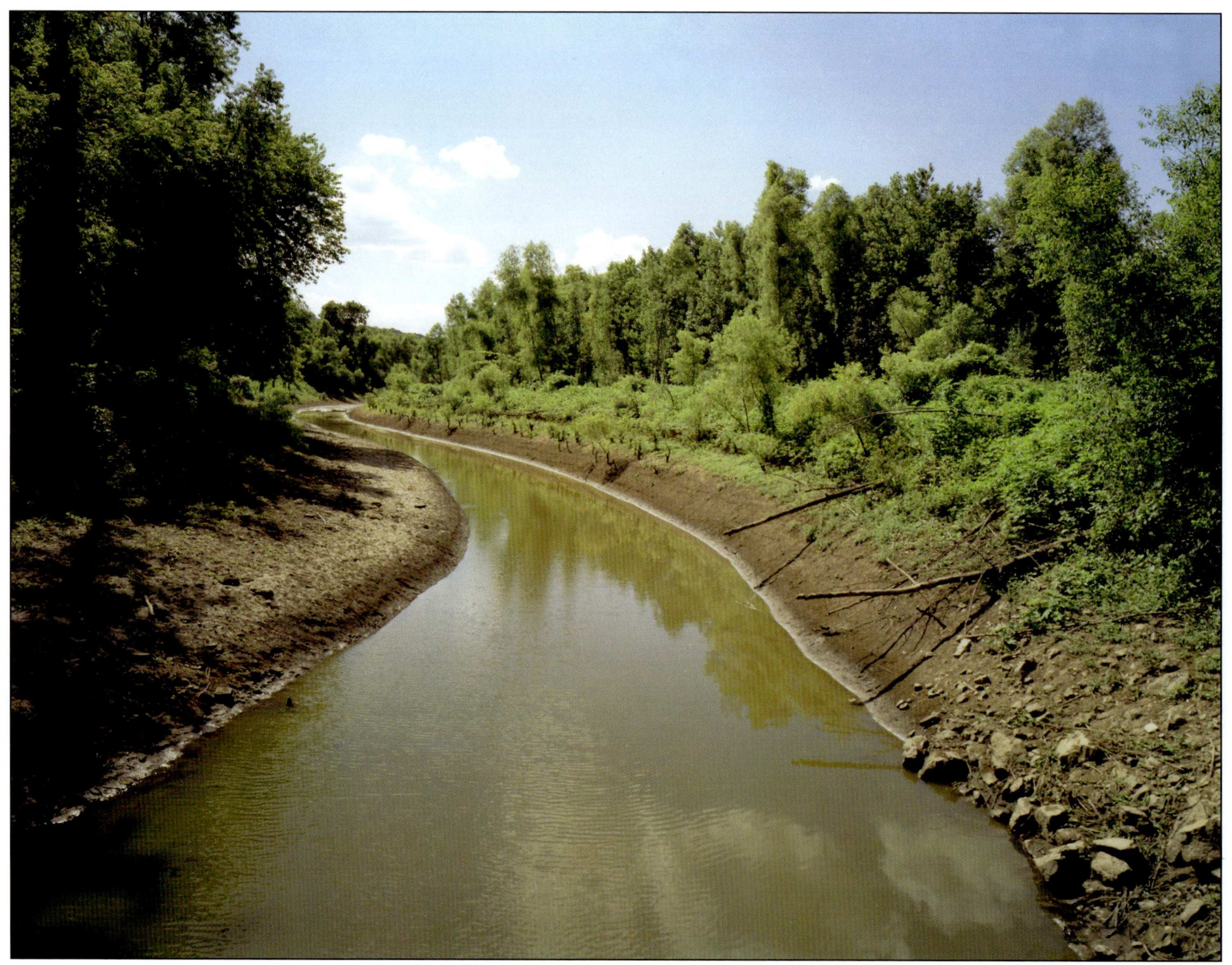

Harlow Island: Harlow Chute
Jefferson County, Missouri

"They are pearls hanging along the river."—Robert Cail, manager, Middle Mississippi National Wildlife Refuge, 2008

"They" are Harlow, Meissner, Beaver, and Wilkinson Islands, 7,000 of the 17,000 acres Congress authorized for the Middle Mississippi River National Wildlife Refuge. In 1993 floodwaters inundated Harlow Island. Three years later the U.S. Fish and Wildlife Service purchased the island and did not repair the breached levee. A young forest took root in the old fields. The service would like to reconnect Harlow Chute to the river and deepen it for overwintering fish.

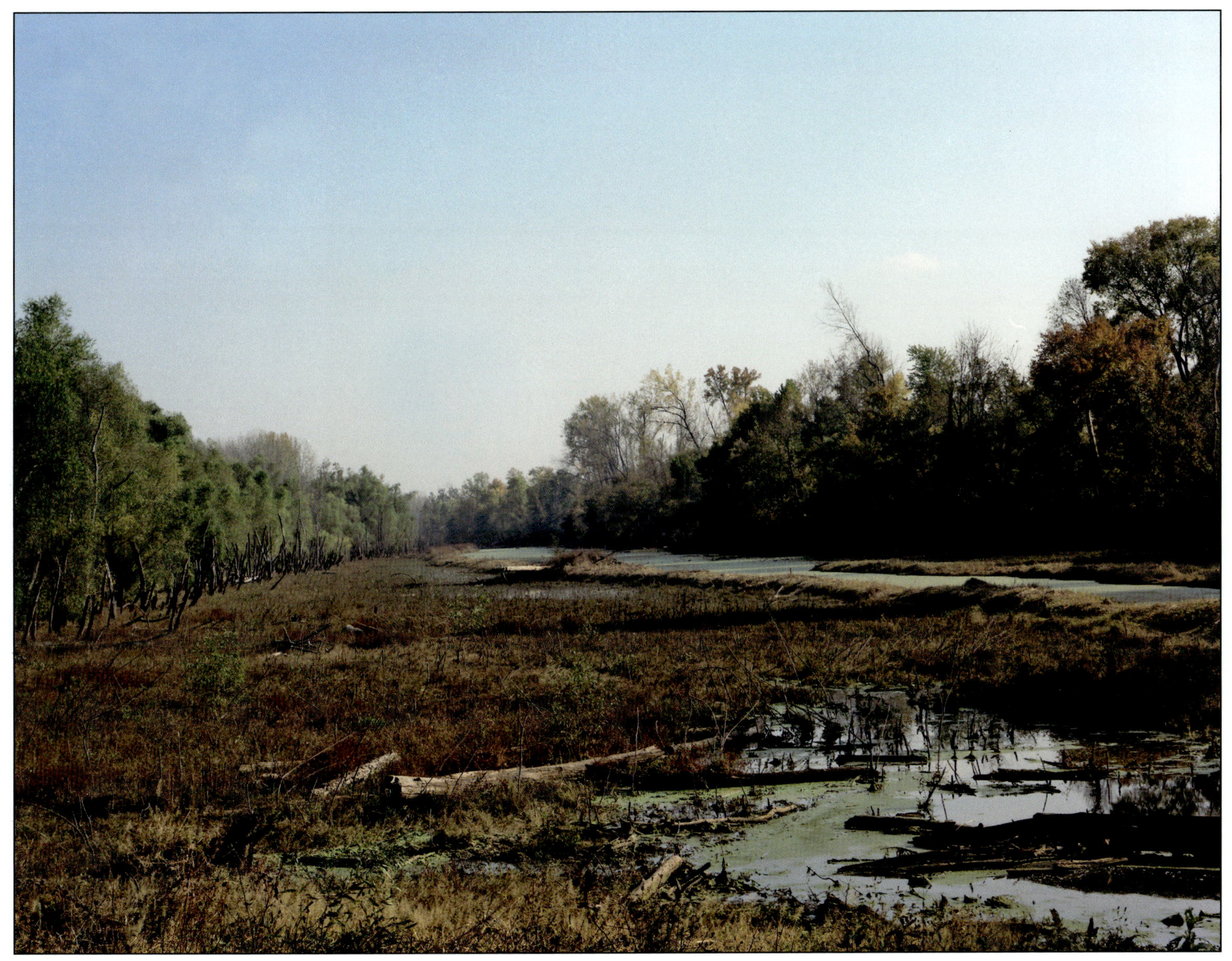

Rockwood Island: Degognia Creek

Jackson County, Illinois

Degognia Creek streams out of the uplands into the batture lands and flows between farm fields and a levee to the Mississippi. Here, Degognia Creek built its own little floodplain, edged by willows and cottonwood, just the kind of batture lands Fish and Wildlife seeks for the refuge. To the south, farmers on Wilkinson Island put 1,900 acres in the WRP in the wake of the 1993 flood. The USFWS purchased 632 acres for the refuge. To the north a $1.10 million grant from the Illinois Clean Energy Community Foundation allowed Southwestern Illinois Resource Conservation and Development and the ALC to purchase land on Rockwood Island for the refuge.

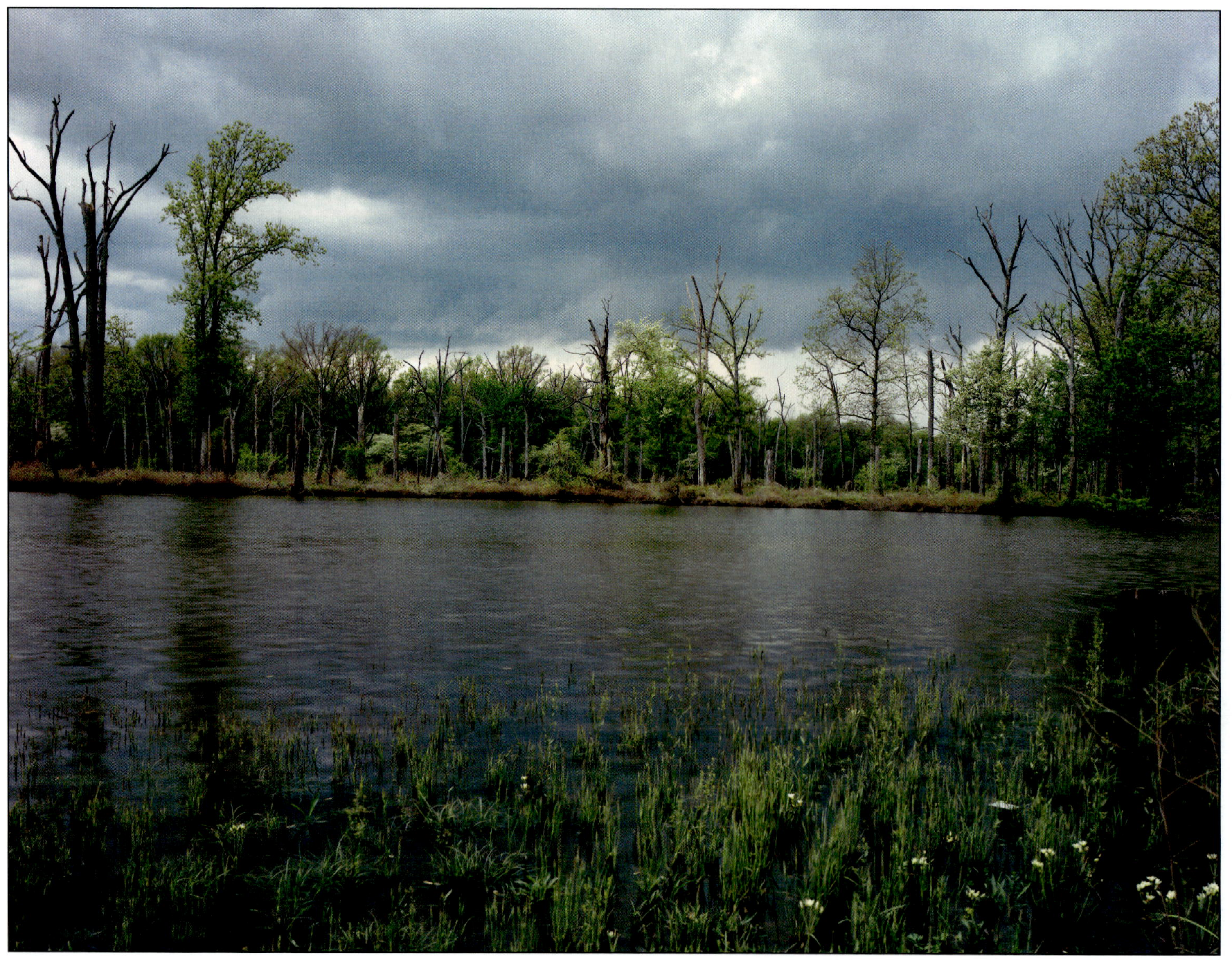

Oakwood Bottoms: Turkey Bayou
Jackson County, Illinois

The U.S. Forest Service purchased Oakwood Bottoms in the 1930s and integrated it into the Shawnee National Forest. Even though it was drained for agriculture, Oakwood Bottoms is a botanical treasure that includes rare and state endangered species: Arkansas manna grass and pole manna grass, known only to the Big Muddy floodplain, and finger dog-shade, found nowhere else in Illinois. Five different forest communities dominate the lowlands: shagbark hickory, pin oak, black willow, pin oak–cherrybark oak, and pin oak–red maple. A 1993 survey of plants scattered across the refuge found swamp red iris, mock bishop's weed, hornwort, Wolf's sedge, and lake cress.

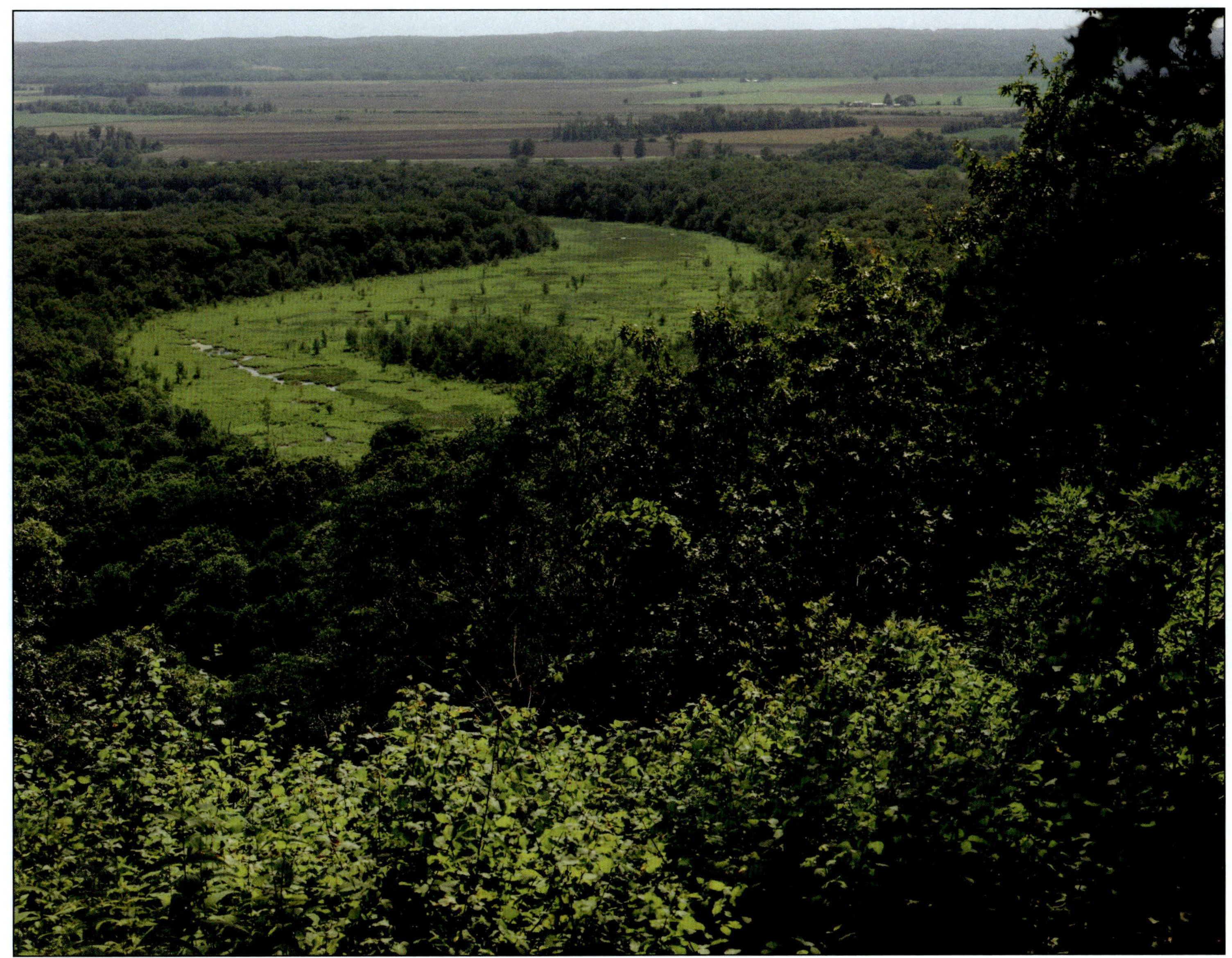

The Big Muddy River: LaRue–Pine Hills Research Natural Area

Union County, Illinois

LaRue Swamp is protected within the Shawnee National Forest, which purchased it in 1937. Big Muddy River flowed out of the uplands and was channelized between levees to its confluence with the Mississippi. Its abandoned channel evolved into a valuable swamp at the base of Pine Hills Bluff, Illinois' Ozarks hills. The Big Muddy flowed into the swamp and out of it. The water level in the swamp varied, allowing soil to dry out and seeds to germinate. Pumpkin ash, water locust, red swamp maple, and cypress took root. Finally, clay plugged the abandoned channel. Runoff from the bluff provided enough water to maintain the swamp, which is surrounded by a levee.

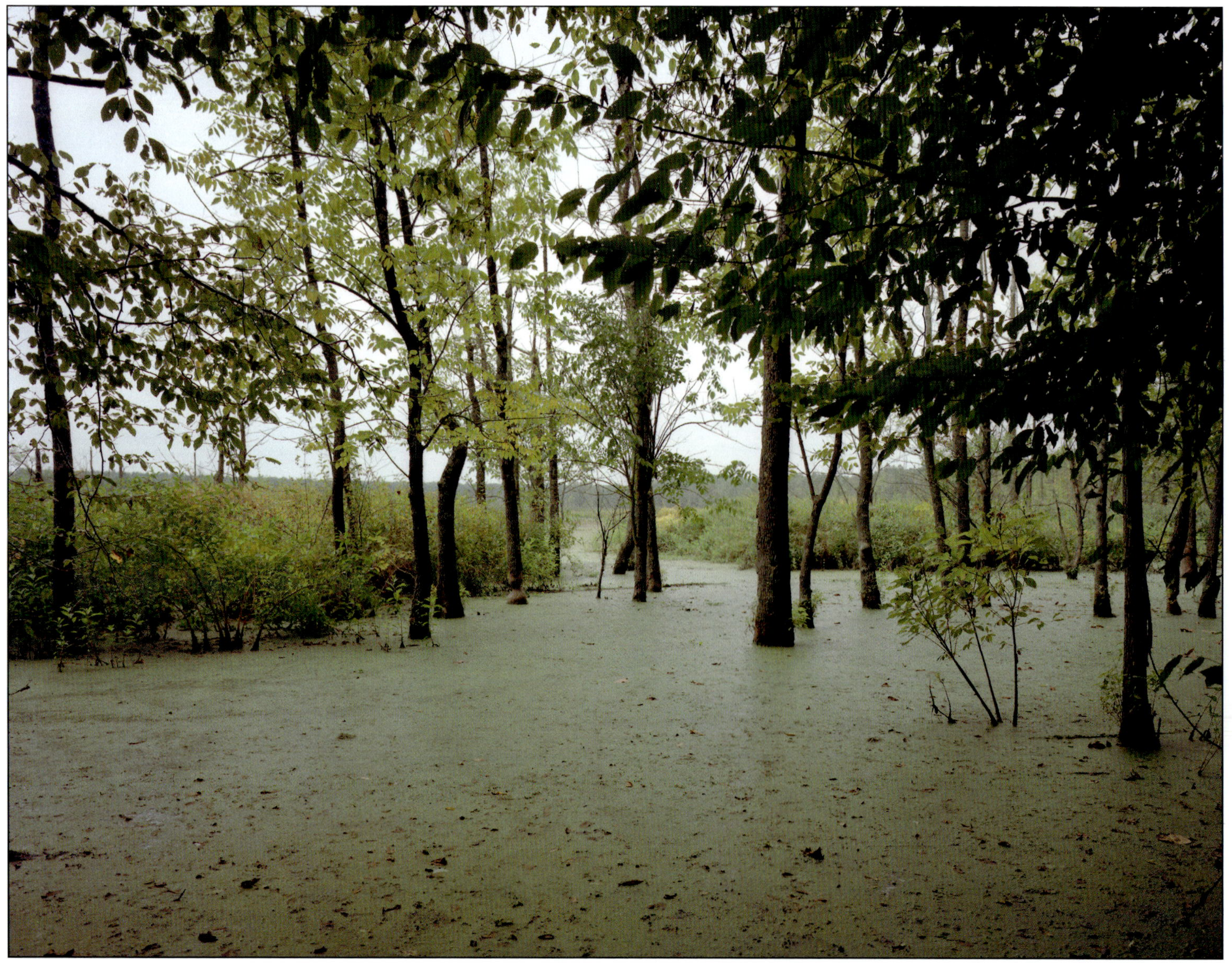

Big Muddy River: LaRue–Pine Hills Research Natural Area

Union County, Illinois

The LaRue–Pine Hills is a biological crossroads. The hills are the southern edge of the natural range of sumac and partridge berry, the northern edge of short needle pine. The swamp is the northern edge of the natural range of the cottonmouth, the rare Mississippi green water snake, the green tree frog, the mole salamander, the mud snake, and the alligator snapping turtle. Virginia willow and the silver bell never crossed the Mississippi from the east, but Missouri primrose and Ozark cornflower crossed from the west. So did the eastern narrowmouth toad, the coachwhip snake, the Great Plains rat snake, and the flathead snake.

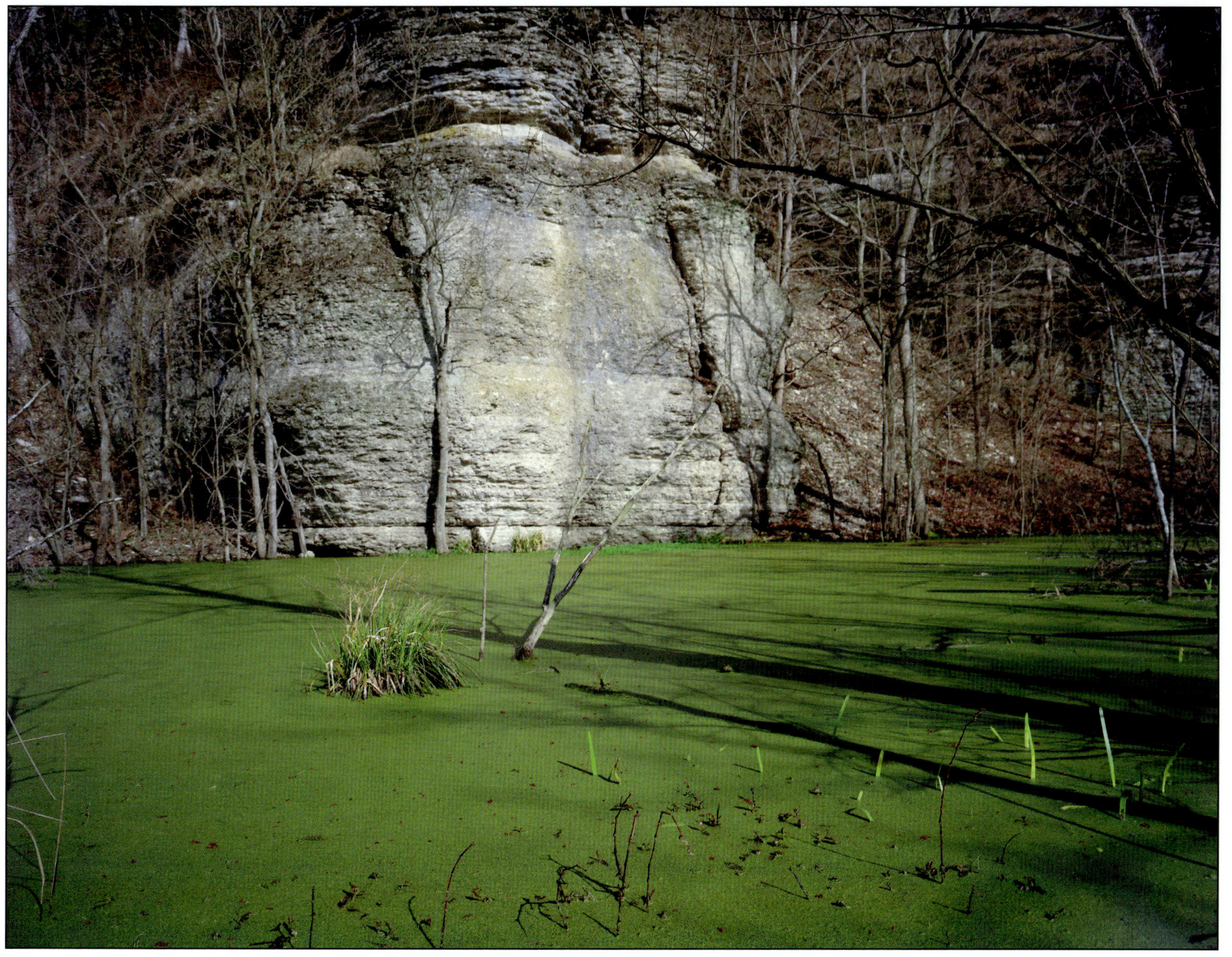

LaRue Swamp: Pine Hills Bluff

Union County, Illinois

Forest Road 345 runs along the base of the bluff and adjacent to the swamp. The Forest Service closes the road between the swamp and the bluff to wheeled traffic from the first of September to mid-October to allow the snakes, toads, lizards, frogs, turtles, and other cold-blooded creatures—half the 102 species of reptiles and amphibians that live in Illinois—to cross the road between the swamp and the bluff unmolested. There they hibernate. The snakes return to the dens their parents occupied before them. The service closes the road again from mid-March to mid-May to allow the creatures to return to the swamp for the summer.

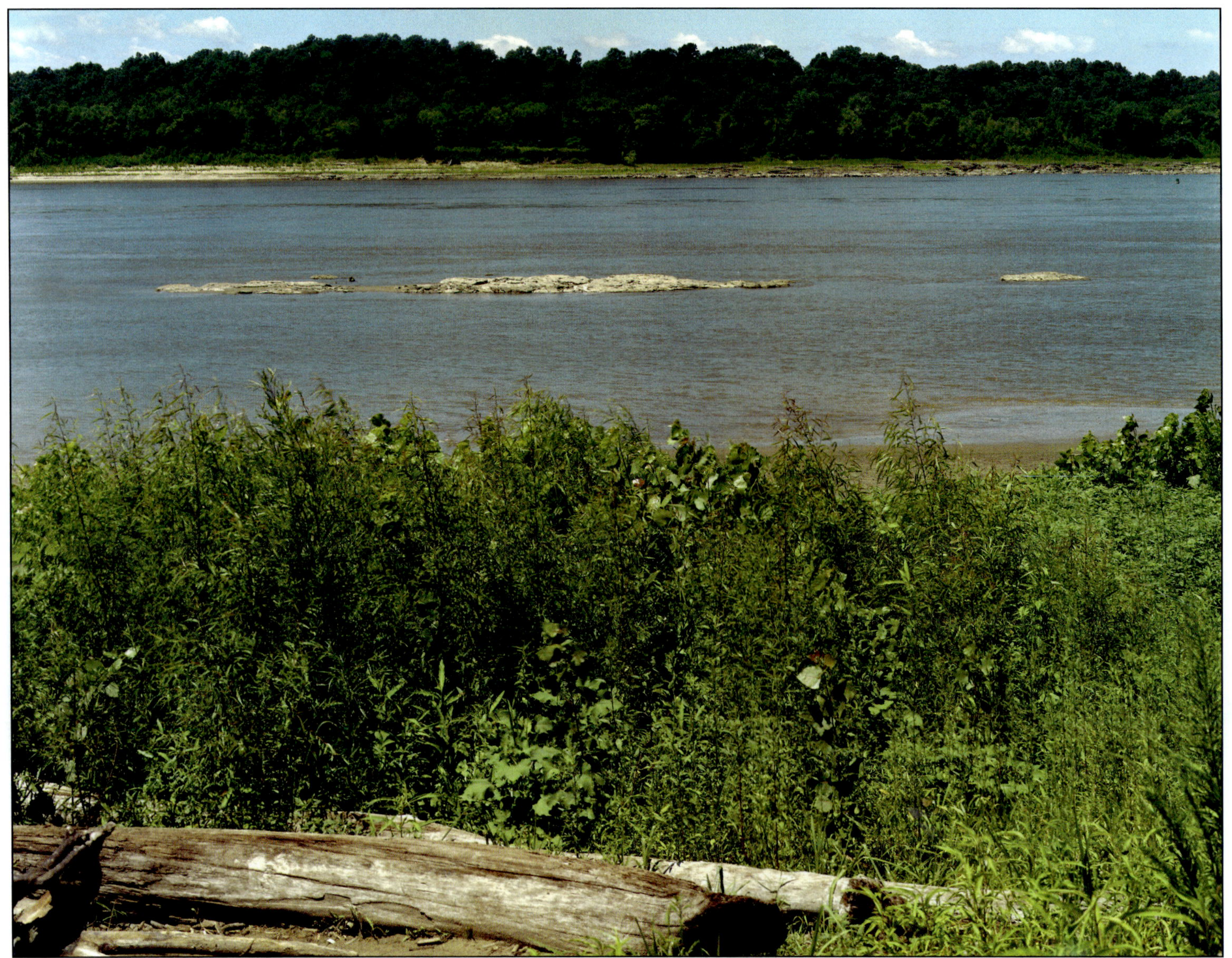

Thebes Gap
Alexander County, Illinois

"Thebes at the head of the Grand Chain and Commerce at the foot of it were towns easily rememberable as they had not undergone conspicuous alteration. Nor the Chain, either—in the nature of things; it is a chain of sunken rocks admirably arranged to capture and kill steamboats on bad nights."—Mark Twain, *Life on the Mississippi*

Thebes Gap is the geological break between the Upper and Lower Mississippi. The river could have diverted through the gap in the series of glacial floods or in a series of earthquakes that opened up the gap in the Benton Hills. River Warren thundered through it and deposited a classical alluvial fan at its mouth.

The Western Lowlands and the White River Basin

> There DeSoto left the Cacique in his own town; and an Indian guided them through an immense pathless thicket of desert for seven days, where they slept continually in ponds and shallow puddles. Fish were so plentiful in them that they were killed with blows of cudgels; and as the Indians traveled in chains, they disturbed the mud at the bottom, by which the fish, becoming stupefied, would swim to the surface, when as many were taken as were desired.
>
> —The Gentleman from Elvas

When Hernando de Soto and his army waded through the Western Lowlands and the White River Basin in 1541, they found a hunting and fishing paradise. In spite of our efforts to drain the lowlands for agriculture, parts of it—particularly the Cache River National Wildlife Refuge, the White River National Wildlife Refuge, and numerous state wildlife management areas—are still fantastic. Even today, these refuges provide a sanctuary for a diverse array of wildlife: the Louisiana black bear, the Prothonotary Warbler, the Pileated Woodpecker, herons, ducks—millions of ducks—and true frogs and tree frogs. The variety of fish—Kentucky bass, gar, sturgeon, pike, sunfish, perch—that astounded de Soto can still be found. And, the big ones can still be landed. In July 2004 an angler hauled a 240-pound alligator gar out of the White River.

Within the Western Lowlands there was little definition between watersheds. Floodwaters washed back and forth between basins. Flooding on the Mississippi backs up into the White; the White backs up into the Cache; the Cache backs up into Bayou De View, ten miles upstream. Underneath it all, a braided network of sandy channels collects and moves shallow groundwater over large areas. The Mississippi alluvial aquifer supplies the groundwater between Crowley's Ridge and Grand Prairie, an ancient terrace that rises thirty to forty feet above the White River and lies between the White and the Arkansas Rivers.

It is the great irony of Arkansas delta lands that the farmers who drained them for agriculture then had to turn around and irrigate them for row crops, particularly for rice, depleting the aquifer. A 2004 U.S. Geological Survey study of groundwater use in Arkansas after 1997 projected that depletion of groundwater in eastern Arkansas for irrigation, particularly for rice farming, could cause parts of the aquifer under the Grand Prairie in Lonoke, Prairie, Jefferson, and Arkansas Counties to go dry by 2009. Depletion would also affect wetlands and the bottomland forests in the Western Lowlands between the White River and Crowley's Ridge, a region where 235,000 acres are given over to wildlife refuges: the White River and Cache River National Wildlife Refuges; the Hurricane Lake, the Bayou De View, the Dagmar, and the Trusten Holder State Wildlife Management Areas. Together, the refuges represent the largest expanse of bottomland forest remaining in the Lower Mississippi Valley. Should farmers continue to withdraw groundwater from the aquifer at the 1997 rates, 275 square miles of it would go dry by 2029, 400 square miles by 2049.

The young century found three projects on the drafting boards at the Little Rock and Memphis Districts of the Corps of Engineers. Environmentalists, who worried about any one of the projects, feared the three together would alter the White River Basin forever. In 2004 the Little Rock District completed the Montgomery Point Lock and Dam on the White half a mile short of its confluence with the Mississippi. The Corps built the dam to maintain a nine-foot navigation channel on the first ten miles of the White, which acts as the first ten miles of the Arkansas River Navigation System. The Arkansas Post Canal connects the two rivers at river mile 10 on the White. Closing the dam could extend spring flooding in the White River National Wildlife Refuge, harming trees and wildlife.

The Memphis District had the White River Navigation Project on its books, a proposal to increase the depth of the navigation channel on the White from eight feet to nine between the Arkansas Post Canal at mile 10 and Newport, Arkansas, at mile 254. The district's Grand Prairie Demonstration Project, a proposal to allow rice farmers on Grand Prairie to pump water out of the White for irrigation, would lower the flowline of White River by one foot at DeValls Bluff, near the critical region where the White, the Cache, Bayou De View, and their attendant wildlife refuges came together. Both the navigation project and the irrigation project could draw water out of the wildlife refuges and divorce the White from its oxbows and side channels.

Fearing that accelerated depletion of groundwater or changes in water levels in the river could change the flow of the White River and its tributaries at a pace faster that the river could repair itself and its wetlands, Arkansans—particularly anglers, duck hunters, and environmentalists—forced the two districts to develop a comprehensive watershed plan for the basin to serve as a framework for sustainable development of its water resources. They also forced the Memphis District to include the 2004 U.S. Geological Survey study of the depletion of groundwater in the Mississippi alluvial aquifer in its environmental impact statement. Against this backdrop, the Nature Conservancy pursued its plan to preserve and augment the remaining bottomland forests in the region the conservancy called the White River–Lower Arkansas Megasite, named the "Big Woods."

The Nature Conservancy breaks down the Big Woods into four sections: the Mississippi River section, the Lower Arkansas River section, the White River section, and the Cache River–Bayou De View section. This last includes forested land on the White north of its confluence with the Cache, patches of forest along the upper Cache River, and the uninterrupted bottomland forest along the narrow floodplain of Bayou De View. Each is isolated from the others by large sections of agricultural land.

In 1988 the Arkansas Natural Heritage Commission contracted with the Nature Conservancy to develop a plan to preserve and augment the Big Woods in the White River Basin. In 1991 the Nature Conservancy outlined an ambitious plan to connect the patches, and since then it has worked with public agencies, timber companies, farmers, and hunters to protect and expand the Big Woods through purchase, gift, or conservation easements. By reforesting marginal farmland, the partners connected patches along the White, Cache, and Bayou De View Rivers. The payoff was the discovery of "Lord God Bird."

On February 11, 2004, when Gene M. Sparling III went kayaking along Bayou De View, he sighted an Ivory-billed Woodpecker in Benson Creek Natural Area, a 299-acre refuge close to the agricultural margin of the Bayou De View floodplain. He returned to the swamp on February 27 with Tim Gallagher, editor of the Cornell Laboratory of Ornithology's *Living Bird* magazine, and Bobby R. Harrison, associate professor of art and photography at Oakwood College in Huntsville, Alabama. The Ivory-bill flew in front of their canoe. They all took notes and later compared them. They had, indeed, seen the bird, thought to be extinct in North America, its habitat lost to the logging of southern swamp forests.

In April the Nature Conservancy formed the Big Woods Partnership with the goal of restoring an additional 200,000 acres of habitat to the Big Woods over ten years. And a group of Arkansas civic leaders and decision-makers, elected officials, and local stakeholders formed the Corridor of Hope Conservation Team to develop and implement plans to conserve habitat for the Ivory-billed Woodpecker in the Big Woods. The federal government redirected $10.2 million dollars—$5 million from the Department of the Interior and $5.2 million from the Department of Agriculture—from other projects to efforts to protect and restore habitat for Lord God Bird.

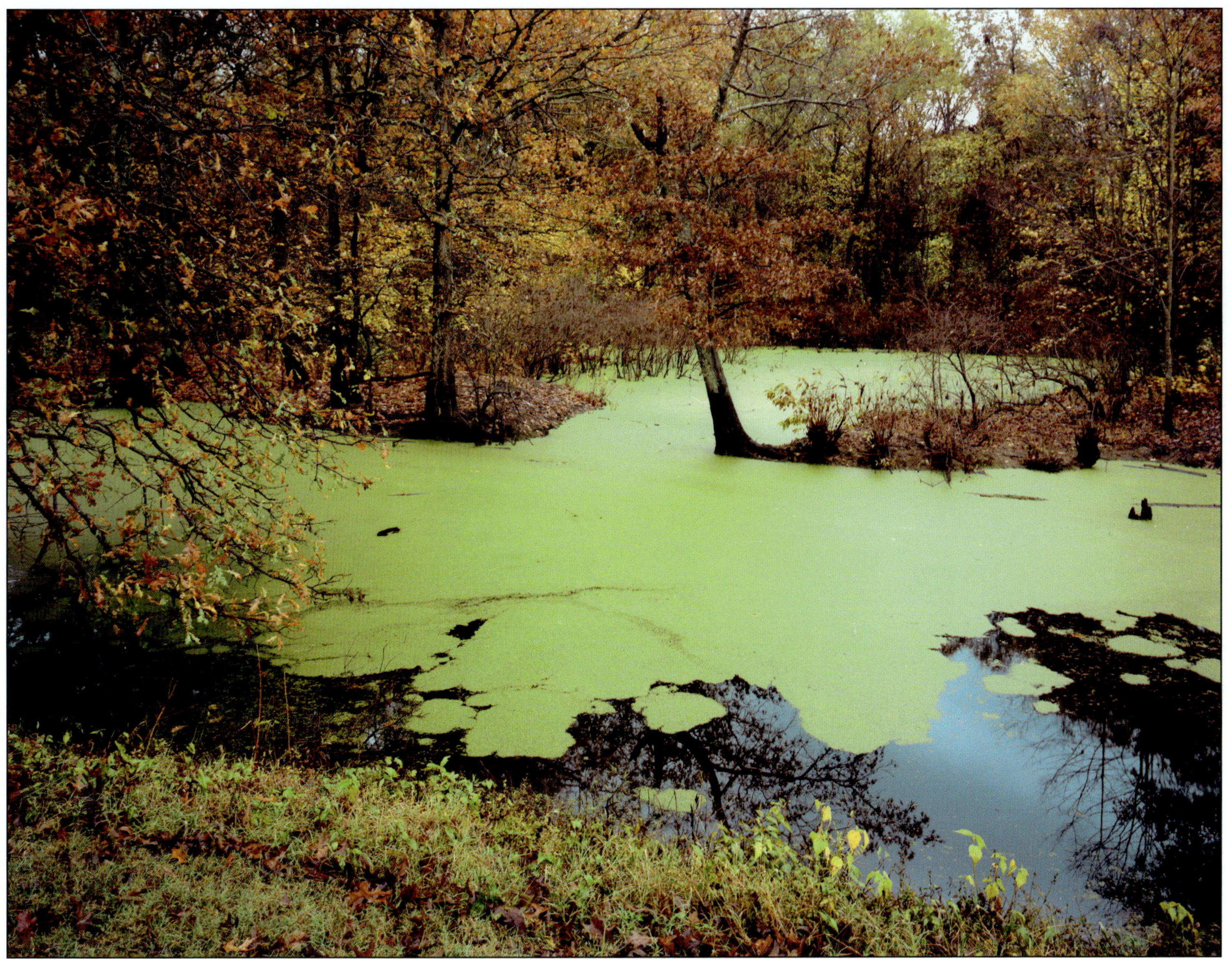

Mingo Swamp: Ditch 10
Stoddard County, Missouri

Mingo: formed when the Mingo River pooled behind the alluvial fan of the St. Francis; a remote, productive swamp in 1800; logged in the nineteenth century; drained, grazed, trampled, burned, and eroded in the early twentieth. In 1945, the U.S. Fish and Wildlife Service purchased a 21,676-acre tract and restored the swamp for a wildlife refuge. L. H. Frederickson and T. S. Taylor developed moist-soil management at Mingo. Over thirteen years they manipulated water levels in different management areas, using drainage ditches to manage four flooding depths to produce food and vegetative cover to draw waterfowl, herons, rails, shorebirds, and upland wildlife.

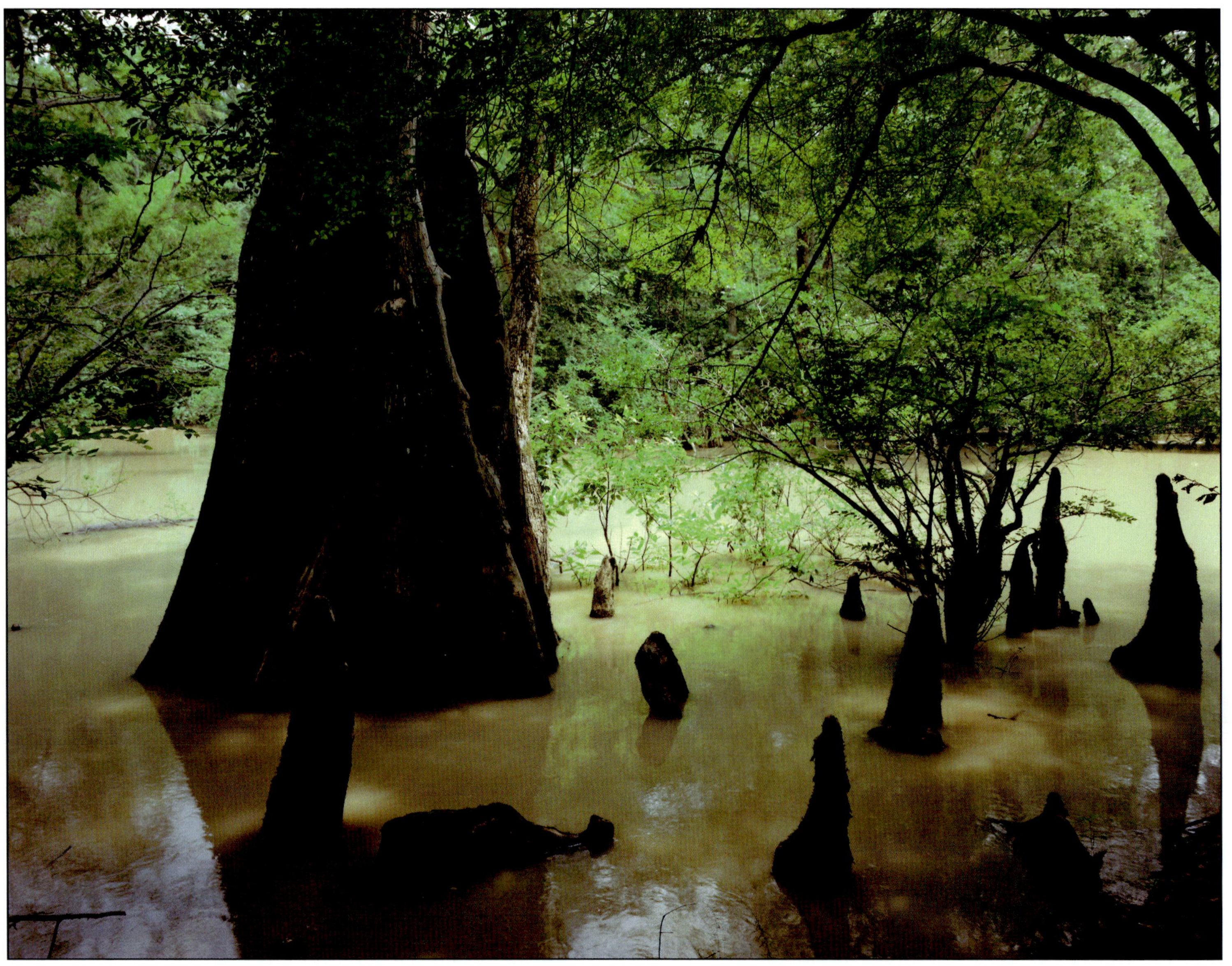

Black River: Dave Donaldson Wildlife Management Area
Randolph County, Arkansas

The Arkansas Game and Fish Commission purchased the Dave Donaldson Wildlife Management Area in the 1950s and '60s in order to salvage 25,000 acres of bottomland forest and Black River wetlands from ever-expanding soybean and rice fields. Cypress and tupelo line the rivers and sloughs that lace the refuge. Oaks—Nuttall, overcup, water, and pin—dominate higher elevations. The refuge provides winter habitat for waterfowl. When the Black comes up in winter, the refuge floods a greentree reservoir for Mallards and Wood Ducks after the oaks have gone dormant. After duck season as the water warms, the refuge drains the reservoir to save the trees.

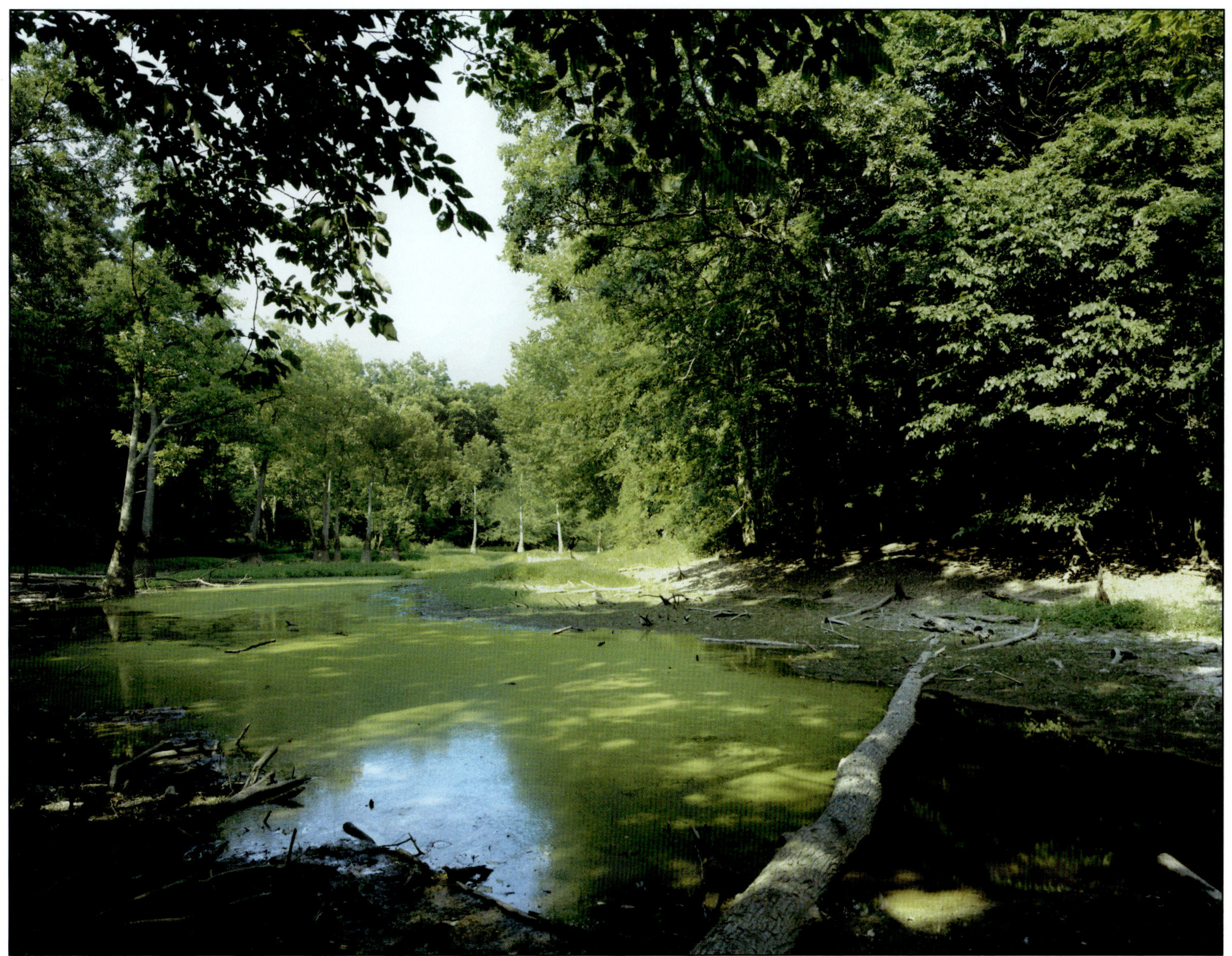

Earl Buss—Bayou De View Wildlife Management Area: Bayou De View

Poinsett County, Arkansas

Bayou De View meanders through a continuous forest from one forested pool to another. The goal of the Nature Conservancy in its Big Woods Project was to acquire and reforest land between the Cache River and Bayou De View. Its second goal was to assure that "umbrella species"—the Swainson's Warbler, the Cerulean Warbler, and the American Swallow-tailed Kite—nest in there. If they do, other species will. The Conservancy added a third goal after February 2004: locate and number Ivory-billed Woodpeckers in the Big Woods and increase habitat for the bird through reforestation of acquired lands.

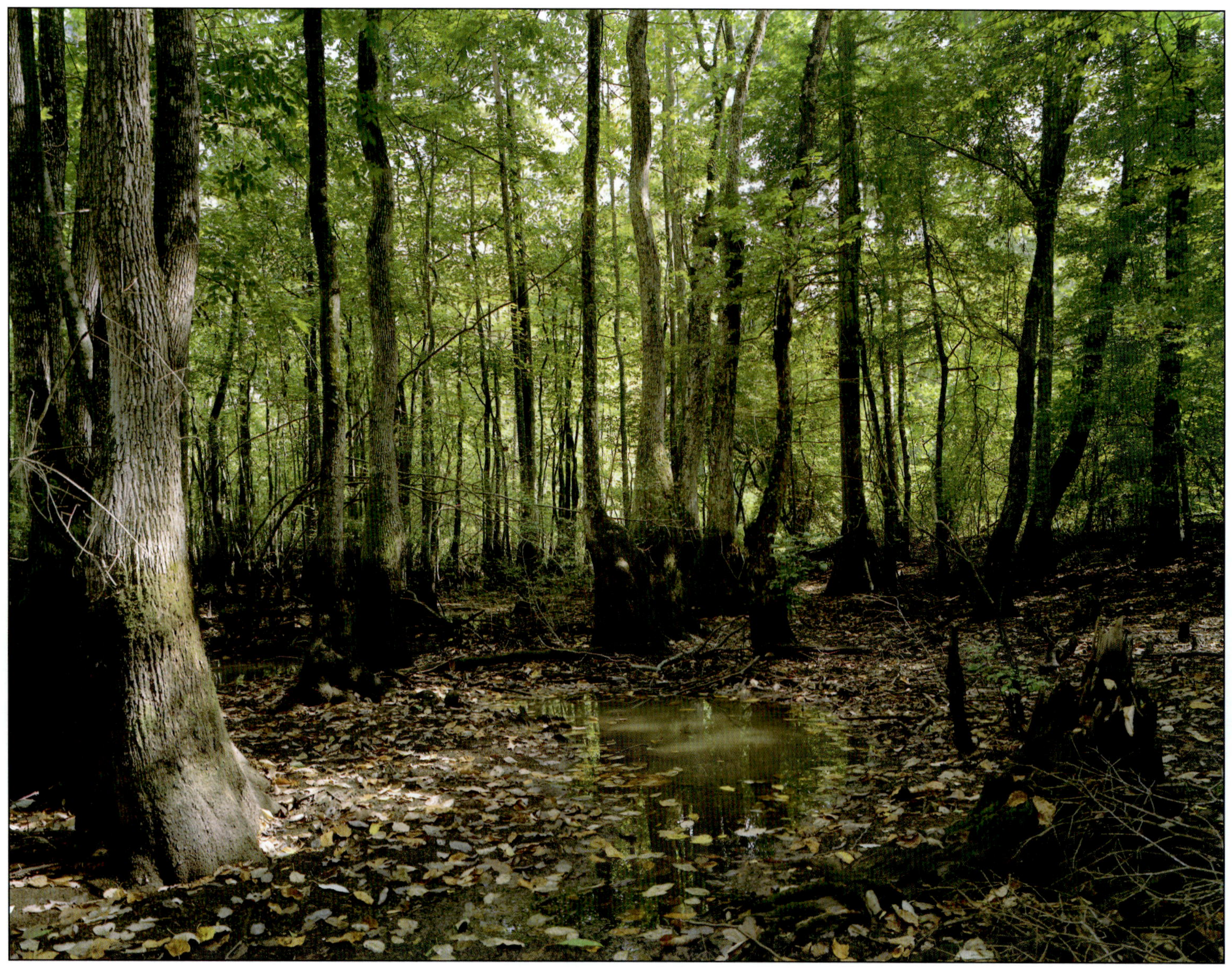

Cache River: Rex Hancock/ Black Swamp Wildlife Management Area

Woodruff County, Arkansas

Scientists studying the Black Swamp identified its forest zones: cypress and tupelo in wet soil close to the Cache; overcup oak and bitter pecan on slightly dryer land; Nuttall oak, willow oak, and sweet gum on high land. Fishery biologists learned that higher spring floods yielded higher rates of spawning. Ornithologists studied the agricultural edge of the swamp and identified Prothonotary Warblers and Great Crested Flycatchers in the cypress forest; Chimney Swifts above the open canopy; Tanagers and Ovenbirds high in the oaks. On the ground, herpetologists learned that the smallest change in elevation was important to amphibians and small reptiles.

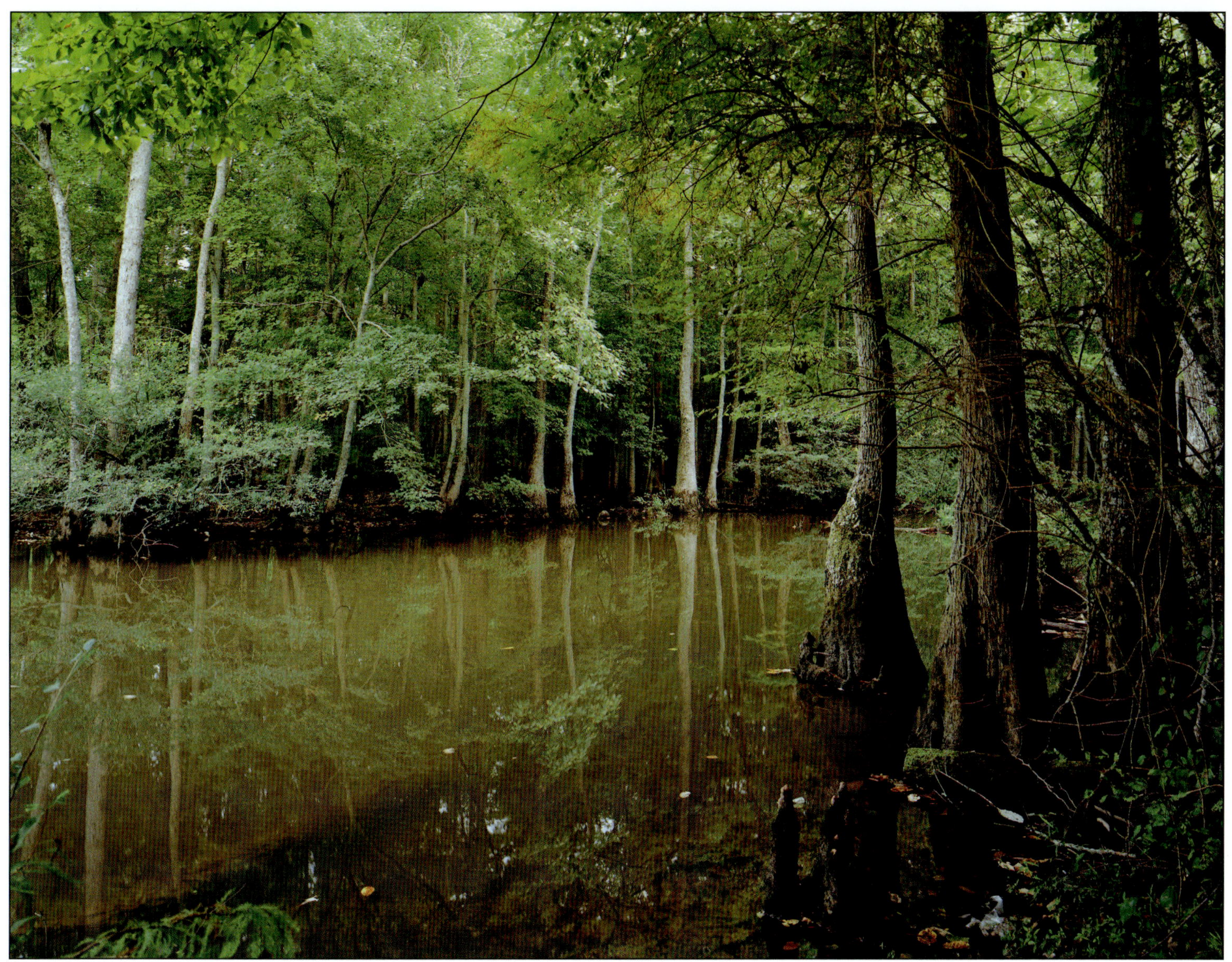

Benson Creek Natural Area: Bayou De View Backwater

Monroe County, Arkansas

No sooner did Brinkley, Arkansas, learn that the Ivory-bill has been spotted on Bayou De View outside of town, than it realized there was cash money to be had in Lord God Bird. The local Super 8 morphed into the Ivory-Bill Inn. Gene's Bar-B-Que handled Ivory-bill coffee mugs, Ivory-bill key rings, and Ivory-bill lapel pins. The Ivory-billed Nest sold only Ivory-bill stuff. The headquarters of the Cache River NWR at Dixie had Ivory-bill T-shirts, gave out Ivory-bill posters, but had no recordings of the bird's call. But the White River NWR at St. Charles sold stuffed Ivory-bill squeeze-me dolls that went "*kent kent*," just like the bird.

The Demands on the White River: White River Navigation Project and the Grand Prairie Demonstration Project

> If the hydrology of a river or stream in the bottomland hardwood forest is changed by either damming the stream or changing land use around the stream and affecting runoff, plant composition in the forest will also change. In mildly affected systems this may shift the dominant tree species from pin oak to overcup oak. Yet, if the hydrology is drastically altered, as in the case of introducing dams or other control structures to hold nearly constant water levels, then the entire forest can be lost. Restoration of such a forest will be impossible, unless the appropriate hydrology is restored.
>
> —Charles W. Downer, 1993

The White River and the Cache River National Wildlife Refuges protect over 200,000 acres of bottomland forest. State wildlife management areas protect 35,000 acres. An additional 115,000 acres are in private hands. Surrounding the refuges are 250,000 acres of rice fields. Winter flooding in the basin provides the most important wintering place in North America for waterfowl. Duck hunting contributes $1 million per day to the economy during its two-month season. Up to 230 species of songbirds migrate to its forests in the breeding season. The White supports 150 species of fish. Recreational fishing contributes $122 million to the local economy.

In 2000, the Corps of Engineers had the White River Navigation Project and the Grand Prairie Demonstration Project on its drafting boards. Both would change the hydrology of the White River and the wildlife refuges that depend on its cycle of flooding and drying to keep their wetland forests and the creatures that depend on them healthy.

The Corps of Engineers came to the White River in 1892 to maintain a four-and-a-half-foot navigation channel in the ten miles between Augusta and Newport and an eight-foot channel 125 feet wide south of Augusta. The Corps stopped maintaining the eight-foot channel in 1950 but resumed in 1961. By 2000 the Memphis District was spending $1.7 million per year to keep it dredged and snagged. Had it been a foot deeper, barge companies using it could have hauled six times as much grain.

So Congress authorized a feasibility study for dredging and diking a nine-foot channel 125 feet wide clear to Newport in the 1986 Water Resources Development Act, deauthorized it two years later, then, under pressure from barge interests, reauthorized it in 1996, and allocated funds for the study in 1998. Environmentalists, anglers, and duck hunters wished it away altogether.

The opposition, including the USFWS, owner of the White River and Cache River Refuges, contended the dikes would force the river to scour a deeper channel, deposit sediment behind wing dams, fill side channels, and turn the White River into a deeply incised stream that would reduce the extent, duration, and timing of winter and spring floods so critical to the maintenance of the forests. The Corps contended that construction of 120 wing dams in 35 dike fields, requiring three sections of paved bank to prevent erosion, would harm neither refuge.

Before European settlement Grand Prairie was just that, a tallgrass prairie growing on a thin layer of loess, which overlaid a bed of clay two feet thick. The land was good for grazing, but not row crops. In 1904 Arkansas farmers discovered that the clay base held water for days, making the land great for rice farming.

Arkansas farmers cultivate 42 percent of the U.S. rice crop. The process is complicated. In early spring they lay out miniature levees, several inches deep and spaced several feet apart, which hold water on the fields at a constant depth of two to three inches during the growing season. When the rice matures, farmers drain the fields and harvest the rice.

While forty inches of rain fall on Grand Prairie between November and May, rice farmers need water between June and August, when it doesn't rain. To fill that need, farmers with fields adjacent to streams used the cheapest form of irrigation available: they dropped in straws, sucked out what they needed, and stored it in reservoirs. Those who lived away from streams tapped the alluvial aquifer.

But, the claypan that held water so well inhibited the surface recharge of the aquifer. Within ten years, it became clear that farmers had drawn more water from the aquifer than was being returned. The aquifer had shrunk, and it continued to shrink as the century went on.

In the late 1980s, threatened with restrictions on water use and fearing shortages, farmers persuaded Senator Dale Bumpers to ask Congress to authorize a diversion of the White River to their storage reservoirs by way of a pump at DeValls Bluff. The Memphis District initiated the Grand Prairie Demonstration Project, even though irrigation projects are not within the Corps mandate. When the district issued its environmental impact plan in September 1999, opponents raised hell.

The statement claimed that tapping the White River for irrigation would lower its flow line no more than a foot at DeValls Bluff and have no impact on backwaters. While it might divorce four oxbows from the river for a short time, the change would not last. Because the reservoirs on the upper reaches of the White maintain the river at summer flows higher than they were in predam days, drawing water from the White during the growing season would return the river to prereservoir conditions. Because ducks don't arrive until after rice is harvested, drawing water from the White during the growing season would have no effect on the water needed during duck season, when the rains would come anyway.

The National Wildlife Federation and Taxpayers for Common Sense objected to the cost: $319 million was too much money for too little benefit and too much habitat destruction. Rice farming, as it was practiced in Arkansas, was unsustainable; it was depleting the aquifers and threatening the region's source of safe drinking water. Dropping the level of the White one foot in the summer months would leave less in the river to recharge the aquifer. Environmentalists urged Arkansas rice farmers to improve their irrigation efficiency beyond the 60 percent level, use on-farm storage reservoirs that would catch and store winter rains, recapture water drained from the rice fields after harvest and return it to the reservoirs. Construction on the pump began in 2004.

In September 2005 the National and Arkansas Wildlife Federations filed suit in federal district court in Little Rock to stop both projects. The plaintiffs claimed that the Ivory-billed Woodpecker, discovered a year earlier, had survived because the Corps abandoned a navigation project on the Cache River in the 1970s. They argued that the Corps and the USFWS had not thoroughly studied the impact of the projects on the bird's habitat. Starting the pump would drop water levels on the White as far south at St. Charles.

On July 20, 2006, U.S. District Judge James R. Wilson ordered the Corps to stop construction and search for signs of woodpecker activity "in all trees 12 inches or greater in areas that will be most affected by changes in water level." In addition, he ordered nesting, roosting, and foraging surveys within two and a half miles of the pump. In May 2008, Judge Wilson postponed his ruling on the suit, noting its complexities.

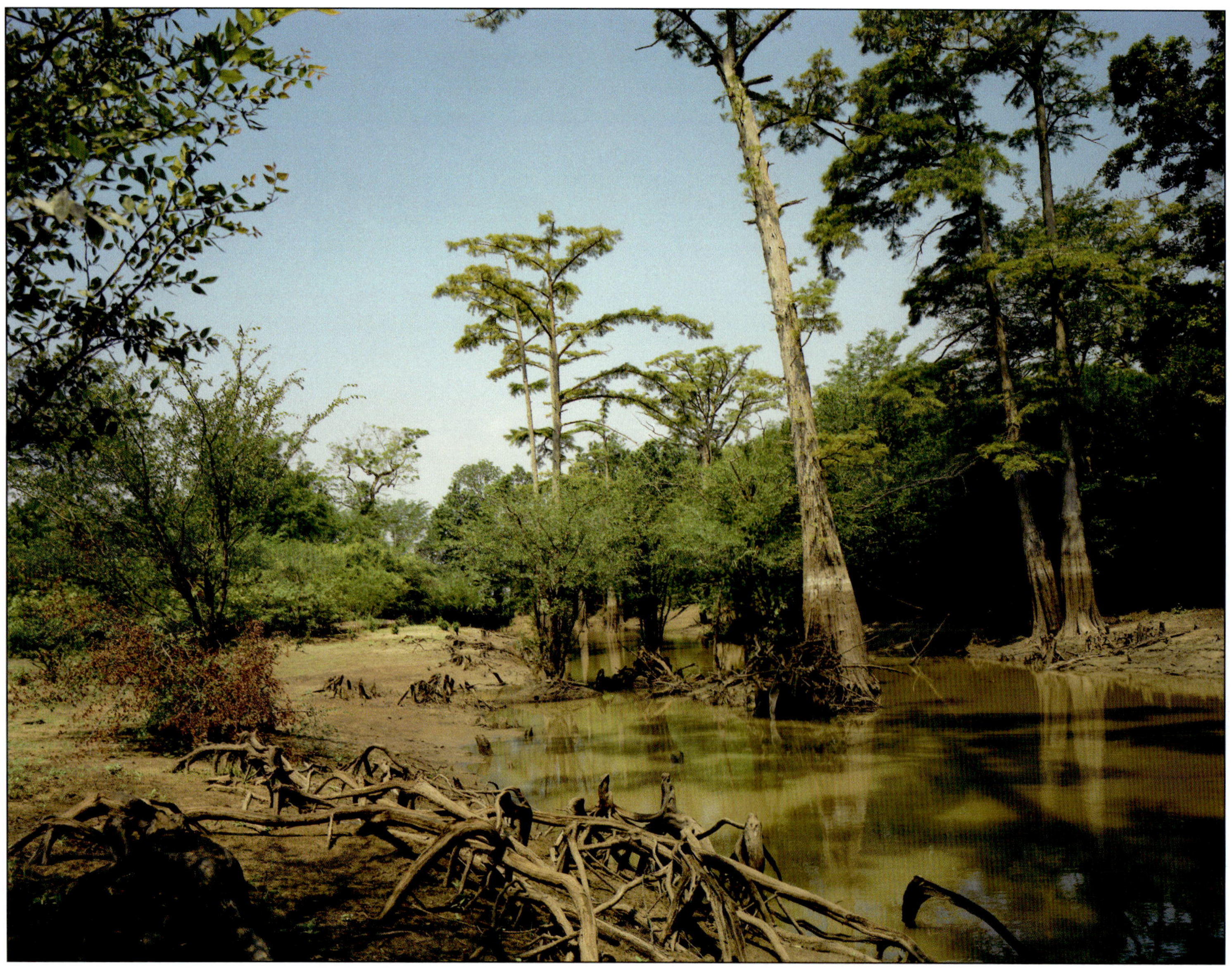

Cache River National Wildlife Refuge: Bayou De View
Monroe County, Arkansas

When the Interior Department revealed sightings of the Ivory-billed Woodpecker, the Corps shut down construction of the pump at DeValls Bluff, located a dozen miles west of the confluence of the Cache and Bayou De View. Within two weeks the Corps issued a biological assessment and Fish and Wildlife agreed: Grand Prairie Demonstration Project would have no adverse effect on the bird's habitat. Construction resumed. The Corps would monitor the effect of pumping from the White on the bird's habitat and adapt its management to the bird's needs. Opponents didn't believe Arkansas's powerful rice industry would allow the pump, once turned on, to be turned off.

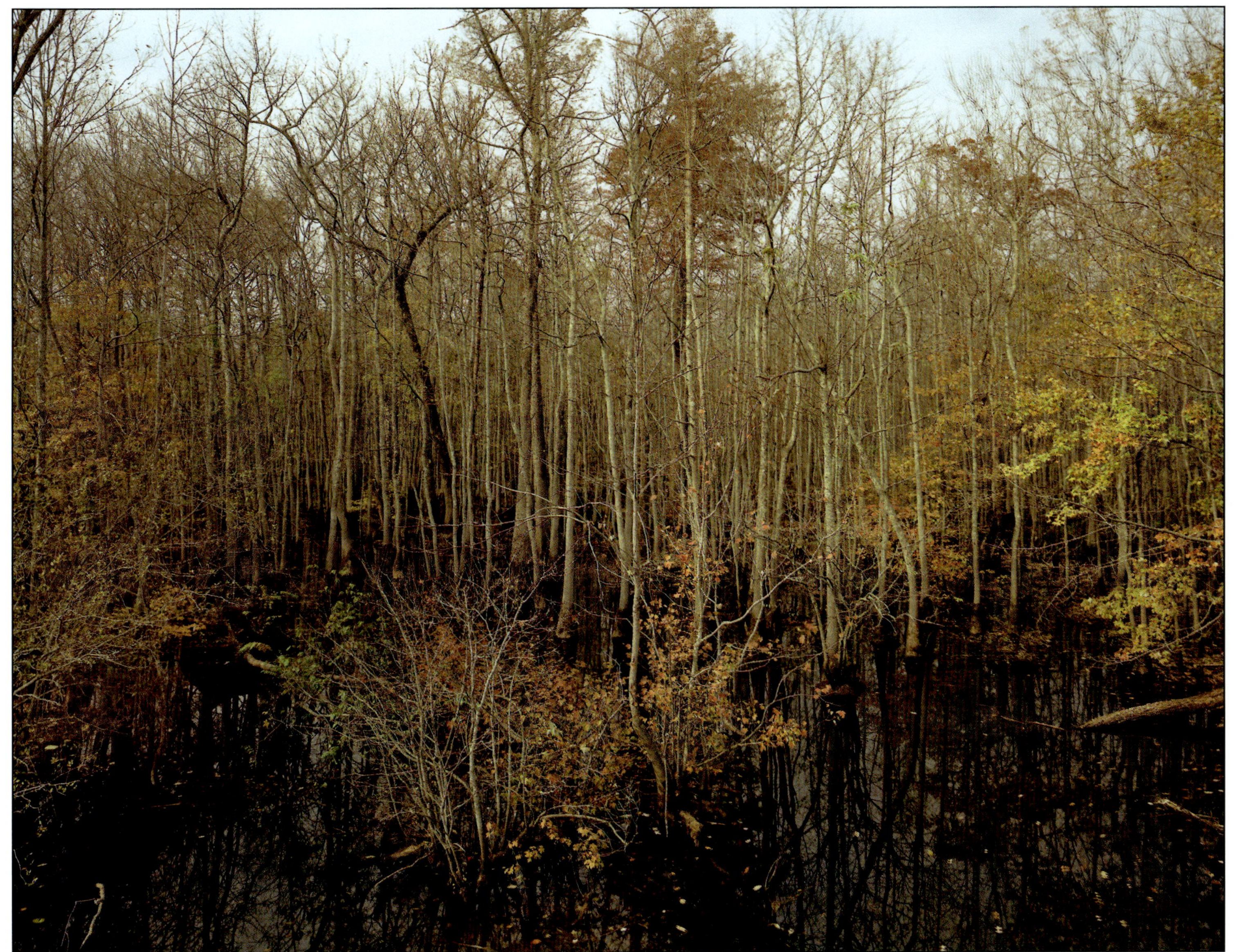

Grand Prairie: LaGrue Bayou
Arkansas County, Arkansas

LaGrue Bayou flows to the White and is within the Big Woods project. The transfer of water from one basin to another is unconstitutional in Arkansas. Nevertheless, the main irrigation canal for the Grand Prairie Project would zigzag south across the prairie, cutting through the natural drainage ridge between the White and Arkansas River Basins. In effect, the project would move water from the White River Basin to the LaGrue Bayou Basin and to the Mill Bayou Basin at the northern end of Grand Prairie. Water in the LaGrue Basin would be returned to the White at the southern end of Grand Prairie, but water in the Mill Bayou Basin would be returned to the Arkansas.

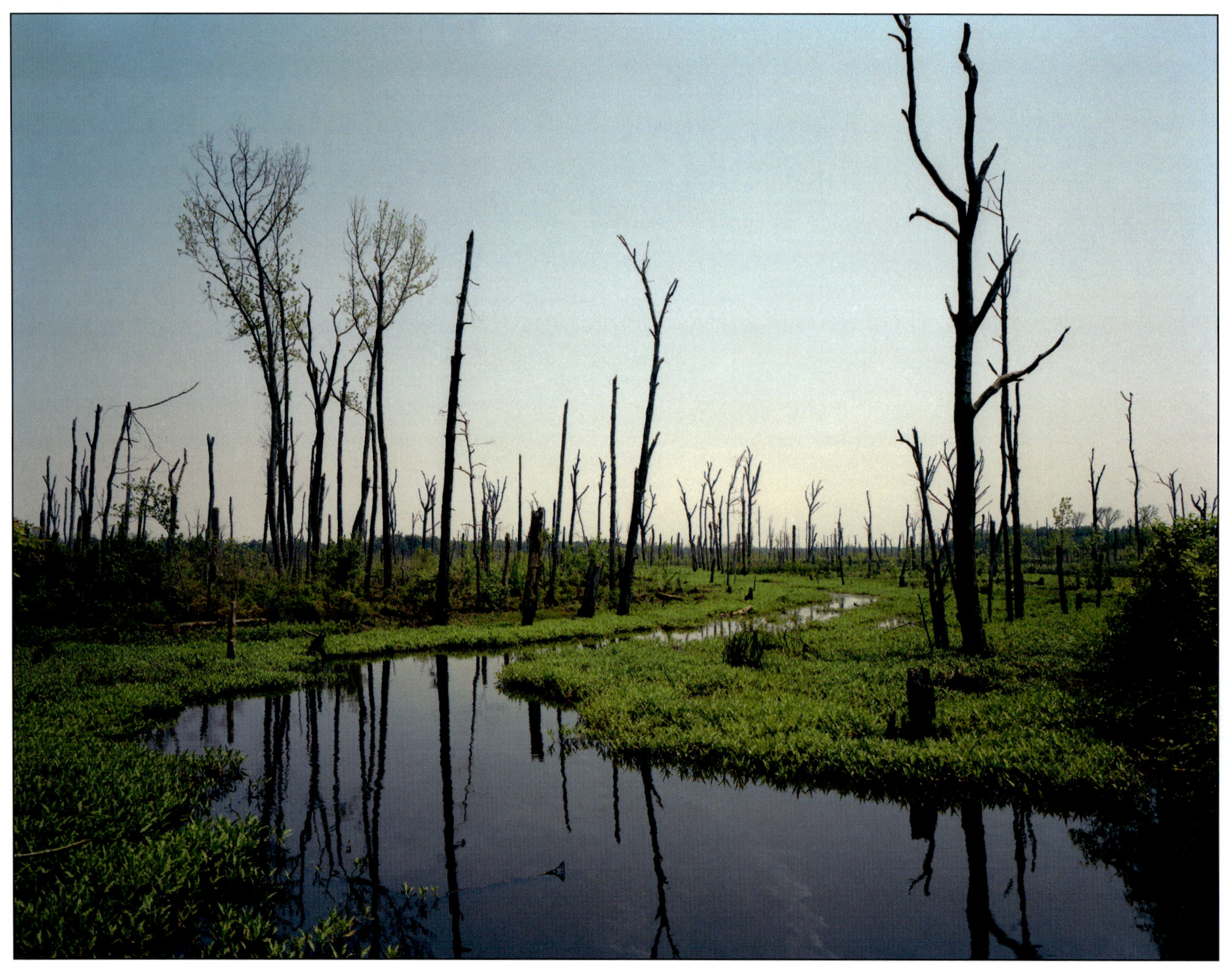

Grand Prairie: Big Creek
Arkansas County, Arkansas

A landscape that hosted 25 million acres of bottomland forest needed the beaver. It opened the canopy and created marshes. A 115,000-acre forest surrounded by rice fields does not. Here, the work of the beaver can create disaster. Trees that can stand periodic flooding cannot survive year-round flooding, their roots soaking for one or more growing seasons. Beaver dammed Big Creek, which drains to the White River Refuge, inundated its forest, and created a marsh. Once a marsh fills with decaying vegetation, the beaver will abandon its dam, the dam will deteriorate, the marsh will drain along the creek, and the forest will grow back.

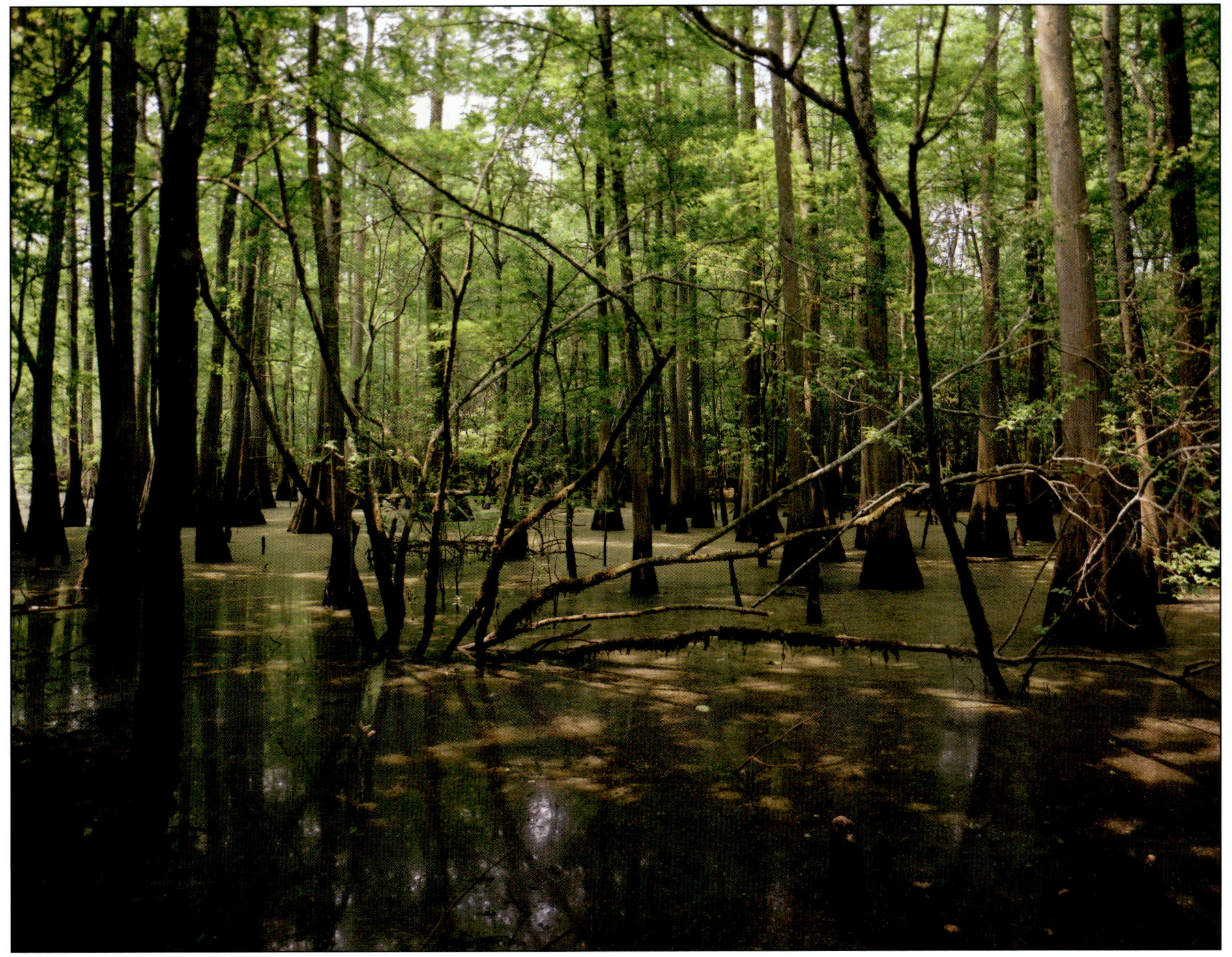

White River National Wildlife Refuge: Backswamp
Arkansas County, Arkansas

"Virtually every ecosystem has at least one bird species that is so intimately tied to that system that the species could be seen as an ecological indicator. The Prothonotary Warbler is found virtually nowhere other than forested wetlands, and that is the primary makeup of this area."—Robert J. Cooper, 2004

Cooper studied the effects of water management on the breeding habits of Prothonotary Warblers. The tiny yellow birds nest over open water, where their eggs are protected from predators—raccoons and rat snakes. If the warbler is breeding successfully, so are Indigo Buntings and Acadian Flycatchers, and the forest is healthy.

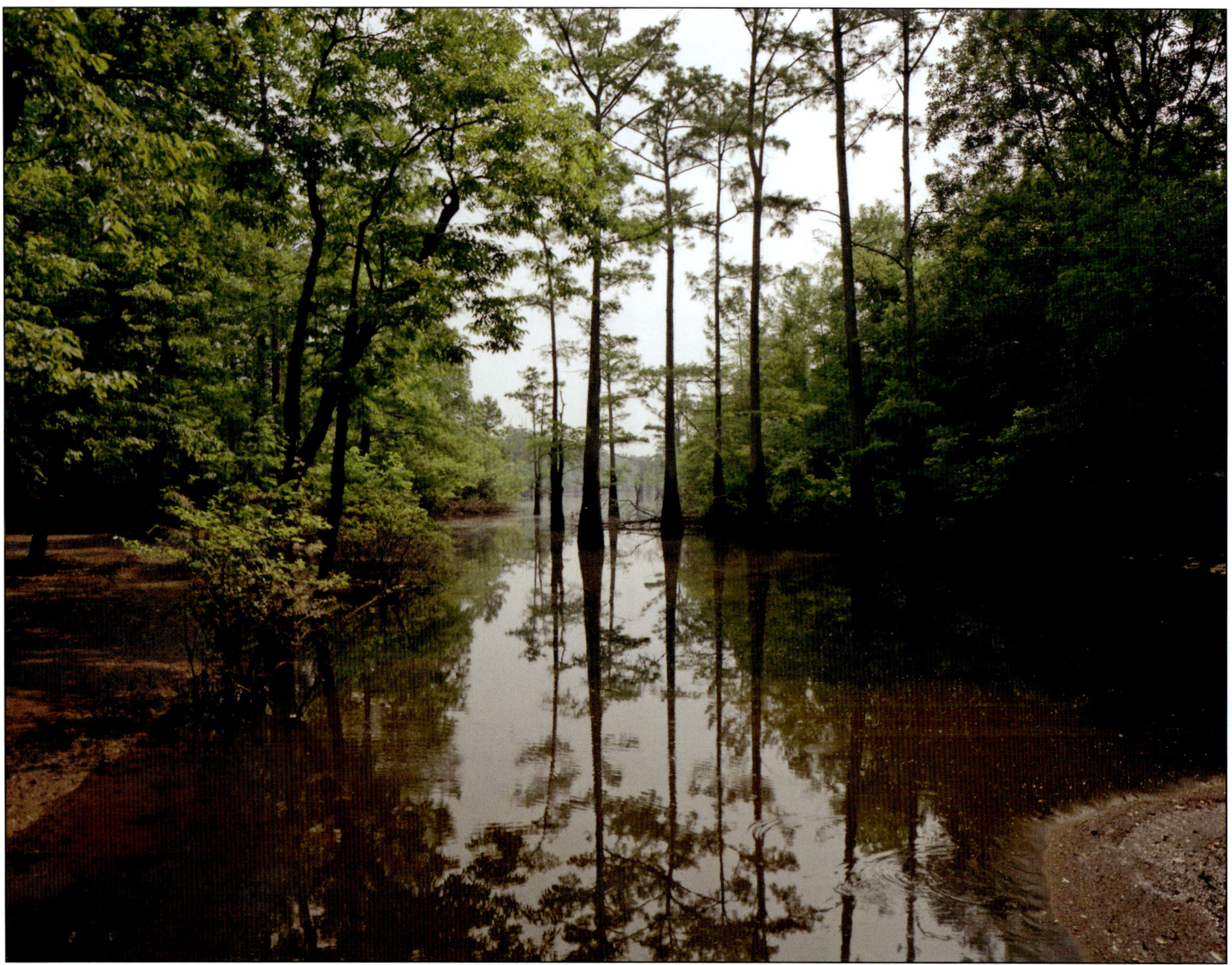

White River National Wildlife Refuge: Frazier Lake

Arkansas County, Arkansas

The White Basin is home to the largest population of black bears in the alluvial valley. American Indians found the bear useful and spiritual. They hunted it in winter by burning it out of its tree and killing it. They wasted none of it. They ate its meat, wore its skin, adorned themselves with its teeth and claws, and made mosquito repellant by mixing its oil with sassafras. Americans hunted the bear, ate its meat, and shipped skins and oil to New Orleans. And they cleared its forests. The bear lost habitat; the bear lost population. By 1928 no more than two dozen survived in the basin. The State of Arkansas prohibited hunting bear in 1927.

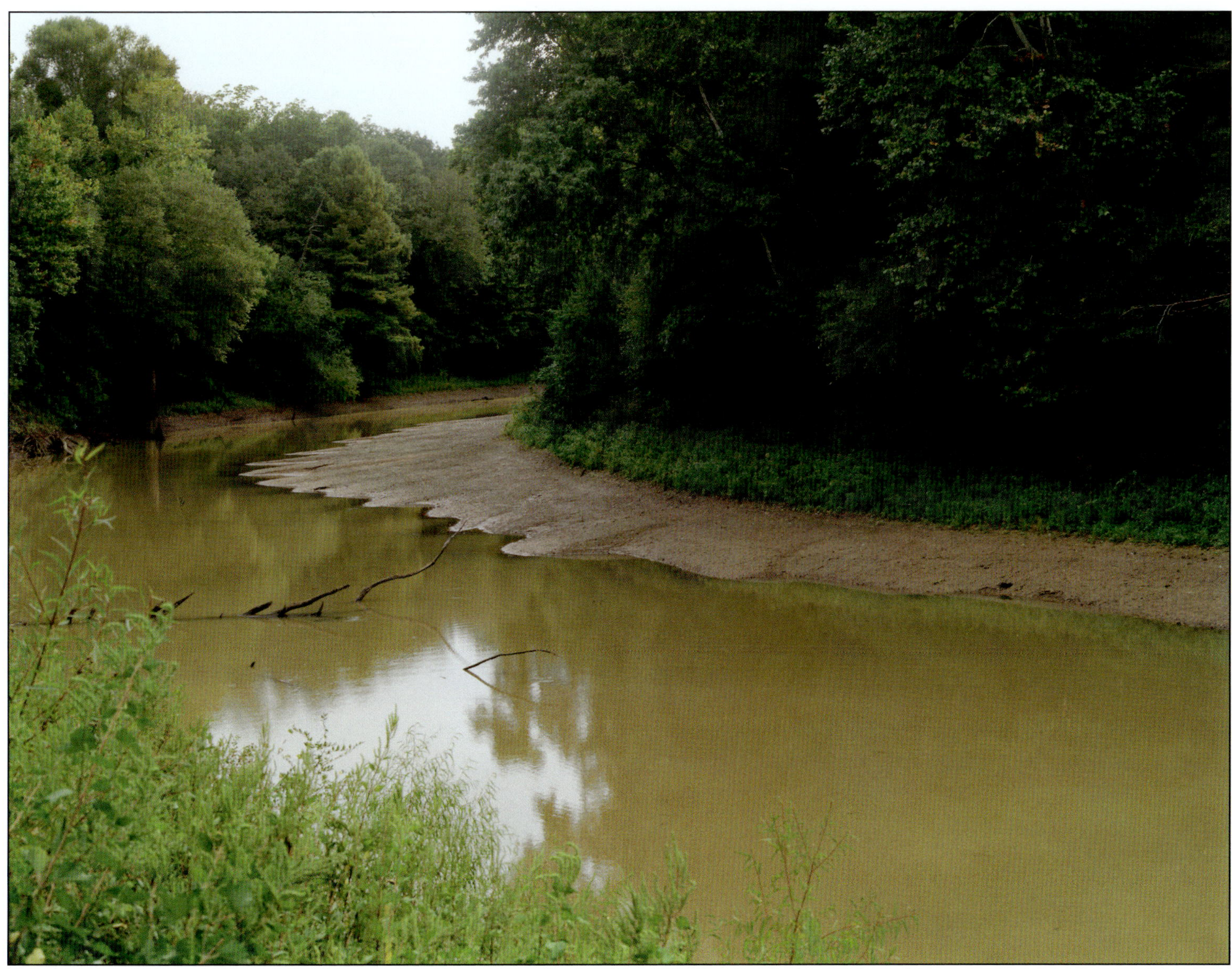

White River National Wildlife Refuge: Big Island Chute

Arkansas County, Arkansas

Big Island Chute breaks away from the White a little south of St. Charles. Before rejoining the White, it breaks up into a swirl of interconnected bayous, which pick up the streams that drain the southern end of Grand Prairie and carry them to the White River. In midsummer, when there is enough water to float a boat in Big Island Chute, the fishing for Kentucky bass is superb. But, the White runs low in midsummer, and Big Island Chute runs lower. Should the Corps of Engineers deepen the White River navigation channel from eight to nine feet, Big Island Chute could be reduced to a series of puddles in midsummer, not good for bass fishing.

Conclusion: Western Lowlands

Finally, no one really knows what will happen to the Cache River and White River Refuges if rice farmers are allowed to draw down the White River one foot during the summer months or if the Memphis District is allowed to scour a nine-foot navigation channel through the two refuges or both. We do know the trickle of water being released from the reservoirs on the upper White has flattened the cycle of flood and drought on the lower White, allowing water into the bottomland forests in the summer when they should be drying out. We will not know the effect of the various Corps projects on the White River and its refuges until we have measured all the demands on the river—navigation, flood control, water supply for agriculture, feedlot runoff, hydropower, drinking water, wildlife, ecosystem restoration and protection, and aquifer protection—with a comprehensive study that integrates all the proposals for the uses of the White River. Then, it might be possible to evaluate the hydrological effects of the Grand Prairie Demonstration and White River Navigation Projects on the wildlife refuges, the bottomland forests, and the underlying alluvial aquifer. Congress authorized 75 percent of the funding for the Water River Basin Comprehensive Study in the Water Resources Development Act of 2007.

The Eastern Lowlands

In establishing the boundary line between Missouri and Arkansas it was first intended to run it all along the parallel of 36 degrees 30 minutes to the Mississippi River, but the early settlers of the peninsula, i.e. the bootheel, strongly opposed the political separation from Missouri on the very good reason that they were entirely cut off from the state of Arkansas by impassable swamps while a few ridges with wagon roads connected them with Missouri. For eight months of the year about one-half of the peninsula is under water and the dry land is cut up into a number islands of all sizes, separated by a network of sloughs and cross-sloughs. The main sloughs run north and south and carry not only the precipitations of the region, but they are also fed by the highwaters of the Mississippi in the east, the Francis in the west, and the Little River in the centre. With the exception of a few narrow ridges, called prairies, running north and south between these, the whole territory is still covered with the original forest, and the comparatively small clearings and deadenings, made for farming purposes on the higher levels of the islands, have not yet changed the woodland character of the region. Even the rivers and sloughs are not free from trees, except in the so-called openings or lakes. Leaving only a narrow channel, there are scattered through the water magnificent cypresses, picturesque tupelos, clusters of waterelms, elbowwood covered with buckvine, flanked by acres upon acres of flags, which in turn are bordered by wide belts of smartweed, patches of lotus, and other aquatic plants. Adjoining the slough, the true home of the cypress and tupelo, is the land of the sweet gum, a tree of formidable size, often over a hundred feet high, with sour gum, hackberry, sycamore, gigantic willows, swamp chestnut oak (cow oak), ash soft maple, sassafras, mulberry, box elder, holly, and as undergrowth, waterbeech, dogwood, redbud, and a variety of small trees and shrubs, as well as climbers, among which we notice with delight the beautiful crossvine and wistaria.

—Otto Widmann, 1895

Excepting the presence of cane-brakes in its southern portion, the Peninsula does not differ essentially from the rest of the alluvial southeast in any of its physical features, but, having escaped the so-called civilization longest, retained the primeval conditions longest, and only since the railroads began to penetrate the region ten years ago is it slowly but surely changing its former peculiarly wild and interesting character into one of devastation and desolation. Not only that the best timber is being removed, but hundreds of thousands of giant trees are girdled in the expectation of making the sandy soil agriculturally available. Levee-building and ditching is going on along the Mississippi River; lakes have been drained and much land has been protected from highwater in the Mississippi; the whole region is in a state of transformation; lumbering and the saw mills have attracted a population whose chief diversion is found in fishing and hunting, in devastating and destroying; surely the Peninsula will soon cease to be the paradise of the naturalist and hunter. Ducks, of which 150,000 were killed in a single winter (1893–94) on the Big Lake and shipped from Hornersville, still visit the region in large numbers, but the resident game birds, such as the Turkey, and summer residents like the Wood Duck, and Hooded Merganser are decreasing rapidly and will, like the Ivory-bill, the Snakebird, the Canada Goose, several kinds of ducks and herons, the Bald Eagle and Osprey, in fact like most birds of larger size, disappear and become as far as the breeding in that part of the Mississippi is concerned, exterminated.

—Otto Widmann, 1907

Locals call it "Swampeast," though the swamp is long gone. Otto Widmann came to the Great Swamp of the Missouri Bootheel, or peninsula, as he called it, in the nick of time, just before loggers cleared its forest, and farmers drained it for row crops. In a series of articles in the *Auk*, a quarterly journal of ornithology, Widmann set the birds that drew him to the Great Swamp in their habitat, the swampy landscape of the Eastern Lowlands. He returned to it repeatedly, always in search of a warbler, or a thrush, or a surprise: "a Yellow-billed Cuckoo alighting on his mate's shoulders and reaching over in an embrace to feed her a willow fly." He noted the changes to the landscape as loggers stripped the swamp of its oak and cypress, took the most valuable parts of each tree, and left the rest to rot where they fell. He watched as the St. Francis Valley and the Little River Drainage Districts drained the denuded land for agriculture. He viewed in horror market hunters killing off his beloved birds. In 1907 he noted in *A Preliminary Catalog of the Birds in Missouri,* "With drainage, deforestation, and settlement of swampy regions the Anhinga is fast receding southward." Ten years earlier it had been a common visitor to Dunklin and Pemiscot Counties. By 1907 it could only be found in a few secluded spots.

The St. Francis River drops out of the uplands into the Mississippi Embayment, crosses the Western Lowlands, cuts through Crowley's Ridge at Chalk Bluff, and enters the Eastern Lowlands, the St. Francis Basin, which extends south from Cairo, Illinois, to Helena, Arkansas. Crowley's Ridge borders it on the west, the Mississippi on the east. The relics of braided channels direct its course in the northern two-thirds of its basin. In the southern third, the St. Francis begins to meander and reaches its confluence with the Mississippi. Sikeston Ridge, a long sliver of the Wisconsinan valley train, rises twenty to twenty-five feet above its surrounding lowlands.

In 1941 the Corps of Engineers completed the Wappapello Dam, set in the gap through which the St. Francis spills from the uplands. Behind it, Lake Wappapello retains floodwater in the event of flooding along the St. Francis or Mississippi. The Corps holds or releases water from the lake: more in the winter to keep the remaining swamp wet enough for ducks; less in the summer to keep agricultural fields dry.

In Arkansas, the Corps turned the lower half of the St. Francis Basin into a complex system of channelized floodways and cutoffs to control flooding along the St. Francis and Little Rivers. At Marked Tree the St. Francis Bay and Oak Donnick Floodway sidestepped the river and ran straight across the landscape.

The Corps reserved 532,000 acres in the lower basin for the storage of Mississippi floodwaters. In 1977 the Corps installed a pump in the levee. When the Mississippi is flowing below flood stage, the gates of the pump stay open and the St. Francis flows to its confluence with the Mississippi. When the Mississippi floods, the Corps closes the gates to keep the Mississippi from backing up into the basin. Should the St. Francis and other streams in the basin pond against the gates, the pump goes to work and dries out the basin.

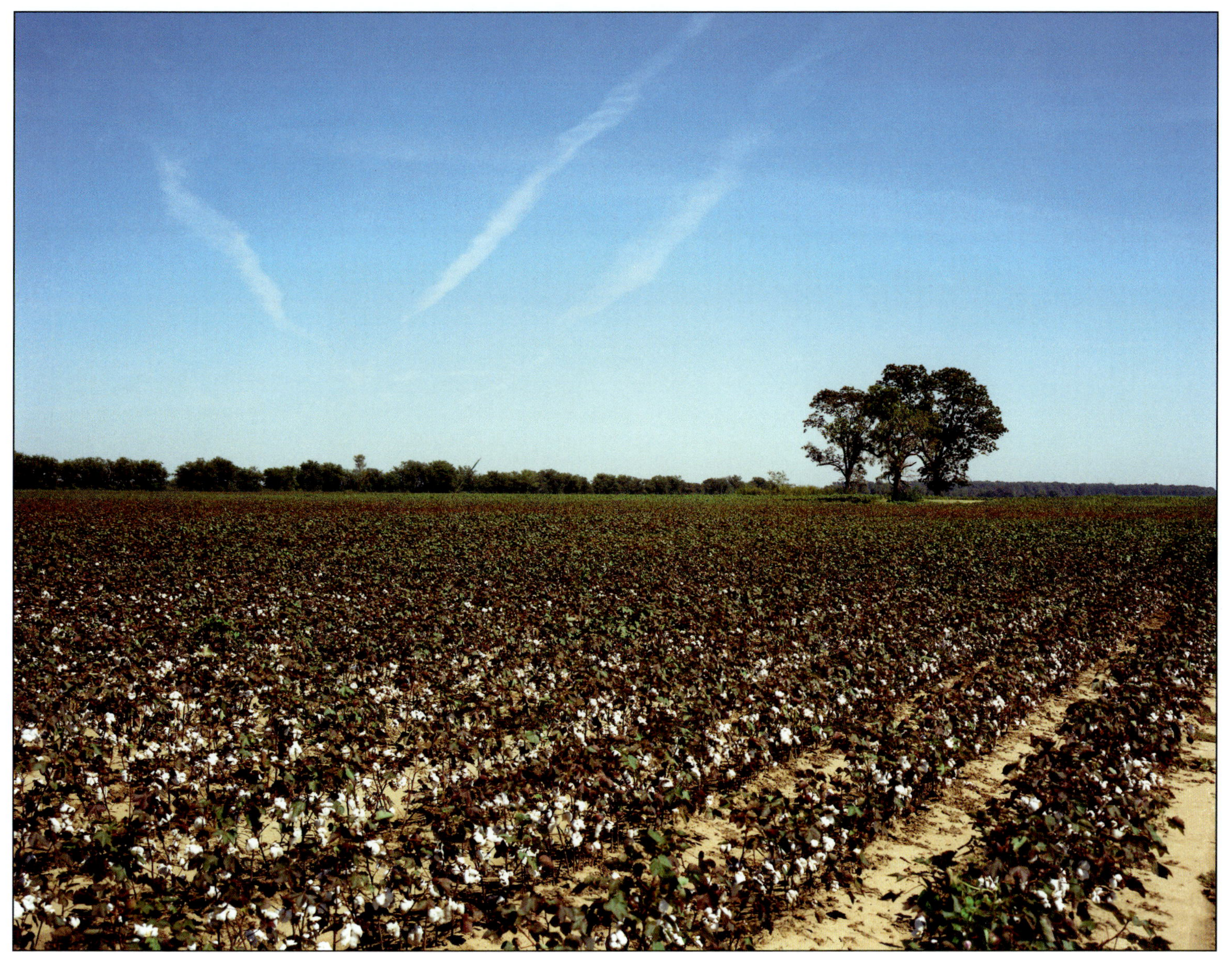

Sikeston Ridge: Cotton Field

Scott County, Missouri

American settlers found a sand prairie rising ten feet or more above the surrounding swamp. Warm-season grasses like switch grass, drought-tolerant plants like prickly pear cactus, and stubby trees like blackjack and post oaks thrived. Illinois chorus and eastern spadefoot frogs, which lived mostly underground, emerged to breed in ephemeral ponds, where their eggs would hatch and tadpoles mature before the ponds dried out. Above ground, racerunner lizards zipped through the grasses. Grassland songbirds like Savannah Sparrows fed on seeds and bugs. When settlers finished clearing land and planting crops, 1 percent of the prairie remained untilled.

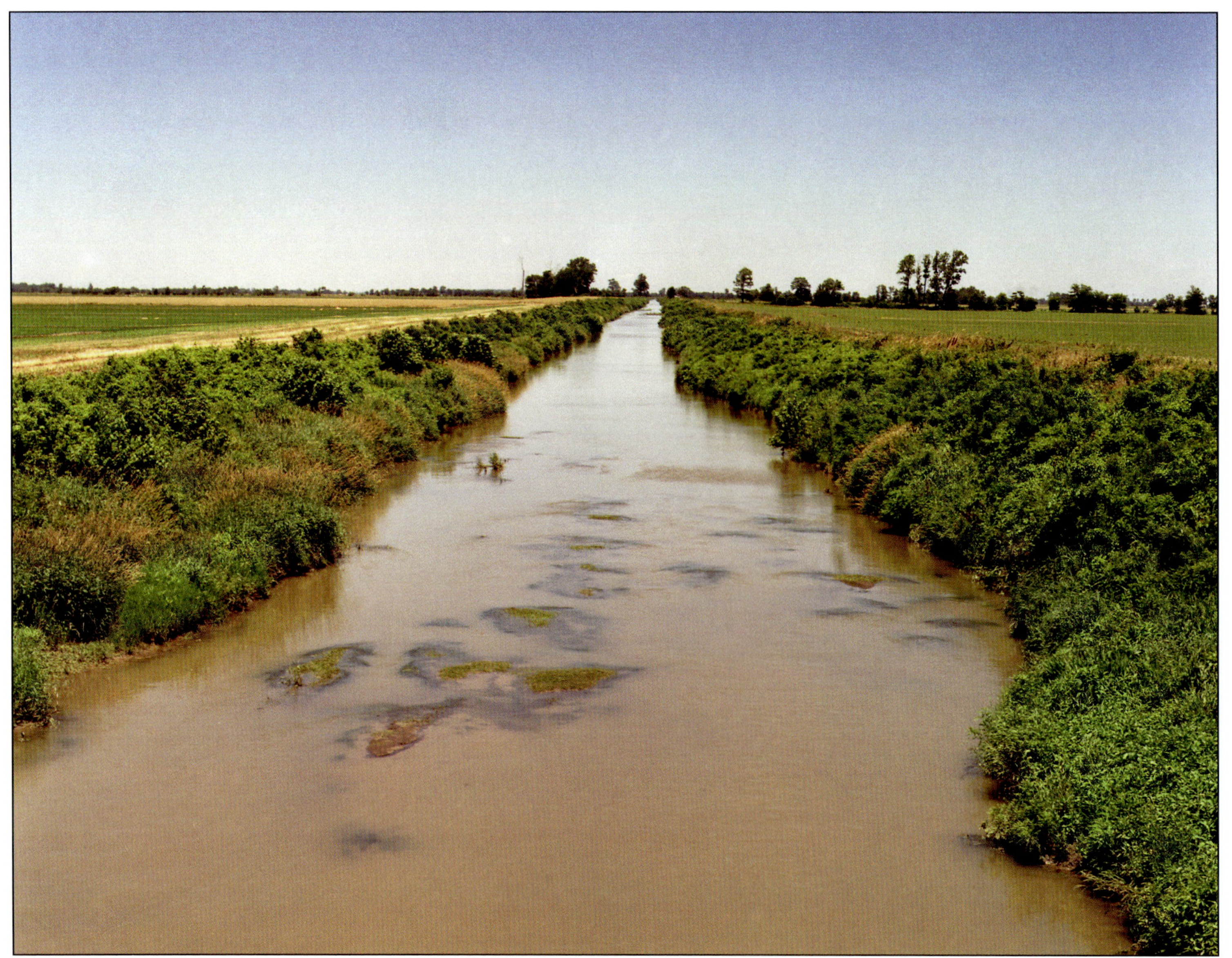

Little River Drainage Canal
Stoddard County, Missouri
Scott County, Missouri

Loggers stripped the Great Swamp of its hardwoods by 1900. Seven years later the Little River Drainage District organized to rob the swamp of its water. It levied a tax of twenty-five cents an acre to implement its drainage plan, completed in 1909. A headwater diversion channel captured the streams that flowed over 1,207 square miles of Ozark hills before they reached the bottomland and carried them thirty-four miles to the Mississippi. Canals drained the 1,710 square miles of bottomland through 849.6 miles of parallel ditches, spaced every mile across the landscape. The district diverted bottomland portions of the streams to the ditches.

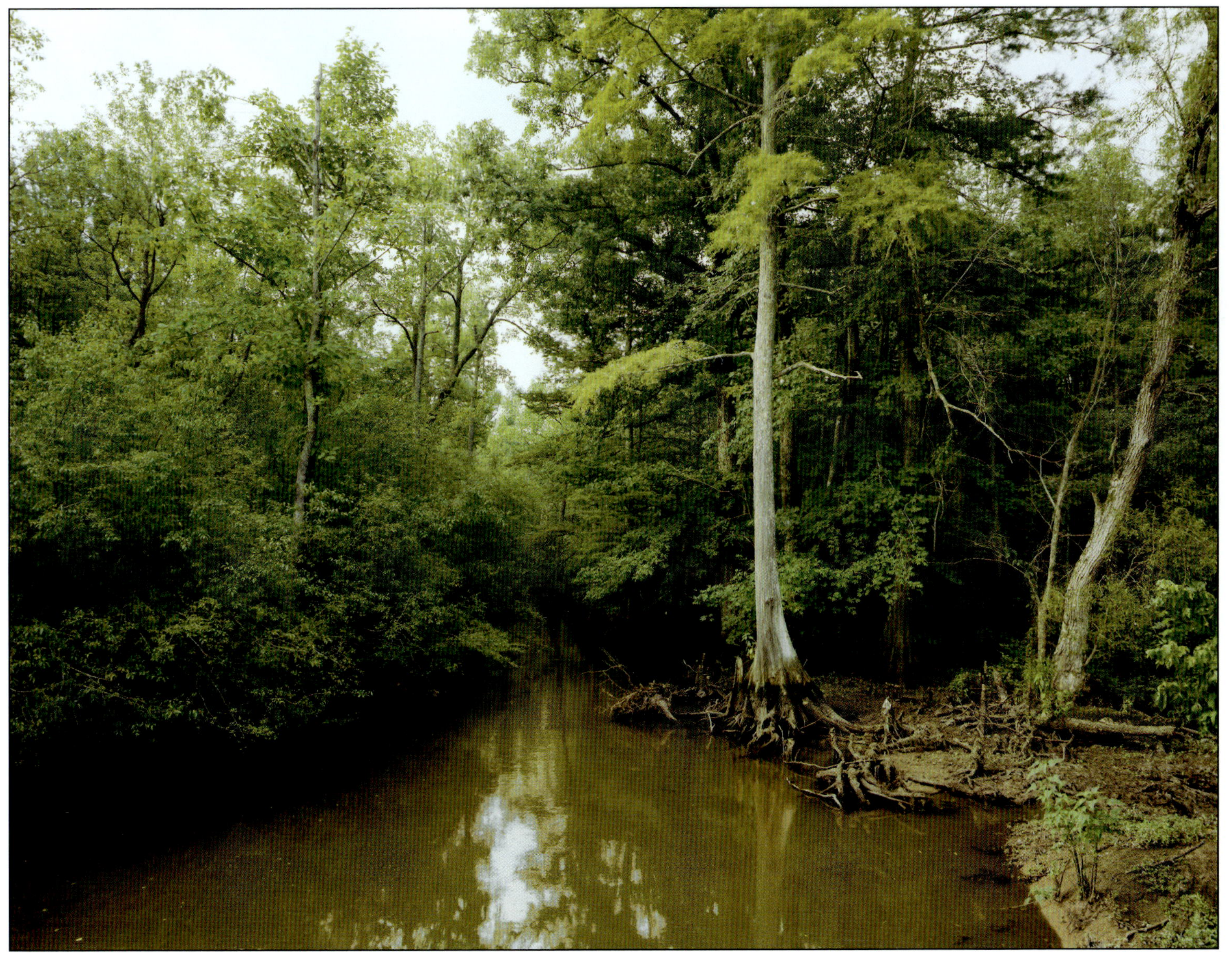

St. Francis River: Sunken Lands

Poinsett County, Arkansas

On December 16, 1811, the first tremors of the 1811–1812 earthquakes struck the St. Francis Basin in Arkansas, 65 miles southwest of New Madrid, Missouri. Church bells rang in Boston. The lands for 120 miles along the St. Francis River subsided six to eight feet and ponded against an uplift downstream. Water filled the depressions, creating the Sunken Lands in which cypress took root. Big Lake formed in similar fashion when Little River subsided. The earth around New Madrid continued to tremble until March 1812, devastating a region that extended from Crowley's Ridge across the St. Francis Basin to Memphis and north to Cairo, Illinois.

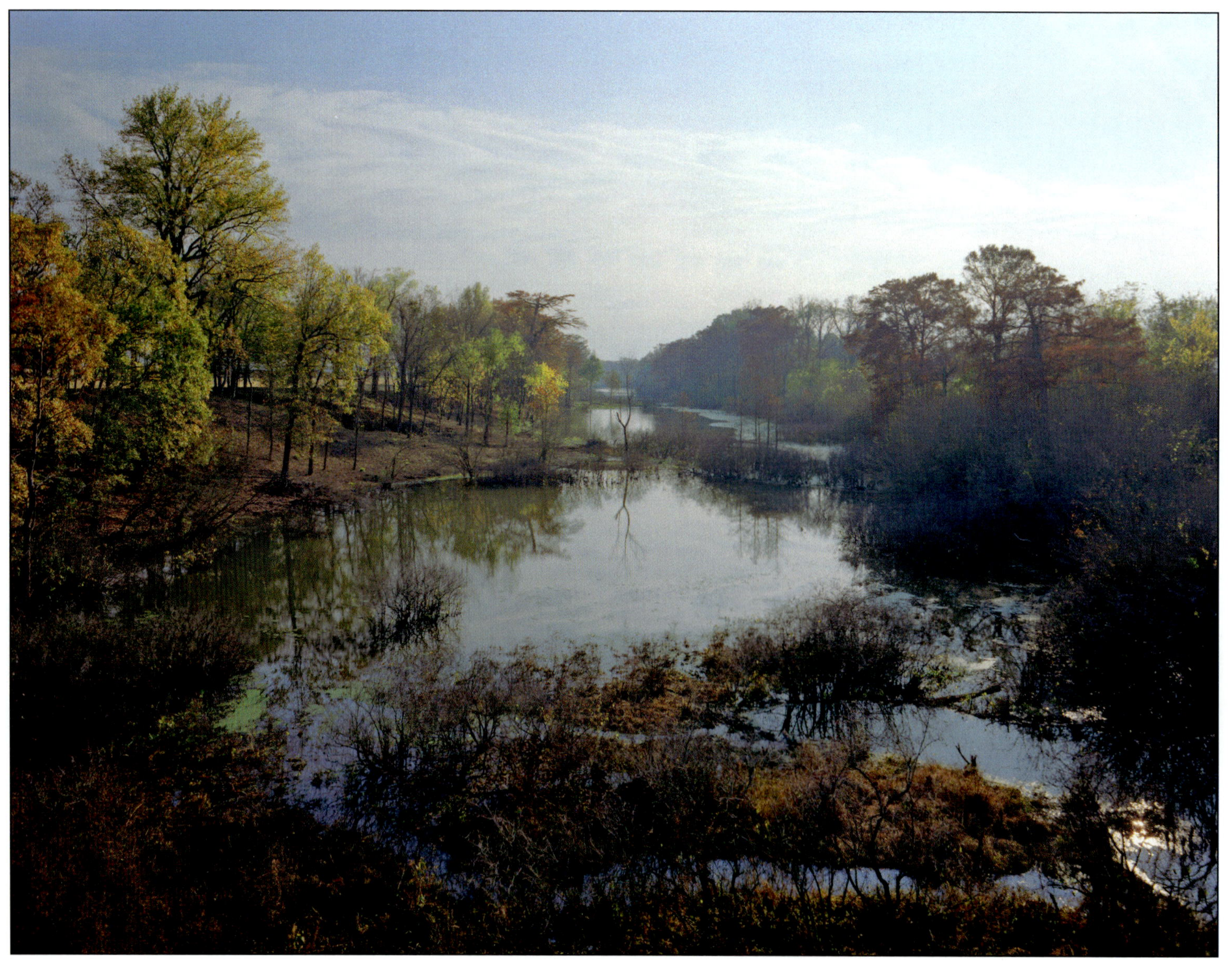

Alligator Bayou: Raggio
Lee County, Arkansas

The alligators that once swam in Alligator Bayou have disappeared, as they did from most of Arkansas. They lost habitat to farmers and government agencies determined to drain land for crops. In the 1920s the leather industry turned their skins into shoes, wallets, belts, handbags, and luggage. The reptiles vanished from the southern wetlands. States began to protect those remaining in the '40s; in 1967 alligators were declared endangered. Within twenty years the alligator returned to its range. Beginning in 1972, Arkansas released 2,800 young Louisiana alligators into its southern wetlands, where the population grew, stabilized, and scattered across the state.

The Yazoo Basin

> The Yazoo Basin presents many advantages for reclamation over the other districts now needing protection from the floods of the Mississippi, on account of the natural drainage afforded by the various streams that flow toward the Yazoo River. Their banks are generally above overflow, while their slope is sufficient to carry off the rain-fall.
>
> —Maj. W. H. H. Benyaurd, United States Engineers, *Report of the Chief of Engineers*, 1875

The Yazoo Basin is the largest in the Mississippi alluvial valley. It extends from Memphis to Vicksburg, reaches from the eastern valley wall to the Mississippi, and encompasses 7,600 square miles. The floodplain slopes about a half foot per mile. All the major streams in the region—the Coldwater, the Tallahatchie, the Yazoo, and the Big Sunflower—have carried the Mississippi in the last ten thousand years. The early streams filled depressions in the valley train and spread mud across the landscape. Then, five thousand years ago, the Mississippi started to meander, first in simple, divided belts, and then in single complex belts. The basin drains along the sluggish major streams and their even more sluggish tributaries.

The Yazoo River flows out of the eastern uplands, along with the Coldwater, Yocona, Little Tallahatchie, and Yalobusha Rivers, and along Cassidy Bayou and other small streams in the bottomlands. The Big Sunflower, Steele Bayou, Deer Creek, and Bogue Phalia all rise in the bottomlands and flow to the lower Yazoo, which carries them to the Mississippi. Under it all in the coarse sands and gravel of glacial outwash lies the Mississippi alluvial aquifer, huge and as heavily used in the Yazoo Basin as it is in the White River Basin. Converting the landscape from bottomland hardwoods to row crops and altering the streams for flood control completely changed the way water flowed through the basin.

With the levees in place along the Mississippi, a five-year flood along the tributaries would inundate 39 percent of the delta, mostly along the upper and lower portions of the Yazoo River and its tributaries, which run along the eastern valley wall. The ridge of the Wisconsinan valley train that rises above the center of the basin and natural levees of the ancient channels would protect most of the rest of the floodplain from flooding along the Yazoo.

While the mainline levees are absolutely necessary to human habitation and agriculture in the Yazoo Basin, levees for flood control along the tributaries in the basin are not. Nonetheless, their construction made it possible to clear, drain, and farm additional bottomland hardwood wetlands in the basin. Without the levees, 1.7 million acres of the basin would still exist as floodplain forest. The Yazoo Headwater Project, the Yazoo Backwater Project, and the Big Sunflower Flood Control Project, all features of the Mississippi River and Tributaries Project, have made it possible to convert one million acres of forested wetlands in the Yazoo Basin to farmland. Of the sixteen million acres of bottomland hardwood forests that have been cleared in the Mississippi Delta, 95 percent have been cleared for agriculture. Of those, two to three million acres produced marginal farmland and should have remained in hardwood to serve the forest products industry.

The forests that have disappeared from the Lower Mississippi Valley were as productive and as diverse as any ecosystem in North America. Water flooded into and withdrew from them, importing, storing, cycling, and exporting nutrients. Different trees took root in different parts of the floodplain. Willow followed by cottonwood anchored the natural levee closest to a stream. Behind them, on the back slope of the levee, grew sweet gum and water oak. Sugarberry and overcup oak grew on the poorly drained flats and backwater basins. Low, poorly drained swales hosted cypress and tupelo. Elm, ash, hackberry, Nuttall oak, sweet gum, and willow oak anchored the adjacent ridges. That complexity disappeared as loggers stripped the forest from the Yazoo Basin, and with the forest they took evidence of what trees grew best where in the landscape, leaving twentieth-century foresters dependent on nineteenth-century surveyors' notes to learn how best to restore the forests to land that was too wet too often for agriculture.

Since the initiation of the Mississippi River and Tributaries Project in 1928, Congress has continually added to it. By 2002, with the project 87 percent complete, the Corps of Engineers had constructed 389 drainage structures, 59 pumping stations, 3,731 miles of flood-control channels, 3,466 miles of levees in the Lower Mississippi Valley, and forty-four flood-control reservoirs in the uplands. Much of the work was done in the Yazoo Basin, where the Corps constructed four flood-control reservoirs on the headwaters of the Yazoo in the uplands; dredged bottomland streams for flood control—including the Big Sunflower and Quiver Rivers; leveed sections of the Coldwater, Tallahatchie, and Yazoo Rivers; built the Whittington Auxiliary Channel to lower flood stages on the Yazoo between Belzoni and Yazoo City, Mississippi; wrapped the Mississippi mainline levee around the Yazoo Backwater Area, and set the Steele Bayou Drainage Structure in the levee to release the resulting interior flooding from backwater streams that ponded against the levee. All this intensive work to reduce flooding left what remained of the forest dependent on rainfall and runoff instead of flooding.

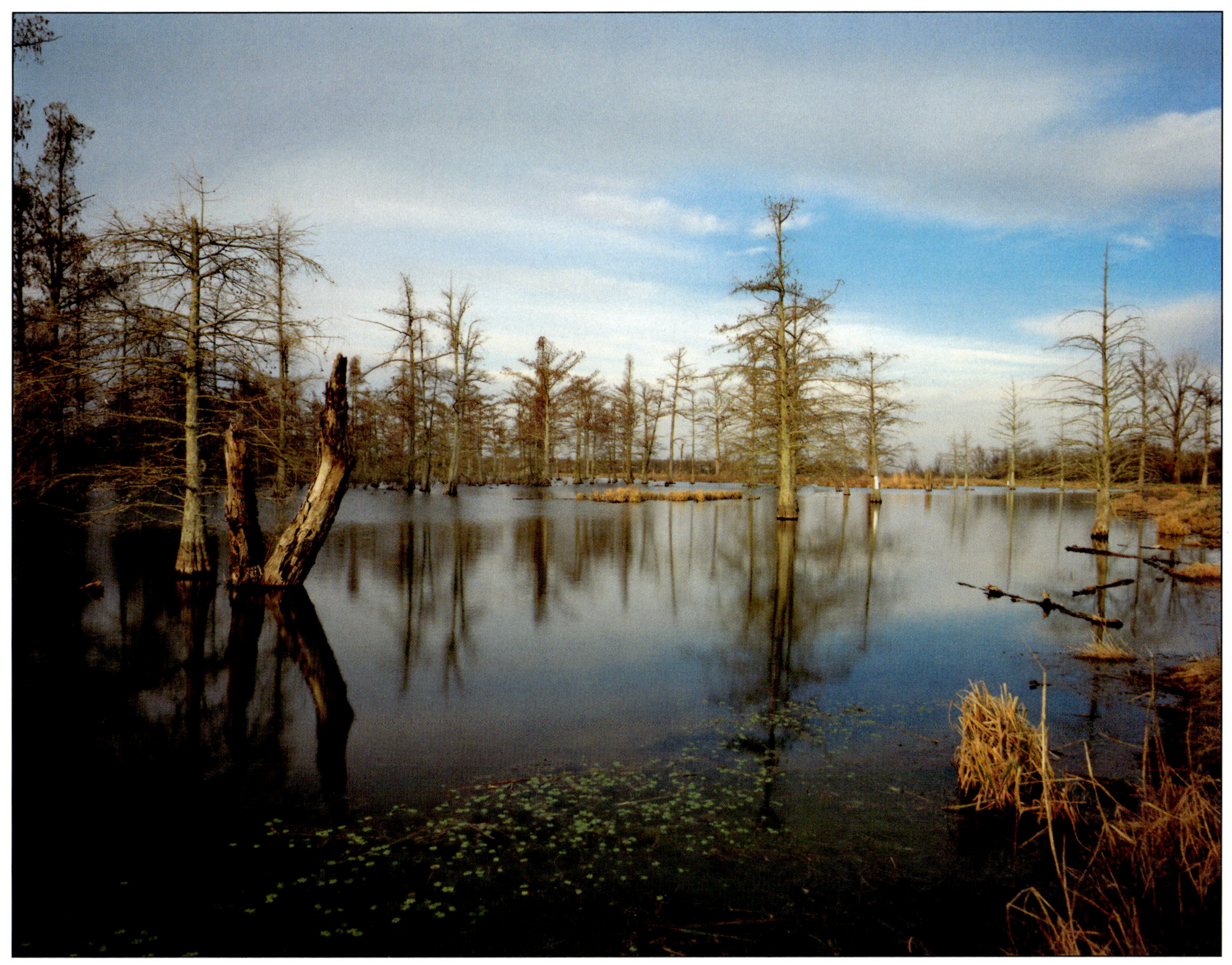

Yazoo Headwaters: Hopson Bayou, Tributary to Cassidy Bayou

Coahoma County, Mississippi

In 1939 the Corps channelized Cassidy Bayou and its tributaries for flood control. By 1999, silt covered their sand-and-gravel beds, where willow and cypress grew. The Corps prepared to dredge selected reaches. The process could disrupt mussel habitat; hence, the Corps needed to find which mussels lived where. Researchers waded the bayous, feeling around the shallows for mussels. They found none in Hopson Bayou, but 983 in Cassidy, and concluded that dredging would destroy habitat for mussels. By narrowing and deepening the bayous, they could increase the current for flood control and maintain habitat for mussels.

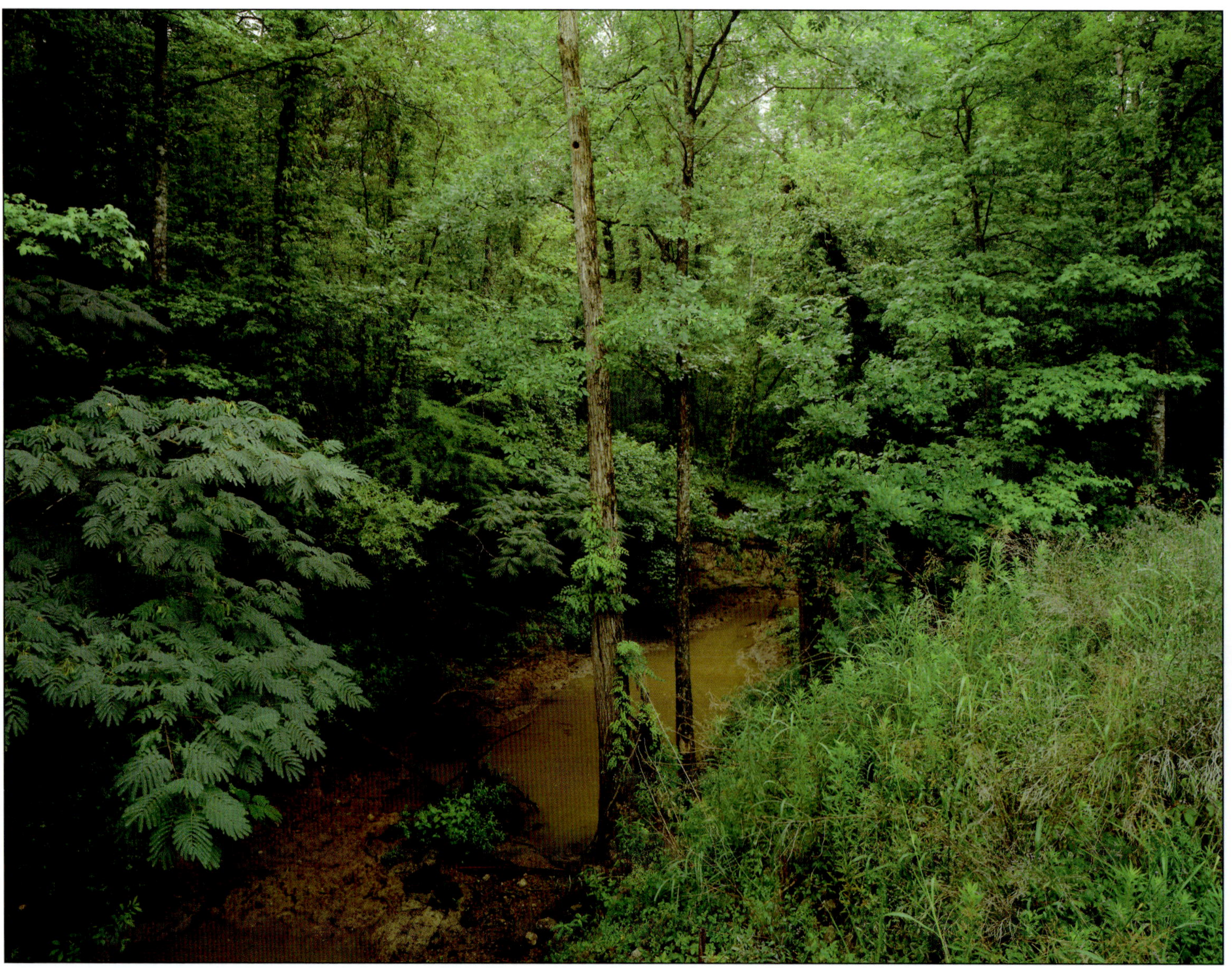

Hillside National Wildlife Refuge: Blissdale Swamp

Yazoo County, Mississippi

In 1975 the Corps of Engineers transferred the Hillside Floodway Project, 15,572 acres, to the USFWS for the Hillside NWR. The project was a sump, designed to catch sediment flowing out from the hills and hold it behind a levee that forms the west boundary of the refuge. As the sump filled, it displaced water with silt and killed many of the bottomland hardwoods. Fish lost habitat; willow and cottonwood replaced hardwoods in the accumulated silt. Even so, an array of herons—Great Blues, Little Blues, Great Egrets, Snowy Egrets, Cattle Egrets, Black-crowned Night Herons, and Tricolored Herons—nest in rookeries, high over deepwater habitat.

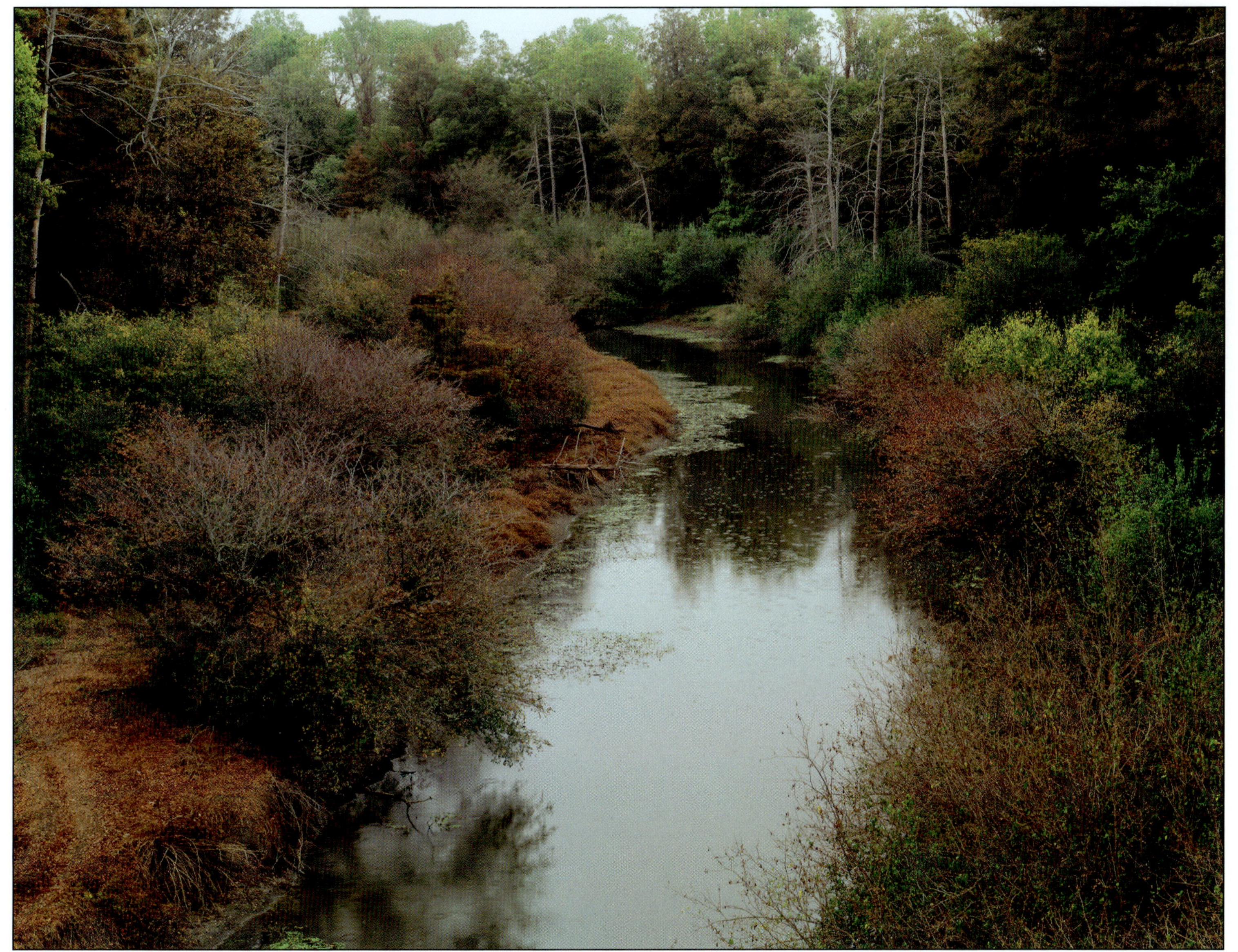

Big Sunflower River: Clarksdale
Bolivar County, Mississippi

The Big Sunflower rises in a series of intermittent streams south of Friar's Point, Mississippi. Its head-water streams flow out of Moon Lake. Increased demands for irrigation led to declines in groundwater levels in the twenty years before 2000 and left the Big Sunflower flowing 80 to 90 percent below its historical low-flow rate. A river that flowed at the rate of 150 cubic feet per second in the 1970s was flowing at 15 cubic feet per second in the 1990s. To boost the amount of water in the Big Sunflower, the NRCS proposed storing water in Moon Lake to be released to the Big Sunflower at low flow, or pumping the Mississippi to the Big Sunflower.

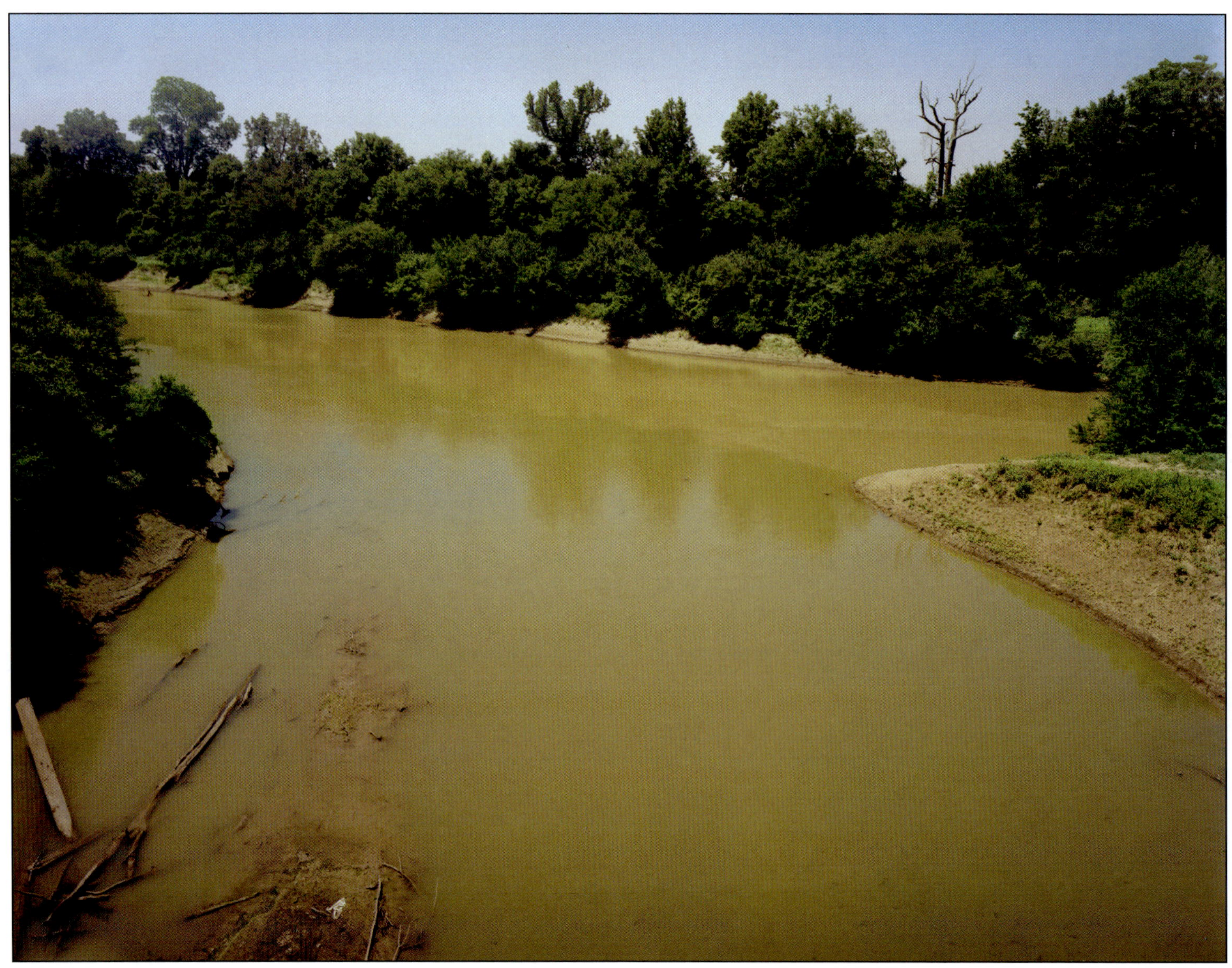

The Big Sunflower at Its Confluence with the Quiver

Sunflower County, Mississippi

Although the Corps finished clearing and snagging the river and its tributaries in 1964, the Big Sunflower remained the one system in the alluvial valley unaltered by flood control. A mussel colony, "believed to be the densest concentration of life on the planet," continued to thrive on its muddy bottom. By 1989 the work needed to be done again. The Corps began to dredge 104.8 miles in 1999, threatening the colony. The Corps removed reaches of the river with the greatest concentration of mussels from the dredging plan and restricted dredging to the center third of the channel in order to leave shallow waters along the banks and their mussels undisturbed.

Deforestation and Reforestation

> Most of this farmland targeted for relief was cleared for soybean production. I witnessed huge Cat dozers clearing dense hardwood forests, much as you and I mow our lawn. It was such a rush, most didn't even harvest the timber, just piled it and burned it.
>
> Turned out to be devastating for the landowners as most not only lost thru farming operations, but many also lost their land.
>
> —FairChase, Mississippi Wildlife Forum, July 22, 2005

In the mid-twentieth century, the price of soybeans shot up, an incentive to landowners who owned forests along low-lying rivers to bulldoze their trees and plant soybeans and only soybeans because spring floods receded from their fields too late for cotton or rice. The price of soybeans fell. Farmers found themselves sitting on land that flooded often and stayed that way up for to six months. In the 1990s landowners, eager to restore their lands to profitability, turned to the possibility of reforesting.

The Yazoo Backwater Area encompasses 926,000 acres in the lower third of the Yazoo Basin, of which 123,000 acres are public lands in national and state wildlife refuges and the Delta National Forest. Private landowners hold 184,000 acres of forested land and 100,000 acres of marginal farmland in the area. At the beginning of the twenty-first century private landowners were engaging in a major effort to reforest these marginal lands, enrolling 36,800 acres in the Wetlands Reserve Program (WRP) and 23,500 acres into the Conservation Reserve Program (CRP).

In 1987, USFWS began reforesting agricultural lands on its refuges and private lands adjoining its refuges. By the end of 1998 the USFWS planned to plant an additional 30,000 acres in the Lower Mississippi alluvial valley. By 2002 the service had reforested over 21,000 acres in its wildlife refuges in Mississippi.

By 1997 the Corps had reforested 6,500 acres along the Yazoo River to mitigate the destruction of fish and wildlife habitat by the Sartartia Area Backwater Levee Projects, completed in 1987. The agency needed to reforest an additional 24,700 acres by 2000 to meet its legal requirements to replace wetlands lost to flood-control projects. The Corps fulfilled part of that obligation when it restored frequently flooded land along Lake George in Mississippi.

Tied to reforestation was the issue of declining populations of neotropical song birds that winter in Central and South America and breed in North America. In the early 1990s resource managers in the Roosevelt NWR Complex turned their attention to the decline. A group of federal, state, and local government agencies, philanthropic foundations, professional organizations, conservation groups, industries, the academic community, and private individuals created Partners in Flight, combining their efforts to address the problem. The group divided the North American continent into regions and wrote conservation plans for the birds that breed in each. In October 2005 the Roosevelt Complex adopted the Partners in Flight conservation plan for the Mississippi alluvial valley as its own.

The plan provided nesting places for birds that breed in the various habitats in the floodplain. Swainson's Warbler, the Prothonotary Warbler, the Cerulean Warbler, and the Swallow-tailed Kite all breed in the forest's core, at least 1.6 miles from the edge. But the Orchard Oriole, the White-eyed Vireo, the Painted Bunting, and the Mississippi Kite breed in scrub on the forest edge. Grassland birds—LeConte's Sparrow, Henslow's Sparrow, the Field Sparrow, the Grasshopper Sparrow, the Loggerhead Shrike, the Dickcissel, the Short-eared Owl, and the Sedge Wren—all winter in the alluvial valley. Finally, birds that breed in nonforested wetlands—shorebirds, long-legged wading birds, bitterns, and rails—need shallow-water foraging habitat.

Partners in Flight established a goal of maintaining or restoring more than 3,705,000 acres of forest (a sum roughly equal to the remains of a forest that spread across twenty-five million acres in the Lower Valley before European settlement), located in 101 patches of contiguous forest; broken down into thirteen patches of more than 100,000 acres each, thirty-six patches of more than 20,000 acres each, and fifty-two patches of more than 10,000 acres each; and distributed among eighty-seven bird conservation areas.

Within the Roosevelt Complex, each of the refuges had a forest core of at least 10,000 acres for the warblers. With the Panther Swamp NWR linked to the Delta National Forest through the reforested Lake George corridor, it had a forest core of 100,000 acres.

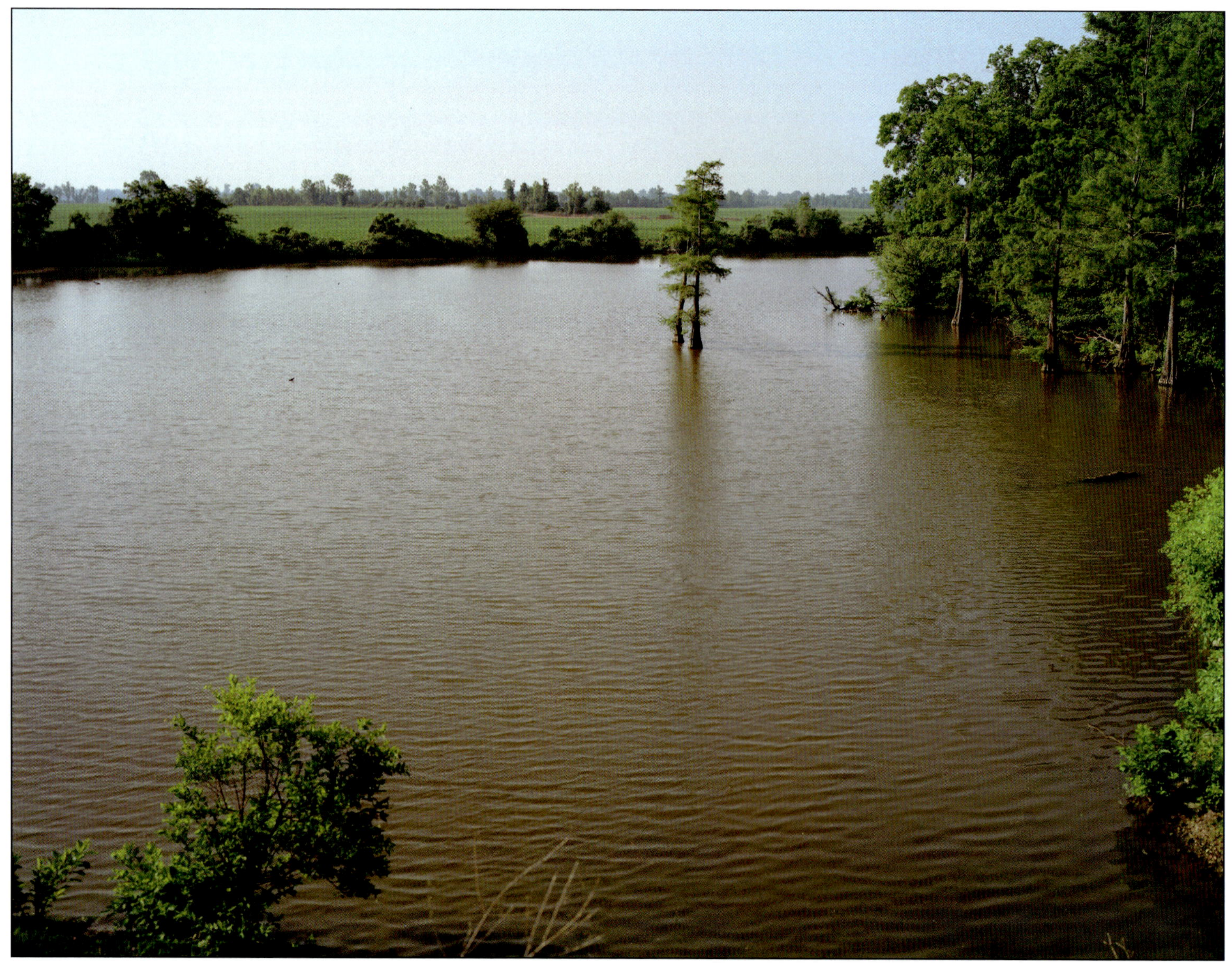

Yazoo Backwater Area: Lake George

Yazoo County, Mississippi

In 1991 the Corps of Engineers, the U.S. Forest Service, and the forestry department of Stephen F. Austin University joined to reforest farmland along Lake George, land the Big Sunflower and the Yazoo flooded regularly. The Lake George Bottomland Hardwood Wildlife and Wetland Restoration Project lies between the Panther Swamp NWR at 38,697 acres and the Delta National Forest at more than 60,000 acres. With the 8,383-acre Lake George project as a forested corridor linking the two, the USFWS reached its goal of establishing 100,000 acres of wildlife habitat in the region of the refuge, possibly enough to provide habitat for the Louisiana black bear as well as the birds.

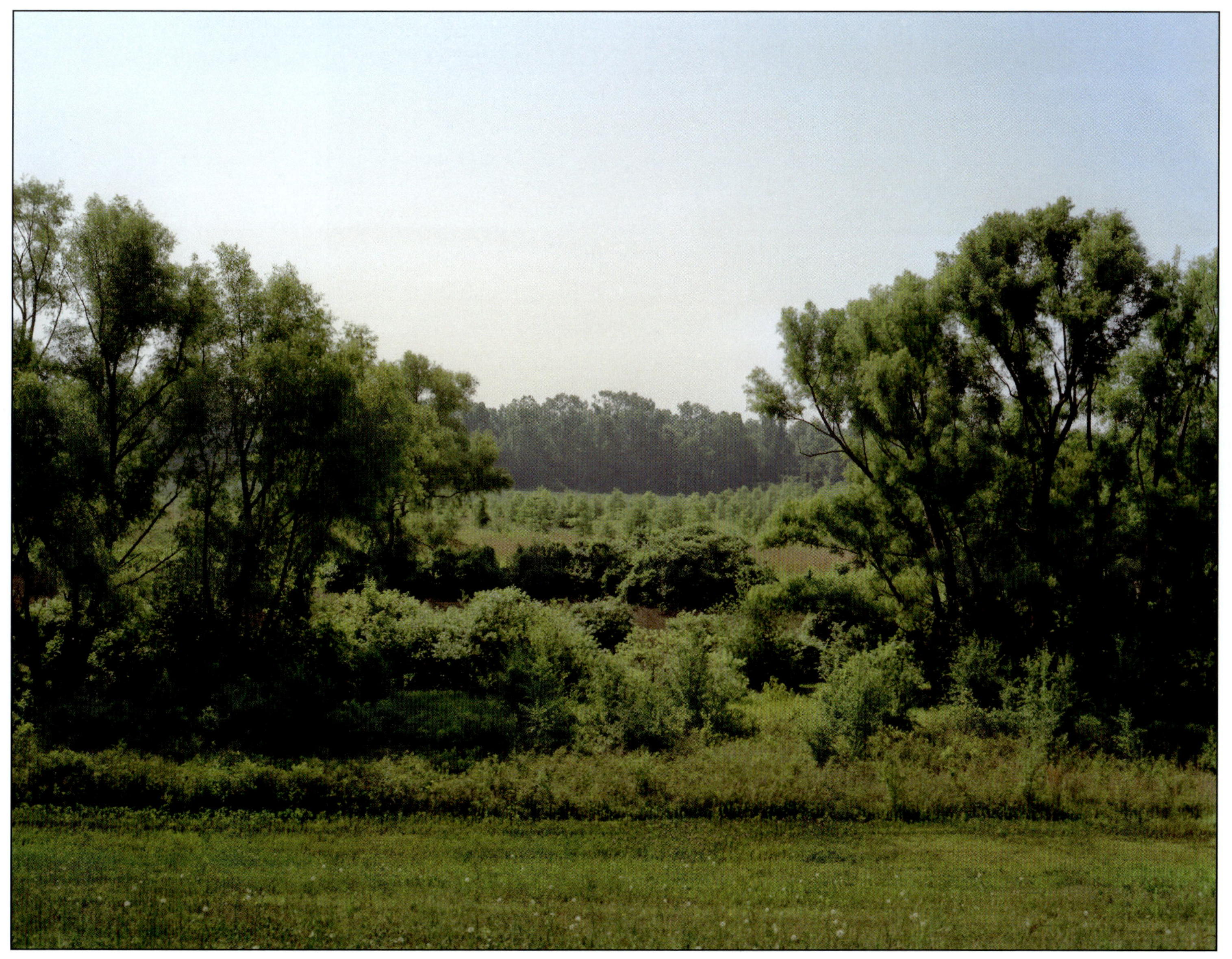

Yazoo Backwater Area: Lake George Reforestation Project

Yazoo County, Mississippi

The collaborators at Lake George studied the soil properties and the planting methods necessary to establish and grow a mixture of common bottomland forest trees: cherrybark, Nuttall's, Shumard, and willow oaks. They planted seedlings according to their ability to tolerate flooding. Nuttall's oak tolerates floods reasonably well; water oak not so well; cherrybark oak not at all. Foresters planted 7,668 acres between 1991 and 1998. To the oaks they added green ash, pecan, sycamore, bald cypress, and water tupelo to bring the total to 8,383 acres. When they measured the forest's progress, they found more than half the young seedlings surviving.

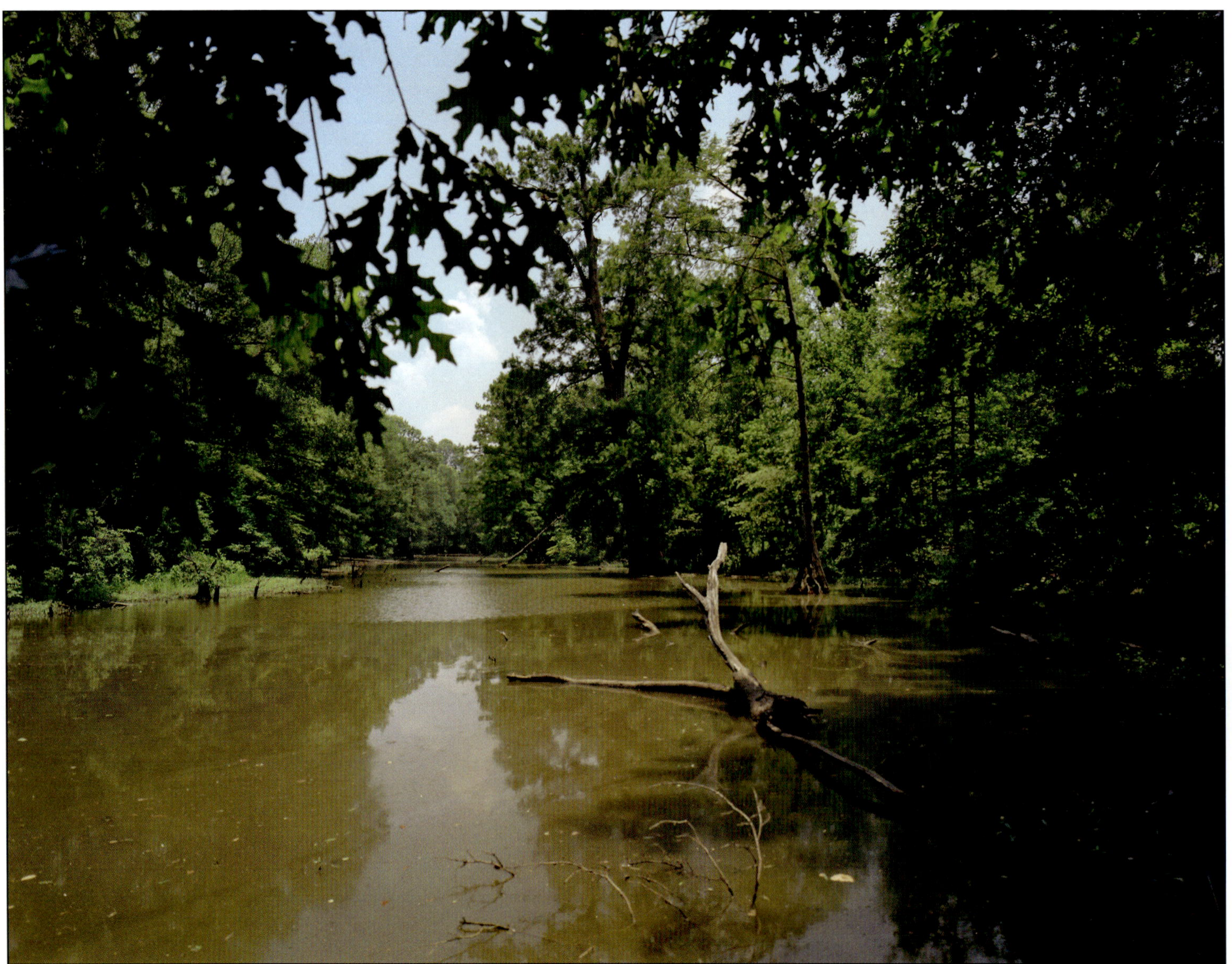

Delta National Forest: Fish Lake

Skarkey County, Mississippi

The Little and Big Sunflower Rivers bracket the Delta National Forest and flood it annually. Beavers built dams. Flooding followed. The year 1994 found 14,000 acres underwater during the growing season. Trees were stunted and 4,000 acres of forest lost. Rangers closed roads and curtailed hunting. Campers pitched tents on muddy sites. Flooding spread to adjacent lands. With help from Ducks Unlimited the Forest Service adopted a beaver-management program to control water on 10,000 acres. Rangers replaced beaver dams with water-control structures, cleared culverts, trapped and killed the beaver, and constructed exclusion devices to keep beaver out.

The Yazoo Backwater Project

When Congress passed the Flood Control Act of 1941, it added the Yazoo Backwater Project to the Mississippi River and Tributaries Project and authorized the Corps of Engineers to extend the Mississippi levee up the west bank of the Yazoo River to protect the Yazoo Backwater Area. When completed, the levee prevented the lower Yazoo and the Mississippi from backing up into the lower third of the Yazoo Basin. However, when streams inside the levee flooded, water pooled behind it. Hence, Congress authorized the installation of floodgates, a drainage structure, in the levee to allow for gravity drainage and of a pump that would be turned on when the Mississippi and Yazoo ran ninety feet above sea level. The levee was built. The drainage structure at the foot of Steele Bayou was built in 1969. A second drainage structure at the foot of the Little Sunflower River was built in 1975. A fifteen-mile-long channel that collected water from the Big and Little Sunflower Rivers, Deer Creek, and Steele Bayou and directed it to the Steele Bayou Drainage Structure was built in 1978. The pump was not.

In 1959 the Corps of Engineers decided that improvements in the ability of the Mississippi to move floods downstream as well as improvements in the Yazoo Backwater Area had rendered the pump unnecessary and cancelled it. However, the pump continued to linger on Corps drafting boards, getting bigger or smaller every time the engineers reexamined it.

In 1982 the Corps reformulated the pump. When Congress added the provision to the 1986 WRDA that beneficiaries of all Corps' projects were required to come up with 25 percent of the cost, the pump's major proponent, the Mississippi Levee Board, lost interest. In 1996, at the behest of Mississippi Senators Trent Lott and Thad Cochran, Congress relieved the levee board of its share of the cost.

The pump would be huge, both in cost, $181 million, and in size, 14,000 cubic feet per second or six million gallons per minute, spewed from the Yazoo backwater into the Yazoo River. Such a pump would be capable of sucking water off the land thirteen times faster than it drains, even in the wettest season, and reducing flood damages to 340,000 acres of farmland. The engineers would switch on the pump only when the water level inside the Steele Bayou Drainage Structure sump reached eighty-seven feet above sea level, three feet lower than the level established by the 1941 act.

Environmentalists, river conservationists, taxpayer watchdogs, the EPA, and the USFWS all objected to the project. It already cost too much, and the price was going up, to $220 million by 2008. The project would drain too many wetlands, even those managed for wildlife habitat in the Delta National Forest, the Panther Swamp National Wildlife Refuge, and the Lake George Reforestation Project. It would undermine the $30 million federal investment that placed 22,500 acres in the WRP and 9,000 acres in the CRP.

The EPA and the USFWS, which, by law, must analyze all Corps of Engineers proposals, urged the Corps to examine the cumulative environmental impact of the Big Sunflower River Channelization Project and the Yazoo Pump, and to turn to nonstructural means of reducing the damage from flooding in the backwater area. They urged the Corps to purchase easements for conservation, for reforestation, and for flooding. In short let the Yazoo backwater and the Big Sunflower flood.

The Corps went back and forth with the EPA and USFWS for years. The Corps issued its impact statement in 2000 and revised it in 2007. Each time, its environmental opponents and the federal agencies raised questions about the validity of the Corps' projections of the costs of the project, both to the nation's pocketbook and to the Yazoo Backwater Area.

When the USFWS submitted its Fish and Wildlife Coordination Act Report to the Vicksburg District in October 2006, the agency stated that the Corps' recommended plan was not "an orderly, balanced, and environmentally sensitive approach to the water and related land resource problems and opportunities of the Yazoo Backwater Area." Because the Corps did not coordinate the plan with the USFWS as required by the Coordination Act to ensure equal consideration of fish and wildlife in the project area, the USFWS threatened to refer the recommended plan to the President's Council on Environmental Quality, where ill-conceived projects go to die. In a letter addressed to the administrator of the EPA and to the secretary of the Interior, a group of wetlands scientists recommended that the USFWS do just that. Actually, under section 404 of the Clean Water Act, the EPA had the power to kill the project to protect the wetlands in the Yazoo Backwater Area.

On January 22, 2008, Lawrence Starfield, deputy regional administrator of the EPA, informed the U.S. Army Corps of Engineers that his agency was initiating a six-month review of the Yazoo Pump. Lawrence noted in his letter to the Corps, "The Yazoo Backwater Area includes some of the richest wetland and aquatic resources in the Nation, including highly productive fisheries, a highly productive yet increasingly rare bottomland hardwood forest ecosystem, hemispherically important migratory bird foraging grounds, habitat for endangered species, and wetlands provided a suite of important ecological support functions." Further, the EPA had "reason to believe that the recommended project plan could result in unacceptable adverse effects on the aquatic ecosystem, particularly to fish and wildlife resources." The review was not the end of the battle over the pump, but environmentalists and the USFWS hoped it was the beginning of the end. Those people who would benefit from the pump and saw it as a part of the cultural framework of the Yazoo Backwater Area hoped otherwise.

On September 2, 2008, the EPA killed the pump. Its supporters in Mississippi threatened litigation.

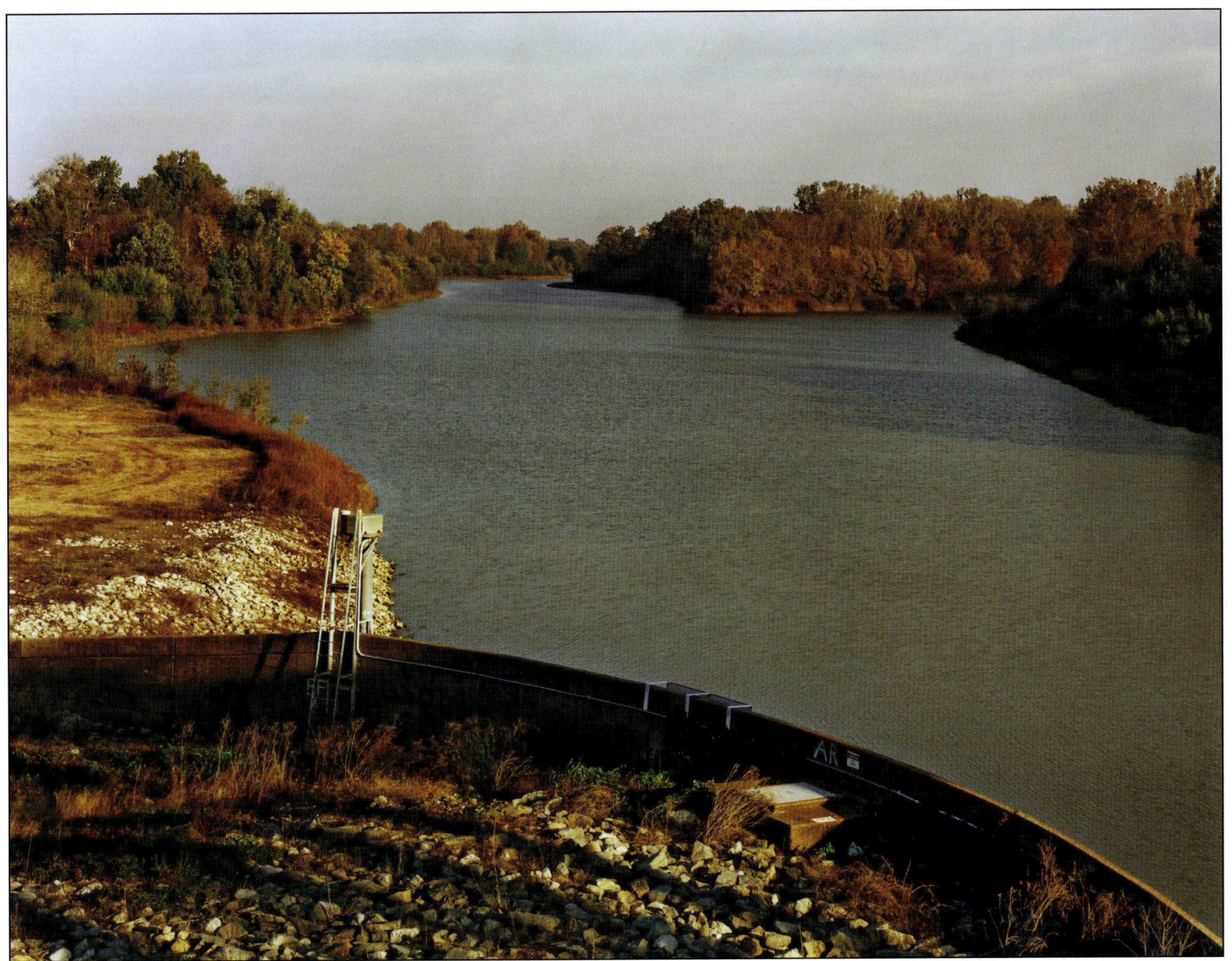

Yazoo Backwater Area: Steele Bayou Drainage Structure
Issaquena County, Mississippi

Directly north of the Steele Bayou Drainage Structure, the site of the Yazoo Pump, a channel that collects the interior flooding from Steele Bayou, Deer Creek, and the Little Sunflower connecting channel and funnels it into the Steele Bayou ponding area or sump, which carries it through the gates in the drainage structure to the Yazoo River and the Mississippi. That's how it works until the Mississippi floods and backs up into the Yazoo, flooding the area south of the structure. The Corps closes the gates. Should the Yazoo tributaries also be in flood, water backs up behind the control structure, flooding in the sump spreads though the backwater area.

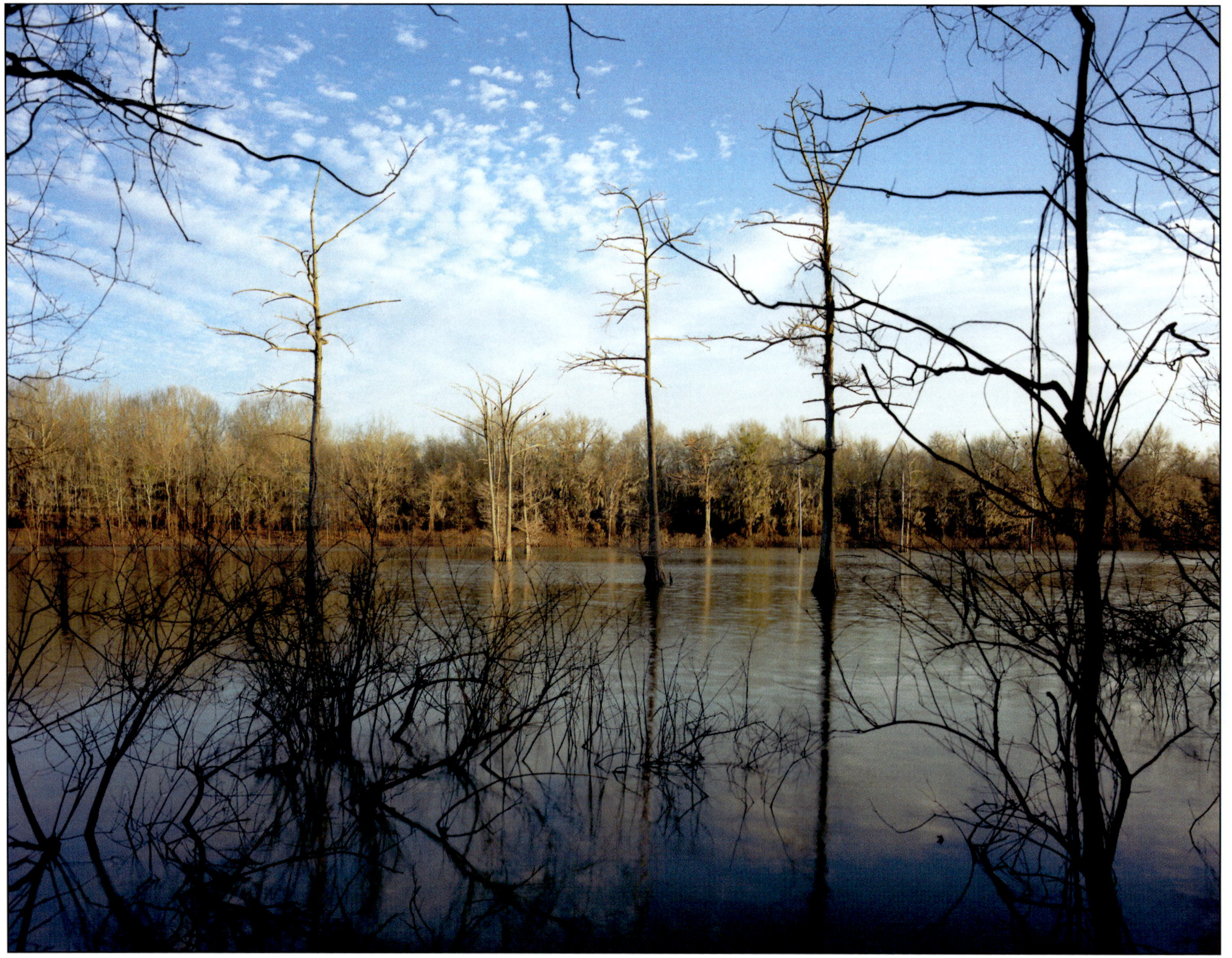

Steele Bayou Ponding Area: Goose Lake

Issaquena County, Mississippi

Goose Lake sits in the forested landscape that is the Steele Bayou ponding area, a place where Louisiana black bears breed. When the Yazoo floods, it refreshes Goose Lake and brings in big river fish. When the EPA filed its intent to review the Yazoo Pump in the *Federal Register,* it noted that of the forested acres the pump would alter: 67,000 would be degraded, and the hydrology of 26,300 so altered they could no longer be defined as wetlands. Reduction of the natural timing and duration of flooding the remaining 40,700 would alter their ecological characteristics and reduce their functions as wetlands. These are the reasons the EPA killed the pump.

The Arkansas Lowlands, the Boeuf Basin, and the Tensas Basin

> During the spring freshes the waters that run out of the Mississippi, by the numerous lagoons or outlets below the Arkansas, are received by the Bayou Macon and Tensaw rivers, and thrown first into Black river, then into the Red river, and finally returned to the Mississippi; but as if proud in the majesty of strength, this mighty stream no sooner receives this great accession of force, than it discharges the auxiliary waters into the Atchafalaya.
>
> —William Darby, 1816

In 1816, William Darby described the natural course of a Lower Mississippi flood below the Arkansas. Gen. Harley Ferguson reiterated Darby's observations in 1940 in his *History of the Improvement of the Lower Mississippi River for Flood Control and Navigation, 1932–1939*. There were any number of ways floodwater could fill the Tensas and Boeuf Basins. It could spill over the levees of the Arkansas, it could stream in via Cypress Creek, it could cross over from the Yazoo Basin.

The modern Arkansas drops into the Bayou Meto Basin at Little Rock and meanders along the southern edge of Grand Prairie to the Mississippi River opposite Rosedale, Mississippi. Before the river adopted its modern channel, it occupied as many as six different meander belts. One flowed along Bayou Bartholomew through the Boeuf Basin, a narrow floodplain between the valley wall and Macon Ridge, a remnant of the early Wisconsinan valley train. A second cut through Macon Ridge along Macon Bayou and extended its course into the Tensas Basin via the Tensas River, east of the ridge. The combined head of the Boeuf and Tensas Basins is in Arkansas at about the latitude of Greenville, Mississippi, and they then run to the mouth of the Red River. Before the construction of artificial levees, the two basins served as floodways to the Atchafalaya when the Mississippi flooded.

When Gen. Edgar Jadwin designed the Mississippi and Tributaries Plan, he intended to use these traditional floodways. The Boeuf Floodway would have delivered water through Boeuf Basin to the Atchafalaya. The Eudora Floodway would have delivered water through the Tensas Basin. Neither was included in the final plan.

The Arkansas River was a major landmark for early explorers. In 1673 Marquette and Joliet descended the Mississippi as far as the mouth of the Arkansas before turning back north. Nine years later La Salle descended the Mississippi, landed at the mouth of the Arkansas on March 14, 1682, claimed its watershed for the King of France, and named it Louisiana. Four years later Henri de Tonti, La Salle's friend and lieutenant, established the Arkansas Post at the mouth of the Arkansas, halfway between the Illinois River and the Gulf of Mexico.

For early traders and adventurers the Arkansas was their route west. At the beginning of the nineteenth century, banned from trading with the Osage Indians along the Missouri River by the Spanish governor of St. Louis, the Chouteau family of traders continued their commerce with the Osage along the Arkansas River in what is now Oklahoma. The Chouteaus and other travelers ascended the White River from the Mississippi to a bayou that connected the White to the Arkansas.

In 1948 Congress authorized the Corps of Engineers to turn the meandering, sand-clogged Arkansas into a nine-foot navigation channel through the construction of a system of eighteen locks and dams that could carry barge traffic 445 miles northwest to Catossa, Oklahoma. The Corps of Engineers formalized the connection between the White and the Arkansas when it completed the Arkansas Post Canal between the two rivers in 1970. The first ten miles of the White became the first ten miles of the Arkansas navigation system. To maintain a nine-foot channel in the White and in the canal, the Corps completed the Montgomery Point Lock and Dam a half-mile upstream from the mouth of the White in 2004. When the Mississippi falls below 115 feet, the Corps closes the dam in order to maintain the channel behind the dam at nine feet.

At the beginning of the twenty-first century the navigation pools behind the dams in the Arkansas lowland served as a tempting source of water for the irrigation of the region south of the river. The Corps had several irrigation projects on its books that would draw water from the Arkansas and funnel it to its ancient courses—Bayou Meto, Bayou Bartholomew, the Boeuf River, and Bayou Macon.

In February 2000 the Corps of Engineers filed its intent to "prepare a draft environmental impact statement to reevaluate the Bayou Meto Irrigation Project." When the Corps finished its Eastern Arkansas Region Comprehensive Study in 1990, the agency concluded that it could improve the supply of water for irrigation on Grand Prairie by drawing water from the Arkansas and pumping it into a system of canals and streams to farms and wildlife refuges. The Bayou Meto Irrigation Project would work in tandem with the Grand Prairie Demonstration Project. In reevaluating the former, the Corps announced that while the focus of the project would be on flood control and irrigation, it would emphasize the creation and restoration of fish and wildlife habitat. The Corps filed a similar statement of intent to improve the supply of water for agriculture with the Southeast Arkansas Irrigation Project the following July.

The aquifer in the Boeuf-Tensas Basin was projected to run out by 2015 and was already contaminated with salt water. Flood-control projects, drainage canals, artificial flooding, moist-soil units, and greentree reservoirs: all changed the way water flowed through the region. Farmers withdrew up to 87 percent of Bayou Bartholomew in the month of August and altered its flow. They plowed to the edge of streams, leaving little or no riparian buffer between stream and cropland, leading to bank erosion, sheet erosion from the fields, and elevated levels of nutrients and turbidity—muddiness.

Soybeans, cotton, and rice covered 86 percent of the land area in the basin. Farmers irrigated 68 percent of their corps. The remaining forests covered 7.5 percent in a region that historically consisted of bottomland hardwoods, meandering bayous, and oxbow lakes. Only forested patches remained, mostly along Bayou Bartholomew, and in the Overflow NWR and the Cutoff Creek WMA.

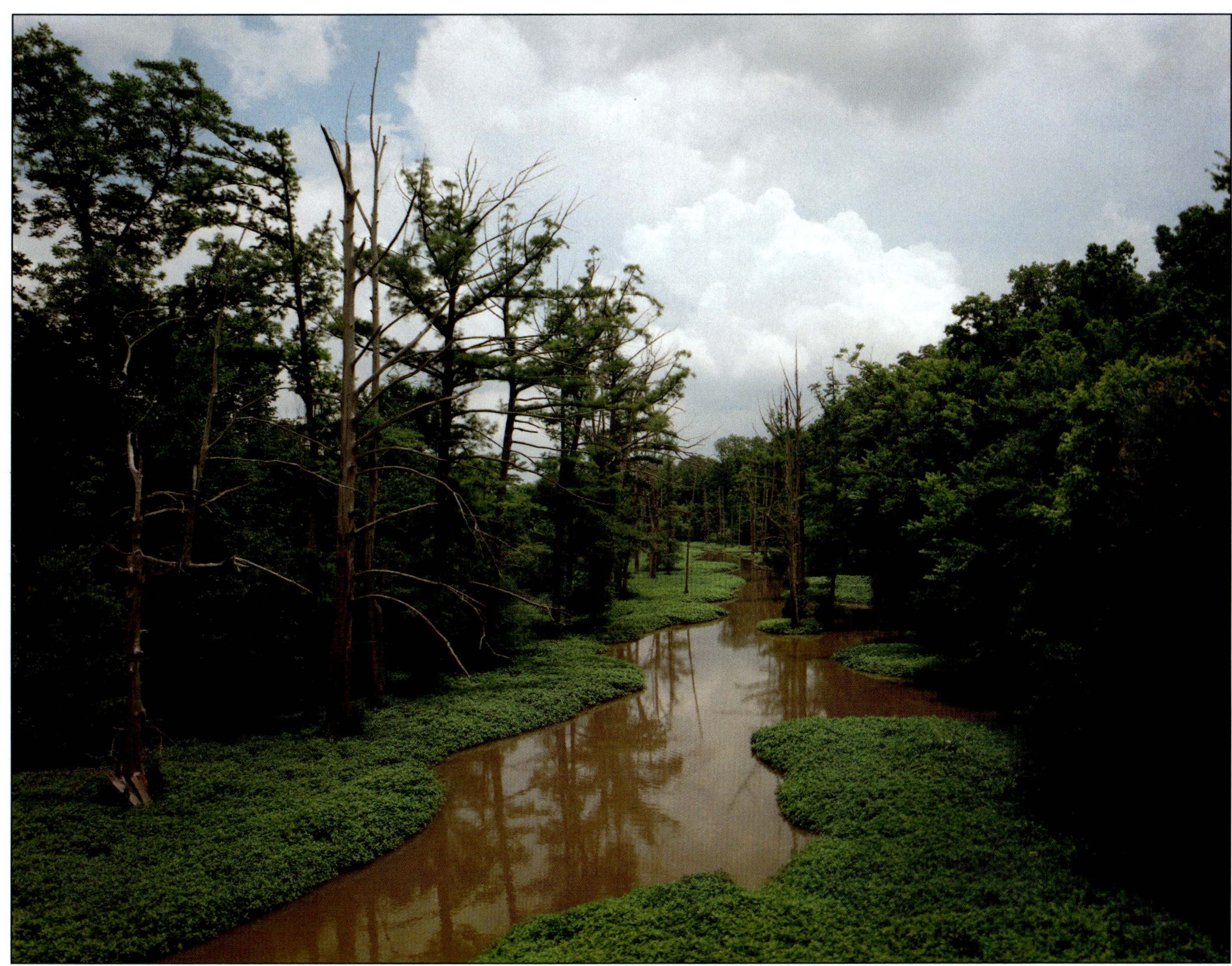

Arkansas River Meander Belt: Moore Bayou
Arkansas County, Arkansas

"The first three villages are situated on the great river (at the mouth of the Arkansas). M. de la Salle erected the arms of the king there; they have cabins made with the bark of cedar; they have no other worship than the adoration of all sorts of animals. Their country is very beautiful, having an abundance of peach, plum and apple trees, and vines flourish there; buffaloes, deer, stags, bears, turkeys, are very numerous. They have even domestic fowls"—Henri de Tonti, 1693

Moore Bayou meanders by the Arkansas Post National Memorial, where Henri de Tonti established an outpost at the mouth of the Arkansas.

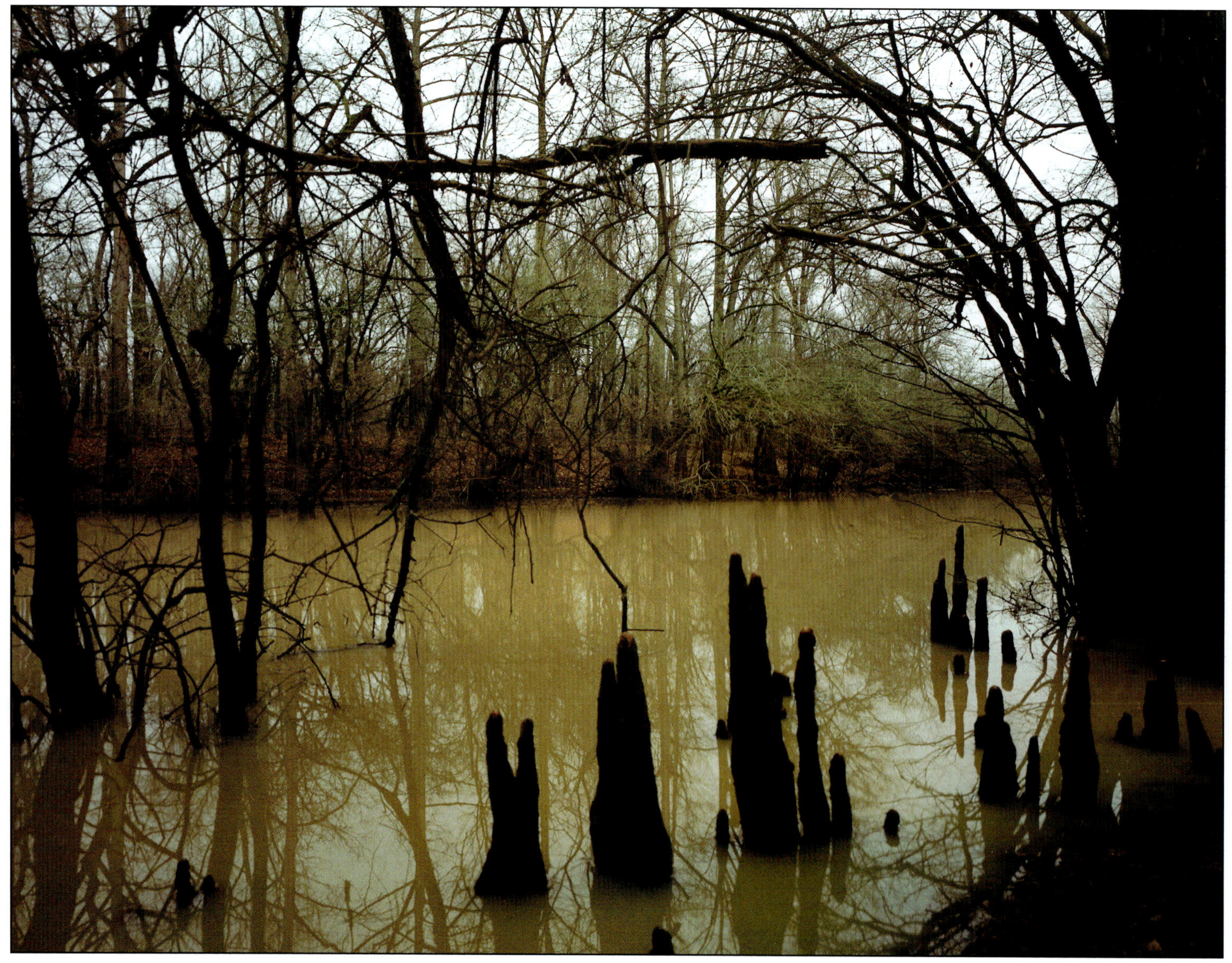

Arkansas River Meander Belt: Bayou Bartholomew

Ashley County, Arkansas

In 1995 a group of people with varied interests in Bayou Bartholomew formed the Bayou Bartholomew Alliance to preserve the water quality and beauty of the bayou. Winrock International—created by Winthrop Rockefeller, a two-term governor of Arkansas—worked with the alliance to restore the bayou and planted 1.5 million trees to stabilize its banks, removed logjams, and monitored its aquatic life. Fish returned to the bayou. In 2002 the alliance started a conservation easement program to save its forests. Once placed under easement, a landowner can control the land, lease it for hunting or other purposes, receive a cut in taxes, but not cut the forest.

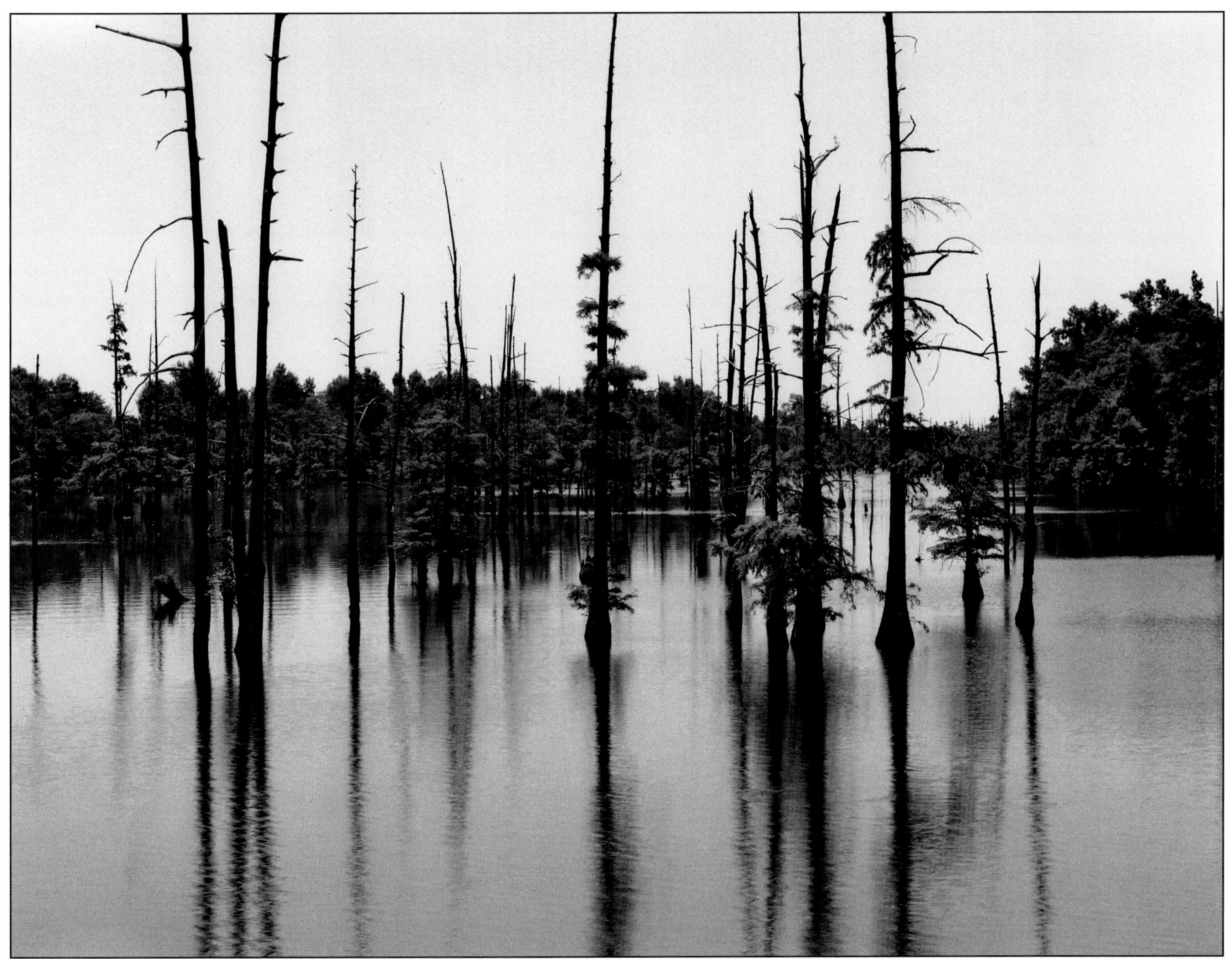

Bayou Bartholomew: Lake Wallace

Chicot County, Arkansas

In 2003 the Bayou Bartholomew Alliance, Winrock International, the Nature Conservancy, and the Arkansas Department of Environmental Quality received $600,000 from the EPA under the agency's Watershed Initiative Program. The collaborators hired a full-time assistant to work with the alliance to oversee conservation easements, volunteer programs, logjam removal, and other activities. The alliance would help landowners renovate weirs to allow for fish and boat passage but stop siltation. Working with the conservancy the alliance documented the bayou's diversity of plants and animals and worked with landowners to develop conservation easement programs.

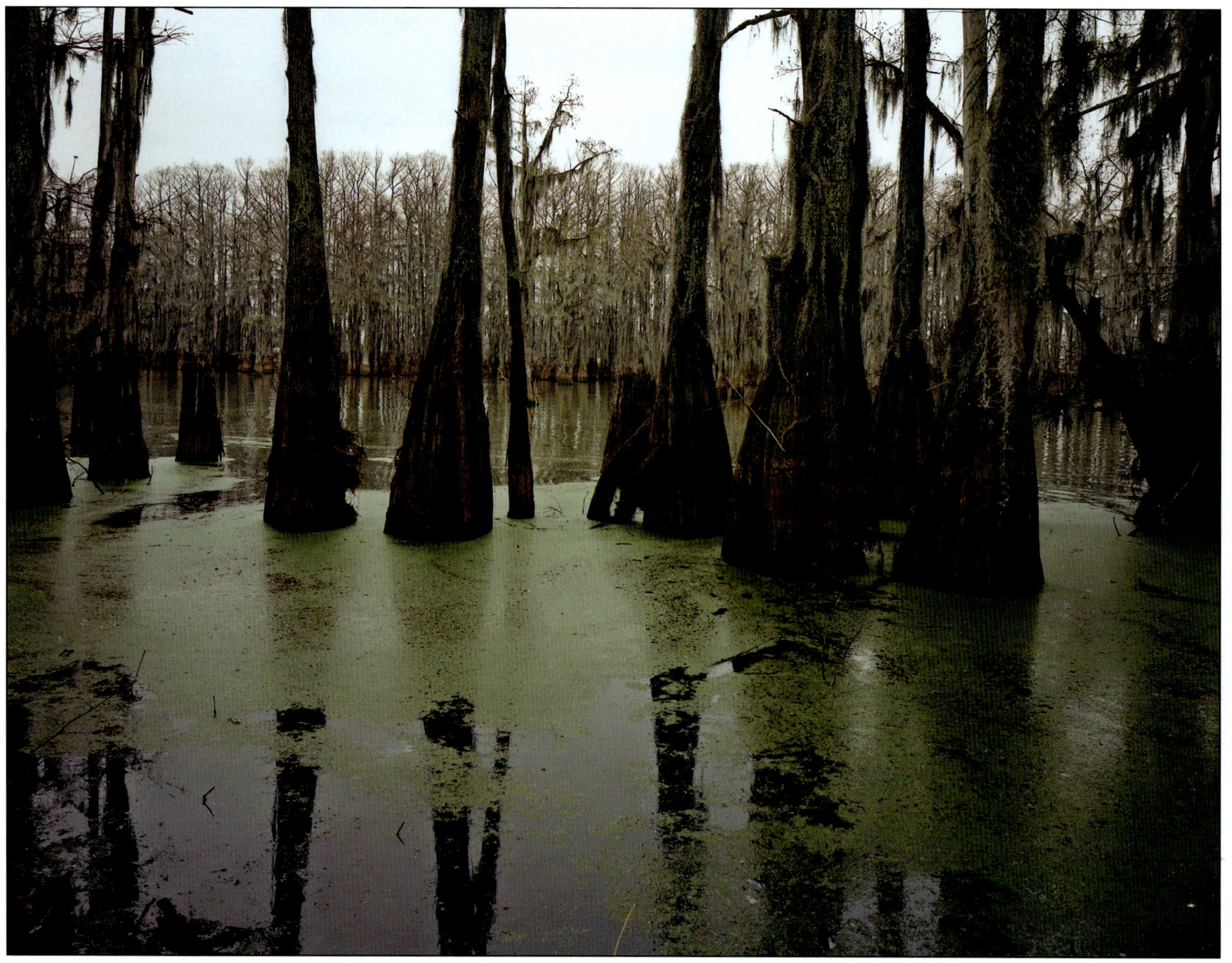

Bayou Bartholomew:
Lake Enterprise

Ashley County, Arkansas

Enterprise, a lake lined with cypress, is ideal habitat for bass and anglers. Underwater, cypress are a labyrinth of roots, which put out knees, which develop their own system of roots. Roots grow from the trunk and reach down into the water, creating a black root-ball, habitat for small fish and crawfish. Cypress knees put out their own system of roots. Bass prowl the maze in search of food. In winter they retreat to the deepest parts of the lake. In spring they move to shallows to spawn among the knees. In summer they find shade under the trees. In fall the bass follow schools of shad into the shallows. So do the anglers. Those who know this routine can fish the lake, its deeps and its shallows, and find their bass.

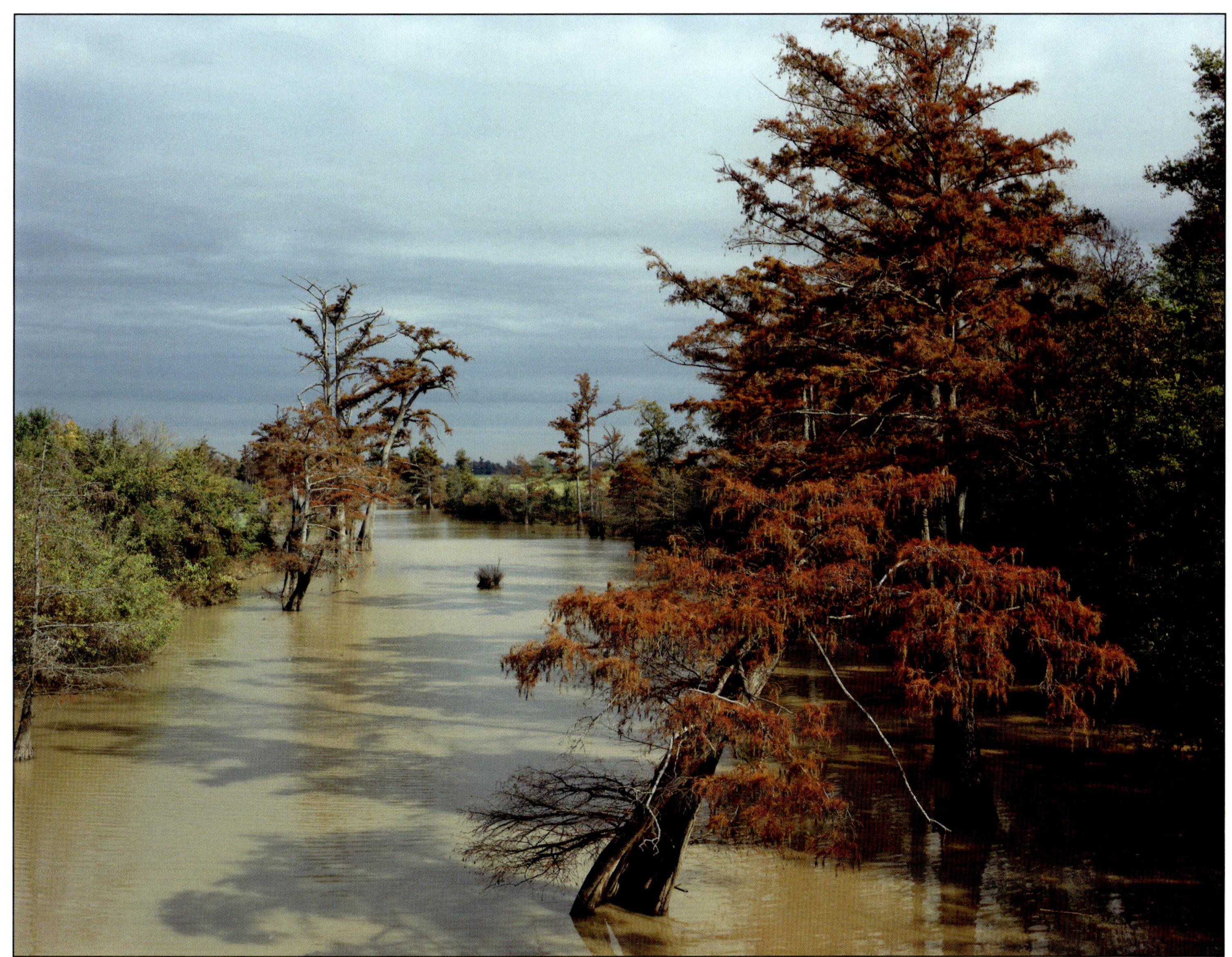

Macon Bayou: Chicot Junction
Chicot County, Arkansas

In September 2000 the USFWS presented the Corps with a list of concerns about replumbing the Boeuf-Tensas Basin: The transfer of water between the Arkansas, the Boeuf, and Bayous Macon and Bartholomew would change the distribution of fish and mussels, creating genetic exchange and competition between individual species. The channelization of streams, the clearing of vegetation from streams, and the construction of weirs might disrupt instream habitat for fish and mussels. The location of irrigation reservoirs might lead to the loss of wetlands. And, lastly, the agency questioned if there was enough water in the Arkansas to irrigate the whole region.

The Tensas Basin

> On the 22nd we reached the Taensa, who dwell around a little lake formed in the land by the river Mississippi.
>
> This whole country is covered with palm trees, laurels of two kinds, plum, peach, mulberry, apple, and pear trees of every kind. There are also five or six kinds of nut trees, some of which bear nuts of extraordinary size. They also gave us several kinds of dried fruit to taste; we found them large and good. Many other kinds of fruit trees which I never saw in Europe are to be found there, but the season was too early to allow us to see the fruit. We observed vines already out of blossom.
>
> —Father Zenobius Membre, 1682

When Father Zenobius Membre accompanied La Salle and his company down the Mississippi, they came upon the Tensas River Basin in 1682, they found a great expanse of wetlands carpeted in freshwater marshes, forested in bottomland hardwoods, and populated by a rich diversity of flora and fauna, possibly the richest in the country.

With settlement 95 percent of the forest gave way to productive agricultural land. Lost were the freshwater marshes, streamside vegetation, bottomland forests, all of which dispersed the energy of heavy floods and provided a stable, healthy, and diverse ecosystem. However, two remarkable tracts of bottomland forest survived.

The Singer Sewing Machine Company purchased a tract along the Tensas River in 1913 with the intention of using wood from its great oaks in sewing machine cabinets. In 1920 Singer contracted with the State of Louisiana to operate the tract as a wildlife refuge. Singer sold its timber rights to Chicago Mill and Lumber in 1937, which began logging it for boxes, caskets, shell boxes, and wagon boxes. On June 28, 1980, in an effort to preserve the remaining portion of the Singer tract forest, Congress authorized the secretaries of the army and interior to purchase 50,000 acres for the new Tensas River NWR and ordered the army to turn over its half to the USFWS for management.

In 1926 the Fisher Corporation of Detroit, maker of auto bodies, owned 160,000 acres of timberlands in the southern United States and sawmills in Ferriday and Wisner, Louisiana. In 1988 the Nature Conservancy purchased 11,255.51 acres of bottomland hardwoods three miles south of Ferriday from Fisher. The tract was the least disturbed remainder of the bottomland forest that once covered the whole of the alluvial valley and included a patch of old-growth forest measuring 750 acres. The Conservancy sold the land to the USFWS over a period of five years for the Bayou Cocodrie NWR, established in 1992.

The modern Tensas River breaks out of the southern arm of Lake Providence through a crevasse in the natural levee of the lake and flows to its confluence with the Ouachita River to form the Black River. By the end of the twentieth century what little remained of the forested wetlands in the basin rubbed up against vast fields of cotton and soybeans. The landscape lost its ability to filter out sediment, nutrients, and pesticides, which poured into a watershed that carried them to Atchafalaya Basin and the Gulf of Mexico. The region was poor, its population in decline, its unemployment high, and its economy dependent on agriculture. By 1998 the Tensas River failed to meet Louisiana's dissolved-oxygen standard, its water quality impaired.

In 1996 people with a stake in the future of the basin formed Partners for Fish and Wildlife, a committee of conservation groups, federal agencies, and local governing boards to develop the Tensas Ecosystem–Based Assistance Pilot Project. Its goal was to revitalize the economy of the basin by creating a sustainable ecosystem where habitat restoration could coexist with improved agricultural practices. Its tools were the education of the populace and the restoration of forested wetlands on marginal cropland adjacent to streams, which would rejuvenate the timber industry. Providing a riparian filter strip would stabilize the banks of streams, capture sediment, filter nutrients and pesticides, improve water quality, create habitat for fish and wildlife, and diversify the landscape. Clear streams and renewed habitat would create recreational opportunities. Large tracts of forested land would provide habitat for the Louisiana black bear and travel corridors for smaller wildlife. A restored habitat along the streams plus best practices—conservation tillage and precision agriculture—would revitalize the soil, increase yields, and enhance the economy of the region. In short, rethinking the use of natural resources would bring in new industry.

By 2000 the efforts of the Partners for Fish and Wildlife had begun to show results. A hardwood seedling nursery that sprouts over a million native trees a year provided saplings for the reforestation of 56,000 acres of farmland. Farmers had enrolled another 48,000 acres in the WRP. The Partners for Fish and Wildlife restored 4,000 acres of bottomland habitat along fifteen miles of riparian corridors.

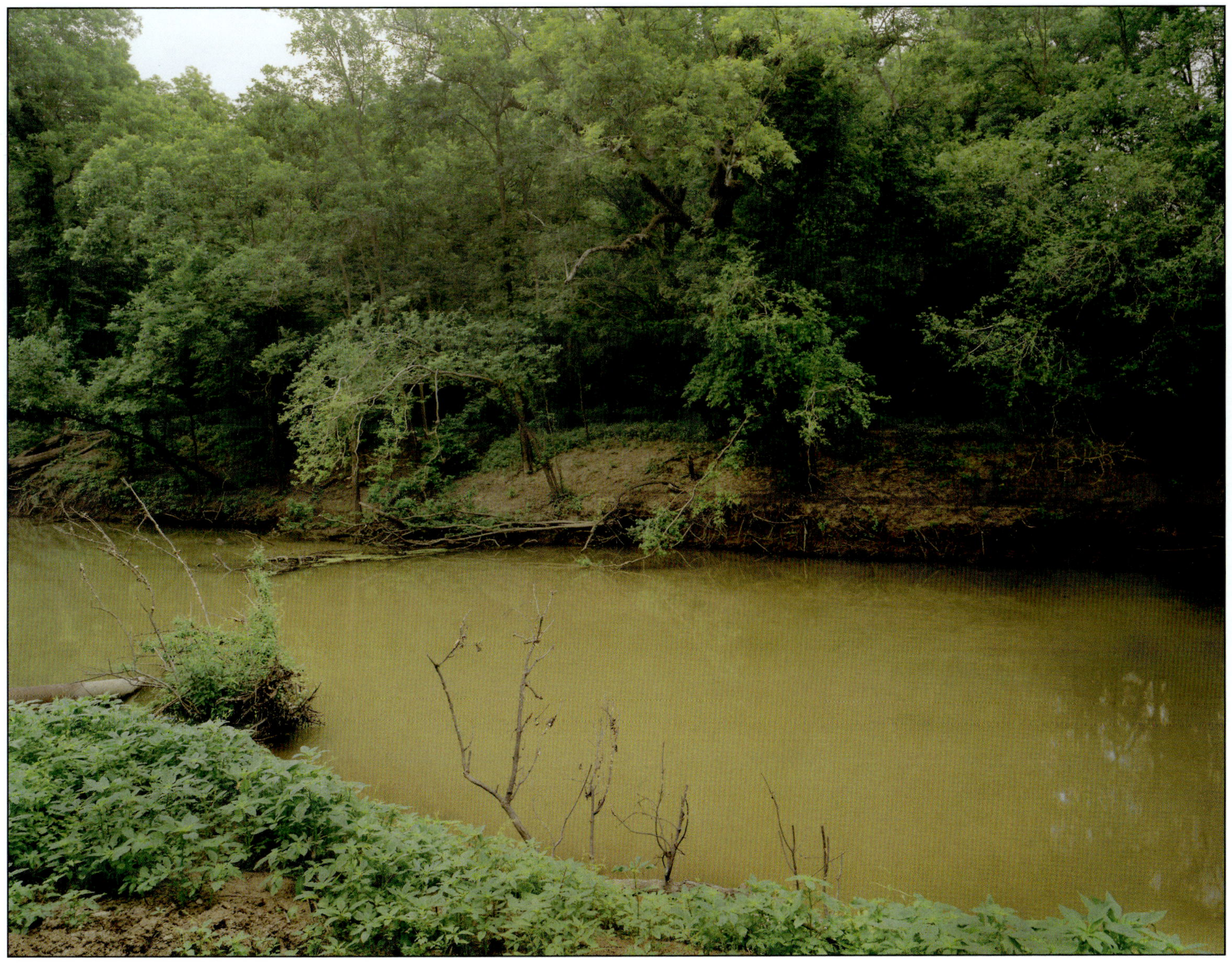

Tensas National Wildlife Refuge: The Singer Tract
Madison Parish, Louisiana

Everything we know about the Lord God Bird we learned from James Tanner, who studied a pair in the Singer Tract for his Ph.D. Tanner arrived in 1937 just as Singer sold timber rights to Chicago Mill, which began logging. Tanner divided the tract into regions where the Ivory-bill should be or had been found and watched the bird's decline. In 1934 he found seven pairs and four young; in 1936 six pairs and six young; in 1937 five pairs, a single male, and two young; in 1938 two pair, two single males, and three young; in 1939 one pair, three single males, one young. As the trees disappeared, the bird lost the sweet gum and Nuttall oak it prized.

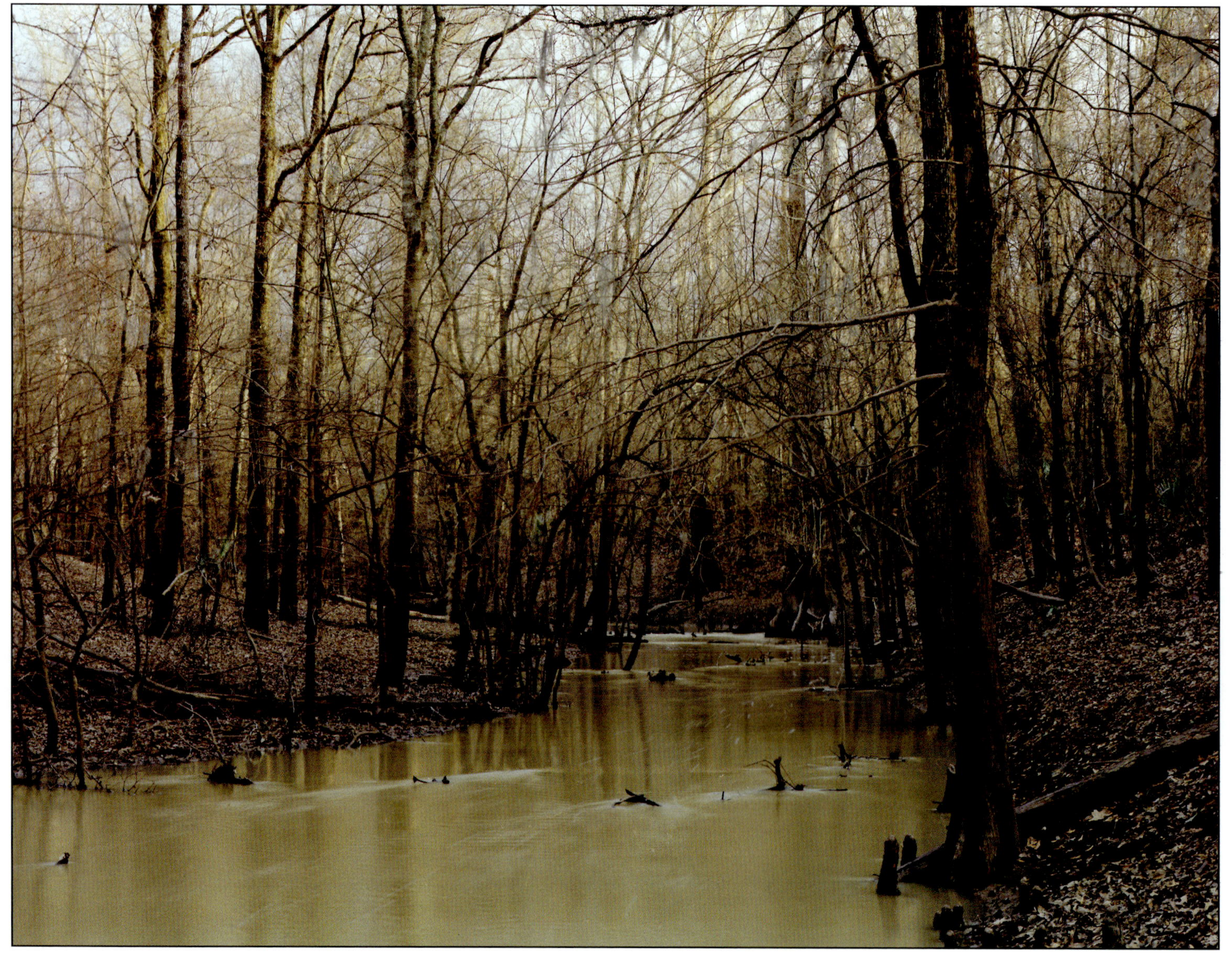

Tensas River: Tensas National Wildlife Refuge
Madison Parish, Louisiana

Tanner left a guide for providing habitat for the Ivory-bill and laid out a plan for 46,000 acres on the Singer Tract: Prohibit logging near Ivory-bill habitat. Log selectively in its extended feeding area. Log the poorest areas. Cut only sound, usable sweet gum. Leave all dead trees. They might contain grubs, woodpecker food. Cut Nuttall oak, valued by many species for their acorns and valued by Ivory-bills, sparingly. Leave hackberry. It has no value as timber. Cut the rest, if sound logs. Girdle trees to kill them, invite in grubs, and increase the supply of food artificially. Prohibit hunting. Transplant the Ivory-bill before destroying its habitat.

The Refuges of Northeastern Louisiana

> The mouth of the red river is accounted to be 75 leagues from New-orleans and 3 miles above the exit of the Chafalaya or Opelousa river which was probably the continuation of the red river, when perhaps its waters did not unite with those of the Mississippi excepting during inundation.
>
> Both banks are clothed with rich Cane-brake, pierced by many creeks fit to carry boats during the inundations: saw many Cormorants and the stately Whooping Crane: Geese and Ducks not yet abundant; they arrive in myriads with the rains & winter cold.
>
> —William Dunbar, 1804

Larto Lake, Saline Lake, Catahoula Lake: Southern Cocodrie Parish is the Dismal Swamp, a network of ridges and swales, bayous, backswamps, flats, and canals, a very wet region and mecca for duck hunters. It is a landscape dotted with refuges both state and national: Grassy Lake, Catahoula Lake, Lake Ophelia, Red River, Spring Bayou, Three Rivers, and Saline.

So many ducks end up in the northeastern Louisiana refuges because they are at the crossroads of the Central and Mississippi Flyways. All along the Mississippi, refuges cater to ducks migrating south from Canada and the Mississippi headwaters. Birds who summer in the Great Plains follow the Red River to northeastern Louisiana. All the rivers that flow south through Louisiana, the Mississippi, the Tensas, the Black, the Red, and the Atchafalaya carry birds south to the Gulf of Mexico. Should the rivers and lakes in the Arkansas refuges freeze over, the birds retreat south to Louisiana. If the weather is hot and dry on the Gulf Coast, the birds move inland to northeastern Louisiana.

Different water bodies attract different birds. Fish-eating diving ducks—Scaup, Ring-necked Ducks, Canvasbacks, and Redheads—flock to open lakes or major rivers. Dabbling ducks—Mallards and Wood Ducks—look for flooded timber. So do Teals, Widgeon, Gadwalls, and Pintails. Wood Ducks, who nest in tree hollows or refuge-supplied nesting boxes, prefer wooded swamps, bottomlands, flooded hardwoods, cypress and tupelo swamps.

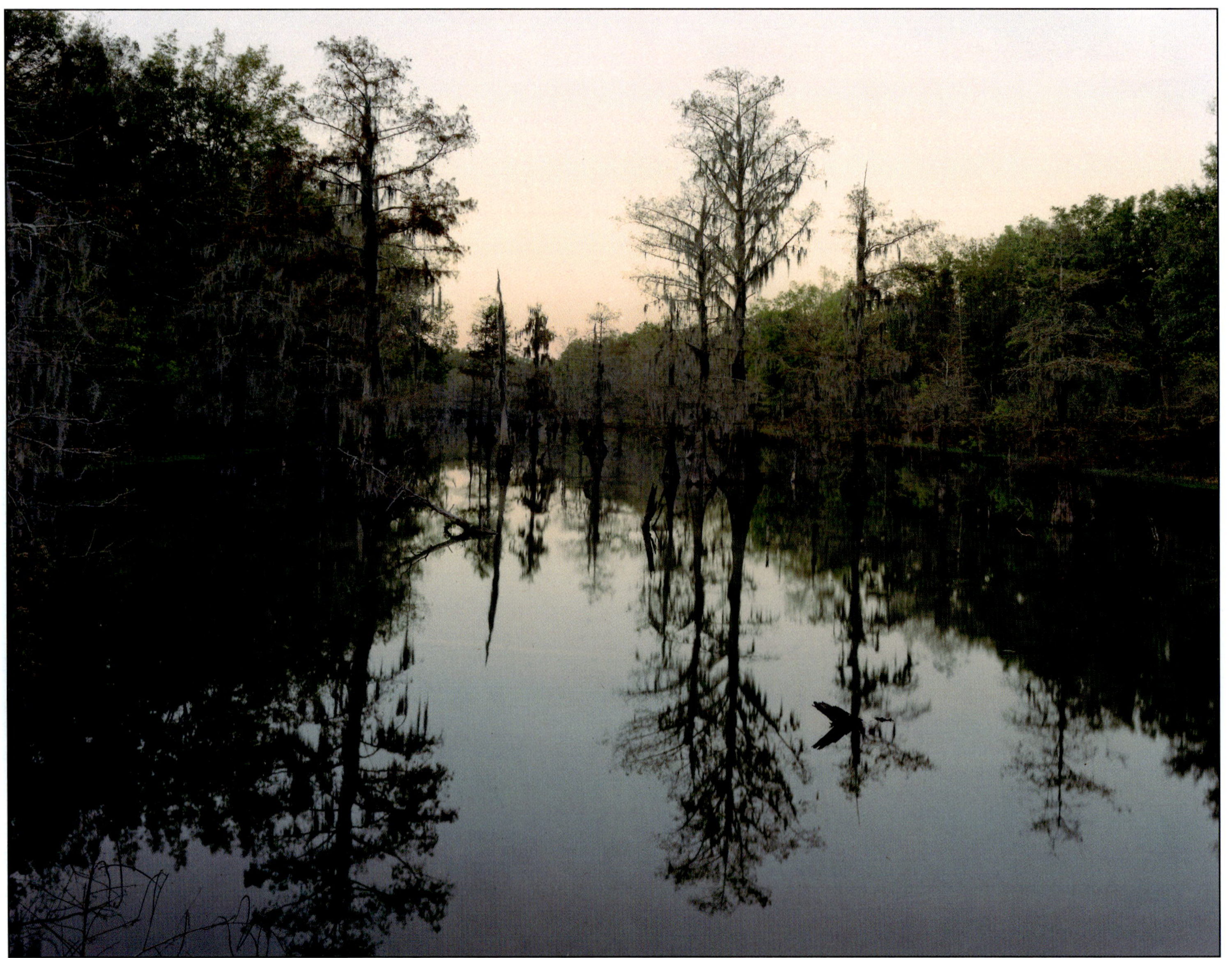

Catahoula National Wildlife Refuge: Cowpen Bayou
LaSalle Parish, Louisiana

In 1814 William Dunbar observed that Catahoula Lake went dry in the summer and grasses rooted, food for wildlife in winter. Each July Louisiana Wildlife and Fisheries draws down the lake by eight feet to expose mudflats and encourage growth of moist-soil plants. Two weeks before duck season, the agency raises the water level, and 100,000 ducks descend on the lake. In 2001 the RAMSAR Convention on Wetlands, a treaty signed in 1971, named the Catahoula refuge a "Wetland of International Importance," where small game mammals, migrating songbirds and ducks, raptors, wading birds, reptiles as large as alligators, and amphibians as small as cricket frogs live.

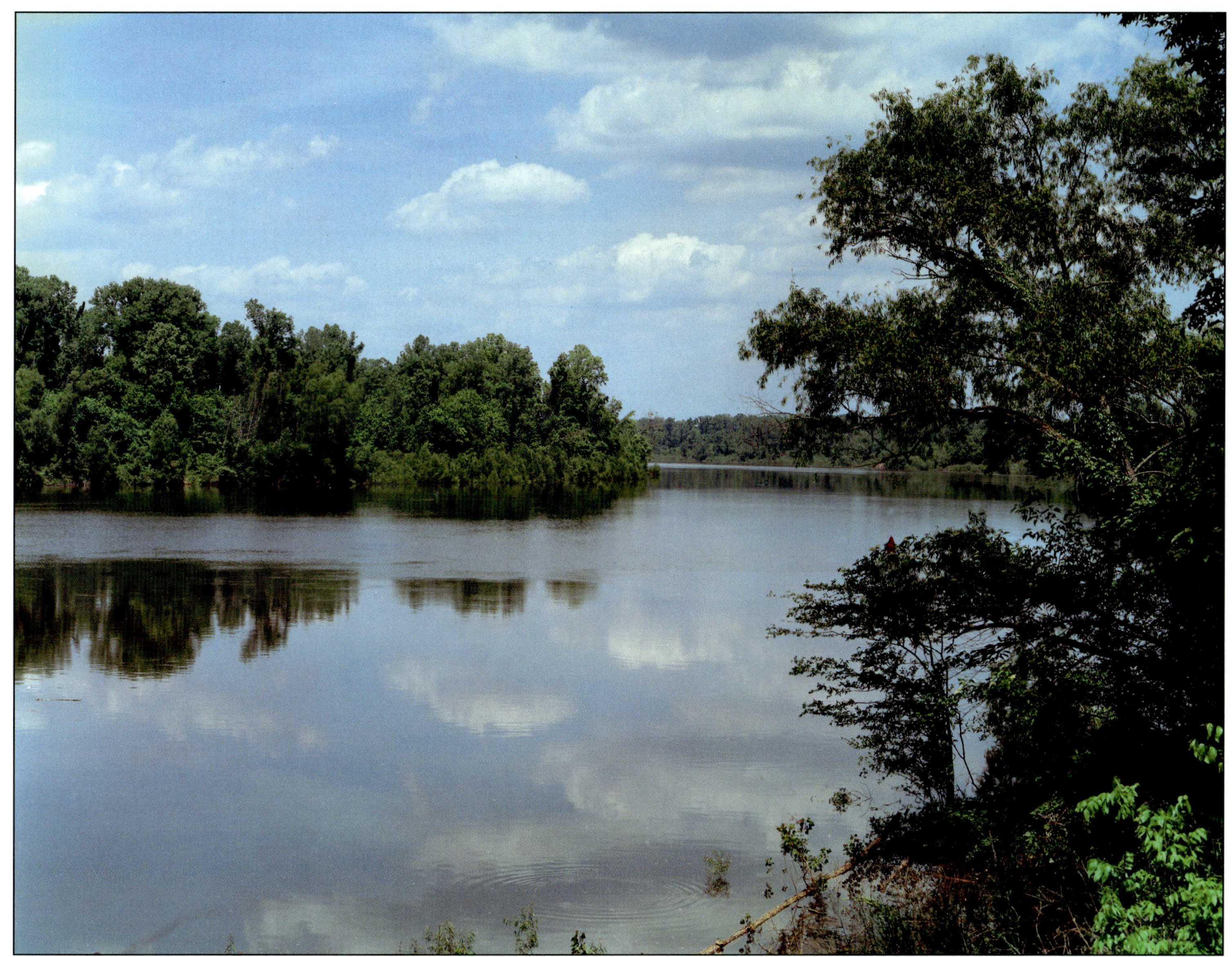

Red River Wildlife Management Area: Red River
Cocodrie Parish, Louisiana

Female Louisiana black bears are unwilling to abandon their cubs and therefore are easier to relocate than males, who head home. In an effort to expand habitat for bears and link the Tensas Basin population with that in the Atchafalaya Basin, the USFWS partnered with the Louisiana Department of Wildlife and Fisheries, the Black Bear Conservation Committee, LSU, and private landowners to move four females, two from the Tensas and two from the Atchafalaya, and their nine cubs to artificial dens in the Red River WMA in March 2001. To track the bears rangers fitted each with a radio transmitter. Three stayed put with their cubs and established home bases.

The Mississippi Meander Belt

> We now turn our attention to the difficulties which embarrass the navigation of the Mississippi. These arise from the impetuosity of its current, and the almost entire absence of rock on its shores from St. Louis to New Orleans. Hence, its constant effort to change its course; and hence the frequent submersion of whole acres of land, covered with trees of the most gigantic growth.
>
> —Army Engineers' Report on the Ohio and Mississippi Rivers, 1823

When the Mississippi initiated its modern meander belt about 2,800 years ago, it simply abandoned the channel occupied by the Yazoo Meander Belt and shifted the western channel a few miles to the east, probably through a series of neck and chute cutoffs. Geologists believe a crevasse near Eagle Lake, Mississippi, north of Vicksburg, developed into a major distributary, picked up the small yazoo streams that flow into the rim swamp, a notch in the bluff between Vicksburg and Natchez, and captured the full flow of the river. At Old River, the river picked up an earlier meander belt and streamed south into the delta. Once the river attained full flow between Memphis and Vicksburg, it meandered through coarse glacial deposits and created an exceptionally large number of cutoffs.

Construction of the mainline levee divorced the Mississippi River from its floodplain and created two entities, the active floodplain on the river side of the levee and the inactive floodplain on the land side. Each must be treated differently when discussing the degradation of habitat and our subsequent efforts at restoration.

Channel-training devices, wing dams, diverted the river's erosive power from the side channels to the main channel, where they scoured the navigation channel south of Alton. Closing dams, installed across side channels, prevented the river from adopting a side channel as its main channel. Sediment, washing off the floodplain, silted in the side channels, damaging habitat for fish and migrating waterfowl. What were once islands became part of the mainland.

The Lower Mississippi River Conservation Committee published its Aquatic Resource Management Plan for the Lower Mississippi in 2000. The ten-year plan addressed declining aquatic resources on the Lower River in its backwater areas and on its active floodplain with a view to restoring aquatic habitat, improving water quality, building partnerships to coordinate management activities, enhancing economic opportunities, and increasing public awareness of the importance of the Mississippi River ecosystem. Similar to the Middle Mississippi Partnership with similar goals, the committee is a coalition of state and federal agencies, dedicated to "promoting the wise use of the natural resources of the Lower Mississippi River through cooperative efforts involving planning, management, information sharing, public education, advocacy, and research."

To this end the committee developed the Lower Mississippi River Conservation Initiative to outline various measures to improve habitat in the active floodplain between the river and the levees. In the early years of the twenty-first century, resource managers from state conservation agencies and representatives from interested conservation groups met with staff from the Corps of Engineers in each of the states bordering the river to examine various possibilities: opening closing dams to return flow through side channels and create improved habitat for fish; notching wing dams to create side channels between sandbars and the floodplain to create nesting places for Least Terns; restoring oxbow lakes and wetlands in the active floodplain to create habitat for fish, migrating waterfowl, and shorebirds; reforesting the active floodplain to create habitat for migratory songbirds.

The Oxbow Lakes

Once the river formed an oxbow lake by cutting through the neck of a point bar, it resumed the process of building its natural levee. In time it buried the channels that connected the oxbow to the river under the natural levee, forcing drainage to flow in and out of the lake by different routes, often into the adjacent basin. Many oxbows formed the headwaters of streams that meander through the basins.

The mainline levee put many of the oxbows in the inactive floodplain. Once loggers and farmers cleared the floodplain for agriculture, bayous and drainage canals streaming to the lakes carried in sediment, nutrients, and pesticides, creating muddy, low-oxygen environments. Often residents flushed raw sewage into the lakes.

Restoration of the lakes entailed employing tools provided by Section 319 of the Clean Water Act of 1972. Conservation tillage, no-till or reduced-till farming practices, reduced erosion in the fields. Grass filter strips around the lakes removed sediment, nutrients, and pesticides before they reached the lakes. Grade stabilization structures held water on the land in winter and allowed sediment to settle in the fields. Adequate septic tanks—or better yet, adequate sewer systems—kept raw sewage out of the lakes.

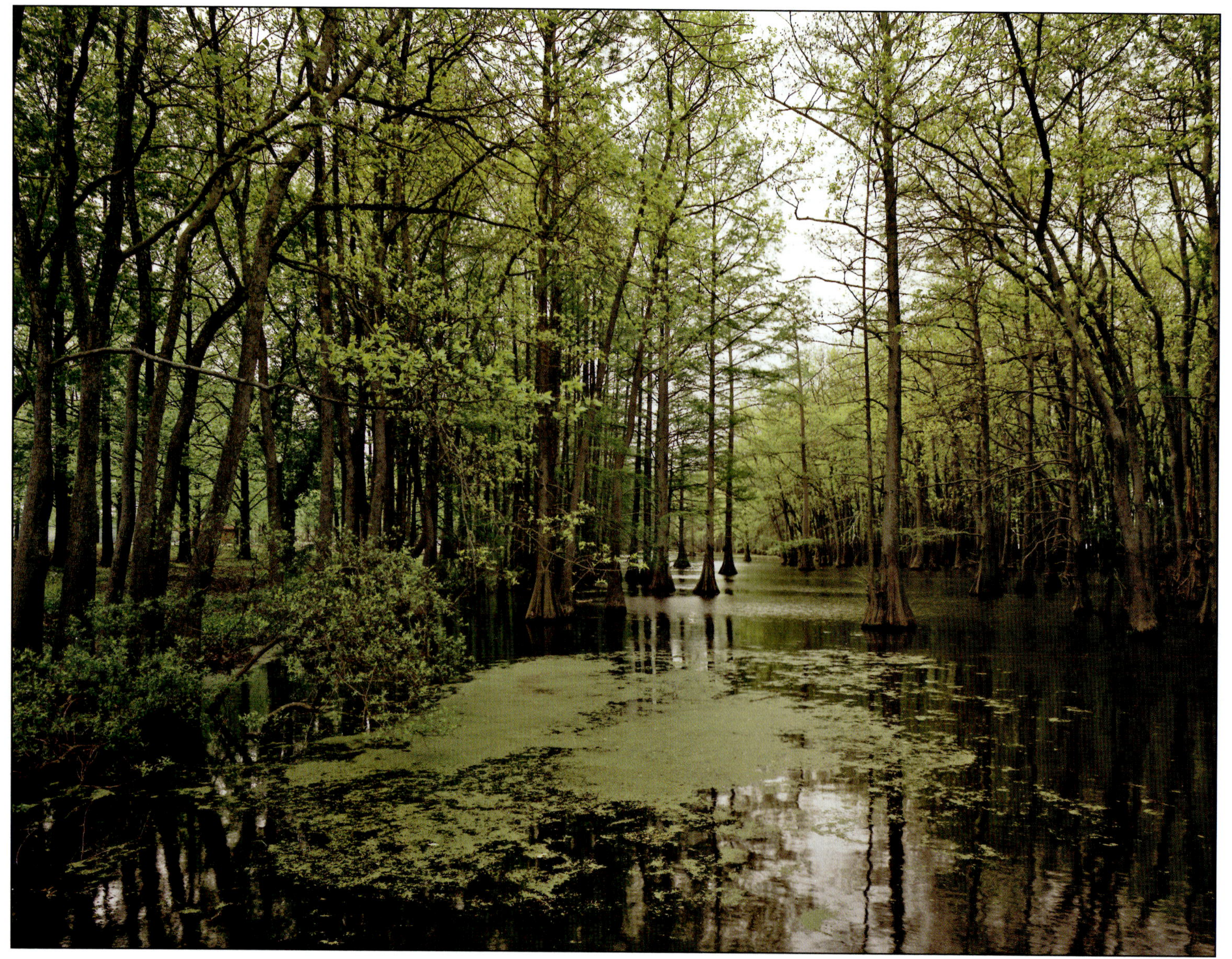

Tywappity Bottom: Horseshoe Lake

Alexander County, Illinois

At 2,400 acres, Horseshoe Lake, just north of Cairo, is the first great oxbow along the Lower Mississippi. The Illinois Department of Conservation purchased the first 49 acres of the Horseshoe Lake Fish and Wildlife Area in 1927 and turned it into a refuge for the giant Canada goose, a species on the wane, and built a stoplog structure that maintained the lake at four feet. The first geese, a thousand of them, discovered the new refuge the following winter. By 1944 their numbers had grown to 40,000. As the state acquired more and more land, more and more geese wintered at Horseshoe Lake, 150,000 on 10,645 acres at last count.

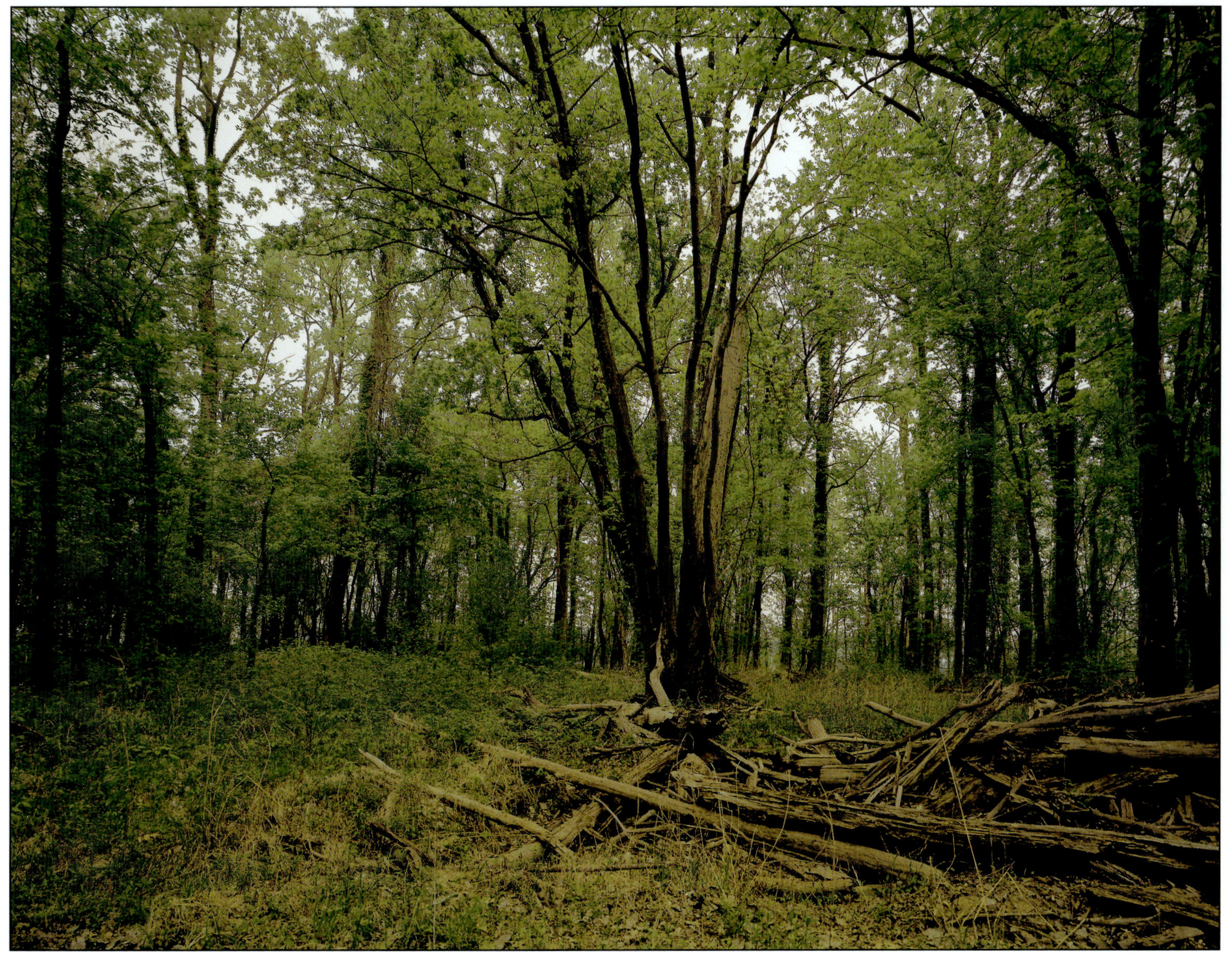

Missouri Sister Island: Dry Bayou/Thompson Bend
Mississippi County, Missouri

Just north of the Ohio, the Mississippi turns in an S, forming two point bars. Should the Ohio be in flood and the Mississippi not, it dams the Mississippi, causing lakelike conditions. Should the Mississippi be in flood and the Ohio not, it rages against the point bar. The distance around Thompson Bend is seventeen miles. Given a big enough flood the Mississippi could cut across the point bar and shorten the distance to a mile and a quarter. Since 1981 the river has been threatening to do just that. Lester Goodin, who farmed the point bar, and Jerry Rapp, a hydraulic engineer with the Corps, worked out a hydraulically sound solution. They planted trees.

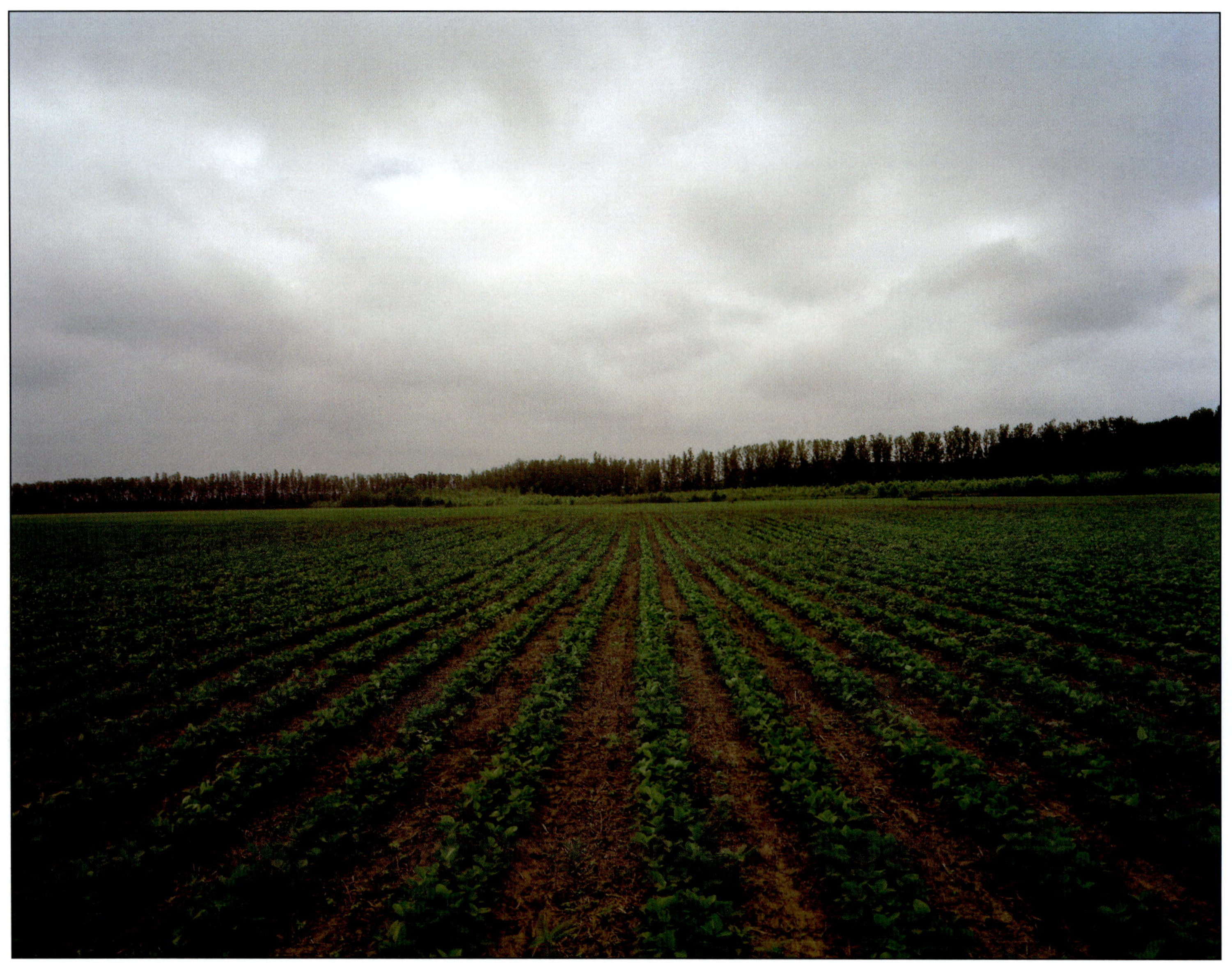

Dry Bayou/Thompson Bend: Lester Goodin's Tree Screen
Mississippi County, Missouri

In January 1986 Goodin and his partners planted 125 acres, forming screens of hard, fast-growing green ash on the upside of the bend to withstand the force of the current and the debris the river would throw at them; then soft, fast-growing cottonwood screens to catch the sediment that made it through the ash. On the eve of the 1993 flood they had trees seventy feet tall, and the Ohio River ran sixteen feet below flood stage. At Thompson Bend the flood surged through the screens, losing half its power against the first screen and depositing more sediment than it scoured. The trees remained standing. The Corps added riparian screens to its toolbox.

The St. Johns Bayou–New Madrid Floodway Project

In 1928 when Gen. Edgar Jadwin left a 1,500-foot gap at the foot of the setback levee of the New Madrid Floodway for the release of floodwater and installed a fuse plug levee at Birds Point at its head. Jadwin and the Corps understood that the lower third would become a backwater storage area. To compensate landowners for the use of their land, the agency purchased flood easements in the upper two-thirds. That wasn't necessary in the lower third, which would flood with the river every time. It was the floodway's role as a backwater storage area that created an uproar at the beginning of the twenty-first century, when the Corps published its plan for the St. Johns Bayou–New Madrid Floodway Project, which promised to eliminate backwater flooding in the floodway.

The 1986 WRDA authorized the dredging of St. Johns Bayou for flood control, the St. Johns Bayou Pump Station, which included a gated culvert across the foot of the bayou, and the New Madrid Pump Station and a gated culvert set in the 1,500-foot gap. The gated culverts would halt backwater flooding from the river but assure interior flooding in both St. Johns Bayou Basin, located between the setback levee and Sikeston Ridge, and in the New Madrid Floodway. The pumps would clear water ponding behind the closed culverts. The culvert across St. Johns Bayou was built. In 1997 the Memphis District of the Corps of Engineers filed its intent to prepare an environmental impact study of the rest of the project.

Environmentalists, river conservationists, the EPA, the USFWS, the Missouri Department of Conservation, the Missouri DNR, and taxpayer watchdogs all objected. They balked at closing the last connection the Mississippi had to its floodplain in Missouri, at the $65 million cost, at the damage that would be done to Big Oak Tree State Park, at the loss of spawning habitat for fishes and wintering places for waterfowl, and at the channelizing of St. Johns Bayou and other drainage ditches. They complained that the project would benefit a handful of big landowners. They noted that East Prairie in the St. Johns Bayou Basin would continue to flood due to runoff from roofs and parking lots. They encouraged the Corps to find nonstructural solutions to the flooding problems, including a ring levee around East Prairie.

The East Prairie Enterprise Community, the local sponsor of the project, and other residents of Swampeast, weren't interested in environmentalists' concerns. East Prairie residents complained that a ring levee would cut them off from the rest of the world. Farmers gave little support to the WRP. They had rejected a 1993 USFWS offer to purchase land in the St. Johns Bayou Basin for a national wildlife refuge at fair market value. Nor were they interested in converting their lands from row crops to timber.

In September 2000 the Memphis District sought to please both the environmentalists and the residents of Mississippi County when it revised its plan. The floodgate and the pumps would stay, but the following changes would be made: the Corps would dredge only the St. Johns Bayou–St. James Bayou drainage ditch, reduce its width from 200 to 120 feet, and excavate only one side to avoid cutting into forests. The engineers would not dredge the upper 3.7 miles of St. James Bayou ditch to avoid the habitat of the golden topminnow, a state endangered fish; would avoid mussel beds or relocate them and set up a ten-year monitoring program. They would set rock structures in the channels to enhance fish habitat; move water in and out of the lower reaches of the floodway and the basin for winter and early spring waterfowl and to allow spawning fish to pass to and from the river; purchase conservation easements on 765 acres of herbaceous land along the channel to replace shorebird habitat; reforest 9,557 acres of seasonally flooded cropland. At Big Oak Tree State Park they would build a control structure to regulate water in its swamps—enough for the cypress, but not too much for the oaks.

The Corps published essentially the same plan in June 2002, but added the construction of the wildlife corridor through the fragmented ecosystem between Big Oak Tree Park and the Ten Mile Pond Conservation Area and riparian buffers along sixty-four miles of streams and drainage channels to filter water flowing to Big Oak Tree. Most important, the engineers committed to the restoration of Big Oak Tree, purchasing and reforesting 1,800 acres surrounding the park and restoring the park's hydrologic connection to the Mississippi with water-control structures in the park, a canal with gated culverts set in the mainline levee to allow water to flow between the park and the river. The cost of the new plan came to $85 million and still did not satisfy the Missouri DNR, owner of the park.

In 2004 the Memphis District issued a contract for the construction of the New Madrid closure and the pump but stopped work when the National Wildlife Federation and the Environmental Defense Fund filed suit in federal court, alleging violations of the Clean Water Act.

In December 2005 the Corps published a second revised supplemental environmental impact statement that would allow fish to spawn in the sumps behind the culverts and would reestablish the hydrological connection between Big Oak Tree and the Mississippi along St. James Bayou through a culvert in the mainline levee.

The Corps pointed out repeatedly that the success of the project depended on finding people willing to sell their land for mitigation to add 1,800 acres to Big Oak Tree State Park or the addition 1,037 acres needed for the wildlife corridor and riparian buffers.

In the fall of 2006 the Corps of Engineers started work on the project, despite being told they would likely lose the federal suit filed two years earlier. That prediction proved true: in September 2007, U.S. District Judge James Robertson of the District of Columbia ordered the project halted and the work already accomplished dismantled.

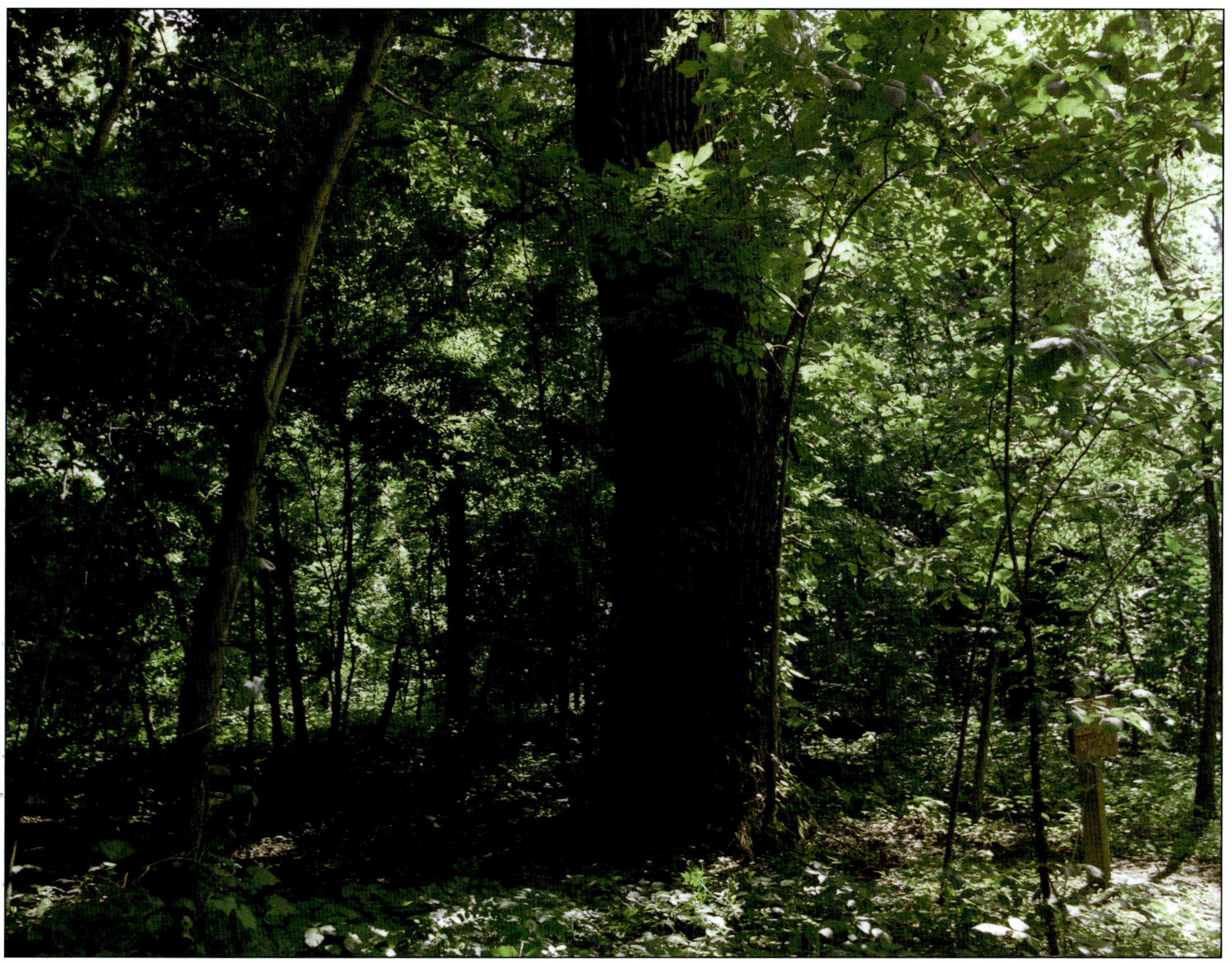

New Madrid Floodway: Big Oak Tree State Park

Mississippi County, Missouri

In 1938 local residents of Mississippi County rescued 1,000 acres, 80 in virgin timber, in the 132,000-acre floodway from logging and draining. The park safeguards the largest tract of uncut bottomland hardwood forest in Swampeast. Its swamp provides habitat to 150 species of birds, 44 species of fishes, and 31 species of reptiles. The National Park Service has made it a National Natural Landmark. The network of drainage channels that made farming in the floodway possible dehydrates the park, stressing its trees. But when the Mississippi floods the lower third of the floodway, it refreshes the wetlands in the park, located near the foot of the floodway.

The New Madrid Earthquakes

> In descending the Mississippi on the night of the 6th of February, we tied our boat to a willow-bar on the west bank of the river, opposite the head of the 9th Island. We were lashed to another boat. About 3 o'clock in the morning of the 7th we were waked by the violent agitation of the boat, attended with a noise more tremendous and terrific than I can describe or any one conceive, who was not present or near to such a scene. The constant discharge of heavy cannon might give some idea of the noise for the loudness, but this was infinitely more terrible, on account of its appearing to be subterraneous.
>
> As soon as we waked we discovered that the bar to which we were tied was sinking, we cut loose and rowed our boats for the middle of the river. After getting out so far as to be out of danger from the trees, which were falling in from the banks—the swells in the river were so great as to threaten the sinking of the boat every moment. We stopped the oarholes with blankets to keep out the water—after remaining in this situation for some time, we perceiving a light on the shore which we left—(we having a lighted candle in a lantern on our boat) were hailed and advised to land, which we attempted to do but could not effect it, finding the banks and the trees still falling in.
>
> At day light we perceived the head of the tenth island. During all this time we had made only about four miles down the river—from which circumstance, and from that of an immense quantity of water rushing into the river from the woods—it is evident that the earth at this place or below, had been raised so high as to stop the progress of the river, and cause it to overflow its banks. We took the right hand channel of the river at this island, an reached within about half a mile of the lower end of the town, we were affrighted with the appearance of a dreadful rapid or falls in the river just below us, we were so far in the suck that it was impossible now to land—all hope of surviving was now lost and certain destruction appeared to await us! We having passed the rapids without injury, keeping our bow foremost, both boats being still lashed together.
>
> —Mathias M. Speed, March 2, 1812

Missourians call it New Madrid Bend; Kentuckians call it Kentucky Bend. Whatever it is called, this is where the Mississippi almost turns back on itself as it rounds Kentucky Point, no more than a mile wide at its neck. The distance around the bend, from the foot of Island 10 to the foot of Island 11 is twenty miles. Under it all, running roughly north to south, lies the Reelfoot fault, one segment in the system of faults that rest within the boundaries of the Reelfoot rift. The rift formed over five hundred million years ago as the earth's crust pulled apart and a block of crust, forty miles wide and three hundred miles long, dropped down. Sediment filled the rift over thousands of years. Then, two hundred million years ago, the region subsided and the Gulf of Mexico flowed in, creating the Mississippi Embayment. The rivers that flow to the northern end of the embayment deposited three thousand feet of sediment. Within the Reelfoot rift are the faults that make up the New Madrid seismic zone, where most of the recorded earthquakes have happened.

Three very large earthquakes struck the upper Mississippi embayment during the winter of 1811–1812. On the night of December 16, 1811, the first quake struck between Blytheville and Mark Tree, Arkansas, leaving the towns—New Madrid, Little Prairie, and Point Pleasant—badly shaken. The saturated floodplain liquefied, causing fissures, fountains, and sand blows. Aftershocks rattled the region for the next five weeks. On January 23, 1812, the second fault ruptured, this time between New Madrid and Cairo, Illinois, breaking up an ice-jam at Louisville, Kentucky. Boats stuck in the ice at Louisville headed down the Ohio to the Mississippi, tying up at New Madrid on the evening of February 6. At 3:45 A.M. the following day the third earthquake cut loose along the Reelfoot fault.

The Reelfoot fault crosses the Mississippi at the foot of Island 9, runs under Donaldson Point, and crosses the Mississippi a second time at the foot of Island 10, runs up Kentucky Point, crosses the Mississippi a third time near New Madrid, and continues north.

The quake created a dam, as high as ten feet, in the bed of a river sixty feet deep at Island 10. The river slammed into it, creating a great wave that flowed upstream as far as Island 8. Downstream of Island 10 the river eroded the dam in a cascade that seemed like a waterfall, carrying along boats that had tied up to the island for the night. Where the Reelfoot fault crossed the river near New Madrid, a second dam rose up, the river crashed against it, and a second wave surged upstream. To the south, in Lake County, Tennessee, where the fault crossed a creek, Reelfoot Lake pooled behind the same dam. The dams eroded quickly; uplifted land did not and is still visible onshore. Geologists call it the Reelfoot scarp.

Geologists and seismologists have sorted out how the New Madrid earthquakes happened, but they have not sorted out why they happened. Nor have they sorted out the rate at which the strain has accumulated since the morning of February 7, 1812.

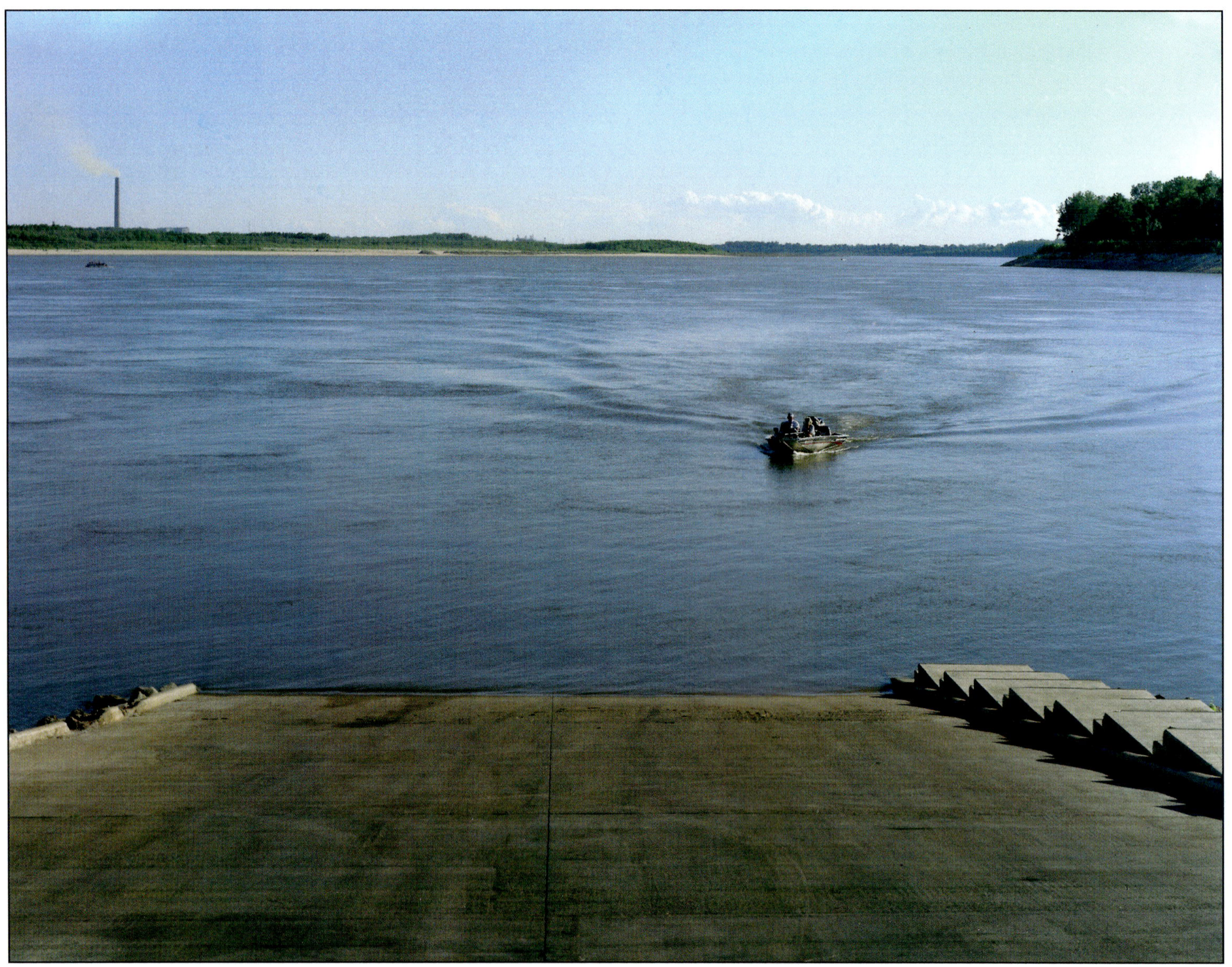

The Old Man: New Madrid Bend

New Madrid County, Missouri

Location, location, location: The City of New Madrid was in trouble long before the earthquakes. A pair of Canadian fur traders established a post at the top of New Madrid Bend in 1783. Six years later at the end of the American Revolution, Col. George Morgan platted a town along four miles of the concave side of New Madrid Bend. Without revetments to armor its banks, the Mississippi continued to shave sediment from the bend, carry it downriver, and deposit it on Kentucky Point. The bank collapsed, taking part of the village with it. The people of New Madrid rebuilt their cabins further inland four or five times in the years before the Civil War.

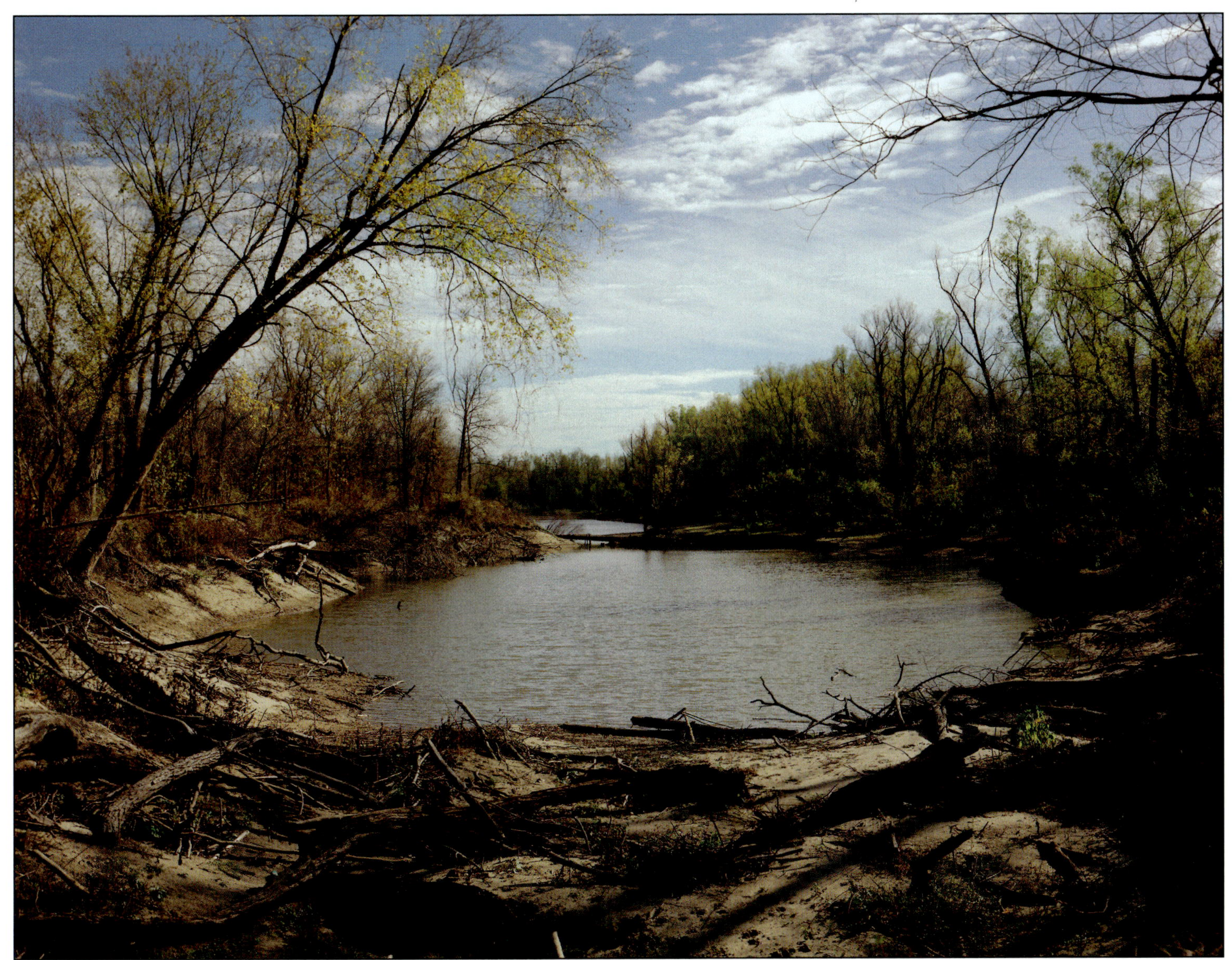

Kentucky Point: Stonewall Lake
Fulton County, Kentucky

Stonewall Lake, a depression in a swale, is long, narrow, and fringed in willows. That there are three parcels of land on Kentucky Point in the WRP is surprising. The Natural Resources Conservation Fund will pay farmers $900 an acre to place land in the program, half to a third of the market value of land in the Kentucky floodplain. One private owner put in 1,358 acres of Kentucky Point and managed it for hunting and fishing, restored 300 acres in bottomland hardwoods, 100 acres in warm-season native grasses and forbs, 264 acres to wetlands, and managed 388 acres as moist-soil habitat for waterfowl.

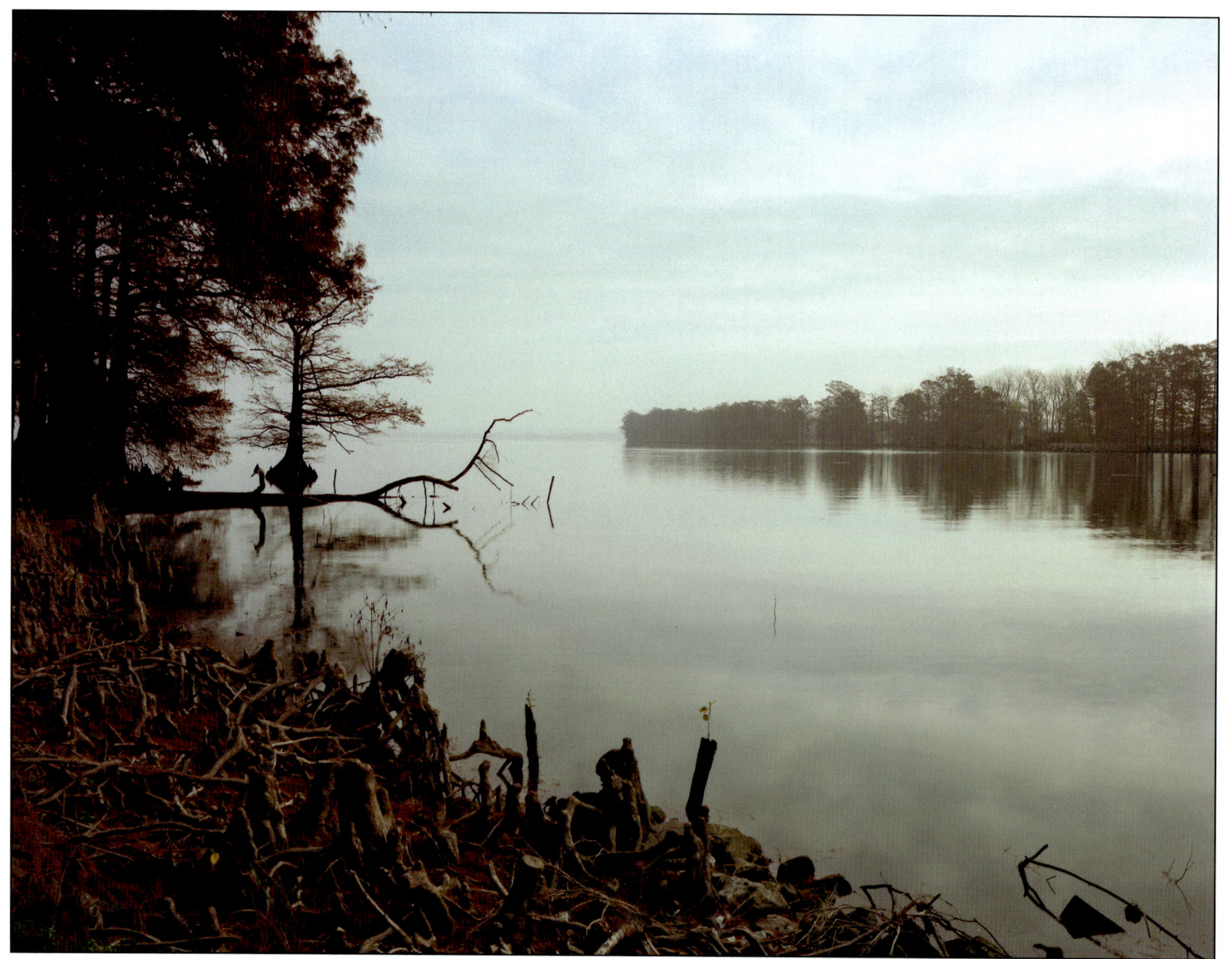

Reelfoot Lake NWR: Cypress Point, 1994
Obion County, Tennessee

Pierre Nichol, a fur trapper hunting beaver on the Obion River on the morning of February 7, 1812, clung to a tree while he watched earth crack and sink, carrying the forest with it. An area thirty miles long and ten miles wide sank fifty feet. The February 7 earthquake thrust up what would become the lakebed of Reelfoot Lake. When the thrust rebounded, the lakebed subsided permanently to a level many feet below its prequake level. The Reelfoot scarp remained permanently uplifted. The Reelfoot River ponded behind it, forming Reelfoot Lake, one of the world's great fish hatcheries. Congress established the Reelfoot Lake NWR in 1941.

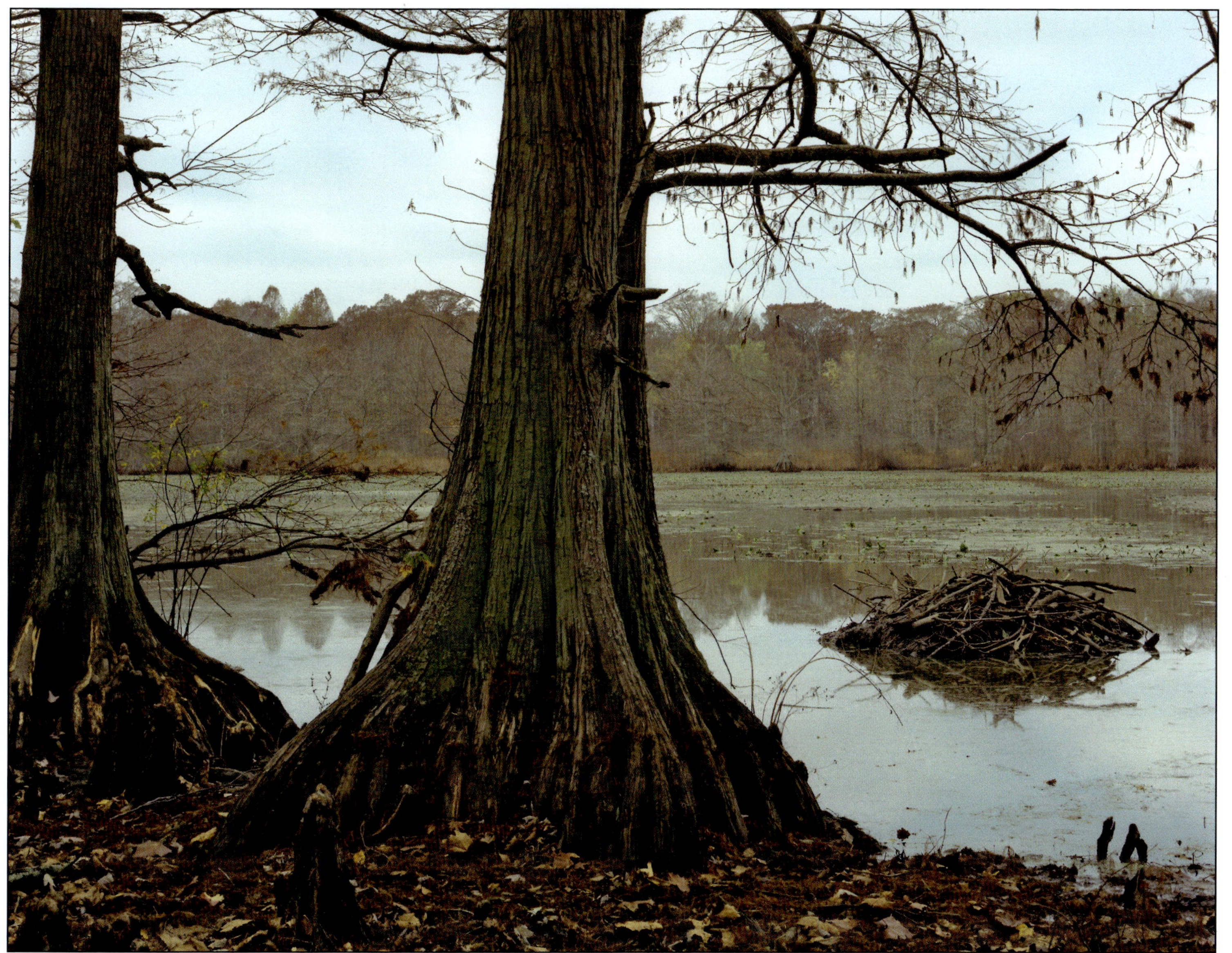

Reelfoot Lake NWR: Mud Basin

Obion County, Tennessee

From its shaky beginning, Reelfoot Lake, the refuge, had a rocky start. In the nineteenth century loggers competed over timber, market hunters clashed over birds, local hunters battled over game. In 1908 the state declared the lands around Reelfoot the property of the citizens of Tennessee. In the 1920s drainage efforts altered its hydrology. Farmers cleared the highly erodible lands on the margins of the lake, sending streams of silt into it, and in the '30s, tried to drain it for row crops. The state settled matters in 1941 by leasing 7,587 acres at the northern end of the lake to the USFWS for the wildlife refuge.

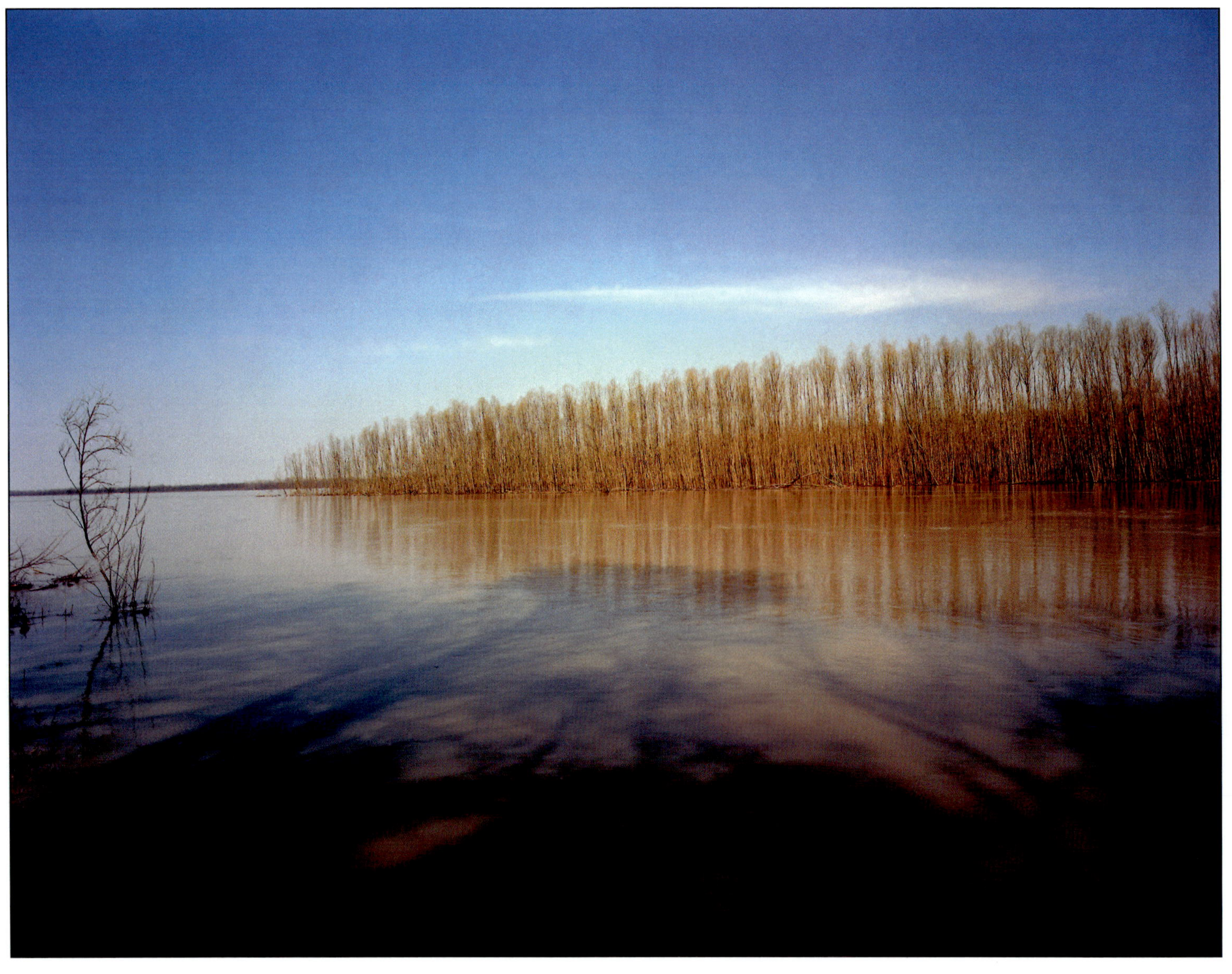

Plum Point Bend: Keyes Point Landing

Lauderdale County, Tennessee

In 1821 the shallow turn around Plum Point was the most dangerous bend on the river. Steamboats had to maneuver through a forest of snags and sandbars. Eight years later Henry Shreve demonstrated the effectiveness of his snagboat at removing the snags. Even today, in spite of the Corps' continual dredging, miles of revetments above the bend to keep the bank from collapsing, and dikes below the bend to deepen the channel, a ridge of sand anchored by sandbar willows can form just upstream of the bend. The Tennessee Wildlife Resources Agency wants to notch the dikes around Plum Point Bend and let the river flow through the channel between the sandbar and the bank.

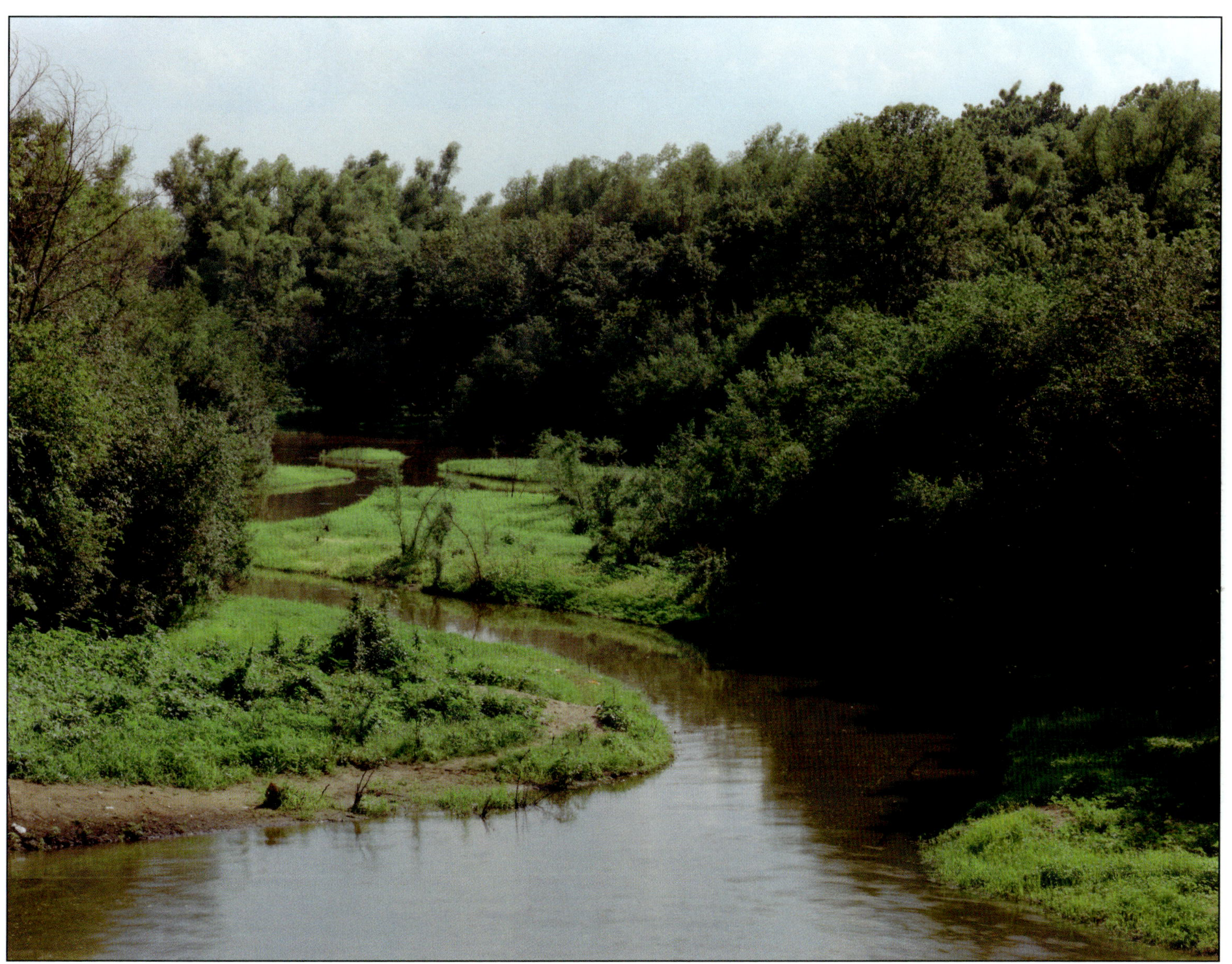

Centennial Island: Devil's Elbow Chute

Tipton County, Tennessee

"On March 7, 1876, the river suddenly and with great violence, within about thirty hours, made for itself a new channel directly across the neck opposite the apex of Dean's Island, so that the old channel around the bend of the elbow (a distance of fifteen to twenty miles) was abandoned by the current, and although it remained for a few years covered with dead water it was no longer navigable except in times of high water for small boats. The old bed immediately began to fill with sand, sediment, and alluvial deposits. In the course of time it became dry land suitable for cultivation and covered with timber."—U.S. Supreme Court, 1918

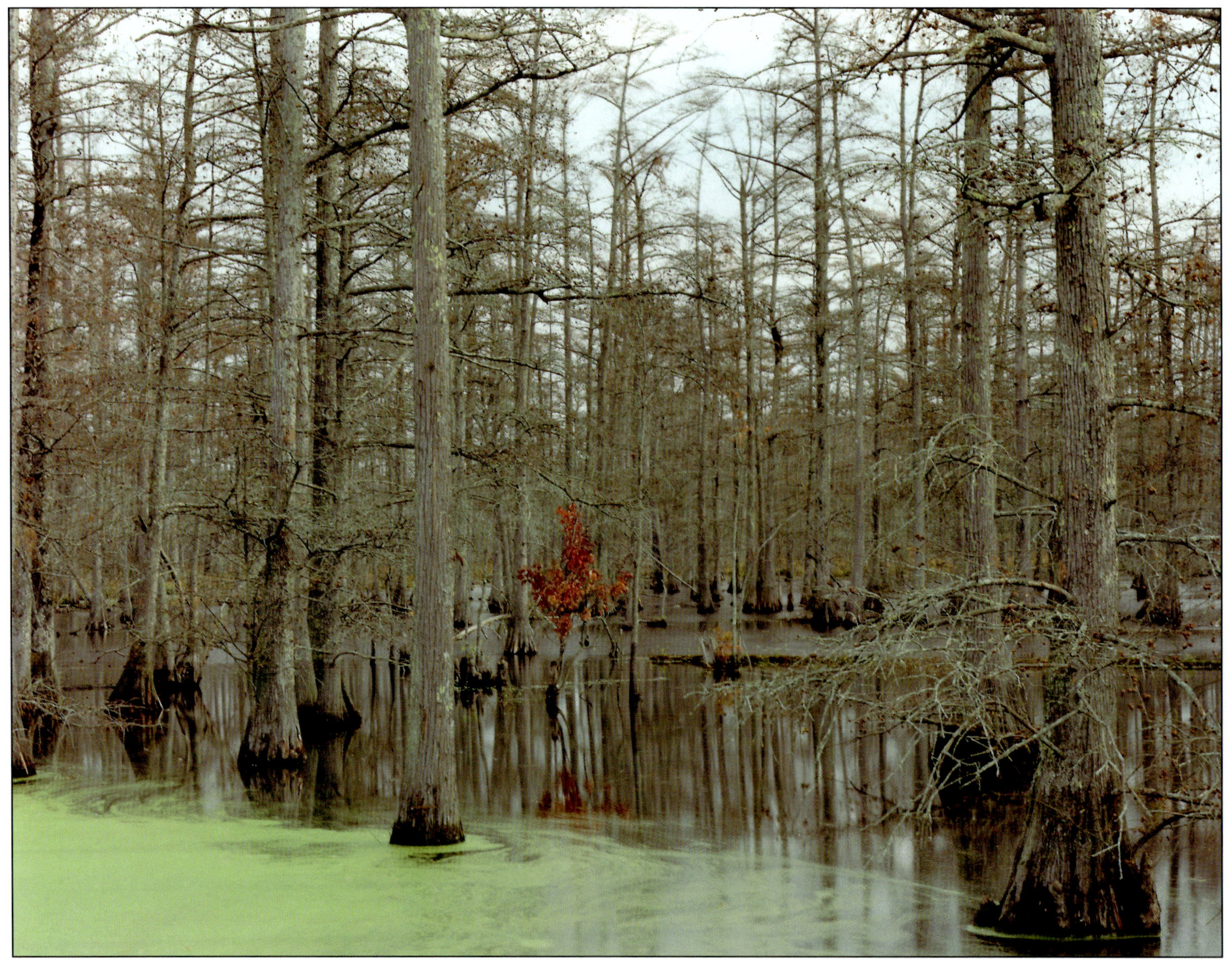

Beaver Dam Lake: Kyles Brake

Tunica County, Mississippi

Beaver Dam Lake formed when the river cut a new channel across a point bar sometime after 1835. A feeder bayou connected Beaver Dam Lake to the Mississippi and deposited fine silts and clays in the ends of the new oxbow with every flood. The oxbow silted in at its ends. A cypress took root in Kyles Brake. The mainline levee cut the feeder bayou from the river, stopping the process. In the early twenty-first century, Beaver Dam Lake still drew ducks and hunters. The ducks—Gadwalls, Mallards, Wigeons, and Teals—came for the duckweed, the hunters for the up-close, personal quality of the hunt, where the ducks are no more than thirty yards away.

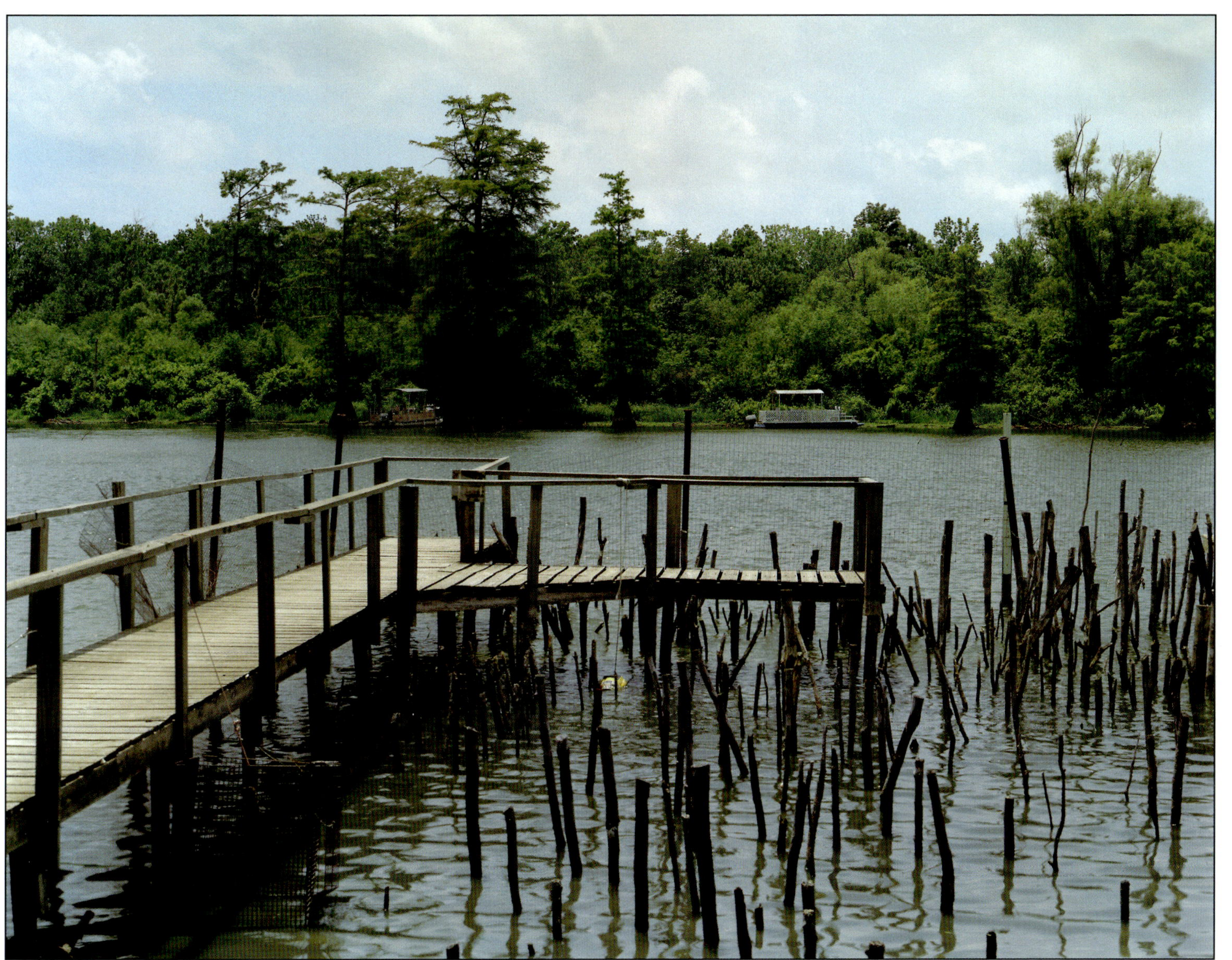

Council Island: Council Lake, Ed's Boat Camp
Tunica County, Mississippi

"The distance was nearly half a league: a man standing on the shore could not be told, whether he were a man or something else, from the other side. The stream was swift, and very deep; the water, always flowing turbidly, brought along from above many trees and much timber, driven onward by its force."—Gentleman of Elvas, 1541

Hernando de Soto and a force of 600 men arrived at a well-timbered spot on the Mississippi's east bank in the spring of 1541. They set up camp, cut the timber, and built houses and barges. They crossed the Mississippi into Arkansas on June 18, 1541, either at Council Bend or Walnut Bend.

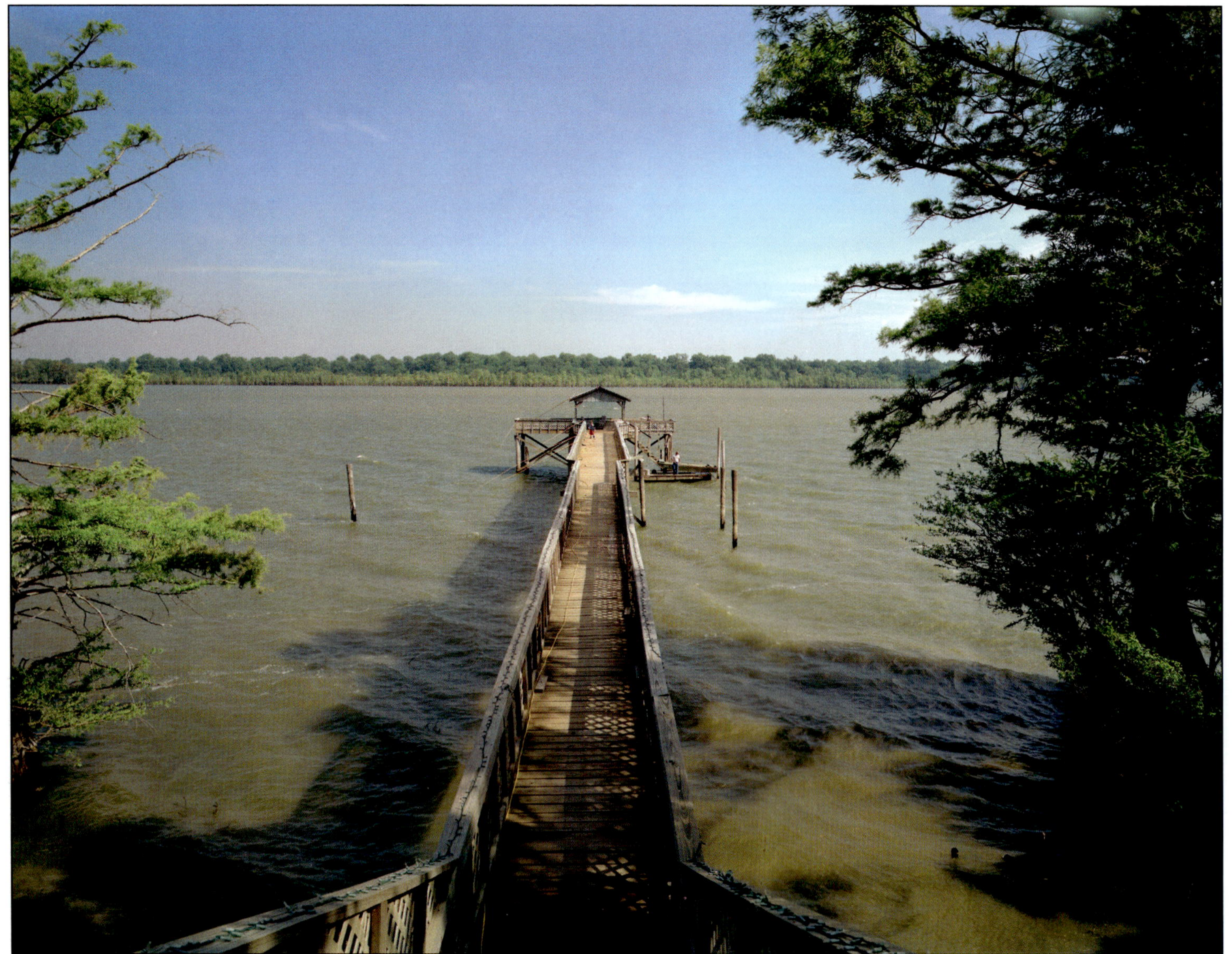

Moon Lake

Coahoma County, Mississippi

Yazoo Pass carries water from Moon Lake to the Coldwater River. The Corps cut the connection. A flooded Coldwater ceased to infuse Moon Lake with fresh water through the pass. Phillips Bayou carried water, sediment, nutrients, and pesticides into Moon Lake, muddying the water, depriving it of oxygen, and adding an inch of sediment every year. The Mississippi Department of Environmental Quality began a Section 319 project to clean up the lake. Farmers adopted best management practices to keep sediment, nutrients, and pesticides out of the lake. The Corps reestablished the flow from the Coldwater and stabilized the water level in the lake.

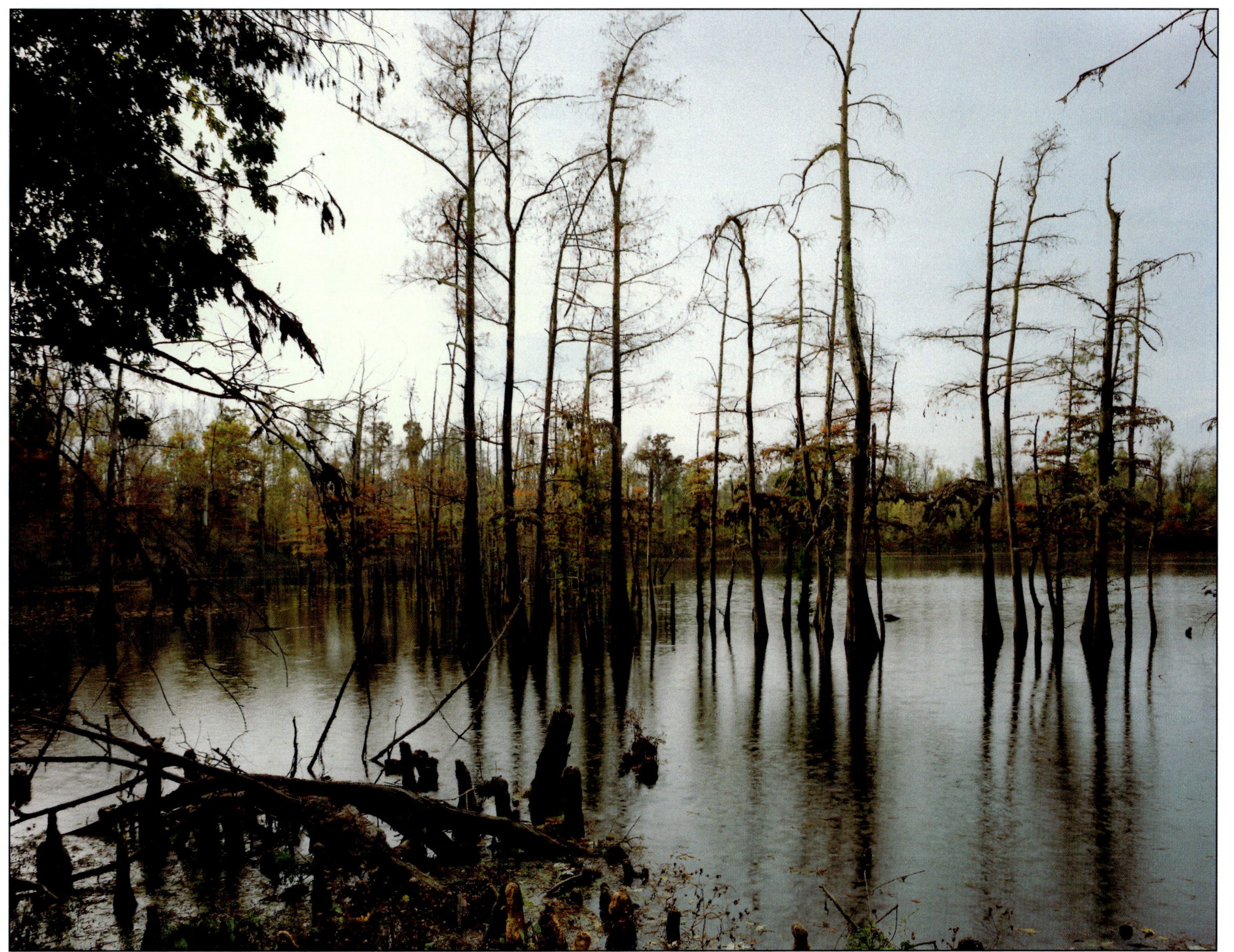

Sunflower Bend: Island 66 and De Soto Lake

Coahoma County, Mississippi

In 1942 the Corps dredged a cutoff across the neck of Sunflower Bend, creating De Soto Lake. When snowmelt swells the Mississippi, it washes across the active floodplain, filling oxbows like De Soto Lake, scattering fish through fields and forests. As the flood recedes, De Soto Lake goes shallow and harbors all those fish in a shrinking lake. Anglers love the concentration of fish, but the lake needs to be deeper. The Lower Mississippi River Conservation Commission suggested dredging deep holes, places fish could retreat to when the lake was too hot or too cold, and building a weir at the outflow of the lake to maintain depth as flooding recedes.

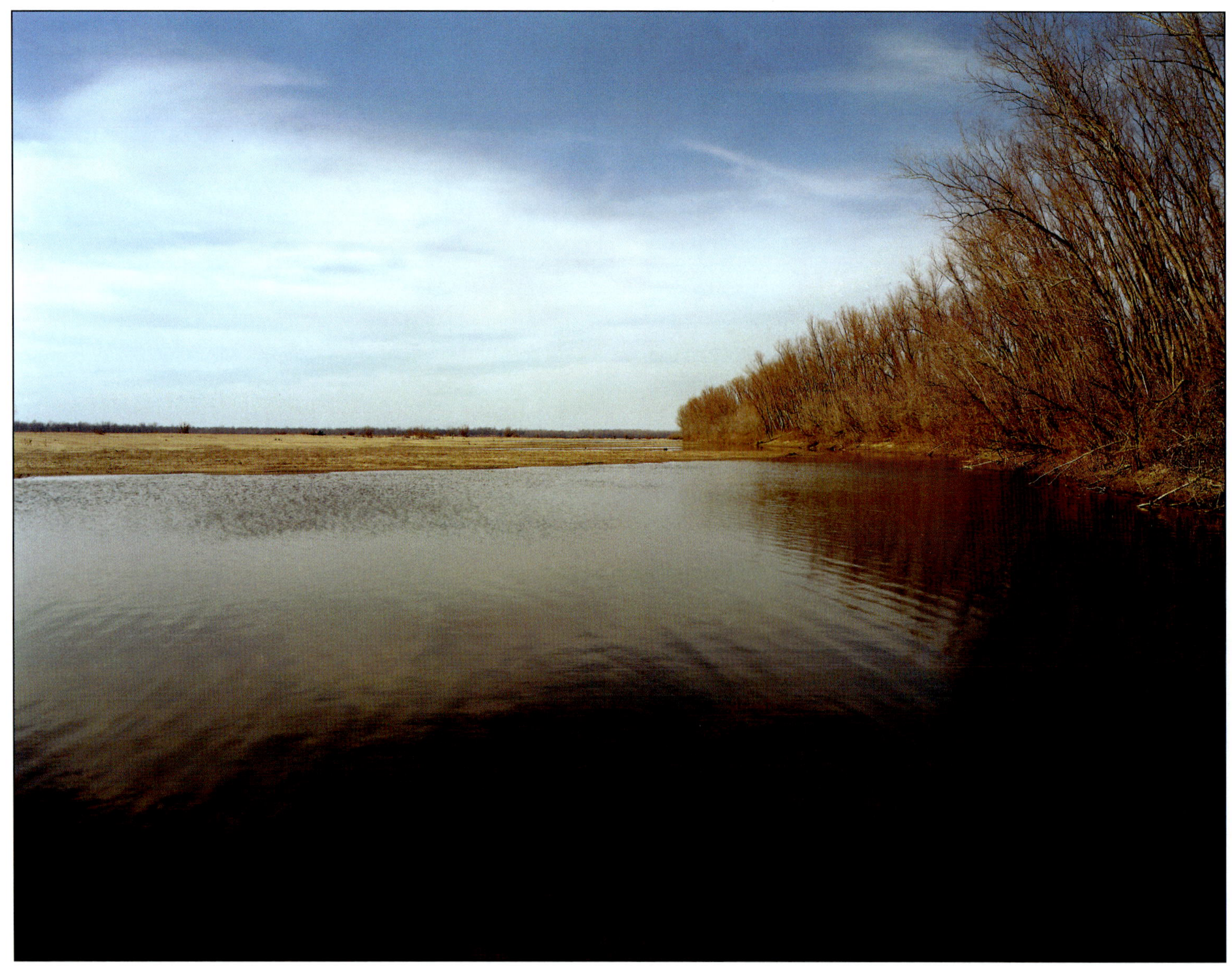

The Old Man: Terrene Dikes Sandbar, Great River Road State Park

Bolivar County, Mississippi

In 1968 the Corps of Engineers set a series of three dikes on the left descending bank of the river between miles 590 and 589 and forced the navigation channel to the opposite bank. The Terrene Dikes captured sediment. A sandbar formed over them. Least Terns took up residence and began nesting, but only a dozen or so, because visitors to the Great River Road State Park walk their dogs on the bar. To give the terns their much-desired privacy, the Corps notched the first two dikes to allow water to flow between the mainland and the sandbar and provide habitat for paddlefish and pallid sturgeon, which are known to swim at mile 590.

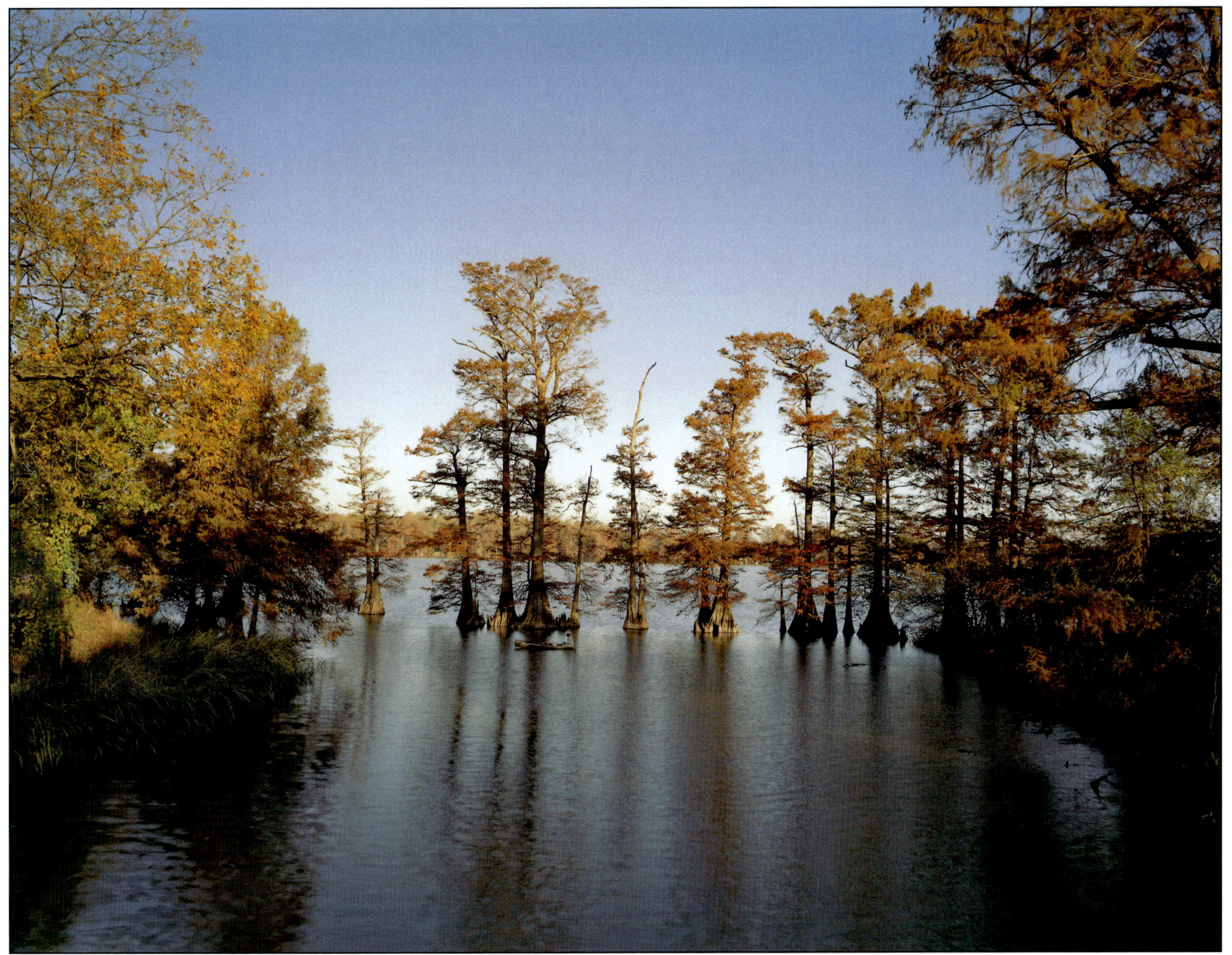

Lake Bolivar: Head of Deer Creek

Bolivar County, Mississippi

Deer Creek—the birthplace of Kermit the Frog—heads in Lake Bolivar, an oxbow. It falls fifty feet in 159 miles to its confluence with the Yazoo. By 2001 its southern reaches dried out in the summer; other reaches barely ran in a trickle. Sediment clogged its channel; nutrients, pesticides, raw sewage fouled its waters, and trash littered its banks. Farmers hoped to tap the Mississippi to restore its historic flows, water that could be used for irrigation. In the fall of 2001 the private Mississippi Fish and Wildlife Foundation joined the USFWS in a plan to restore Deer Creek by engaging schoolchildren in cleaning it up and monitoring its water quality.

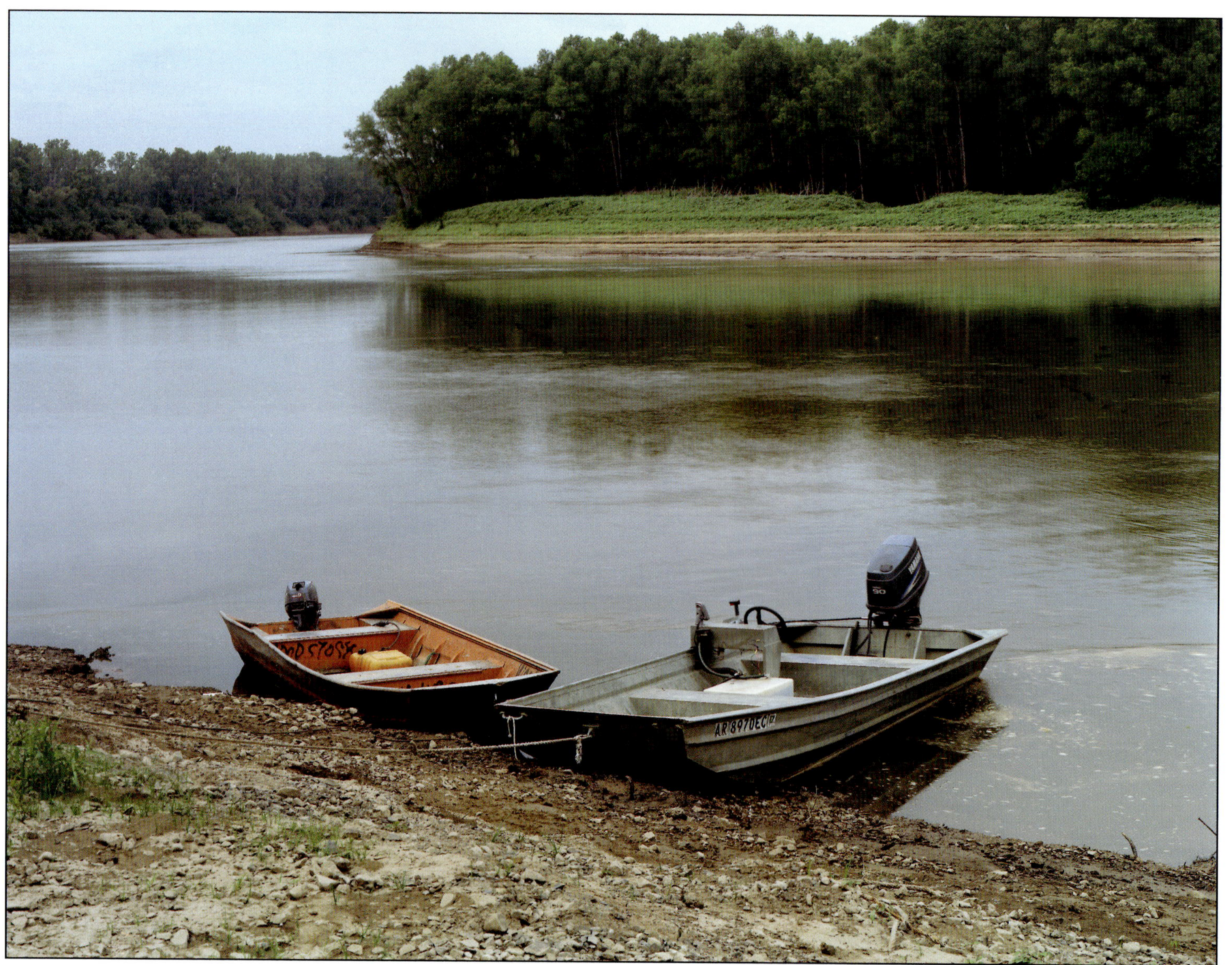

Greenville Bends: Old River at Luna Landing

Washington County, Mississippi

Rowdy Bend, Miller Bend, Spanish Moss Bend, and Bachelor Bend: the river zigged and zagged between Arkansas City and Greenville, Mississippi. River pilots called them the Greenville Bends. It was fifteen land miles between the head of Rowdy Bend and the toe of Bachelor Bend, fifty by river. They were shallow and meandered through resistant and cohesive clay. In a flood the river pooled in the bends, which acted like dams. Water backed up to Arkansas City. The Corps worked to prevent the river from cutting across the point bars that formed bends, only to have Gen. Harley Ferguson include them in his cutoffs to shorten the river and speed floods downstream.

General Ferguson's Cutoffs

A meandering river works to maintain a fairly constant length. Natural cutoffs are its means. When the river becomes too long and its slope too flat, it searches out a steeper, more efficient slope and makes a cutoff across the narrow neck of a point bar. Having made a cutoff, the river increases its slope and speed above the cutoff and erodes its banks and its bed, adding to its load of sediment. Below the cutoff the river remains unchanged. It moves slowly down a shallow slope, forcing the river speeding through the cutoff to slow down and deposit its sediment downstream of the cutoff, creating a new sandbar, around which the river meanders, restoring its length. In its natural state the Lower Mississippi made a cutoff once every seven to ten years. After each cutoff, the river took thirty to eighty years to recover and regain its width, its bar sequence, and its flow regimen.

Before Ferguson made his cutoffs, the average length of the Lower Mississippi River was about 1,080 miles. It varied up and down as the river made cutoffs and created bars, but it always came back to the average. Ferguson lopped 116 miles off the average in the 330 miles between the Arkansas and the Red Rivers. Overall, the increased carrying capacity of the river yielded flood levels two to five feet lower between the Arkansas River and Natchez and lowered flood heights in the White, the Yazoo River, and the Red River backwaters.

Because Ferguson's intent was to speed floods downstream, he needed to prepare the river for the rush of water that would stream through each new cut. Hence, he began work on the southernmost cutoff and worked upstream. The Greenville Bends were to be the fourth step in Ferguson's plan. After 1880 the river added seven miles in the bends as it shaved sediment off the concave bends, deposited it on the heads of the point bars, and threatened to chew away the levees on both banks. In Ferguson's view the bends had to go. Bachelor Bend, on which the City of Greenville was located, volunteered to go first.

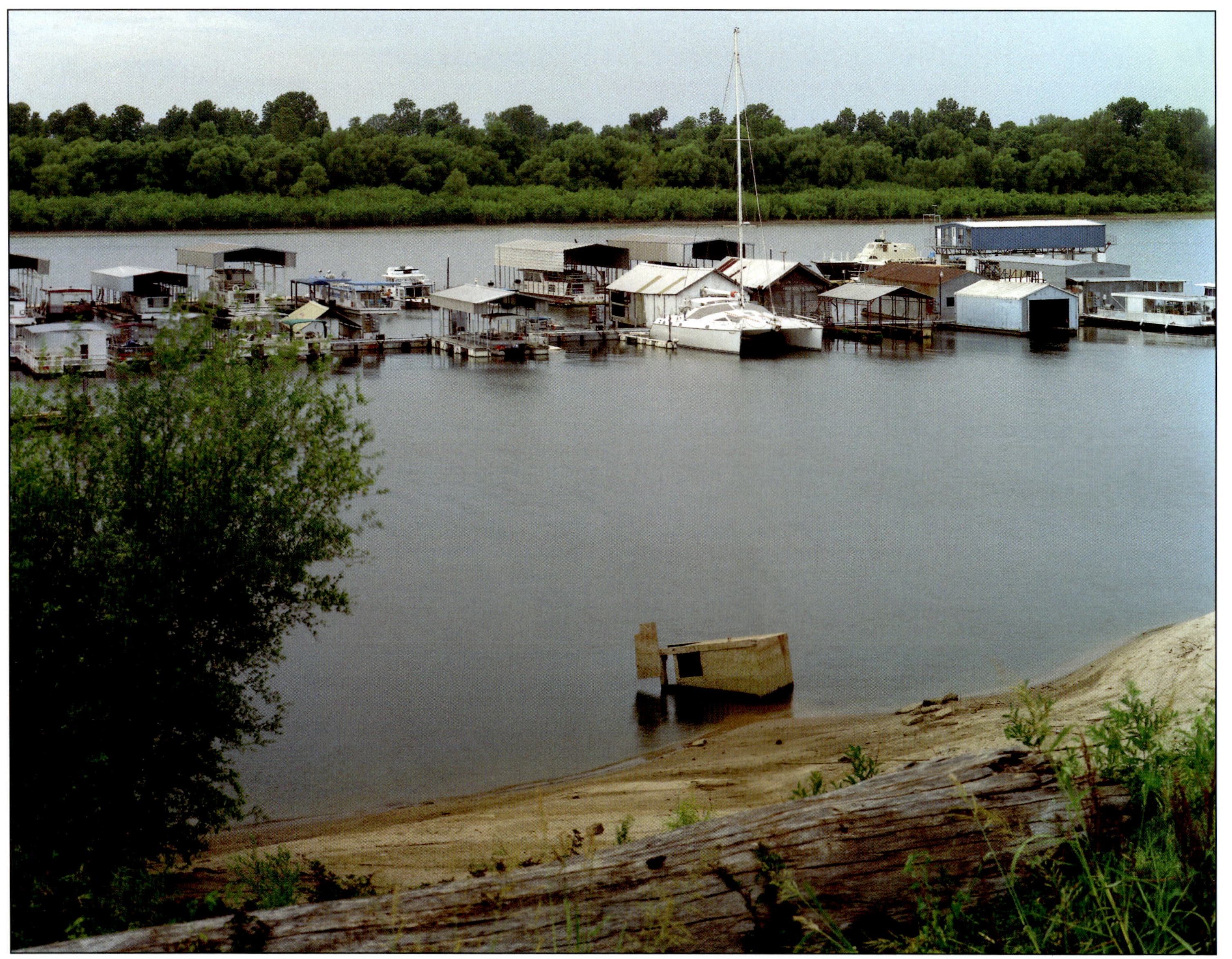

Bachelor Bend: Lake Ferguson
Washington County, Mississippi

Ferguson only planned two cutoffs at the Greenville Bends. Bachelor Bend was not one of them. The bendway wrapped itself around Point Chicot. The river broke through the dike that protected the point from scour on July 8, 1933, and forced Ferguson to redraw his plans for the Greenville Bends. Ferguson and his engineers finished the work the river had started across Point Chicot and aligned it properly, leaving Greenville on the shores of Lake Ferguson, old Bachelor Bend. The new channel, the Leland Cutoff, carried 50 percent of the flow during the low-water season in 1933. Ferguson made the Ashbrook and Tarpley Cuts in the Greenville Bends in 1935.

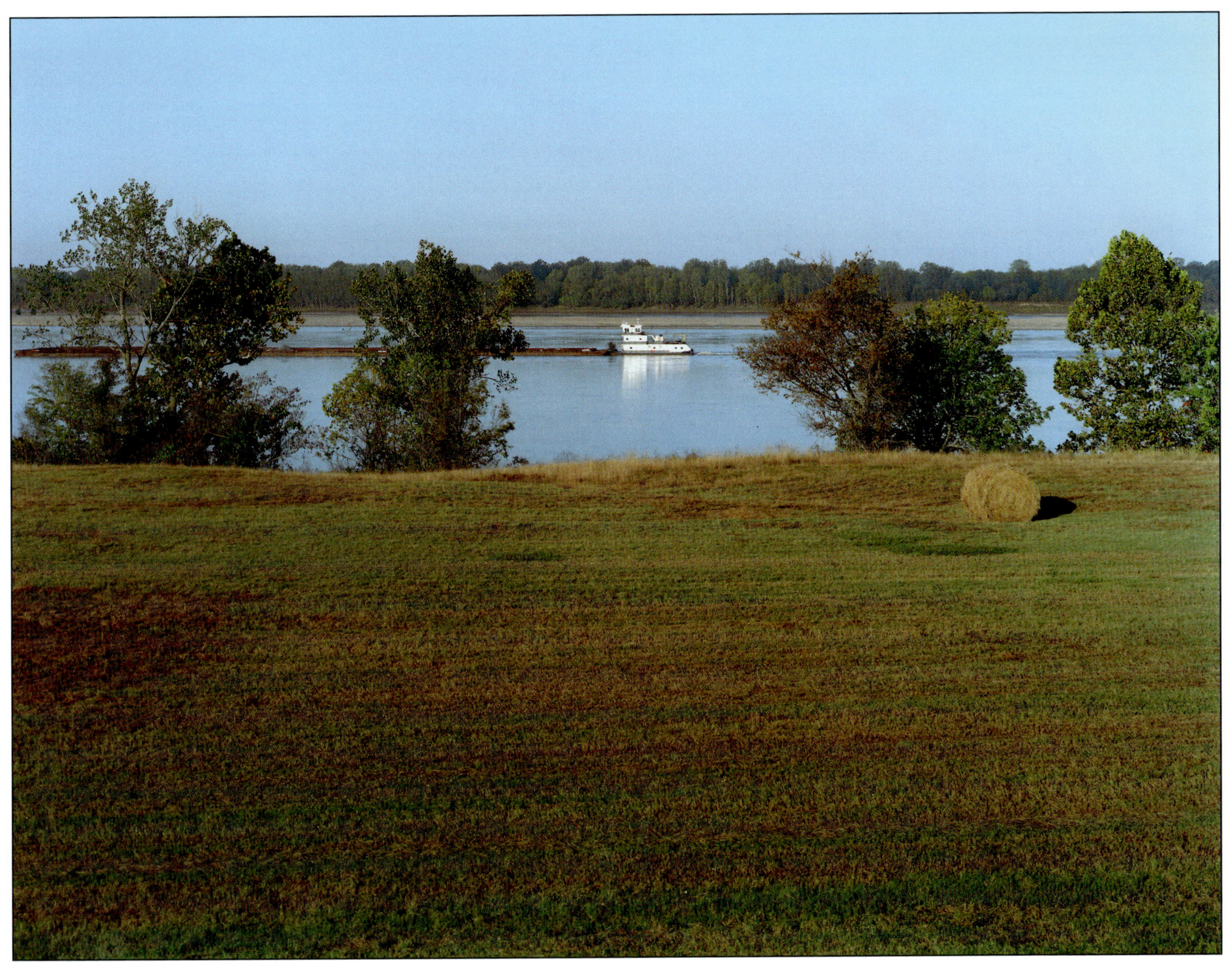

The Old Man: Greenville Bends, Tarpley Cutoff
Washington County, Mississippi

The new reach through the old bends continued to vex the Corps. The old sinuosity allowed the Mississippi fifty-three miles to negotiate the steep grade between the top of Askbrook Cutoff and the foot of Leland Cutoff and allowed the river to deposit sediment on the point bars. Ferguson created a straight channel, but the steep grade required constant dredging. The Corps laid revetments to discourage meander, built dikes to catch sediment, reducing the need for dredging. But the navigation channel shifted constantly, leading one engineer to suggest training structures to create a sinuous channel that would allow the river to meander.

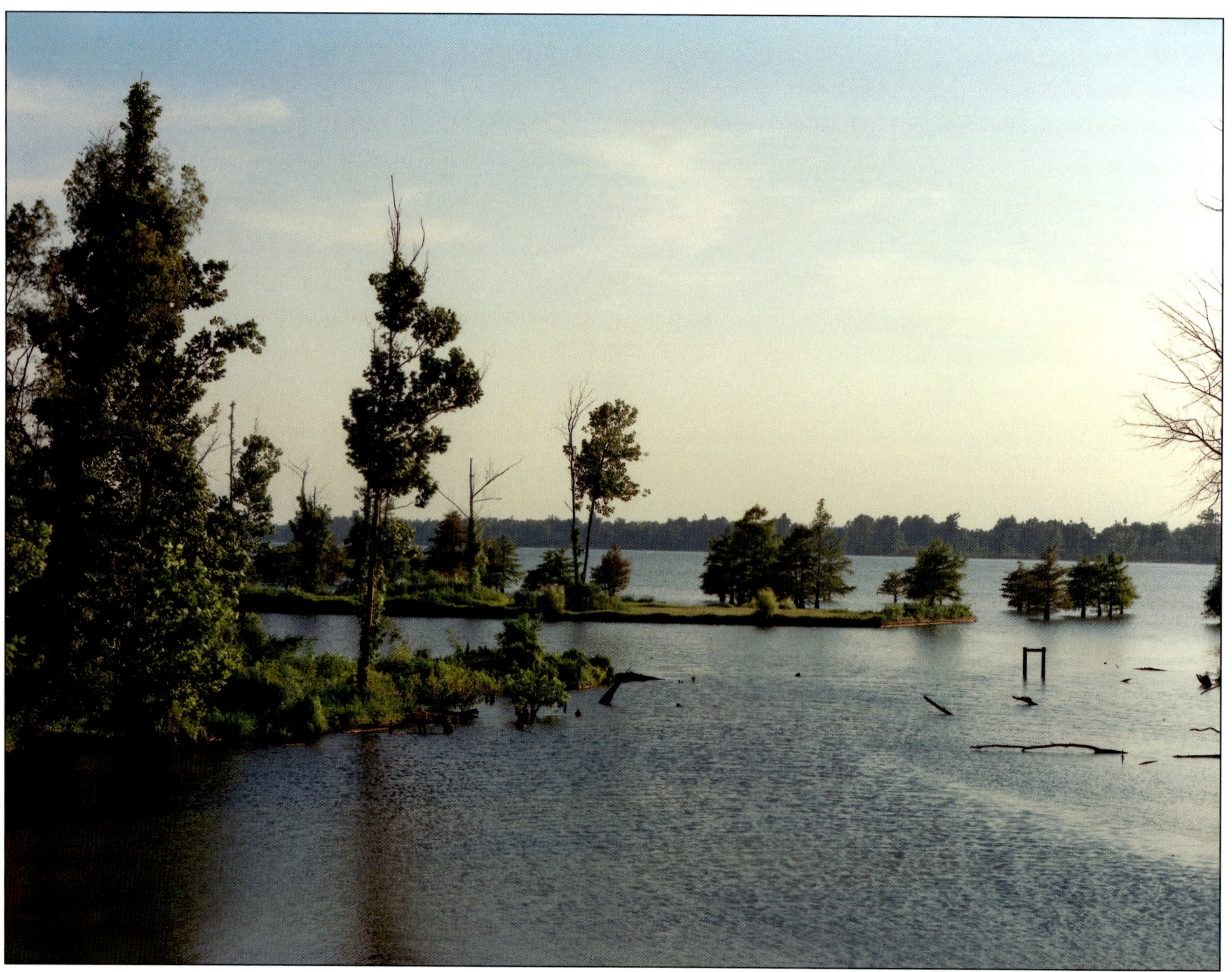

Chicot Lake: At the Causeway across the Lake
Chicot County, Arkansas

Five hundred years old, Chicot, twenty miles long, and nearly a mile wide, is the largest oxbow lake in North America. In 2000, cormorants and largemouth bass, which have a taste for crappie, were decimating its beloved crappie fishery. The Arkansas Game and Fish Commission developed the Lake Chicot Management Plan in March 2001 to improve fishery quality and increase the abundance of crappie: Reduce the loss of shoreline riparian habitat. Maintain aquatic vegetation. Thin populations of cormorant, bass, and catfish. Maintain below 40 percent the number of commercial species—gar, carp, sucker, buffalo, drum, catfish, and paddlefish.

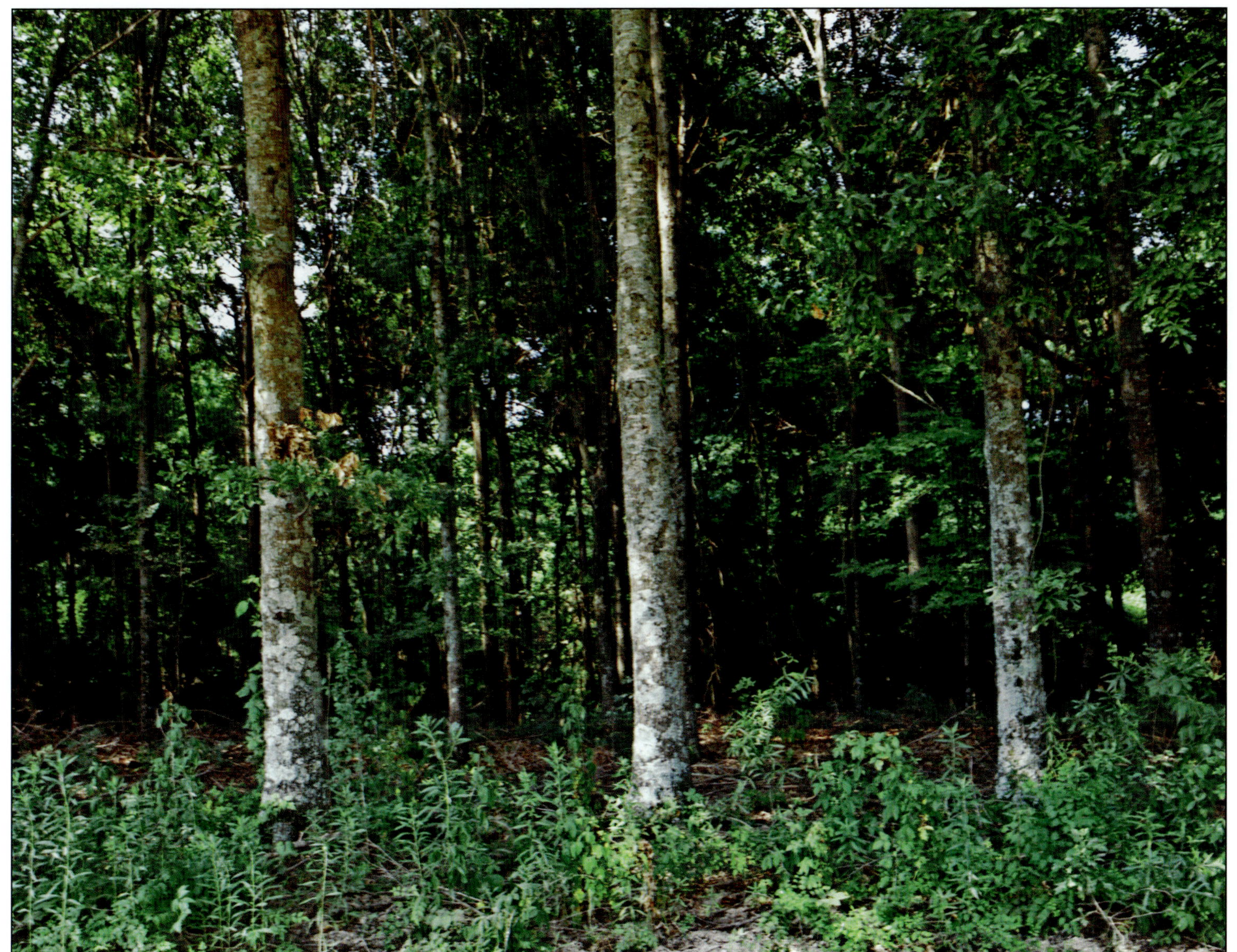

Yazoo National Wildlife Refuge: Swan Lake Reforestation

Washington County, Mississippi

Since 1968 foresters have seeded acorns or planted seedlings on approximately 3,000 acres of marginal farmland on the Yazoo NWR. At first foresters had little information to go on other than the survey maps that noted what witness trees were located where when the land was first surveyed. They assumed any tree anyplace would do. It took years of trial and error to learn what trees did best where; how the hydrologic cycle must be managed to mimic the flood cycles that characterize bottomland forests historically; that timber must be harvested to increase tree diversity; and that small, isolated tracts provided little habitat for migrating songbirds.

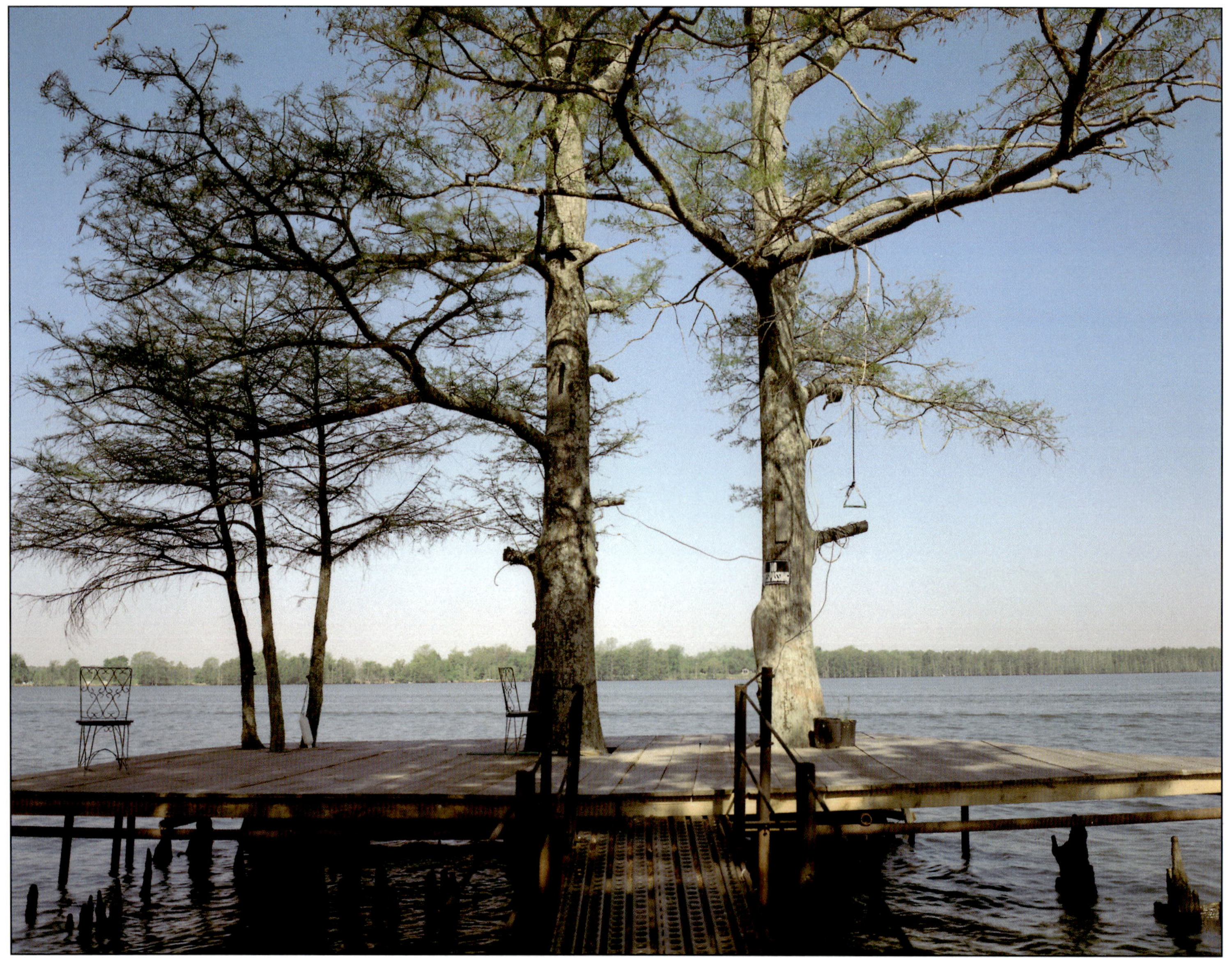

Lake Washington

Washington County, Mississippi

Lake Washington: cut off from the Mississippi seven hundred years ago, drainage ditches altered the flow of water to the lake. The 11,000 acres of farm fields that surround it eroded twelve tons of soil per acre per year into 3,200 acres of open water and cypress swamp. With the soil came pesticides and nutrients. Hundreds of cottages and house trailers lined its banks, few with adequate septic tanks. The lake was muddy, its water stagnant. Pesticides closed the lake to commercial fishing in the 1970s. Low-oxygen conditions produced fish kills in 1986. A toxic blue-green algal bloom in 1990 killed fourteen neighborhood dogs that drank the water.

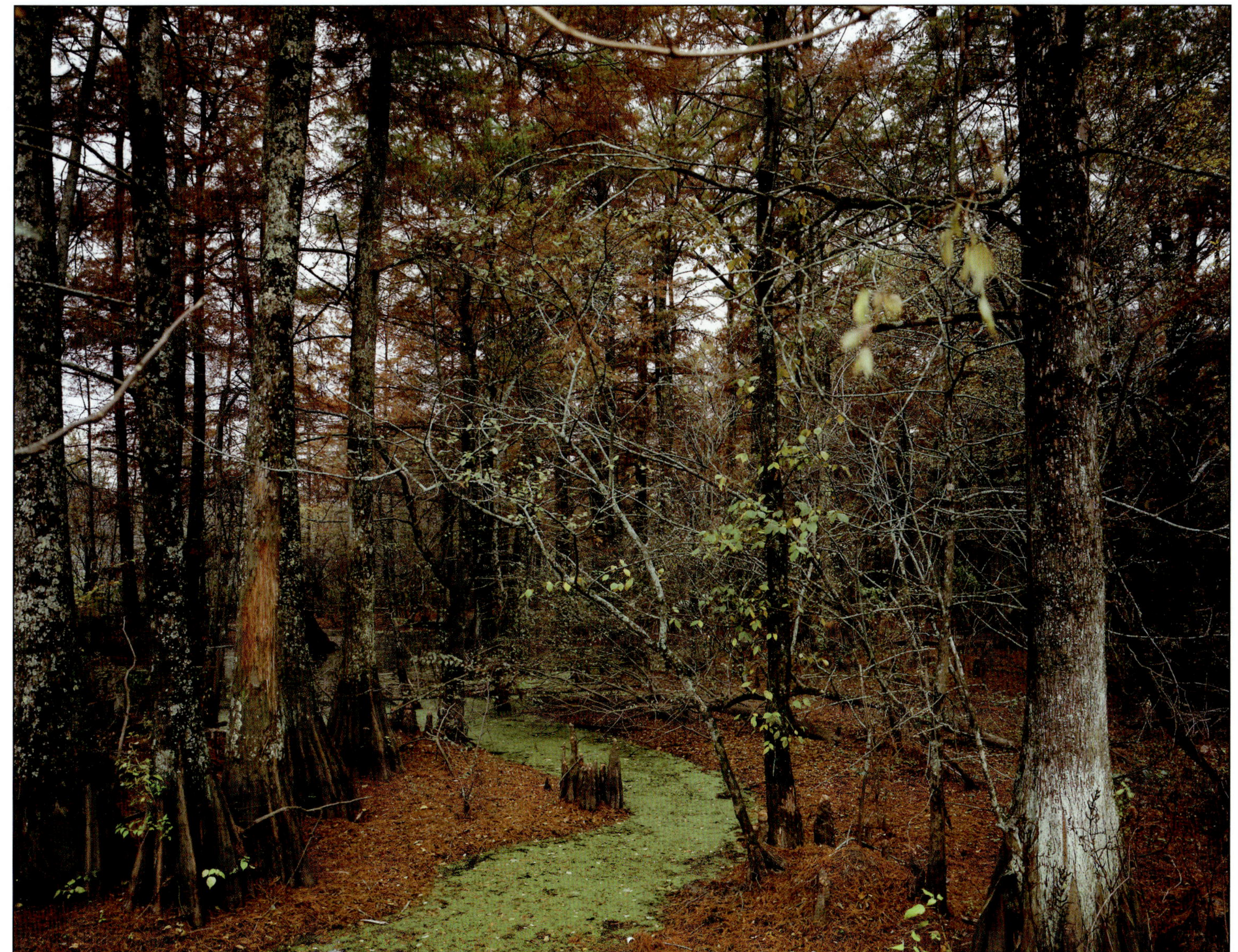

Lake Washington: Intermittent Stream from Washington Bayou
Washington County, Mississippi

The first attempt to clean up Lake Washington in the early 1990s failed. By 1996 the lake had more of everything—more sediment, more nutrients, more sewage, more algal blooms, more cormorants—except oxygen. In 2003 with good state and local support, Mississippi enrolled the lake in the Gulf of Mexico hypoxia-reduction program and adopted a watershed program to develop a plan: Identify and quantify water-quality issues affecting the lake. Estimate the cost and describe the means for restoring water quality. Educate the public about the need. Schedule the work. Define targets. Set criteria for success. Monitor the lake to keep it clean.

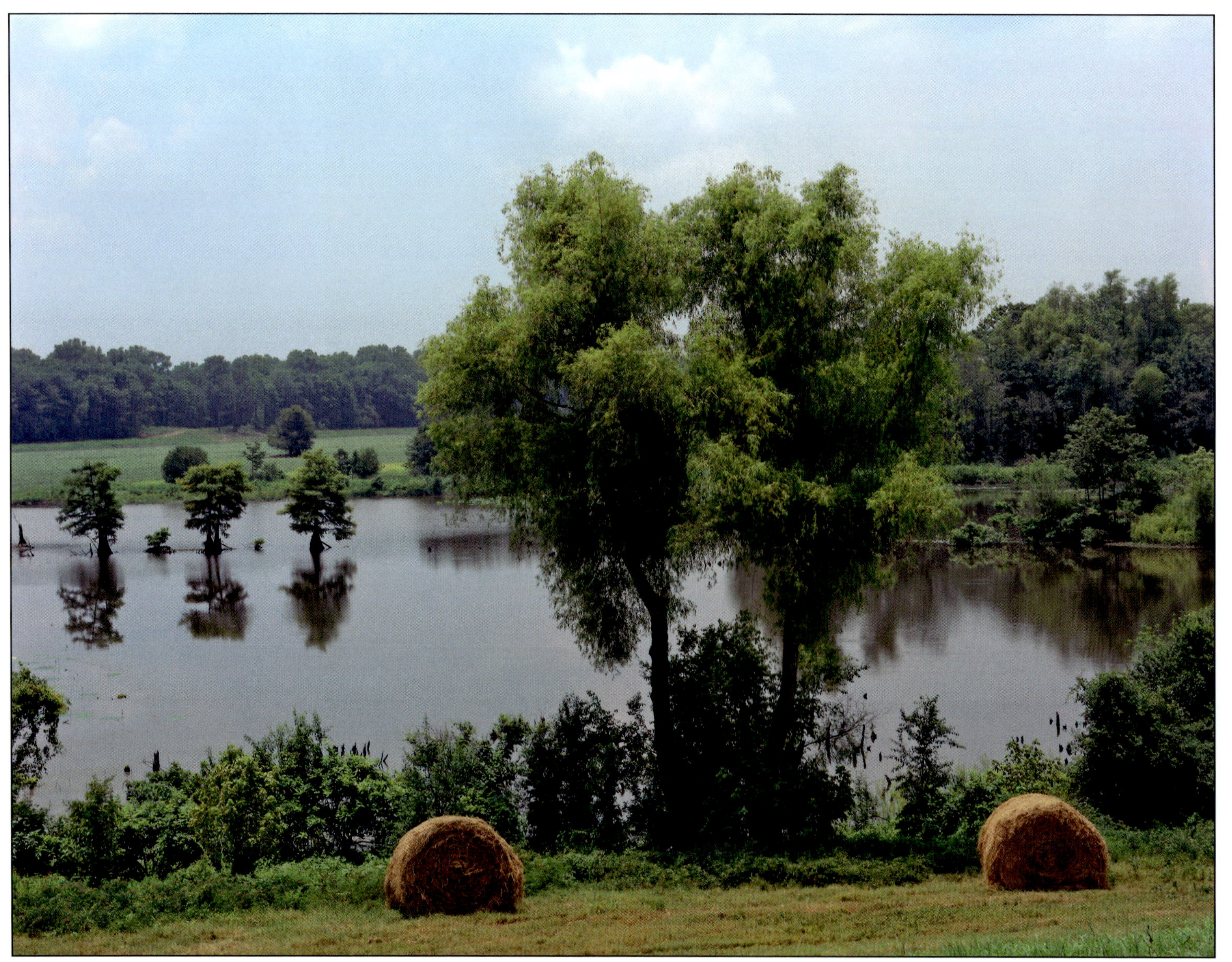

Arcadia Point: Borrow Pit

Issaquena County, Mississippi

The soil to build a levee comes from pits on the river side of the levee. The pits fill with water and water-tolerant plants and trees take root. In 2000 the Corps acknowledged that borrow pits evolve into wetlands and wrote new specifications. A pit should be located so it fills slowly when the river rises and drains fully when the river falls in order to minimize scour, encourage siltation, and promote the growth of vegetation. Some areas within a borrow pit can remain unexcavated to preserve standing trees and existing vegetation. The old borrow pit at Arcadia evolved into a wetland. A willow soaked up soggy soil next to the levee.

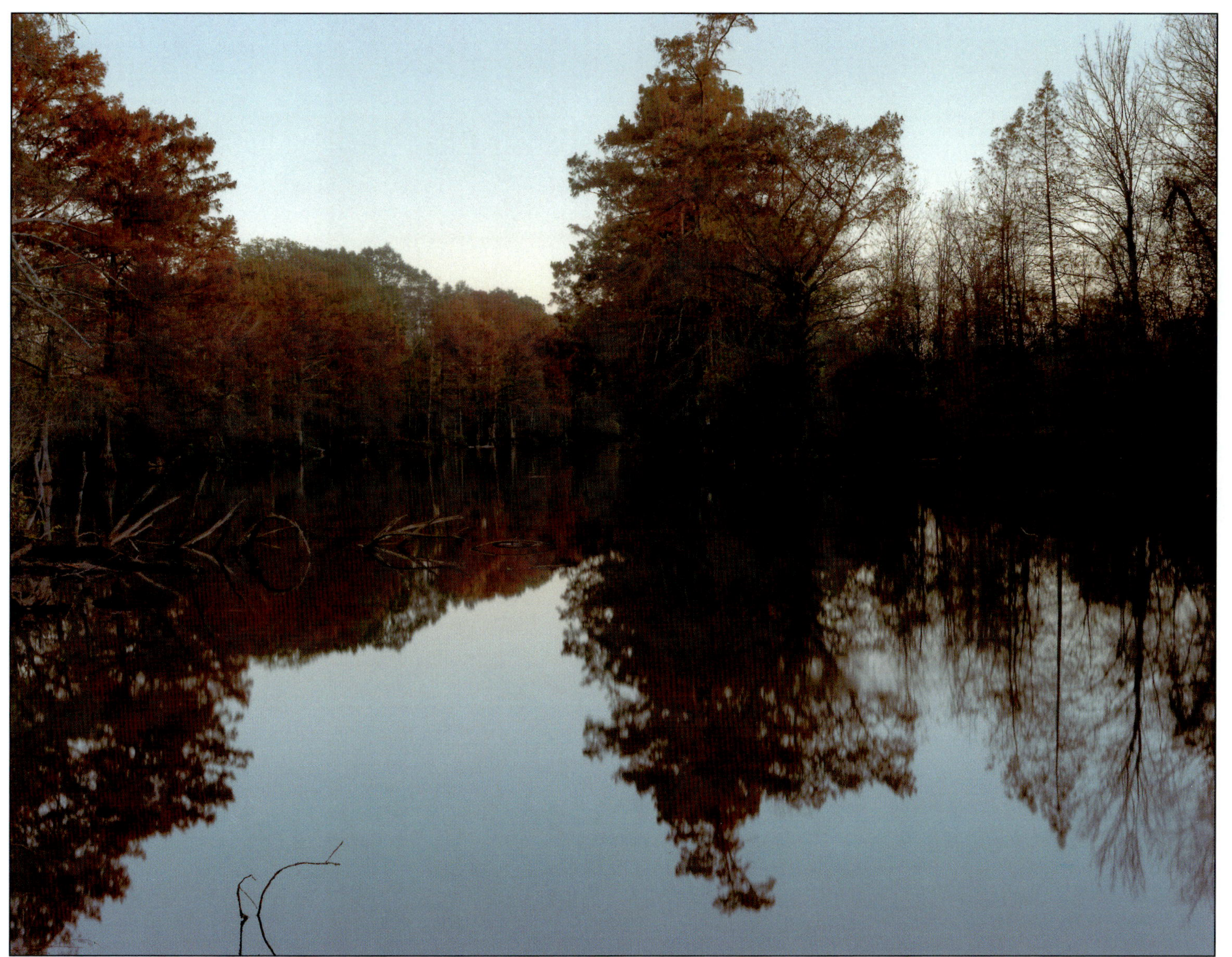

Yazoo Basin: Five Mile Lake

Issaquena County, Mississippi

For years anglers came to Five Mile Lake for white crappie and bass. In 2002 its owner, Billy VanDevender, enrolled 8,000 acres in the WRP, restored the hydrology to 3,000 acres, and managed the land for hunting. Working with the Mississippi Fish and Wildlife Foundation, he created moist-soil units for waterfowl and shorebirds, dammed a slough for a "natural duck hole," and planted cottonwoods and oaks. He invited researchers to study the cottonwood beetle on his adjacent tree farm; those from the Patuxent Wildlife Research Center tested plastic-coated paper birdhouses attached to trees, houses for cavity-nesting birds.

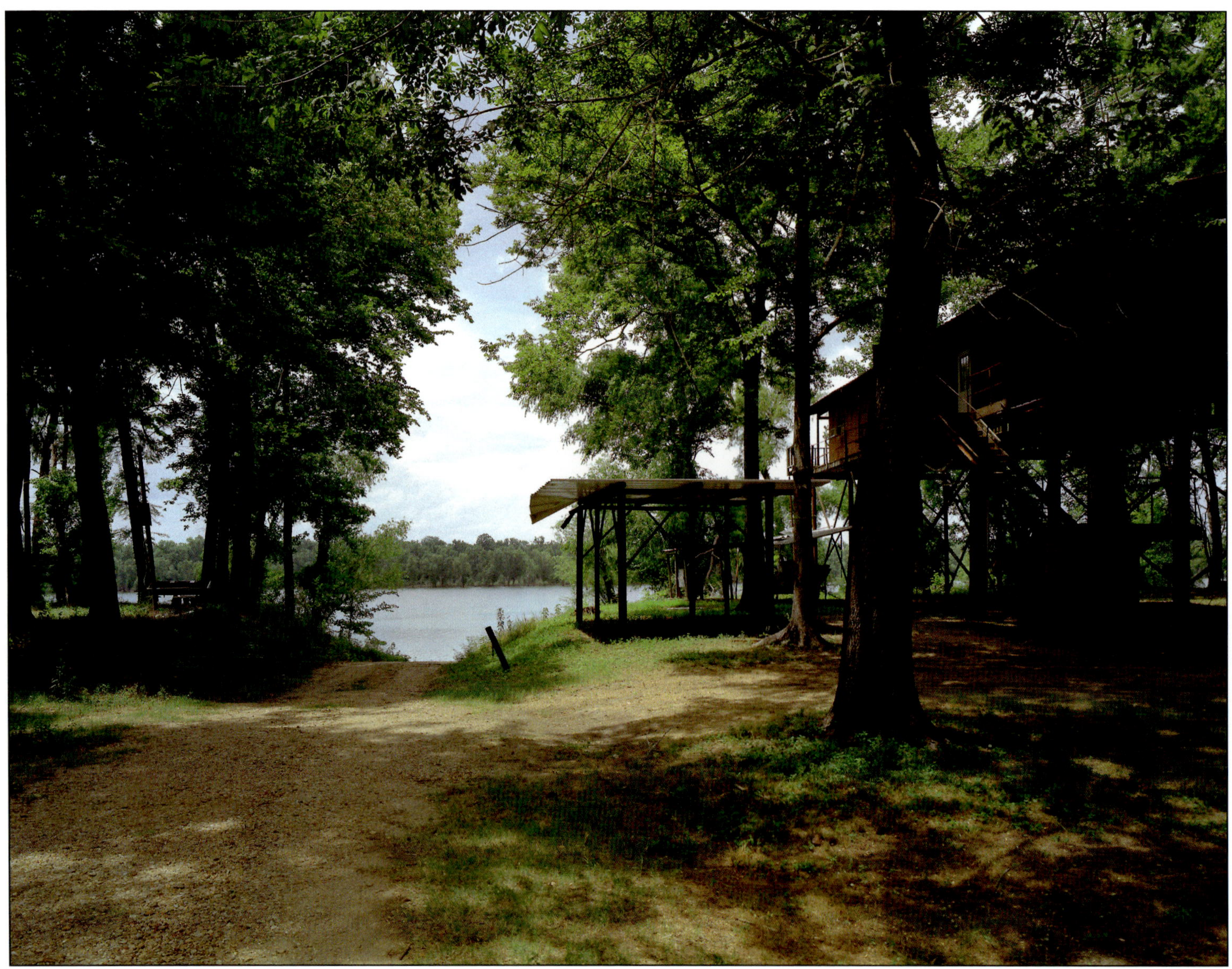

Chotard Lake: Fishing Camp

Issaquena County, Mississippi

Coming upon Chotard Lake is like approaching a busy intersection. Cormorants, egrets, great blues, and anhingas streak back and forth between Chotard Lake on the outside of the levee and Jones Lake on the inside. The fishing brings birds to Chotard Lake. The fishing brings the anglers to Chotard Lake. When the Mississippi runs low, Chotard is a prime fishing lake for crappie. When the Mississippi runs high, bass anglers can risk maneuvering their big boats through its shallow, narrow batture channel to the river, where the big sea-run striped bass swim.

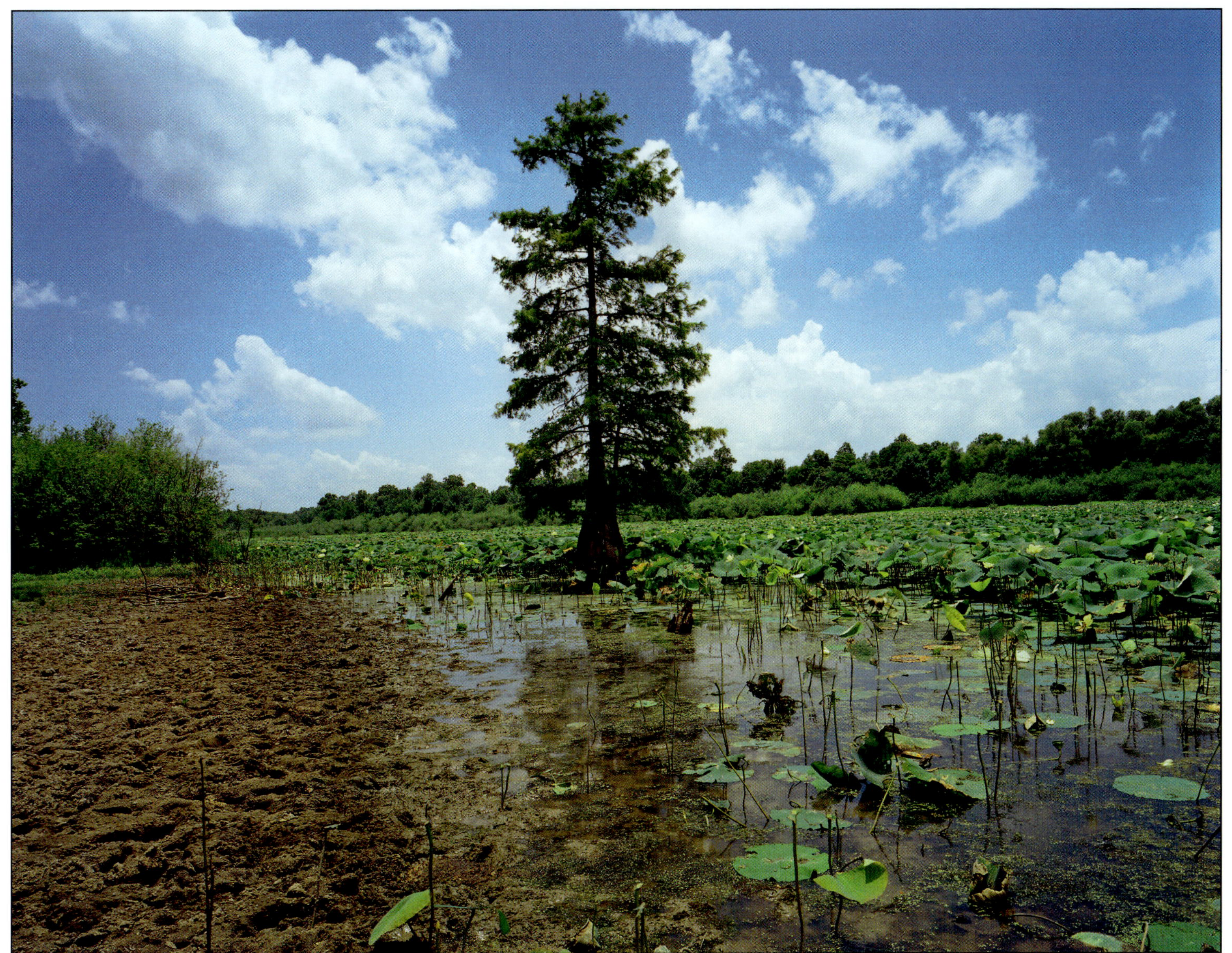

Island 102: Buck Chute/ Eagle Lake Pass
Warren County, Mississippi

In 2006 the USFWS partnered with nineteen others, including private landowners, like Tara Wildlife, to form the Mississippi Partners for Fish and Wildlife to encourage conservation on private lands. The group hoped to build on earlier work and initiate bottomland reforestation projects, manage timber, reestablish the hydrology of wetlands, and plant riparian buffers along streams to absorb nutrients flowing off fields. In the region around Buck Chute, private landowners made great strides in restoring the landscape. When they finished they put their land in the WRP or conservation easements with Ducks Unlimited to assure that it stay restored.

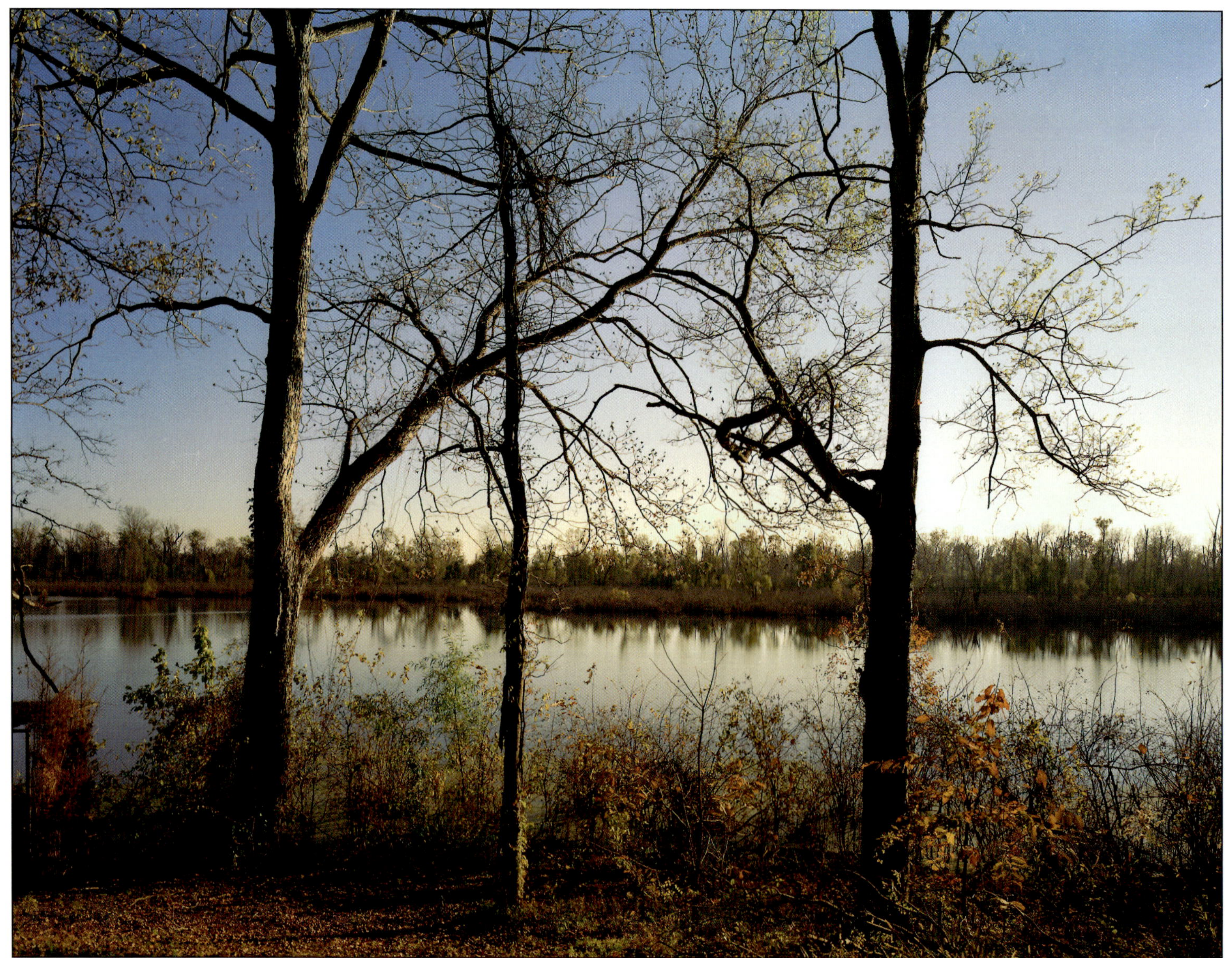

Tara Wildlife: Halpino Lake
Warren County, Mississippi

Maggie Bryant inherited 20,000 acres of cropland, bottomland hardwood forest, and swamp, fronting along twelve miles of Mississippi shoreline. She decided conservation was the best way to make the land pay for itself. She built a conference center, invited anglers to fish in her lakes, and bow-hunters to track deer in her woods. She took her cropland out of production and put in timber. Louisiana black bears returned to Tara, forty sightings in 2001 led wildlife biologists to hope that this private refuge would one day support a breeding population. In December 2001 she placed 17,200 acres under conservation easement to Ducks Unlimited.

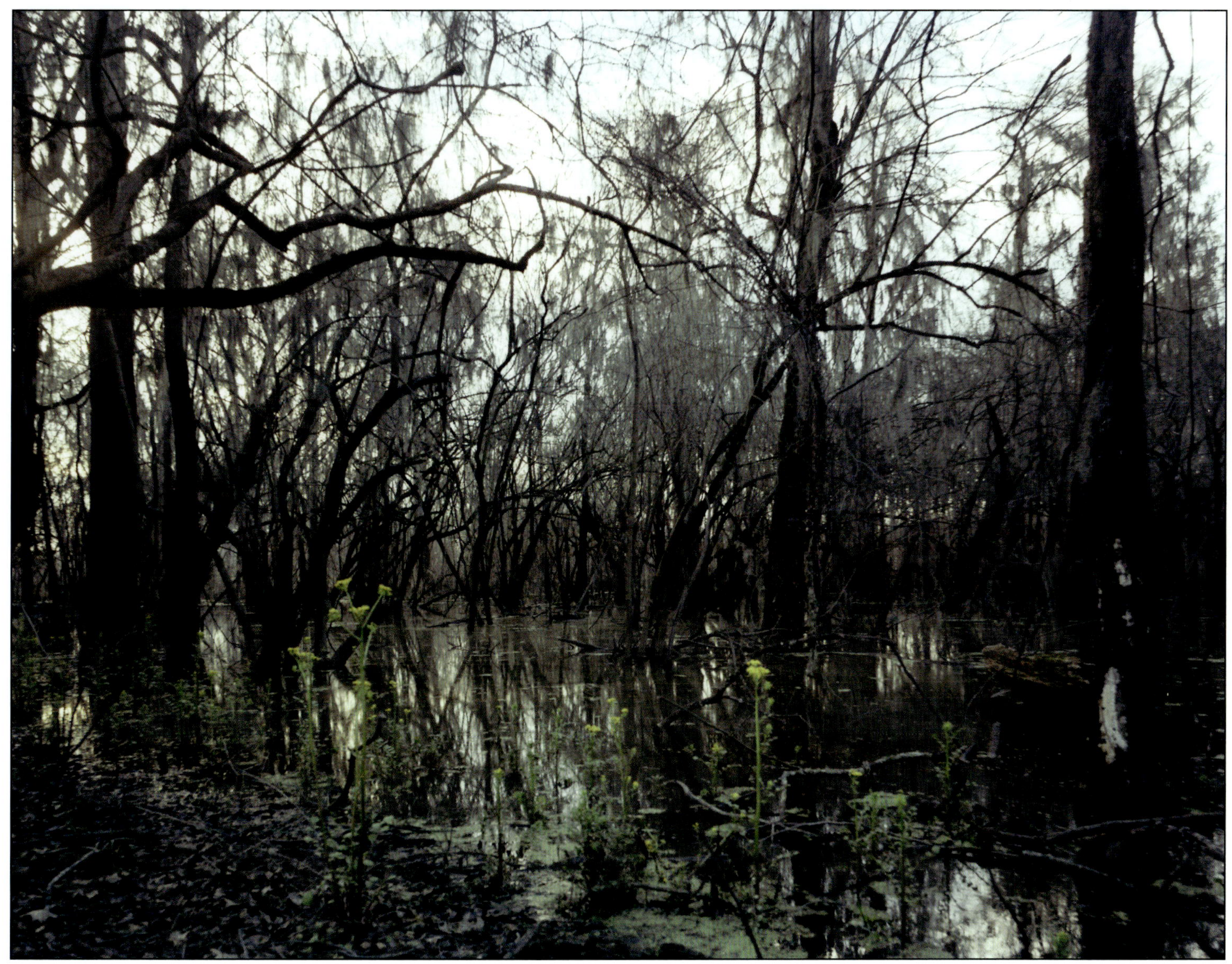

Old Channel: Yazoo River

Warren County, Mississippi

Vicksburg, atop a bluff, has a commanding view of the Mississippi. In 1863, he who controlled the Mississippi and Confederate troops controlled Vicksburg, bombarding the Union fleet every time it rounded De Soto Bend. In January, Gen. Ulysses S. Grant tried to divert the river through a canal across Young's Point opposite Vicksburg and bypass the city. In 1876 the Mississippi did what Grant failed to do and cut across De Soto Point, leaving Vicksburg without access to the river. In 1903 the Corps diverted the Yazoo River to the old Mississippi bed in front of Vicksburg, leaving the bed of the Yazoo to turn to swamp.

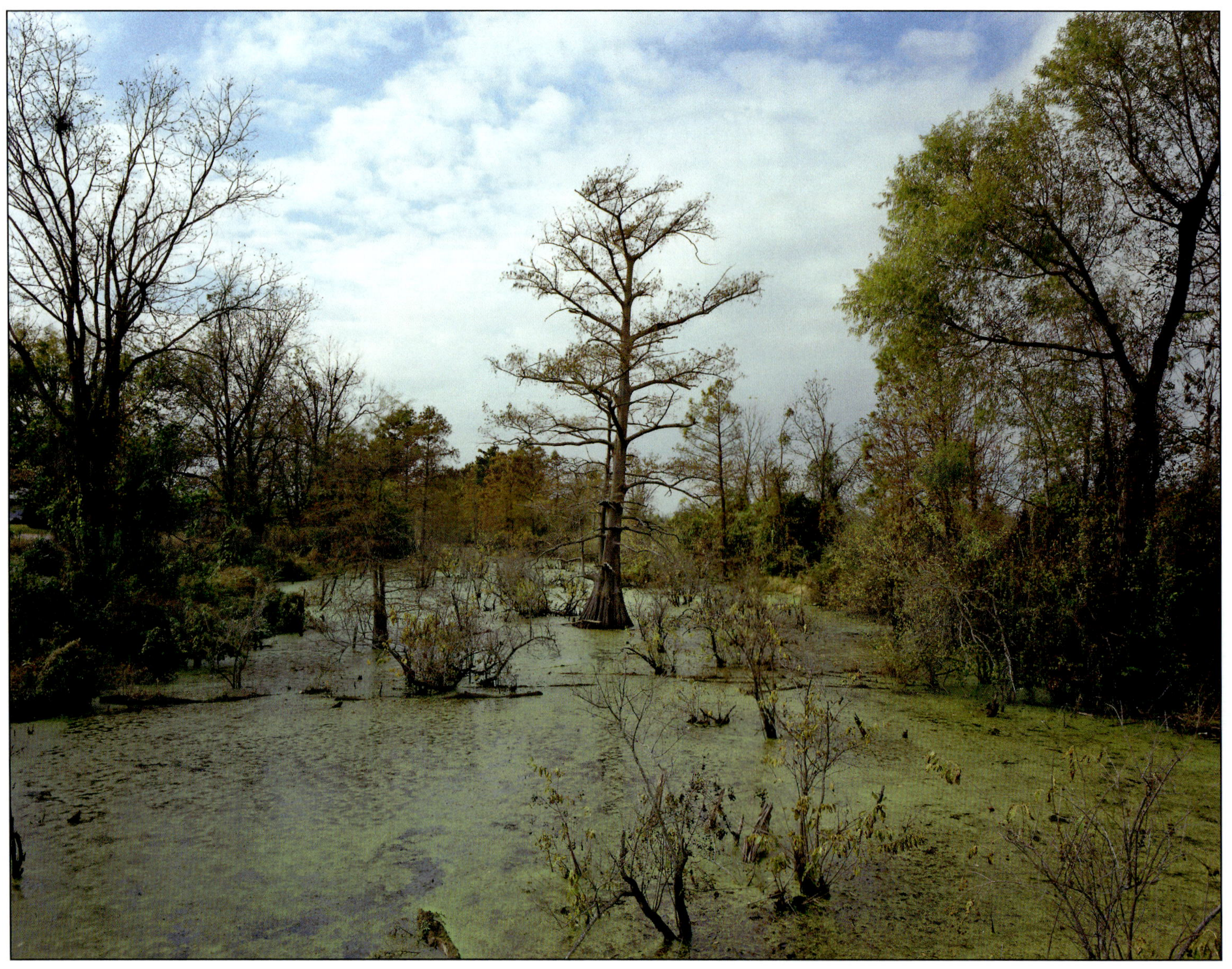

Walnut Bayou Meander Belt: Walnut Bayou

Madison Parish, Louisiana

In March 1863, Gen. William T. Sherman took advantage of the fact that Walnut Bayou headed close to the Mississippi above Vicksburg and returned to the Mississippi below Vicksburg and diverted the river to the bayou, bypassing the city. Soldiers dug a canal from river to bayou and removed snags and trees. On April 13 workers broke through the levee, allowing four dredges to move into the canal to deepen it. However, the river only trickled into the bayou and then fell, leaving two dredges and twenty barges stranded. On April 25 all work on the canal stopped. One barge reached its destination. Grant's army followed on foot.

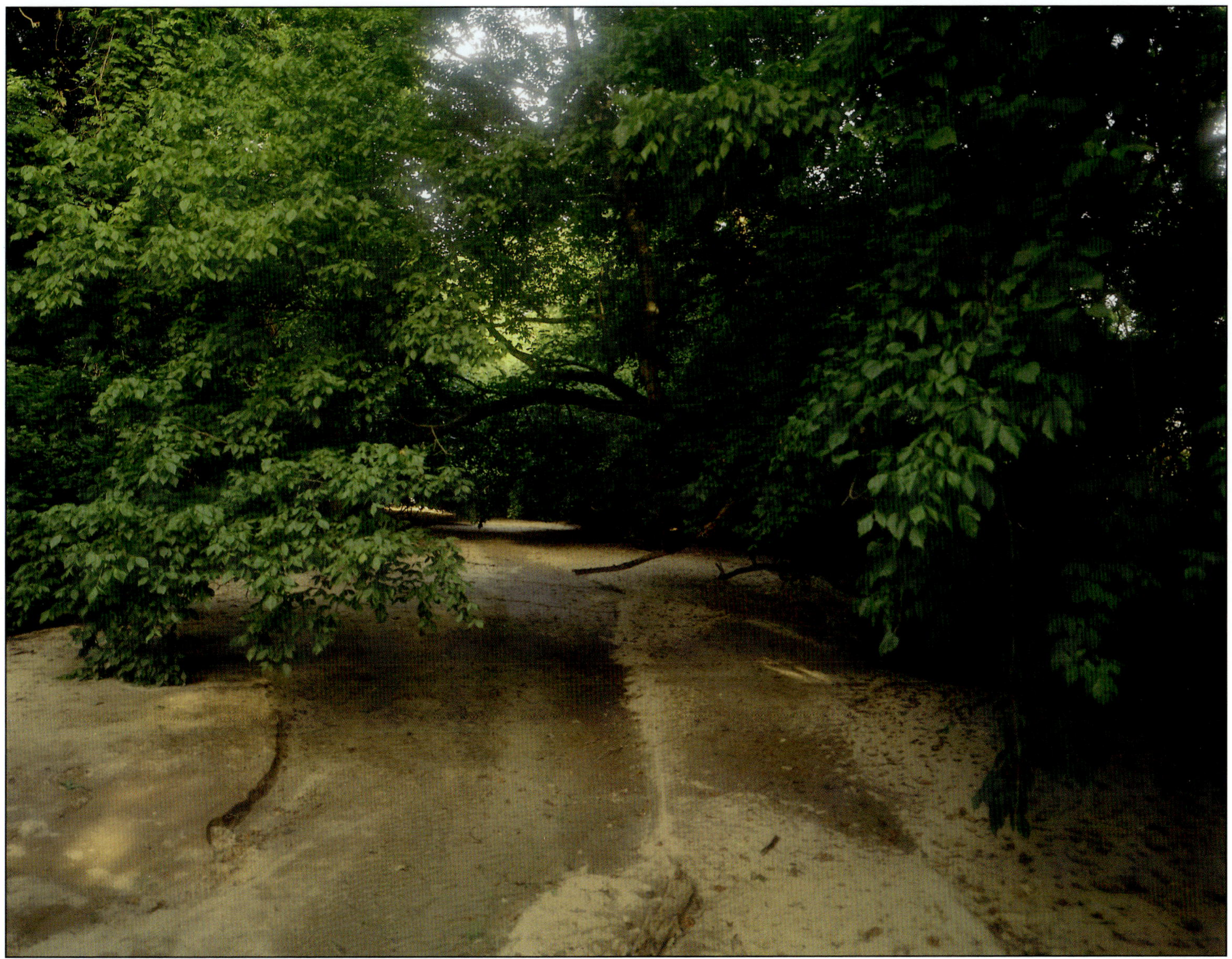

St. Catherine Creek National Wildlife Refuge: St. Catherine Creek
Adams County, Mississippi

The U.S. Fish and Wildlife Service purchased land for the refuge from farmers tired of farming a rim swamp, where they built levees to fend off floods, installed pumps to dry out fields, and had airplanes seed their crops. The service used the levees and pumps to create 1,700 acres of moist soil and jump-started a forest with cypress, ash, and overcup and Nuttall oaks. Willows followed every flood, grew rapidly, and shaded out seedlings. Foresters mowed the willows, which grew back. They tried herbicides, which killed seedlings. Left to nature, willow, cottonwood, and sycamore would have colonized the swamp, followed by ash and sugarberry, then oak.

The Atchafalaya

> Line of Demarkation, this line was agreed upon between Spain and the United States several years prior to the latter government taking possession of Louisiana as ceded to it by France. It crosses the river in 31 degrees north latitude.
>
> About one mile below the line is what is called the Great Cutt-off, which is only five miles across, and is reckoned as the river runs fifty-four miles round.
>
> Red river, 9 miles below the line, This is a very considerable river entering in at a large bend on the right shore.
>
> Bayou Chaffalio, 3 miles below Red river, be careful that you keep pretty close to the left shore from Red river below this place, to avoid being drawn into this current, which runs out of the right shore with great rapidity. This is the first large body of water which leaves the Mississippi, and falls by a regular and separate channel to the Gulf Mexico, owning to an immense floating bridge, or raft across it, of many leagues in length, and so firm and compact in some places that cattle and horses are driven over it. This astonishing bridge is constantly augmented by the trees and rubbish which the Chaffalio draws out of the Mississippi, which leaves in the westernmost part of that remarkable bend just below the boundary, and has every appearance of having been formerly a continuation of the Red river, when the Mississippi washed the high lands from Clarksville to the Bayou Tunica (or Willings creek,) the traces of which are yet visible by the lakes through which a large current passes when the river is high. The distance on a straight line from Clarksville to the Bayou Tunica is not more than eight miles, but by the present course of the river, it is about fifty.
>
> —Zadok Cramer, 1814

Zadok Cramer depicted the future when he described Turnbull's Bend. The Red River and the Atchafalaya River both joined the Mississippi in Turnbull's Bend on the Louisiana side of the river. The Red, a tributary, carried water to the Mississippi; the Atchafalaya, a distributary, carried water away from the Mississippi, in such a rush that it sucked drift into its channel at its head.

In 1831, Henry Shreve dredged a new channel across the neck of Turnbull's Bend in an effort to improve navigation. In doing so he shortened the distance between the upper and lower bends. The upper end silted up and almost disappeared from the landscape. The lower bend, renamed Old River, remained open as the mouth of the Red and the head of the Atchafalaya. In 1860, after years of picking away at the raft that blocked the head of the Atchafalaya, the State of Louisiana succeeded in breaking it open. The Mississippi poured through Old River into the Atchafalaya, enlarging and deepening its channel with every flood after 1880. Twelve years later the Red joined itself to the head of the Atchafalaya, and Old River became a two-way street, flowing to or from the Red/Atchafalaya, depending on the flood levels on the Mississippi. In 1945 the Atchafalaya captured the full flow of the Red. From then on Old River flowed in one direction only: to the Atchafalaya. Five years later a flood made it clear that the Atchafalaya would one day capture the Mississippi, and there was no way to stop it. Congress thought differently and authorized the Corps to build the Old River Control Structure.

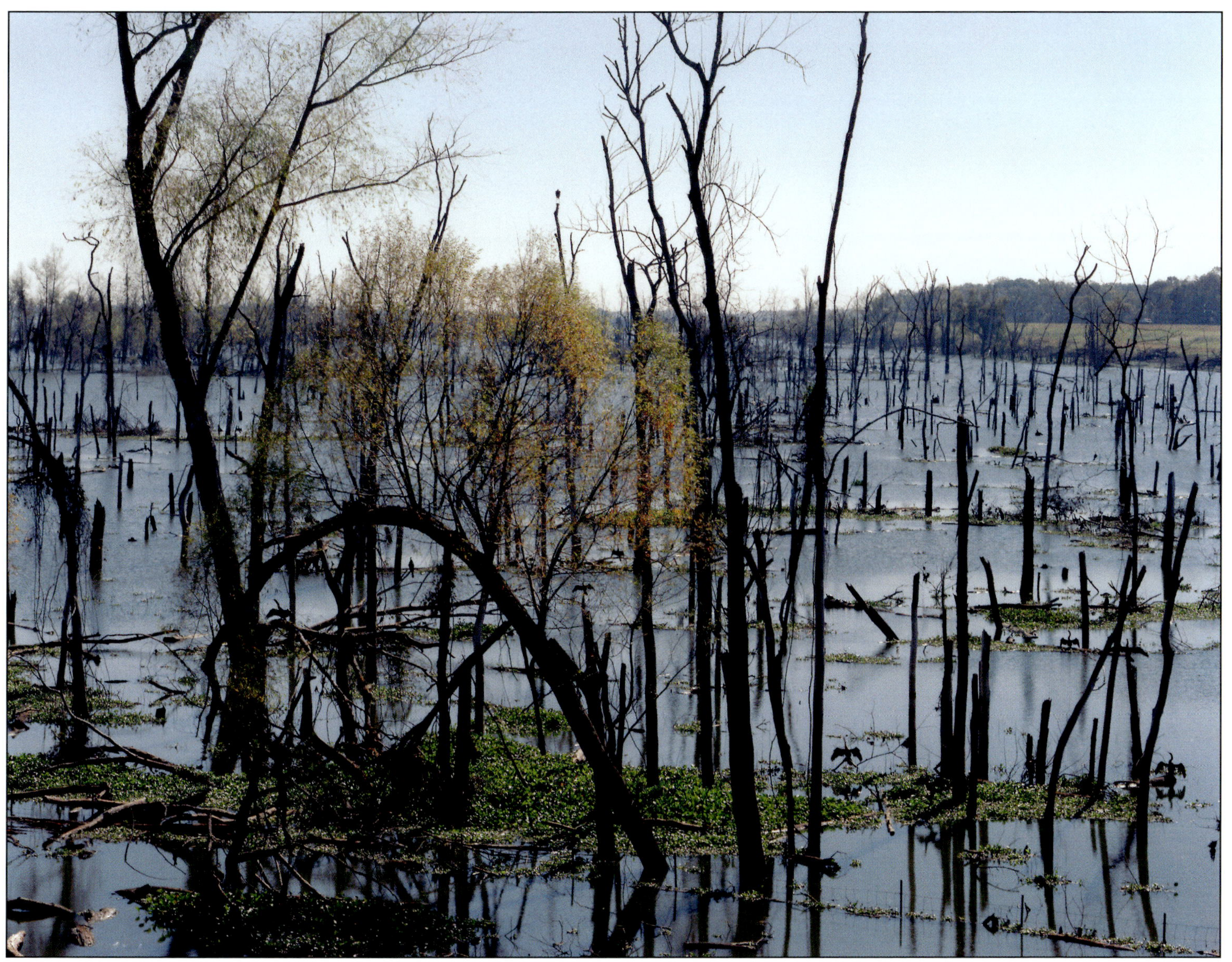

Morganza Floodway: Forebay

Pointe Coupe Parish, Louisiana

It made sense to turn Morgan's Bend into the head of a floodway. Louisianans made repeated attempts to maintain a levee at Morgan's Bend, only to see it destroyed by floods. In 1874 the Mississippi blew a mile-wide crevasse in the levee. Ten years later the state closed the gap, only to see the levee collapse in the 1884 flood. Repaired again, it collapsed again in the 1890 flood. After the flood of 1928, the Army Corps of Engineers installed a 125-gate weir in the mainline levee just north of Morgan's Bend at the head of the Morganza Floodway. Guide levees funnel floodwater to the East Atchafalaya Floodway. The Corps has opened the weir once, during the Flood of 1973.

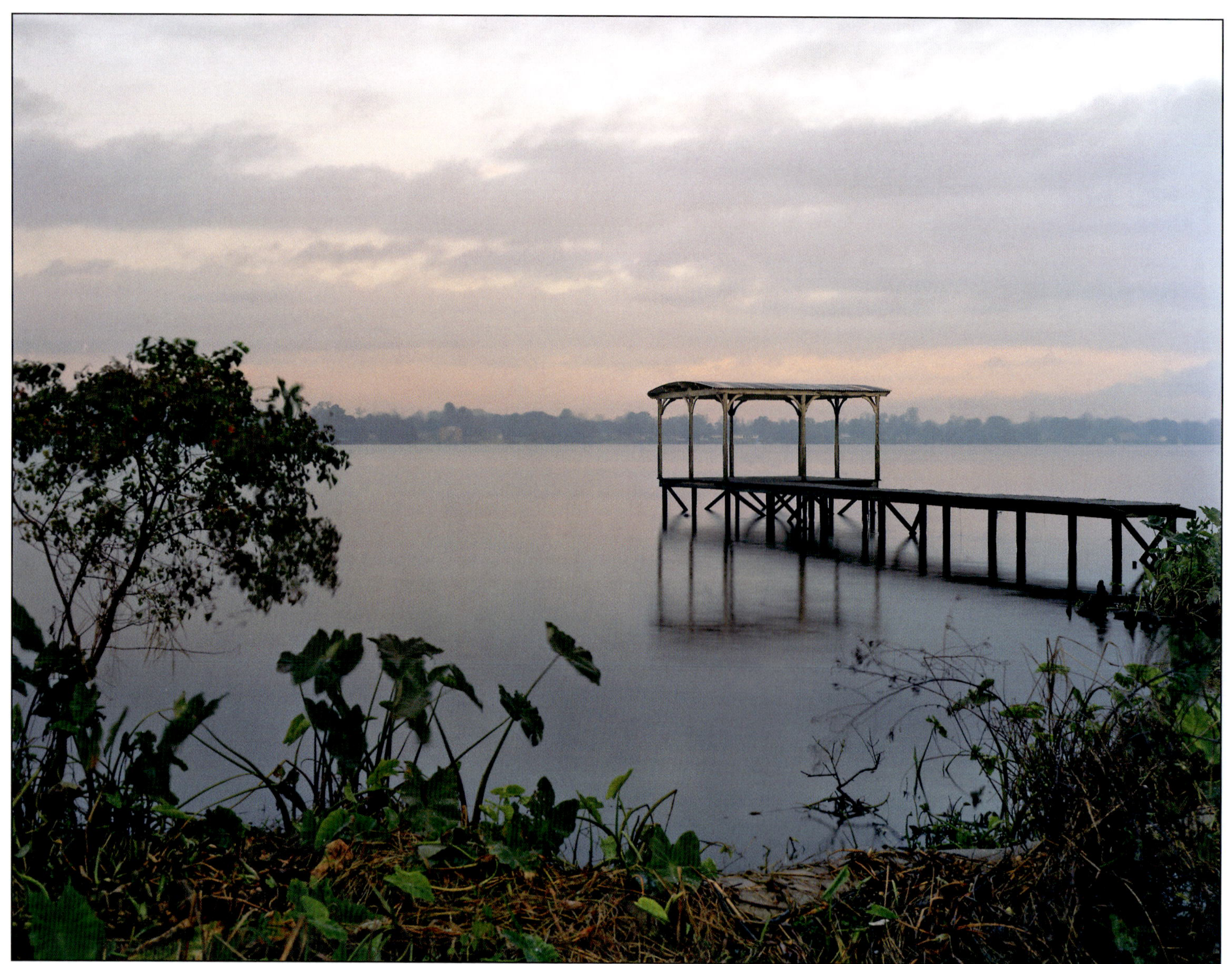

False River: New Roads

Pointe Coupe Parish, Louisiana

In the eighteenth century wealthy sugar growers built their plantations along False River. In the nineteenth people from Baton Rouge and New Orleans came to fish, swim, and boat, but by the end of the twentieth century, the quality of one of the most popular lakes in southern Louisiana was declining. Fifty miles of drainage canals in its watershed delivered excessive amounts of silt, nutrients, and pesticides. The diversity of the aquatic population declined. In 2002, the Corps initiated the False River Aquatic Ecosystem Restoration project that reduced sedimentation and restored water quality to False River by reconfiguring drainage to the lake.

The Atchafalaya Basin

> The Mississippi is known to seek new channels; and there is good reason to believe, that it has from time to time varied its course from one extreme of its valley to the other. The channel of the Chafalia, a few miles only from the head of it, is completely obstructed by logs and other materials. Were it not for these obstructions, the probability is, that the Mississippi would soon find a much nearer way to the gulf than at present; particularly as it manifests a constant inclination to very its course.
>
> —Maj. Amos Stoddard, 1812

When the French first settled in Louisiana at the beginning of the eighteenth century, the Atchafalaya was a small distributary of the Mississippi, a river of no importance that carried away the big river's overflow. After the French sold Louisiana to the United States in 1803, Maj. Amos Stoddard, the army officer who took charge of the Mississippi, observed that only a log dam, near the head of the Atchafalaya, built as the Atchafalaya sucked Mississippi debris into its channel, prevented the Mississippi from diverting to the shorter, steeper Atchafalaya.

The Atchafalaya Basin is the transition between the Mississippi alluvial valley and the Gulf coastal plain. It is the northern part of the Barataria-Terrebonne estuarine system, which lies between the west bank of the Mississippi and the east bank of the Atchafalaya River. In short, the Old River Control Structure is the head of the Mississippi Delta.

The history of the basin is one of human intervention in natural geological processes. Henry Shreve's cutoff at Turnbull's Bend in 1831 and the opening of the log dam in 1860 hastened the threatened capture of the Mississippi at Old River. General Jadwin isolated his floodway in the center of the basin, which overwhelmed the floodway with sediment, started the construction of the delta lobe, and cut off the flow of water and sediment to the fringes of the basin outside the floodway, leading to subsidence and the drowning of bottomland forests in its lower regions.

As the Atchafalaya siphoned more and more water and sediment from the Mississippi and Red Rivers, it formed a meander belt with a well-defined channel and natural levee in the upper third of the basin. When the Atchafalaya and its bayous reached the still waters of the great lake in the southern two-thirds of their basin, they deposited their loads of sediment in the lake and constructed a series of deltas, building land and creating smaller lakes between the bayous. Between 1917 and 1930 the Atchafalaya built a delta that covered 4.63 square miles of Grand Lake at the head of the lake. It continued building land in Grand Lake at the rate of three-fourths of a square mile per year. By 1989 the delta covered more than ninety-two square miles.

Between 1930 and 1968 the Corps of Engineers accelerated the process of delta building in Grand Lake by dredging a forty-foot navigation channel on the upper Atchafalaya River, sending more water and sediment to Grand Lake, turning it into a network of bayous separated by willow bars. Further, the Corps closed distributary bayous—Bayou Courtableau, Little Alabama, and Indian Bayou—to increase the flow of water down the Atchafalaya, which also increased the amount of sediment filling Grand Lake. The great basin lake, which had once covered more than 230 square miles, was reduced to a collection of small, shallow lakes—Six Mile Lake and Upper and Lower Grand Lakes—which now cover only 50 square miles and huddle at the base of the basin, just north of Morgan City.

By 1950 the Atchafalaya River had begun to bypass the lakes and deposit sediment in Atchafalaya Bay at the mouth of the lower Atchafalaya River, and the mouth of the Wax Lake Outlet, an artificial channel located ten miles to the west. For twenty years the river formed a marine delta below the surface of the bay. The delta first appeared above the surface after the Flood of 1973 sent a huge load of sediment into the bay. In the years since, the delta has added about sixteen thousand acres of new land to Atchafalaya Bay.

Today, the Atchafalaya Basin comprises four regions: Between Old River and about U.S. 190, which crosses the basin, the land is solid. Bayous lined with oak, pecan, and sweet gum meander between soybean and rice fields, much like the backswamp regions of Mississippi and Arkansas that have been drained and turned over to row crops. The Atchafalaya River itself is an efficient navigation channel running between levees. Between U.S. 190 and Morgan City the basin hosts the great lake, still the largest river swamp in North America. It is a network of bayous, lakes, and swamps where patches of land are underwater much of the year and stands of cypress and tupelo dot a watery landscape. South of Morgan City the coastal wetlands of Atchafalaya Bay progress from freshwater swamps to brackish and then saline marshes. Finally, at the mouth of the Atchafalaya, the river is building its delta, the only geomorphic event happening in the Mississippi valley in modern times. There is a fifth region, the lands outside the floodway, where south of I-10 the land is subsiding for lack of flooding and new sediment.

At the beginning of the twenty-first century, the Atchafalaya Basin was still a river of trees, with 885,000 acres of forested wetlands and 517,000 acres of marsh. That translates into 25 percent of Louisiana's commercial forests and 51 percent of its hardwood forests. Its trees and twenty-nine rookeries were alive with 170 species of birds, including six endangered or threatened species. Forty species of mammals prowled its understory; forty species of reptiles and twenty species of amphibians depended on its wetlands. One hundred species of fish or shellfish lived in its waters, producing more than a thousand pounds of finfish per acre in some lakes in the lower part of the basin. Sport fishing takes up 500,000 user-days, and hunting, 164,000 user-days in the basin, contributing $123 million a year to Louisiana's economy. Commercial fishing for finfish and crawfish adds five to six million dollars a year.

The basin holds more than three hundred active oil and gas wells in the Plumb Bob Oil Field, and the Happytown Oil and Gas Field. Pipelines crisscross the basin, disrupting its hydrology. Morgan City, at the foot of the floodway, is the basin's major port.

The history of the Atchafalaya in the late twentieth century is way more complex than stopping the diversion of the Mississippi. It is about saving the river of trees between Krotz Springs and Morgan City. It is about real estate transactions. It is about the reluctance of the Corps of Engineers to allow federal support for recreation and wildlife in the Atchafalaya Floodway.

The 1982 Environmental Impact Statement, the plan for the Atchafalaya Floodway, allowed for the continued dredging of the river between river mile 90 and river mile 116. Once dredging stopped in 1968 between Alabama Bayou at Sherburne and Six Mile Lake near Morgan City, it was never resumed. The engineers concluded that the river itself could scour and maintain the channel to the desired width and depth. In addressing recreation and wildlife, the plan afforded the purchase of 50,000 acres in the floodway for three wildlife refuges and boat ramps, the construction of recreation facilities, and it broke the Atchafalaya Basin into thirteen management units, each with distinct environmental and hydrological characteristics that were the result of natural processes and human actions, and detailed the construction of two pilot units. The plan satisfied environmentalists, the EPA, and the USFWS, all of whom had protested the Corps' 1968 plans for the Atchafalaya. Congress authorized the plan in a Supplemental Appropriations Act in 1985 and reauthorized it in the 1986 WRDA.

Real estate acquisition for the wildlife areas and flowage easements—the right to flood the land whenever the Corps needed to open the gates of either the West Atchafalaya or the Morganza Floodway—required additional authorization from Congress and set off another struggle, this time between local landowners and the Corps, the USFWS, and the State of Louisiana, who would own the wildlife area jointly. Local landowners feared that given federal support for wildlife, the USFWS would turn the whole of the basin into a wildlife refuge and stop all oil exploration and timber harvesting.

The State of Louisiana purchased its 12,000 acres for the Sherburne WMA in 1983. Congress authorized the establishment of the Atchafalaya NWR in 1984, and over the next two years the USFWS purchased a little over 15,000 acres adjacent to the Sherburne refuge and formally established the refuge in 1986. All sellers retained mineral rights under the refuges. Once the state and USFWS had purchased their 27,000 acres, the Corps insisted that its commitment was restricted to the 23,000 remaining acres. It held to that position until 1994, when it agreed to purchase 50,000 acres for recreation and wildlife, including 16,000 acres adjacent to the Sherburne and Atchafalaya refuges.

The lower Atchafalaya Floodway, south of U.S. 190, spreads across 595,000 acres. The State of Louisiana owns 150,000 acres of water bottoms and accreted land—that is lakes and land formed by the deposits of sediment in lakes—30,000 acres of land donated by the Dow Chemical Company, and 12,000 acres purchased for the Sherburne WMA. The USFWS owns 15,000 acres in the Atchafalaya NWR. Of the 388,000 acres remaining, the Corps had the authority to purchase 50,000 for recreation and wildlife protection.

On the remaining 338,000 acres, the Corps purchased flowage easements. The state threw in its 192,000 acres and USFWS its 15,000 acres as flowage easements. The Corps had developmental control and environmental-protection easements on the remaining 279,000 acres. Developmental control meant that the Corps had the right to prohibit construction of permanently habitable buildings and require permits on all other structures in the floodway, including hunting and fishing camps. Environmental protection meant that the Corps had the right to prohibit the conversion or development of land in the floodway to new uses and to prohibit certain timber-harvesting practices without permit. In short, the Corps controlled the floodway. And like the Mississippi River south of St. Louis, where the Corps' primary authority is navigation and flood control, its primary authority on the Atchafalaya is flood control. All other needs are secondary.

Those who cherished the Atchafalaya and its river swamp were not completely satisfied with the outcome of the 1982 plan and the controlling authority for the Atchafalaya Basin. Hence, organizations like the Audubon Club, the Sierra Club, the Atchafalaya Basinkeepers, and Ducks Unlimited closely monitored the health of its wetlands, sent out the alarm when need be, and developed the Atchafalaya Basin as a National Heritage Area.

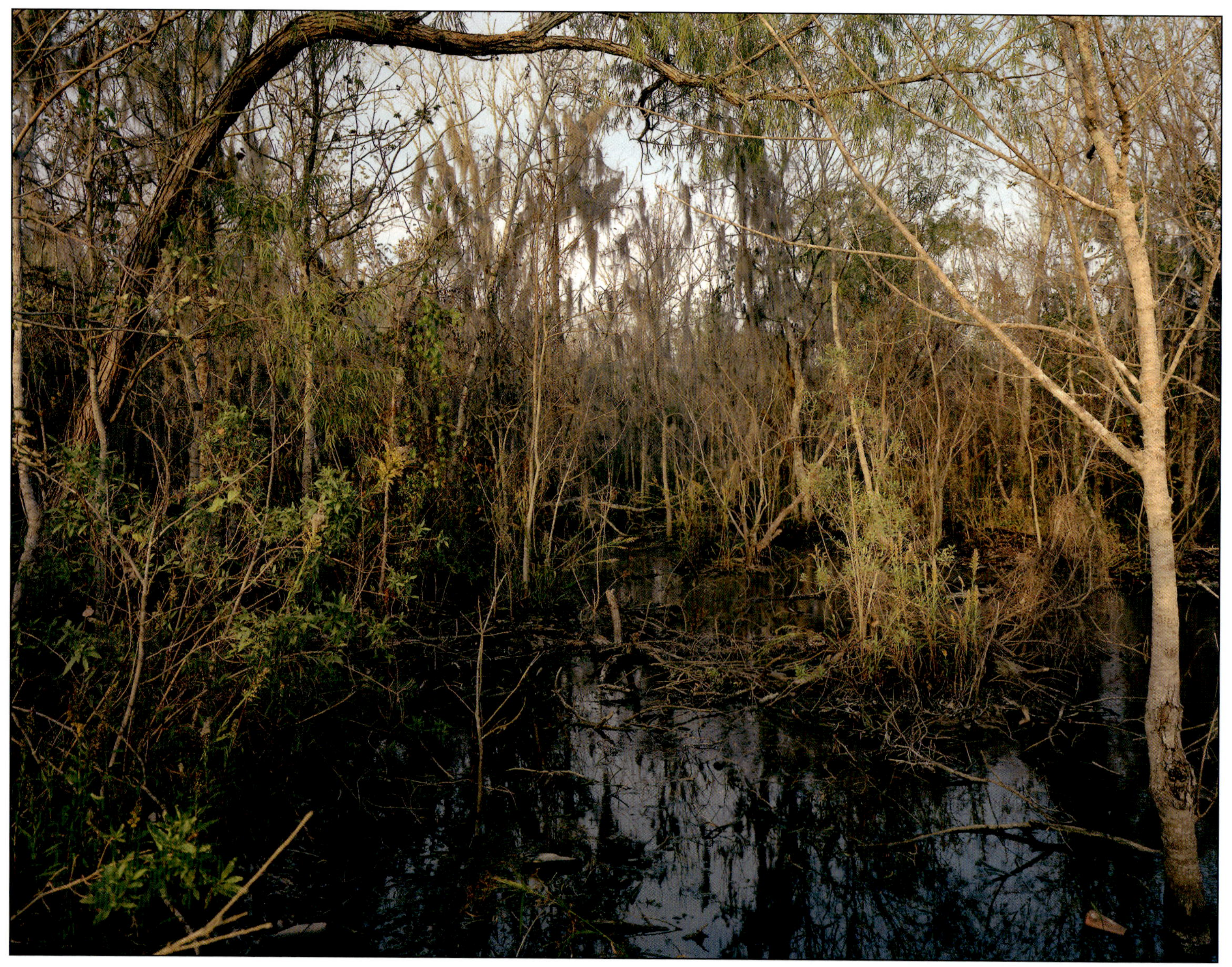

Sherburne Wildlife Management Area: Forest
Iberville Parish, Louisiana

Sherburne's swamp is a birding paradise for waterfowl, wading birds, and songbirds. But of all the birds that flock to Sherburne, the Swallow-tailed Kite is the species of special concern. The kite nests in the tallest trees, preferring cypress swamps and savannas and cypress-hardwood swamps, close to open water. A black-and-white raptor with a four-foot wingspan, it feeds on the fly, slowly circling the treetops, nipping at insects with its hooked beak, snatching lizards from tree trunks, barely moving its wings, but guiding its flight with the rotation of its deeply split tail. It skims the surface of a pond or marsh for a drink of water or a bath.

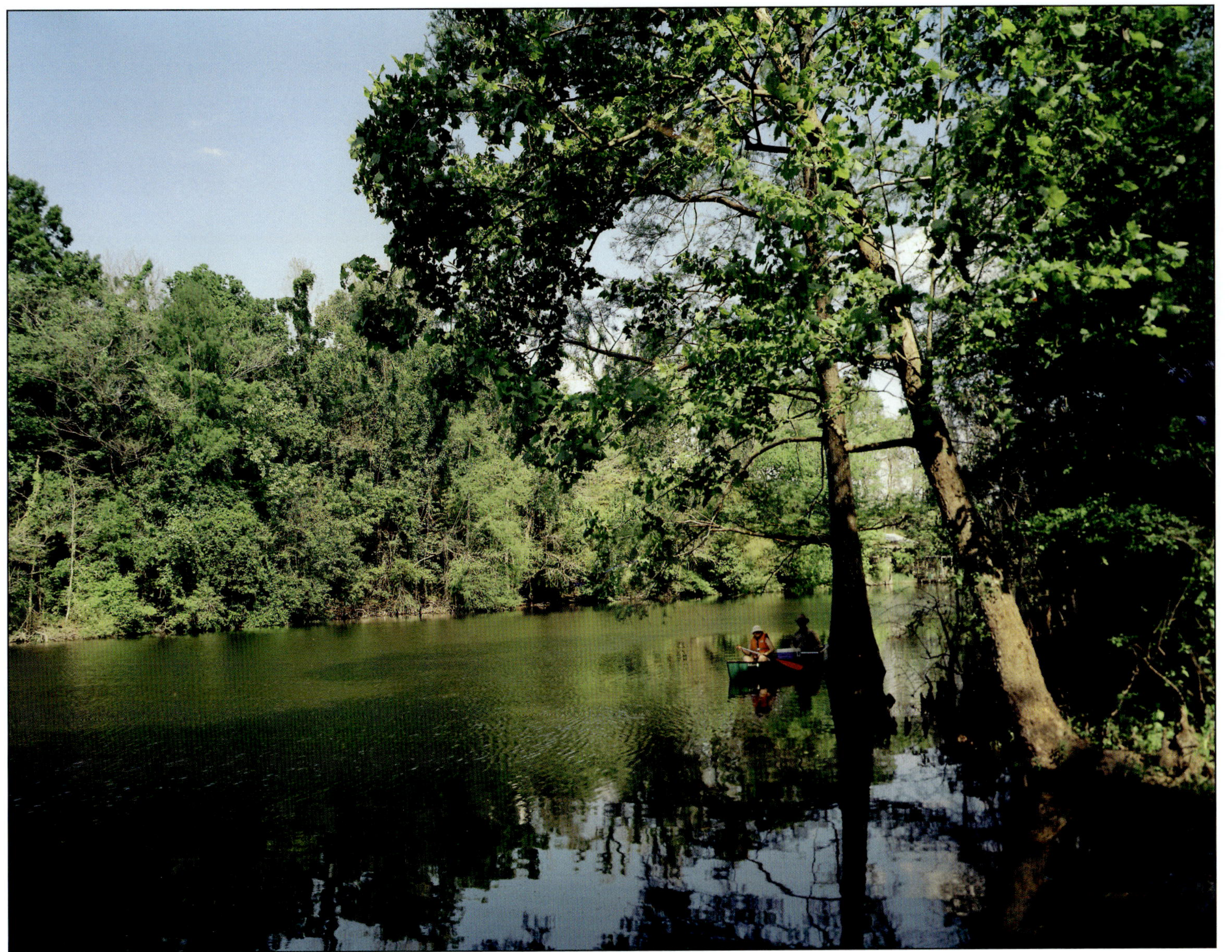

Sherburne Wildlife Management Area: Little Alabama Bayou

Iberville Parish, Louisiana

The Corps used dredge material from the Atchafalaya River to build the East Atchafalaya River Levee and cut the flow of water to Alabama and Little Alabama Bayous and to Des Ourses Swamp. The two bayous silted in at their southern ends. As part of its 1982 plan the Corps intended to reconnect Little Alabama Bayou to the Atchafalaya through a gravity structure set in the levee. It never happened. But given the right water levels past the end of the levee, the Atchafalaya backs up into the Sherburne WMA. Canoeists following the Sherburne Paddle Trail Network can paddle clear south into Upper Flat Lake through a maze of bayous.

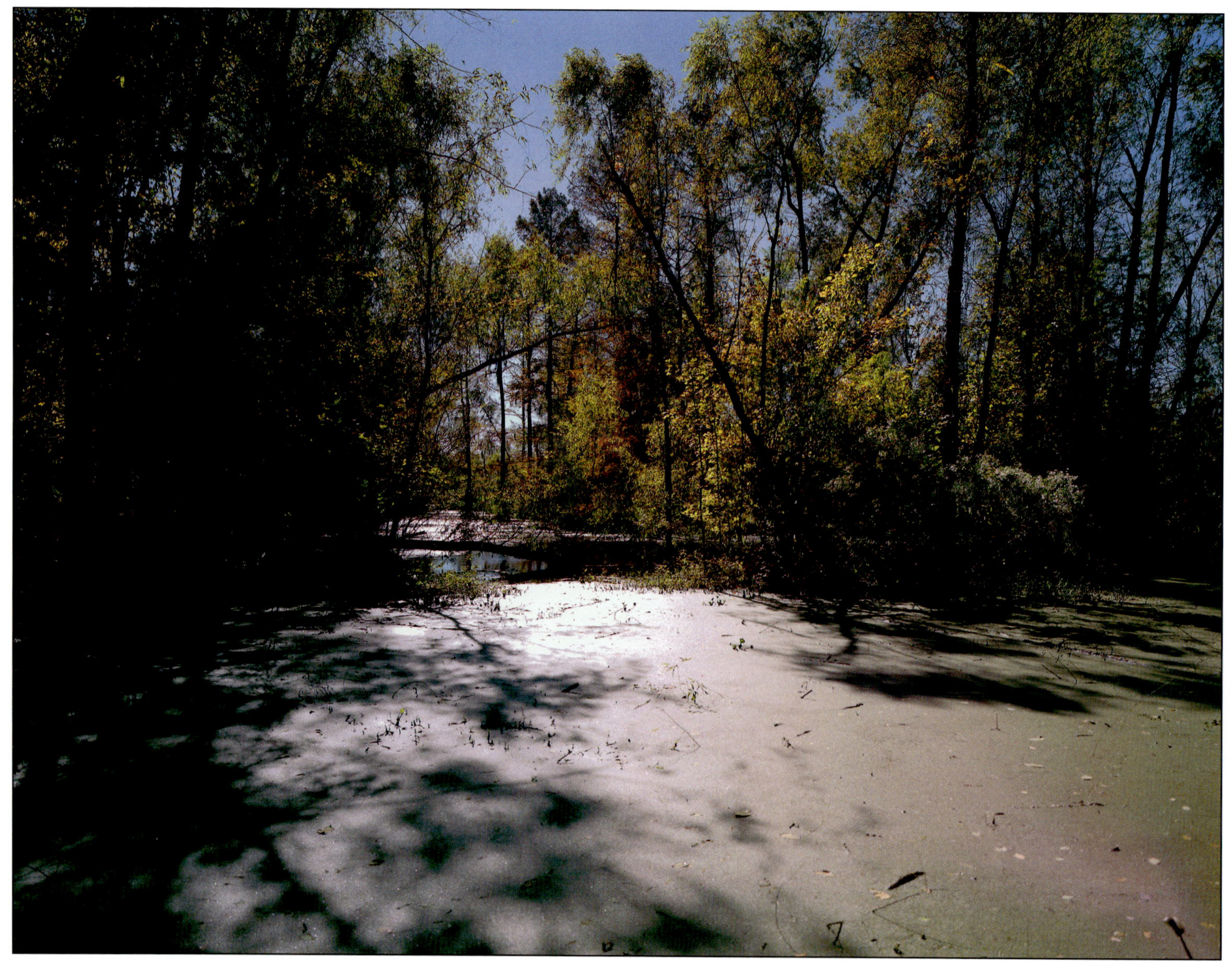

Sherburne Complex: Bayou des Ourses Natural Area

Iberville Parish, Louisiana

Willows took root in new sediment on the edge of Des Ourses Swamp, one of the many lakes in the river swamp. Sedimentation slowed when the Corps cut Alabama Bayou from the Atchafalaya. Instead of too much water and sediment, the swamp suffered from too little water. To draw ducks and wading birds to the swamp, Ducks Unlimited, Exxon, the North American Wetlands Conservation Council, the Louisiana Department of Wildlife and Fisheries, and the Corps developed a 2,400-acre moist-soil unit in 1994. DU and Exxon came up with half the $986,000 cost as required by the North American Wetlands Conservation Act. Access to the area is only by foot, bike, or ATV.

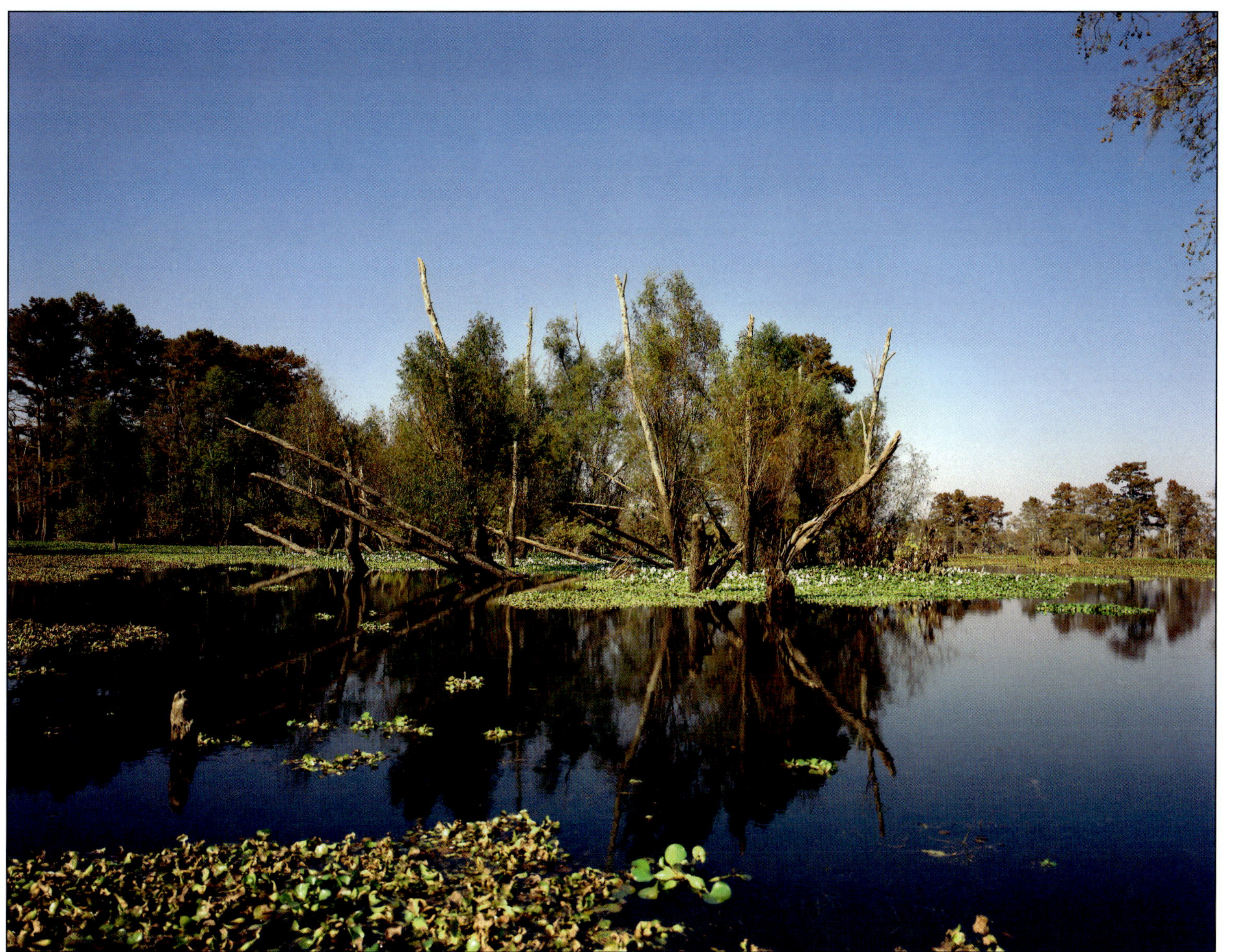

Atchafalaya Basin: Upper Flat Bayou
Iberville Parish, Louisiana

The termination of its river levees at the Whiskey Bay Pilot Channel leaves the Atchafalaya River free to flood the region between the protection levees. And its floods are the lifeblood of the swamp, distributing fresh water and oxygen, fish and crawfish, plankton and invertebrates, reptiles and amphibians throughout the river swamp. Where the Upper Flat Bayou flows across Upper Flat Lake, it is an ephemeral stream: discernible when the water is down, it disappears when the water is up, its banks inundated.

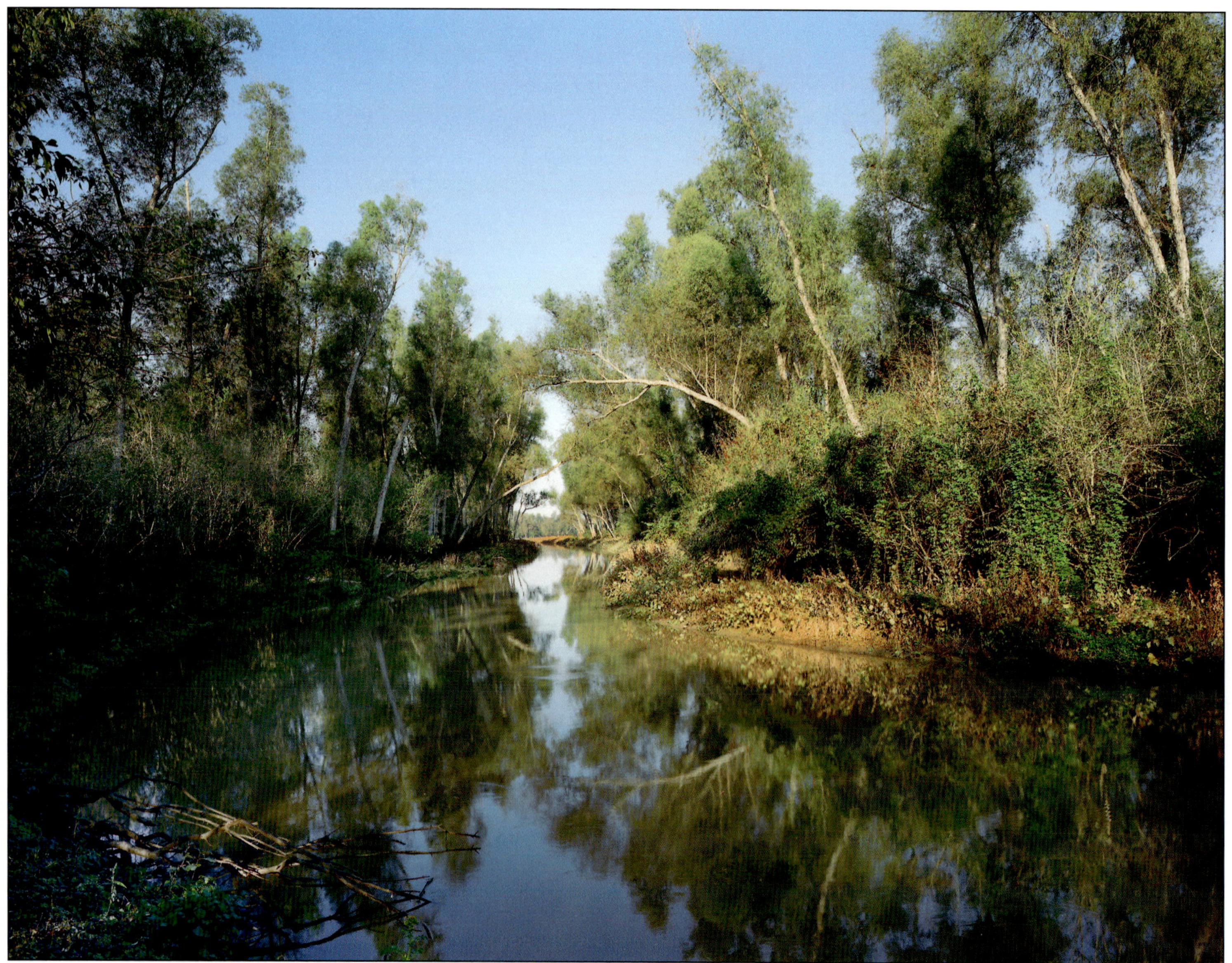

Atchafalaya Basin: Slough to Upper Flat Lake
Iberville Parish, Louisiana

So, too, the narrow slough, lined with willows and carpeted with cocklebers, runs between the river and the lake. Sometimes the slough flows to the lake, sometimes to the river. This is a pioneer forest rooted on new deposits of sediment. As more sediment accumulated and the land dried out, pioneer forests evolved into productive bottomland hardwood forests, treed in oak, pecan, ash, and red maple: habitat for wildlife, gold to the timber industry. Without the 1982 plan, which forbad the conversion of land south of U.S. 190 to agriculture, the bottomland forests would have been logged and the land turned over to agriculture.

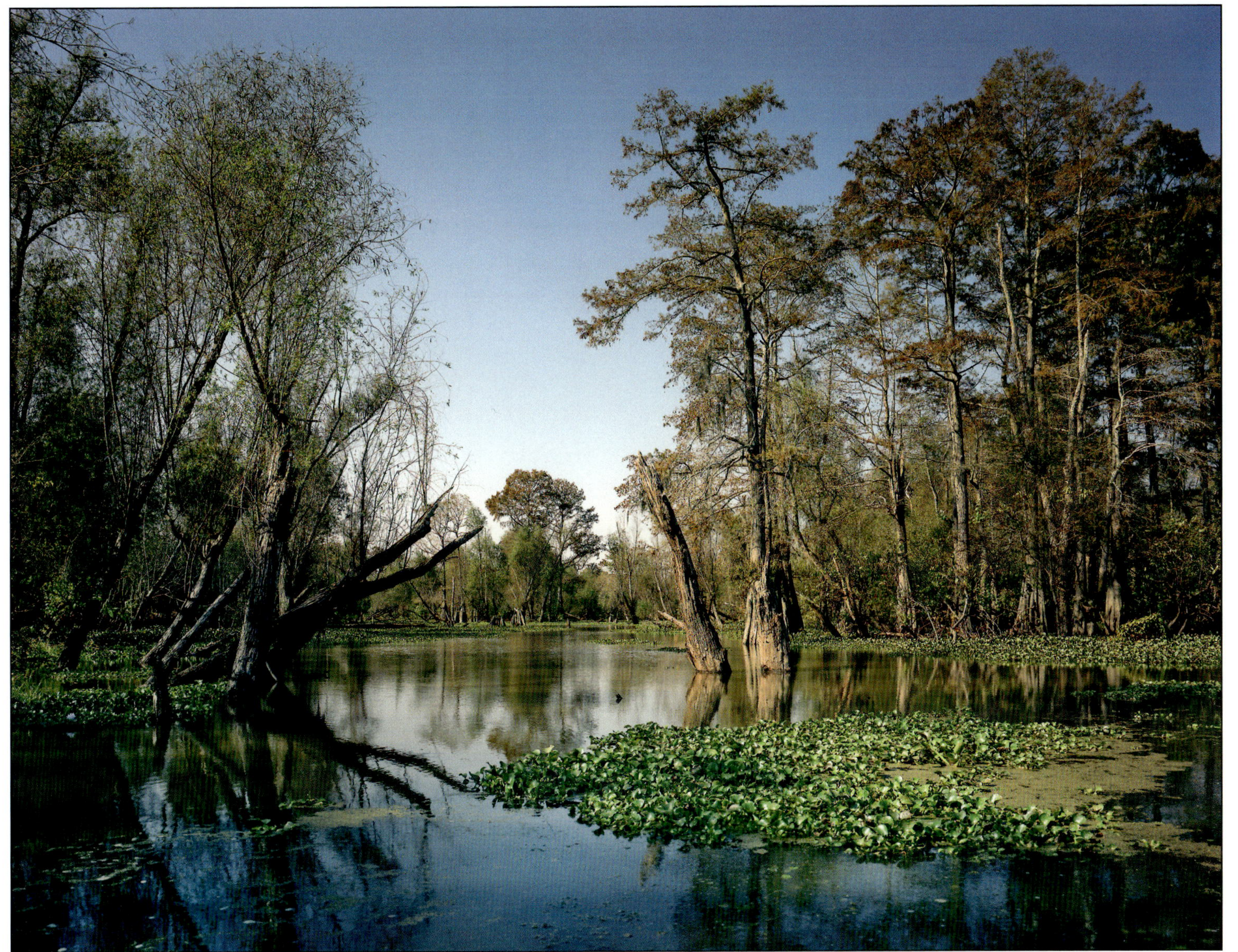

Atchafalaya Basin: Upper Flat Lake

Iberville Parish, Louisiana

Periodically, Upper Flat Lake dries out enough for cypress to germinate. The seeds require oxygen to germinate and flowing water to disseminate. Cypress produce seeds in fall and winter. Spring flooding disperses winter seeds. Seeds produced in fall sprout in the dry season, when the lake is drawn down but soil remains moist. Seedlings grow rapidly, keeping their tips above the rising water, and do best after a short drawdown followed by shallow flooding, when they shoot up. Mature trees develop buttresses at their bases, and knees that grow above the water from the roots support the tree.

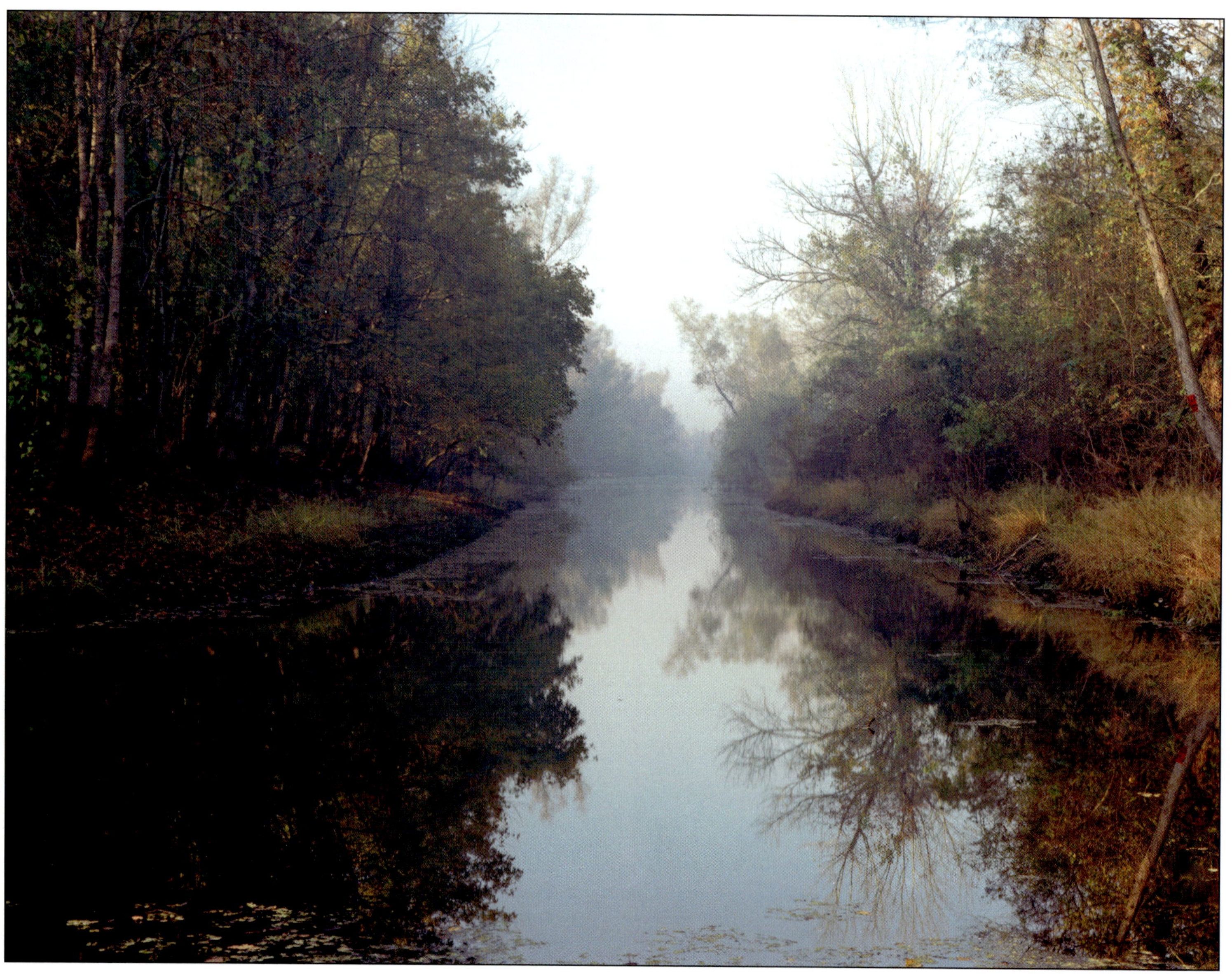

Opelousas Bay: Henderson Environmental Management Unit

St. Martin Parish, Louisiana

The Corps of Engineers' 1982 plan broke the basin into thirteen experimental management units, where the Corps could test theories that could reduce sedimentation and restore hydrology. The statement detailed plans for the Henderson Pilot Unit: Restore its water regime to historic overflow patterns. Flush water through the unit. Restrict the movement and deposition of sediment. The plan listed the tools: Impound the unit behind low levees and dikes. Dredge entrance channels. Control the flow of water with weirs at its inlets and outlets. Close canals that deliver sediment to backwaters. Open spoil banks to improve water-flow patterns.

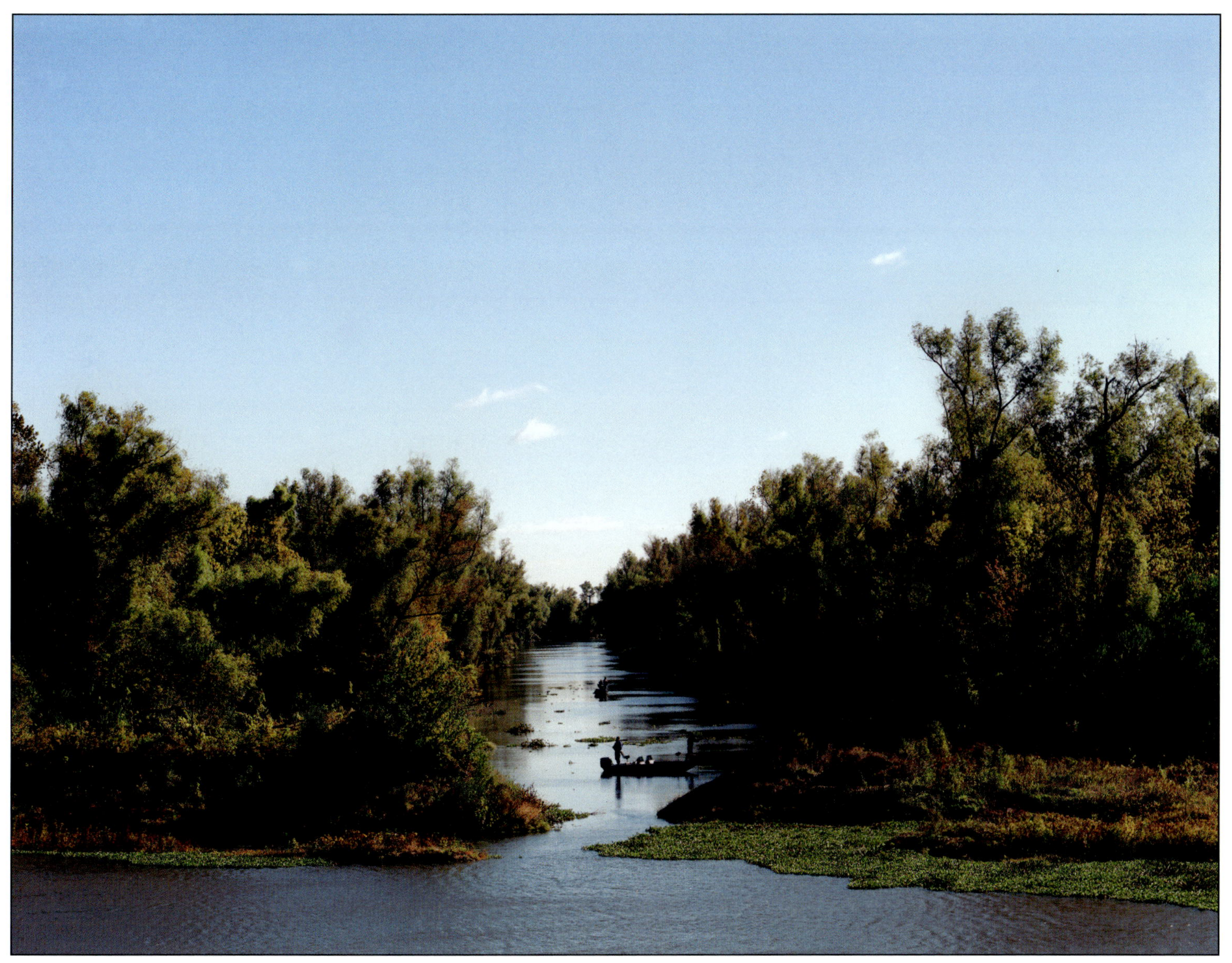

Opelousas Bay: Henderson
St. Martin Parish, Louisiana

In October 2006 locals expressed their hopes for the Henderson unit in a Corps scoping report: Do something about flooding inside and outside the unit. Remove the water-control structure that holds water at the southern end, floods the northern end, and keeps cypress and oak from regenerating. Protect old-growth cypress and cypress/tupelo swamps from harvesting for mulch. Restore the flood/dry cycle. Let plants that feed ducks and crawfish grow. Restore old watercourses that bring in water. Control and return sediment to the Atchafalaya to restore coastal wetlands. Lower or take out oil spoil banks. Create a self-sustaining system.

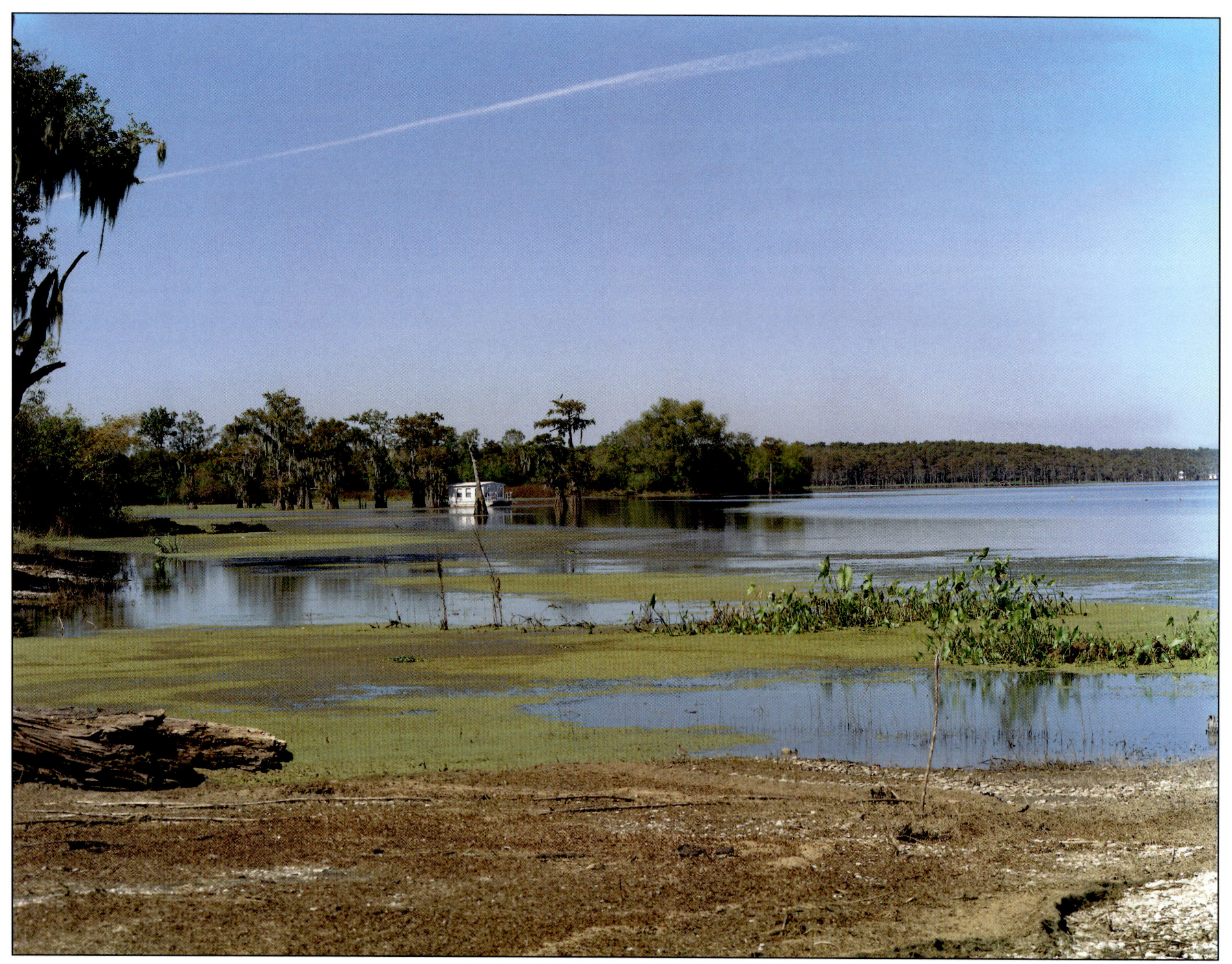

Atchafalaya Basin: Grand Lake
St. Mary Parish, Louisiana

In 1917, Grand Lake covered 136 square miles. After initiation of the floodway project, the Corps ran the Atchafalaya navigation channel through the lake and installed wing dams to train it. Oil companies dredged canals in the 1960s and '70s. Water levels had increased at its southern end and decreased at its northern end, reducing the current's velocity. Bayous flowing into the lake deposited sediment and formed deltas. New bayous meandered through the deposits. All bayous lost depth, and their natural levees gained elevation. By 2005, when construction on the Buffalo Cove Management Unit began, Grand Lake was half its former size.

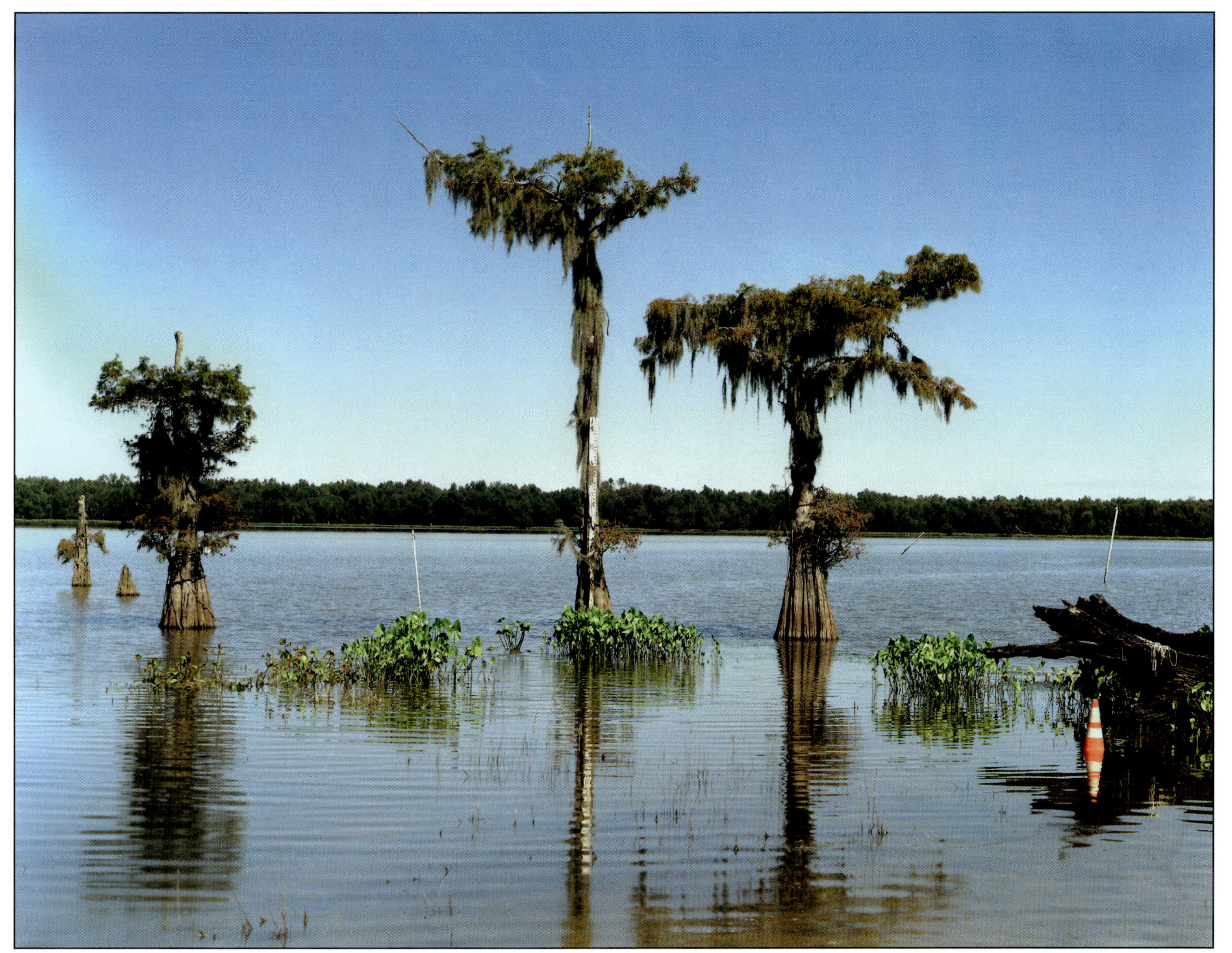

Atchafalaya Basin: Grand Lake

St. Mary Parish, Louisiana

The Corps used passive water-management techniques to restore north-to-south flow through the Buffalo Cove unit. Rather than creating an artificial impoundment behind levees, engineers modified the heights of natural and artificial levees by shaving banks to reduce barriers to water input; closed, opened, or realigned existing channels; created or restored natural or artificial channels to improve water circulation; experimented with the length and depth of channels and their configurations—sinuous or straight; constructed traps to keep sediment out of some areas and directed sediment to places that were already accreting.

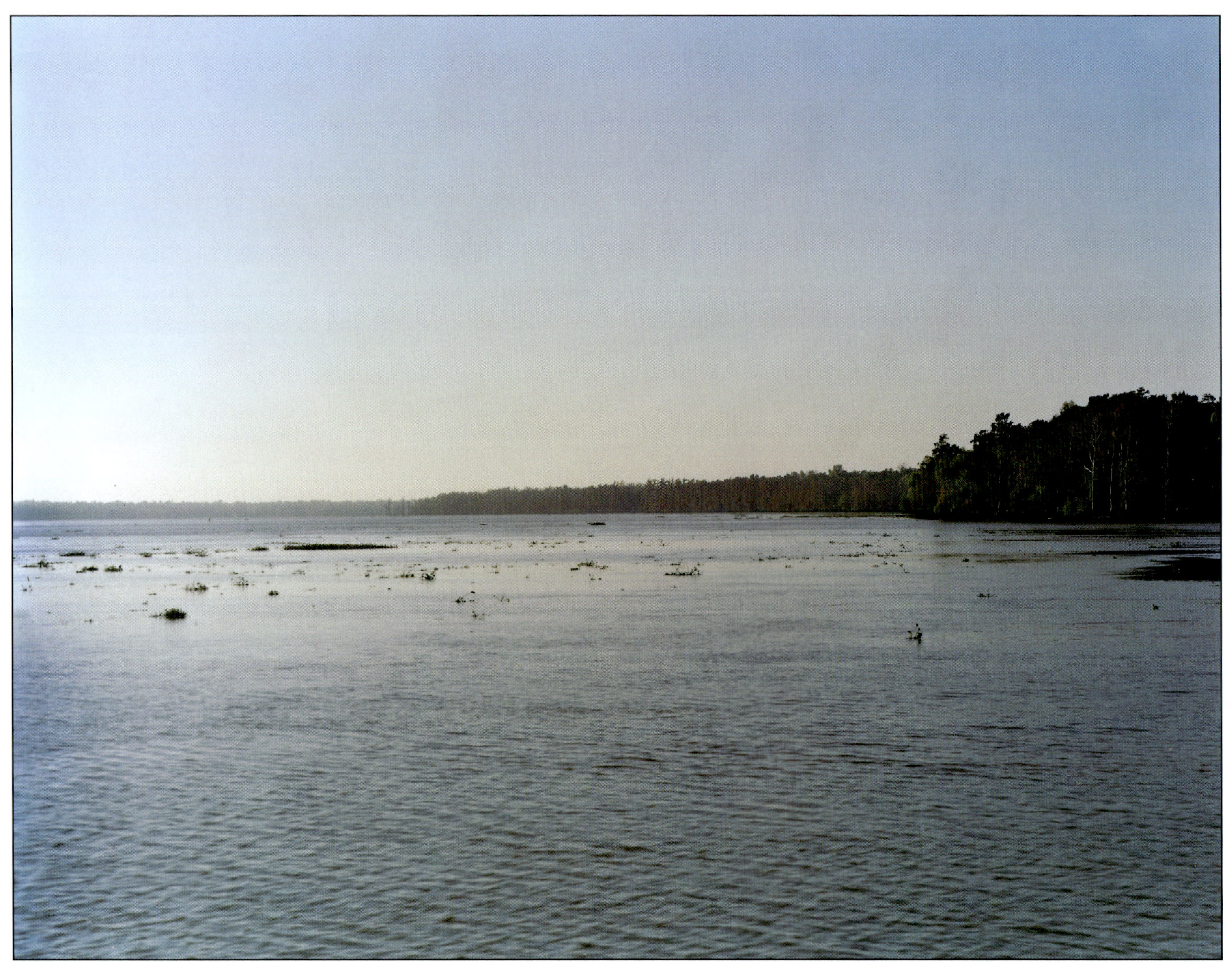

Lower Atchafalaya River at the GIWW: Berwick

St. Mary Parish, Louisiana

"The Atchafalaya River is the great under-used branch of the Mississippi River in terms of restoration"—Dr. Paul Kemp, 2007

River stages along the Atchafalaya rose steadily between 1940 and 2000, about two feet higher at its crossing with the GIWW. With this head the Atchafalaya drives water in the GIWW eighty miles to the east and fifty miles to the west. The GIWW distributes freshwater and sediment to coastal wetlands to the south. If we better understood the flow of water through the GIWW and its relationship to the Lower Atchafalaya, we could formalize the waterway's role in refreshing the wetlands.

The Delta: Introduction

The Deltaic Plain

The headwaters of the Mississippi River were the holy grail for American explorers until 1832, when Oza Windib, an Ojibway Chippewa from Cass Lake, guided Henry Rowe Schoolcraft to Lake Itasca. The explorers wrote histories of their expeditions. They all described the landscape they explored. Not so the Louisiana deltaic plain. Eighteenth- and nineteenth-century explorers made the obligatory trip to the head of passes and the mouth of the Mississippi, described their trips and the landscape, and dismissed every place east and west of the river. As late as 1816, William Darby, a surveyor, geographer, and gazetteer who did explore Louisiana between 1812 and 1814, published a detailed map of the state based on his surveys and said of the marshes that span West Cote Blanche Bay between Bayou Cypremort and Bayou Sale: "like other parts of the coast of Louisiana, is morass." The exception was Antoine Simon Le Page du Pratz, who spent sixteen years, eight of them living among the Natchez along St. Catherine's Creek in Mississippi, exploring French Louisiana. He described the intricacies of the Lafourche subdelta: "In going still farther west, we meet much thicker woods, because this country is extremely well watered; we here find numbers of rivers, which fall into the sea; and what contributes to the fertility of this land, is the number of brooks, that fall into these rivers."

Americans paid little attention to the Mississippi or the Louisiana coast until after the Louisiana Purchase in 1803. And of the people President Thomas Jefferson sent out to explore the territory—Pike to the Upper Mississippi, Lewis and Clark along the Missouri to the Pacific, Dunbar along the Red—he sent no one to the Louisiana coast. In 1807 the army sent Maj. Amos Stoddard to New Orleans. In his sketches of Louisiana he described the salt domes—Weeks Island, Cote Blanche Island, and others—rising out of West and East Cote Blanche Bays, and he explored the reaches of Bayou Terre aux Bouefs in St. Bernard Parish. Otherwise, he was more interested in the Atchafalaya. William Darby expanded our knowledge of the Louisiana coast, particularly the Chenier Plain, when he explored the region in 1812 and published his findings in *The Emigrant's Guide to the Western and Southwestern States and Territories* in 1818.

Every change we have made to the Mississippi since French settlers built the first levee at New Orleans in 1718 has contributed to the loss of the coastal wetlands. The levees, extending to the Gulf of Mexico, broke the seasonal exchange between freshwater and salt water and shifted the wetlands from river-dominated to tidal-dominated systems. Before the levees, the Mississippi, fed by winter snowmelt and spring rains, washed over its banks, flushed out salt water that crept into the marshes in the fall and winter when the river stayed within its banks. And it delivered sediment to the wetlands. The levees prevented the river from flooding the wetlands with freshwater and sediment. The wetlands became dependent on rain for freshwater. Gulf tides washed salt water into brackish and freshwater marshes.

Revetments reduced erosion of the river's banks, a major source of sediment. Eads's shipping channel through South Pass delivered sediment to very deep water at the continental shelf, where it was useless for land building, and where it disrupted the westward flow of currents in the Gulf of Mexico. Closure of old distributaries cut the flow of freshwater and sediment to the coastal marshes. Channel dams on the Upper Mississippi and the Missouri retained sediment north of St. Louis. By the end of the twentieth century the coastal marshes were receiving 80 percent less sediment than they had at its beginning.

The construction of navigation channels and oil and gas canals through the marshes broke down the zones between freshwater and salt water and disrupted the flow of water across the marshes. Salt water bled into freshwater marshes, destroyed vegetation that anchored sediment, and forced out fish and wildlife. Oil extraction in the marshlands increased the rate of subsidence. Marshes submerged under as much as three feet of water.

And the problematical happened: global climate change caused eustatic sea levels to rise as measured against the worldwide average. And the uncontrollable happened: faults lying deep in the rock under the coast slipped in blocks, which caused relative sea level to rise, as measured against local benchmarks. On top the marshes subsided.

In 1998 the Coast 2050 proposal broke the Louisiana coast into four regions: the wetlands formed by the Calcasieu, Sabine, and Mermentau Rivers at the western edge of the coast; the Terrebonne, Atchafalaya, and Teche/Vermilion region that encompassed the wetlands east of Freshwater Bayou and west of Bayou Lafourche in parts of the Teche and Lafourche Deltas; the Breton, Barataria, and Mississippi River region that encompassed the wetlands laying east of Bayou Lafourche and those west of the Mississippi River and Gulf Outlet (MRGO) in parts of the Lafourche, St. Bernard, and Modern Deltas; and the Pontchartrain region than encompassed the wetlands surrounding Lake Pontchartrain and parts of the St. Bernard Delta.

The 2050 proposal detailed the habitat and historic land loss in each region, projected its future land loss, described fish and wildlife resources, specified infrastructure (roads, oil and gas pipelines), noted previous strategies for restoring wetlands in each basin, and outlined proposed strategies for restoring wetlands.

Conventional wisdom has long held that this intricate web of natural levees and basins containing marshes and swamps soaked up the power of storm surges produced by hurricanes and reduced the flooding that followed. Until 1992 it was just that: conventional wisdom with no data to back it up. On August 26, 1992, while Americans focused on the damage Hurricane Andrew produced in Homestead, Florida, the storm surged across the Gulf of Mexico, made a second landfall as a category three storm at Point Chevreuil, Louisiana, and racked up numbers on continuous-water-level recorders in the Terrebonne marshes south of Houma. A storm surge that measured 9.3 feet at Cocodrie swept across the Houma Navigation Canal at Houma, twenty-three miles to the north, at 3.3 feet. That translates into an amplitude loss of 3.1 inches per mile of marsh and open water between Cocodrie and Houma. Between Oyster Bayou and Kent Bayou, the storm surge was reduced by 2.8 inches per mile across nineteen miles. Clearly, conventional wisdom was correct, even allowing for different hurricanes following different storm tracks across different coastal landscapes. Coastal wetlands soak up the power of hurricanes. Hence, when Katrina's storm surge ripped across Breton Sound and Lake Borgne thirteen years later and wiped out the string of lovely towns on Mississippi's coastline, it demonstrated the destructive power of a Category Three storm unimpeded by healthy marshes.

Before Katrina and Rita tore through Louisiana's coastal marshes, the environmental and economic necessity of a healthy system of wetlands was little understood outside the state. After Katrina and Rita, we finally understood that Louisiana's coastal wetlands act as a buffer against storms. But we still needed to learn that they absorb nutrients, sediment, and contaminants. They serve as the breeding, spawning, feeding, and nursery grounds for fish and shellfish at some time in their life cycles. Summer flounder, spotted seatrout, snook, tarpon, and others spawn in the Gulf, migrate to their freshwater nurseries in the summer, and return to the Gulf when temperatures drop in the fall. So do juvenile brown and white shrimp. Migratory birds rest on Louisiana's barrier islands on their annual migration from Central and South America. Waterfowl, wading birds, and shorebirds colonize its freshwater marshes, attracted by their diverse menu of fish and shellfish, broad-leaved plants, tall grasses, and shrubs. The marshes provide habitat for the endangered brown pelican and at least seventy pairs of bald eagles. Furbearers—nutria, muskrat, mink, raccoon, otter, bobcat, beaver, coyote, and opossum—thrive in the marshlands.

The American alligator—once endangered, now abundant—nests along the banks of coastal freshwater marshes.

Louisiana's commercial fishermen harvest 1.1 billion pounds of fish and shellfish, including shrimp, crabs, crayfish, oysters, and finfish, up to 20 percent of the nation's catch, valued at $2.2 billion a year to Louisiana's economy. Recreational anglers contribute $944 million. More than 40 percent of the nation's fur harvest comes from Louisiana. Louisiana's alligator farmers take eggs from the wild, and after the alligators hatch, they return some to the wild, keeping the rest until they are large enough to harvest, netting $9.3 million in skin and meat.

Louisiana's three million acres of coastal wetlands are more productive than many agricultural lands, and they are disappearing at the rate of twenty-five to thirty-five square miles a year. If the loss continues at that rate, commercial and recreational fish would decline by 30 percent, putting up to 70,000 jobs at risk statewide. Migratory birds dependent on the marshes might decline, having an impact on the rest of the country, on duck hunters, on bird watchers, on the numbers of pests. Fur trappers would see the loss of a $1.3 million industry. The cost of treating drinking water would rise, along with the cost of salt and other minerals taken from the coast. Alligator meat might once again become a delicacy.

Even before Katrina and Rita devastated 217 square miles of Louisiana's coastal wetlands, New Orleans, and Mississippi's Gulf Coast, the question at the beginning of the twenty-first century was: What should we do about the wetlands that, were they healthy, would protect New Orleans and Mississippi's coastal towns? And, who was going to pay for it? Like the Upper Mississippi Pool Plans and the Lower Mississippi Conservation Initiative, the $14 billion Coast 2050 proposal laid out a restoration plan that was more wish list than reality.

The Teche Delta and the Vermilion Basin

> Southwest of the Teche, a number of small bayous rise, and flow into the Vermilion and Atchafalaya bays. The most remarkable of these streams are, the Petite Anse, Bayou Cypriere Mort (dead cypress) Bayou Caroline, Bayou Sale, and the Myrtle Bayou. Some good arable land lies upon the Bayou Cypriere Mort, and Bayou Sale, rendered more valuable, as being within the climate suitable for sugar cane. The intermediate space between those water courses, like other parts of the coast of Louisiana, is morass.
>
> —William Darby, 1816

Bayou Teche carried the Mississippi along the western valley wall for a very long time and initiated the first of the Mississippi delta lobes, beginning with the Maringouin Complex about 7,000 years ago. Distributaries broke off from the Mississippi and delivered its sediment into what are now deep Gulf waters. As sea level continued to rise over the next thousand years, the Gulf submerged or eroded the outer margins of the new delta. The river abandoned its distributaries.

Submerged portions of the Maringouin can be found on the Tiger, Ship, and Trinity shoals, ridges of sand under the Gulf, sources of sediment for rebuilding barrier islands. The Mississippi formed new distributaries—to the south along Bayou Cypremort and Bayou Sale; and to the east along Bayou Black. The new channels deposited their sediment on top of a poorly drained swamp, the remnants of the earlier complex.

Bayou Cypremort deposited its ridge between Vermilion Bay on the west and West Cote Blanche Bay on the east. Bayou Sale pushed its ridge out between East Cote Blanche Bay and Atchafalaya Bay. Distributaries, which developed to the east, deposited their sediment in very shallow water south of Morgan City and Bayou Black. These deposits subsided and were later covered by sediment delivered to the Gulf by distributaries in the Lafourche subdelta.

Vermilion Bay and West and East Cote Blanche Bays encompass the Teche-Vermilion Basin, 243,000 acres of wetlands in Vermilion, Iberia, and St. Mary Parishes, which progress from fresh to intermediate to brackish. Marsh Island—a 170,000-acre barrier island composed of bayous, lakes, and dunes, and encircled by live and relict oyster reefs—separates and buffers the three bays from the saltier water of the Gulf of Mexico.

Unlike the later delta lobes, the Teche subdelta is fairly stable and its marsh loss low. Most of the more delicate marshes in the basin eroded or submerged centuries ago, after its distributaries stopped delivering fresh sediment to its delta front. The remaining sediments have had centuries to compact and become stable. The basin, as a whole, lost 42,293 acres, or 14.8 percent, of its wetlands after 1932, with over half the loss coming between 1951 and 1974. At the end of the twentieth century the basin was profiting from fresh water and sediment being delivered to West Cote Blanche Bay and Vermilion Bay from the Atchafalaya River and the Wax Lake Outlet through the GIWW and Bayou Cypremort. East and West Cote Blanche Bays were slowly filling with sediment. Navigation channels, oil and gas access canals, spoil banks, and levees changed the way water and sediment flowed across the basin and caused erosion.

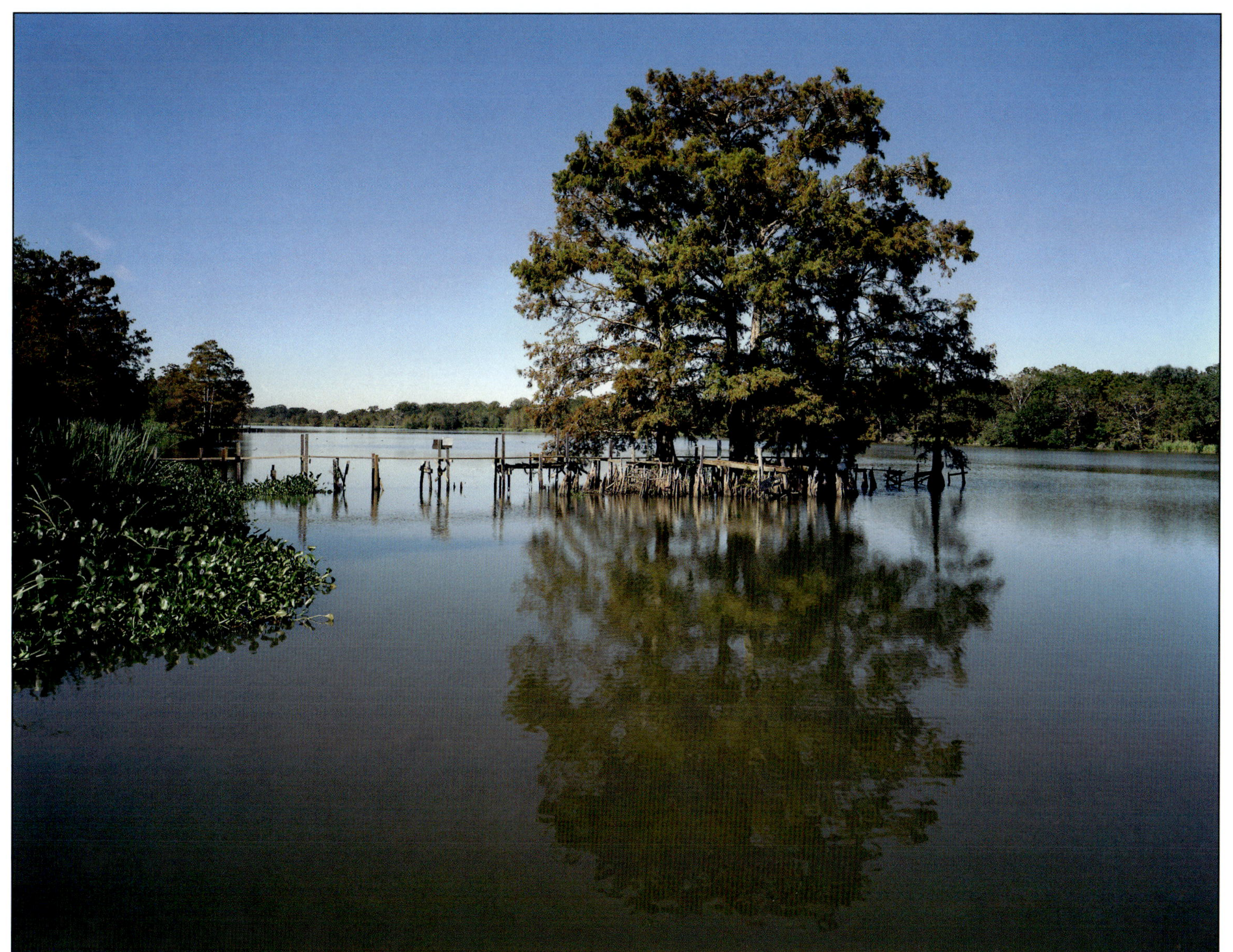

Bayou Teche: Avalon

St. Mary Parish, Louisiana

The snake: That the Chitimachas took their word for "snake" to name the meandering river had nothing to do with its serpentine shape. Tribal legend has it that the Chitimachas killed a great snake, which thrashed out the Teche channel as it died. Modern Bayou Teche rises at Bayou Courtableau and meanders south through multiple changes to its confluence with the lower Atchafalaya. How much water flowed to Teche depended on how much water was flowing to Courtableau through a complex system of flood-control structures in the West Atchafalaya Floodway that diverted water from the Atchafalaya through Bayou Courtableau and into Bayou Teche.

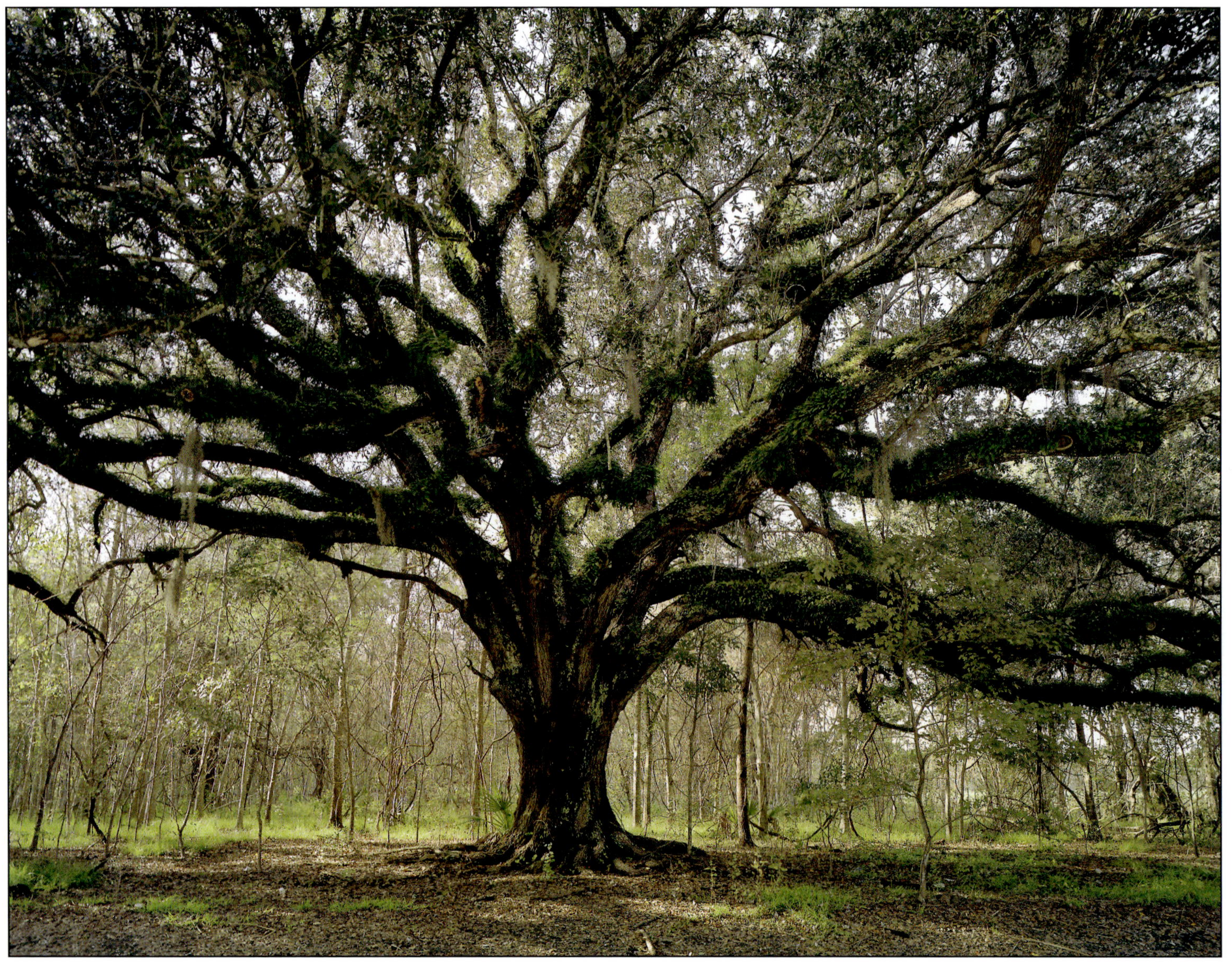

Bayou Sale Natural Levee: Ellerslie

St. Mary Parish, Louisiana

Dense live oak forests rooted on the natural ridges, the highest and driest land that knitted together the coastal wetlands. European settlers cleared the oaks for their fields and pastures. The live oak remained intact on the narrow Bayou Sale ridge, where the natural levee gave way to cypress swamp and there was no room for agricultural fields. When forests disappeared, so did songbirds that rested in them after their migration across the Gulf of Mexico. In 2005 the Louisiana Department of Wildlife and Fisheries listed the Prothonotary Warbler, which breeds above flooded streams in the White River National Wildlife Refuge, as a species of concern.

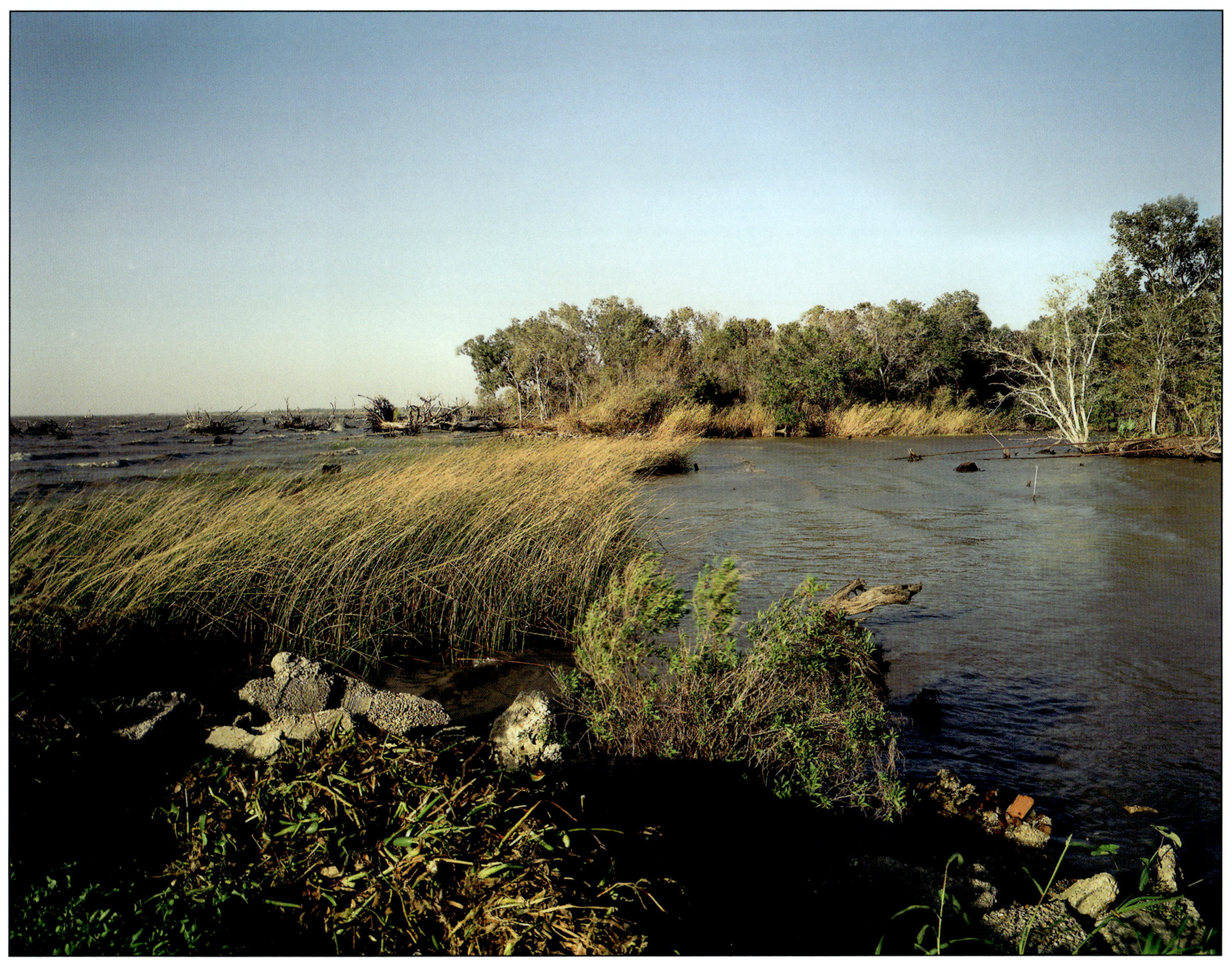

Bayou Sale: East Cote Blanche Bay

St. Mary Parish, Louisiana

By 2004 wind fetch, driving waves across East Cote Blanche Bay and into the Bayou Sale ridge, had eroded its shoreline. Waves battered the emergent marsh out front of the ridge first, then the ridge and its live oak forest. Skeletons of the drowned forest sank into the bay. Fish and wildlife, including the Louisiana black bear, lost habitat. The CWPPRA Task Force, working with the NRCS, approved the engineering and design phase of the Bayou Sale Shoreline Protection Project to try to reduce and reverse the retreat of the Bayou Sale ridge. Engineers planned a rock dike, 35,776 feet long and 150 feet out from the scoured shoreline of East Cote Blanche Bay.

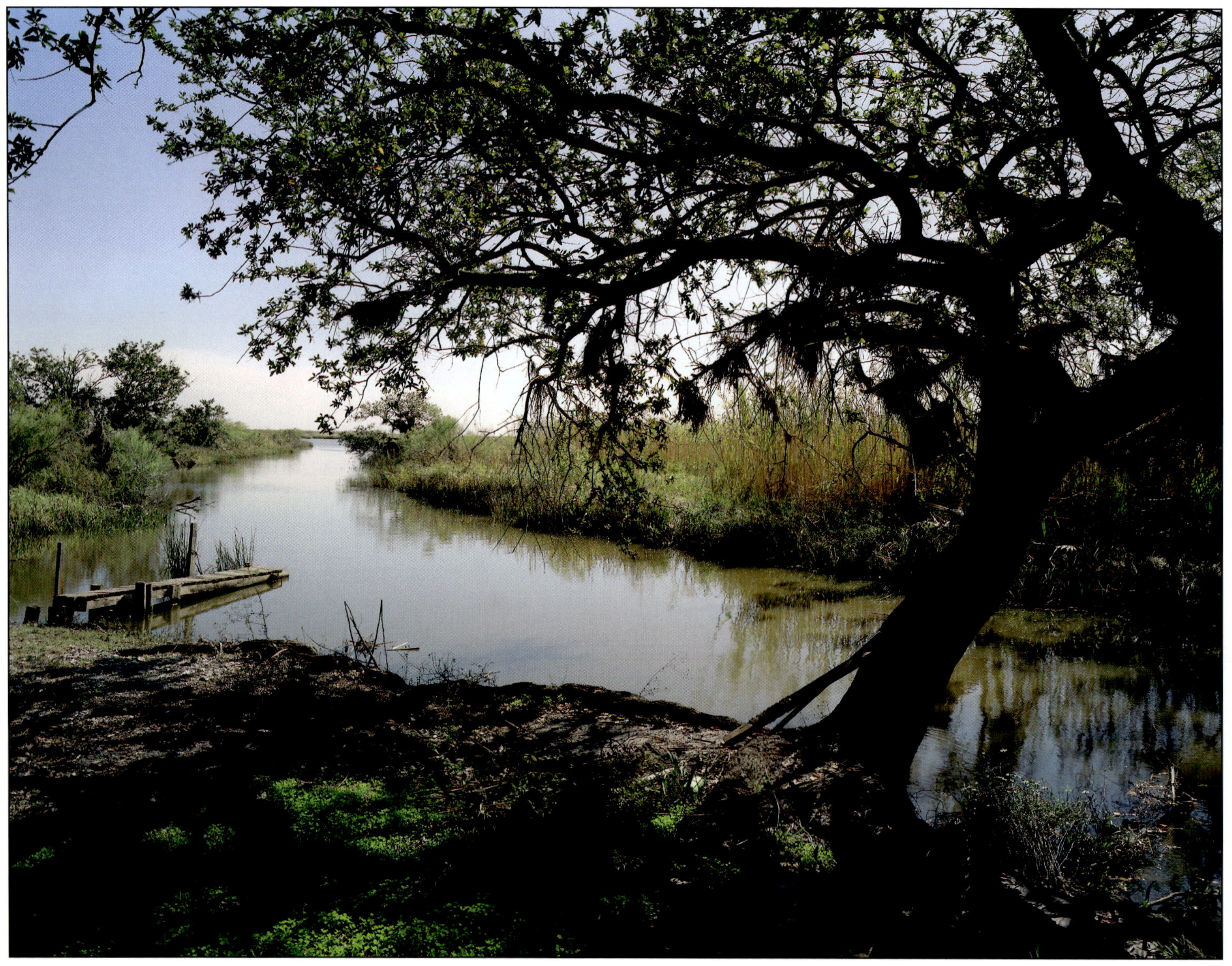

Bayou Cypremort: Outlet to West Cote Blanche Bay

St. Mary Parish, Louisiana

In 1998 the Louisiana DNR held a series of meetings to develop goals for restoring the Louisiana coast: Slow tidal exchange and maintain the Cote Blanche Bays as brackish. Use marshes to slow the flow of freshwater and sediment from the GIWW. Protect bay shorelines. Stabilize the banks of canals running through the marshes with dredge. Whatever strategies restorers take in the Cote Blanche wetlands will produce winners and losers. Too little sediment would keep waterfowl and freshwater fish happy but reduce the wetlands' ability to buffer storms. Too little freshwater would increase salinity, bad for freshwater fish, alligators, and waterfowl.

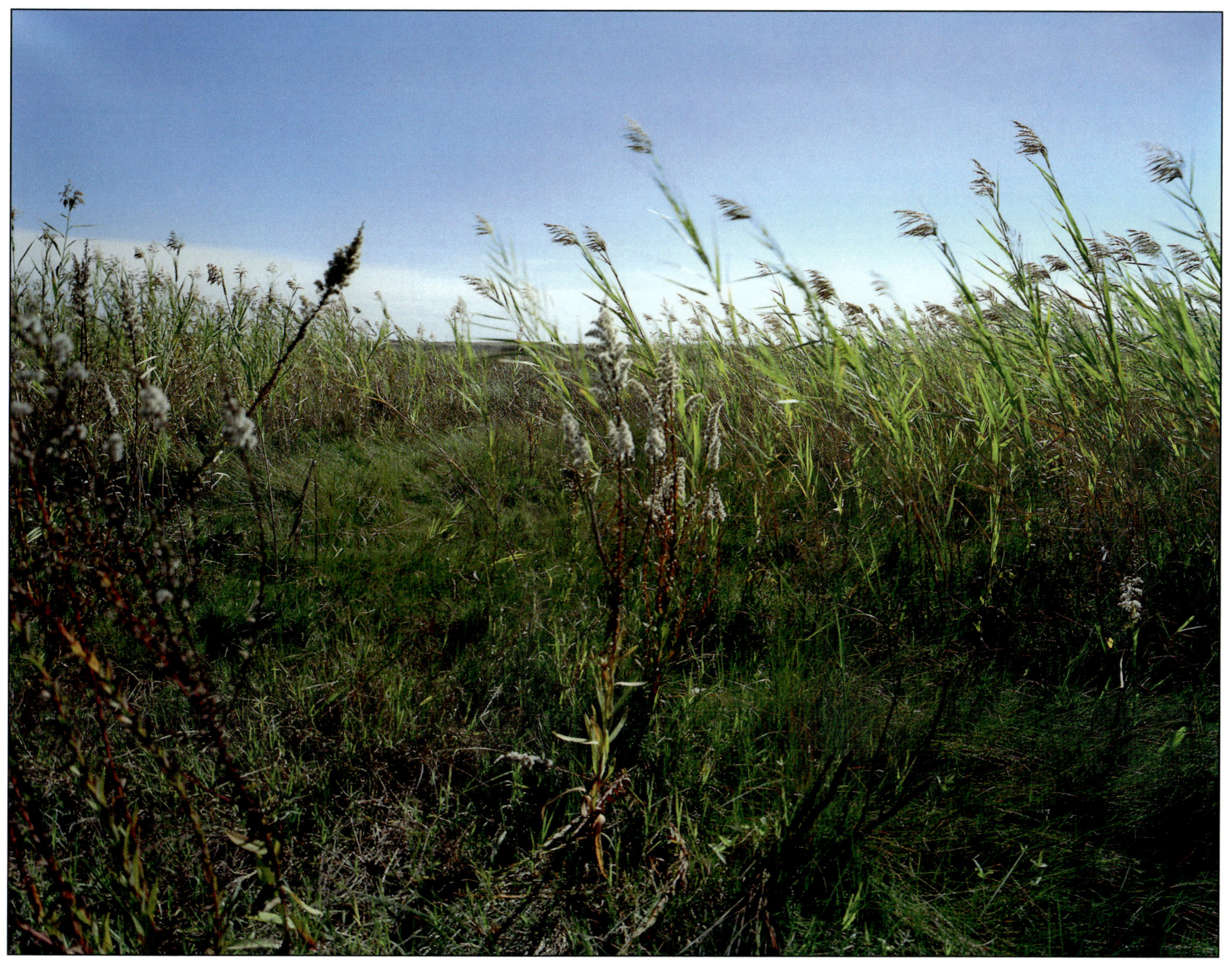

Cypremort Point: West Cote Blanche Wetlands

St. Mary Parish, Louisiana

Marsh muck and peat anchored the brackish marshes, lying between the tip of Cypremort ridge and Hammock Lake, a pond in the wetlands. A wide array of marsh grasses bound the soils together: marshhay corgrass, leafy three-square, roseau cane, black needle rush, and smooth cordgrass. By 2000 the marshes were freshening and turning intermediate. Wave energy breached a narrow strip of marsh between the lake and the bay. With the strip gone, the Louisiana DNR feared wave energy would erode the marsh clear to the ridge. To restore the strip the DNR built a 1,532-foot tree fence, stocked it with recycled Christmas trees, and regained 1.7 acres of marsh.

The Terrebonne Basin

The Terrebonne Basin lies between Bayou Lafourche on the east and the Atchafalaya East Protection Levee and lower Atchafalaya on the west. Bayou Black, a distributary of the Teche Delta delivered sediment to the basin 4,500 years ago and built a ridge that ran west to east. A thousand years later the Mississippi diverted to the eastern side of its alluvial valley and began depositing its sediment in the St. Bernard Delta along Bayou Terre aux Boeufs southeast of New Orleans. The old Teche Delta continued to deliver freshwater from the whole of the Atchafalaya and Verret Basins to the Terrebonne Basin, and sediment flowed to it from the Red River. Not quite 2,500 years ago the Mississippi formed a distributary along Bayou du Large, initiated the Lafourche Delta, and began depositing freshwater and sediment into the Terrebonne Basin, sometimes along the old Teche distributaries. The river shifted to Bayou Terrebonne 1,270 years ago, Bayou Grand Caillou, 900 years ago, and Bayou Petit Caillou, 700 years ago. Together they knitted a web of natural levees, where bottomland hardwood forests took root, which protected the freshwater swamps that took shape in the backwaters. And freshwater continued to flow south from the Atchafalaya and Verret Basins. The freshwater swamps and marshes occupied the upper three-quarters of the basin. In the lower quarter of the basin the natural ridges extended southward. Delta building exceeded subsidence at the edge of the Gulf of Mexico

By the time Americans began settling along Bayou Lafourche 200 years ago, the Mississippi had abandoned the Lafourche Delta but continued to deliver 15 percent of its flow to Bayou Lafourche, not enough to sustain the delta front, which eroded inland. Longshore currents reworked loose sediment into barrier islands, the Isles Derniers.

After Bayou Lafourche was closed at its head in 1904, the freshwater swamps and marshes retreated, but continued to occupy two-thirds of the basin. The cycle of growth and decay in the marshes equaled subsidence, but the ridges started to shrink. Farmers cleared the bottomland forests for fields; loggers cleared the cypress from the swamps. In 1830, R. R. Barrow dredged the Barataria Canal from the Mississippi River to Houma, cutting across the ridges and silted-in distributaries in the basin, which reopened and began to flow. Hurricanes lashed the lower third of the basin and opened up saltwater bays, but the barrier islands increased in size and elevation as longshore currents redistributed sand.

By the beginning of the twentieth century the wetlands in the lower basin had deteriorated. The freshwater swamps and marshes in the upper half were stressed, but the marshes remained unbroken as they had been for hundreds of years. By 1950 the lower third was deteriorating rapidly, and deterioration had expanded to one-half the basin. The barrier islands diminished in size and elevation. Tidal channels expanded between the islands, allowing more and more salt water into the bays. The bays expanded, enlarged by storms. Even with the dam across the head of Bayou Lafourche and no water and sediment from the Mississippi flowing along the distributaries in the basin, the growth and decay of the marshes overcame subsidence. The natural levees however, continued to decrease in width and elevation.

After 1950 the barrier islands collapsed; the deteriorating lower half expanded to cover two-thirds of the basin as the shore zone moved inland. Bays expanded; tidal marshes retreated. The Louisiana DNR attempted to restore the deteriorating barrier islands in the 1990s. Freshwater swamps and marshes retreated to the upper third. The growth and decay of the marshes lost out to subsidence.

The Terrebonne Basin and the Barataria Basin to the east have suffered the greatest lost of wetlands. Oil extraction from the sands deep under the wetlands pulled them down. Down deeper, the faults that underlie coastal Louisiana dropped down in blocks and dragged them down. Open water replaced wetlands. Depending on which geologist you read, land-loss hot spots—Bay St. Elaine, Madison Bay, du Large, Pointe au Chien, and Bully Camp—in the basin have been attributed to oil extraction or faults, possibly both: The faults may have been activated by intense oil extraction. Finally, Katrina and Rita, the hurricanes of 2005, reduced 19.4 square miles of wetlands to open water in the Terrebonne Basin.

The Verret Basin

Between the natural levees of the Mississippi and Bayou Lafourche and the Atchafalaya East Protection Levee lie the combined backswamps of the Mississippi and Atchafalaya Rivers. This is the fringe of the Atchafalaya Basin, the Lake Verret watershed, which extends clear north to Morganza. Historically, Lake Verret lay in the Atchafalaya floodplain even though it is no more than two or three miles from the western edge of the Bayou Lafourche ridge. Construction of the East Atchafalaya Basin Protection Levee cut it off from the Atchafalaya Basin.

The Verret watershed is an estuarine basin that drains into the lower Atchafalaya and filters water through the western Terrebonne marshes to the Gulf of Mexico. Water drains off its natural levees, through its hardwood forests and cypress swamps, and into the bayous and canals that lead to Lake Verret. Bayou Boeuf carries water out of the watershed to the lower Atchafalaya River and into the western Terrebonne Basin marshes.

The Atchafalaya East Protection Levee runs down the GIWW and wraps itself around Morgan City—almost. Water sneaks around Avoca Island, south of Morgan City, and into Boeuf Bayou, flooding towns east of Morgan City, its eastern neighborhoods, and the Lake Verret watershed.

The 1982 plan for the Atchafalaya Basin guides flooding, navigation, recreational development, and environmental issues in the floodway. Not until April 2005 did the New Orleans District of the Corps of Engineers initiate the Atchafalaya River Backwater Study to alleviate flooding in Morgan City and the Lake Verret Watershed and propose the construction of a barrier, a large water-control structure and pumping station on Boeuf Bayou east of Morgan City. However, such a structure would induce headwater flooding. All the water draining out of the Lake Verret watershed would back up behind the structure and have to be pumped out. However, pumping out the surplus might help the bottomland hardwoods and the cypress/tupelo swamps, which were drowning in excess water.

Before the construction of the East Protection Levee, the Atchafalaya spread sediment across a basin that stretched from the Mississippi west to Bayou Teche. Once cut from its source of sediment, the landscape subsided. East of the levee the Lake Verret watershed depended on rainfall, backwater flooding, and subsidence for water. Subsidence was bringing in too much water, drowning the bottomland hardwoods found on the natural ridges. By 2000, forests throughout the watershed, whether they grew on ridges or in swamps, were in trouble. And the water level was increasing at the rate of a half-inch a year.

In April 2006 the USFWS weighed in on plans for the Verret wetlands. Fish and Wildlife would like to see the Verret wetlands included in the floodway where they could receive deposits of sediment coming down the Atchafalaya. Such a solution would entail running the East Protection Levee up the western flank of the ridge created by Little Black Bayou and enclosing all the communities in the extended floodway in ring levees, elevating structures, relocating people, or simply buying them out.

Should that alternative prove impractical or unfeasible, the Corps would need to manage water levels behind the new Boeuf Bayou structure to mimic as closely as possible the natural rise and fall of the Atchafalaya River, high in the spring, low in the late summer and fall. Such a regime would increase the productivity of both the bottomland hardwood forests and the cypress/tupelo swamps.

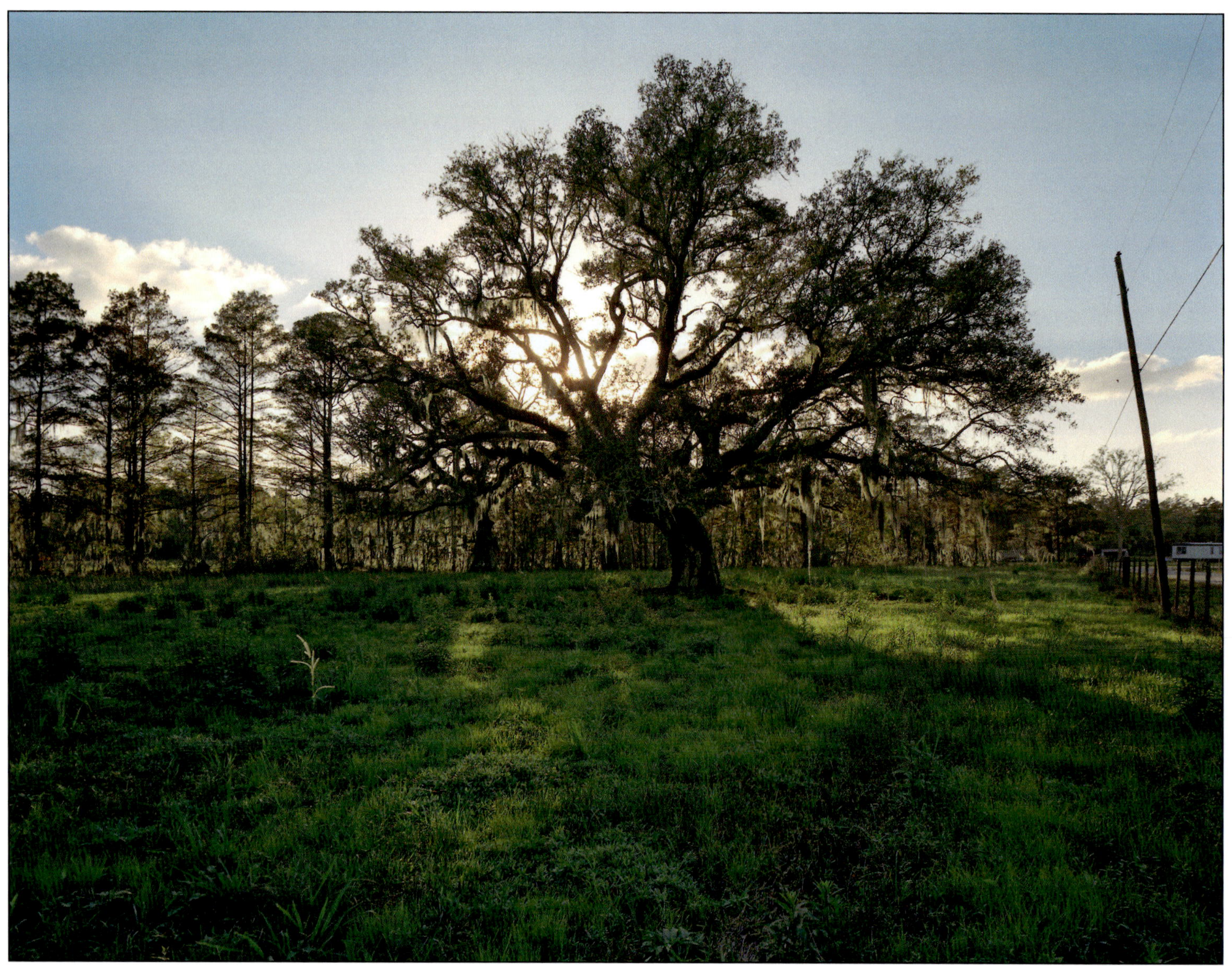

Atchafalaya Basin: Upper Texas
Assumption Parish, Louisiana

A live oak survives on a high spot in a submerged, wooded swamp. Live oaks and oaks common to bottomland hardwood forests don't tolerate standing water. Nor do they tolerate wet, oxygen-depleted soil. Their productivity depends on a reliable wet-dry cycle, wet in late winter and early spring, drier the rest of the year with enough moisture to thrive. Change the cycle, and the trees become stressed. Their productivity falters. With subsidence, water levels rise, the forest becomes wetter, the hardwoods—green ash, bitter pecan, and Nuttal oak—disappear. Cypress and tupelo replace them. But the cypress and tupelo are not doing well either.

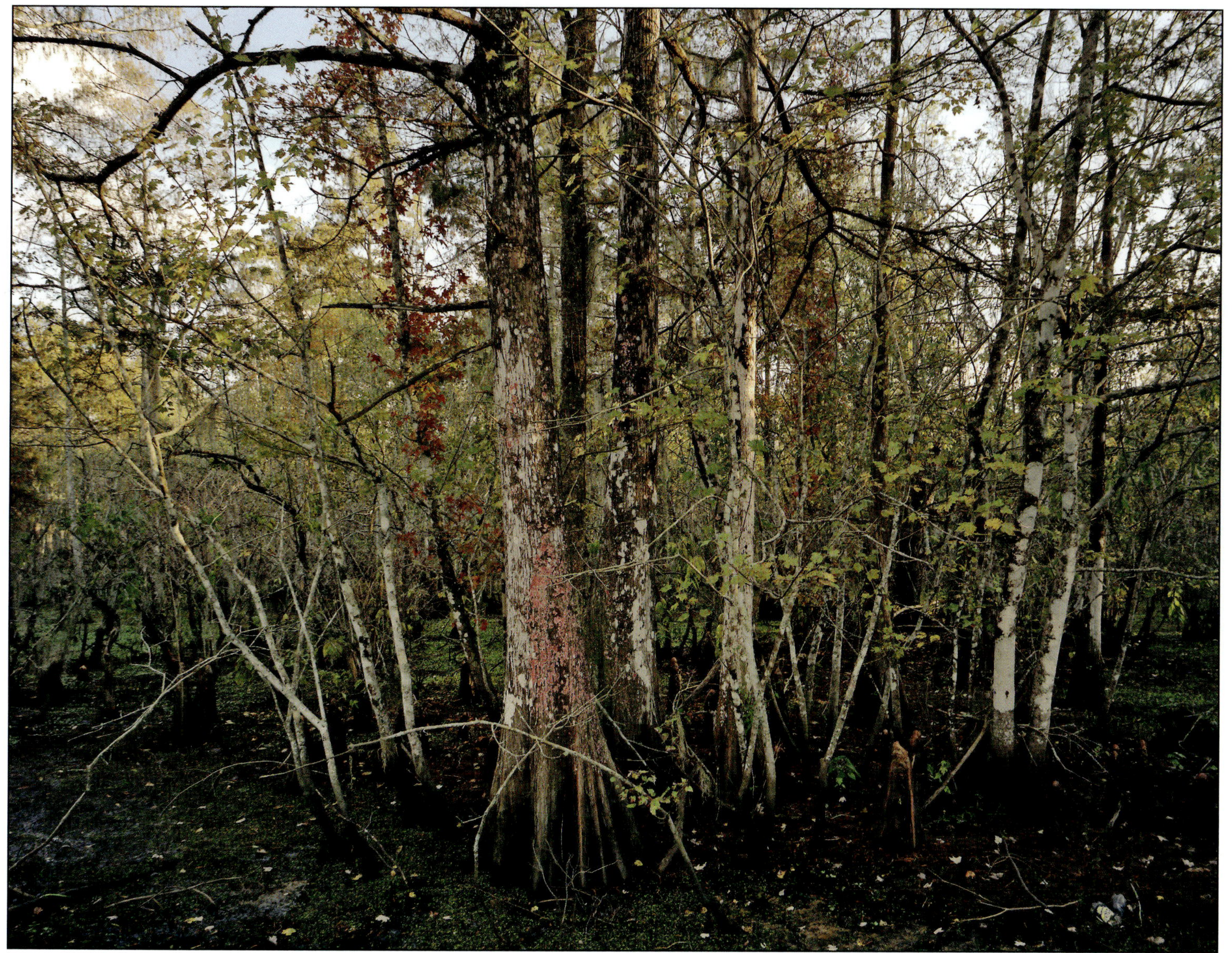

Atchafalaya Basin: Bayou Crab
Assumption Parish, Louisiana

In the 1980s, LSU researchers studied the interaction between cypress growth and flooding. They planted two plots, flooding one early in the growing season and the second nearly all season. After twenty-five years, on the flooded plot, 14 percent of the trees had died, and the rest had grown very little. On the other plot, 37 percent of the trees had died, but the rest had grown large and filled the spaces. Researchers concluded that forests flooded most of the growing season would lose cover, marsh plants would creep in, and forest would give way to open water. In addition, thinning natural stands of cypress would promote the growth of large trees.

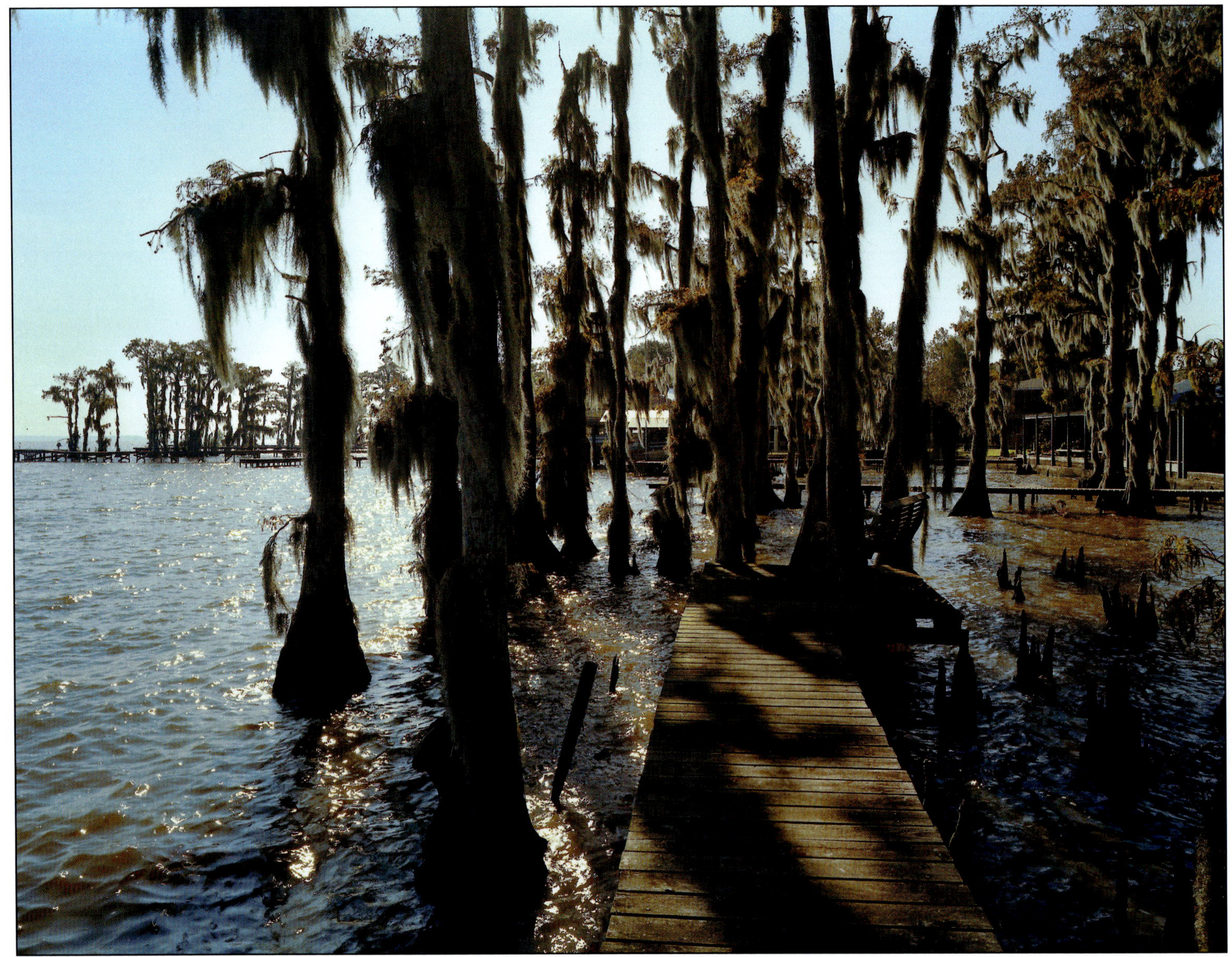

Lake Verret: Shell Beach
Assumption Parish, Louisiana

Though not an oxbow, Lake Verret suffers from many of the same ills as Lake Washington—pollution and sedimentation with the addition of subsidence. Its sole source of freshwater was rainfall and runoff from the surrounding landscape. With the runoff came sediment. Little tributaries deposited sediment and formed deltas. Anglers complained that the lake was growing more shallow and water temperatures higher. In 2005 the Corps of Engineers evaluated the possibility of dredging to increase depth, of trapping sediment on the surrounding landscape, diverting it to regions in the basin where it was needed, or confining it to specific areas with a jetty.

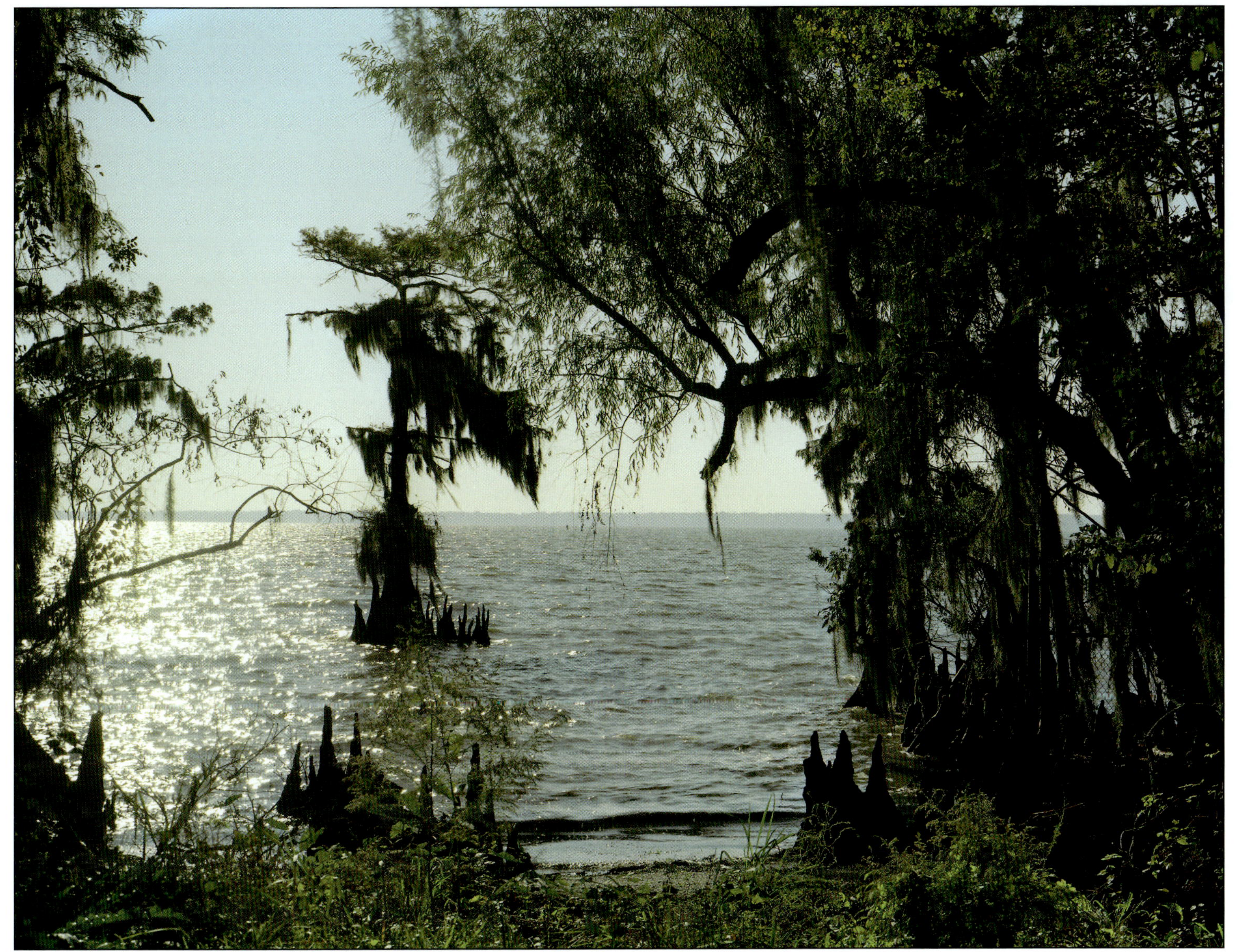

Lake Verret Watershed: Lake Palourde

St. Martin Parish, Louisiana

In the wake of Katrina, coastal scientists began to formalize their ideas for delivering Atchafalaya water and sediment to the Terrebonne marshes. Drs. G. Paul Kemp and Emily Hyfield, coastal scientists at LSU, noted the Atchafalaya used only 10 percent of its sediment for land building. The rest streamed into Atchafalaya Bay and the Gulf of Mexico. Tapping the river at Lake Palourde and sending it through an outfall channel into the Penchant Basin in the western Terrebonne marshes would let its water and sediment sustain cypress swamps and flotant marshes in the basin but not hinder delta building at the river's mouth.

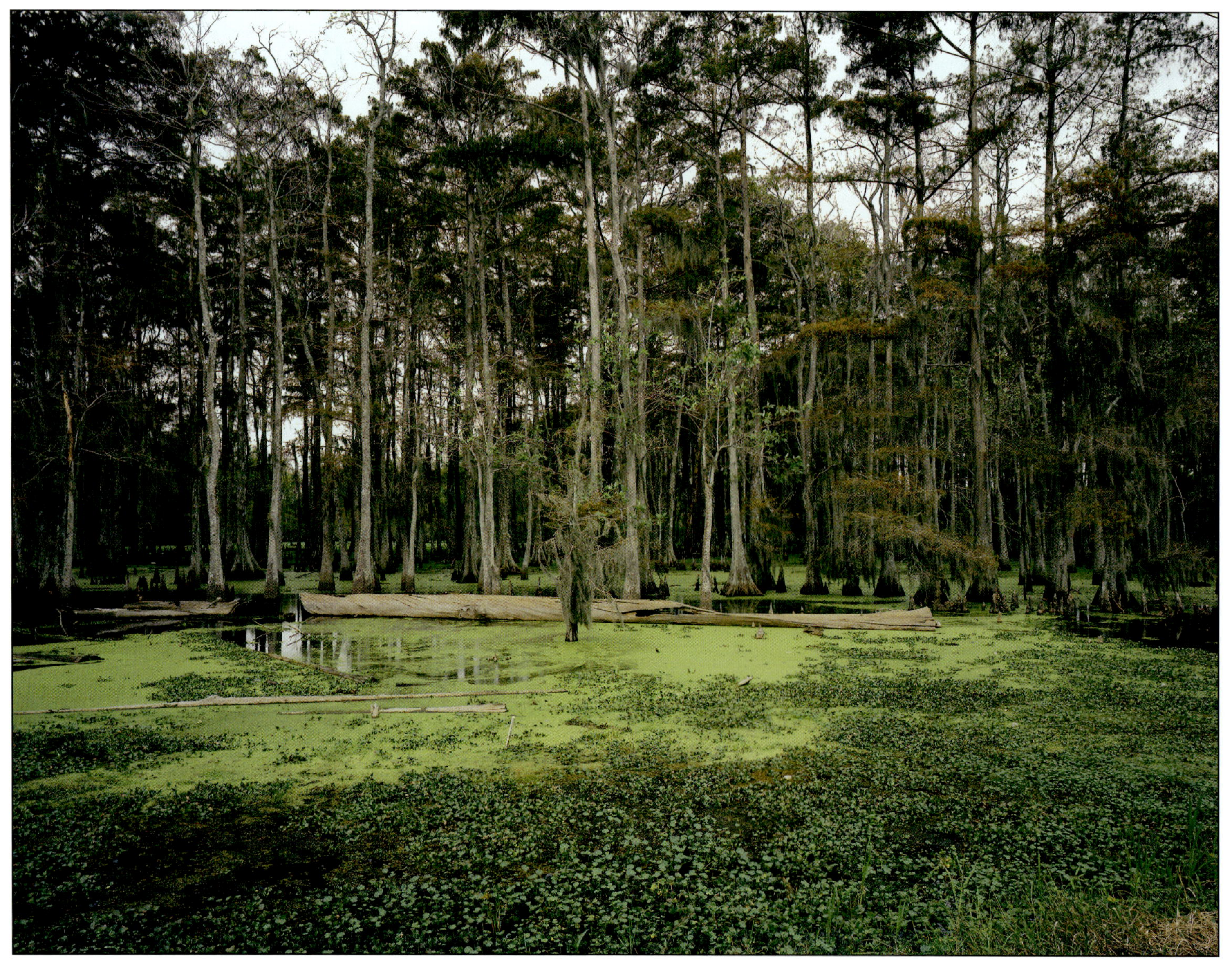

Lake Verret Watershed: Swamp Forest Adjacent to Bayou Boeuf

Assumption Parish, Louisiana

The pair proposed altering the 70/30 split between the Mississippi and Atchafalaya and sending more water down the latter. A diversion structure set in the east guide levee could discharge water directly into Lake Palourde at the rate of 140,000 cfs but would operate at an average of 20,000 cfs. A floodway would carry water and sediment across the lake and deposit it in swamps north of the GIWW. From there it would seep down into the Penchant Basin. In April 2007 the Multiple Lines of Defense Assessment Team upped the ante and suggested to the Louisiana DNR a "near complete" diversion of the Atchafalaya through the spillway.

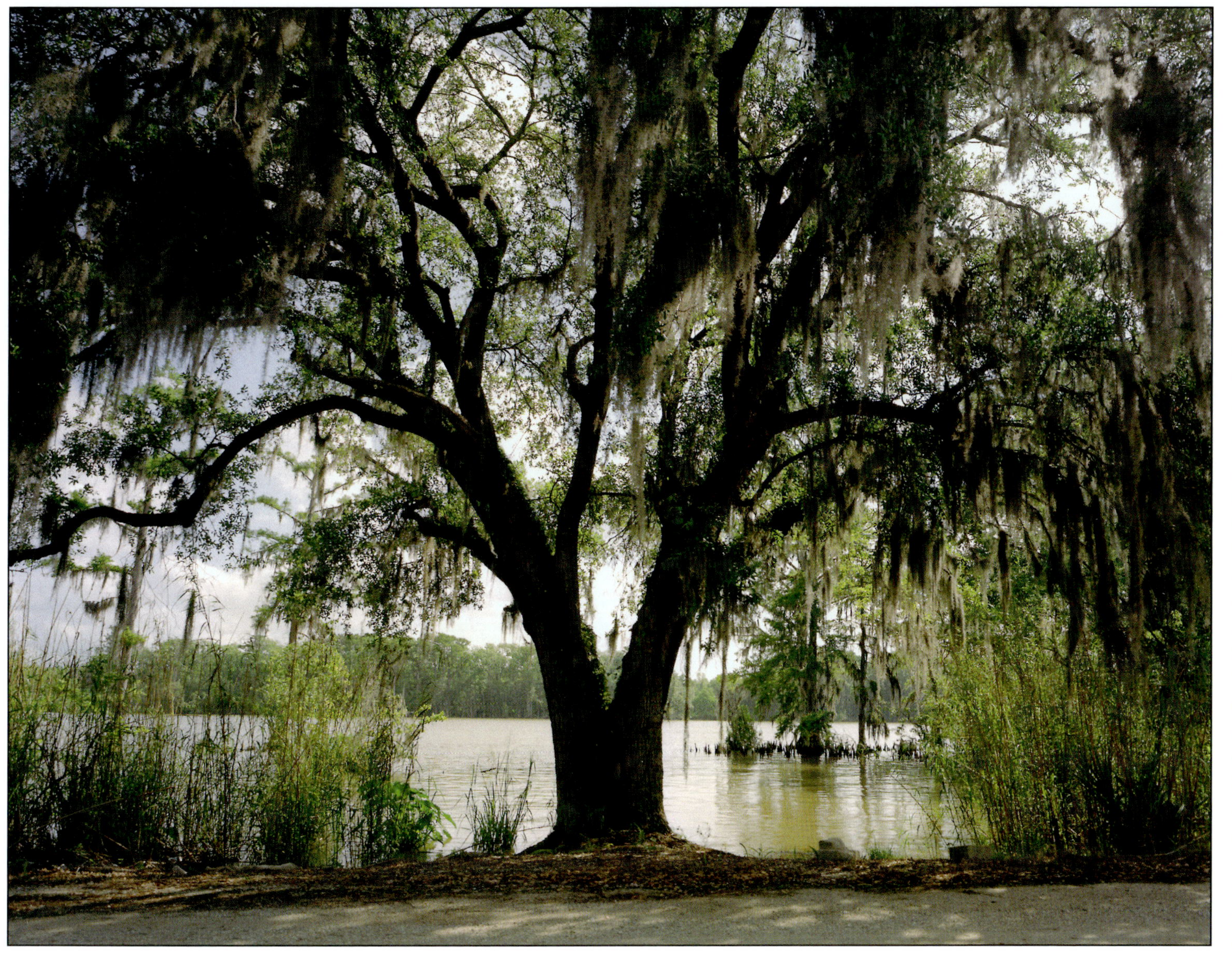

Avoca Island: Bayou Chene at the GIWW

St. Mary Parish, Louisiana

Without the infrastructure around Morgan City, water and sediment from the lower Atchafalaya would flow east to the western Terrebonne marshes, but a lock on the GIWW at Morgan City prevents that. A levee along the west edge of Avoca Island prevents water from the lower Atchafalaya from flowing east to the marshes and northeast to the GIWW. The Avoca Island Cutoff Channel, running to the northeast from the end of the levee, delivers water from the lower Atchafalaya to Bayou Chene and the GIWW to the east of Morgan City and to Bayou Penchant in the western Terrebonne marshes. It's a roundabout way to move water to where it's needed.

Penchant Watershed

Before completion of the GIWW, before completion of the Old River Control Structure and the Atchafalaya Floodway, before construction of the Avoca Island Levee along the lower Atchafalaya, and before construction of the Houma Navigation Canal, flooding along the Atchafalaya sent freshwater and sediment into the Penchant watershed to the east through Bayou Cocodrie via Bayou Boeuf at Morgan City and through Bayou Penchant via Bayou Shaefer and Bayou Chene. Construction of all of those changed the way water flowed to and through the Penchant watershed.

The Old River Control Structure rationed the Atchafalaya to 30 percent of the Mississippi's water and sediment. The Bayou Boeuf Lock on the GIWW blocked the flow to Bayou Cocodrie. The Avoca Island Levee blocked the flow to the east. The construction of the numerous canals throughout the basin cut across the natural ridges of Bayous Mauvais Bois and Marmande and exposed the basin to tidal influence from the south. Freshwater flowed out along the canals; salt water flowed in on tides and was blown in by strong southwesterly winds; the erosion of natural ridges accelerated, allowing in more salt water; interior marshes eroded; hurricanes had rolled marshes up like rugs; and finally, subsidence set in.

However, in 1973 after the Atchafalaya Delta broke the surface of Atchafalaya Bay, higher river stages led to increased flows of freshwater to the east and increased rates of sedimentation in the marshes. Freshwater, sediment, and nutrients entered the western Terrebonne marshes via the Avoca Island Cutoff Channel, Bayou Chene, and Bayou Penchant. By 1978 the influx of freshwater into the Penchant watershed began to be felt. Brackish marshes turned fresh. By 1982 too much freshwater was getting the basin. The trees along the Bayou Penchant were drowning. Between 1988 and 1997, heavy flooding along the Mississippi and Atchafalaya hastened the transition to fresh marsh.

There was a time when floating marshes, flotants, covered 75 percent of the western Terrebonne marshes. By 1998 thick-mat maidencane flotants had converted to fragile thin-mat floating marshes, vegetated in spikerush with no evidence as to why. Louisianans had lumped flotants with attached marshes and, therefore, had no idea how to preserve and restore them.

This much was known: Maidencane grows from rhizomes, which can form a dense, floating mat up to two feet thick, capable of supporting a person's weight. The cycle of growth and decay builds organic soil and thickens the mat. It becomes a self-sustaining unit. Woody plants, even small cypress, can take root. Because flotants are rooted in organic soils, they are buoyant, rise and fall with the water level, and seldom flood. Should a flotant hit bottom, its roots could anchor it in the mud; should water levels rise, the anchored flotant drowns. And nutria, whose appetite for maidencane can reduce healthy stands of the grass to mudflats, prefer flotants above all other marshes.

The thin-mat flotant is very different. Spikerush grows from fine roots and produces a mat that is half the thickness of a maidencane mat. It is fragile, easily torn, not as buoyant, and unable to support a person. Before 1968 it was rarely found along the Louisiana coast. By 1992, 41 percent of the maidencane marsh east of the Atchafalaya had converted to spikerush marsh.

In 1998 the Louisiana DNR and the NRCS proposed a demonstration project: Reverse the loss and learn to turn thin-mat floating marshes into thick-mat marshes. Researchers transplanted healthy plugs of maidencane into spikerush marsh on four sites east of the Avoca Island Cutoff, each in a different sediment regime—high, medium, or low, depending on their distance from Bayou Chene, the source of sediment. They fertilized the plugs and used fences to keep out the nutria. In 2001 they began monitoring the project using measurable goals: Increase the maidencane and other plants associated with thick-mat flotant; increase the mat's buoyancy, its height, and its strength; increase nutrient levels in the plants and their roots. They set up control sites similar to the selected sites, where they did not plant maidencane, did not fertilize the marsh, and made no effort to control nutria. Where researchers fertilized maidencane and protected it from nutria, it established itself and thrived. They concluded that protecting flotants from nutria had been more critical to the success of the demonstration than fertilization, which seemed to take care of itself.

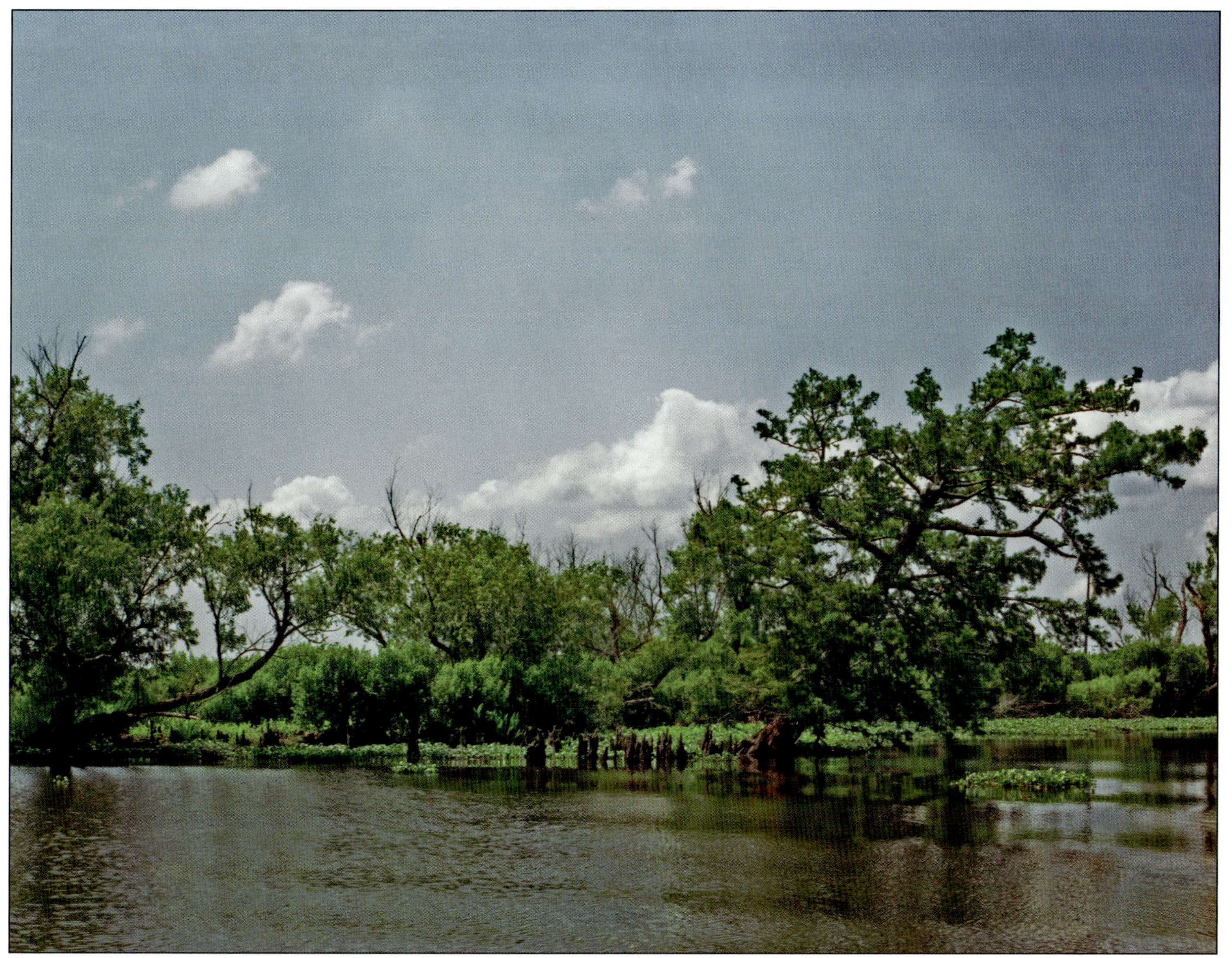

Bayou Penchant: Freshwater Marsh

Terrebonne Parish, Louisiana

Before Europeans arrived, freshwater marshes covered up to two million coastal acres. Roughly half has been lost to salt water intrusion, canal dredging, and urban development. Over ninety species of freshwater plants have been identified in coastal fresh marshes, including maidencane, spikerush, cattail, and coontail, tall roseau cane, pickerelweed, arrow arum, pennyworts, water lilies, bladderworts, and tiny duckweed—all food for nutria and muskrats. The ridges that run through the marsh host cypress, sweet gum, water oak, and other bottomland trees. The rich variety of trees, shrubs, grasses, and seeds attracts a rich variety of wildlife.

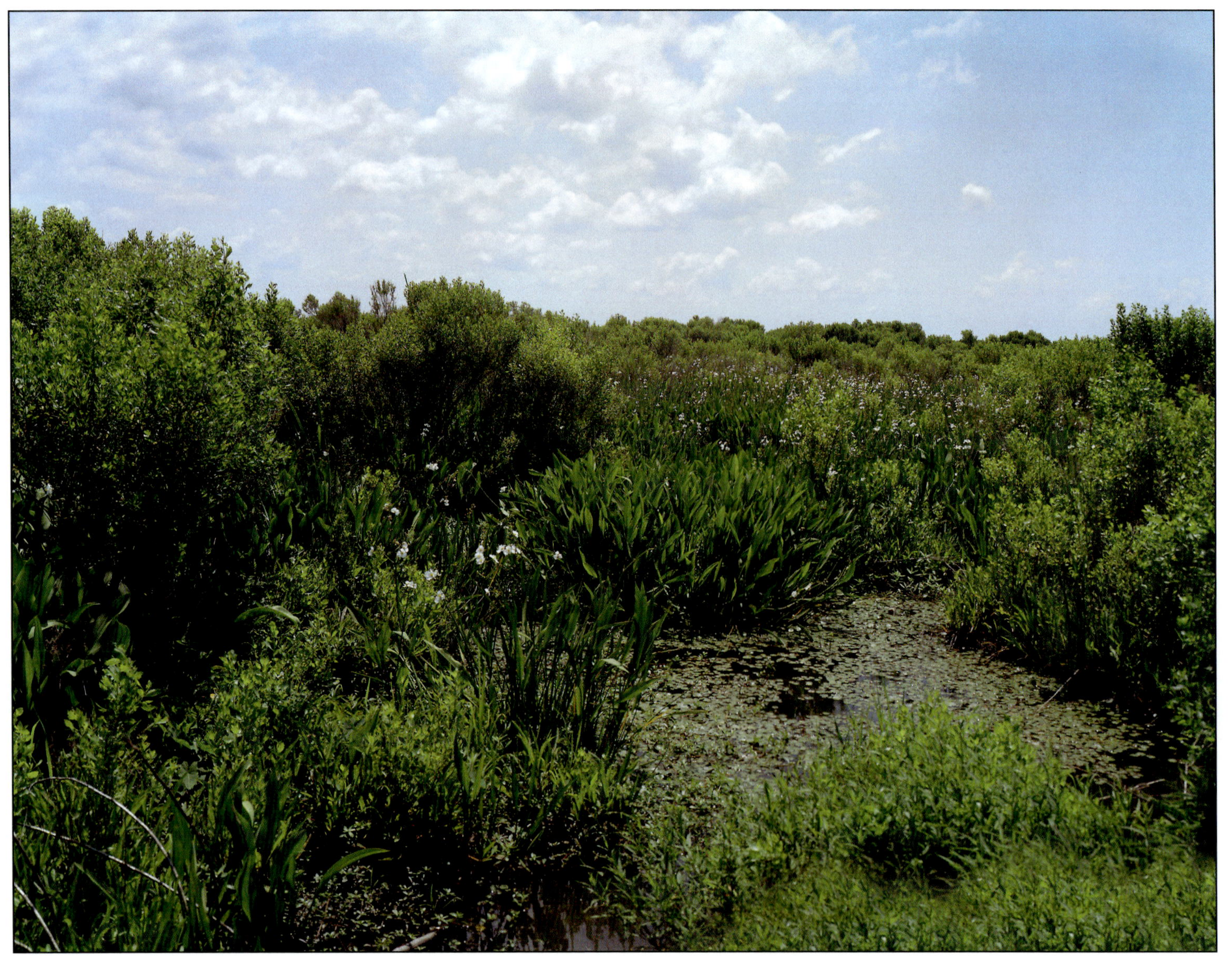

Big Bayou Carencro: Freshwater Marsh

Terrebonne Parish, Louisiana

Waterfowl—Canvasbacks, Northern Pintails, Redheads—winter in the marshes. Rails, herons, and bitterns wade in the shallows. Eagles and Osprey swoop down and snatch fish, marsh rats, and swamp rabbits. Terns follow meandering creeks in search of fish—seatrout, drum, and flounder, and white and brown shrimp, which spawn in salt water, migrate to fresh as young, and return to salt as adults. Butterflies feed on vegetation. Bacteria decompose litter; nematodes feed on bacteria; amoebae on nematodes; snails on amoebae; birds on snails. American alligators swim in the bayous, nest on the banks, and feed on rabbits, snakes, fish, birds, and baby alligators.

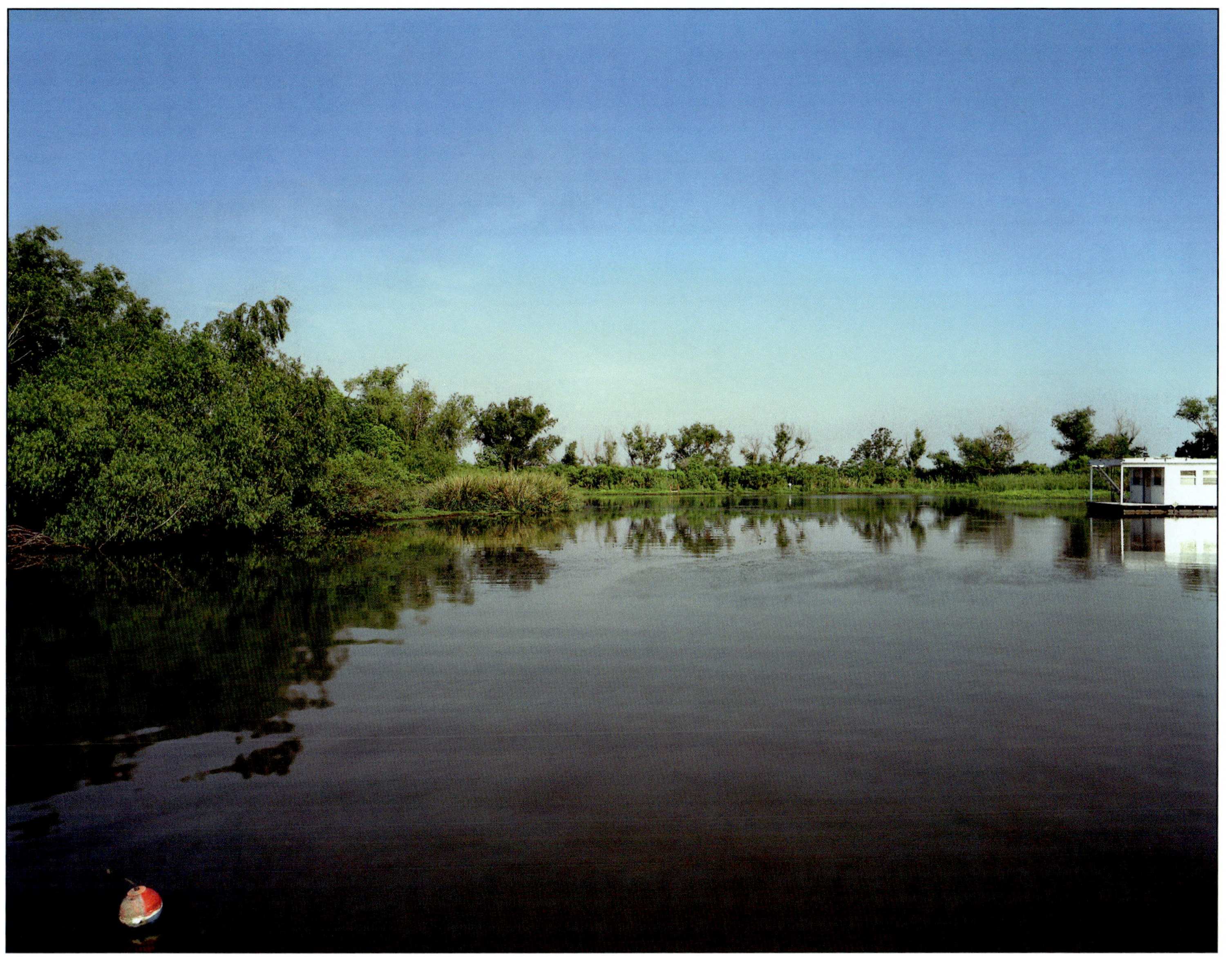

Marmande Ridge: Fishing Camp Next to Marmande Ridge
Terrebonne Parish, Louisiana

In 1909 the Minor Family, nineteenth-century sugar barons, dredged a canal through their land in order to transport goods south. The Houma Navigation Channel replaced it in 1962. A century later the canal channeled freshwater from the GIWW to Lake de Cade. Anglers in search of largemouth bass and speckled trout put in at Bayou Black near Waterproof for the trip to Lake de Cade. Its cut through Marmande Ridge reveals the progression of freshwater marshes to cypress swamps to bottomland hardwoods. Together, the Marmande and Mauvais Bois ridges form the boundary between freshwater marsh to the north and fresh to intermediate to brackish marsh to the south.

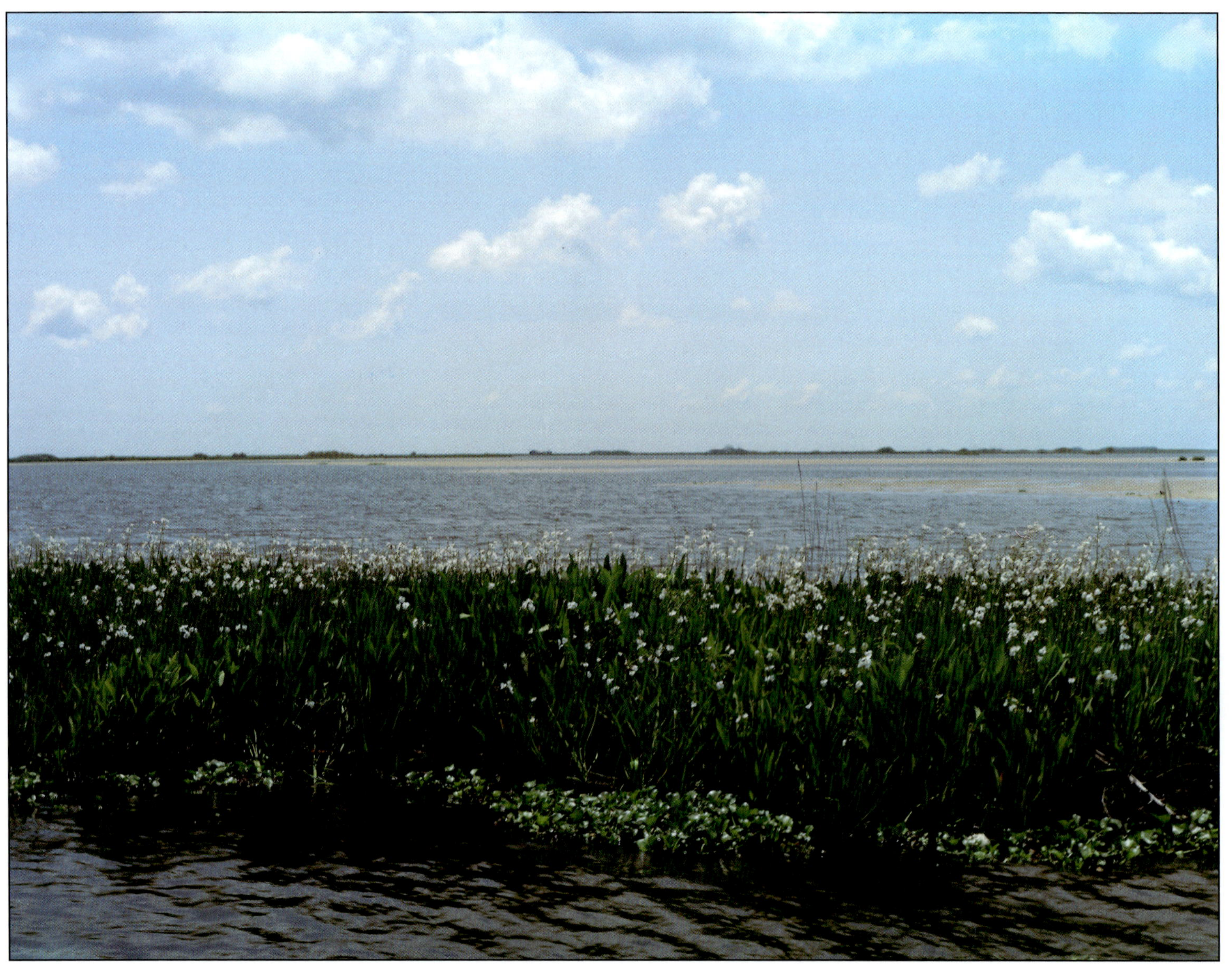

Bayou de Cade: Apache Minerals Shoreline Restoration

Terrebonne Parish, Louisiana

Apache Minerals owns 267,000 acres of coastal land, including the north bank of Bayou de Cade. It owns surface rights to the marshes and mineral rights underneath. It manages its surface rights to protect its mineral rights. Should its marshes erode to open water, the State of Louisiana would take ownership of its mineral rights. In 1959, Apache began rebuilding of the bank of Lake de Cade to maintain its interior marshes, a chore that had to be done year after year. In 2004 the company extended its work to Bayou de Cade, where it planted California bulrush, smooth cordgrass, seashore paspalum, roseau cane, and cattail along the north bank to stop erosion.

The Houma Nav and the Central Terrebonne Wetlands

The western Terrebonne wetlands have a reliable source of freshwater from the Atchafalaya via Bayou Penchant and the GIWW. The central Terrebonne wetlands, those east of Bayou du Large, do not. The key to getting freshwater to the central Terrebonne Basin is the Houma Nav, as the locals call it, which has delivered salt water since its construction in 1962.

Bigger than Minor's Canal, the Houma Nav was longer (thirty miles from Houma to the Gulf), wider (150 feet), and deeper (15 feet). In 1974 the Corps deepened it to 18 feet and widened its bottom to 300 feet from Mile 0 just north of Timbalier Island to the Gulf of Mexico. The difference between the wetlands in the western Terrebonne marshes around Lake de Cade to the east of Bayou de Large and those adjacent to the Houma Nav to the west could not be more striking. The Houma Nav is the Terrebonne Basin's answer to MRGO. And, like MRGO, it has killed acres and acres of cypress swamp.

The first loss came with the dredging, straight through the vegetative zones—forested wetlands, fresh marshes, and salt marshes; the second with the placement of the spoil banks, which disrupted the flow of water through the wetlands; the third with its size, which allowed larger vessels dragging larger wakes behind them, creating greater amounts of edge erosion; the fourth with salt water intrusion as southerly winds pushed water north from the Gulf of Mexico, leading to rapid changes in habitat. Breaks in its bank let in even more salt water. Fresh marshes converted to intermediate, intermediate to brackish, brackish to open water, particularly in the southern regions of the basin.

At the end of twentieth century, the quality of water moving through the Houma Nav depended on stages in the Lower Atchafalaya River and how much freshwater flowed into the GIWW from the Verret watershed. The higher the Atchafalaya, the more freshwater delivered to the Houma Nav. More freshwater draining out of the Verret watershed meant more in the Houma Nav. Several proposed restoration projects depended on the ability of the channel to deliver freshwater to the wetlands on either side of it.

Residents of the Terrebonne Basin looked forward to the construction of a lock on the Houma Nav, designed to block salt water intrusion and storm surges and located just to the south of Cocodrie. In the event of a hurricane, the lock would block a storm surge coming up the Houma Nav. On an ordinary day, it would limit salt water intrusion into the channel. The Louisiana Coastal Area Ecosystem Restoration Study, issued in November 2004, proposed modifying the design of the lock to increase the retention time of Atchafalaya water, sediment, and nutrients in the central Terrebonne wetlands. Doing so would nourish the full spectrum of wetlands—forested to fresh to intermediate to brackish marshes—adjacent to the lock and channel, in the Lake Boudreaux wetlands to the north, the Lake Merchant wetlands to the west, and the Grand Bayou wetlands to the east.

The Houma Nav lock was a part of the Morganza-to-the-Gulf Hurricane Protection Project, which languished on the Corps' drafting table after Congress authorized the feasibility study in 1994. Congress authorized parts of the plan, including the lock on the Houma Nav in the 2007 Water WRDA.

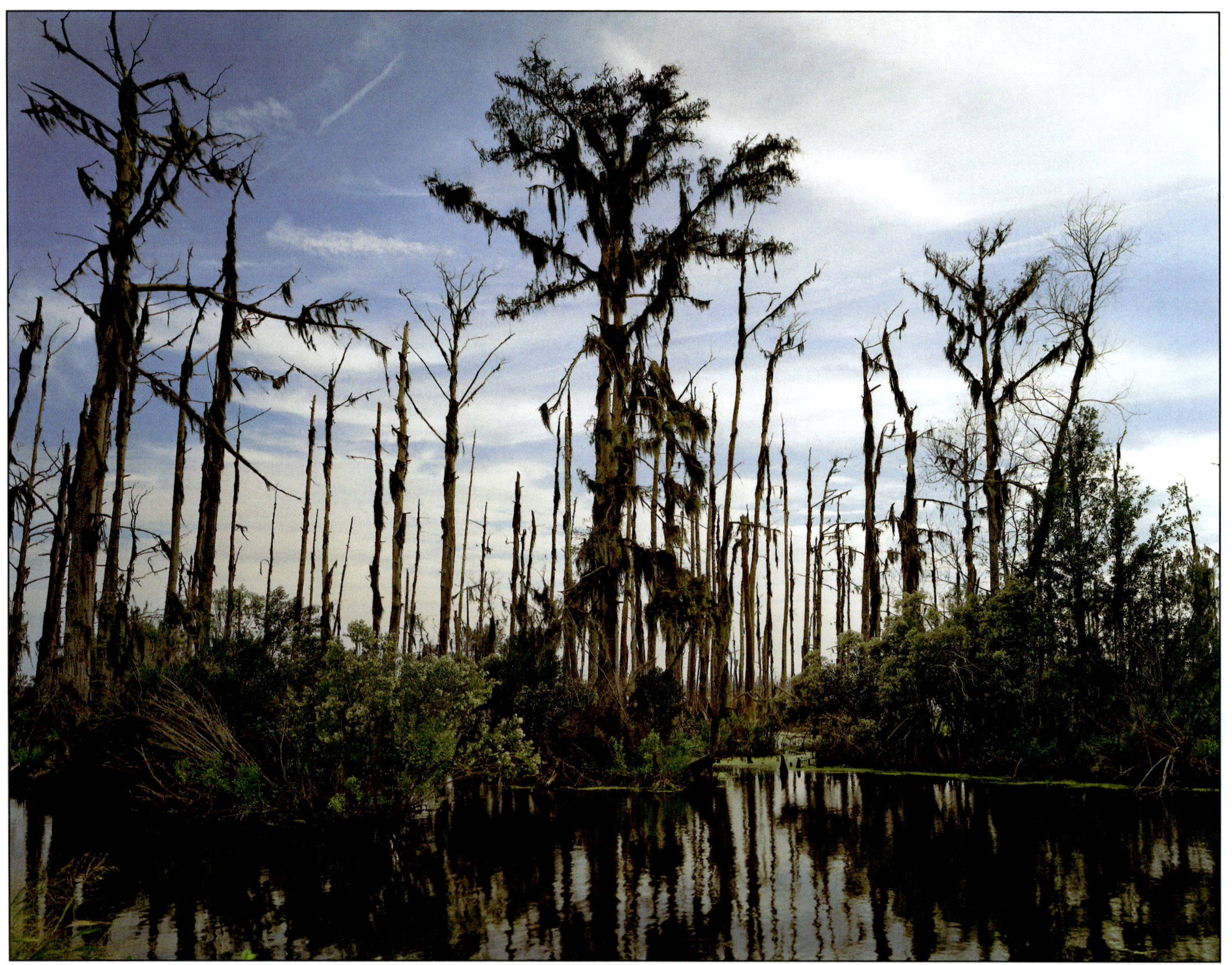

Falgout Marshes: Theriot

Terrebonne Parish, Louisiana

Douse a cypress swamp with seawater; the trees become stressed in eight hours. Soak the trees in salinity levels of ten parts per thousand; they die. Construction of the Falgout Canal in 1909 impounded 7,423 acres between Bayous du Large and Grand Caillou. In 1956 cypress dominated the north half, marshes the south half. Hurricanes Betsy (1965) and Camille (1969) swept in salt water. The trees died. In 2006 Terrebonne Parish proposed introducing freshwater from the Atchafalaya into the north end of the marshes via a water-control structure in the bank of the Houma Nav. Success depended on restoring the GIWW bank and construction of the Houma Nav lock.

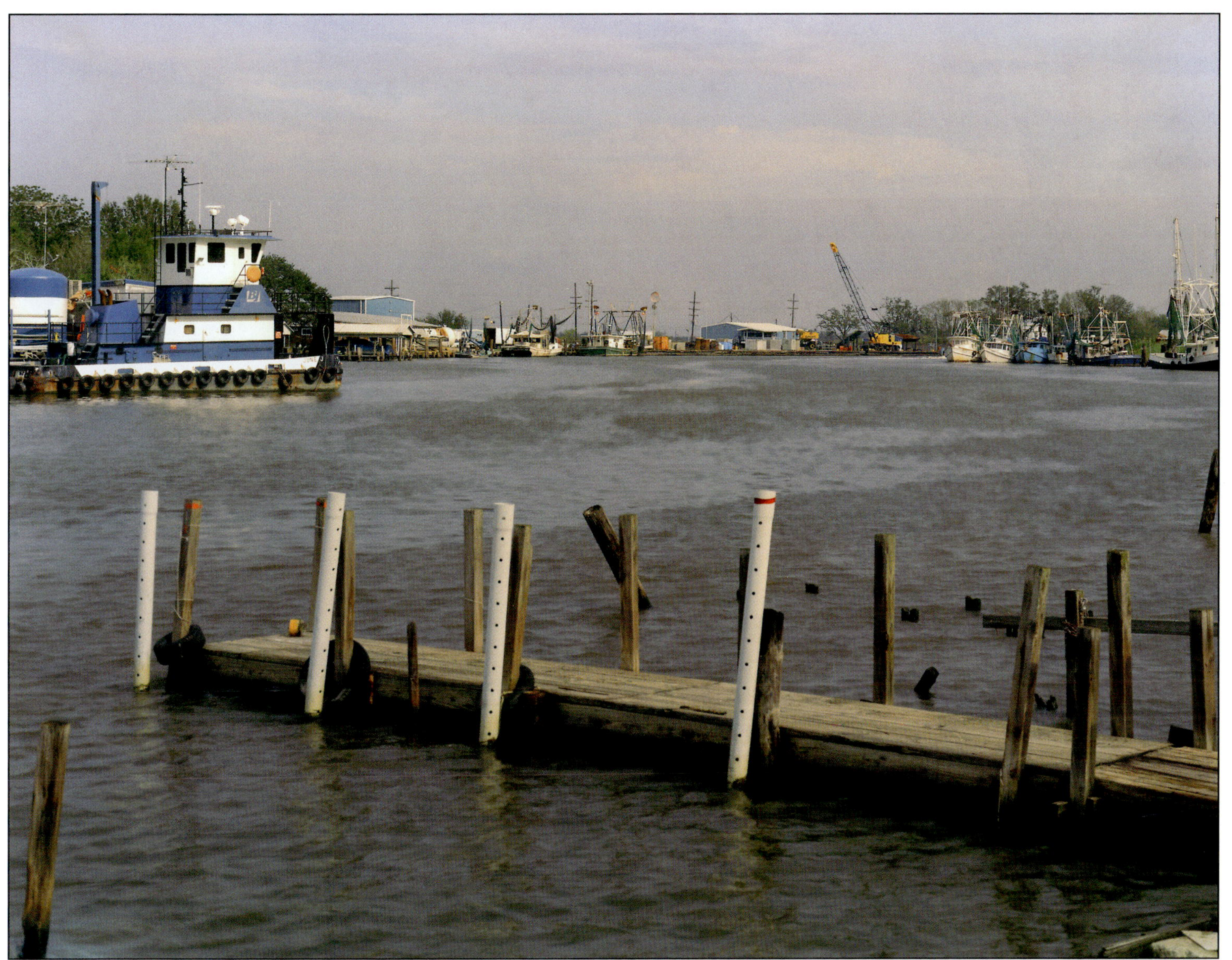

Bayou Grand Caillou: Dulac

Terrebonne Parish, Louisiana

During the fall of 2006 it was apparent at Dulac that the activities the marshes generate disguised the disaster that happened the year before and the one happening underfoot. Rita generated an eight-foot surge that tracked up the Houma Nav to Dulac, heaved shrimp boats into yards, washed mud into homes, rolled marsh grass into balls, and left hundreds of snakes to slither back to the marsh. There was nothing out in front of Dulac to absorb the surge. The wetlands in the Caillou and Boudreaux marshes had submerged. If two miles of wetlands can reduce a surge by a half-foot, twenty miles of wetlands would have left Dulac soaked, not trashed.

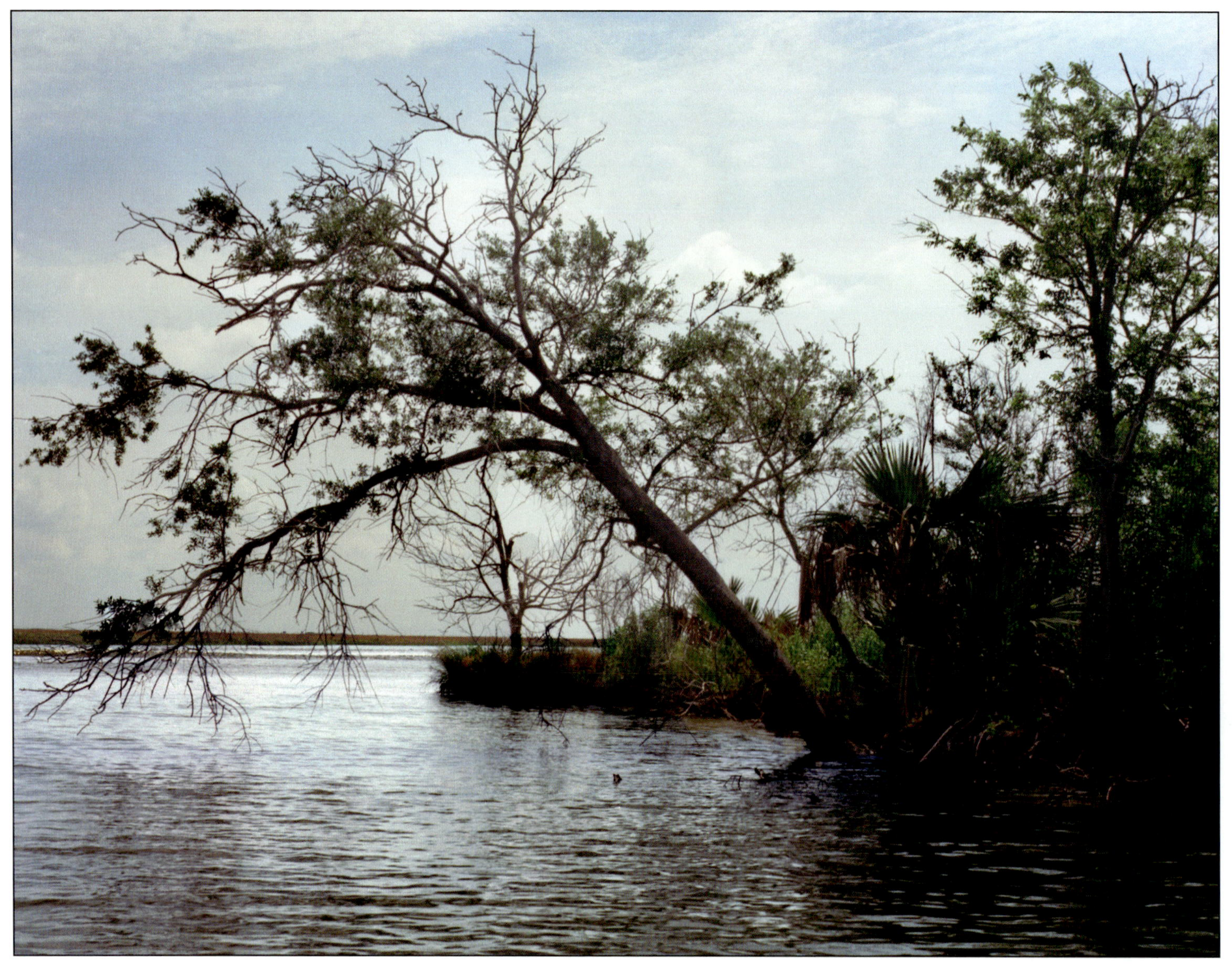

Bayou Petit Caillou: At Sevin Canal

Terrebonne Parish, Louisiana

In the 1920s, shrimper Dolephus Sevin broke through the Bayou Petit Caillou ridge and dug a canal that measured the width of his shovel. Afterward, he could float his boat across the marsh at high tide to a pond and play out his weighted net in a circle. He dragged the bottom, herding shrimp into the net's pouch. He took the full net home, unloaded, and started over. By 2007 the eroded canal had widened and was three feet deep at high tide. It gave commercial and recreational anglers easy access to wetlands lying between Bayous Petit Caillou and Terrebonne, so easy that, in 1995, they were able to halt a restoration project that would have plugged it.

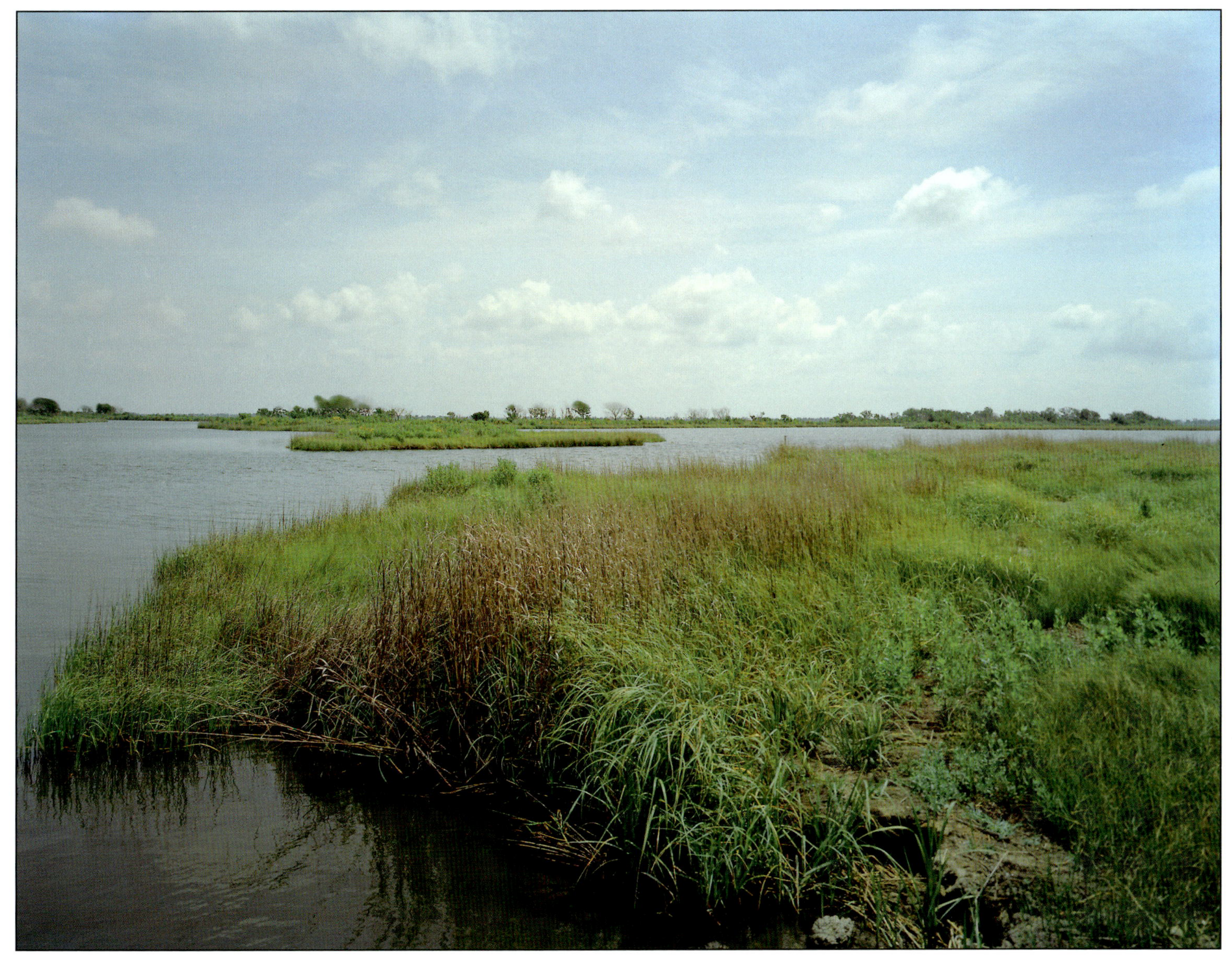

Boudreaux Marshes: Lake Boudreaux/Robinson

Terrebonne Parish, Louisiana

Motor up Bayou Petit Caillou, turn into Robinson Canal, and pass under the LA 56 bridge into Lake Robinson. What's a handy route for boats is a handy route for salt water. Until folks dredged canals through the Petit Caillou ridge around 1900, it and the Grand Caillou ridge isolated Lakes Robinson and Boudreaux from salt water intrusion. The canals let in salt water, stressing fresh and intermediate marshes, making them susceptible to waves and storm surges. By 1997 a cypress swamp north of Lake Boudreaux was as dead as the Falgout Marshes; Boudreaux had swallowed up Robinson; its shoreline had eroded into islands. The DNR and the USFWS proposed restoring it.

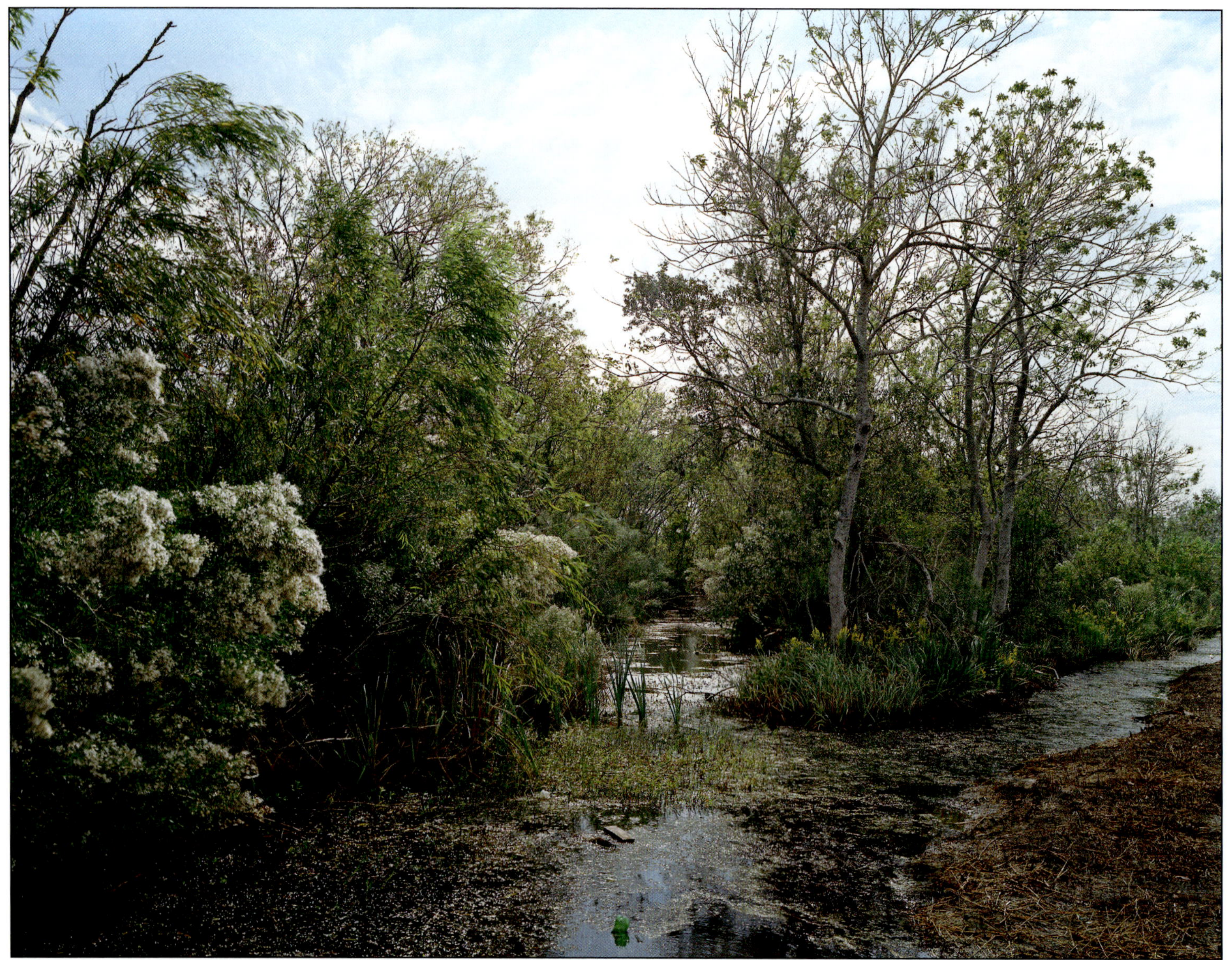

Bayou Grand Caillou: Backwater, Bayou Pelton
Terrebonne Parish, Louisiana

First: Introduce freshwater into the dying wetlands north of Lake Boudreaux from the Houma Nav through Bayou Pelton. The USFWS and the Louisiana DNR would dredge 6,700 feet of Bayou Pelton to 70 wide and 8 feet deep. Run freshwater through sluice gates set in the Grand Caillou ridge. Connect it to a 3,200-foot outfall channel dredged through private land in the wetlands. When complete the project would increase the flow of freshwater to marshes north of Lake Boudreaux and enhance wildlife and fish productivity. Success of the project depended on shoring up the banks of the GIWW, the completion of the lock on the Houma Nav, and willing sellers.

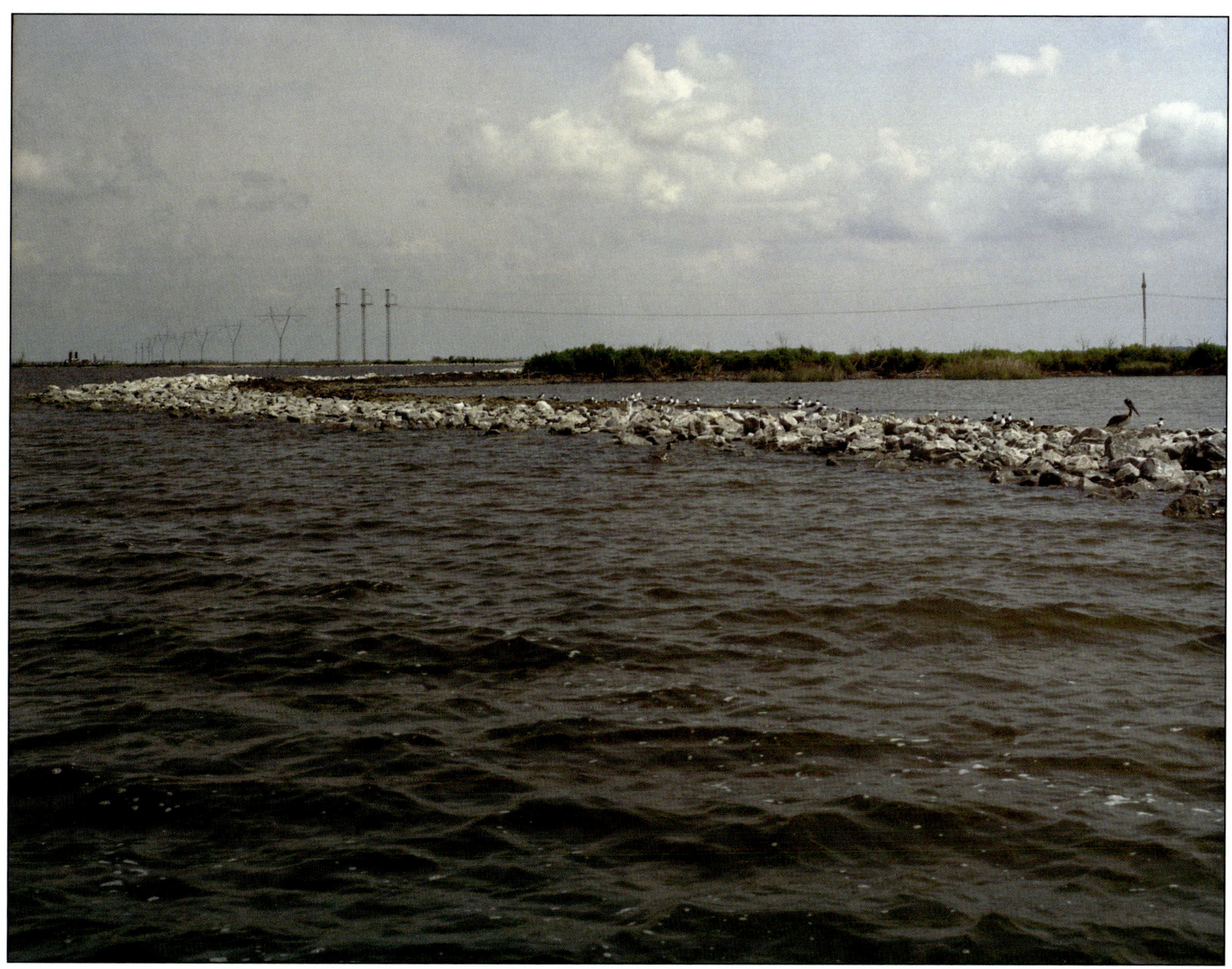

Lake Boudreaux: East Shoreline Restoration Project

Terrebonne Parish, Louisiana

Second, third, and fourth: Reinforce the Boudreaux shoreline with 14,000 feet of foreshore rock dike running parallel to the western shore of the lake to stop wave fetch in normal weather and reduce storm surges in abnormal weather. Doing so halted erosion, but not subsidence. Mud, 15,000 acres of mud, pumped from the lakebed into areas of open water and fragmented marshes behind the dike would create 284 acres of brackish to intermediate marsh in three to five years. Earthen dikes surrounding the marshes protected them. The DNR and the Terrebonne Parish Levee and Conservation District constructed a 6,800-foot rock dike along the lake's eastern shoreline.

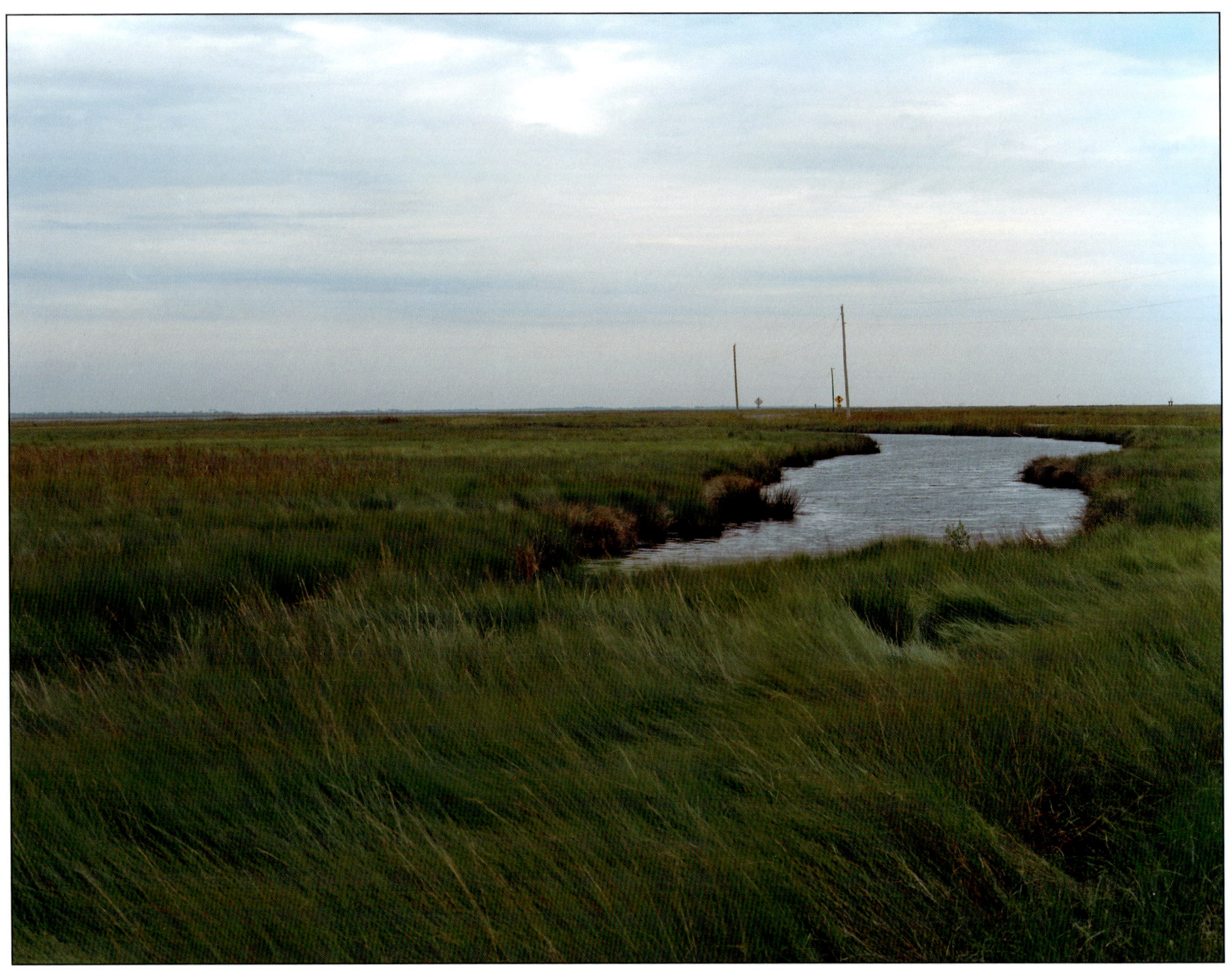

Pelto Marshes: Grassy Bayou

Terrebonne Parish, Louisiana

Grassy Bayou flows in and out with the tide through a salt marsh dominated by smooth cordgrass. Leaf-chewers—insects, butterflies, squareback crabs—feed on its leaves; sap-sucking insects, on its stems. Birds weave nests from its stems and feed on the insects and crabs. When it dies, the invertebrate larvae feed on the bacteria and fungi. Blue crabs browse the larvae and decaying grass. Oysters filter food particles. Fish feed along the edges of creeks. Wading and diving birds feed on the fish. Nutria and muskrat may prefer fresh marsh but will eat the growing salt grass in the summer and rip up and feed on the tubers in the winter.

Marsh Deterioration in Billy Goat and Madison Bays

The Bayou Terrebonne distributary system included Bayou Grand Caillou, Bayou Petit Caillou, and Bayou Barre. For 800 years (beginning 1,200 years ago) they deposited their loads of sediment in the Gulf of Mexico and formed a delta lobe that extended out to the Isles Dernieres and the Timbalier Islands, the barrier islands that protect the wetlands that edge Caillou Bay and Terrebonne Bay.

As Bayou Terrebonne washed over its banks, it deposited fine sediments in shallow water. The mud surfaced about 950 years ago. Freshwater plants took root: the first marsh. Over the next 300 years the marsh increased its elevation at the rate of a little less than a tenth of an inch a year. Vegetation grew and died and decayed and added its bulk to the marsh in the form of peat. This process continued until 650 years ago, shortly after delta building had switched to Bayou Lafourche.

As natural subsidence set in, the growth and decay of the marsh sustained the wetlands in the bay, building up layers of peat, even after the marsh turned saline 150 years ago. The marshes rose an average of nine inches above sea level. A series of small open lakes, oblong in shape, dotted the edge of the Bayou Terrebonne ridge. Tidal creeks meandered through a dense salt marsh that covered all of Madison Bay. This was the state of the marsh in 1956. By 1969 the first evidence of wetland loss in Madison Bay showed up on aerial photographs.

Madison Bay lies just off the east bank of Bayou Terrebonne and south of the village of Lapeyrouse. Since the 1970s it has been a hot spot for wetland loss. For decades after Louisianans realized their coastal wetlands were disappearing, hot spots, like Madison Bay where marsh loss was extreme, perplexed them. They found Madison Bay particularly perplexing because oil companies had dredged few canals through the bay to disrupt the flow of freshwater and invite in salt water. By 1990 the delta lobe that embraced the two bays was in the advanced stages of delta decay. Salt marshes were migrating inland. Marshes that had been brackish in the 1940s had turned saline by 1988. Stands of marsh grasses, anchored in peat, sank below the water level, became waterlogged, and died. Once the roots died, the peat fell apart, and the wetlands converted to open water, even though tides and storms washed in new mud.

Three deep reservoirs of oil surround Madison Bay. All three were active in the 1940s and 1950s, but at moderate, even low, levels of production. When rates of extraction of gas, oil, and water increased in the 1970s, so did rates of subsidence. And, wetland loss continued, even after activity in the oil fields decreased.

When producers drill down through the wetlands and suck oil, gas, and water out of an oil field, the sediments that hold the reservoir of hydrocarbons compact, pulling the wetlands on the surface underwater. In addition, once-active faults may slip, in this case the Golden Meadow fault, pulling the wetlands even deeper.

In 2002 the USGS scientists measured the rates of subsidence in Madison Bay and the subsidence along the Bayou Lafourche and Bayou Petit Caillou ridges and linked the changes to oil extraction.

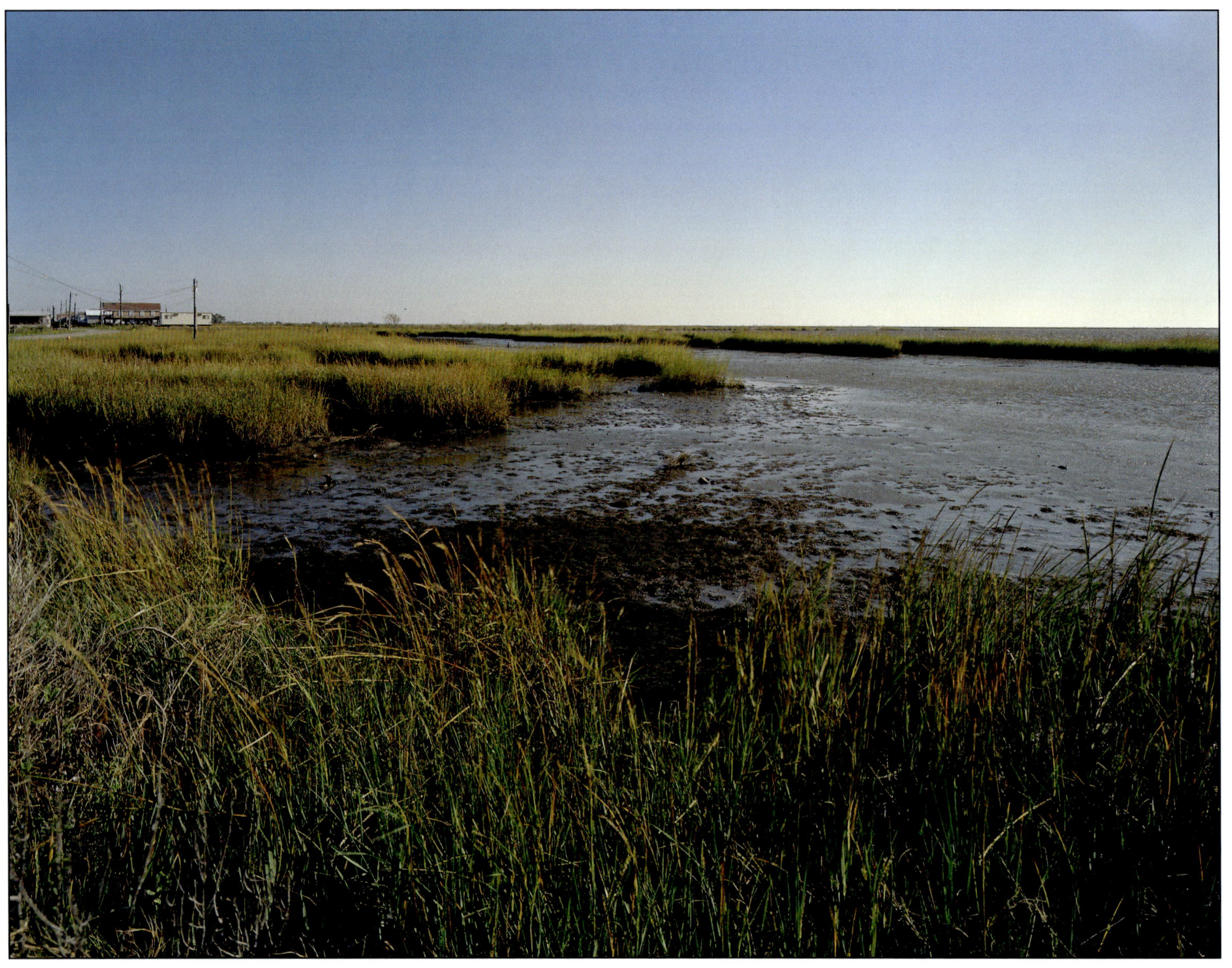

Bayou Terrebonne Ridge: Madison Bay

Terrebonne Parish, Louisiana

USGS scientists compared aerial photographs of Madison Bay from 1969, 1974, and 1998 and drilled cores in 2002, circling the edge of the bay with four pairs and a fifth in open water, reaching down through peat, mud, and sand, through the history of the marsh's construction. As production in the oil fields increased in the 1970s, the land began to sink. The loss of wetlands was noticeable on aerial photographs as early as 1974. Tidal creeks that laced the bay and small lakes that dotted its edge along Bayou Terrebonne enlarged as the marsh at their edges drowned and submerged. By 1998 most of Madison Bay was open water, right up to the Bayou Terrebonne ridge.

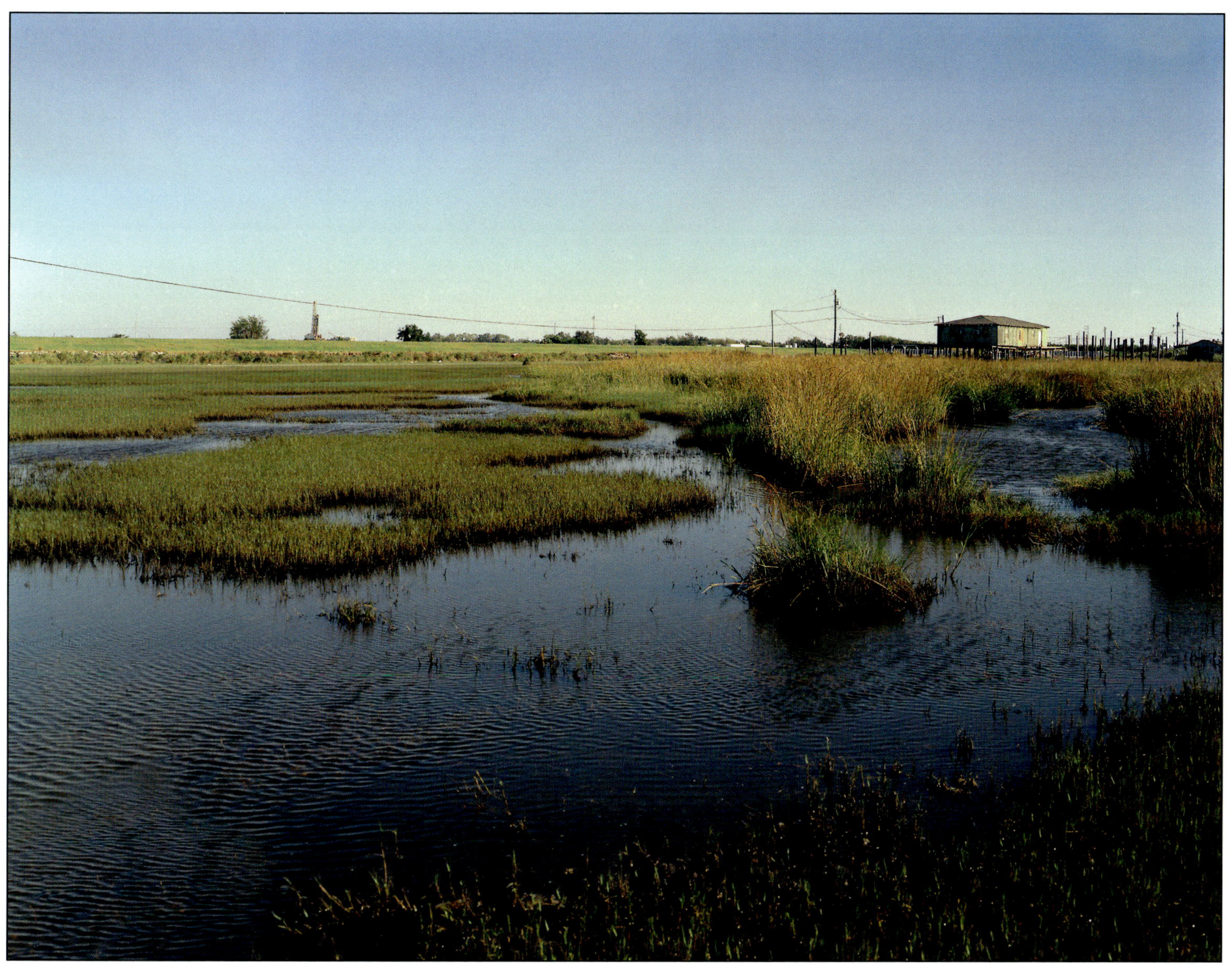

Terrebonne Ridge: Madison Bay

Terrebonne Parish, Louisiana

The USGS scientists who measured the rate of subsidence in Madison Bay also measured subsidence along the Lafourche and Petit Caillou ridges and concluded that increased oil extraction had caused them to sink. The ridges along Bayous Terrebonne and Petit Caillou were wider north and south of the zone of greatest wetland loss. The Terrebonne ridge was fragmented. To restore it engineers would mimic how a stream deposits its sediment and strategically place, probably in phases, dredged sediments along the bayou's margins. Coarse sediments would settle closest to the stream; finer sediments would wash into the marsh and be transported across it.

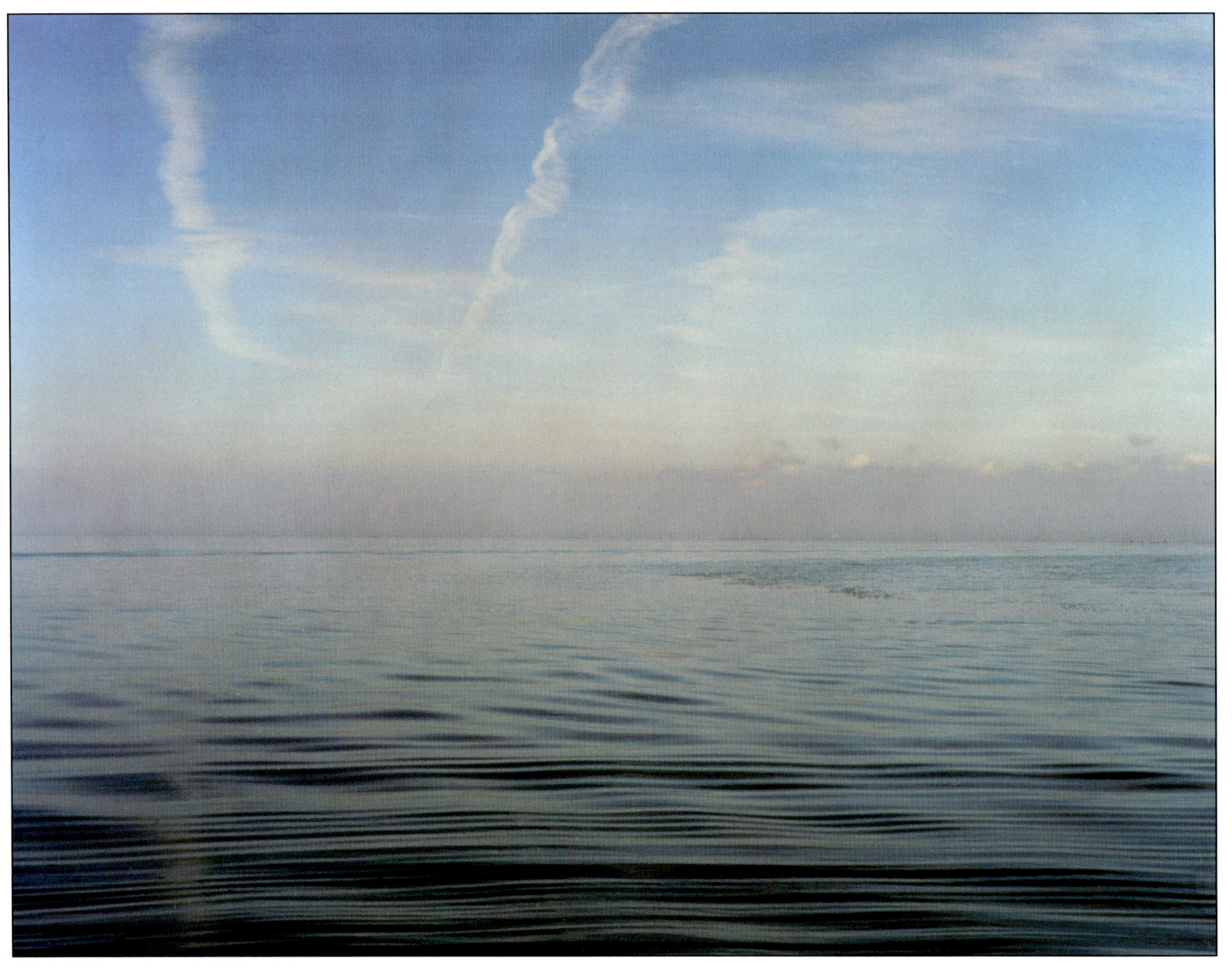

Terrebonne Bay: Lake Barre

Terrebonne Parish, Louisiana

In 2004 participants in an EPA workshop brainstormed about increasing marshes in Lake Barre, the inlet to Terrebonne Bay: Build a subtidal barrier, a "first line of defense" to salt water intrusion, using coarse materials to reduce wave and tidal energy. Build a berm on the north shore with piped sediment, filling breaks that allow wave energy into the marshes, a "second line of defense." Rebuild the Jean Baptiste Ridge. Create experimental oyster reefs. Rebuild islands. Pipe sediment into open water to fill low spots and allow it to spread across the marsh. Leave open tidal creeks. Leave the pipe and pipe in freshwater to sustain the new marsh.

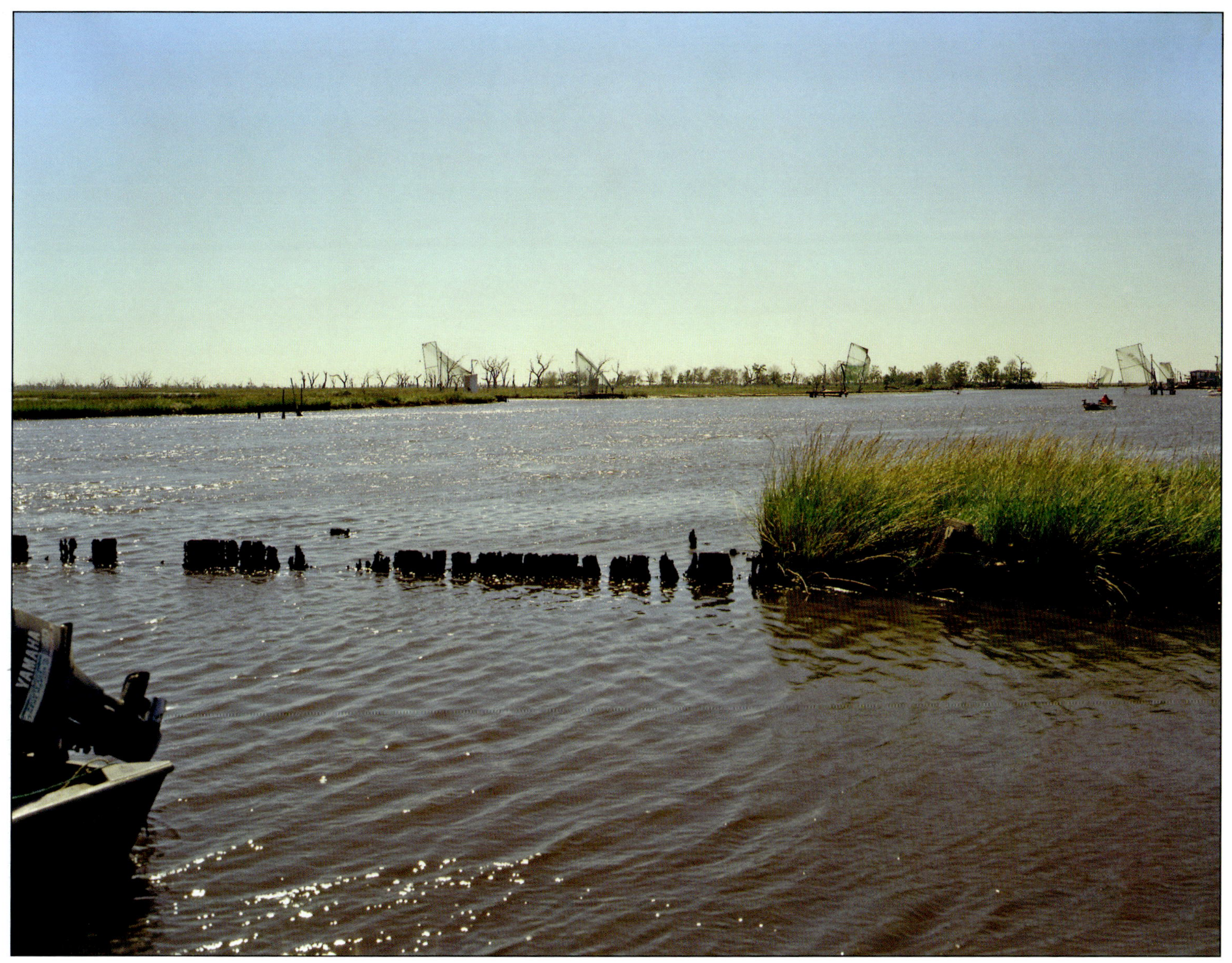

Pointe aux Chenes Wildlife Management Area: Billy Goat Bay

Terrebonne Parish, Louisiana

When the State of Louisiana purchased the Pointe aux Chenes WMA in 1968 in the upper part of the Terrebonne marshes, it was the best it would ever be. Over the next six years the refuge became a hot spot for subsidence, where production in three oil fields went into full gear. The marshes subsided close to three feet. Terrebonne Parish proposed diverting stormwater to an impoundment in the WMA to push back salt water, stimulate the growth of aquatic plants, which would capture and hold sediment, allow it to settle, and build new land. Only a few pumping stations in the parish discharged stormwater into wetlands. The rest funneled it to the Gulf of Mexico.

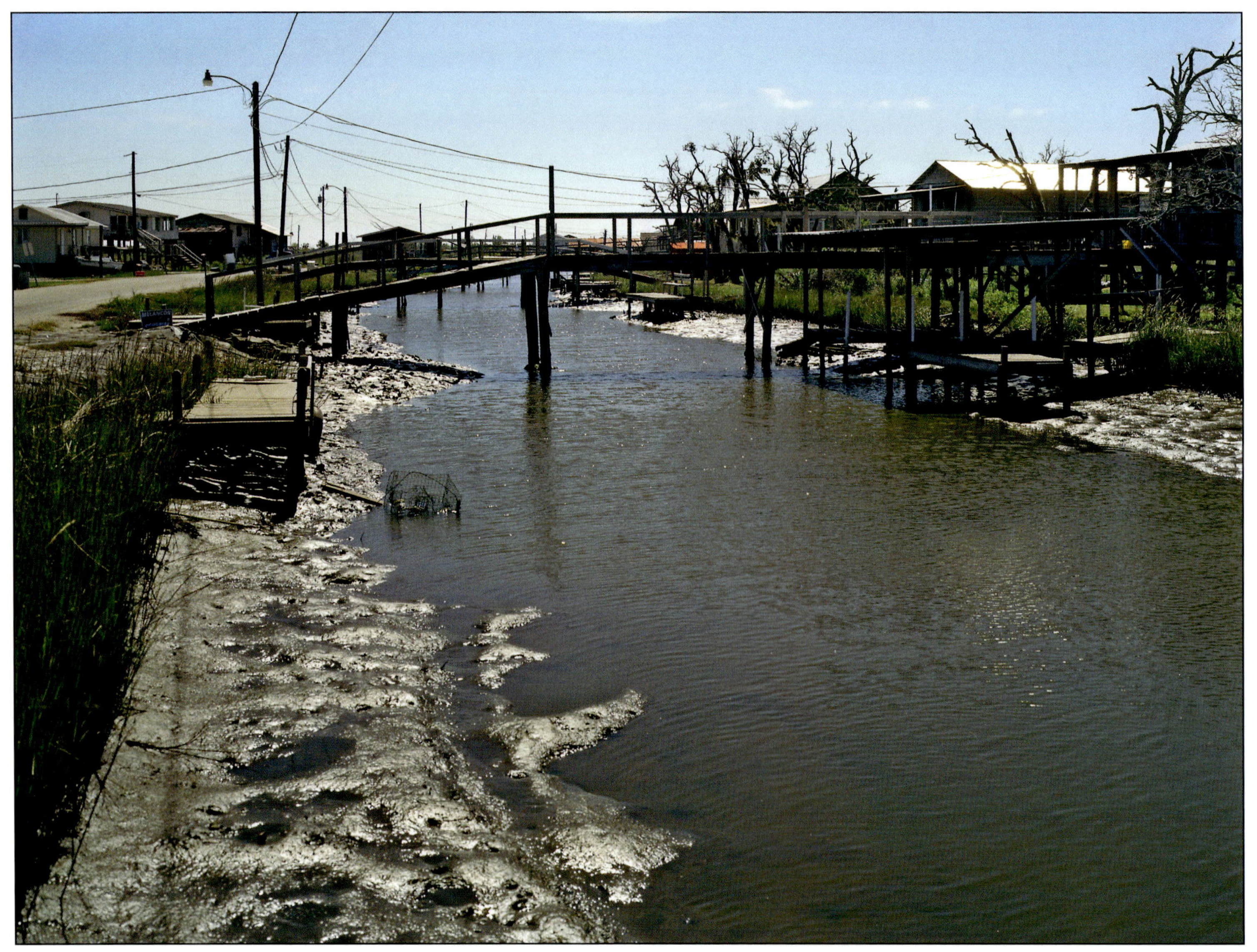

Isle de Jean Charles: Bayou St. Jean Charles

Terrebonne Parish, Louisiana

Dangling at the end of a thread in the Point aux Chenes WMA is Isle St. Jean Charles, home of a group of Biloxi-Chitimacha-Choctaws. Fiddler crabs drag their single claws along its muddy bank. Its wooden houses line Bayou Jean Charles. Rickety wooden walks over the bayou connect houses to the island's only road. Until a road connected them to the outside world, villagers came and went by boat and made a living from the marshes. They measured years by what hurricane hit when. 2002: Lili battered houses. 2005: Rita swept in four feet of water. Their community fragmented with their marshes. Half the 240 people living on the island in 1997 were gone by 2006.

The Barataria Basin and the Lafourche, St. Bernard, and Modern Deltas

When the Lafourche delta lobe began pushing into the Gulf of Mexico fifteen hundred years ago, the trunk channel between Donaldsonville and New Orleans that had serviced the St. Bernard lobes shriveled, but the Mississippi did not abandon it completely. About thirteen hundred years ago, when the Bayou Lafourche began carrying silt to the Gulf, so did the older St. Bernard channel, initiating the Plaquemine Delta lobe. As discharge along Bayou Lafourche decreased, discharge through the Plaquemine complex increased in direct proportion. It took four hundred years for the Plaquemine lobe to capture the full flow of the Mississippi. The Plaquemine complex pushed south between the deteriorating lobes of the St. Bernard Delta—the Bayou des Familles on the west and the Bayou La Loutre on the east. It formed the eastern edge of the Barataria Basin and the western edge of Breton Sound.

The Barataria Basin received its sediment from three distributaries, Bayou des Familles south of New Orleans, Bayou Lafourche on the west side of the basin, and the Mississippi and a few small distributaries in the modern Delta on the east. The construction of the GIWW segregated the freshwater swamps and bottomland hardwoods in the northern half of the basin from the tidally influenced salt marshes in the southern half. Water draining from the swamps flows to several large lakes in the middle of the basin—Lac des Allemands, Lake Cataoutche, Lake Salvador, and Little Lake—which act as a sump. The landbridge that stretches across the basin from Bayou Lafourche to the Mississippi—marshes and the swamps progressing inland from Barataria Bay—absorbs storm surges and protects the towns and villages along the Mississippi, Bayou des Familles, and Bayou Lafourche. And the cypress swamps in the northern reaches of the basin protect the V-shaped hurricane levee that guards New Orleans. Its barrier islands, Grand Isle, Grand Terre, Shell Island, and others at the foot of Barataria Bay, speed bumps for hurricanes, protect the wetlands.

No streams flow to the Barataria Basin. Lafourche Parish closed off Bayou Lafourche at its head in 1904. The construction of the Mississippi main line levee after 1927 cut off its annual influx of freshwater and sediment that came with spring flooding, which flushed out salt water that had intruded in the late summer and fall. Until the Davis Pond Freshwater Diversion Structure was completed on the west bank of the Mississippi near Luling in 2001, the basin depended on rainfall and runoff from the adjacent ridges and on small diversions along the Mississippi south of New Orleans for freshwater to hold back the increasing levels of salinity that were killing its fresh marshes and swamps.

Like the Terrebonne Basin to the west, wetlands disappeared from the Barataria Basin at a great rate, 5,700 acres a year between 1974 and 1990, with the greatest loss coming in the Grand Cheniere and Bay regions just west of the Mississippi River. Katrina and Rita converted 17.6 square miles of wetlands in the basin to open water.

The four barrier islands had a combined area of 1,800 acres in 1990. As they were reshaped by wind and breached by waves, passes between them widened, more salt water poured into the basin, and tidal action increased in the central part of the basin. Fresh and intermediate marshes shifted to saline marshes or disappeared altogether. The Louisiana DNR expects the barrier islands to shrink to a thousand acres by 2015, and expects East Grand Terre and Grand Pierre to disappear altogether by 2045.

When the State of Louisiana laid out the Coast 2050 plan to cover restoration in all nine basins on the Louisiana coast, the Louisiana DNR and the Corps of Engineers made the decision to start with the Barataria Basin because of its extreme loss of wetlands. In 2001 the two agencies signed a contract to develop a feasibility study for the basin that would address barrier shoreline restoration and wetlands creation and restoration from the perimeter to the center. And their engineers would develop a hydrologic-hydrodynamic computer model of water circulation and salinity patterns in the basin as a guide for freshwater diversions.

Diverting freshwater to the coastal marshes in the adjacent basins first appeared as a concept in the 1993 Louisiana Coastal Wetlands Restoration Plan. The many restoration plans for the Barataria Basin focus on diversions from the Mississippi. Two small diversions at Naomi, opened in 1993, and West Pointe a la Hache, opened in 1991, delivered freshwater to the wetlands on the eastern edge of the Barataria Landbridge. The Davis Pond Diversion Project, completed in 2001, was the largest of several diversions planned around its perimeter.

For years people in the Barataria Basin held out hope that the Davis Pond Diversion Project would heal their wetlands. In July 2002 the Corps of Engineers and the Louisiana DNR opened iron gates in the four 14-foot square box culverts set in the Mississippi main line levee at the site of an 1884 crevasse. The Corps designed the $120-million project to divert water at the rate of 10,650 cubic feet per second through an outflow channel guided by levees 11,000 feet long set 120 feet apart and running through forested swamps and spilling into a 10,084-acre ponding area. Sheet flow—water flowing ever so slowly down a low grade and through shallow wetlands, made slower when it encountered submergent and emergent vegetation—would spread it into the fresh and intermediate marshes of the Barataria Basin.

The aim of the diversion is to mimic springtime overbank flooding from the Mississippi, push back intruding salt water, preserve 33,000 acres of marsh, and benefit 777,000 acres of marsh and bays. At its maximum flow the diversion would raise water levels three inches in Lake Cataouatche south of the ponding area and one inch in Lake Salvador south of there. It didn't work that way.

A two-mile-long rock weir separates the ponding area from flotant marsh at the edge of Lake Cataouatche. The Corps designed the weir to settle a foot and a half so water would spill over it. The rocks didn't settle. Water didn't spill over. Instead, it backed up behind the weir. What did spill over spilled into buoyant flotant, which drifted up with the water level, forming a higher dam. Water did spill over the guide levees into the swamps, which didn't need the water.

The Corps made cuts in the weir to improve drainage. On December 1, 2003, the engineers opened the gates to divert water at the structure's full rate. Again water backed up and spilled over the guide levees. The Corps made nine more cuts in the weir and raised the guide levees, which had settled. In the four years after it was dedicated, the project seldom operated at more that 2,000 cubic feet per second. The ponding area turned wet most of the year, alligators and nutria moved in, and at least nine pairs of eagles set up household in the trees. And the water was not getting to where it was needed—the fresh and intermediate marshes to the south.

After Katrina and Rita washed salt water into the basin, the Corps opened the gates and released water at the rate of 4,400 cubic feet per second. It did so during a rainstorm that dumped two inches on the basin. Water again spilled over the guide levees. Since then the Corps has backed off to 4,000 cubic feet per second, a rate that has reduced salinity in the basin.

The Louisiana DNR proposed other diversion. The small, 1,000 to 1,500-cubic-feet-per-second diversion, through a new pump at the head of Bayou Lafourche at Donaldsonville, would reduce salinity along Bayou Perot and Bayou Rigolettes, just west of Lafitte. The Pikes Peak diversion would freshen declining cypress swamps between the Lafourche and Mississippi natural levees along Bayou Chevreuil. Two projects would divert freshwater into the swamps north of Lac des Allemands. The Davis Pond project would be modified to introduce more sediment. The Myrtle Grove diversion, along the Mississippi south of New Orleans, would introduce freshwater and sediment into the landbridge in the vicinities of Bayou Dupont and Little Lake. All the projects could be enlarged at a later date to introduce more sediment into the basin.

In 1998 the 2050 proposal outlined several alternative diversions that would reduce the rate of wetland loss by 50 percent, maintain the wetlands, or increase wetland gain by 50 percent a year. The first alternative would minimize changes in salinity in Barataria Basin, the second would be a continuous reintroduction of freshwater, and the third would mimic historic hydrology. It included the big one, the Third Delta Conveyance Channel.

The Third Delta project would deliver massive amounts of water and sediment to Terrebonne and Barataria wetlands. In 1993 Sherwood M. Gagliano and Johannes L. van Beek saw the ability of the Wax Lake Outlet to build land with freshwater and sediment from the Atchafalaya as a good model of land building in the Terrebonne and Barataria Basins and proposed their Third Delta Conveyance Channel.

Some agency, ostensibly the Corps of Engineers, would tap the Mississippi just downstream of the Sunshine Bridge to the east of Donaldsonville and install a control structure with a navigation lock in the main line levee. Excavators would dredge a channel along the eastern toe of the Bayou Lafourche ridge. At thirty miles the channel would split. One branch would continue along the eastern toe of the Lafourche ridge for thirty-five miles, cross the GIWW, and enter Little Lake, where it would form its subdelta. The second branch would cut across Bayou Lafourche, follow the toe of the western ridge, veer away from the levee south of the GIWW, and form its subdelta thirty miles southwest of the split. Engineers would have to dam Bayou Lafourche at its crossing with the second channel and build a pumping station to remove excess water from the bayou. A 1955 diversion structure at Donaldsonville would continue to feed freshwater from the Mississippi and supply drinking water to the towns along the bayou.

Gagliano and van Beek expected their new channel to mimic natural development of a distributary. Like a distributary it would scour a deeper, wider channel as it carried off more and more water from the Mississippi. Like a distributary it would build a natural levee. And like a distributary it would deposit its sediment in the shallow, still waters of the Terrebonne and Barataria Basins and replace what had been lost to erosion and subsidence.

More realistic is the Bayou Lafourche diversion at Donaldsonville, but even that has problems. Three siphons pump water from the Mississippi through the dam at the head of the bayou at the rate of 200 cubic feet per second, about as much as the bayou could handle in 2000, enough to make it silt in, lose depth, and lose width, but not enough to nourish the wetlands. Pump any more, and Bayou Lafourche would flood the homes and businesses that grew up along the bayou in Donaldsonville after 1904. Hence, a diversion of 1,000 to 1,500 cfs would entail dredging 2.9 million yards of sediment to deepen the bayou between Donaldsonville and Thibodaux and building a new pump at Donaldsonville and would cost $180 million, half of which would go into dredging. The Bayou Lafourche diversion was one of the five near-term projects laid out in the Louisiana Coast Area Ecosystem Restoration Study in November 2004 and approved in the 2007 WRDA.

Lac des Allemands Watershed

Historically, Bayou Chevreuil carried the excess water from the northern Barataria swamps to Lac des Allemands. Ten feet deep, twelve thousand acres, surrounded by fresh marshes and cypress swamps—Lac des Allemands is a glory hole for catfish. Its waters range from fresh to brackish. It is connected to Lake Salvador through Bayou des Allemands. Salvador is connected to Little Lake through Bayou Perot, which connects to Grand Bayou, and so on to the Gulf of Mexico. When salt water intruded, this is the track it took.

The fresh marshes that surrounded the edges of the lake have been lost to erosion. While the Davis Pond diversion does not flow directly into Lac des Allemands; inputs of freshwater into the Barataria Basin from the Mississippi freshen the waters of Lac des Allemands as well as those of Lake Cataouache and Lake Salvador to the east, which do receive diverted waters from the Davis Pond project. The small diversions at Pikes Peak or along the Dredge Boat Canal or Bayou Lafourche into the Lac des Allemands watershed, should they ever happen, would also freshen it. In the meantime the Lac des Allemands watershed will depend on rainfall and whatever freshwater makes its way in from the Davis Pond Diversion Project.

Finally, like the forests of the Verret watershed in the Terrebonne Basin, the forests in the Lac des Allemands watershed are subsiding and becoming waterlogged.

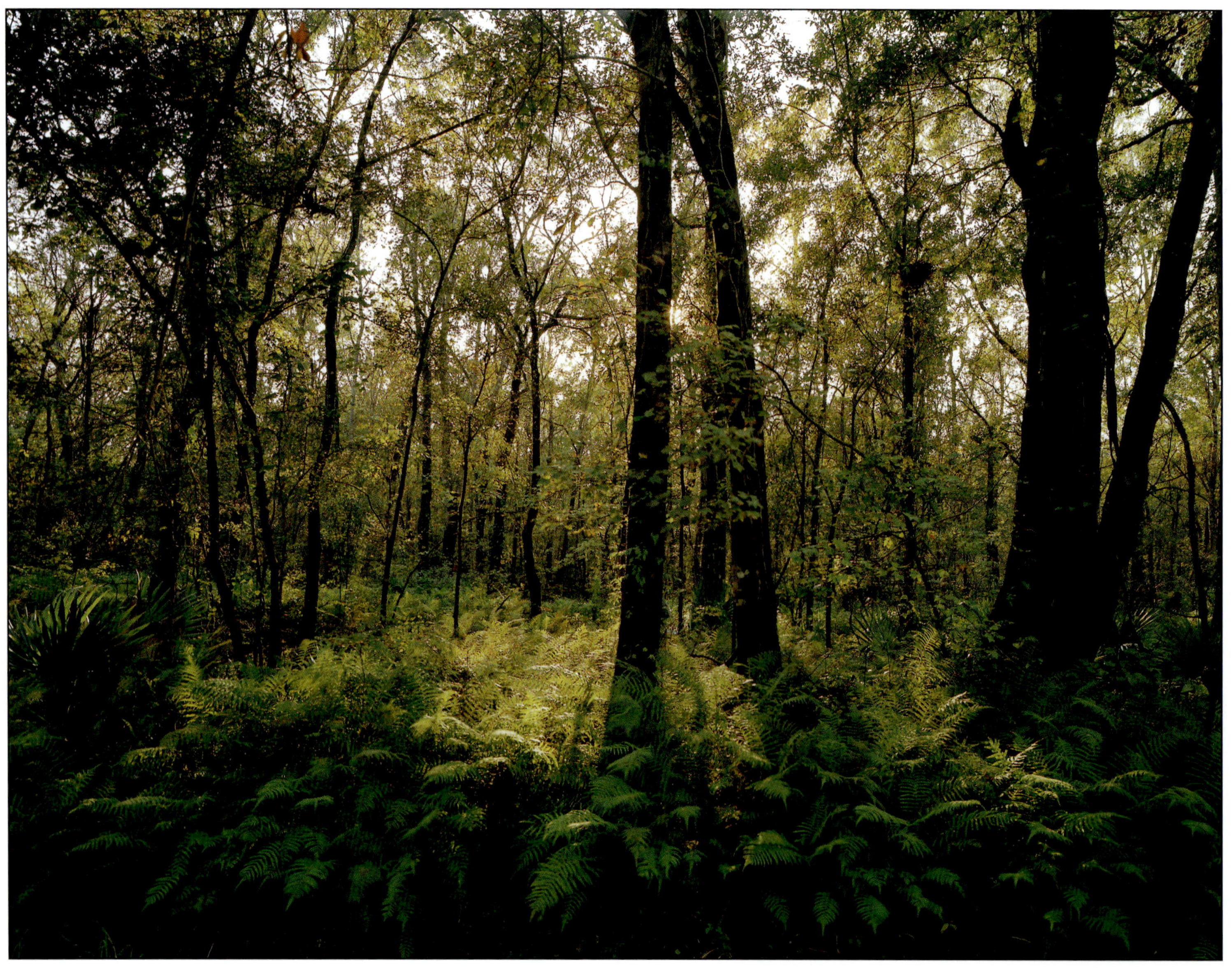

Lac des Allemands Watershed: Laurel Valley Swamp

Lafourche Parish, Louisiana

In 1927 the bottomland hardwoods of the northern Barataria served as storage areas for floodwater, captured sediment, and soaked-up nutrients. Deciduous trees contributed an annual load of litter, which decayed into organic sediment, counteracting subsidence. The Mississippi levees disrupted the seasonal flooding/drying patterns and deprived the forests of freshwater and sediment. Without sediment to counteract subsidence and rising water levels, Barataria's forests became waterlogged year-round and declined by 38 percent between 1972 and 1992. Should that rate continue, the bottomland forests of the upper Barataria Basin would disappear by 2025.

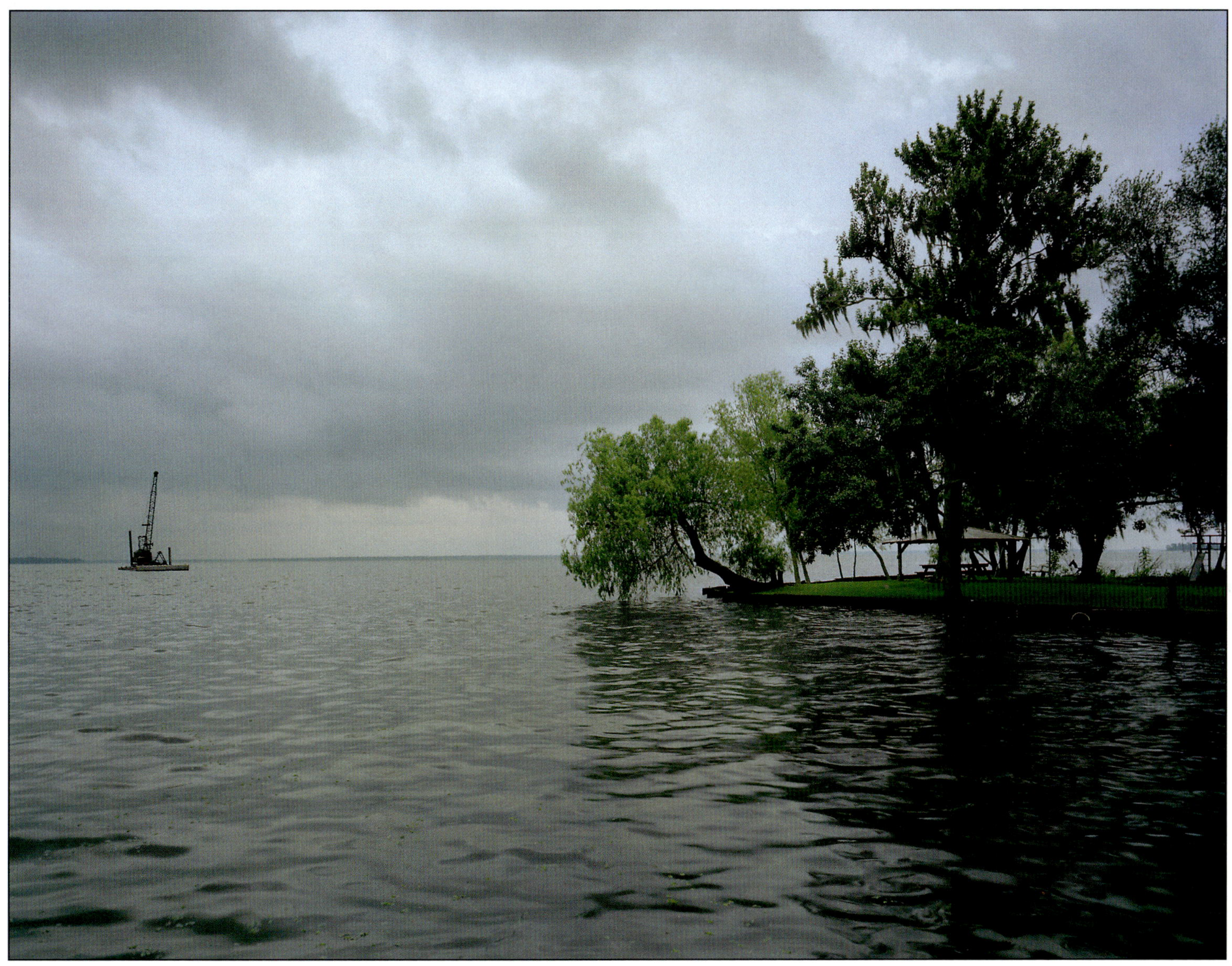

Lac des Allemands: Chenier's Camp

St. John the Baptist Parish, Louisiana

In 1963 Lou Chenier built a camp at the mouth of Vacherie Canal, where it empties into Lac des Allemands, and watched 300 yards of fresh marsh on his lakefront disappear over the next several years. He shored up his lake frontage with rocks and his canal frontage with a wooden bulkhead. Lac des Allemands is losing its fresh marsh, the place where its famed catfish and bass breed and feed. In 2000 and 2001 drought and salt water intrusion decimated the cats and bass. Blue crab and shrimp turned up where they had never been before. Recreational anglers, expecting cats and bass, hooked redfish and speckled trout, fish which prefer salt marshes to fresh.

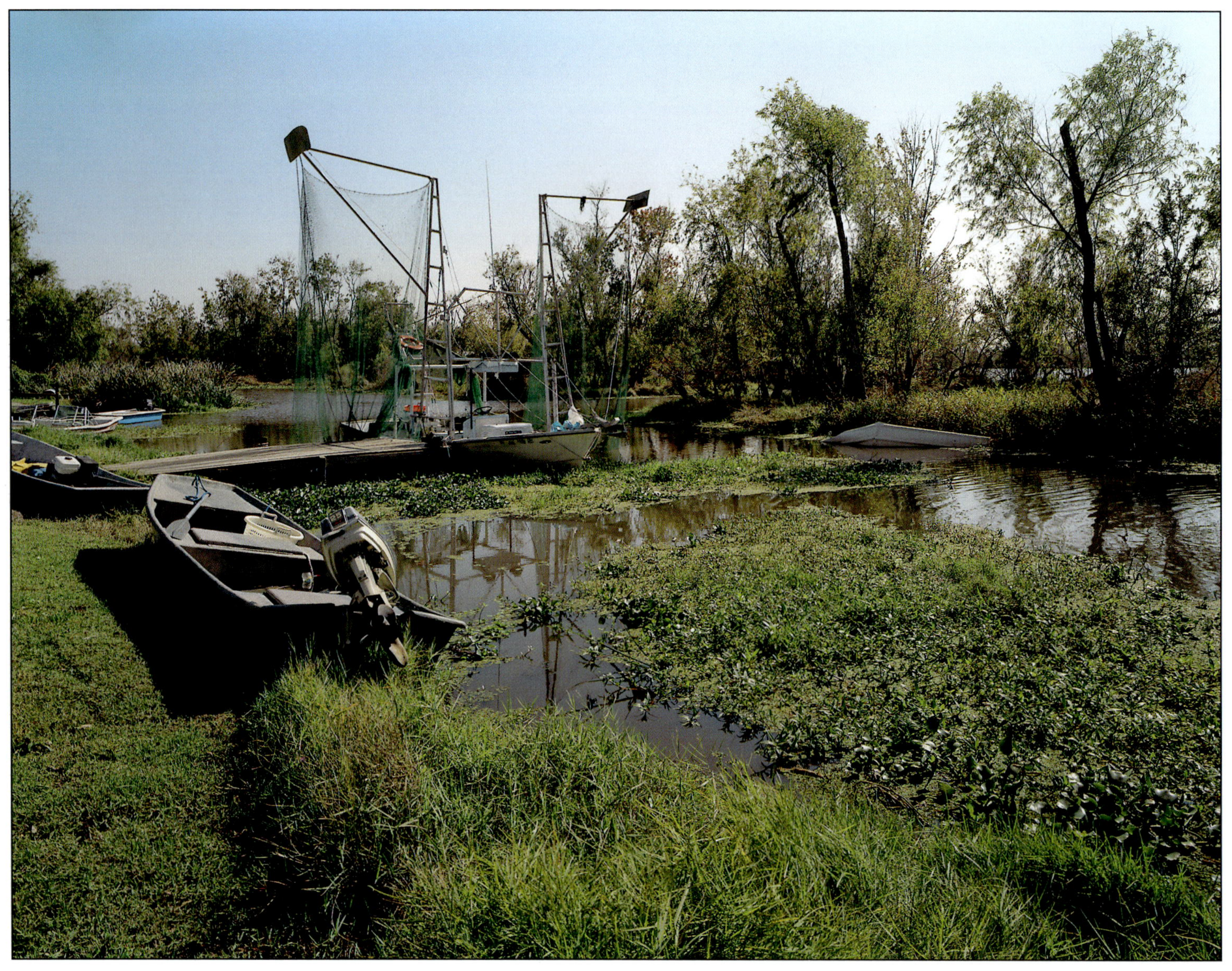

Lac des Allemands Watershed: Bayou Gauche

St. Charles Parish, Louisiana

The Louisiana year: People who draw their living from the coastal marshes live by the seasons—brown shrimp in May; white shrimp in August; alligators in September; oysters December to April; crabs all year long; mink, nutria, muskrat, and waterfowl in winter. The way of life is threatened. In 2000 the price shrimpers got fell to $.15 a pound as they competed with imports from Asia. Pollution fouled oyster beds. Alligator harvesting required a permit. People for the Ethical Treatment of Animals put a crimp in the fur industry. To rid the coast of nutria the State of Louisiana offered $5.00/seven-inch tail, no match for the value of the lost mink pelts.

The Barataria Landbridge

> Bayou Rigolets is a sea-marsh bayou, widening out at almost a lake in places. Its length measured down the center is 10 miles and 3,000 feet.
>
> The banks are low sea-marsh, averaging about a foot above low tide. A great deal of it is prairie flotant, and in places the motion of the waves could be noticed 50 feet back of the apparent bank. This bayou is what may be called a dying one, as every year the banks advance their line of reeds; and wherever a duck hunter constructs a blind, an island is commenced which rapidly grows.
>
> —H. S. Douglas, Assistant Engineer,
> U.S. Army Corps of Engineers, 1881

A marshy landmass bridges the Barataria Basin between Bayou Lafourche ridge and the Mississippi ridge south of the cypress forests of the Lac des Allemands watershed and north of the saline marshes in the lower Barataria Basin. Historically, a quartet of narrow bayous—Perot, Barataria, Dupont, and Villars—meandered through a landmass between Lake Salvador on the north and Little Lake on the south. The landbridge thwarted tidal exchange and served as a barrier to salt water intrusion from the lower basin. Little salt water made its way into the narrow bayous.

Wave erosion, tidal energy, subsidence, and the rise in sea level eroded the bayous and their interior marshes. The elimination of overbank flooding from the Mississippi and the closure of Bayou Lafourche shifted the basin from a river-dominated system to a tidal-dominated system. The dredging of the various waterways—the GIWW, the Barataria, the Harvey Cutoff, and the oilfield access channels—allowed in salt water. Salty tides washed away the organic soils, peat, and root mats that composed the landbridge. Summer storms blowing in from the south could raise water levels several feet above the marshes. Winter winds from the north could push the water out and expose mudflats to erosion.

Bayou Rigolettes connects to the Barataria Waterway, at Lafitte; Bayou Perot, its twin to the west, flows out of Lake Salvador. H. S. Douglas found true bayous in 1881. Today, they are elongated lakes separated by a long peninsula of marsh. At their southern ends, they come together and flow through a narrow passage, bordered by marsh, into Little Lake.

It took a hundred years for Bayous Perot and Rigolettes to widen into lakes. In 1892 the pair were narrow, meandering streams that carried freshwater south. By the 1940s they had elongated into a pair of oblong pools. A few long, narrow point bars defined what remained of the bends in bayous. Those eroded over the next twenty years. By 1965, Perot and Rigolettes had evolved into broad, elongated lakes. And the process continued at the rate of up to a hundred feet of shoreline a year in some places. By 1990, 1,550 acres of interior marsh had disappeared from the ridge between the two, and the narrow passage to Little Lake had widened.

A work group—made up of people from the academic community and local, state, and federal conservation and restoration agencies—formed in April 1996 to investigate the possibility of arresting the deterioration of the landbridge and preserving its function of retarding the intrusion of salt water to the north. The group decided to protect the 76,000 feet of shoreline. The work would shore up the narrow passage to Little Lake at the foot of the bayous, the shoreline of the bayous, and the entrance into Harvey Cutoff from Bayou Rigolettes.

They tested four techniques: rock dikes that retained and compacted the underlying organic soil; two different rock dikes that used a lightweight core material; and concrete sheet pile structures. None had been used before to protect erodible organic soils. All offered potential cost savings. And all but the concrete sheet pile structures settled two to four feet after a year of testing.

The brackish to intermediate marshes in the Barataria Landbridge provide habitat to estuarine-dependent fish and shellfish: brown and white shrimp, blue crab, southern flounder, black and red drum, and, speckled trout, important to both recreational and commercial fishing. Ducks—Gadwalls, Green-winged Teals, Blue-winged Teals, Ring-necked Ducks, Lesser Scaup—settle in for the winter in the open areas in the marshes. Mottled ducks are permanent residents. Furbearers—mink, raccoon, muskrat, otter, and nutria—feed and nest in the marshes.

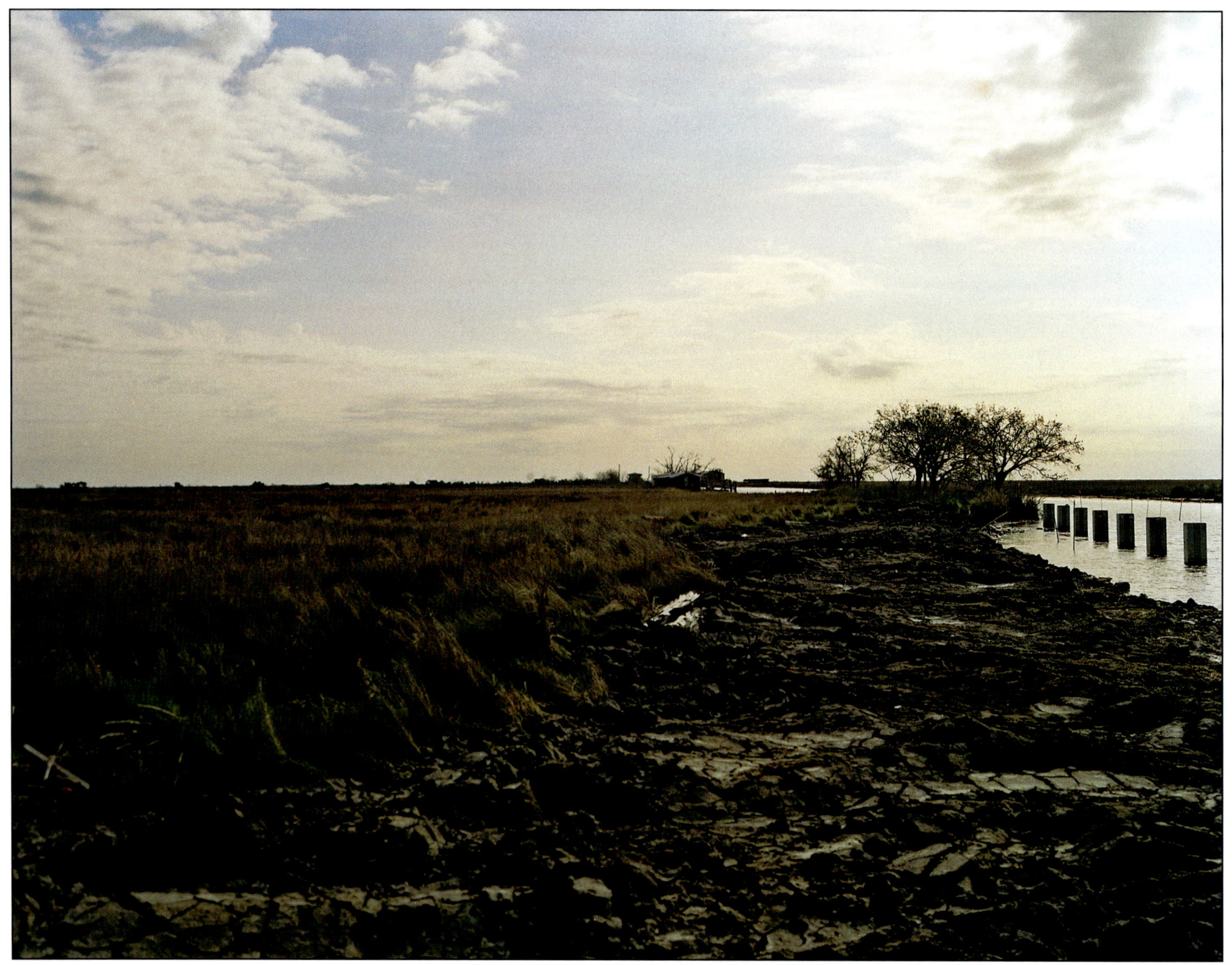

Barataria Landbridge: Bayou Rigolettes
Jefferson Parish, Louisiana

Precast slabs of concrete, eight feet wide, twenty feet long, and six inches thick, set vertically between sixty-foot-long concrete piles having an H-configuration in the top twenty feet: these are the parts of the concrete sheet pile structure. Contractors set the piles 8.5 feet on center and drove them into the muck out front of the 31,500 feet of bayou shoreline to be protected. Then they slid the panels between the piles. They left overlapping gaps for marine creatures to go to and from the marshes. When complete, the concrete panels rose 3.5 feet above sea level and served as containment walls for dredge material pumped in for marsh creation.

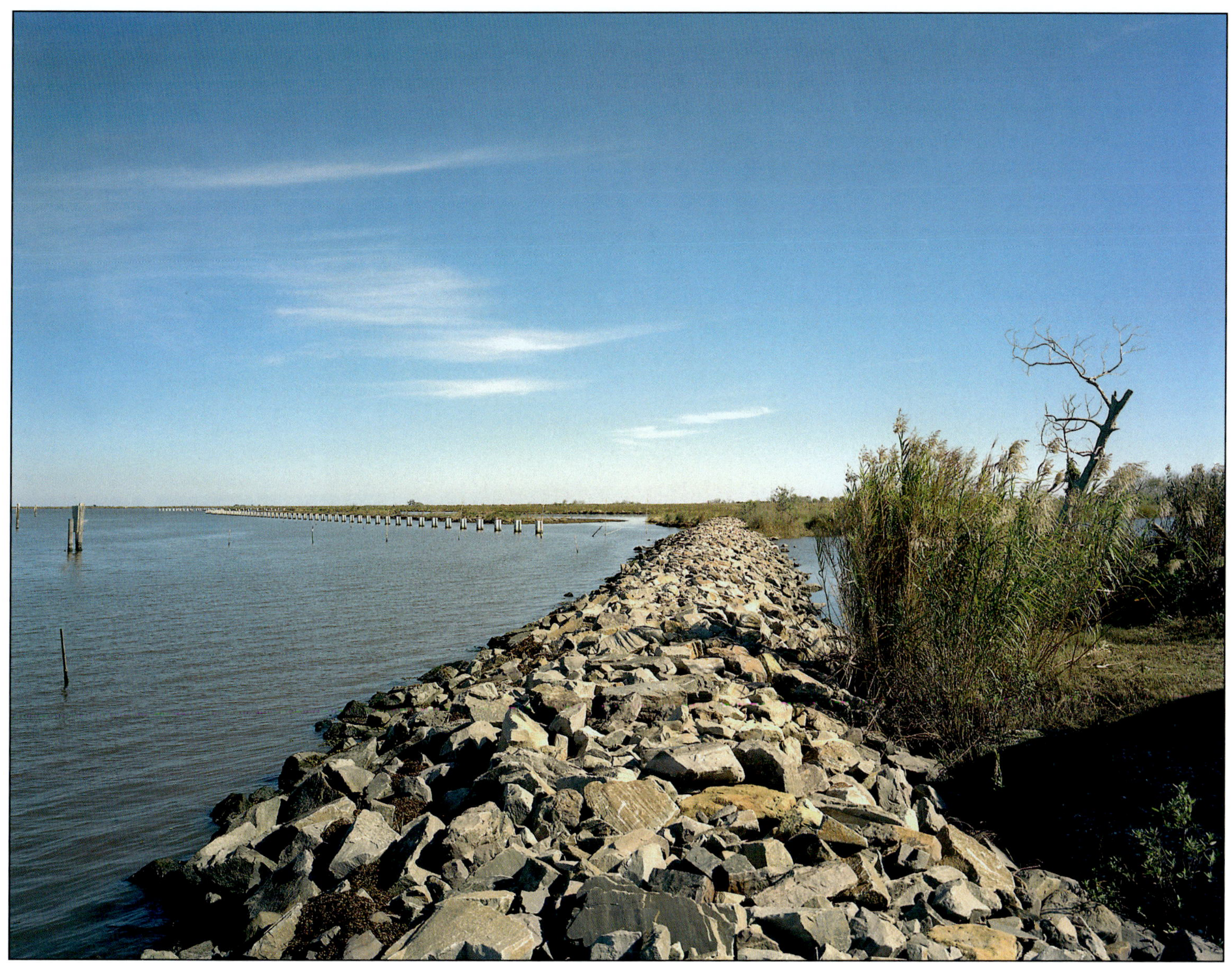

Barataria Landbridge: Bayou Perot at Little Lake

Jefferson Parish, Louisiana

To stop the erosion of the shore of Little Lake at Bayou Perot, engineers determined that the soils could support a rock revetment to baffle wave action instead of the more expensive sheet pile. Once installed on top of permeable geotextile cloth to increase the stability of the soil, the rock wrapped around the Little Lake entrance to Bayou Perot. It reached 3.5 feet above sea level. Dredge spoil filled the ponds in the marsh behind it. Fish dips allowed marine organisms to pass through it. Should the dike sink to the level of the constructed marsh, NRCS engineers would raise it. Sheet pile did protect the shore of Bayou Perot at Little Lake.

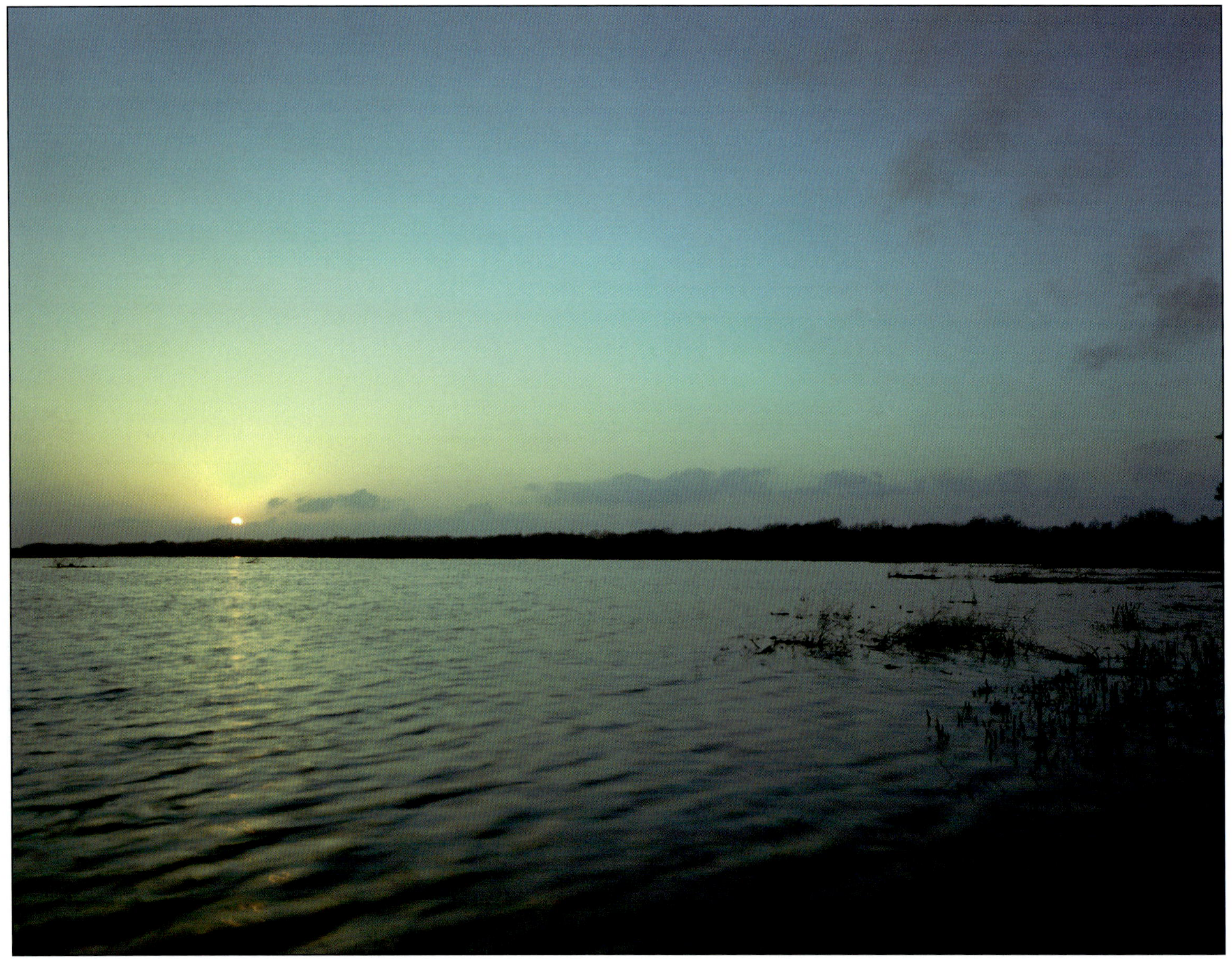

The Pen: LaFitte

Plaquemines Parish, Louisiana

Leave decomposing plant litter underwater, where free oxygen can't get to it, and it accumulates faster than it decomposes. This is how organic soil is built, at the rate of a few inches per 100 years. Organic soil supports the fresh and intermediate marshes of the Louisiana coast. Drain it, expose it to air—free oxygen—and it oxidizes. Oxygen combines with carbon in the plant tissues, is converted to carbon dioxide and water, and decomposes, fast. This is how drained organic soil subsides at the rate of a few inches per year. Farmers constructed a levee around the Pen and drained it. The levees failed, water poured in, turning it into a shallow lake.

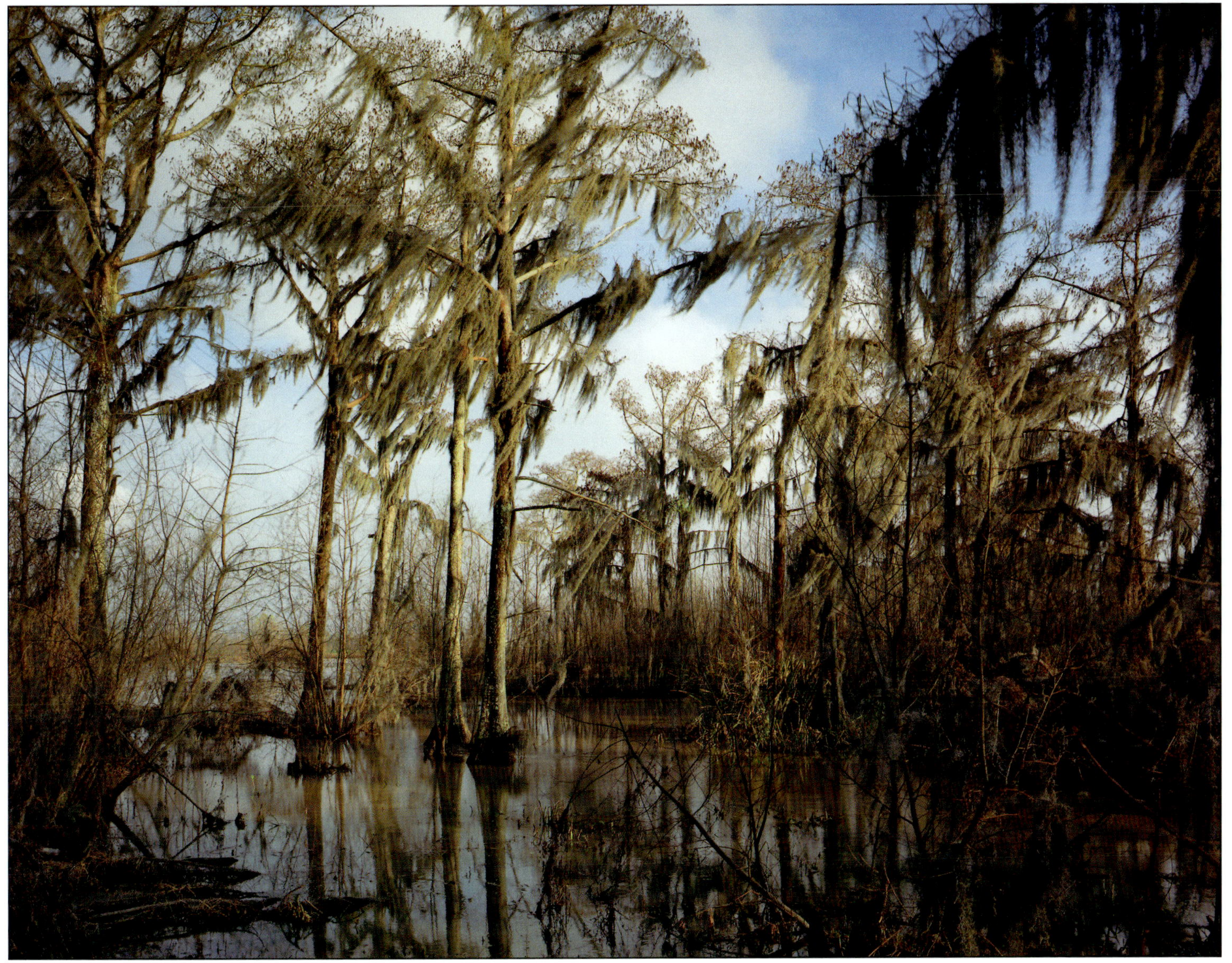

Barataria Landbridge: Naomi Siphon Outfall Area

Plaquemines Parish, Louisiana

To mimic the Mississippi flooding and reduce levels of salinity in Barataria Basin, Plaquemines Parish and the Louisiana DNR primed the Naomi siphons in 1993 and delivered freshwater to 13,000 acres of marshes between the toe of the hurricane protection levee along the west bank of the river and eastern edge of the Pen. Eight tubes draw water from the river and discharge it into a pond. A 30-foot-wide, 3,300-foot-long channel carries it to the marshes, where sheet flow diverts it to meandering bayous, which do a better job of depositing sediment than the straight canals, which carry it to the Pen. Even so, the siphons reduced salinity in the wetlands.

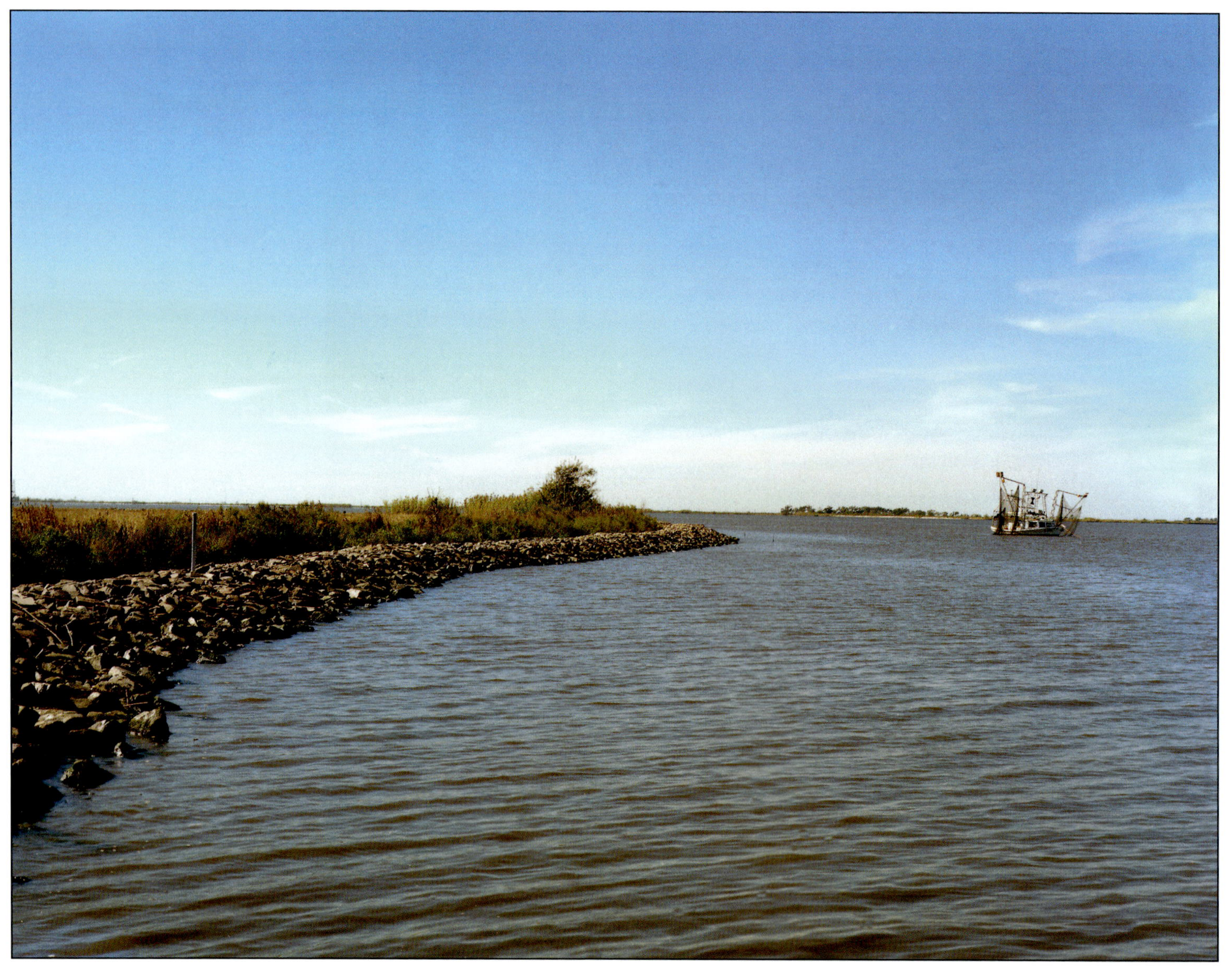

Barataria Landbridge: Little Lake

Jefferson Parish, Louisiana

Freshwater diversions yielded little sediment needed for marsh building. The Louisiana DNR studied sediment traps, excavated pits in the Mississippi riverbed that would capture suspended sediment flowing along the bottom. Once trapped, sediment could be pumped through a pipeline to places it was needed most and used for marsh building and ridge restoration. A long-distance pipeline would start at Myrtle Grove, reach a dozen or so miles across the Barataria Basin to generate marsh at the upper end of Little Lake, sustain the surge-reduction function of the landbridge, and complement shoreline restoration along Bayous Rigolettes and Perot.

The Wetlands West of the Mississippi Ridge

Buras, built along Louisiana 23 on the narrow ridge of the Mississippi, was protected from the river by the main stem levee on one side, from the Gulf by a hurricane levee on the other, and by neither when Hurricane Katrina made landfall at 6:01 A.M. on August 29, 2005. The storm surge swept away much of the town, salt water pooled between the levees and hung around for months.

Over forty thousand acres of degraded marsh and open water protected the Buras hurricane levee in August 2005. In 1932 the region between the Empire Navigation Channel, a shortcut from the Mississippi to the Barataria Basin, and the Grand Liard ridge to the south, contained 27,555 acres of marsh. By 1974, 8,025 acres had slumped underwater, lost to subsidence, oil-field canals, the navigation channel, and the deep borrow pits necessary for the construction of the hurricane levee. By 1990, 15,320 more acres disappeared, these lost to the tidal energy allowed in by subsidence. With the tides came wind erosion, augmented by the grid of canals dredged through the landscape. Only 4,210 acres remained in 1990. Of that, 3,990 acres would be reduced to open water by 2050 if nothing were done to rebuild the marshes. For Buras and all the marshes west of the Mississippi ridge, marsh restoration was critical.

South of the Barataria Landbridge, the Mississippi deposited its sediment in hundreds of feet of water. Small distributaries—Bayou Grande Cheniere, Bayou Grand, Bayou Grand Liard, Bayou Schofield, and Bayou English—broke off from the trunk channel and created subdeltas. Their ridges formed hydrological barriers between marshes and protected freshwater swamps that grew up along the toe of the ridge of the trunk channel.

Before the Corps of Engineers ran the Mississippi River levee to Venice, halting the annual overflows of water and sediment into the marshes, eight miles of wetlands protected by barrier islands protected the villages of Plaquemines Parish from storm surges. When the State of Louisiana published its Comprehensive Master Plan for a Sustainable Coast in February 2007, the plan discussed the need for large diversions from the Mississippi in Lower Plaquemines Parish.

In 1991 the West Point a la Hache siphons started diverting freshwater into 16,297 acres of brackish marshes and open water between the Bayou Grande Cheniere Ridge and the toe of the hurricane levee. The goal of increasing the ratio of marsh to open water was not met. Between 1991 and 1999 the project area lost 460.4 acres of land at the rate of 1.03 percent of the 1991 acreage per year—not great, but slower than the 1.29 percent-per-year loss rate before the completion of the siphons.

The Coast 2050 proposal suggested continuous diversions of freshwater, sediment, and nutrients at Empire, Bastian Bay, and Main Pass in lower Plaquemines Parish would yield a 50 percent increase in the rate of wetland creation. Doing so would require relocating the main navigation channel on the Mississippi.

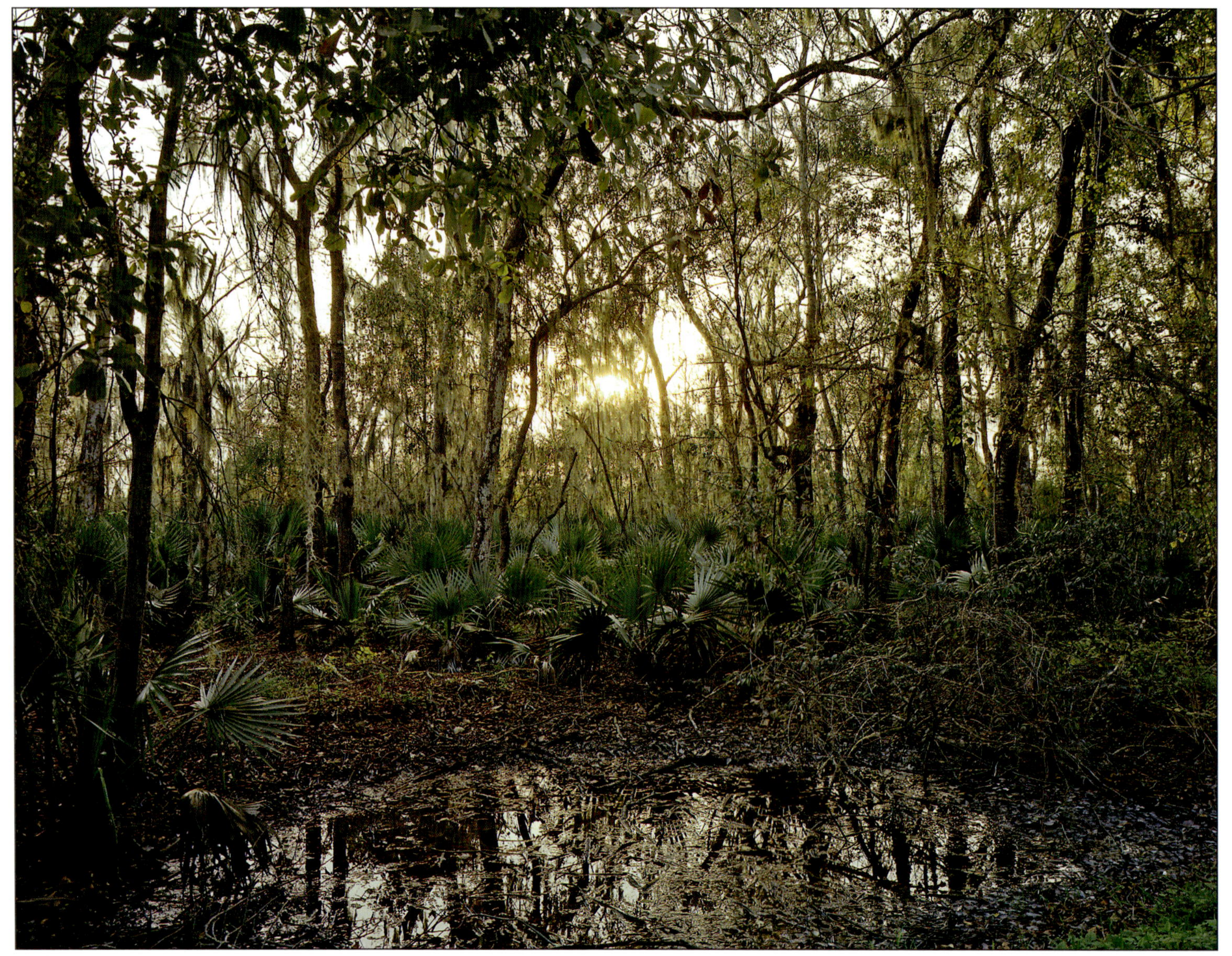

Bayou Grande Cheniere Ridge: Lake Hermitage
Plaquemines Parish, Louisiana

About 950 years ago Bayou Grande Cheniere broke away from the Mississippi and formed a subdelta. A bottomland hardwood forest—treed in sycamore, sweet gum, ash, and pecan—grew up on the ridge, palmetto covered the understory, a cypress-tupelo swamp took root in the back-swamp, with freshwater marsh grading to brackish beyond that. People from the Coles Creek culture settled on the Bayou Grande Cheniere ridge 300 years later and erected twelve mounds set in a circle. The forest, the swamp, and the marshes supplied their needs. They hunted alligators, migratory ducks, swamp rabbits, and deer and caught southern flounder, speckled trout, and drum.

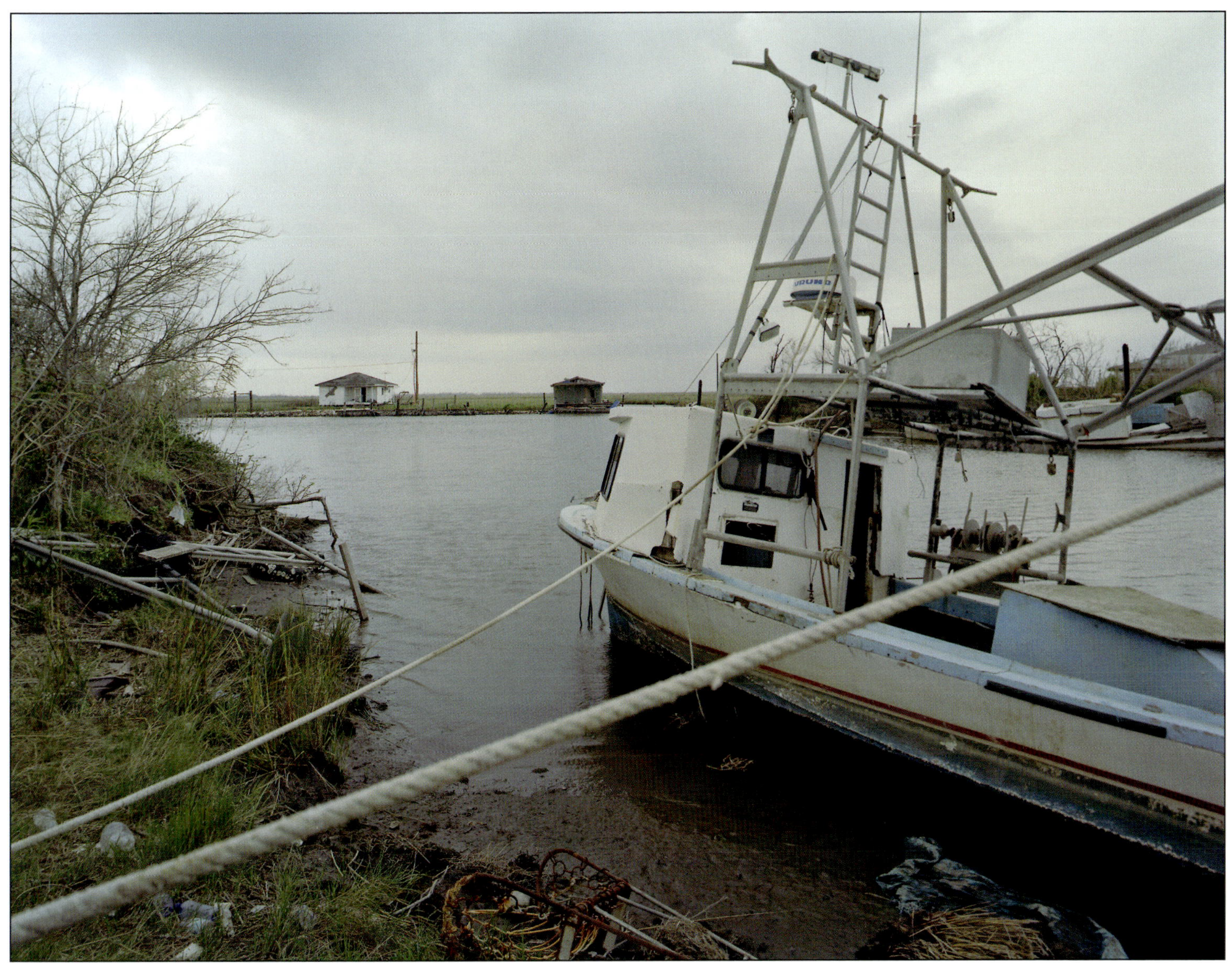

Grand Bayou: At Fosters Canal
Plaquemines Parish, Louisiana

The twenty-five families who live at Grand Bayou descend from Houma and Atakapa Indians and have inhabited these wetlands for 300 years. The bayou is their main drag, their rowboats their sidewalk, their fishnets—suspended from docks to catch seafood—their supermarket. They live the Louisiana year—fishing, crabbing, shrimping, and trapping. Their possibilities are dwindling along with their marshes. They live in 19,000 acres of brackish water and marsh between the Mississippi and the Bayou Grand Cheniere ridge, which prevents Gulf waters from swamping their homes, is sinking. Of the 13,400 acres of marsh mapped in 1932, 8,360 acres remained in 1990.

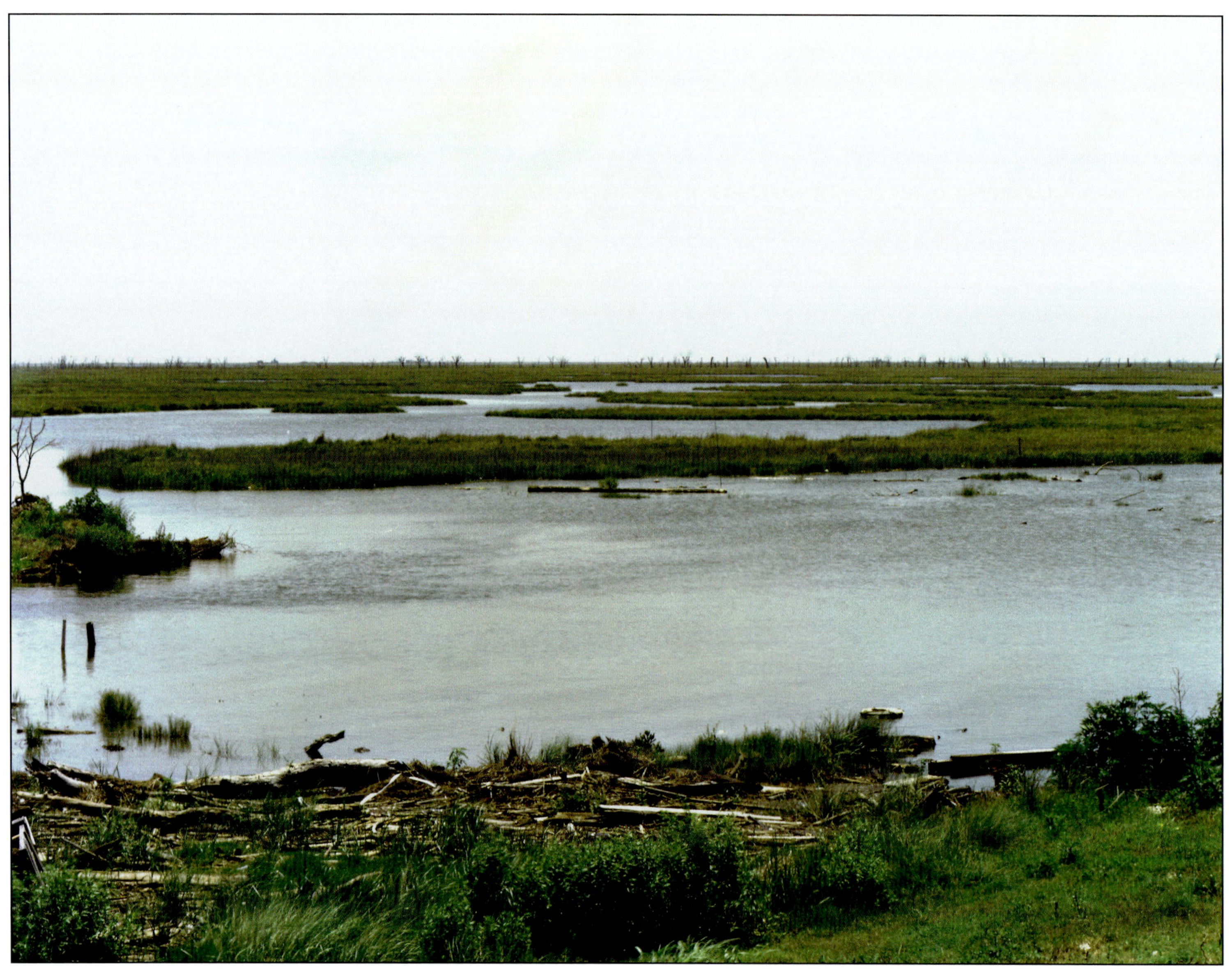

Bayou L'Eau Noire: Homeplace

Plaquemines Parish, Louisiana

A square mile of healthy marsh has four miles of edge habitat, where land meets water, oysters settle, small marine animals hide, fish and reptiles feed on small creatures, and waders and waterfowl feed on fish and reptiles. Dredge a canal through the marsh; you have two more miles of habitat, places for critters to flourish, but less marsh. Dredge another canal: more water, more edge, more critters, less marsh. The marsh erodes and breaks into ponds and then more and bigger ponds—no more edges, no more habitat, different critters. Species that thrive in open water move in; shrimp, crabs, red drum, speckled trout move out. So do the waders and waterfowl.

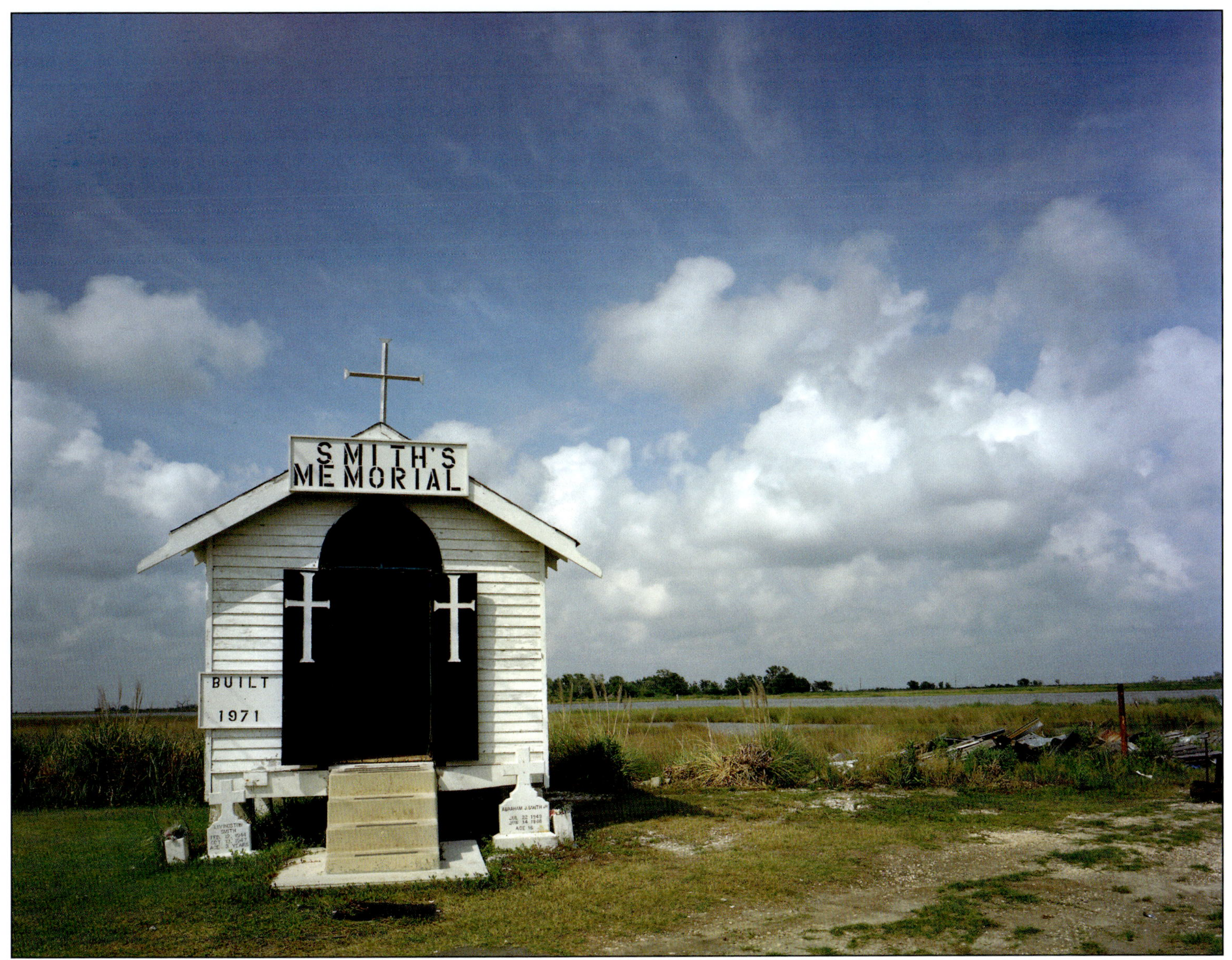

Bayou Lafourche: Smith Memorial Shrine

Lafourche Parish, Louisiana

Golden Meadow to Larose hurricane levee, completed in 1986, ends in floodgate across Bayou Lafourche. So does the broad expanse of the Bayou Lafouche natural levee. In 1971 the Smith family built a memorial shrine on the Bayou Lafourche ridge a mile and a half south of Golden Meadow. Here, the ridge is narrow and the bayou wide. The Corps of Engineers keeps the bayou dredged to nine feet deep and a hundred feet wide from Golden Meadow to Leeville. The firm mineral soils of the ridge have subsided. The forest that once anchored the western ridge has disappeared. A few trees and upland shrubs anchor the eastern ridge. Here, the ridge is at or near sea level.

Barrier Islands of the Lafourche Delta

When the Corps of Engineers and the Louisiana Department of Natural Resources published the LCA Study in November 2004 they did identify the restoration of the Barataria Barrier Shoreline, specifically Caminada Headland and Shell Island to the east, as "near-term critical features for the Louisiana Coastal Area Plan." That is, the restoration of the headland and the barrier island were projects that could be accomplished in the ten years following the publication of the study. The shoreline-restoration project would protect vital oil and gas infrastructure at Port Fourchon on the Caminada Headland and has the potential to prevent future land loss in the Barataria Basin.

Louisiana's barrier islands buffer storm surges, reduce flooding in the bays and erosion in the marshes behind them, and preserve estuarine systems by maintaining the gradient between salt water and freshwater in the basins they protect. The processes that build barrier islands—waves, tides, and the circulation of coastal waters—also erode and fragment them.

As each distributary of the Mississippi builds its delta lobe, it continues to deposit sediment in the Gulf of Mexico. Interdistributary bays form between distributaries. The Lafourche lobe, which took the form of a horsetail delta, formed bays between each of its several distributaries. Caillou Bay flanks the deteriorated Bayou Petit Caillou headland on the west, Terrebonne Bay on the east. Terrebonne Bay flanks the deteriorating Lafourche headland on the west; Caminada Bay and Barataria Bay flank it on the east. The backswamps of the overlapping web of natural levees within the Lafourche Delta contained interdistributary swamps and marshes clear up to the delta front. The process of deterioration begins once the river shifts to a new distributary and ceases to deliver sediment to its delta front.

As each delta lobe deteriorates, it evolves first into an erosional headland with an interdistributary marsh at its core. Waves and currents winnow sand from the headland and mold it into beaches and a flanking barrier arc. The headland beach migrates slowly inland. The barrier arc migrates inland and sideways. Storms create tidal inlets in the arc, which enlarge over time and break the arc into distinct barrier islands. After the headland breaks from the mainland, the interdistributary marsh ceases to form its core. Storms surge through larger and larger tidal channels between the islands until they are completely destroyed, leaving only submerged shoals of sand, as with Ship Shoal and Trinity Shoal.

Storms, subsidence, and longshore currents reconfigure barrier islands continually. Storm surges attack from the south, cold fronts from the north. In gentle weather sand moves onshore in the summer, pushed by prevailing winds from the south, and offshore in the winter, with prevailing winds from the north. And islands move sideways with swash and back-swash. Incoming waves—swash—strike the beach at an angle and carry water and sediment onto the beach. Back-swash flows at the steepest grade, at right angles to the shoreline, and carries water straight down the beach and back into the Gulf. In this way longshore currents erode the island at one end while depositing new sediment at the other. The process creates spits that encircle open water at the end that is receiving new deposits.

The Louisiana Gulf beaches can be divided into three interrelated environments: the shoreface, the foreshore, and the backshore. The shoreface slopes gently down into the Gulf from the low-tide line. The foreshore slopes up from the Gulf to the crest of the beach berm. The backshore lies between the berm and the dunes. Sparse vegetation grows on the backshore, none on the foreshore. Storms can eliminate the berm and the backshore.

Next comes the dune zone. It varies and is shaped by waves, wind, currents, and human intervention. It may consist of a single ridge of dune, several parallel ridges, or curved ridges. They tend to be narrow and long, composed of sand or other coarse sediments, blown up by the wind. Vegetation may or may not hold them in place.

When storm-generated waves wash over barrier islands, they can cut through the dunes and spread out into overwash fans, flat terraces located between or behind the dunes. Vegetation takes root on the flats and evolves into shrub thickets, marshes in saline and freshwater ponds or lagoons behind the dunes, and maritime forests.

Louisiana's barrier islands are low and narrow; their dunes low, discontinuous, sparsely vegetated, and broken by numerous washover channels. They are the first line of defense for the inland bays, the wetlands, and the mainland from storms. Each of Louisiana's barrier systems—the Isles Dernieres, the Timbaliers, the Plaqueimines, and the Chandeleur Islands—protect about eleven square miles of estuarine habitat behind them, prevent the intrusion of salt water, and maintain the gradients between saline and freshwater. They are the speed bump a storm must cross before surging inland and therefore can reduce coastal flooding. Without them ocean waves would attack coastal wetlands directly and erode them more quickly.

Restoration of the Caminada Headland would start at Ship Shoal, the remnant of the Maringouin Complex that was active about 7,000 years ago. It is a source of sand from outside the Barataria Basin. With the permission of the Minerals Management Service, the Louisiana Department of Natural Resources and the Corps of Engineers would mine between nine and ten million cubic yards of well-graded quartz sand from Ship Shoal and place it along thirteen miles of gulf shoreline.

To maintain the restored shoreline, the agencies had to understand the forces they were up against. They would have to replace 190,000 cubic yards a year to make up for sand lost to erosion and the rise in sea level. To put it another way, the agencies would start with the 430 acres of dune and berm habitat on the headland in 2000; they would add 529 acres of dune, bringing the total to 959 acres. But within the first year, forty-nine acres would be lost to erosion and sea level rise. At the end of ten years the dunes would be down to 750 acres, and would have to be nourished with the addition of two million cubic yards of new sand to bring the dunes back to 910 acres.

To add stability to the headland, they would measure the existing marsh elevation to establish design grade in the lagoons lying behind the dune. They would create a continuous marsh platform, up to five miles long and 1,200 feet wide. In 2000 the lagoons represented 1,200 acres and were growing ever larger year by year. The DNR and the Corps would add 400 acres.

In creating the marsh, once again, the agencies would have to consider the forces that are acting on the headland. Created marshes lose elevation three ways. Within the first year water seeps out of the new land and it compacts; within the next five years its own weight compacts it more; sea level rises. Grade stakes in the marsh would help the restorers maintain elevation as the fill was compacting.

To stabilize the dune, the agencies would run sand fencing the length of the headland and then plant native vegetation, bitter panicum and seaoats. After allowing the marshes to compact for six months to a year, they would plant smooth cordgrass.

Restoration of the dunes and the marsh platform behind would help preserve the cheniere live oak forests, the black mangrove thickets, and the coastal dune shrub thickets on the headland, all resting places for migratory birds and habitat for small mammals. The marshes would provide additional nursery for fish and shellfish, which would attract gulls, terns, pelicans, and wading birds. Leaf litter in the marshes would feed the marine worms, crustaceans, and insects, food for the Piping Plover and Kemp's Ridley sea turtle. Over all, restoration of the headland would help preserve the marshes to the north, the western boundary of the Barataria Basin. Sand eroding from the headland would nourish the beaches along Grand Isle to the east. And restoration would protect the valuable infrastructure at Port Fourchon and the evacuation route along Louisiana Highways 1 and 3090.

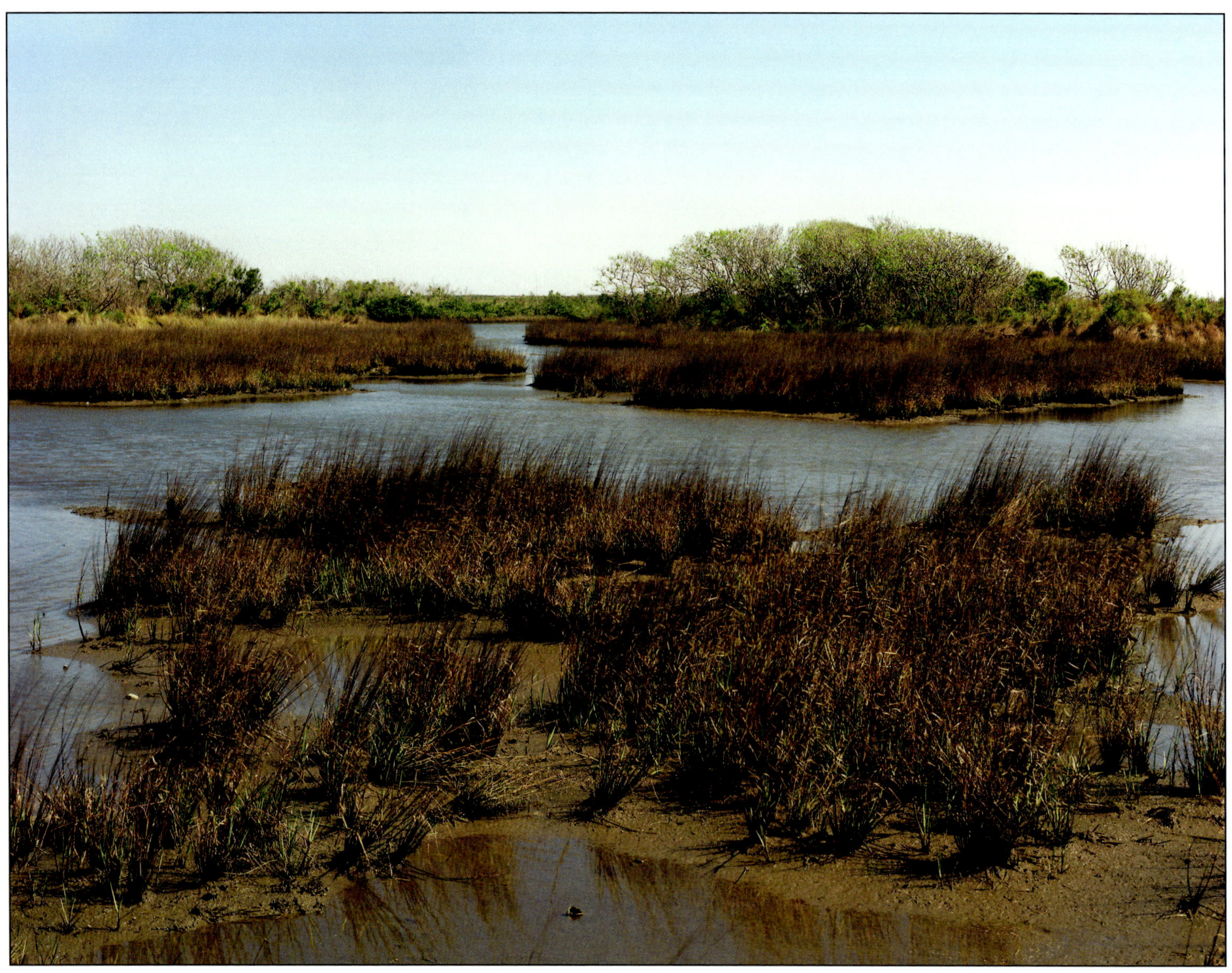

Caminada Headland: Mudflats South of Bayou Tartellon
Lafourche Parish, Louisiana

The Caminada Headland, the largest on the Louisiana coast, stretches from Belle Pass on the east to Caminada Pass. No other Louisiana headland remains attached to the distributary that formed it. A five-foot sand dune confronts the Gulf of Mexico, its front slope steep, its back slope gentle, grading into shallow marshes anchored in fine sediments in the back-barrier. One large lagoon and several ponds lie behind the dunes. Small bayous, like Bayou Tartellon, lace the back-barrier wetlands. Thickets of black mangrove, interspersed with smooth cordgrass, provide a nursery for fish and shellfish and a feeding, nesting, and resting area for birds.

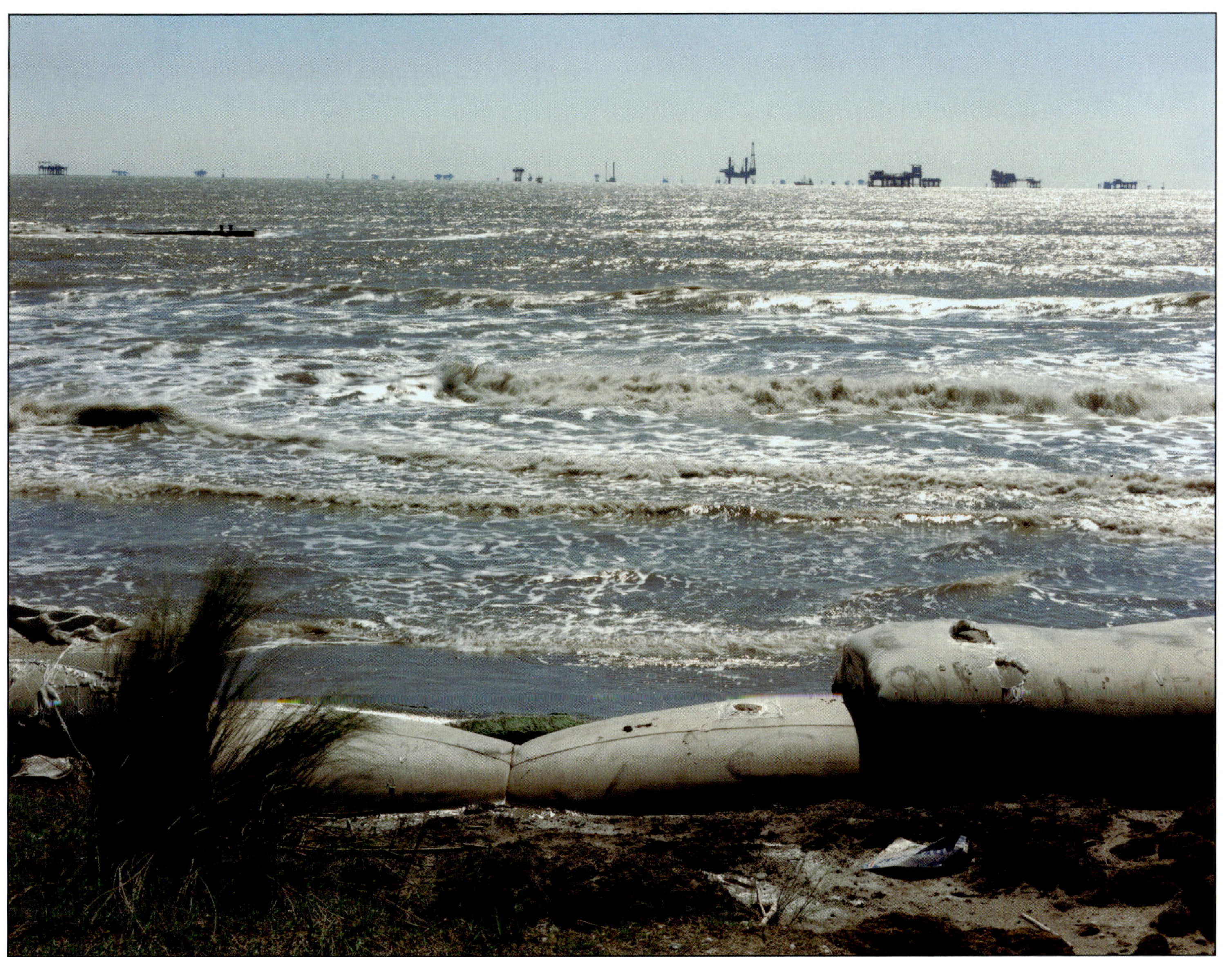

Caminada Headland: Gulf of Mexico

Lafourche Parish, Louisiana

Offshore breakwaters in front of the headland stop waves from dragging the beach into the Gulf during storms. Boudin bags, cement-filled geotubes, which line 5,000 feet of shoreline, do the same. Armored mats under 1,800 feet of boudin bags keep them from washing away. Shorebirds patrol the beach. Speckled trout, Florida pompano, and blue crabs attract gulls, terns, pelicans, and skimmers to the surf zone. Kemp's Ridley sea turtle feeds near the shore and in protected bays. Without headland restoration the surf zone would survive, but the saline ponds and lagoons—important to fish, shellfish, and their predators—would be much smaller.

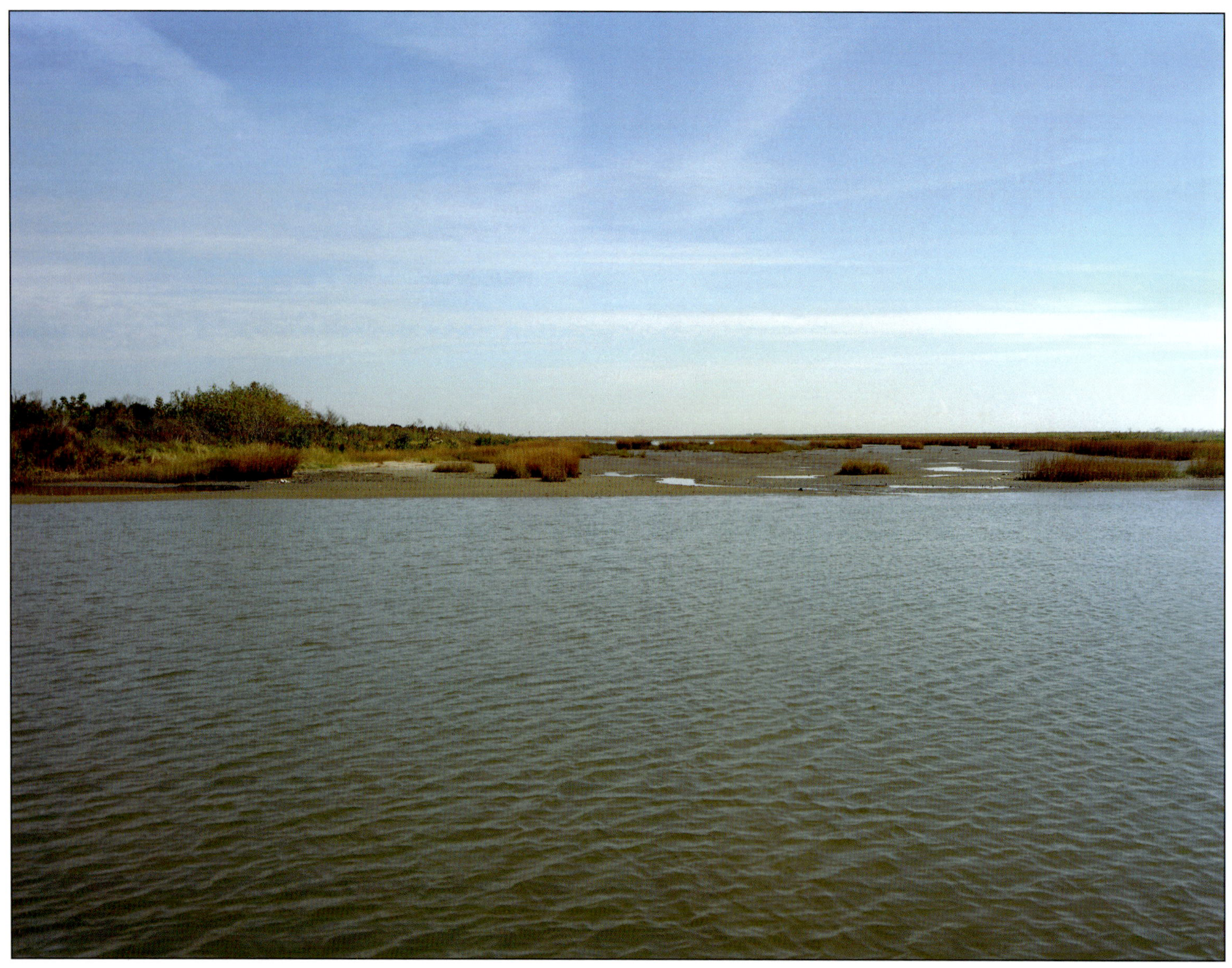

Inlet off Caillou Pass: Timbalier Island

Terrebonne Parish, Louisiana

Sand eroding from the Caminada Headland supplied sediment to the Timbalier Islands, a barrier arc. That stopped when the Corps of Engineers extended the jetties at the mouth of Belle Pass to 722 feet in 1969, blocking the transport of sediment to the islands, which eroded on their eastern flanks. Longshore currents carried eroded sediment to their western flanks. By 1996 Timbalier was a skinny island, measuring 1,114 acres, pinched between Caillou Pass and the Gulf of Mexico, 70 percent of its 1887 landmass gone. Its highest dunes measured less than seven feet above sea level, so low that storms could wash over it, break open tidal inlets, and fragment it.

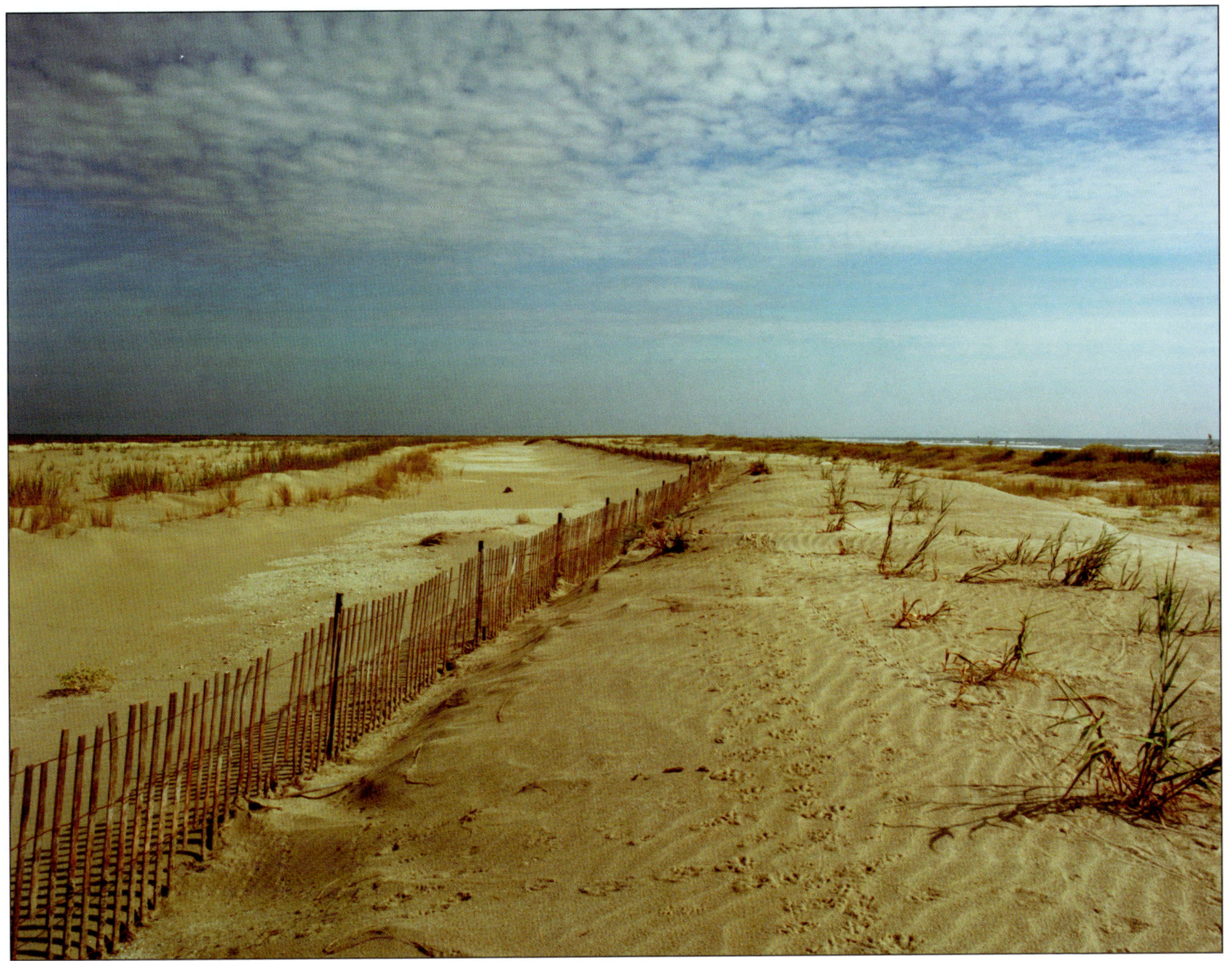

Timbalier Island: East Flank Marsh and Dune Restoration
Terrebonne Parish, Louisiana

In 1995 the Louisiana DNR and the NRCS set 7,390 feet of sand fencing parallel to Timbalier's shoreline to trap blowing sand and increase the dune elevation. They planted 17,250 plugs each of marshhay cordgrass and Atlantic panicgrass in rows on the bayside of the fence to trap more sediment and stabilize fine sands. But dunes rely on beaches for their sand, and beaches rely on dunes to hold sand in reserve and release it to the beach during high water. The fences do not add sand; they simply build dunes higher and hold it in reserve until it is released to the beaches. With so little sand available to build dunes, more sediment needed to be added.

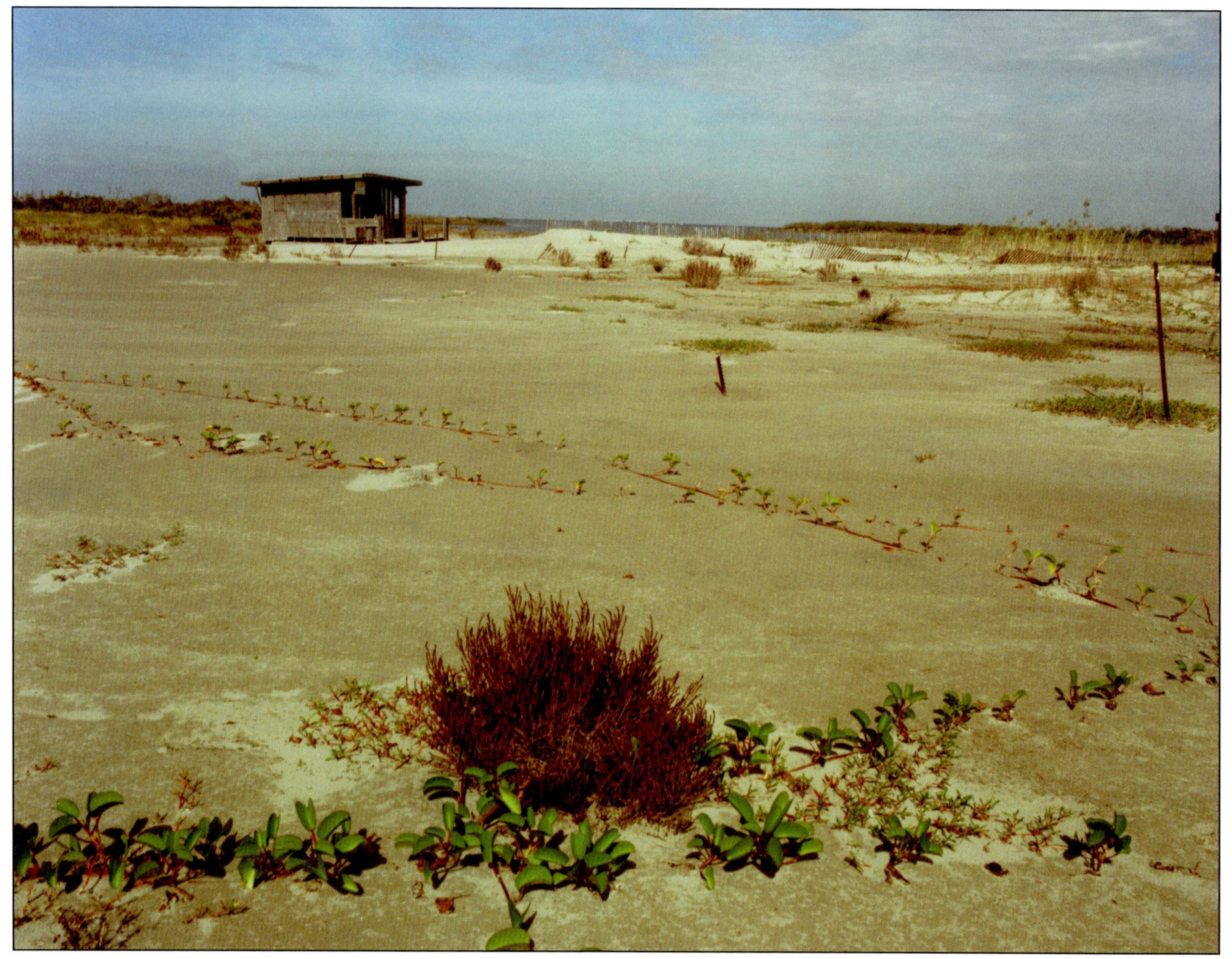

Timbalier Island: Marsh and Dune Restoration
Terrebonne Parish, Louisiana

The agencies returned to the east end of Timbalier Island in 2004 to pipe 4.6 million cubic yards of sand from the Gulf to create dune and marsh. They built 8-foot dunes, 400 feet wide on top, low and narrow to allow overwash to deposit sediment in the rear marshes. A back-bay berm, raised to four feet, protected the dune from assault from the bay. They constructed a low marsh platform, 1.4 feet, to allow bay-generated waves to create channels, edge habitat, and to let overwash sand come to rest. They anchored it with sand fencing and vegetation. The dunes done, sand eroding from the east end of Timbalier could nourish its west end.

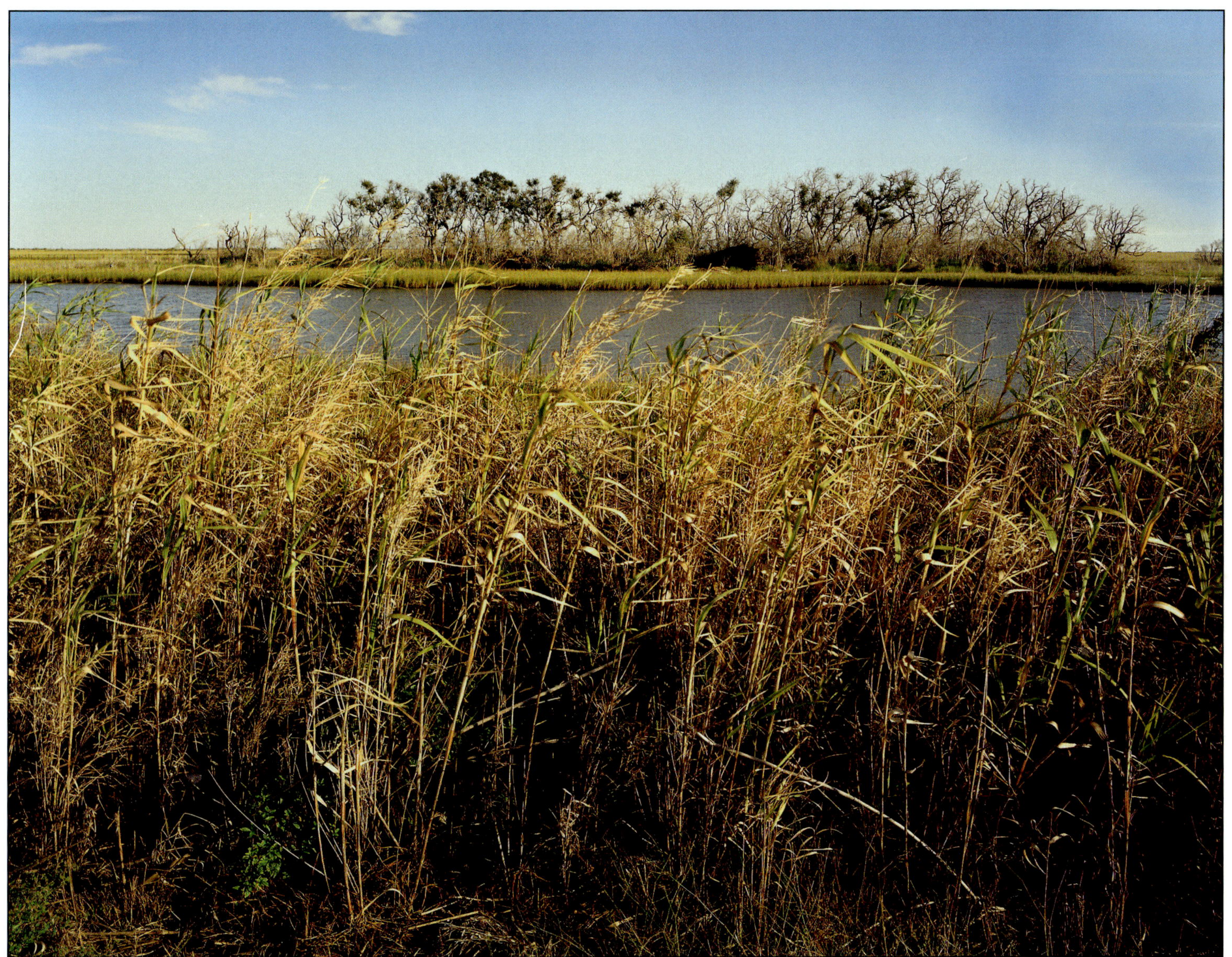

Cheniere Caminada: Fer Blanco

Lafourche Parish, Louisiana

Behind the dunes that front the Gulf of Mexico lie the cheniere ridges, parallel ridges hosting a rare cheniere maritime forest, treed in live oaks and hackberries. Saline marshes, linear ponds, and small lagoons occupy the watery spaces between the ridges. Migratory birds depend on the forests as resting places after crossing the Gulf of Mexico. Diving and dabbling ducks feed on the ponds and lagoons. The ridges are subsiding and eroding. Salt spray is killing the trees. Birds, already stressed by loss of breeding habitat in the northern U.S. and wintering habitat in Central and South America, are losing resting and feeding habitat on the Louisiana coast.

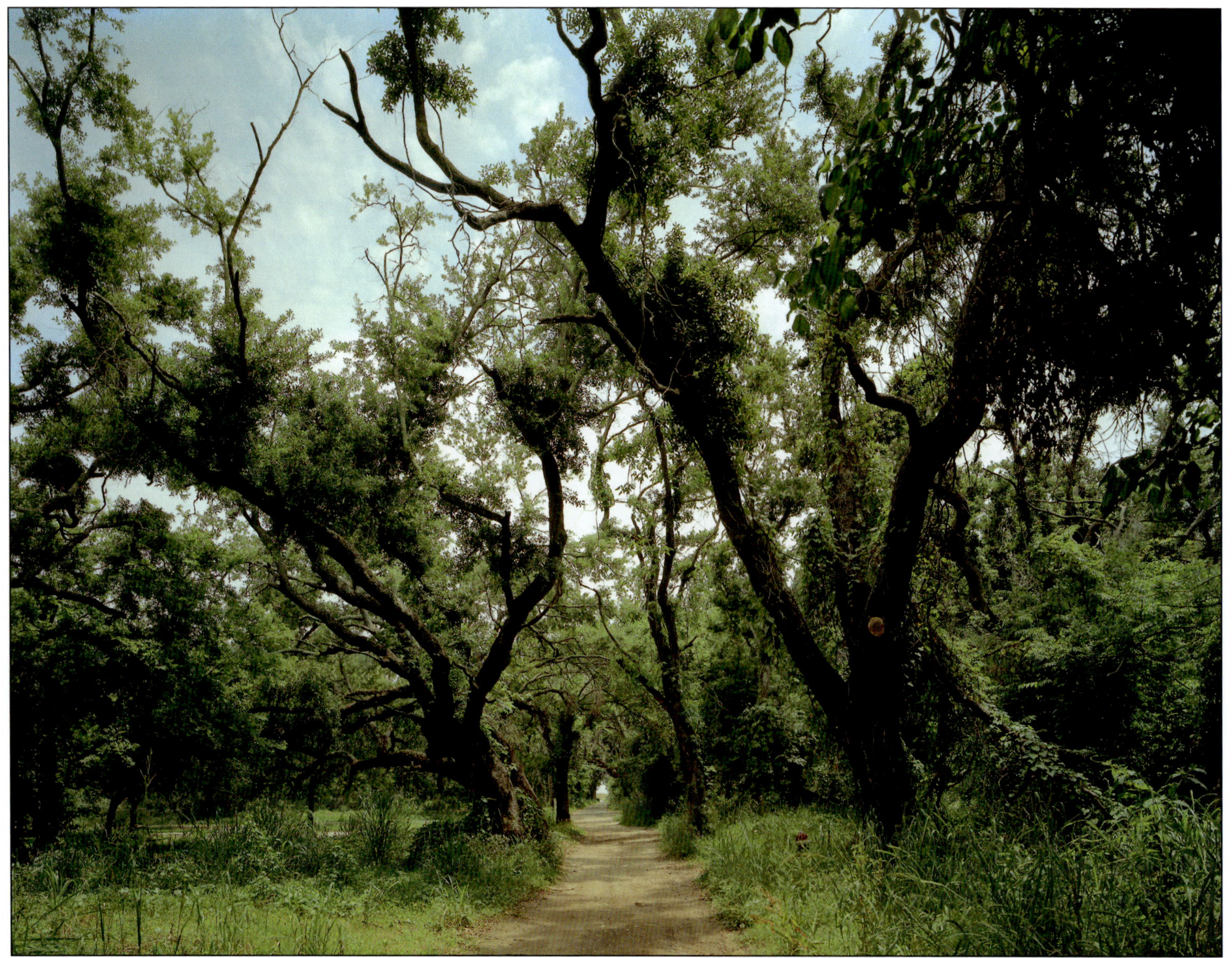

Grand Isle: Sureway Forest
Jefferson Parish, Louisiana

Grand Isle is the last place in Louisiana where we can find a maritime forest like Sureway Woods. Island development and the assault of exotic species left it fragmented. Salt spray left it stunted. Its rarity left our knowledge of it incomplete. The live oak forest has protected island residents from its earliest settlement. Farmers planted orange groves, blackberry and melon patches, and vegetable fields within it. In 1893 a ten-foot storm surge destroyed the great beachfront hotels. Houses built in the shelter of the trees survived. Katrina whipped across the island, stripped leaves from the trees, but the woods acted as a windbreak and saved the island.

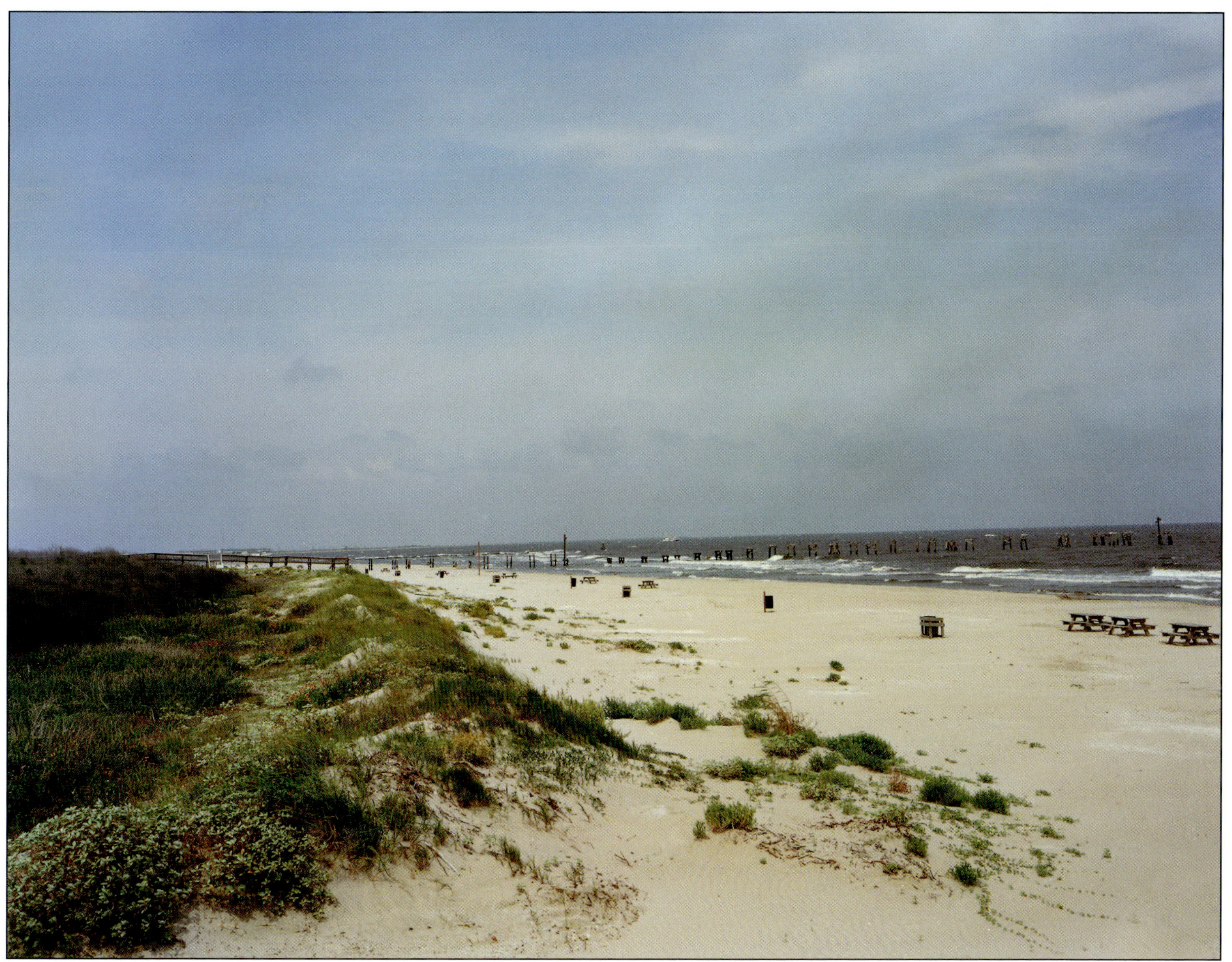

Grand Isle State Park: Dune and Thicket

Jefferson Parish, Louisiana

Dunes, elevated above high tide, are well drained, desertlike. The grasses—wiregrass, seaoats, and others—that take root tolerate salt spray and blowing sand. So do the forbs—frog-fruit, butterfly pea, and others. Vegetation root from fragments or seeds washed in by the Gulf. Some are succulents, able to retain water in a dry environment. Some creep under the sand, put down roots, and form a dense, stabilizing mat. Shrubs form thickets of wax myrtle, marsh elder, saltbush, and acacia. Human activity can be destabilizing. A foot trail, or worse, an off-road vehicle trail, can trample the mat and create openings for storm surges to do real damage.

The Lake Pontchartrain Basin

At the end of the glacial era as the ice sheet retreated and advanced, streams of meltwater, laden with glacier debris, oozed from its southern margins and filled the Upper Mississippi gorge with a series of valley trains, that extended clear to the Gulf of Mexico. Each downcut through the last. North of Lake Pontchartrain they are reflected in three east-west trending terraces that descend to the edge of the lake. Each is younger than the one above it. The lowest terrace slopes southward from sixty feet above sea level to the point where it slips below sea level.

When the rising sea reached about thirty feet below its present level 7,000 years ago, it flooded part of the exposed Pleistocene terrace in the vicinity of New Orleans. A thousand years later, when it reached ten to fifteen feet below the present level, sand washed into the Gulf of Mexico from the Pearl River westward on longshore currents and settled next to the exposed terrace. Sand accumulated and emerged from the Gulf as a beach ridge. With a temporary cessation of shoreline retreat, the ridge shifted to the southwest. In another thousand years the rising seas flooded more of the terrace but left the ridge exposed. The beach now measured five to ten feet above sea level and thirty-five miles long, a barrier island out front of the Pontchartrain Embayment. Soon after, the Mississippi diverted to the eastern side of its valley and flowed along the Bayou Sauvage. It buried the beach in sediment and formed the East Orleans Landbridge between Lakes Pontchartrain and Borgne.

The greater Pontchartrain Basin includes the Pearl River alluvial plain, which extends clear north to Jackson, Mississippi. It takes in 19 percent of Louisiana's land area. It holds 46 percent of its population, many of whom live in New Orleans and Baton Rouge. With the Pearl River swamps, the basin holds 2,100 square miles of marshes and swamps. When you take into account open water, the Pontchartrain estuary covers 5,800 square miles and includes the rivers that flow to Lake Maurepas and Lake Pontchartrain, the two lakes themselves plus Lake Borgne, Breton Sound, Chandeleur Sound, and the eastern half of the Birdfoot Delta.

When the Lake Pontchartrain Basin Foundation published its *Comprehensive Habitat Management Plan,* it broke the basin into four parts. North of I-12 pine forests followed by flatwood savannas dominate the Upland subbasin. Small rivers and bayous deliver freshwater to Lakes Maurepas and Pontchartrain. Its riverine swamps, Lake Maurepas and its wetlands, lie on or adjacent to the natural levee of the Mississippi.

Lake Pontchartrain and its surrounding wetlands make up the Middle subbasin. Lake Borgne and wetlands in Breton Sound and Chandeleur Sound form the Lower subbasin. They receive freshwater only indirectly and grade south through brackish and saline marshes laced by tidal channels and dredged canals to the Gulf of Mexico. Only the Upland subbasin is not influenced by tides. In the last decades of the twentieth century, the parishes in the Upper subbasin, particularly St. Tammany Parish, lost forests and wetlands to urbanization.

The piney forest along the north shore of Lake Pontchartrain startles the newcomer expecting cypress. Habitats that surround Lake Pontchartrain range from upland pines to alluvial swamps to submerged aquatics along the lakeshore. Rangia clams, which filter phytoplankton, bacteria, suspended leaf particles, silt, and clay, are abundant and clear the lake. Fish reflect the variety of habitats in the basin—largemouth bass and catfish in freshwater rivers; red fish and southern flounder in more saline waters; brown and white shrimp in the estuarine nurseries; American oysters in the transition zones. True sea grasses grow in Breton Sound and Chandeleur Sound, offering habitat to pink shrimp, hard clams, and scallops.

At the beginning of the nineteenth century the Pontchartrain Basin was in balance. The Mississippi and a distributary, Bayou Manchac, poured freshwater into the basin with each spring flood, flushing out salt water that had eased north during the fall and winter lows. Estuarine-dependent fish and shellfish lived out their lives according to the changing levels of salinity.

Infrastructure changed its hydrology. In 1814 Andrew Jackson closed the Bayou Manchac distributary at its head, cutting off the flow of freshwater from the Mississippi. However, the river did continue to flood the basin with freshwater until the construction of the levees in the wake of the Flood of 1927, leaving only the spring-fed rivers, rising in the Pleistocene terraces that rim the north shore of Lake Pontchartrain to carry freshwater to the lake.

The Bonnet Carre Floodway is the head of the Lake Pontchartrain estuary. The Corps has opened the stop-log structure about once every ten years, sending Mississippi water into Lake Pontchartrain and Lake Borgne. Though the initial response to the influx of freshwater to the brackish lakes is negative, for several years after, both lakes experience increased levels of oyster, crab, and fishery production. When the Mississippi runs high, but the spillway is not needed and remains closed, water seeps through between the stop-log timbers at a rate of less than 10,000 cubic feet per second, stimulating the natural cycle of spring flooding to the estuary and leaking small amounts of freshwater to the lake.

The East Orleans Landbridge is a wave absorber. Its marshes absorb storm surges that sweep out of Lake Borgne into Lake Pontchartrain and protect three parishes along its shoreline from flooding. It supports a nursery for estuarine fish, the Bayou Sauvage NWR, major transportation corridors (I-10, U.S. 11, U.S 90, and the tracks of the Louisville and Nashville Railroad), the primary evacuation routes, and a protection levee. The GIWW cuts through it, running parallel to U.S. 90.

The Manchac Landbridge between Lakes Pontchartrain and Maurepas supports its own infrastructure, which changed the way water flows across it. An elevated I-55 runs south on its piers, U.S. 51 and Illinois Central Railroad run on embankments, which isolate the eastern half of the landbridge from any freshwater that may be introduced from the Mississippi into Lake Maurepas.

The Mississippi River and Gulf Outlet, completed in 1965, connected Lake Pontchartrain to the Mississippi through the Inner Harbor Navigation Canal and completely altered the hydrology of the basin. The Corps of Engineers designed the deep-draft navigation channel to be 650 feet wide and 36 feet deep with a bottom width of 500 feet. The sides of the channel sloped at a twenty-five-degree angle, too steep for the soft soils to hold. The sides sloughed off into the bottom of the channel. Oceangoing ships dragged wakes behind them, which washed against the sides, eroding them. By 2005 wave-wash, propeller backwash, and tidal flows along MRGO had eroded its width to 2,200 feet. The Corps spent $22 million a year maintaining its depth to forty feet, dredging the eroded soil from the bottom and returning it to the spoil bank.

MRGO extended seventy-six miles into the wetlands. It cut through the cypress swamps that protected New Orleans and St. Bernard Parish from storms, shredded brackish and saline marshes that slowed and reduced storm surges, broke through the Bayou la Loutre ridge—a speed bump and the hydrologic barrier between Breton Sound and Lake Borgne—ripped up submerged aquatic vegetation that anchored the floor of the marshes west and south of Lake Borgne, and breached the Gossier Barrier Island chain.

MRGO had no flow that could counter daily tides from the Gulf, much less storm tides. Once it breached the Bayou la Loutre ridge, it reversed the natural north-to-south flow of water, tilted the basin out of balance, conveyed salt water from Breton Sound and the Gulf of Mexico into the freshwater swamps in the northern part of the basin, and converted 20,000 acres of wetlands to open water.

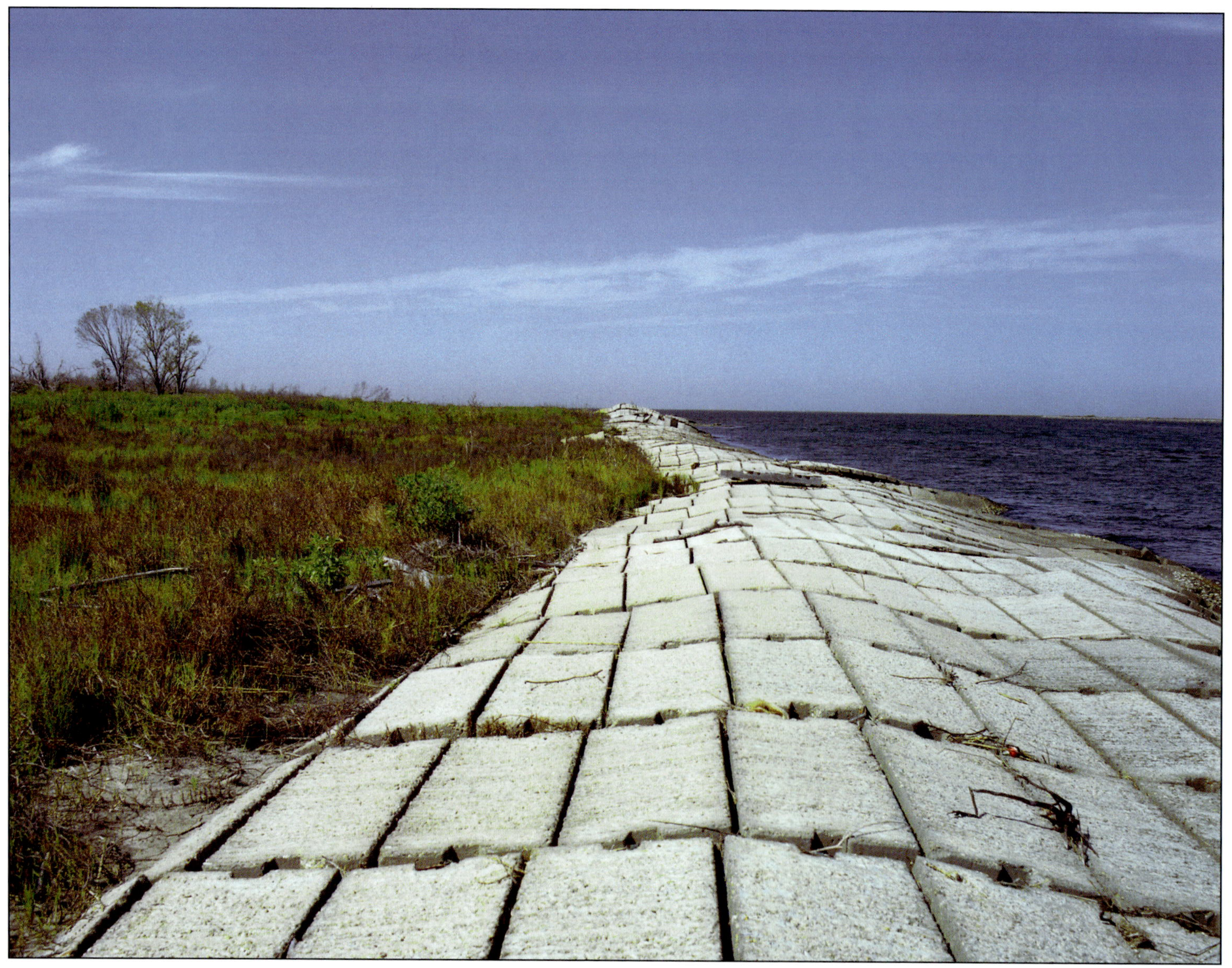

Mississippi River Gulf Outlet: Shell Beach

St. Bernard Parish, Louisiana

In all, MRGO had a negative impact on 618,000 acres of the basin. It caused major shifts in habitats and fisheries, created a 100-square-mile dead zone in Lake Pontchartrain, destroyed 1,500 acres of cypress swamp, converted 11,000 acres of fresh and intermediate marsh and cypress swamp to brackish marsh and 19,000 acres of brackish marsh to saline marsh, and finally, wiped out 4,000 acres of saline marsh. Rangia clam, the primary food for blue crabs and shrimp and Pontchartrain's natural filter, declined. Brown shrimp replaced white. Oysters moved inland to less salty waters. Furbearers lost habitat. A quarter million wintering ducks went elsewhere.

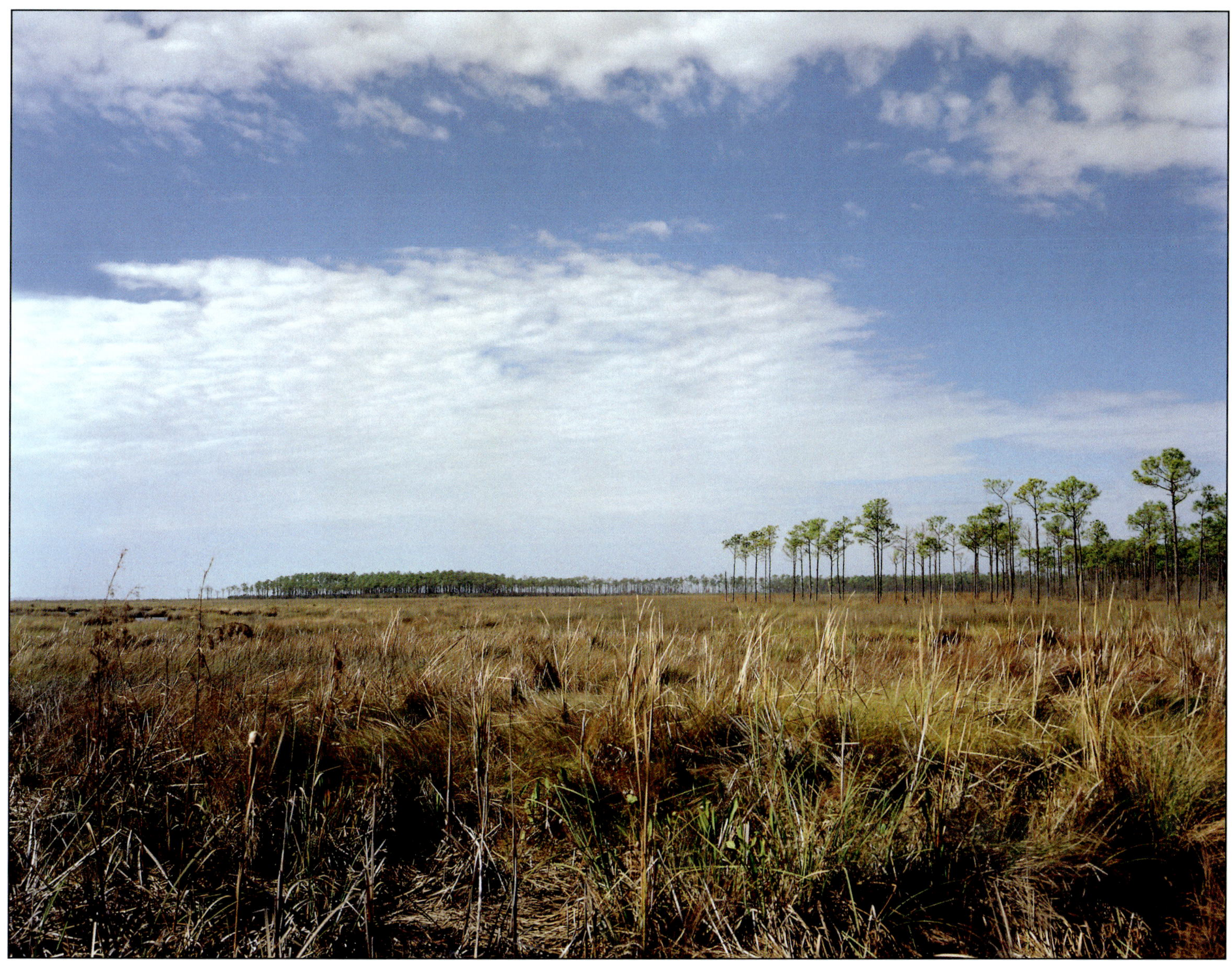

Big Branch Marsh National Wildlife Refuge: Marsh Adjacent to Bayou Lacombe

St. Tammany Parish, Louisiana

Between U.S. 190 and the lush beds of submerged grass in Lake Pontchartrain the Big Branch NWR contains 13,000 acres of open water and coastal marsh grading from brackish to fresh with salinities that depend on proximity to the lake, wind direction, and rainfall. Where the landscape rises five feet above sea level, slash pine, loblolly pine, and pockets of longleaf pine anchor the ridges. Coastal marshes spread under pinelands that fall below five feet. Scattered throughout 5,000 acres of forest are hummocks of hardwoods. Cypress swamps border the bayous. Katrina passed directly over the refuge, ripping through the woods, leaving few trees standing.

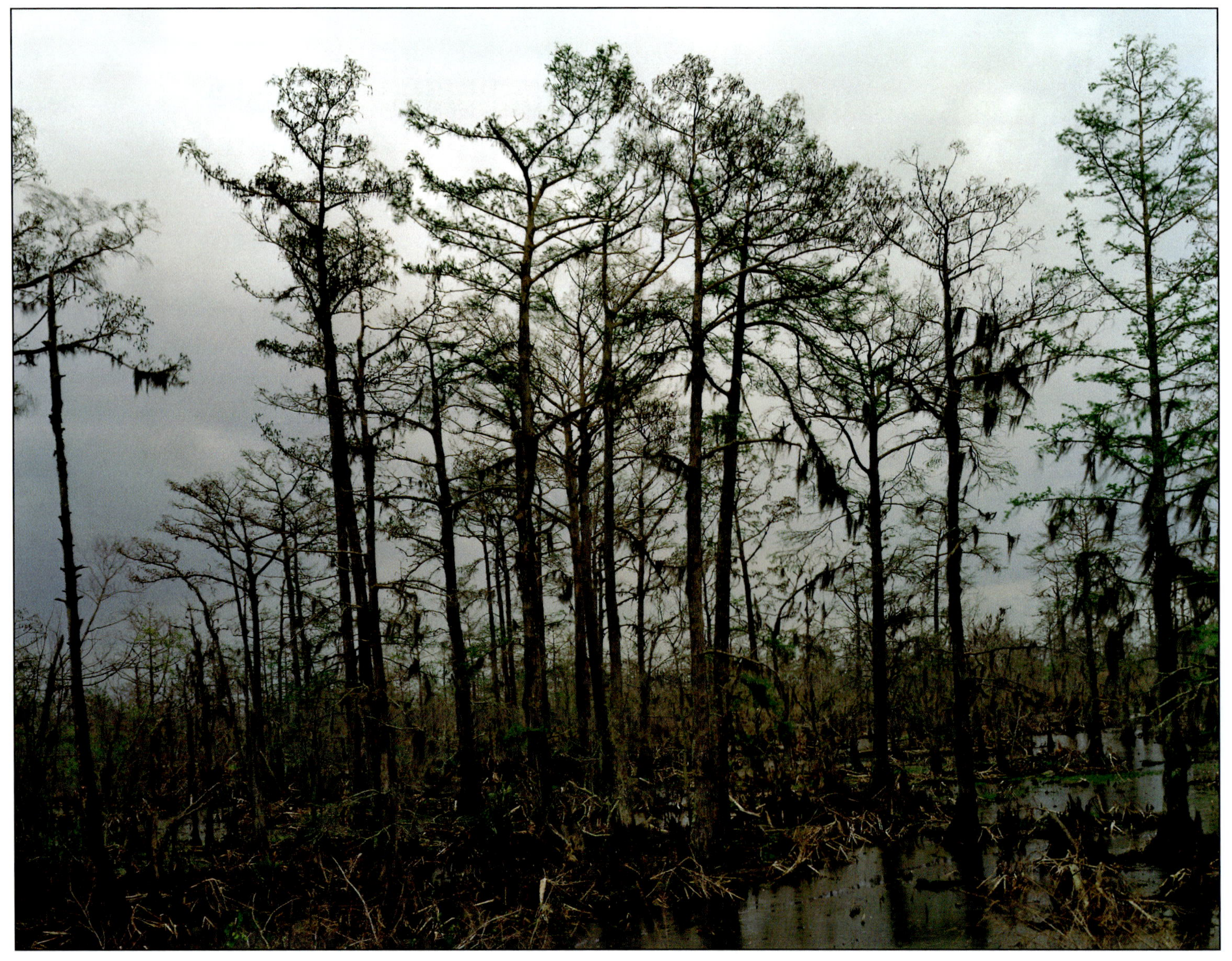

Manchac Land Bridge: Between Lakes Maurepas and Pontchartrain

St. John the Baptist Parish, Louisiana

When Europeans explored the landbridge between Lakes Maurepas and Pontchartrain in the 1700s and 1800s, they found a canopy of ancient cypress spreading over a healthy understory that supported indigenous swamp creatures. Commercial logging had decimated the forest by 1930. Loggers moved cut trees out of the swamp along ditches and canals that changed its hydrology and invited in salt water. MRGO raised salinity an average of 0.4 parts per thousand in Pass Manchac, stressing the cypress. By 2007 what forest remained was a flooded relic swamp, where young trees would not replace dying cypress and intermediate and brackish marshes replaced the trees.

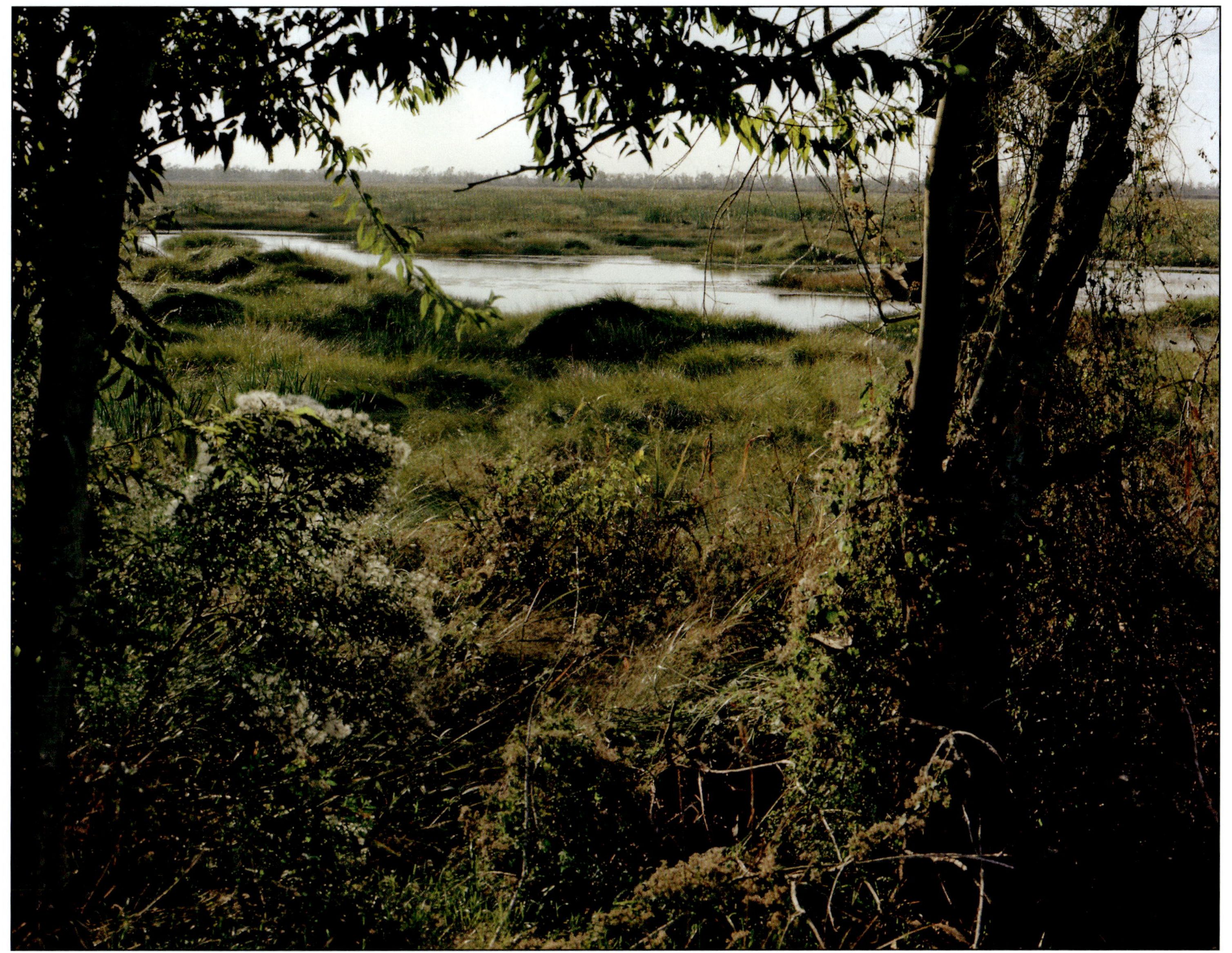

East Orleans Landbridge: Bayou Sauvage National Wildlife Refuge

St. Bernard Parish, Louisiana

The Bayou Sauvage NWR is located in New Orleans, its marshes confined to a bowl, surrounded by hurricane levees, and dependent on rain for freshwater. The USFWS manages it for cypress reforestation and moist-soil habitat for winter waterfowl. Should midsummer drought dry out the marshes, managers pump in brackish water from Pontchartrain, damaging freshwater vegetation. Urban birders drop by in spring or fall to track migrating birds. Wading birds nest in the swamp. So do Brown Pelicans, Mottled Ducks, and Wood Ducks. Anglers come for freshwater fish—bass, crappie, bluegill, and catfish. Katrina drowned its marshes and swamps in salt water.

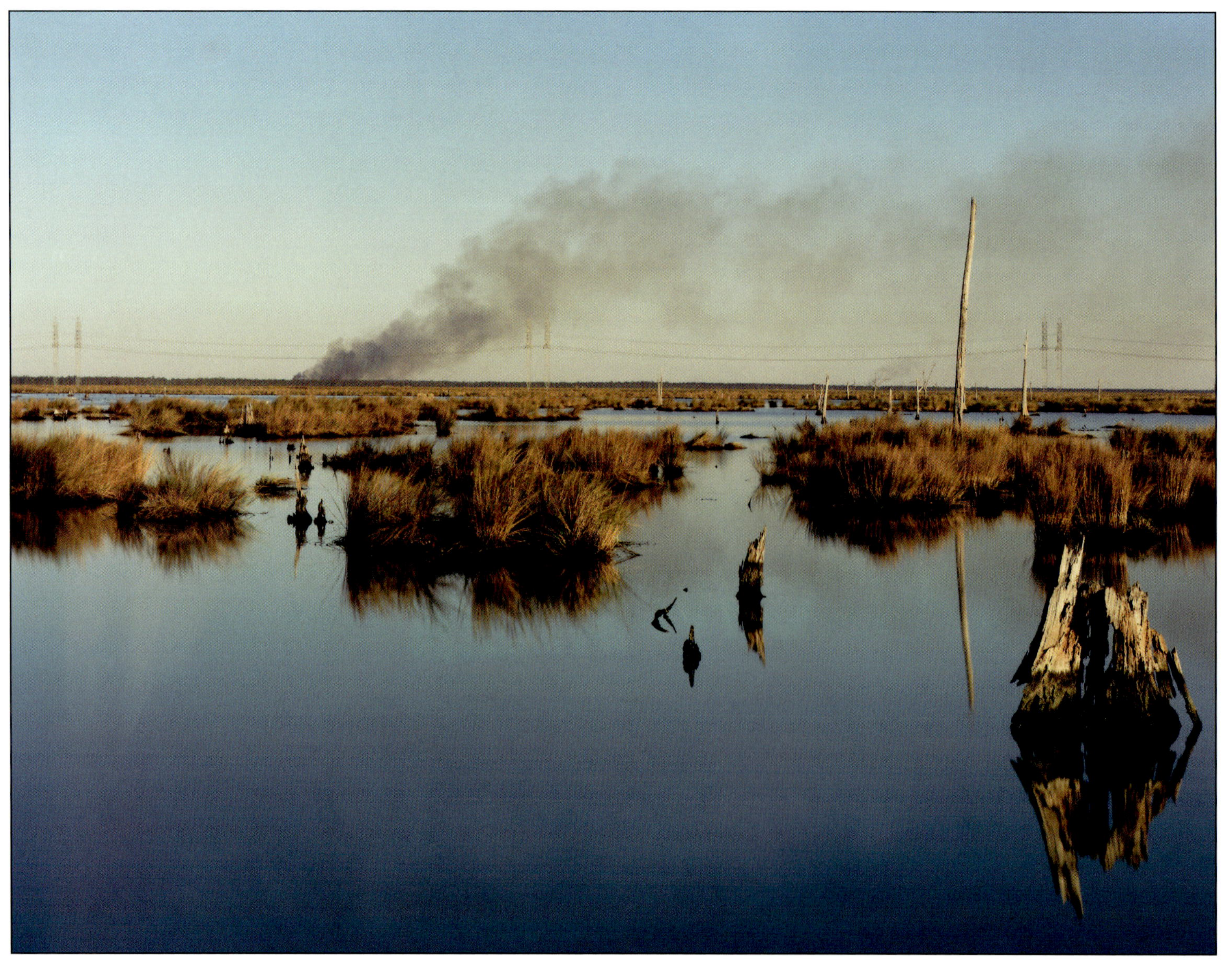

Bayou Bienvenue: North of Chalmette

St. Bernard Parish, Louisiana

In 1718 Bayou Bienvenue meandered through a dense cypress forest between New Orleans and Lake Borgne, which buffered hurricanes coming from the southeast. Lethal doses of salt water, ushered in on MRGO, killed off its wetlands impounded behind the MRGO spoil bank, leaving tufts of marsh broken by open water. In October 2006 LSU ecologists proposed pumping millions of gallons of treated wastewater from local sewage plants into the wetlands to fertilize 10,000 acres and push back salt water coming in from MRGO. Foresters would plant trees. In ten years a 30-foot cypress forest would protect the Lower Ninth Ward. The cost would be $40 million.

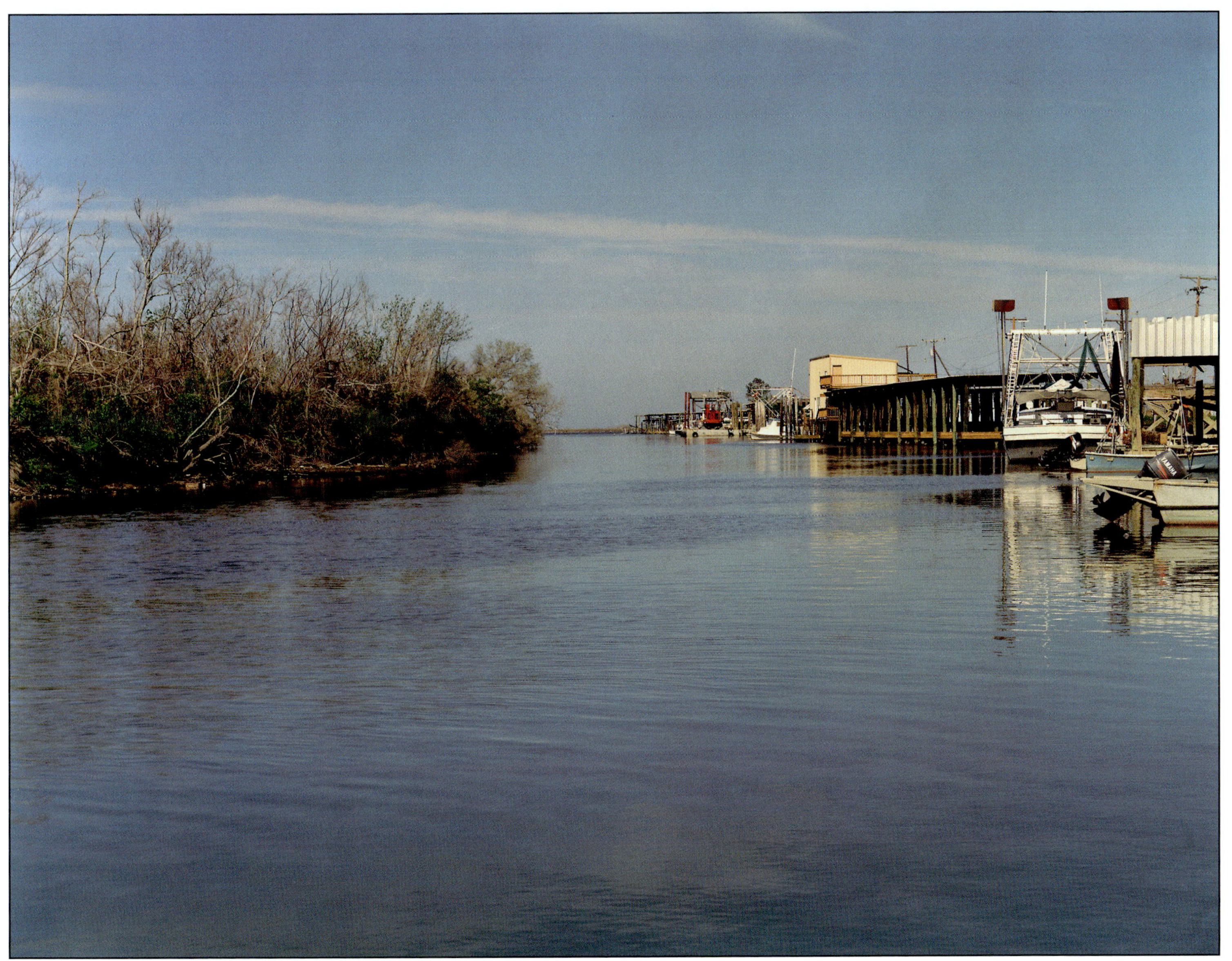

Bayou Yscloskey: Yscloskey

St. Bernard Parish, Louisiana

"As a whole, our fishing communities east of the Mississippi River are out of business. There are no docks to land the product, no ice houses, no fuel, no electricity, no cold storage, no marinas, no bait and tackle shops, no communities meaning no welders, no mechanics, no deckhands and on."—Ewell Smith, November 7, 2005

On the eve of Katrina, anglers moved their commercial fishing boats to the protection of the Violet Canal levee and saved their boats. Katrina's 18-foot surge leveled their houses and docks and washed them into the bayous along with their fishing gear, their infrastructure, and their vehicles—a loss of $943 million.

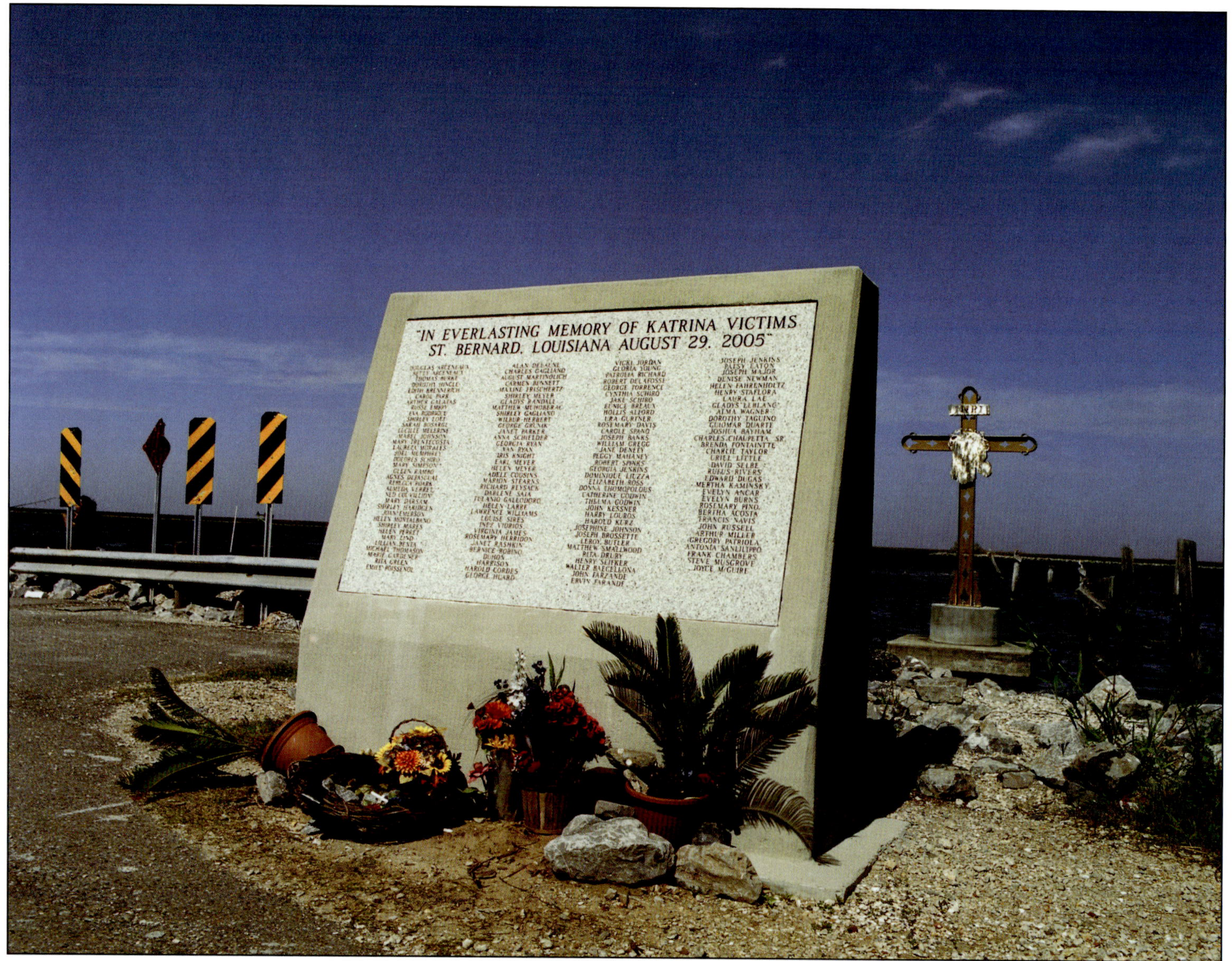

Bayou la Loutre: Intersection with MRGO

St. Bernard Parish, Louisiana

Residents of St. Bernard Parish put their memorial to those who died during Katrina at the intersection of Bayou la Loutre and MRGO. The cut through the Bayou la Loutre ridge changed everything in the Pontchartrain Basin. In January 2008 the Corps announced that it would close MRGO with a rock dike across la Loutre ridge, enlarge the Industrial Canal Lock, and dredge Baptiste Collette Bayou to sixteen feet by the start of the 2009 hurricane season. This would require navigation coming from the west on the GIWW to go down the Mississippi, out Baptiste Collette, through Breton and Mississippi Sounds to the GIWW east of the Port of New Orleans.

Breton Sound and the Birdfoot Delta

Three thousand years ago Breton Sound gathered its sediment from the deposits of the St. Bernard subdelta along Bayou Terre aux Boeufs on the east. Beginning about six hundred years ago, the sound gathered sediments from the Plaquemines subdelta along the Mississippi and the River aux Chenes, a small distributary on the west. When a distributary deposits sediment into very shallow water, it builds land very quickly. When Bayou la Loutre and other distributaries of the eastern St. Bernard complex deposited sediment in Gulf waters no more than fifty feet deep, they built a lobe that went past the Chandeleur Islands and extended another twenty miles to the east. That the Chandeleur Islands are only a thin chenier, the remnant of the front of the St. Bernard delta, lying about twenty miles from the mouth of Bayou la Loutre, demonstrates how much the Bayou la Loutre lobe has deteriorated since it was abandoned about two thousand years ago.

The Mississippi and the Gulf of Mexico performed their annual two-step year after year, exchanging freshwater for salt in the Breton Sound estuary: Salt water streamed into the basin on Gulf tides in the late fall and early winter; during its spring rise the Mississippi flooded the basin with freshwater and sediment and flushed out salt water. In the 1930s the Corps of Engineers ran their flood-protection levees down the west bank of the Mississippi to Bohemia. From then until 1991, when the Louisiana Department of Natural Resources opened the Caernarvon Freshwater Diversion Structure, Breton Sound depended on rainfall for freshwater.

From 1812 to 1960, brackish marshes in Breton Sound moved a little bit inland. After 1960 the pace stepped up. Oil and gas companies dredged numerous canals that crisscrossed the region, gobbled up 8,256 acres of marsh, extended to the Gulf, changed the way water flowed through the marshes, and allowed salt water into fresh and intermediate marshes. Erosion increased to 270 acres a year. In 1965 Hurricane Betsy washed in salt water and destroyed the forested wetlands in the backswamp of the Mississippi ridge close to the head of the sound, turning the area to open water. By 1986 brackish marshes with a salinity of five parts per thousand reached clear north to the Big Mar, an impoundment just off the Mississippi at Caernarvon. Oysters moved inland with the marshes. By the late 1980s rising levels of salinity and disease in Breton Sound were killing the oysters. Black drum and conch, saltwater predators, feasted on them. By 1990 salt water had destroyed 50,000 acres of private oyster beds, which ringed the southern rim of the marshes and lined the marshes off the east bank of the Mississippi. Oysters and levels of salinity have been an issue in Breton Sound ever since Slavonian immigrants found an abundance of oysters east of the Mississippi in the 1840s.

Louisianans began discussing the need for freshwater diversions through their levees as early as 1900. They first considered diverting Mississippi water into Breton Sound in 1914 to restore oyster beds. Each flood brought levee breaks that killed the oysters in the first year but boosted production in the following years. Beginning in 1926, the state tapped the Mississippi with small siphons designed to increase oyster production. In 1955 oyster farmers in Breton Sound requested a freshwater diversion. Four years later the U.S. Fish and Wildlife Service informed the Corps of Engineers that diversions would be advisable. Congress authorized diversions in 1965 and held public hearings in 1968 and 1969, when a diversion at Caernarvon was proposed. For a dozen years the state, the Corps, Fish and Wildlife, and oyster farmers discussed the pros and cons of a diversion. In 1982 the state signed on.

In 1986 Congress authorized a freshwater diversion structure to be built at the Caernarvon crevasse, located just short of the English Turn on the Mississippi fifteen miles south of New Orleans. It was at Caernarvon that the city of New Orleans blasted a crevasse in the levee on May 9, 1927, that released floodwaters from the swollen Mississippi to take pressure off its levees and save the city from a levee break. The purpose of the new diversion was to reduce salinity in Breton Sound and to increase habitat for fish and wildlife, including nutria and muskrat for the fur trade. Over the years Louisianans put more and more demands on Caernarvon as they learned how to use this new reconstruction tool and recognize its possibilities.

In February 1991 the Corps of Engineers and the Louisiana Department of Natural Resources opened gates in the Caernarvon Freshwater Diversion Structure for the first time. The Corps designed the structure to flow at the rate of 8,000 cubic feet per second. In addition to controlling salinity in Breton Sound, the project aimed to preserve 16,000 acres of marsh and benefit an additional 77,000 acres of marshes and bays. It must be noted that Congress did not authorize Caernarvon for marsh creation, but rather for salinity reduction. Marsh creation, it seems, was a by-product.

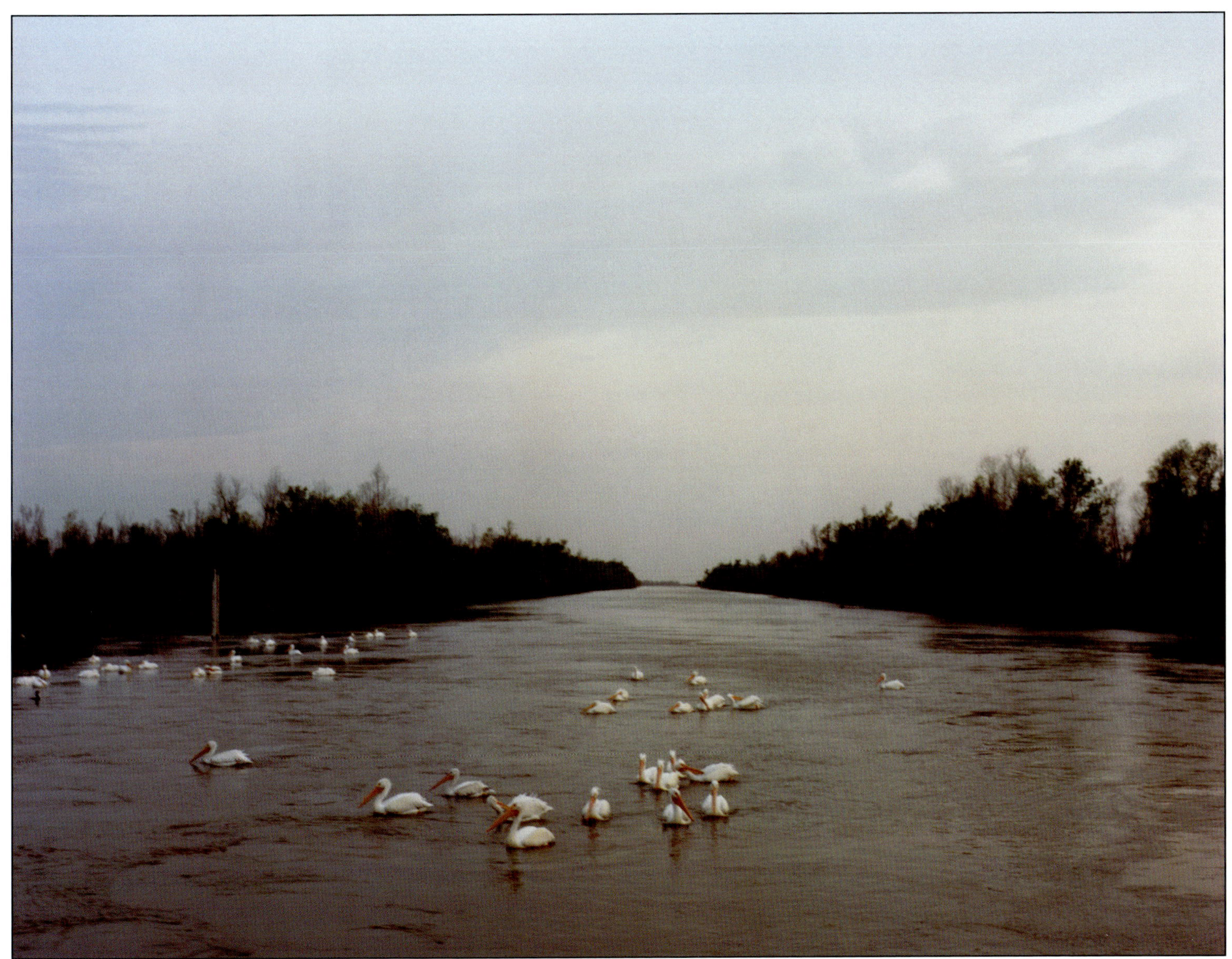

Caernarvon Freshwater Diversion Project: Outfall Channel

St. Bernard Parish, Louisiana

Over the years, the DNR changed the operations plan of the structure. At first the agency operated the structure to maintain salinity of state oyster seed grounds. From 1994 through 1996, the DNR kept the gates open in winter to maximize the sediment flowing to the outfall region and nourish vegetation. The third plan provided more consistent patterns of salinity at the five-parts-per-thousand line, which had been pushed south to the edge of 1986 oyster leases. The fourth delivered high and low pulses of water in the spring to mimic actual flooding, to hasten recovery after Katrina, and to manage the five ppt salinity line.

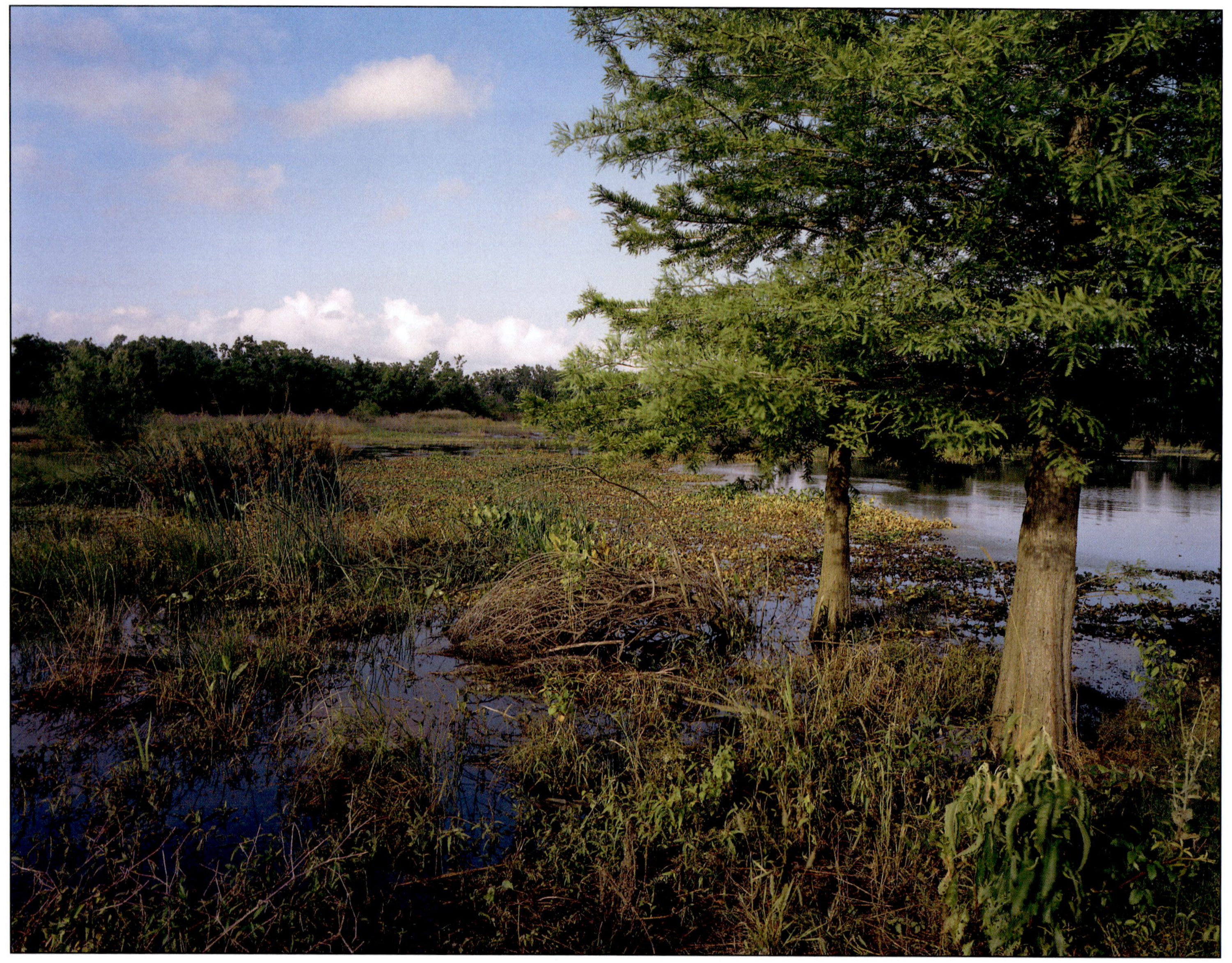

Caernarvon Freshwater Diversion Project: Delacroix Fresh Marsh

Plaquemines Parish, Louisiana

By 1998 freshwater marsh plants had increased seven-fold; salt marsh plants had decreased by half. Fresh marsh appeared near Big Mar and around Lake Lery to the east. Thousands of new oysters and 406 acres of new marshes removed nitrogen from the water before it reached the Gulf. Sedimentation kept pace with sea level rise. As salinity dropped, anglers caught twice the bass. Upward of 25,000 ducks wintered in the marsh. Muskrats and alligators built nests. White shrimp increased; brown shrimp, blue crabs, and redfish declined. Speckled trout stayed even. All this occurred with no fish kills, no algal blooms, and no decrease in water quality.

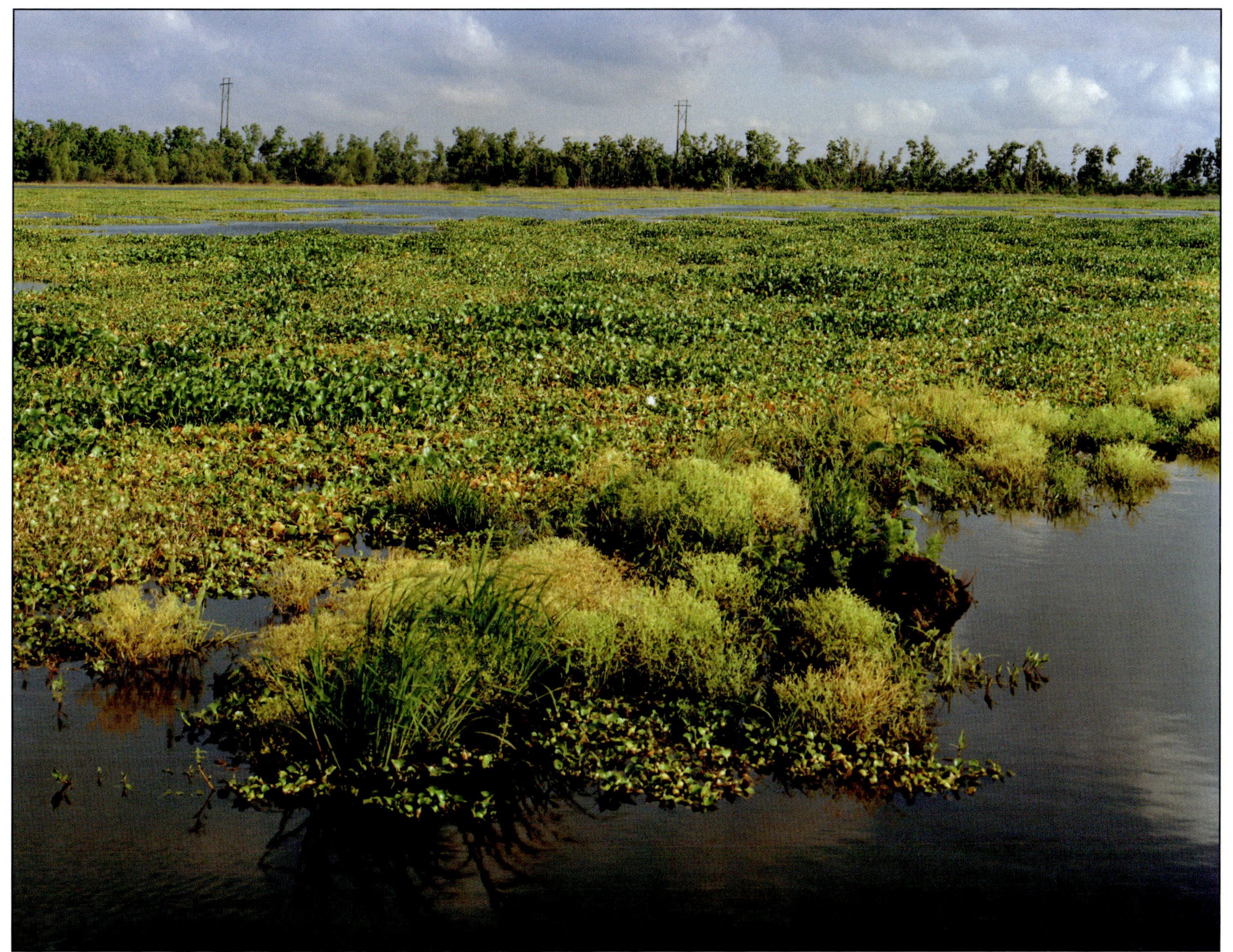

Caernarvon Freshwater Diversion Project: Wind Shear Area

Plaquemines Parish, Louisiana

Katrina's storm surge ripped across the fresh marshes, sheared them down to the root mat, pushed them into accordion pleats, then skidded them across the basin until they hit elevated ridges and dropped. Her winds rolled them into balls and scattered them across newly created, shallow ponds. She left behind forty-one square miles of open water, three feet deep in some places. But, for the most part, water merely skimmed mudflats. Possibly the marsh balls, made up of buoyant organic soils, would anchor in the mudflats and reestablish the marsh. The DNR opened the structure wide to deliver water and sediment to the most heavily damaged areas.

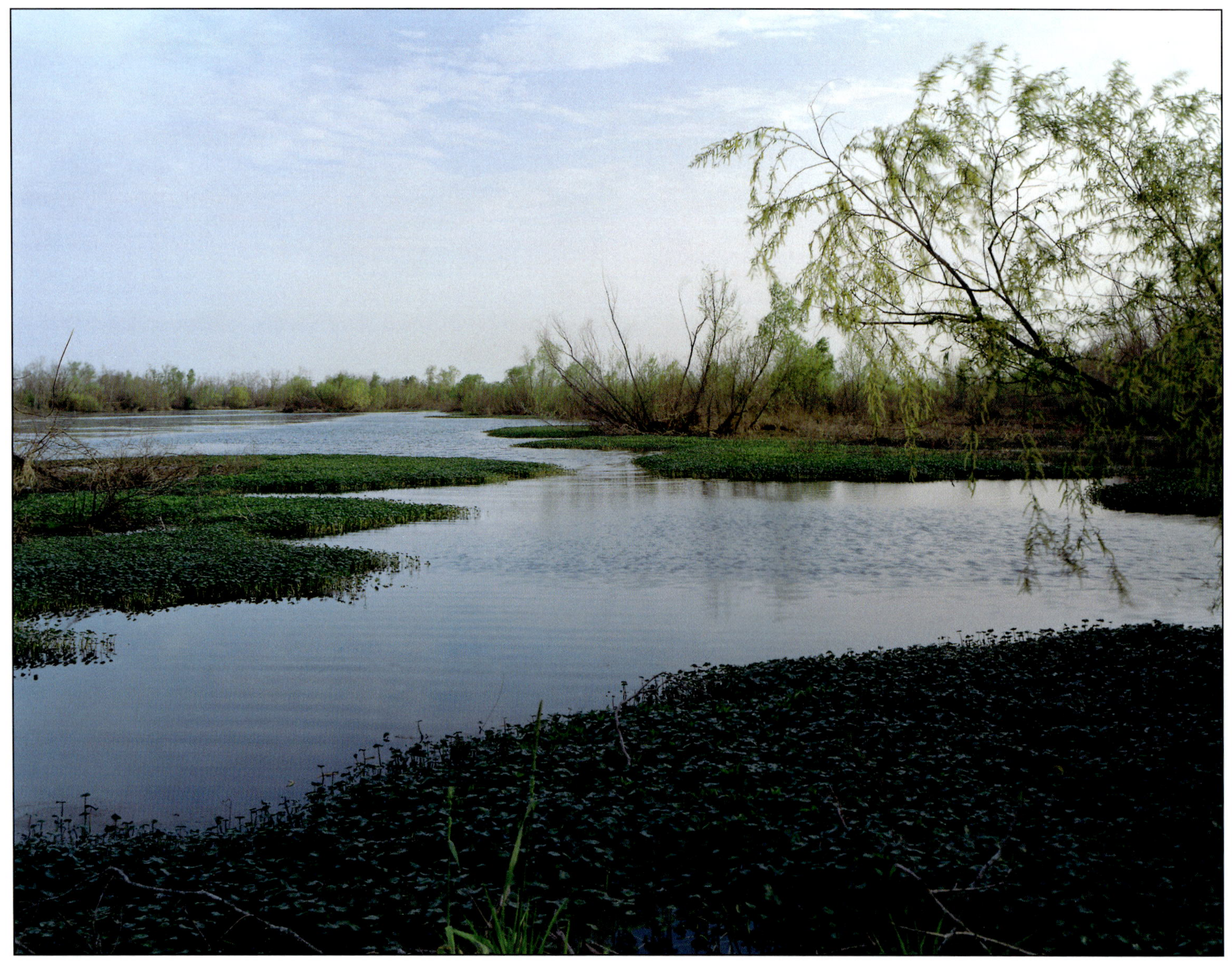

Caernarvon Freshwater Diversion Project: Recovering Marsh

Plaquemines Parish, Louisiana

In early 2006, USGS Landsat maps displayed the areas of open water and new growth in Caernarvon marshes. Trees along the Mississippi's natural levee were leafing out. Marshes were recovering near the outfall canal and Lake Lery. The rest looked dead. That all changed by September when the marshes along the Mississippi ridge began to thrive. Congress looked at future land loss in light of Katrina's damage and voted to spend $10.1 million to modify the structure. To deliver more sediment to the marshes, the Corps would dredge the river and run it through a pipeline threaded through the structure to the wetlands where it was most needed.

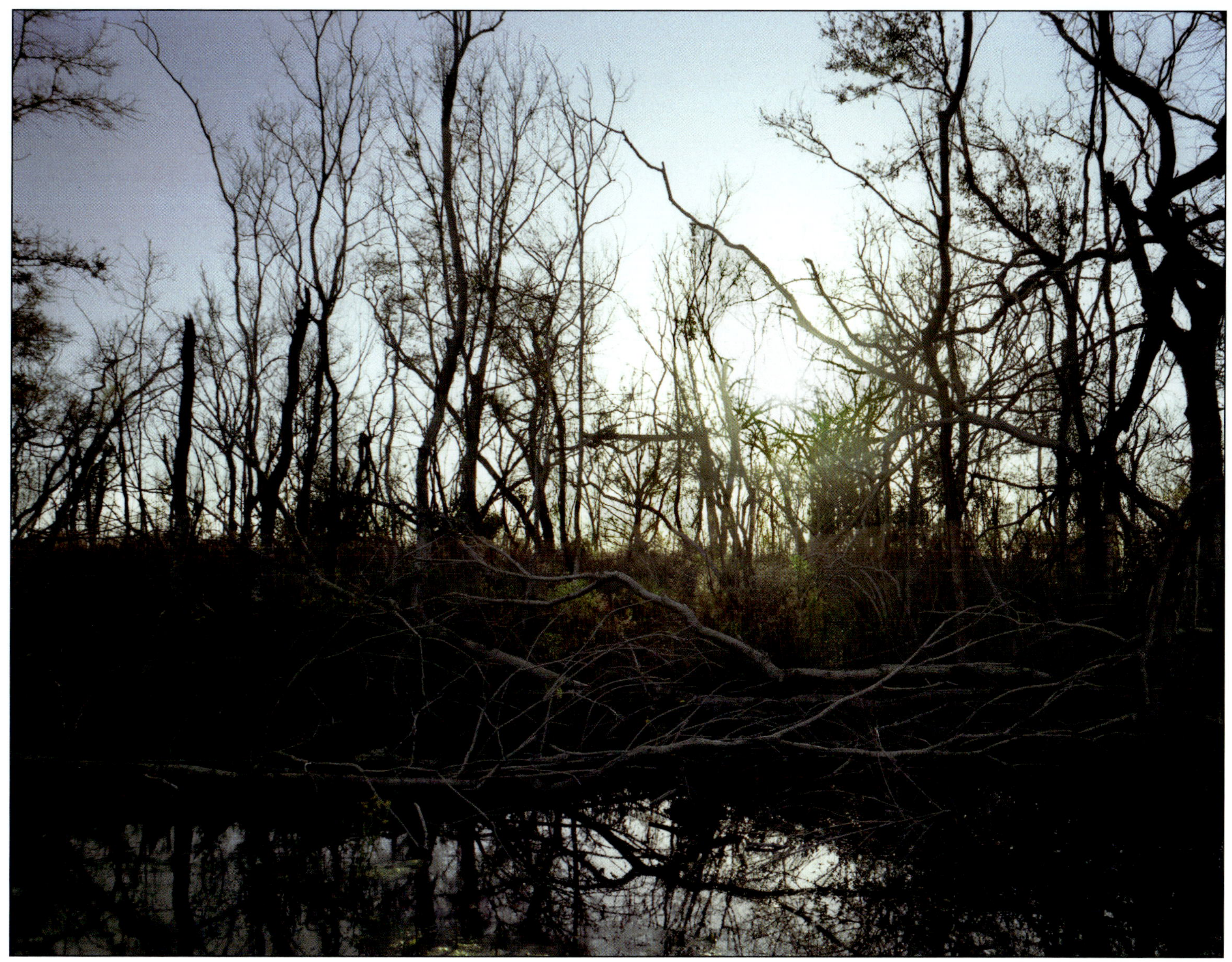

Mississippi River Ridge: Pointe a la Hache Relief Outlet

Plaquemines Parish, Louisiana

The 2004 LCA Study emphasized diverting freshwater and sediment into Breton Sound. So did the post-Katrina 2007 Comprehensive Master Plan and Corps' post-Katrina proposal. The coastal scientists and engineers who published the multiple lines of defense strategy in August 2007 recommended allowing the Mississippi to wash over its banks, at rates of up to 100,000 cubic feet per second, over the twenty miles south of Bohemia, where the mainline levee ends, thus allowing scientists to observe how the river develops its natural levee, a habitat unique to Louisiana, where all other ridges were under intense development.

The Birdfoot Delta

> Nothing is more certain than that the Delta has gradually risen out of the sea, or rather that it has been formed by alluvious substances, precipitated by the waters from the upper regions. It is calculated that, from 1720, to 1800, a period of eighty years, the land has advanced fifteen miles into the sea; and there are those who assert that it has advanced three miles within the memory of middle aged men.
>
> —Maj. Amos Stoddard, 1814

Venice, like Port Fourchon, serves as a base for oil exploration and fishing expeditions. Katrina washed over the ring levee that surrounds it and roared through town, scattering oilfield vessels, fishing boats, and barges across the landscape and leaving wrecked boats both outside and inside the levee. Venice lies northwest of the Head of Passes, where the Mississippi breaks into its Birdfoot Delta. Several small distributaries break off from the Mississippi at Venice.

There was a time when Spanish Pass, Red Pass, and Tiger Pass, all small distributaries, broke away from Grand Pass, a large distributary, and delivered water and sediment to the bay to the west. Levees, roads, and other infrastructure cut Spanish Pass and Red Pass from Grand Pass, their source of water and sediment. To the west hurricanes wiped out flotant marshes. Newly dredged canals in the Venice Oil Field changed the way water flowed across the marshes and invited in salt water. The land subsided at the rate of 3.5 feet per century.

In 1949 freshwater marshes and swamps, including flotant marshes, spread across the small basins bordered by the ridges of the distributaries, large and small, west of the river and between Venice and Southwest Pass. Within twenty years they evolved into a mix of fresh and intermediate marshes. In the next twenty years more and more salt water crept into the wetlands. Intermediate marshes turned saline; fresh marshes turned intermediate. Still, in 1988, 30 percent of the marshes remained fresh.

The land loss was astounding: 38,400 acres out of 59,640 gone between 1932 and 1974. By 1990 only 7,980 acres remained. At that rate another 1,870 acres would disappear by 2050. In 2005 Hurricane Katrina came along and transformed 17.8 square miles of fresh and intermediate marshes in the Birdfoot Delta to open water.

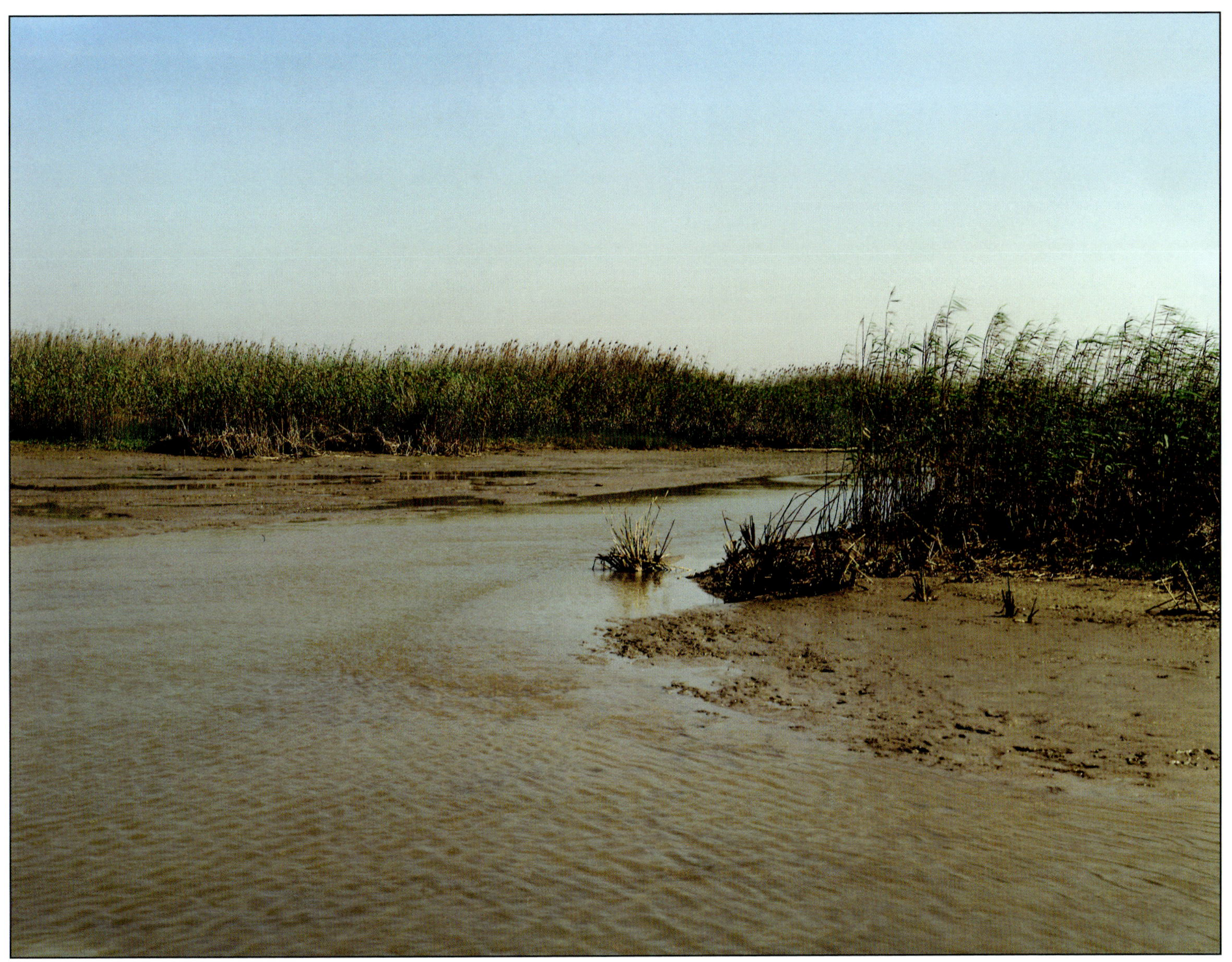

Delta National Wildlife Refuge: Crevasse

Plaquemines Parish, Louisiana

In 1935 the USFWS purchased 48,000 acres from the Delta Duck Club in the triangle between Main and Raphael Passes. Within forty years 75 percent of the refuge had submerged, on its way to becoming open water. In 1978 a crevasse opened in Brant Bayou in the refuge; freshwater and sediment poured through and built a square mile of emergent marsh. Refuge engineers noticed and added the crevasse to their restoration toolbox. By 1995 they had opened up twenty-four crevasses, producing 711.7 acres of new land. The DNR created four crevasses in its Pass-a-Loutre WMA, producing over 400 acres. One in South Pass yielded 353.1 acres; one on Loomis Pass 113.7 acres.

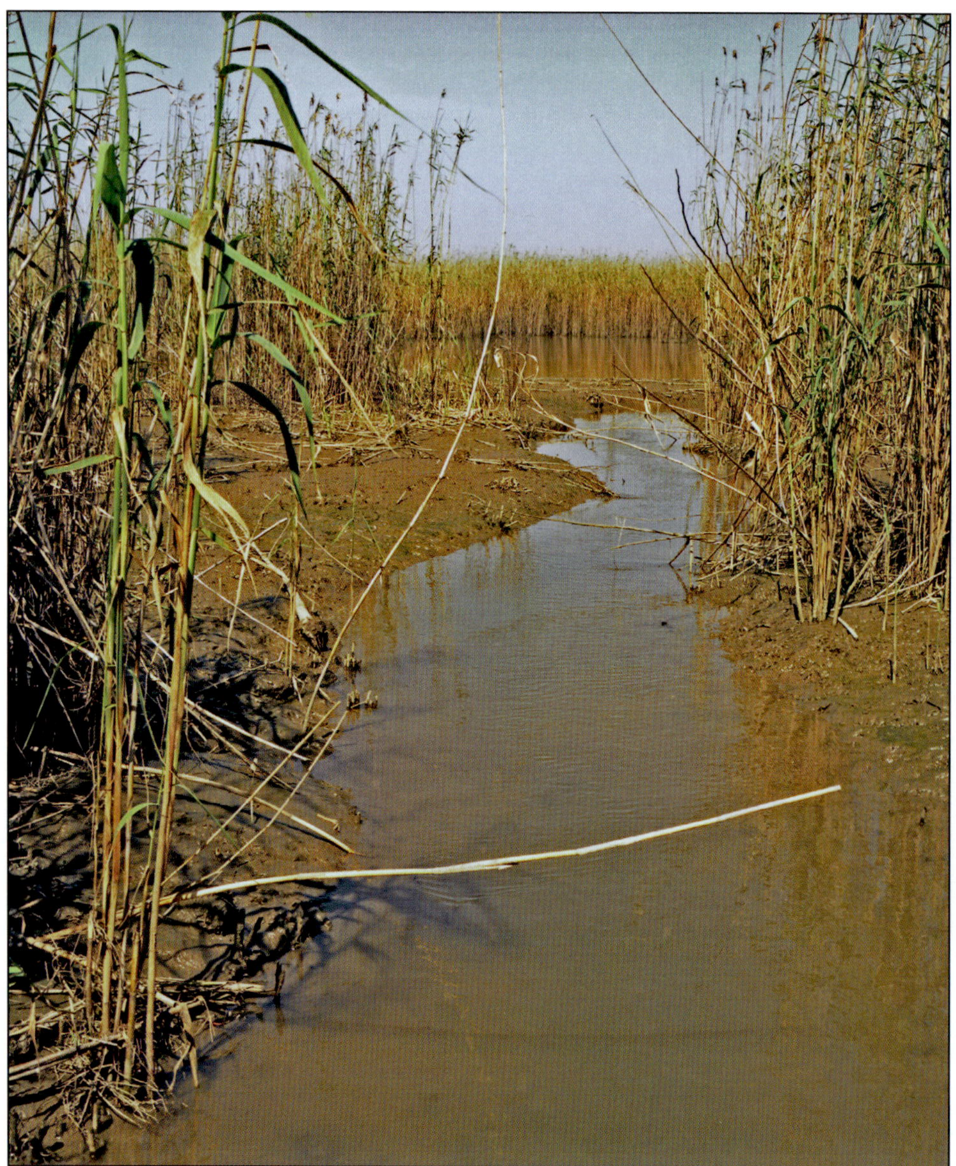

Delta National Wildlife Refuge: Roseau Cane

Plaquemines Parish, Louisiana

Crevasses are old and simple, cheap and easy to construct. And maybe, design engineers found out, not so simple. Designers needed to consider the angle of the cut in the bank; the size of the receiving bay, its gradient, its depth, and its outflow ability; the size of the cross-sections of the parent channel and the crevasse; the depth of the crevasse; its slope; and the number of bifurcations (how many times it splits into two smaller channels). Then there are the uncontrollables—river stage, flow velocity, sediment load in the water column, distance from the main channel—that govern the growth of new land once a crevasse splay is created.

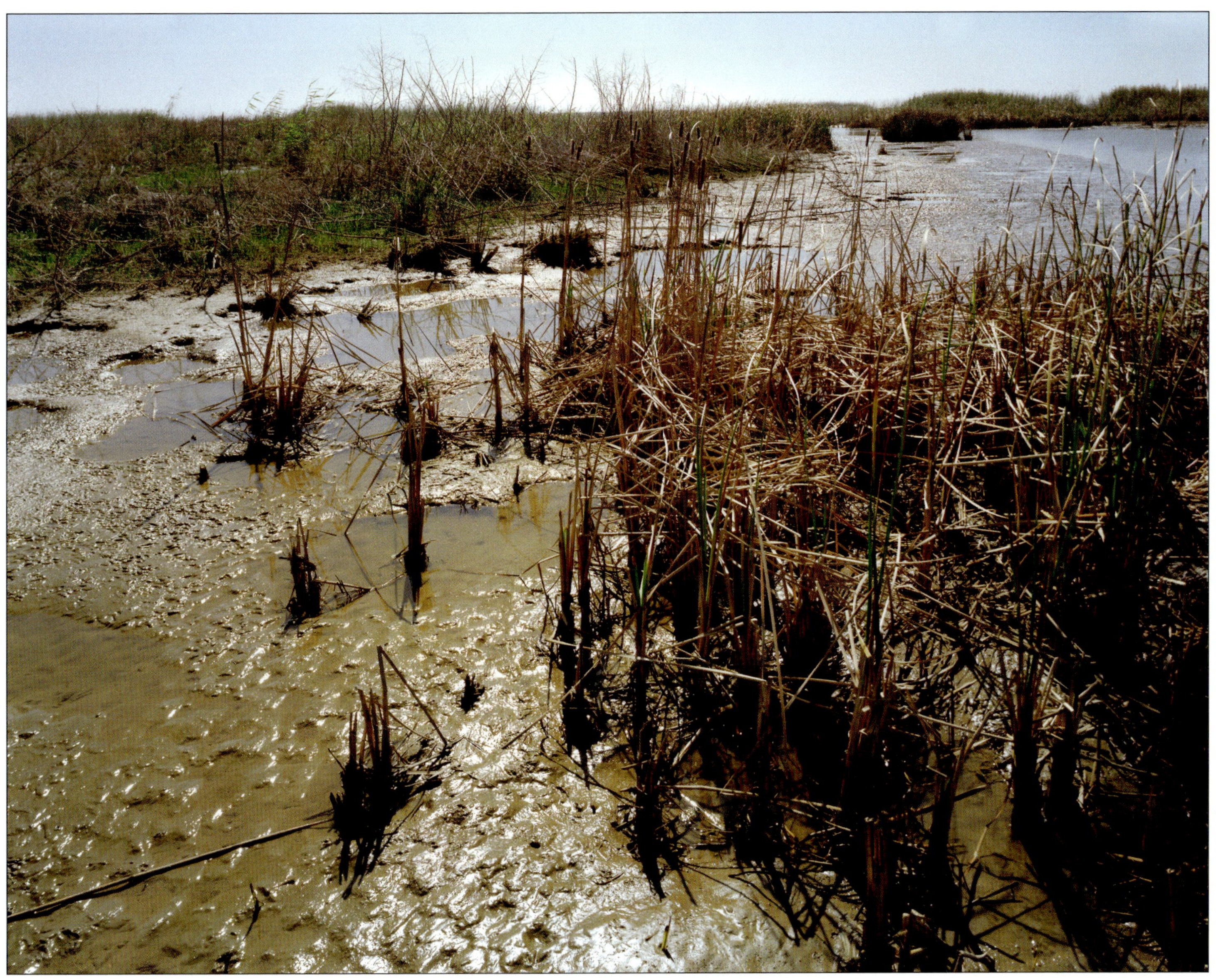

Delta National Wildlife Refuge: Mud

Plaquemines Parish, Louisiana

"Manchac down to the sea, it is probable, and even some degree certain, that all the lands thereabouts are brought down and accumulated by means of the ooze, which the Mississippi carries along with it in its annual inundations; which begin in the month of March by the melting of the snow to the north, and last for about three months. Those oozy or muddy lands easily produce herbs and reeds; and when the Mississippi happens to overflow the following year, these herbs and reeds intercept a part of this ooze, so that those a distance from the river cannot retain so large a quantity of it, since those that grow near the river have stopt the greatest part; and by a necessary consequence, the others farther off, and in proportion as they are distant from the Mississippi, can retain a much less quantity of mud. In this manner the land rising higher along the river, in process of time the banks of the Mississippi became higher than the lands about it. In like manner also these neighbouring lakes, on each side of the river, are remains of the sea, which are not yet filled up."—Antoine Simon Le Page du Pratz, 1718–1734

Mud and the Mississippi

> Relocating the Mississippi River sediment distributary system out of the deep draft navigation channel is needed to prevent loss of sediment off the continental shelf and provide long-term sustainability and create new marsh in the lower basin.
>
> —U.S. Army Corps of Engineers, Louisiana Comprehensive Coastal Protection Master Plan, May 2007

Mud: it's the most important ingredient the Mississippi has to contribute to coastal restoration. Where the river deposits these mineral soils in still waters, they settle and build land. Freshwater and nutrients come with the mud and nourish the vegetation that takes root in it. The vegetation holds mud in place, filters more mud out of the water column, grows, dies, and decays into organic soil, and sustains the new land against subsidence and rising sea levels.

Mississippi mud came from windblown loess—rock flour—deposited on the uplands overlooking the Upper Mississippi and returned to the river by its tributaries. It came from the limestone and sandstone canyons of the Upper Mississippi, from the glacial debris that lined the banks of the Ohio, from the shale and sandstone cliffs of the Upper Missouri, from the eroded banks of the Lower Mississippi. And in the twentieth century when we built dams on the Upper Mississippi, on the Upper Missouri, and on the Ohio, when we built headwater dams on all the tributaries of the Lower Mississippi, when we built revetments on the Lower Mississippi to straighten its channel and stop its meandering ways, and when we diverted a third of the river's water and mud to the Atchafalaya, we deprived the river of this most valuable ingredient. At the beginning of the twenty-first century the river delivered 80 percent less sediment to the Gulf of Mexico than it had at the beginning of the twentieth. And because we turned Southwest Pass into a deep-draft navigation channel, what mud was left in the water column poured out of the pass and drifted westward, driven by the wind, away from the delta and over the continental shelf.

The Corps of Engineers may have put what needs to be done about Mississippi mud in eye-crossing bureaucratese, but "relocating the Mississippi River sediment distributary system out of the deep draft navigation channel," defined the issue in a nutshell. In May 2007, two years after Katrina and Rita, it was just as important to abandon the Birdfoot Delta, and redirect the Mississippi's freshwater, nutrients, and sediment into Breton Sound to the east and the Barataria Basin to the west, as it was to abandon MRGO and its destructive ways. The caveat was that it was also necessary to maintain a deep-draft navigation channel along the river. Plaquemines Parish wanted to solve that problem by turning Bayou Baptiste Collette into a deep-draft channel through Breton Sound to the Gulf of Mexico, and in January 2008 the Corps announced plans to do so, at least temporarily, while it enlarged the Industrial Canal.

Three years before the release of the Corps' response to Katrina, the 2004 draft of the LCA Study did not really consider abandoning the Birdfoot Delta, even though the notion had been in the air since Ivor van Heerden proposed abandonment in 1994. Instead, the plan put a Mississippi River Delta Management Plan, a study to maximize the use of sediments, nutrients. and freshwater in Breton Sound and the Barataria Basin, off into the future. It was something that would require Congressional authorization.

The state's *Comprehensive Master Plan for a Sustainable Coast,* released in May 2007, put the Mississippi Delta Management Plan right up front. It recommended the study of very large diversions that would pour the majority of the river's water and sediment in Breton Sound and the Barataria Basin, build new delta lobes, and nourish existing wetlands. The state developed two scenarios: The first would create the diversions at Myrtle Grove on the west bank and at Phoenix on the east bank, which would make maximum use of the river's sediment but would also create shifts in salinities and therefore of commercially important species. Think oysters, redfish, and speckled trout. While residents of lower Plaquemines Parish feared that without the river, and the commerce it brought them, their towns would dry up, the plan noted that barrier-island restoration and massive diversions to create new delta lobes would bring them added protection.

The second scenario would create the diversions farther downstream, near Boothville and Venice, which would minimize changes in salinity but would diminish the amount of land that could be built in Breton Sound and the Barataria Basin. The state noted that massive sediment diversion was an untested concept, and researchers needed to examine its impact on ecosystems and hydrology, as well as on fisheries, flood control, and navigation. Without such diversions, however, the adjacent basins would continue to deteriorate, leaving New Orleans and other communities more and more vulnerable to storm damage and navigation on the river more and more difficult to maintain.

In June 2009, a pair of coastal scientists issued a report that noted that the system of more than 40,000 dams on the Mississippi and its tributaries that retain sediment in the upper basin and deprive the Mississippi of 50 percent of the sediment it had for land building 7,000 years ago. Because the Mississippi can contribute so little mud to delta building, coastal deterioration and the rise in sea level will drown the whole of the Louisiana coast by 2100. The scientists concluded that Louisiana needed to concentrate on diversions where sediment retention would be maximized and enhance existing fresh and brackish wetlands in the northern reaches of the Louisiana coast. Doing so would protect New Orleans and other population centers.

Afterword

Just as I finished this manuscript, the Flood of 2008 rolled down the Upper Mississippi and hurricanes ripped the Louisiana coast, proving that the Mississippi and its wetlands, including the coastal wetlands, are all of a piece. The Corps of Engineers described the flood as shorter in duration than that of 1993 but more intense. South of the Iowa River, farm levees that had collapsed in 1993, and some that hadn't, failed. Farmers in the American Bottom were grateful that the Missouri was not also in flood, because sand boils were erupting landside of the new levee, which replaced the one that had burst in 1993. The new one held.

Many factors contributed to the 2008 flood. Congress mandated an increase in ethanol in the 2005 energy bill and a five-fold increase in the production of ethanol in the 2007 energy bill. Farmers responded by taking highly erodible land out of the Conservation Reserve Program and planting it in corn, sending more water and sediment into the rivers. Just as farmers fertilized their fields in 2008, rain flooded them. Runoff washed huge amounts of sediment and nutrients into the river. At the mouth of the river the Mississippi spewed all that sediment into the Gulf of Mexico, where it was lost to ecosystem restoration. Scientists from the Louisiana Universities Marine Consortium and Louisiana State University, who receive funding from the National Oceanic and Atmospheric Administration, predicted that the Dead Zone in the Gulf could grow to the size of New Jersey, 8,800 square miles, the largest ever. It did not. Hurricane Dolly mixed in a bit of oxygen and reduced its size to 7,988 square miles.

In light of Katrina, the Bush administration asked for and got a $30 million supplemental funding request to initiate a national levee inventory and assessment program to be conducted by the Corps of Engineers. The engineers began work in 2006. Congress formalized the program in 2007 with the National Levee Safety Act but provided no funds to continue the work.

The drowning of Cedar Rapids, Iowa, on the Cedar River reminded me that during the course of this project we Americans watched as four of our cities went underwater: Grand Forks, North Dakota, on the Red River of the North, in 1997; Davenport, on the Upper Mississippi, in 2001; New Orleans in 2005; and Cedar Rapids in 2008.

By August the Flood of 2008 had ceased to be a threat, but the fields in the batture lands between the levees and the rivers were still flooded. Egrets, who normally fish my pond in the uplands during the summer, were hanging out in the flooded fields, where the water was shallow, the fish crowded, and the pickings easy.

Then came the hurricanes, two in the Gulf of Mexico after two years of quiet. Gustav, a mild Category Two storm, missed New Orleans, blew roofs off houses in Houma, Louisiana, turned out the lights as far north as Baton Rouge, but it did not flood the little towns on Louisiana's coastal bayous. It did not, because Gustav tracked across Louisiana's coastal wetlands, which took the energy out of its storm surge. It crossed Grand Isle on September 1 with a twelve-foot storm surge, but Grand Isle took some of the punch out of the surge. So did the levees and the ridge of Bayou Lafourche at Larose, after it crossed the Barataria Landbridge. The hurricane levees at Montegut on Bayou Terrebonne held back an eight-foot storm surge. Crossing the other ridges and levees reduced the surge more. There was little flooding in the unprotected villages in lower Terrebonne Parish. What was left, when it reached Houma, was wind, lots of wind and rain. The wetlands did what they should do: took the energy out of the storm surge.

Not so with Hurricane Ike two weeks later, on September 12 and 13.

Ike wiped out Galveston Island in Texas and took our focus away from the Louisiana coast, which received extreme flooding from Plaquemines Parish along the Mississippi River to the Sabine River on the Texas border. Those who lived through the hurricanes of 2005 and returned to coastal Louisiana said the flooding from Ike in 2008 was worse than that from Hurricane Rita.

But Ike was not finished with us when it left Texas and Louisiana. It tracked northeast through Arkansas, into Missouri, through my hometown of Waterloo, Illinois, where its winds stirred and flattened the corn crop. It continued across Indiana and Ohio, where it put out the lights in Cleveland.

On its way to Cleveland, Ike hit a cold front at St. Louis and dumped between three and five and a half inches of rain on the Midwest. Little creeks that lace the St. Louis region rose ten to twenty feet above their normal flows in a hundred-year flood. In St. Louis County, 302 commercial properties and 1,932 residences experienced flooding, enough to seek help from FEMA. Friends from Rochester, New York, visiting relatives along the DuPage River, outside Chicago, found themselves stacking sandbags. Which brings us to the second Flood of 2008 on the Upper Mississippi. All that rain drained to the Mississippi, reflooded the fields, and washed in more fish for the egrets, which stayed through October to be replaced by gulls through November.

While the egrets and the gulls found plenty in the flooded fields, the ducks who migrate along the Mississippi did not. Moist-soil plants, duck food, could not germinate where mudflats stayed flooded. Whatever plants managed to grow on mudflats that drained were drowned in September, leaving the ducks to depend on moist-soil units maintained behind levees in wildlife management areas, both public and private.

The new year brought the inauguration of President Barack Obama and the discussion of a very large stimulus package focused on infrastructure to pull the U.S. economy out of a very serious recession. I would stipulate that floodplain forests and wetlands and coastal barrier islands and marshes are infrastructure. Lester Goodin demonstrated that when he planted a 125-acre tree screen on Missouri Sister Island and stopped the 1993 flood from cutting a new channel across the point bar. *Sharing the Challenge* illustrated the value of wetlands in the Upper Mississippi Basin in storing floods. The Floods of 2008 reinforced the need. Water-level recorders in the Terrebonne marshes measured the height of Hurricane Andrew's 1992 storm surge and proved the conventional wisdom that coastal marshes soak up the power of hurricanes. Gustav's track across the marshes and levees reinforced the wisdom. Katrina, Rita, and Ike reinforced the need.

Common Acronyms in Captions

BRNEP Barataria-Terrebonne National Estuary Program

cfs cubic feet per second

CRP Conservation Reserve Program

CWPPRA Coastal Wetlands, Planning, Protection, and Restoration Act projects—The Breaux Act

DNR State Department of Natural Resources

EMP Environmental Management Program (Upper Mississippi)

GIWW Gulf Intracoastal Waterway

HREPS Habitat Rehabilitation and Enhancement Projects (Upper Mississippi)

LCA Study Louisiana Coast Area Ecosystem Restoration Study

LACPR Louisiana Coastal Protection and Restoration Study

LMRCC Lower Mississippi River Conservation Committee

LSU Louisiana State University

LTRMP Long-Term Resource Monitoring Program

NAWCA North American Wetlands Conservation Act

NAWCC North American Wetlands Conservation Council

NOAA National Oceanic and Atmospheric Administration

NESP Navigation and Ecosystem Sustainability Program (Upper Mississippi)

NRCS Natural Resources Conservation Service

NWR National Wildlife Refuge

UMRCC Upper Mississippi River Conservation Committee

USFWS U.S. Fish and Wildlife Service

USGS U.S. Geological Survey

WMA State Wildlife Management Area

WRDA Water Resources Development Act

WRP Wetland Reserve Program

Bibliography

Indigenous Americans and European Explorers

Ambrose, Stephen. *Undaunted Courage.* New York: Simon and Schuster, Touchstone Books, 1996.

Ashe, Thomas. *Travels in America.* Newburyport: William Sawyer and Co., 1808.

Audubon, Marie. *Audubon and His Journals,* with zoological and other notes by Elliott Coues. New York: Charles Scribner's Sons, 1897.

Beltrami, J. C. *A Pilgrimage in America*. Chicago: Quadrangle Books, 1962.

———. "Giacomo Beltrami's Summer of Discovery." http://home.rconnect.com/~matisse/beltrami.html, October 3, 2002.

Brackenridge, Henry Marie. *Views of Louisiana.* 1814. Reprint. Chicago: Quadrangle Books, 1962.

Bray, Martha, ed. *The Journals of Joseph N. Nicollet: A Scientist on the Mississippi Headwaters, with Notes on Indian Life, 1836–37*. Translated from the French by Andre Fertey. St. Paul: Minnesota Historical Society, 1978.

Brower, Jacob V. *The Mississippi River and Its Source*. Minneapolis: Harrison and Smith, 1893.

Cramer, Zadok. *The Navigator.* Ann Arbor: University Microfilms, 1966.

Darby, William. *Geographic Description of the State of Louisiana.* Philadelphia: John Melish, 1816.

Dunbar, William. *Journal of a Voyage.* Philadelphia: John Vaughan, 1817.

Flint, Timothy. *The History and Geography of the Mississippi Valley*. Cincinnati: E. H. Flint, 1833.

Hennepin. Louis. *A New Discovery of a Vast Country in America*. Second London edition, 1698. Reprint. Chicago: A. C. McClurg and Co., 1903.

Iberville, Pierre Le Moyne. *Iberville's Gulf Journals.* Translated and edited by Richebourg Gaillard McWilliams. Introduction by Tennant S. McWilliams. Tuscaloosa: University of Alabama Press, 1981.

Kelly John E., Andrew C. Fortier, Steven J. Ozuk, and Joyce A. Williams. *The Range Site: Archaic through late Woodland Occupations*. Urbana: Illinois Department of Transportation by the University of Illinois Press, 1987.

Kniffen, Fred B. "Bayou Manchac: A Physiographic Interpretation." *Geographical Review,* vol. 25, no. 3 (July 1935).

Le Page du Pratz, Antoine Simon. *The History of Louisiana.* Translated from the French of M. Le Page du Pratz. Edited by Joseph G. Tregle, Jr. Facsimile reproduction of the 1774 edition. Baton Rouge: Louisiana State University Press, 1975.

Lewis, Theodore H., ed. "The Narrative of the Expedition of Hernando de Soto by the Gentleman of Elvas." In *Spanish Explorers in the Southern United States, 1528–1543*. New York: Barnes and Noble, 1907.

Membre, Father Zenobius. "Narrative of La Salle's Voyage down the Mississippi." In *The Journeys of Rene Robert Cavelier, Sieur de LaSalle,* by Isaac Joslin Cox. New York: Allerton Book Co., 1905.

Nuttall, Thomas. *Travels into the Arkansa Territory in the Year 1819*. Ann Arbor: University Microfilms, 1966.

Pathfinders and Passageways: The Exploration of Canada. "Louis Joliet and Jacques Marquette, Finding the Mississippi." http://www.nlc-bnc.ca/2/24/h24–1470-e.html.

Pike, Zebulon M. *Sources of the Mississippi and the Western Louisiana Territory.* Ann Arbor: University Microfilms, 1965.

Pittman, Captain Philip. *The Present State of the European Settlements on the Mississippi.* 1770. Reprint. Cleveland: A. H. Clark, 1906.

Sabo, George, III. "The Indians of Arkansas." University of Arkansas, Department of

Archeology. http://arkarcheology.uark.edu/indiansofarkansas/index.html.
Schilling, Timothy M. "Excavations at the Bayou Grande Cheniere Mounds (16PL159): A Coles Creek Period Mound Complex." Master's thesis, Louisiana State University, May 2004.
Schoolcraft, Henry Rowe. *Expedition to Lake Itasca; the Discovery of the Source of the Mississippi*. East Lansing: Michigan State University Press, 1958.
Stein, Anthony. "The Mississippian Moundbuilders and Their Artifacts," http://www.mississippian-artifacts.com/.
Stoddard. Major Amos. *Sketches, Historical and Descriptive of Louisiana.* Philadelphia: Mathew Carry, 1812.
Tanner, James, T. *The Ivory-Billed Woodpecker.* 1942. Reprint. Mineola, N.Y.: Dover Publications, 2003.
Thwaites, Reuben Gold, ed. *Jesuit Relations and Allied Documents*. Cleveland: Burrows Brothers Co., 1896–1901.
Tonti, Henri Memoir de. "Tonti on the Illinois and Mississippi." In *The Journeys of Rene Robert Cavelier, Sieur de LaSalle,* by Isaac Joslin Cox. New York: Allerton Book Co., 1905.
Twain, Mark. *Life on the Mississippi*. New York: Modern Library, 1994.
U.S. Department of the Interior, National Park Service. "Effigy Mounds." http://www.nps.gov/efmo/index.htm.
U.S. Department of the Interior, National Park Service, U.S. World Heritage Sites. "Cahokia Mounds State Historic Site, Illinois." http://www.cr.nps.gov/worldhaeritage/cahokia.htm.
Widmann, Otto. *A Preliminary Catalog of the Birds in Missouri.* St. Louis: Academy of Science of St. Louis, 1907.

Assembling the Basin and Building the Master River—Headwaters

Hobbs, H. C. "Drainage Relationships of Glacial Lakes Aitkin and Upham in Early Lake Agassiz in Northeastern Minnesota." In *Glacial Lake Agassiz,* by James T. Teller and Lee Clayton. Geological Association of Canada Special Paper 26, 1993.
Hudak, G. Joseph, Elizabeth Hobbs, Allyson Brooks, Carol Ann Sersland, and Crystal Phillips, eds. *A Predictive Model of Precontact Archaeological Site Location for the State of Minnesota.* Final Report, "St. Croix Moraines and Outwash Plains Subsection Model Results and Interpretation." St. Paul: Minnesota Department of Transportation. http://www.mnmodel.dot.state.mn.us/chapters/twch.htm.
Ojakangas, Richard W., and Charles L. Matsch. *Minnesota's Geology*. Minneapolis: University of Minnesota Press, 1982.
Patterson, C. J., and H. E. Wright, Jr., eds. *Contributions to Quaternary Studies in Minnesota.* St. Paul: Minnesota Geological Survey Report of Investigations 49 (1998).
Ruddiman, W. F., and H. E. Wright, Jr., eds. *North American and Adjacent Oceans during the Last Deglaciation*. In Geology of North America, vol. K-3. Boulder: Geological Society of America, 1987.
Teller, James T., and Lee Clayton. *Glacial Lake Agassiz*. Geological Association of Canada, Special Paper 26, 1983.
Wright, H.E., Jr. *Geologic History of Minnesota's Rivers*. St. Paul: Minnesota Geologic Survey Education Bulletin-7, 1990.
Wright, H.E., Jr. "History of the Landscape in the Itasca. Region." In *Elk Lake, Minnesota: Evidence for Rapid Climate Change in the North-Central United States,* edited by J. P. Bradbury and W. E. Dean. Boulder, Colorado: Geological Society of America, Special Paper 276, 1993

Assembling the Basin and Building the Master River—Upper Mississippi

Anderson, Jeffrey D., E. Arthur Bettis II, and James S. Oliver. *Landform Sediment Assemblage Units in the Upper Mississippi River Valley*. Vol. 1. United States Army Corps of Engineers, Rock Island District, 1996.
Benn, David W., Jeffrey D. Anderson, Robert C. Vogel, and Lawrence Conrad, eds. *Archaeology, Geomorphology, and Historic Surveys in Pools 13–14, Upper Mississippi River*. Springfield, Missouri: Center for Archaeological Research, Southwest Missouri State University, September, 1989.
Bettis, E.A., III and Autin, Whitney J. "Complex Response of a Midcontinent North America Drainage System to late Wisconsinan Sedimentation." *Journal of Sedimentary Research*, Vol. 67, No. 4, July, 1997.
Bettis, E. A, III, Baker, Richard G., Green, William R., Whelan, Mary K., Benn, David W. *Late Wisconsinan and Holocene Alluvial Stratigraphy, Paleoecology, and Archaeological Geology of East-central Iowa*. Guidebook Series no. 12, Iowa City: Iowa Department of Natural Resources, April 1992.
Esling, Steven P., and Blum, Michael, eds. *Quaternary Sections in Southern Illinois and*

Southeast Missouri, Carbondale, Illinois: Midwest Friends of the Pleistocene, 1995.

Fortier, Andrew C. Lacampagne, Richard B., and Finney, Fred A. *The Fish Lake Site* Urbana: Published for the Illinois Department of Transportation by the University of Illinois Press, 1984.

Goodfield, Alan Granger. *Pleistocene and Sufical Geology of the City of St. Louis and the Adjacent St. Louis County.* Ph.D. Dissertation. University of Illinois, Urbana-Champaign, 1965.

Hajic, Edwin R. "Geomorphology of the Northern American Bottom as Context for Archaeology," in *Highways to the Past: Essays on Illinois Archaelogy*, *Illinois Archaeology*, Vol. 5, Nos. 1 and 2, 1993.

Hajic, Edwin R. *Late Pleistocene and Holocene Landscape Evolution, depositional subsystems, and stratigraphy in the lower Illinois River Valley and adjacent Central Mississippi River Valley*. Ph.D. Thesis. Urbana-Champaign: University of Illinois, 1990.

Hajic, Edwin R., Sheena K. Beaverson, and Andrea K. Freeman. "Archaeological Geology of the Ringering Site and Vicinity." In Evans, J. Bryant, and Madeleine G. Evans, *The Ringering Site and the Archaic-Woodland Transition in the American Bottom*, Illinois Transportation Archaeological Research Program Transportation Archaeological Research Reports, No. 8, November 2000.

Johnson, Scot. *Geomorphic Evolution of the Mississippi River During the Pleistocene (Glacial) and Holocene (Recent) Epochs*. Lake City, Minnesota: Minnesota DNR, May 28, 1993.

Martin, Lawrence. *Physical Geography of Wisconsin*, Madison: University of Wisconsin Press, 1965.

Madigan, Thomas, and Schirmer, Ronald C. *Geomorphological, Mapping and Archaeological Sites of the Upper Mississippi Valley, Navigation Pools 1–10, Minneapolis, Minnesota to Guttenberg, Iowa*. Minneapolis: Hemisphere Field Services, April, 2001.

Nelson, John C., Sparks, Richard E., DeHaan, Lynne, Robinson, Larry. "Land Use History of North America: Presettlement and Contemporary Vegetation Patterns Along Two Navigation Reaches of the Upper Mississippi River." U.S. Geological Survey, LUHNA Program. http://biology.usgs.gov/luhna/program.html.

Peck, John Mason. *A Guide of Emigrants.* Boston: Lincoln & Edmands, 1831. Reprint, Ayer Publishing, 1975.

Peck, John Mason. *A Gazetteer of Illinois in Three Parts.* Philadelphia: Grigg & Elliot, 1837.

Prior, Jean C. *Landforms of Iowa*. Iowa City: University of Iowa Press, 1991.

Ramsey, Cynthia Russ. "Water: Time's Relentless Sculptor," in *Powers of Nature*. Washington, D.C.: Special Publications Division, National Geographic Society, 1978.

Rubey, William W. *Geology and Mineral Resources of the Hardin and Brussels Quadrangles (in Illinois)*. Washington, D.C.: United States Geological Survey Paper 218, 1952.

Thomson, Betty Flanders. *The Shaping of America's Heartland.* Boston: Houghton Mifflin Company, 1977.

U.S. Geological Survey. "Evidence of Climate Change in the last 10,000 years in the Sediment of Lakes in the Upper Mississippi Basin." U.S. Geological Survey Fact Sheet FS-059–99, April 1999. http://geology.cr.usgs.gov/pub/fact-sheets/fs-0059–99/index.html.

Weisman, Alan. *The World Without Us.* New York: Thomas Dunne Books, St. Martin's Press, 2007.

Yarbough, Ronald E. "The Physiography of Metro East." *Illinois Geographical Society Bulletin*, vol. 16, no. 1.

Assembling the Basin and Building the Master River—Lower Mississippi

Asland, Andres and Autin, Whitney. "Evolution of the Holocene Mississippi Floodplain, Ferriday, Louisiana: Insights on the Origin of Fine-grained Floodplains." *Journal of Sedimentary Research*, Vol. 69, No. 4, July, 1999.

Blum, Michael, ed. "Late Pleistocene Evolution of the Lower Mississippi Valley, South Missouri to Arkansas." Final manuscript to be submitted to the *Geological Society of America Bulletin*, May 18, 1999.

Fisk, Harold N. *Geological Investigation of the Alluvial Valley of the Lower Mississippi River*. Vicksburg: Mississippi River Commission, 1945.

Guccione, Margaret J., Hehr, Lynne J., and Van Arsdale, Roy, B. "Prigin and age of the Manila high and associated Big Lake 'sunklands' in the New Madrid seismic zone, northeastern Arkansas," *Geological Society of America Bulletin, 2000,* Vol. 112. http://www.gsajournals.org/gsaonline/?request=get-abstract&doi=10.1130%2F0016–7606(2000)112%3C579:OAAOTM%3E2.0.CO%3B2.

Johnston, Arch C., and Schweig, Eugene S. "The Enigma of the New Madrid Earthquakes of 1811–1812." Annual Review, *EarthPlanet Science,* 1996. http://www.ceri.memphis.edu/compendium/enigma.pdf.

Knox, James. "Late Quaternary Upper Mississippi alluvial episodes and their significance to the Lower Mississippi River System." *Engineering Geology 45* (1996).

Saucier, Roger. *Geomorphology and Quaternary Geologic History of the Lower Mississippi Valley.* Vicksburg: U.S. Army Corps of Engineers Waterways Experimental Station, 1994.

Tye, Robert S., and Coleman, James M. "Evolution of the Atchafalaya lacustrine deltas, south-central Louisiana." *Sedimentary Geology*, 65, 1989.

Wailes, Benjamin Leonard Covington. *Report on the Agriculture and Geology of Mississippi: Embracing a Sketch of Social and Natural History of the State.* Philadelphia: Lippincott, Grambro and Co., 1854.

Assembling the Basin and Building the Master River—Louisiana Coast

Muth, David. "Historic Flora and Fauna of the Old Barataria-Des Familles Distributary." In Swanson, Betty, *Terre Haute de Barataria,* Gretna, Louisiana: Jefferson Parish Historical Commission, 1991.

Penland, Shea, et al. "Shoreline Changes in the Timbalier Barrier Island Arc-1887 to 1996, Terrebonne Parish, Louisiana," U.S. Geological Survey, 2003, http://pubs.usgs.gov/of/2003/of03–398/posters/pdf/cont_pdf/ti_atlas.pdf.

Penland, Shea, and Andrew Beall. "Geologic Setting of the Big Branch Shoreline." In *Environmental Atlas of the Lake Pontchartrain Basin.* U.S. Geological Survey Open File Report 02–206, 2002. http://pubs.usgs.gov/of/2002/of02–206/geology/geologic-setting.html.

Penland, Shea, and Andrew Beall. "Recent Stratigraphy of Lake Pontchartrain." In *Environmental Atlas of the Lake Pontchartrain Basin.* U.S. Geological Survey Open File Report 02–206, 2002. http://pubs.usgs.gov/of/2002/of02–206/geology/stratigraphy.html.

Saucier, Roger. *Geomorphology and Quaternary Geologic History of the Lower Mississippi Valley.* Vicksburg: U.S. Army Corps of Engineers Waterways Experimental Station, 1994.

Tornqvist, Torbjorn E., Kidder, Tristram R., Autin, Whitney J., van der Borg, Klaas, De Jong, Arie F.M., Klerks, Cornelis, J.W., Snijders, Els, M.A., Storms, Joep E.A., van Dam, Remke L., and Wiemann, Michael C. " A Revised Chronology for Mississippi River Subdeltas," *Science*, Vol. 273, September 20, 1996.

Changing the River and Its Floodplain—General

National Research Council. *River Basins and Coastal Systems Planning within the U.S. Army Corps of Engineers.* Washington, D.C.: The National Academies Press, 2004.

Trotter, Julie and Slack Paul, eds. *Managing Water Resources, Past and Present*. Oxford: Oxford University Press, 2004.

Vileisis, Ann. *Discovering the Unknown Landscape*. Washington, D.C.: Island Press, 1997.

Wright, James M. *The Nation's Responses to Flood Disasters: A Historical Account.* Madison, Wisconsin: Association of State Floodplain Managers, April 2000.

Changing the River and Its Floodplain—Headwaters

Blegen, Theodore C. "'The Headwaters of the Mississippi River,' a reprint from "Discovery of Lake Itasca." Pamphlet issued by the Minnesota Historical Society in 1931. In the *Itasca Guide Book*, St. Paul: Minnesota Department of Natural Resources, Division of Parks and Recreation, 1995.

Holling, Holling Clancy. *Minn of the Mississippi.* Boston: Houghton Mifflin Company, 1951.

MacGregor, Molly. *Headwaters Guide*. Walker, Minnesota: Mississippi Headwaters Board, 1995.

U.S. Forest Service. *Cass Lake and Lake Winnibigoshish: Ecosystem Analysis at Watershed Scale*. http://www.fs.fed.us/r9/chippewa/plan/aquatics/watershed/assessment/final_assessment.pdf.

Waters, Thomas F. *The Streams and Rivers of Minnesota*. Minneapolis: University of Minnesota Press, 1977.

Wright, H.E., Jr. "History of the landscape in the Itasca region." *Geological Society of America*, Special Paper 276 (1993).

Wright, H.E., Jr. "Physiography of Minnesota," in *Geology of Minnesota: a Centennial Volume*. Minneapolis: Minnesota Geological Survey, 1972.

Changing the River and Its Floodplain—Upper Mississippi

Anfinson, John O. *The River We Have Wrought: A History of the Upper Mississippi*. Minneapolis: University of Minnesota Press, 2003.

Cronan, William. *Nature's Metropolis*. New York: W.W. Norton and Company, 1991.

Davis, Norah Deakin, and Holmes, Joseph. *The Father of Waters.* San Francisco: Sierra Club Books, 1982.

Fremling, Calvin R. *Immortal River: The Upper Mississippi in Ancient and Modern Times.* Madison: University of Wisconsin Press, 2005.

Gard, William T. *The Sny Story*. Texas: Smithfield Press, 2002.

Great Rivers Habitat Alliance. "Summary Position of Opposition to the Expansion of Smartt Airport, St. Charles County, Missouri." http://grha.net/news/smartt__airport.pdfhttp://www.nos.noaa.gov/pdflibrary/hypox__t3final.pdf.

Guenther, Joseph R. "Floodplain Connectivity Restoration Opportunities and Suitability Modeling Utilizing GIS Technology." Minnesota Department of Natural Resources, Lake City, Minnesota, nd, http://www2.smumn.edu/ra/gis/Pages/GradProjects/JGuenther.pdf.

Hunter, Louis C. *Steamboats on the Western Rivers, An Economic and Technological History.* New York: Dover Publications, 1993.

Hurley, Andrew, *Common Fields: An Environmental History of St. Louis.* St. Louis: Missouri Historical Society, 1997.

Madsen, John. *Up on the River: An Upper Mississippi Chronicle*. New York: Viking Penguin, 1985.

Madigan, Thomas and Schirmer, Ronald C. *Geomorphological Mapping and Archaeological Sites of the Upper Mississippi Valley, Navigan Pools 1–10, Minneapolis, Minnesota to Guttenberg, Iowa*. Minneapolis: Hemisphere Field Services, April 2001.

Merritt, Raymond. *The Corps, the Environment, and the Upper Mississippi River Basin.* Washington, D.C.: Office of Administrative Services, Office of the Chief of Engineers, 1984.

Minnesota Department of Natural Resources. Kellogg-Weaver Sand Dunes SNA. http://www.dnr.state.mn.us/snas/sna00979/index.html.

Minnesota Department of Natural Resources. "Mississippi Yields Record Turtle, September-October 2002." http://www.dnr.state.mn.us/volunteer/sepocto2/turtles.html.

Morgan, Arthur E. *Dams and Other Disasters: A Century of the Army Corps of Engineers in Civil Works* Boston: Parter Sargent, Publisher, 1971.

Norman, Dennis E. "Headwater Diversion Watershed: Inventory and Assesment." Missouri Department of Conservation. http://www.conservation.state.mo.us/fish/watershed/headwater/contents/150cotxt.htm.

O'Neill, Karen M. *Rivers by Design: State Power and the Origins of U.S. Flood Control* Durham, North Carolina: Duke University Press, 2006.

Primm, James Neal. *Lion in the Valley.* Boulder, Colorado: Pruett Publishing Company, 1990.

Prince, Hugh. *Wetlands of the American Midwest: A Historical Geography of Changing Attitudes*. Chicago: University of Chicago Press, 1997.

Scarpino, Philip. *Great River: An Environmental History of the Upper Mississippi, 1809–1950*. Columbia, Missouri: University of Missouri Press, 1985.

Scott, Quinta, and Miller, Howard S. *The Eads Bridge: Photographic Essay by Quinta Scott; Historical Appraisal by Howard S. Miller*. Columbia, Missouri: University of Missouri Press, 1979.

Smith, Dawn M., David C. Gordon, Aron M. Rhoads, Robert D. Davinroy. "Sedimentation Study of the Middle Mississippi River at Jefferson Barracks, River Miles 176.0 to 166.0, Hydraulic Micro Investigation. "U.S. Army Corps of Engineers, St. Louis District, Hydrologic and Hydraulics Branch, Applied Engineering Center, November 2001. http://www.mvs.usace.army.mil/eng-con/expertise/arec/Model%20Study%20Report%20PDFs/JB%20Bridge%20CD/JB-BridgeReport.pdf.

U.S. Army Corps of Engineers. "The Evolution of Federal Flood County Policy." http: //www.usace.army.mil/inet/usace-docs/eng-pamphlets/ep870–1013/c-4.pdf.

Upper Mississippi River Conservation Committee. "FACING THE THREAT: An Ecosystem Management Strategy for the Upper Mississippi River."http://www.mississippi-river.com/umrcc/Call-for-Action.html.

Wisconsin Department of Natural Resources. Rush River Delta State Natural Area. http://www.dnr.state.wi.us/org/land/er/snas/snas202.htm.

Changing the River and Its Floodplain—Lower Mississippi

Barry, John M. *Rising Tide: The Great Mississippi Flood of 1927 and How it Changed America*. New York: Simon and Schuster, 1997.

Bragg, Marion. *Historic Names and Places on the Lower Mississippi River*. Vicksburg: Mississippi River Commission, 1977.

Beorkrem, Mark, and Sarthou, Cynthia. *Destruction by Design: The U.S. Army Corps of Engineers' Continuing Assault on America's Environment*. Gulf Restoration Network, December 14, 1999.

Camillo, Charles A., and Pearcy, Matthew T. *Upon Their Shoulders.* Vicksburg, Mississippi River Commisssion, 2004.

Corthell, E.L. *A History of the Jetties at the Mouth of the Mississippi River*. New York: John Wiley&Sons, 1881.

Czarnecki, John B., Clark, Brian R., Reed, Thomas B. "Conjunctive-Use Optimization Model of the Mississippi River Valley Alluvial Aquifer of Northeastern Arkansas, U.S. Geological Survey, Water-Resources Investigation Report 03–4230." http://www.water.usgus.gov/pubs/wri/wri034230.

Daniel, Pete. *Deep'n as it Come: The 1927 Mississippi River Flood*. New York: Oxford University Press, 1977.

Eads, James B. *Mouth of the Mississippi: Jetty System Explained*. Pamphlet. St. Louis, 1874.

Eads, James B. *Physics and Hydraulics of the Mississippi River*. Pamphlet. New Orleans, 1876.

Eads, James B. *Review of Humphreys and Abbot Report*. Pamphlet. Washington, D.C., 1878.

Ellet, Charles. *The Mississippi and Ohio Rivers: containing plans for the protection of the delta from inundation; and investigations of the practicability and cost of improving the navigation of the Ohio and other rivers by means of reservoirs, with an appendix, on the bars at the mouths of the Mississippi.* Philadelphia: Lippincott, Grambo, and Co., 1853.

Ferguson, Harley, B. *History of the Improvement of the Lower Mississippi River for Flood Control and Navigation, 1932–1939*. Washington, D.C.: War Department, Corps of Engineers, U.S. Army, 1940.

Galuski, Ed. "Underground Aquifers Damaged, says Geologist." *Lonoke Democrat*, April 7, 2004. http://www.lonokedemocrat.com/Pages/14-07-04/Underground%20quifers.htm.

Gillmore, General Quincy Adams. *Remarks, Official Report of the Proceedings of the Mississippi River Improvement Convention, St. Louis, Missouri, October 26–28, 1881.* St. Louis: Great Western Printing Company, 1881.

Gideon School District #37, Gideon Public Schools, Gideon, Missouri. "The Little River Drainage District," http://gideon.k12.mo.us/town/river3.htm.

Humphreys, A.A. *Report on the Physics and Hydraulics of the Mississippi River*. Washington, D.C.: U.S. Government Printing Office, 1876.

Mississippi River Commission. "The Mississippi River: A Short Historic Description of the Development of Flood Control and Navigation on the Mississippi River." Vicksburg: the Office of the President, Mississippi River Commission, nd.

Payne, B.S. "An Investigation of Mussel Resources in Selected Bayous, Northwestern Mississippi." Vicksburg: U.S. Army Engineers Research and Development Center, 2001.

Ramcer, C.E. "Flow of Water in Drainage Channels: The Results of Experiments to Determine the Roughness Coeffiecient *n* Kutter's Formula." U.S. Department of Agriculture, Technical Bulletin, #129, November 1929.

U.S. Army Corps of Engineers. "Mississippi River Navigation: Federal participation in Waterways Development." http://www.mvn.usace.army.mil/PAO/history/MISSRNAV/federal.asp.

U.S. Army Corps of Engineers. *Report of the Commission of Engineers Appointed to Investigate and Report a Permanent Plan for the Reclamation of the Alluvial Basin of the Mississippi River Subject to Inundation.* Washington: Government Printing Office, 1875.

U.S. Army Corps of Engineers, Memphis District. *Draft Environmental Assessment, Grand Prairie Demonstration Project, Post General Reevaluation Design Changes*. March 2, 2004. http://www.mvm.usace.army.mil/grandprairie/pdf/Draft%20EA.pdf.

U.S. Army Corps of Engineers, Vicksburg District. "Yazoo Backwater Area Reformulation, Main Report." September 2000. http://www.mvk.usace.army.mil/offices/pp/Yazoobackwater/docs/oomain/pdf.

U.S. Department of War. *Annual Report of the Secretary of War for the Year 1881.* Volume II, Part 2. Washington, D.C.: Government Printing Office, 1882, 1289–1292.

U.S. Fish and Wildlife Service, Division of Ecological Services. "The Relationship of Federal Flood Control and Drainage to the Agricultural Development of Wetlands in the Lower Mississippi Valley, A Case History: The Yazoo Basin." Vicksburg, Mississippi: October, 1986.

U.S House of Representatives. Hearings before the Committee on Flood Control, House of Representatives, 77th Congress. H.R. 4911, A Bill Authorizing the Construction of Certain Public Works on Rivers and Harbors for Flood Control, and for Other Purposes, April 21 to May 14, 1941. Washington, D.C.: United State Government Printing Office, 1941

U.S. House of Representatives. *The Executive Documents of the House of Representatives for the Second Seession of the Fifty-third Congress,* 1893–1894. Washington, D.C.: U.S. Government Printing Office, 1895, 1846–1848.

U.S. Senate. *Report of the Inland Waterways Commission* Senate Documents, 50th Congress, 1st Session, December 1907–May 30,1908. Washington, D.C.: U.S. Government Printing Office, 1908, 304.

Changing the River and Its Floodplain— Atchafalaya River

Goolsby, D.A. et al. "Flux and Sources of Nutrients in the Mississippi-Atchafalaya River Basin: Topic 3 Report," in Gulf Hypoxia Scientific Papers submitted to the White House Office of Science and Technology Policy, May 1999, xv–xvii, 23–24.

McBrayer, Mickey C. "1973, the Atchafalaya Strikes Back," in *The River War: the Mississippi vs. the Atchafalaya.*

McPhee, John. "Atchafalaya." *The Control of Nature.* New York: Farrar, Straus and Giroux, The Noonday Press, 1989.

Reuss, Martin. *Designing the Bayous: The Control of Water in the Atchafalaya Basin*. Alexandria: Office of History, U.S. Army Corps of Engineers, 1998.

Changing the River and Its Floodplain—Louisiana Coast

Barataria-Terrebonne National Estuary Program. "Sediment Reduction: Less Deposits Available to the Natural System." www.btnep.org/pages/sediment1.html.

Barataria-Terrebonne National Estuary Program. "State of the Estuary, Hydrological Modifications," http://www.btnp.org/hydro.htm.

Gagliano, Sherwood M. "Effects of Earthquakes, Fault Movements, and Subsidence on the South Louisiana Landscape." *Louisiana Civil Engineer,* Vol. 13, No. 2, 1–7. http://www.coastalenv.com/Publications/Effects%20of%20Earthquakes%20Fault%20Movement.pdf.

Hallowell, Christopher. *Holding Back the Sea.* New York: Harper Collins, Publishers, 2001.

Harrison, Richard W. *Levee Districts and Levee Buildings in Mississippi.* Stoneville, Mississippi: Delta Council, nd.

Johnson, Carrie. "Wetland Loss in Louisiana," http://www.geology.uno.edu/~serpa/geo1000/carrie_johnson.html.

LaCoast. "CWPPRA, Louisiana Loses Justification for Action." www.lacoast.gov/CWPPTAIntro/JustificationforAction.htm.

LaCoast. "Wetlands' Decline Fuels Unsustainable Harvests, Burgeoning Productivity Disguises Disaster in the Wetlands." *Watermarks,* June 2006. http://www.lacoast.gov/watermarks/200606/1disaster_in_the_wetlands.

Lohman, Sarah, "Scientists blame corn for growning 'dead zone.'" *St. Louis Post-Dispatch,* June 11, 2008.

Louisiana Mid-Continent Oil and Gas Industry. "Historical Highlights for the Louisiana Oil and Gas Industry." http://www.Imoga.com/history.htm.

http://www.ce.utexas.edu/stu/mcbraymc/ceproposal.html#2.3.

Mississippi Riverwide Partnership. "The Gulf of Mexico Dead Zone." June 1999. www.beachbrowser.com/archives-99/HYPOXIA-IN-THE-GULF-OF-MEXICO.htm.

Morton, Robert A., Buster, Noreen A., and Krohn, M. Dennis. "Subsurface controls on historical subsidence rates and associated wetland loss in southcentral Louisiana." Transactions, Gulf Coast Association of Geological Societies, 2002. http://coastal.er.usgs.gov/gc-subsidence/gcags-paper/GCAGS02.pdf.

Morton, Robert A., Bernier, Julie C., Barras, John A. and Ferina, Nicolas F. "Rapid Subsidence and Historical Wetland Loss in the Mississippi Delta Plain: Likely Causes and Future Implications." U.S. Geological Survey Open-file Report 2005–1216. http://pubs.usgs.gov/of/2005/1216/ofr-2005–1216.pdf.

Morton Robert A. Tiling, Ginger, Ferina, Nicholas F. "Primary causes of wetland loss at Madison Bay, Terrebonne Parish, Louisiana," St. Petersburg: U.S. Geological Survey, Center for Coastal and Watershed Studies, Open File Report 03–06. http://pubs.usgs.gov/of/2003/of03–060/ofr0360.pdf.

PIANC. "Case Study: Mississippi River-Gulf Outlet (MRGO)(USA)." http://www.pianc-aipcn.org/envicom7/13%20-%20mississippi.pdf#search=%22MRGO%20%22.

Sevin, Carl, and Wendy Wilson Billiot. Conversation, Cocodrie, Louisiana. May 2, 2007.

Sevin, Carl. Telephone Conversation. LUMCON, Cocodrie, Louisiana. June 30, 2007.

Seed, R.B. etal. *Investigation of the Performance of the New Orleans Flood Protection System in Hurricane Katrina on August 29, 2005.* Berkeley: July 31, 2006, Chapter 4, 24–28.

Tidwell, Mike. *Bayou Farewell: The Rich Life and Tragic Death of Louisiana's Cajun Coast.* New York: Vintage Books, a Division of Random House, 2003.

U.S. Army Corps of Engineers, Galveston District. "Closing the Mississippi River Gulf Outlet: Environmental and Economic Considerations." http://www.swg.usace.army.mil/mrgo/Documents/Publications/Closing%20the%20MRGO%20environmental%20and%20economic%20considerations.pdf.

U.S. Geological Survey. "Drainage of Organic Soils," in *Land Subsidence in the United States,* Circular 1182, Part II, July 2001. http://pubs.usgs.gov/circ/circ1182/pdf/10Part2.pdf.

Beginnings of the Restoration Movement

Audubon. "Audubon Centennial: 100 Years of Conservation, Timeline." http://www.audubon.org/centennial/timeline_intro.php#.

Ducks Unlimited. "Ducks Unlimited's History" Major Milestones. http://www.ducks.org/About_DU/AboutDucksUnlimitedHome/2093/Timeline.html.

Ducks Unlimited. "How Ducks Unlimited Conserves." http://www.ducks.org/Page1598.aspx.

Institute of Public Law. University of New Mexico School of Law. " The Lacey Act." May 25, 1900. http://ipl.unm.edu/cwl/fedbook/laceyact.html.
The Izaak Walton League of America. "Who We Are." http://www.iwla.org/index.php?id=9.
Jordan, William R. *The Sunflower Forest.* Berkley: University of California Press, 2003.
Leopold, Aldo. *A Sand County Almanac*. New York: Ballantine Books, 1949.
Price, Jennifer. "Hats Off to Audubon," *Audubon,* December 2004.
The Nature Conservancy. "About Us: History and Milestones of The Nature Conservancy." http://www.nature.org/aboutus/history.
U.S. Fish and Wildlife Service. "Federal Aid in Wildlife Restoration (Pittman-Robertson)." http://federalaid.fws.gov/wr/fawr.html.
U.S. Fish and Wildlife Service. "Federal Aid to Sport Fish Restoration." http://permanent.access.gpo.gov/lps52835/fa.r9.fws.gov/sfr/fasfr.html.
U.S. Fish and Wildlife Service. "A Guide to the Laws and Treaties of the United States for Protecting Migratory Birds." http://www.fws.gov/migratorybirds/intrnltr/treatlaw.html.
U.S. Fish and Wildlife Service. Lacey Act, Title 18. http://www.fws.gov/invasives/Index.LaceyAct.html.

Restoration—Upper Mississippi River

Benjamin, Gretchen, American Rivers. "Peck Lake Drawdown Yields Benefits." *Mississippi Monitor.* Vol. 3, No. 11, November, 1999.
Darylrymple, Ken. "Wetland Reforestation, a Prescription for a Wetland Mast Tree Planting System." http://www.mvr.usace.army.mil/forestry/planting.htm.
Davinroy, Robert D., Gordon, David C., Hetrick, Robert D., Redington, Steven L., Strauser, Claude H. "River Restoration Measure in Four Secondary Channels of the Mississippi River, An Interagency Success Story." Los Alomos National Laboratory, U.S.-Chine Water Resource Management Program. http://www.lanl.gov/chinawater/documents/rrestoration.pdf.
Great Rivers Habitat Alliance. "The McKnight Foundation Awards $800,000 to The Nature Conservancy for Its Mississippi River Work," Emailed Newsletter, March 2008.
Jordan, William R., III. "'Sunflower Forest:' Ecological Restoration as the Basis for a New Environmental Paradigm." In Baldwin, A. Dwight, Jr., DeLuce, Judith, and Pletsch, Carl, *Beyond Preservation, Restoring and Inventing Landscapes."* Minneapolis: University of Minnesota Press, 1994.
Lane, John J. and Jensen, Kent D. *Moist-Soil Impoundments for Wetland Wildlife* Technical Report EL-99–11. Vicksburg, Mississippi: U.S. Army Corps of Engineers, Research and Development Center, October 1999.
Low, Jim. "Ten Shanks Redemption." *Missouri Conservationist Online*, March 20, 2003, http://www.mdc.missouri.gov/conmag/2003/03/20.htm.
Low, Jim. "Ted Shanks: Rising Tide Floats New Hopes," Missouri Sportsmen Information Network. http://www.mosportsmen.com/hunting/waterfowl/shanks.htm.
Meadows, James S., and Nowacki, Gregory J. "An Old-Growth Definition for Eastern Riverfront Forests." U.S. Department of Agriculture, U.S. Forest Serivce, General Technical Report SRS-4.
Ortego, Brent, Fentress, Carl, Haucke, Hayden, and Rose, Julie Hogan. *Green Tree Reservoir Management*. Austin: Texas Department of Parks and Wildlife. http://www.tpwd.state.tx.us/conserve/publications/media/greentree__reservoir__mgmnt.pdf.
Roush, Deborah. "East St. Louis and Vicinity Interior Flood Control and Ecosystem Restoration Project," *Esprit*, U.S. Army Corps of Engineers, St. Louis District. August 1999.
Southwestern Illinois Resource Conservation and Development, Inc. *The Middle Mississippi River Partnership Coordination Plan—2005.* http://www.swircd.org/swircd/middle%20mississippi/Vision%20Plan.pdf.
Upper Midwest Environment Sciences Center. "Habitat Rehabitation and Enchancement Project, Small Scale Drawdown." www.umesc.usgs.gov/http__data/hrep__projects/small__scale__drawdown/small__scale__drawdown.html.
Upper Midwest Environmental Sciences Center. Vegetation Response to a Water-Level Drawdown of Pool 8 of the Upper Mississippi River." http://www.umesc.usgs.gov/aquatic/drawdown__p8__veg.html.
Upper Midwest Environmental Science Center. "Whitewater River Habitat Rehabilitation and Enhancement Project." www.umesc.usgs.gov/httpp__data/hrep__projects/whitewater__river.html.
The Upper Mississippi River Basin Association. The Upper Mississippi River System Environmental Management Program, Meeting the Challenge. www.umec.usgs.gov.
Upper Mississippi Environment Sciences Center. Habitat Rehabilitation and Enhancement Project Fact Sheets for Water Project along the Upper Mississippi River. www.umec.usgs.gov.
U.S. Army Corps of Engineers, Rock Island District, Public Affairs Office. "Mississippi Valley Division Improves Environment Along the Mississippi River." September 20, 2000. www.mvr.usace.army.mil/PublicAffairsOffice/

NewReleases/MVDImprovesEnvironmentAlongMississippiRiver.htm.
U.S. Army Corps of Engineers, Rock Island District. "Mississippi Valley Division Improves Environment Along Mississippi River." New Release, September 26, 2000. www.mvr.usace.mil/PulbicAffairsOffice/NewsRelease/2000NewsRelease/MVDimprovesEnvironmentAlongMississippiRiver.htm.
U.S. Army Corps of Engineers, Rock Island District. "Silvicultural Characteristics and Management Techniques of the Mississippi River Floodplain Forests." www.mvs.usace.army.mil/forestry/silvics.htm.
U.S. Army Corps of Engineers, Rock Island District. *Upper Mississippi-Illinois Waterway System Navigation Study Environmental Impact Statement*. http://www.mvr.usace.army.mil/pdw/nav__study/env__reports/Env7-Ch/7chptr5.pdf.
U.S., Army Corp of Engineers, St. Louis District, Applied Engineering Center. "Micro Modeling," http://www.mvs.usace.army.mil/engr/ed/river/MicroModel/MainFrame.htm.
U.S. Army Corps of Engineers, St. Louis District. *East St. Louis and Vicinity, Illinois Ecosystem Restoration and Flood Damage Reduction Project*, November 2003.
U.S. Army Corps of Engineers, St. Louis District. *Environmental Pool Management*. http://mvs-wc.mvs.usace.army.mil/epm/epmindex.html.
U.S. Army Corps of Engineers, St. Louis District. "Middle Mississippi River Side Channels: A Habitat Rehabilitation and Conservation Initiative." no date.
U.S. Army Corps of Engineers, St. Louis District. *River Projects, Master Plan*. http://www.mvs.usace.army.mil/pm/riverplan/Section4.html.
U.S. Army Corps of Engineers, St. Paul District. "Environmental Management Projects and Studies, Mississippi River." http://www.mvp.usace.army.mil/environment/.
U.S. Army Corps of Engineers, St. Paul District. *Mississippi River Environmental Pool Plans*. September 2001.
U.S. Army Corps of Engineers, St. Paul District. "Trempealeau National Wildlife Refuge, Trempealeau, Wisconsin." http://www.mpv.usace.army/environment/defaul.asp?pageid=261.
U.S. Fish and Wildlife Service. Mark Twain National Wildlife Refuge Complex, *Comprehensive Conservation Plan and Environmental Assessment*, 2004. http://www.fws.gov/lmre/strategic__plan.htm.
U.S. Fish and Wildlife Service. Upper Mississippi National Wildlife and Fish Refuge. http://www.fws.gov/cacheriver/.
U.S. Fish and Wildlife Service. *Upper Mississippi National Wildlife and Fish Refuge Comprehensive Conservation Plan*. http://www.fws.gov/Midwest/Planning/uppermiss/index.html.
U.S. Fish and Wildlife Service, and the U.S. Army Corps of Engineers, St. Louis District. "Middle Mississippi River Side Channels: A Habitat Rehabilitation and Conservation Initiative." No Date.
U.S. Geological Survey, Biological Resources Division. *Habitat Needs Assessment for the Upper Mississippi River System, Technical Report*, October 2000. http://www.umesc.usgs.gov/habitat__needs__assessment/tech__report.html.
Webber, Eileen. "Grey Cloud Island: Suburb or Park, You Can Make the Difference." North Star Chapter, Sierra Club, http://www.northstar.sierraclub.org/Sprawl__grey__cloud__island.htm.

Restoration—The White River Basin, Western Lowlands

Arkansas Department of Environmental Quality, Water Division. *Physical, Chemical, and Biological Characteristics of Least-Disturbed Reference Streams in Arkansas' Ecoregions*, Volume 1: Data Compilation, June 1987.
Arkansas Game and Fish Commission. AGFC Wildlife Management Areas. http://www.agfc.com/data-facts-maps/maps/wildlife-mgt-areas.aspx.
Arkansas Nature Conservancy. *The Big Woods of Arkansas: A Proposal for the Conservation of the Great Wetland Ecosystems of the Cache River, Bayou DeView, White River, and Lower Arkansas River of the Mississippi River Alluvial Plain*. Little Rock, Arkansas, 1992.
Arkansas Soil and Water Conservation Commission. *Draft: White River Allocation, Bull Shoals Dam to the Mississippi River*. http://www.state.ar.us./aswcc/WhiteRiver.pdf.
Black Bear Conservation Committee. "Black Bear Repatriation of Unoccupied habitats." http://www.bbcc.org/Repatriation/repatriation.html.
Cornell Lab of Ornithology. "The Search for the Ivory-Billed Woodpecker," December 12, 2005. http://www.birds.cornell.edu/ivory/press__room/mediaeventrelease/document__view.
Cooper, Robert J., et al. "Response of Songbirds to Natural and Anthropogenic Disturbances in the White River National Wildlife Refuge." Southern Division, Arkansas Chapter of the American Fisheries Society, http://www.sdafs.org/arkafs/pdffiles/2001/meet/wrabstracts.pdf.
Downer, Charles W. *Hydrology and Hydraulic Design Criteria for the Creation and Restoration of Wetlands*. Vicksburg: USACE Waterways Experiment Station, Wetlands Research Program, Technical Note HY-RS-3.1, August 1993.
Eilperin, Juliet. "Bird's Advocates Challenge Corps." *Washington Post*, September 8, 2005.
Flinn, Tim. "White River Basin Comprehensive Study," found in Southern Divi-

sion American Fisheries Society, Large River Fisheries Symposium, February 3, 2004. http://www.sdafs.org/arkafs/pdf/2004__meeting/lg__river__fish__agenda.pdf.
Foley, Larry(Producer); Briuer, Elke(Director); and Kleiss, Dr. Barbara A.(Principal Investigator). *The Black Swamp*. Video, Waterways Experiment Station, Vicksburg, 1995.
Foti, Thomas. "Presettlement Forests of the Black Swamp Area, Cache Richer, Woodruff County, Arkanasas, from Notes of the First Land Survey." http://www.srs.fs.usda.gov/pubs/gtr/gtr__srs042/gtr__srs042-foti01.pdf.
Klimas, Charles V., Murray, Elizabeth, O., Pagan, Jody, Langston, Henry, and Foti, Thomas. *A Regional Guidebook for Applying the Hydrogeomorphic Approach to Assessing Wetland Functions of Forested Wetlands in the Delta Region of Arkansas, Lower Mississippi River Alluvial Valley*. Ecosystem Management and Restoration Research Program. Vicksburg: U.S. Army Engineer Research and Development Center Environmental Laboratory, September 2004. http://el.erdc.usace.army.mil/wetlands/pdfs/trel04–16.pdf.
Kokes, Gina. "Arkansas Bears Achieving Their Natural State." http://www.arkansas-travel.com/archives/printable__popup__botframe.asp?id=143.
Luneau, David. "Report on the Search for the Ivory-billed Woodpecker in the White River National Wildlife Refuge." January 16, 2003.
Multi-Agency Wetland Planning Team, *Arkansas Wetland Stratagy*, 35. http://www.mawpt.org/pdfs/Strategy.pdf.
National Resources Conservation Service. U.S.D.A., Arkansas. "Grand Prairie/White River Irrigation Project, http://www.ar.nrcs.usda.gov/irrig/gpweb/grand.htm.
National Wildlife Federation. "What's at Stake? "Stop the Grand Prairie Project—for good." http://action.nwf.org/campaign/grandprairie20060808/explanation.
U.S. Fish and Wildlife Service. "History of Mingo Swamp." http://midwest.fws.gov/Mingo/history.html.
U.S. Fish and Wildlife Service, Division of Endangered Species. "Louisiana Black Bear." http://endangered.fws.gov/i/a/saa9e.html.
U.S. Army Corps of Engineers, Memphis District, "White River Navigation to Newport, Arkansas; General Investigations." September 1, 2000. http://www.mvm.usace.army.mil.whiteriver?FactSheet/WRNavSept1.htm.
U.S. Army Corps of Engineers. "White River Basin Comprehensive Study, (Arkansas and Missouri)." http://corpslakes.usace.army.mil/employees/watershed/pdfs/whiteriver.pdf.
U.S. Fish and Wildlife Service. *The Ivory-billed Woodpecker*. December 2005.
U.S. Fish and Wildlife Service. Cache River National Wildlife Refuge. http://www.fws.gov/cacheriver/.
U.S. Fish and Wildlife Service. White River National Wildlife Refuge. http://www.fws.gov/whiteriver/.

Restoration—Arkansas Meander Belts

Arkansas.gov. Bayou Bartholomew Alliance. http://www.arkansas.gov/bba/photos.htm.
Bayou Bartholomew Alliance. "Bayou Bartholomew Alliance, Winrock International, ADEQ, and The Nature Convervancy Receive Grant, Conservation Easements Pick Up Steam." Newsletter, Summer 2003, Vol. 14, 1–6, http://www.arkansas.gov/bba/files/BBnews14.pdf.
Brooks, Jeff A., George, Steven G., Hayes, David M., Minton, Russell L. Pezold, Frank, and Ulmer, Ronnie. "Diversity and Distribution of Freshwater Mussels In Bayou Bartholomew, Arkansas." Freshwater Mollusk Conservation Society, 4th Biennial Symposium, May15–18, 2005, http://ellipse.inhs.uiuc.edu/FMCS/Symposium/FMCS2005ProgramandAbstracts04–26–2005.pdf.
CWPA Watershed Success Stories. "The Tensas River Watershed: Reversing the Adverse impacts of Agricultural Development." http://www/usgs.gov/owq/clearwater/success/tensas/html.
Felsher, John N. "North Louisiana Early Ducks," Louisiana Game and Fish. http://www.lagameandfish.com/hunting/la__aa112404a/index.html.
Hoose, Phillip. *The Race to Save the Lord God Bird*. New York: Farrar, Straus and Girous, 2004.
Layher, William G., Phillips, Jason W. *Bayou Bartholomew Wetland Planning Area Report*, Little Rock: Arkansas Multi-Agency Wetland Planning Team, 2002. http:/www.awrims.cast.uark.edu/wetland__resources/wpar/bbarth/Chapters__1&2.pdf.
Pew Center for Global Climate Change. "Entergy Carbon Sequestration and Offsets." http://www.pewclimate.org/companies__leading__the__way__belc/company__profiles/entergy/entergy__carbon.cfm.
Rogers, Susan. "Planning Aid Letter on the Boeuf-Tensas Basin, Southeast Arkansas Feasibility Study. U.S. Fish and Wildlife Service, Arkansas Field Office, Conway, Arkansas. September 2000.
U.S. Department of Agriculture. National Resources Conservation Service. "Ecosystem-Based Assistance Pilot Projects, FY-96, Summary." http://www.nrcs.usda.gov/technical/ECS/ecosystem/ebapilot96.html.

U.S. Department of Energy, Office of Science. "Carbon Sequestration." http://cdiac2.esd.ornl.gov/
U.S. Environmental Protection Agency. Environmental Sciences: Tensas River Basin, Tensas River Basin- A Landscape Approach to Community Based Environmental Protection." http://epa.gov.nerlesd1/land-sci/tensas/exe-summary/newexsun.pdf.
U.S. Fish and Wildlife Service. "Bayou Cocodrie National Wildlife Refuge: Draft Comprehensive Conservation Plan." March 2001.
U.S. Fish and Wildlife Service. "Relocation of Black Bears to the Red River and Three Rivers Wildlife Management Area: SoFar-SoGood." http://www.fws.gov/southeast/news/2001/r01–062.html.
U.S. Fish and Wildlife Service. Tensas River National Wildlife Refuge. http://www.fws.gov/tensasriver/.
U.S. Fish and Wildlife Service. "Terrestrial Carbon Sequestration to Benefit Fish and Wildlife: Questions and Answers." http://www.fws.gov/southeast/carbon/Q-As.html.
Winrock International. "From Arkansas Roots, a Global Mission, Little Rock, Arkansas: Winrock International, 2005." http://www.winrock.org/common/files/publications/winrock__mag__AR__roots.pdf.
Winrock International. "Protecting and Restoring a Jewel of the Delta, 2007." http://www.winrock.org/Ecosystems/solution__story1.asp.

Restoration—Yazoo Basin

"EPA Halts Corps' Yazoo Pump Project." Water and Wastewater News. February 8, 2008, http://www.wwn-online.com/articles/58289/.
"EPA weights in against Mississippi Flood Project." Cox News Service, Sunday, February 3, 2008. http://www.coxwashington.com/reporters/content/reporters/stories/2008/02/03/YAZOO__PUMPS03__COX.html.
Humphrey, M.N., Lin, J.P., Kleiss, B.A. and Evans, D.E. "Monitoring Wetland Functional Recovery of Bottomland Hardwood Sites in the Yazoo Basin, MA." WRAP Technical Notes Collection (ERDE/EL TN-04–01). U.S. Army Engineer Research and Development Center, Vicksburg, MS.
Mississippi Forest and Wildlife Research Center, Department of Forestry Research. "Restoration of Bottomland Hardwood Forests." http://www.cfr.msstate.edu/fwrc/forestry/restore.htm.
Shabman, Leonard, and Laura Zeep. *An Approach for Evaluating Nonstructural Actions with Application to the Yazoo River (Mississippi) Backwater Area*. A report prepared in cooperation with the United States Environmental Protection Agency, Region 4, Under Grant #X984355–98. http://www.vwrrc.vt.edu/pdf/report.pdf.
Turner, R. Eugene, to Stephen L. Johnson, Administrator, U.S. Environmental Protection Agency, and Dirk Kempthorne, Secretary, U.S. Department of the Interior. Re: Yazoo Backwater Pumping Plant, Mississippi, November 2007. http://www.americanrivers.org/site/DocServer/Yazoo__Pumps__Scientist__Letter.pdf?docID=6941.
Twedt, Daniel, Pashley, David, Hunter, Chuck, Mueller, Allen, Brown, Cindy, and Ford, Bob. "Partners in Flight Bird Conservation Plan for the Mississippi Alluvial Valley." http://www.blm.gov/wildlife/plan/MAV__plan.html.
U.S. Environmental Protection Agency. "Yazoo Backwater Area: Technical Review of the Draft Reformulation Report: Cumulative Impacts in the Yazoo Basin." November 2, 2000. http://www.epa.gov/region4/water/specialprojects/yazoo/review.htm#t1.
U. S. Environmental Protection Agency, Region 4, Special Projects. "Lower Yazoo River Basin Economic and Environmental Restoration Initiative." http://www.epa/gov/region4/water/specialprojects/yazoo/investment/htm.
U.S. Fish and Wildlife Service. *Draft Comprehensive Conservation Plan and Environmental Assessment, Theodore Roosevelt National Wildlife Refuge Complex.* Hollandale, Mississippi, October 2005.
U.S. Fish and Wildlife Service, Ecological Services. "Fish and Wildlife Coordination Act Report: Yazoo Backwater Area, Mississippi, Reformulation Study. Submitted to Vicksburg District, U.S. Army Corps of Engineers, Vicksburg, Mississippi, October 2006, 36–37. http://www.americanrivers.org/site/DocServer/Fish__and__Wildlife__Service__Coordination__Act__Report.pdf?docID=6961.
Williams, Hans M., Kliess, Barbara A., Humphrey, Monica N., Klimas, Charles,V. "First-year Field Performance of Oak Species with Varying Flood Tolerance Planted on Hydric and Non-hydric Soils." Proceedings of the Seventh Biennial Southern Silvicultural Research Conference, Mobile, Alabama, November 17–19, 1992.
Williams, Hans M., and Craft, Monica N. "First-Year Survival and Growth of Bareroot, Container, and Direct-seeded Nuttall Oak Planted on Flood-prone Agricultural Fields." Proceedings of the Ninth Biennial Southern Silvicultural Research Conference, Clemson, South Carolina, February 25–27, 1997.

Restoration—Lower Mississippi River

American Rivers. "River Budget: National Priorities for Local River Conservation. Fiscal Year, 2007, http://www.americanrivers.org/site/DocServer/RB__07.pdf?docID=2961.

Davis, Angela A., Kleiss, Barbara A., O'Hara, Charles G., and Derby, Jennifer S. "The Development of a Decision Support System for Prioritizing Forested Wetland Restoration Areas in the Lower Yazoo River Basin, Mississippi." United States Environmental Protection Agency, Special Projects. http://www.epa.gov/region4/water/specialprojects/yazoo/dssdocument.htm.

King, Marcus D., and Sarria, Palomo. "U.S. Business Actions to Address Climate Change: Case Studies of Fine Industry Sectors." Washington, D.C.: Sustainable Energy Institute, and Numarck Associates, November 2004, 6, 50–55, http://www.getf.org/file/toolmanager/CustomO16C45F54636.pdf.

Longmire, David. "Vicksburg tracks the birds." *Engineer Update*, Vol. 20, No. 11, November 1996. www.hq.usace.army.mil/cepa/pubs/oldpubs/nov/story12.htm.

Lower Mississippi River Conservation Committee. "Lower Mississippi River Conservation Initiative." http://www.lmrcc.org/MRCI.htm.

Lower Mississippi River Conservation Committee. "Who We Are." http://www.lmrcc.org/who__we__are.htm.

Mitchell, W.A., Guilfoyle, M.P., and Walters, M.S. "Riparian shorebirds potentially impacted by USACE reservoir operations." EMRRP Technical Notes Collection (ERDC-EMRRP-SI-17). Vicksburg, Mississippi: U.S. Army Corps of Engineers, 2000, 6–7.

Pingleton, Mike. "Notes from the Field: A Journal of Amphipians and Reptiles, The Great Moccasin Migration." http://spongebob.ncsa.uiuc.edu/mike/field/mocs/moc2.htm.

Robinson, Dr. Michael C., Chief of Public Affairs. "An Environmental Tapestry." A Briefing to the Headquarters, U.S. Army Corps of Engineers, Civil Works Directorate, April 6, 1995.

Smith, R. Daniel, and Klimas, Charles V. *A Regional Guidebook for Applying the Hydrogeomorphic Approach to Assessing Wetland Functions of Selected Regional Wetland Subclasses, Yazoo Basin, Lower Mississippi Alluvial Valley.* Vicksburg: U.S. Army Corps of Engineers, Wetlands Research Program, April 2002.

U.S. Fish and Wildlife Service. "Lower Mississippi River Ecosystem: Final Draft, Lower Mississippi River Ecosystem Plan, September 10, 2002."

U.S. Fish and Wildlife Service. *Bayou Cocodrie National Wildlife Refuge: Draft, Comprehensive Conservation Plan. March 2001.* http://library.fws.gov/CCPs/bayoucocodrie__draft.pdf.

U.S. Fish and Wildlife Service, Southeast Region. "Terrestrial Carbon Sequestration to Benefit Fish and Wildlife." http://www.fws.gov/southeast/carbon/QandAs.html.

Restoration—Atchafalaya Basin

Atchafalaya Commission. *The Atchafalaya Trace: Heritage Area Management Plan,* Executive Summary, Baton Rouge, 2001. http://www.atchafalaya.org/office/execsumm.pdf.

Demas, Charles R., Brazelton, Sebastian R., and Powell, Nancy J.. "The Atchafalaya Basin—River of Trees." U.S. Geological Survey, U.S.G.S. Fact Sheet 021–02, November 2001, http://la.water.usgs.gov/pdfs/rivertree-web.pdf.

Environmental Research Group, LLC. *Scoping Report for the Supplemental Environmental Impact Statement for the Henderson Water Management Unit and the Recreational Development Feature of the Atchafalaya Basin Floodway System, Louisiana.* Prepared for the U.S. Army Corps of Engineers, New Orleans District, October, 2006. http://www.mvn.usace.army.mil/pd/projectsList/ProjectData/118002/Reports/Complete%20Scoping%20Report-final.pdf.

Conner, William J., Day, John W, and Slater, Wayne R. "Bottomland Hardwood Productivity: Case Study in a Rapidly Sudsiding Louisiana, U.S.A., Watershed." *Wetlands Ecology and Management,* Vol. 2, No. 4, 1993.

Coulson, Jennifer. "Timber Activity on Sherburne WMA and Swallow-Tailed Kite Use: 2002." *Newsletter of the Louisiana Ornithological Society*, September 2003. http://losbird.org/news/0309__202__news.pdf.

Fryling, Charles. Conversations. Baton Rouge, Louisiana, November 12, 1996.

Lockwood, C.C. *Atchafalaya: America's Largest River Basin Swamp*. Baton Rouge: Claitor's Publishing Division, 1981.

Mississippi River Commission. *Atchafalaya Basin Floodway System, Louisiana, Feasibility Study: Main Report and Final Environment Impact Statement.* Vicksburg: Mississippi River Commission, 1982, EIS-80–81.

Narvratilova, Juliette. "Sherburne Paddle Trail Network." Bayou Haystackers Paddling Club. http://www.bayouhaystackers.com/TrpsFrame.htm.

U.S. Environmental Protection Agency. "Intent to Prepare a Draft Supplemental Environmental Impact Statement for the Atchafalaya Basin Floodway System, Louisiana Project, Including Flat Lake Management Unit, Beau Bayou Management Unit, And Possible Modificiations or Additions to the Buffalo Cove

Management Unit, Located in St. Martin, St. Mary, Iberville, and Iberia Parishes, LA. August 3, 2005, Vol. 70, No. 148, 44586–44588. http://www.epa.gov/fedrgstr/EPA-IMPACT/2005/August/Day-03/i15298.htm.

U.S. Army Corps of Engineers, New Orleans District. "Buffalo Cove Engineering Documentation Report." July 15, 2004. http://www.mvn.usace.army.mil/pd/projectsList/reports.asp.

Restoration—Louisiana Coast

Brass, Agaha, and Bethany Krumrine. "Ecological Review: Timbalier Island Dune/Marsh Restoration," Baton Rouge: Louisiana Department of Natural Resources, Februrary 17, 2003. http://data.lacoast.gov/reports/er/ER%20(TE-40).pdf.

America's Wetland. "Habitats of America's Wetlands: Flotants." http://www.americaswetlandresources.com/background__facts/detailedstory/habitat.html.

Barataria-Terrebonne National Estuary Program. "State of the Estuary, Hydrological Modifications," http://www.btnp.org/hydro.htm.

Beall, Andrew D., Shea Penland, and Felix Cetini, Jr.. *Urbanization Effects on Habitat Change in St. Tammany Parish, 1982–2000.* New Orleans: 2001. http://www.saveourlake.org/pdfs/St-Tamanystudy2000.pdf.

Belhadjoli, Karim, Balkum, Kyle F.. "Ecological Review, Barataria Basin Landbridge Shoreline Protection Project." August 2004, CU4–2. http://data.lacoast.gov/reports/er/ER%20Barataria%20Basin%20Landbridge%20SP.pdf

Brown, Michael. "Davis Pond not meeting its projections." *New Orleans Times-Picayune,* Tuesday February 21, 2006. http://www.nola.com/weblogs/print.ssf?/mtlogs/nola__tpupdates/archives/print114833.html.

Brown, Matthew. "Sewage may be coast's savior." *New Orleans Times-Picayune,* October 16, 2006. http://www.nola.com/news/t-p/frontpage/index.ssf?/base/news-6/1160978422135610.xml&coll=1&thispage=1.

CH2Mhill. "Mississippi River Water Reintroduction into Bayou Lafourche: Phase 1 Design Report." Prepared for the Louisiana Department of Natural Resources, December 2005. http://data.lacoast.gov/reports/project/BA-25b/phase__1__section__1.pdf.

Chenier, Lou. Conversation, May 4, 2007. Lac des Allemands, Louisiana.

Conner, William H., Gosselink, James G., and Parrondo, Roland T. "Comparison of the Vegetation of Three Louisiana Swamp Sites with Different Flooding Regimes." *American Journal of Botany,* Vol. 68, No. 3, March, 1981, http://links.jstor.org/sici?sici=0002–9122%28198103%2968%3A3%3C320%3ACOTVOT%3E2.0.CO%3B2-S&size=LARGE&origin=JSTOR-enlargePage.

Day, John W., Faulkner, Stephen, Hyfield, Emily, Howard, Jenny. "Monitoring Response to the Stormwater Discharge at the Proposed Pointe au Chien Pumping State, Pointe au Chien Game Management Area, Terrebonne Parish, LA." Submitted to the Barataria-Terrebonne National Estuary Program, March 28, 2005.

Day, John, Mark Ford, Paul Kemp, and John Lopez. "Mister Go Must Go: A Guide for the Army Corps' Congressionally-Directed Closure of the Mississippi River Gulf Outlet." Environmental Defense Fund et al., December 4, 2006. http://www.environmentaldefense.org/documents/5665__Report%20-%20Mister%20Go%20Must%20Go.pdf.

Ducks Unlimited, "Marsh Terraces as a Conservation Practice." http://www.ducks.org/Louisiana/LouisianaConservation/1724/MarshTerracesasaConservationPractice.html.

Duplechain, Josh. "Scientists work to save 300-year-old community of Grand Bayou from a disaster." *LSUToday,* Vol. 20, No. 12, February 20, 2004. http://www.lsu.edu/lsutoday/040220/pageone.html.

Georgiou, Ioannis, Duncan M. Fitzgerald, Gregory W. Stone. "Physical Processes along the Louisiana Coast." In Ecosystem Restoration Study, U.S. Army Corps of Engineers, New Orleans District, November 2004, Chapter D.2, http://data.lca.gov/Ivan6/app/app__d__ch2.pdf.

Gilbert, Tony. "The Dead Zone: Closing MRGO could return life to a part of Lake Pontchartrain that is barren because of saltwater intrusion." Best of New Orleans.com May 8, 2007. http://www.bestofneworleans.com/dispatch/2007–05–08/news__feat.php.

GovTrak.us. "Authorization of the Morganza to the Gulf of Mexico Hurricane Protection Project." http://www.govtrack.us/congress/record.xpd?id=110-s20070104–92&bill=s110–202.

LaCoast, "Louisiana Coastal Wetland Functions and Values," http://lacoast.gov/cwppra/reports/EvaluationReport1997/4htm.

Kemp, P. and E. Hyfield. "The East Atchafalaya River Restoration Spillway." New York: Environmental Defense Fund, 2006.

LaCoast. Coastal Louisiana Basins. http://www.lacoast.gov/landchange/basins/index.htm.

LaCoast. CWPPRA's Restoration Projects. http://www.lacoast.gov/projects/list.asp.

LaCoast. Priority Project Lists. http://www.lacoast.gov/reports/multiproject/PPL/index.htm.

LaCoast. "From water to wetlands, Pipeline Projects Building New Marsh." http://www.lacoast.gov/watermarks/2005–08/4pipelineProjects/.

LaCoast. "Mississippi River Sediment Trap (MR-12)." http://www.lacoast.gov/reports/display.asp?projectNumber=MR-12&reportType=general.

Lake Pontchartrain Basin Foundation. *Comprehensive Habitat Management Plan for the Lake Pontchartrain Basin.* February 28, 2006, http://www.saveourlake.org/pdfs/JL/CHMP__final__%2022706.pdf.

Lane, Robert R., John W. Day, Jr., Burnell Thibodeaux. "Water Quality Analysis of a Freshwater Diversion at Caernarvon, Louisiana." Estuaries, Vol. 22, No. 2A, June 1999. http://estuariesandcoasts.org/cdrom/ESTU1999__22__2A__327__336.pdf.

Louisiana Coastal Wetlands Conservation and Restoration Task Force and the Wetlands Conservation and Restoration Authority. *Coast 2050: Toward a Sustainable Coastal Louisiana*. Baton Rouge: Louisiana Department of Natural Resources, 1998. http://www.coast2050.gov.

Louisiana Coastal Wetlands Conservation and Restoration Task Force. "Caernarvon Diversion Outfall Management (BS-03a)." October 2003. http://data.lacoast.gov/reports/gpfs/BS-03a.pdf.

Louisiana Department of Natural Resources, Executive Summary, "Draft Louisiana Coastal Impact Assistance Plan," February 2007. http://dnr.louisiana.gov/crm/ciap/ciap.asp.

Louisiana Department of Natural Resources. "History of the Christmas Tree Program." http://dnr.louisiana.gov/crm/coastres/pcwrp/history.asp.

Louisiana Department of Wildlife and Fisheries. "Wildlife Management Areas and Refuges." http://www.wlf.state.la.us/experience/wmas/.

Louisiana Department of Wildlife and Fisheries. "Natural Communities of Louisiana." http://www.wlf.state.la.us/experience/naturalheritage/natural communities/.

LSUResearch. "Preserving a Fragile Habitat: Coast Research Optimizing Breton Sound Diversion for Continued Preservation." Louisiana State University Office of Research and Economic Development, Summer 2004. http://www.research.lsu.edu/newsletter/archives/2004summer/cable.htm.

Marine Protected Areas of the United States. "Pointe aux Chenes Wildlife Management Area." http://www3.mpa.gov/exploreinv/SiteProfile4.aspx?SiteID=LA7.

Massimi, Michael. "Critique of Proposal to Redirect River," Rebuilding Louisiana Coalition, May 19, 2006. http://rebuildinglouisianacoalition.org/index.php?option=com__content&task=view&id=84&Itemid=64.

McGraw, Molly J. "The Effect of Environmental Forcing on the Suspended Sediment within the Naomi Wetlands as Reflected in Turbidity Data." Ph.D. Dissertation, Louisiana State University, August 2005.

McInnis, Nelwyn, and Bryan Rogers. *Priority Conservation Areas in the Lake Pontchartrain Estuary Zone.* The Nature Conservancy. http://www.nature.org/wherewework/northamerica/states/louisiana/files/estuary__zone__final__s.pdf.

McLeod, Ken, and Will Conner. "Rising sea level making conditions tougher for survival of forested coatal wetlands." News Release, Savannah River Ecology Laboratory, University of Georgia, March 19, 1996. http://www.uga.edu/srel/searise.htm.

Naomi, Al and Fredine, Jack. "District works to tame Ol' Man River." *Engineer Update*, Vol 24, no. 2, February, 2000. http://www.hq.usace.army.mil/cepa/feb00/story14.htm.

National Oceanic and Atmospheric Adminstration. "Coastal Wetlands Planning, Protection and Restoration Act, Myrtle Grove Freshwater Diversion Project." http://www.photolib.noaa.gov/habrest/cwppra.html.

National Research Council. *Drawing Louisiana's New Map.* Washington, D.C.: The National Academies Press, 2006.

Nelson, S.A., Soranno, P.A., and Qi, J. "Land-cover Change in Upper Barataria Basin Estuary, Louisiana, 1972–1992: Increases in Wetland Area." *Environ Manage*, May 2002, http://www.ncbi.nlm.nih.gov/entrez/query.fcgi?CMD=Display&DB=pubmed.

Paganie, David, Senior Editor. "Port Fourchon positions for future GoM E&P," *Offshore.* Vol. 66, No. 3, March 2006. http://www.offshore-mag.com/articles/article__display.cfm?Section=ARTCL&ARTICLE__ID=250818&page=1.

Quaid, John. "Written Off: The Gulf is slowly swallowing Isle de Jean Charles and other south Louisiana towns." Special Edition: Washing Away, 1997, *New Orleans Times-Picayune.* http://www.nola.com/hurricane/index.ssf?/washingaway/writtenoff__4.html.

Penland, Shea, S. Jeffers Williams, Donald W. Davis, Asbury H. Sallenger, Jr., and C.G. Groat. "Chapter 1, Barrier Island Erosion and Wetland Loss in Louisiana," in *Louisiana Coastal Area (LCA), Louisiana, Ecosystem Restoration Study,* New Orleans: U.S. Army Corps of Engineers, November 2004. http://coast2050.gov/reports/bia/BarrierIslandAtlas11x17.pdf.

Roy, Kevin J. "Final Environmental Assessment, Dedicated Dredging on the Barataria Basin Land Bridge, BA-36, Jefferson Parish, Louisiana, U.S. Fish and Wildlife Service, November 2005. http://lacoast.gov/reports/env/Barataria%20Basin%20BA-36.pdf.

Saveourwetlands.org. South Louisiana's Environmental Watch Network. http://saveourwetlands.org/.

Shleifstein, Mark, and McQuaid, John. "Washing Away." A five part series. *New Orleans Times-Picayune,* June 2002. www.nola.com/hurricane/content.ssf?/washingaway/index.html.

Swarenski, Christopher M. *Surface-water hydrology of the Gulf Intracoastal Waterway in South-central Louisiana, 1996–99.* U.S. Geological Survey Professional Paper 1672. http://pubs.usgs.gov/pp/pp1672/pdf/pp1672.pdf.

Swarzenski, Christopher M.. "Resurvey of Quality of Surface water and Bottom Material of the Barataria Preserve of Jean Lafitte National Historical Park and Preserve, Louisiana, 199–2000." Baton Rouge: U.S. Geological Survey, Water-Resources Investigations Report 03–4038 in Cooperation with the National Park Service, 2004. http://la.water.usgs.gov/pdfs/WRI__03–4038.pdf.

Swarzenski, Christophe. "The Intracoastal Waterway as a Distributary of Freshwater and Sediments to Coastal Louisiana. " Paper delivered to AUG, 1998 Meeting. http://www.agu.org/cgi-bin/SFgate/SFgate?&listenv=table&multiple=1&range=1&directget=1&application=sm98&database=%2Fdata%2Fepubs%2Fwais%2Findexes%2Fsm98%2Fsm98&maxhits=200&="OS42B-02.

Tate, J.N., A.R. Carrillo, R.C. Berger, and B.J. Thibodeaux. *Salinity Changes in Pontchartrain Basin Estuary, Louisiana, Resulting from Mississippi River-Gulf Outlet Partial Closure Plans with Width Reduction,* Vicksburg and New Orleans: U.S. Army Corps of Engineers, Coastal and Hydraulics Laboratory, August 2002.http://mrgo.swg.usace.army.mil/Documents/2002%20August%20Salinity%20Changes%20in%20Pontchartrain.pdf.

The Nature Conservancy. "The Preservation of Migratory Bird Habitat on Grand Isle, Louisiana." http://www.nature.org/wherewework/northamerica/states/louisiana/preserves/art16540.html.

U.S. Army Corps of Engineers, New Orleans District. "Caernarvon Freshwater Diversion Project." http://www.mvn.usace.army.mil/prj/caernarvon/caernarvon.htm

U.S. Army Corps of Engineers, Galveston District. "Closing the Mississippi River Gulf Outlet: Environmental and Economic Considerations."http://www.swg.usace.army.mil/mrgo/Documents/Publications/Closing%20the%20MRGO%20environmental%20and%20economic%20considerations.pdf

U.S. Army Corps of Engineers, New Orleans District. "Davis Pond Freshwaterr Diversion Structure." http://www.mvn.usace.army.mil/pao/dpond/davispond.htm.

U.S. Army Corps of Engineers, New Orleans District. *Louisiana Coastal Area (LCA), Louisiana: Ecosystem Restoration Study, Final Report.* November 2004. http://www.lca.gov/main__report.aspx.

U.S. Army Corps of Engineers, New Orleans District. *U.S. Army Corps of Engineers Response to Hurricanes Katrina & Rita in Louisiana, Environmental Assessment, EA #433.* Draft, No Date, EA-28. http://www.mvn.usace.army.mil/hps/Items%20of%20Special%20Interest/Final%20Draft%20Katrina%20EA.pdf.

U.S. Department of Agriculture. Natural Resources Conservation Service, "Plant Guide: Maidencane," http://plants.usda.gov/plantguide/pdf/pg__pahe2.pdf.

U.S. Environmental Protection Agency. "River Corridor and Wetland Restoration: Myrtle Grove Freshwater Diversion Project." http://yosemite.epa.gov/water/restorat.nsf/80721365528c5f00852565840 06a4bc2/21c91233da4d6b0985256c6a006c567f!OpenDocument.

U.S. Environmental Protection Agency, Gulf of Mexico Program. "Monitoring Response to the Stormwater Discarge at the Proposed Pointe aux Chenes Pumping Station, Project #MX974605," http://www.epa.gov/gmpo/projects/stormwater__intro.html.

U.S. Fish and Wildlife Service. "Big Branch Marsh National Wildlife Refuge." http://www.fws.gov/southeast/pubs/bigtear.pdf.

U.S. Fish and Wildlife Service. *Big Branch Marsh National Wildlife Refuge, Draft Comprehensive Conservation Plan and Environmental Assessment.* Atlanta: Southeast Region, April 2007.

U.S. Fish and Wildlife Service. "Southeast Louisiana National Wildlife Complex: Bayou Sauvage National Wildlife Refuge." http://www.fws.gov/bayousauvage.

U.S. Geological Survey. National Wetlands Center. "Salt Tolerance of Southern Baldcypress." Lafayette, Louisiana, June 1997. http://www.nwrc.usgs.gov/climate/fs92__97.pdf.

van Heerden, Ivor. "Coast Land Loss: Hurricanes and New Orleans," Center for the Study of Public Health Impacts of Hurricanes." LSU Hurricane Center, Louisiana State University, 2003. http://www.publichealth.hurricane.lsu.edu/Adobe%20files%20for%20webpage/Coastal%20Land%20Loss%20-%20Hurricanes%20and%20New%20Orleans.pdf.

van Heerden, Ivor. "Louisiana Wetland News: Long-term Coastal Restoration Plan Recently Released by LSU," Louisiana Sea Grant College Program, Louisiana State University Agricultural Center. http://www.seagrantfish.lsu.edu/pdfs/lwn/1994/summer__94.pdf.

Wilhite, L.P. and Toliver, J.R., "Baldcypress," U.S. Deparment of Agriculture, U.S. Forest Service, Northeastern Area, State and Private Forestry. http://www.na.fs.fed.us/pubs/silvics__manual/Volume__1/taxodium/distichum.htm.

Wilkins, Jim and Walter Keithly. "Louisiana Natural Resource Policy: Coastal Restoration versus Oysters?" New Orleans, Louisiana Sea Grant Legal Program,

Louisiana State University, May 22, 2007. http://www.lsu.edu/sglegal/pdfs/CNREP__oyster.pdf.

Williams, S. Jeffress, Penland, Shea, and Sallenger, Asbury H., Jr. eds. *Atlas of Shoreline Change in Louisiana from 1853 to 1989*, U.S. Geological Survey, 1992. http://www.coast2050.gov/reports/bia/ch4c.pdf.

The Flood of 1993

Changnon, Stanley A, ed. *The Great Flood of 1993: Causes, Impacts, and Responses*, Boulder, Colorado: Westview Press, 1996.

Committee to the Administration Floodplain Management Task Force. *Sharing the Challenge: Floodplain Management into the 21st Century*, Report of the Floodplain Management Review. Washington D.C.: U.S. Government Printing Office, June 1994.

Conrad, David, Stout, Martha, McNitt, Ben. *Higher Ground: A Report on Voluntary Property Buyouts in the Nation's Floodplains*. Washington, D.C.: National Wildlife Federation, July, 1998.

Dyhouse, Gary R. "Myths and Misconceptions of the 1993 Flood." http://www.mvs,usace.army,mil/dinfo/fl93info.htm.

Galloway, Gerald E. Jr. "Corps of Engineers Responses to the Changing National Approach to Floodplain Management Since the 1993 Midwest Flood. *Journal of Contemporary Water Research and Education*, Issue 130, March 2005, 5–12.

Galloway, Gerald E., Jr. "New Directions in Floodplain Management." *Water Resources Bulletin*, Vol. 31, No. 3, June 1995, 351–357.

Galloway, Gerry; Cunniff, Shannon; Kelmelis, John; Robinson, Mike; Shoudy, Harry. "What's happened in Floodplain Management since the "93 Mississippi Flood." http://www.colorado.edu/hazards/o/may098.htm/may098a.htm#Galloway.

Frankie, W.T., et al. *Guide to the Geology of the Columbia and Waterloo Area, Monroe County, Illinois*. Illinois State Geological Survey. Field Trip Guidebook 1997a, April 19, 1997.

Kolva, James R. "Effects of the Great Midwest Flood of 1993 on Wetlands." U.S. Geological Survey, Water Supply Paper 2425. http://water.usgs.gov/nwsum/WSP2425/flood.html.

Larson, Lee W. "The Great USA Flood of 1993." Paper presented at IAHS Conference, *Destructive Water: Water-Caused Natural Disasters-Their Abatement and Control*, Anaheim, California, June 24–28, 1996. http://www.wnrfc.noaa.gov/floods/papers/oh__2/great.htm.

Lovelace, James T., Strauser, Claude N. "Upper Mississippi Flood," http://lms1.mvs.usace.army.mil/93.html.

Phillipi, Nancy S. "Revisiting Flood Control: An Examination of Federal Flood Control Policy in Light of the 1993 Flood Event on the Upper Mississippi River." The Wetlands Initiative. http://www.wetlands-initiative.org/pub/revisiting.html.

Pinter, Nicholas. "One Step Forward, Two Steps Back on U. S. Floodplains." *Science*, Vol. 308, April 8, 2005, 207–208.

Saulny, Susan. "Development Rises on St. Louis Area Flood Plains." *New York Times*, May 15, 2007. http://www.nytimes.com/2007/05/15/us/15flood.html.

U.S. Army Corps of Engineers. St. Louis District. *Upper Mississippi River Comprehensive Plan.* Draft for Public Review, May 2006.

Wahl, K.L., Vining, K.C., Wiche, G.J. "Flood Discharges in the Upper Mississippi River Basin, 1993." U.S. Geological Survey Circular 1120-A. http://www. geo.mtu.edu/department/classess/ge404/flood/background/1120-a.

Yin, Yao, Nelson, John C., Swenson, Gary V., Langgrehe, Heidi A., and Blackburn, Theresa A. " Tree Mortality in the Upper Mississippi River and Floodplain Following an Extreme Flood in 1993." http://www.mvr.usace.army.mil/forestry/Publications/1994%20tree%20mortality%20report.htm.

Flood of 2005 and Post-Katrina Restoration

Bahr, Len. "Corps outshines state at river diversion summit." lacoastpost.com. March 5, 2009. http://lacoastpost.com/blog/?p=3927.

Barataria-Terrebonne National Estuary Program. "Healthy Estuary, Healthy Economy, Healthy Communities: Environmental Indicators in the Barataria-Terrebonne Estuary System" http://www.nationalestuaries.org/publications/nepspotlight/btnep/PDFs/IndicatorsReport02.pdf.

Barras, John. "Caernarvon Diversion Post-Katrina, Illustrating Some Recovery after Spring Flows from the Caernarvon Diversion." In Lopez, John, "Hurricane Protection: Where Do We Stand?" Powerpoint to the Tulane Engineering Forum, May 11, 2007. http://tef.tulane.edu/presentations/lopez__john.pdf.

Bowser, Betty Ann. "Investigating Broken Levees." *A NewsHour with Jim Lehrer* Transcript, October 20, 2005. http://www/pbs.org/newshour/bb/science/july-dec05/levees__10–12.html.

Buskey, Nikki. "Louisiana Officials criticize Corps report." *Thibodaux Daily Comet*. March 6, 2009. http://www.dailycomet.com/article/20090306/ARTICLES/

903069935/1030/OPINION02?Title=La-officials-criticize-corps-report.
Coast 2050, Press Release. "Corps of Engineers and State of Louiaiana sign historic Coast 2050 study agreement." February 18, 2000. http://www.coast2050.gov/press/02–18–00.htm.
Coastal Protection and Restoration Authority of Louisiana. "Gaining Ground: Coastal Restoration a Big Winner after Legislative Session." Newsletter, July 18, 2007. http://lacpra.org/index.cfm?md=pagebuilder&tmp=home&nid=41&pnid=4&pid=34&fmid=0&catid=0&elid=0.
Colton, Craig E. *An Unnatural Metropolis: Wresting New Orleans from Nature.* Baton Rouge: Louisiana State Unversity, 2005.
Conner, William H., Brody, Michael. "Rising Water Levels and the Future of Southeastern Louisiana Swamp Forests." *Estuaries,* Vol. 12, No.4, December 1989. http://estuariesandcoasts.org/cdrom/ESTU1989__12__4__318__323.pdf.
Conner, William J., Day, John W, and Slater, Wayne R. "Bottomland Hardwood Productivity: Case Study in a Rapidly Sudsiding Louisiana, U.S.A., Watershed." *Wetlands Ecology and Management,* Vol. 2, No. 4, 1993.
Day, John W., Jr., et al. "Restoration of the Mississippi Delta: Lessons from Hurricanes Katrina and Rita." Science, Vol. 315, March 23, 2007. http://www.clear.lsu.edu/clear/web-content/Web__items/Science%20Paper.pdf.
Department of Defense, Emergency Supplemental Appropriations to Address Hurricanes in the Gulf of Mexico, and Pandemic Influenza Act of 2006. 109th Cong. 1st Session. H.R. 2863.
Energy and Water Development Appropriations Act of 2006. 109th Cong. 1st Session. H.R. 2419.
Drew, Christopher, and Revkin, Andrew C. "Design Shortcomings Seen in New Orleans Flood Walls" *New York Times,* September 21, 2005. http://www.nytimes.con/national/nationalspecial/21walls.html?hp=&pagewanted=print.
Ewing, Philip. "'Illinois' next big export product could be…mud." *St. Louis Post-Dispatch.* January 6, 2006.
Gagliano, Sherwood M. "Coastal Restoration in Louisiana: Striving for a Higher Level." A Position Paper of the Louisiana Landowners Association, 2002. http://www.coastalenv.com/Publications/LLA%20Position%20Paper.pdf.
Gagliano, S.M., and van Beek, J.L.. A "A Third Branch for the Mississippi River: Lafourche Conveyance Channel," Baton Rouge: Coastal Environments, 1999. http://www.coastalenv.com/Publications/THIRD%20DELTA%20CONVEYANCE.pdf.
Grunwald, Michael, and Glasser, Susan D. "Experts Say Faulty Levees Caused Much of Flooding." *Washington Post,* September 21, 2005. http://www.washington-post.comwp-dyn/content/article/2005/09/20/AR005092001894__pf.html.
Houck, Oliver. "Comments on Preliminary Draft of the Comprehensive Coastal Protection Master Plan for Louisiana." Letter to Sidney Coffee, Office of the Governor, Randy Hanchey, Louisiana Department of Natural Resources. http://saveourwetlands.org/commentsonccpmp.html.
Keim, Richard F., Chambers, Jim L., Dean, Thomas J. "Baldcypress Site Relationships and Silviculture." *Louisiana Agriculture,* Spring 2006. http://www.lsuagcenter.com/en/environment/conservation/wetlands/Baldcypress+Site+Relationships+and+Silviculture.htm.
Louisiana Coastal Protection and Restoration Authority. http://www.lacpra.org/.
Louisiana Coastal Protection and Restoration Authority. Louisiana's Comprehensive Master Plan for a Sustainable Coast. http://www.lacpra.org/index.cfm?md=pagebuilder&tmp=home&nid=24&pnid=0&pid=28&fmid=0&catid=0&elid=0.
Louisiana Recovery Authority.http://www.lra.louisiana.gov/.
March, Leslie, Delta Chapter Sierra Club. Letter to The Honorable Kathleen Blanco and Lieutenant General Carl A. Strock. March 2007. http://louisiana.sierraclub.org/pdf/DeltaChap__Coastal__comments__March__2007.pdf.
McQuaid, John and Marshall, Bob. "Officials knew about weak soil under levee, 17th Street Canal was just above soft peat." *New Orleans Times-Picayune,* October 22, 2005. http://www.nola.com/printer/printer.ssf?/base/news-4–1129960640235820.xml.
McQuaid, John, Walsh, Bill, Barnett, Jim, and Schleifstein, Mark. "Levees' weakness well-known before breaches, Lack of political will, funds cited in failure." *New Orleans Times-Picayune*. http://www.nola.com/weblogs/print.ssf?/mtlongs/nola__tporleans/archives/print76025.html.
Maygarden, Benjamin D., Yakuik, Jill-Karen, and Weiss, Ellen. *National Register Evaluation of New Orleans Drainage System, Orleans Parish, Louisiana.* New Orleans: U.S. Army Corps of Engineers, New Orleans District, 1999.
McKinney, Lee. "To build or not to build." *St. Louis Post-Dispatch,* September 20, 2005.
Melancon, Charlie. "Melancon Votes for Water Projects Bill Authorizing of $2 Billion for Louisiana." News Release, April 19, 2007. http://www.melancon.house.gov/news.asp?ARTICLE3337=7420.
Multiple Lines of Defense Assessment Team. *Comprehensive Recommendations Supporting the Use of The Multiple Lines of Defense Strategy to Sustain Coastal Louisiana.* Lake Pontchartrain Basin Foundation, August 17, 2007. http://www.saveourlake.

org/pdfs/JL/LPBF%20-%20CRCL%20Final%20Draft%20MLODS%20report%208-17-07%20for%20release%20part1.pdf.

National Acedemies Press. *Fourth Report of the National Academy of Engineering/National Research Council Committee on New Orleans Regional Hurricane Protection Projects: Review of the IPET Volume VIII*. April, 2008. http://www.nap.edu/openbook.php?record_id=12167.

"Pumping the floodwater out...." *St. Louis Post-Dispatch,* September 4, 2005.

Revkin, Andrew C. "Gazing at Breached Levees, Critics See Years of Missed Opportunties." *New York Times*, September 2, 2005. http://www.nytimes.com/2005/09/02/national/nationalspecial/02levee.htm?pagewanted=print.

Russo, Edmond J., Jr. U.S. Army Corps of Engineers, New Orleans District. "Louisiana Coastal Area, Louisiana—Ecosystem Restoration Feasiblity Study." in *Planning Ahead: Notes for the Planning Community*, February, 2000. http://www.usace.army.mil/inet/functions/cw/cecwp/news/v3i2.pdf.

Scheifstein, Mark. "Land Lost: Hurricanes Katrina and Rita turned 217 square miles of coastal land and wetlands into water." *New Orleans Time-Picayune,* October 11, 2006. http://www.nola.com/recovery/t-p/index.ssf?/recovery/articles/land_lost.html.

Schleifstein, Mark. "Laying the Groundwork." *New Orleans Times-Picayune,* March 6, 2007. http://www.nola.com/speced/lastchance/t-p/index.ssf?/speced/lastchance/articles/day3layinggroundwork.html.

Schleifstein, Mark. "Last Chance: The fight to save a disappearing coast." *New Orleans Times-Picayune*. March 4, 2007. http://www.nola.com/speced/lastchance/.

Schleifstein, Mark. "Corps works to climb mountain of flood projects." *New Orleans Times-Picayune*. May 26, 2007. http://blog.nola.com/stormwatch/2007/05/corps_works_to_climb_mountain.html.

Schleifstein, Mark. "Save Our Wetlands Plans to Sue Over 'Leaky Levee.'" *New Orleans Time-Picayune*, June 7, 2007. http://saveourwetlands.org/sowlplan2sueleaky.html.

Schleifstein, Mark. "Big Plans." *New Orleans Times-Picayune*. July 29, 2007. http://www.nola.com/news/t-p/frontpage/index.ssf?/base/news-8/118570214516450.xml&coll=1&thispage=1.

Schleifstein, Mark. "Category 5 hurricane protection plan is delayed again." *New Orleans Times-Picayune*. December 6, 2008. http://www.nola.com/news/index.ssf/2008/12/category_5_hurricane_protectio.html.

Schleifstein, Mark. "Army Corps of Engineers delays outrage." *New Orleans Times-Picayune*. January 14, 2009. http://www.nola.com/news/t-p/frontpage/index.ssf?/base/news-12/1231914123231780.xml&coll=1.

Schleifstein, Mark. "Sense of urgency grips coastal restoration summit." *New Orleans Times-Picayune*. March 5, 2009. www.nola.com/news/index.ssf/2009/03/sense_of_urgency_grips_coastal.htm.

Schleifstein, Mark. "Corps releases Category 5 hurricane protection study, but document contains no action plan." *New Orleans Times-Picayune*. March 5, 2009. http://www.nola.com/news/index.ssf/2009/03/corps_releases_storm_study_but.html.

Shleifstein, Mark, and McQuaid, John. "Washing Away: The Big One." Part 2 of a five part series. *New Orleans Times-Picayune,* June 2002. http://www.nola.com/printer/ptinter.ssf?/washingaway/thebigone_1.html.

Smith, Ewell. Testimony on "Revitalizing the Economy of South Louisiana: Empowering the Region for Recovery and Growth." before the Senate Commerce Committee, Science and Transportation Committee, New Orleans Supreme Court Chambers, November 5, 2005. http://commerce.senate.gov/pdf/Smith%20Senatetestimony.pdf.

Seed, R.B. etal. *Investigation of the Performance of the New Orleans Flood Protection System in Hurricane Katrina on August 29, 2005.* Final Report, Berkeley: July 31, 2006.

Sparks, Richard E. "Rethinking, Then Rebuilding New Orleans," *Issues in Science and Technology.* Winter 2006. http://www.issues.org/22.2/sparks.html.

Team Louisiana. *The Failure of the New Orleans Levee System during Hurricane Katrina.* Report prepared for Secretary Johnny Bradberry, Louisiana Department of Transportation and Development, Baton Rouge, Louisiana, State Project No. 704-92-0022, December 6, 2006. http://www.publichealth.hurricane.lsu.edu/Adobe%20files%20for%20webpage/Team%20LA%20indiv/Team%20Louisiana%20-%20cov,%20toc,%20exec%20summ,%20intro.pdf.

U.S. Geological Survey. "USGS Reports Latest Land Change estimates for Louisiana Coast." News Release, October 3, 2006. http://dnr.louisiana.gov/sec/execdiv/pubinfo/newsr/2006/1003usgs-coast-land-change.pdf.

U.S. Army Corps of Engineers. Performance Evaluation of the New Orleans and Southeast Louisiana Hurricane Protection System. Final Report of the Interagency Performance Evalution Task Force. Final Draft. June 1, 2008. https://ipet.wes.army.mil/.

U.S. Army Corps of Engineers, New Orleans District. "Atchafalaya Bacwater Study." http://www.mvn.usace.army.mil/pd/projectsList/home.asp?projectID=100.

U.S. Army Corps of Engineers, New Orleans District. "CAP—Lake Verret Ecosystem Restoration." http://www.mvn.usace.army.mil/pd/projectsList/home.asp?projectID=88&directoryFilePath=ProjectData%5C.

U.S. Army Corps of Engineers. New Orleans District. IPET Risk and Reliability Report. http://nolarisk.usace.army.mil.

U.S. Army Corps of Engineers, New Orleans District. *Louisiana Coastal Protection and Restoration, Preliminary Technical Report to United States Congress,* July 2006. http://lacpr.usace.army.mil/PreliminaryReport/LACPR%20Preliminary%20Technical%20Report%20to%20United%20States%20Congress.pdf.

U.S. Army Corps of Engineers. New Orleans District. Louisiana Coastal Protection and Restoration Study (LACPR). Draft Final Technical Report. http://lacpr.usace.army.mil/Report/DTR/Draft%20LACPR%20Technical%20Report%20Mar%2009.pdf.

U.S. Army Corps of Engineers, New Orleans District. Draft, Louisiana Coastal Protection and Restoration. Plan Formulation Atlas. http://lacpr.usace.army.mil/default.aspx?p=s&t=15&i=28.

U.S. Army Corps of Engineers, New Orleans District. *Lake Pontchartrain and Vicinity Hurricane Protection Project in St. Bernard, Orleans, Jefferson, and St. Charles Parishes.* Project Fact Sheet, Updated May 23, 2005. http://www.mvn.usace.army.mil/pao/visitor/index.htm.

U.S. Army Corps of Engineers, New Orleans District. "Scoping Report: Wetland Creation and Restoration, Louisiana Coastal Area, Louisiana, Ecosystem Restoration, Barrier Island Restoration, Marsh Creation and River Diversion, Barataria Basin Feasibility Study." June 2000, http://www.coast2050.gov/reports/wet__scoping__rep.pdf;

U.S. Army Corps of Engineers. New Orleans District. *Water Marks,* March 2006.

Van Heerden, Ivor. *The Storm.* New York: Viking, 2006.

Westrink, J.J. and Luettich, R.A. "The Creeping Storm." *Civil Engineering Magazine,* June 2003, 1–3. http://www.pubs.asce.org/ceonline/ceonline03/0603feat.html.

Wold, Amy. "Scientists, Engineers Caution State, Long Levees Could Damage Coast." Baton Rouge *Advocate,* March 17, 2007. http://www.louisianaspeaks.org/news/3128.html.

WETMAAP.ORG. "Cocodrie Background Information, Barataria-Terrebonne Estuary: The Houma Navigation Channel and the Gulf Intracoastal Waterway, Louisiana."http://www.wetmaap.org/Cocodrie/Supplement/co__background.html.

Working Group for Post-Katrina Planning for the Louisiana Coast. *A New Framework for Planning the Future of Coastal Louisiana after the Hurricanes of 2005.* Cambridge, Maryland: University of Maryland, Center for Environmental Science, January 2006. http://www.umces.edu/la-restore/New%20Framework%20Final%20Draft.pdf.

The Upper Mississippi-Illinois River Waterway

American Rivers. "The Nation's Most Endangered Rivers of 2000." http://www.amrivers.org/mer00miss.html.

Duyvejonck, Jon, Editor. "Draft Supplement to the April 2002 *Draft, U.S. Fish and Wildlife Coordination Act Report for the Upper Mississippi and Illinois River System Navigation Feasibility Study*. April 2004. In the U.S. Army Corps of Engineers, Rock Island. *Final Integrated Feasibility Report and Programmatic Environmental Impact Statement for the UMS-IWW System Navigation Feasibility Study*, September 24, 2004.

Faber, Scott. "Scandal Rocks Navigation Study." American Rivers. *Mississippi Monitor*, Vol. IV, no. 3, March 2000.

Grunwald, Michael. "How Corps Turned Doubt into a Lock." *Washington Post,* February 13, 2000.

Lambrecht, Bill. "Corps officials rejected study, urged expansion of river locks." *St. Louis Post-Dispatch*, February 13, 2000.

Lambrecht, Bill. "One economist traded security for uncertainty when he blew the whistle on an Army Corps of Engineers study." St. Louis *Post-Dispatch*, March 19, 2000.

National Research Council. *Inland Navigation System Planning: The Upper Mississippi—Illinois Waterway*, Washington, D.C.: National Academy of Sciences, 2001.

National Research Council. *Restructured Upper Mississippi River-Illinois Waterway, Feasibility Study*. Washington D.C.: National Academies Press, 2004.

Shipley, Sara. "Corps says locks aren't needed, shifts decision to Congress." *St. Louis Post-Dispatch*, Janaury 24, 2004.

Spitzack, Charles. Regional Program Director, Navigation and Ecosystem Sustainability Program for the Upper Mississippi River System, Rock Island District, U.S. Army Corps of Engineers. Telephone conversation. April 1, 2008.

Thorne, Christopher. "Early Corps of Engineers' report rejects rebuilding lock system." *St. Louis Post-Dispatch*, December 2, 1998.

Pogue, Jim. "District to do a half million dollar river study. *River Watch Online*. U.S. Army Corps of Engineers, Memphis District. January 18, 2008.

U.S. Army Corps of Engineers, Rock Island District. *Interium Report for the Restructured Upper Mississippi River-Illinois Waterway Navigation Feasibility Study.* October 2002.

U.S. Army Corps of Engineers. "Construction gets green light; funding want begins," Navigation and Ecosystem Sustainability Program for the Upper Mississippi River System." January 2008,

U.S. Army Corps of Engineers, Rock Island District. *Final Integrated Feasibility Report and Programmatic Environmental Impact Statement for the UMS-IWW System Navigation Feasibility Study*. September 24, 2004.

Upper Mississippi River Basin Association. "Upper Mississippi River System: Environmental Management Program." Testimony to the U.S. Army Corps of Engineers, October 29, 2003. http://www.umbsn.org/stewardship__legislation/NavigationStudy.shtml#umbsnnavstudycomment.

Vanderpool, Ginger. "Navigation Debate Pits Farmers, Shippers Against Environmentalists." American Rivers: *Mississippi Monitor*, Vol. 3., no. 7, July 1999.

Congress, the Corps of Engineers, and Restoration

Blum, Michael D., and Roberts, Harry H. "Drowning of the Mississippi Delta due to insufficient sediment supply and global sea-level rise." Nature Geoscience, Vol. 2, No. 7, July, 2009, 488-91.

Brinson, Mark et al. *A Guildbook for Applications of Hydrogeomorphic Assessments of Riverine Wetlands*. Washington, D.C.: U.S. Army Corps of Engineers, Wetlands Research Program, Technical Report WRP-DE-11, December 1995.

Buskey, Nikki. "Local levees face experts' scrutiny." houmatoday.com, April 29, 2008. http://www.houmatoday.com/article/20080429/ARTICLES/804290327/1211/Local__levees__face__experts____scrutiny.

Carter, Nicole. "IB10133-Water Resources Development Act (WRDA) and Other Army Corps of Engineers Legislation." Congressional Research Service Reports, April 12, 2005. http://www.ncseonline.org/NLE/CRS/abstract.cfm?NLEis=53747.

Department of the Army, Office of the Inspector General. Report of Investigation (Case 00–19) on the Upper Mississippi Navigation Study. http://www.osc.gov/Documents/ArmyRol/p1–10.pdf.

Galloway, Gerald E. "Restoring Coastal Louisiana: Planning without a National Water Policy," *The Bridge*, Vol. 36, No. 1, Spring 2006.

Galloway, Gerald E. Statement before the Committee on Transportation and Infrastructure, Subcommittee on Water Resources and the Environment. U.S. House of Representatives. October 27, 2005. http://www.umimra.org/documents/galloway.pdf.

Galloway, Gerald E. "Water Resources and Climate Change." Testimony, U.S. House of Representatives, Committee on Transportation and Infrastructure. May 16, 2007.

Grunwald, Michael. "Army Corps Suspends Mississippi River Projects. *Washington Post*. February 28, 2001.

Grunwald, Michael. "The Corps Cored." *Washington Post*, May 5, 2003.

Grunwald, Michael. "Corps of Engineer Reforms Suspended." *Washington Post*. April 7, 2000.

Grunwald, Michael. "New Twist in River Wars: Recreation View with Navigation for Commercial Use," *Washington Post*, January 10, 2000.

Grunwald, Michael. "Public Works Study Halted." *Washington Post*, March 1, 2001.

Grunwald, Michael. "Senators Seek to Block Corps of Engineers Reforms. *Washington Post*. May 13, 2000.

Grunwald, Michael. "Working to Please Hill Commanders." *Washington Post*, September 11, 2000.

Hutchinson, Tim, United States Senator. "Senate Passes Bill Containing $20 mill for Delta Regional Authority: Energy and Water Appropriations Bill Has Millions for Arkansas Projects." http://www.senate.gov/~hutchinson/9–8-00__press__release.html.

Lambrecht, Bill. "Army takes steps to rein in Corps of Engineers, Changes are designed to bolster civilian control." *St. Louis Post-Dispatch*, March 31, 2000.

Lambrecht, Bill. "Corps of Engineers commander defends his embattled agency." *St. Louis Post-Dispatch*, March 16, 2003.

Lambrecht, Bill. "Scientists recommend against lock construction on Mississippi River," *St. Louis Post-Dispatch*, March 1, 2001.

Marshall, Bob, and Mark Schleifstein. "Last Chance, a three part series." *New Orleans Times-Picayune*, March 4–6, 2007. http://www.nola.com/speced/lastchance/.

Marshall, Bob, and Mark Schleifstein. "Losing Ground: Bureaucratic Barrier Islands." *New Orleans Times-Picayune*, March 5, 2007. http://www.nola.com/speced/lastchance/t-p/index.ssf?/speced/lastchance/pdf/BureaucraticBarrierIslands.pdf.

National Research Council, *U.S. Army Corps of Engineers Water Resources Planning: A New Opportunity for Service*, Washington, D.C.: National Academy Press, 2004,

Isikoff, Michael. "Logjam breaking up at Alton Locks and Dam." Illinois Periodicals Online: *The Alton Telegraph*. January 1979. http://www.lib.niu.edu/1979/ii790117.html. http://www.nae.edu/nae/bridgecom.nsf/weblinks/MKEZ-6MYT5R?OpenDocument.

Kazmann, Raphael. *Modern Hydrology*. New York: Harper and Row, 1972.

Marshall, Bob. "Last Chance: The fight to save a disappearing coast." *New Orleans Times-Picayune*, March 4, 2007. http://www.nola.com/speced/lastchance/t-p/index.ssf?/speced/lastchance/articles/day1.html.

National Research Council. *New Directions in Water Resources Planning for the U.S. Army Corps of Engineers*. Washington, D.C.: National Academy Press, 1999.
National Research Council. *U.S. Army Corps of Engineers Water Resources Planning: A New Opportunity for Service.* Washington, D.C.: National Academy Press, 2004.
National Research Council. *Wetlands: Characteristics and Boundaries*. Washington D.C.: National Academy Press, 1995.
National Wildlife Federation. "Greening the Corps: Eastern Arkansas Irrigation Projects." http://www.nwf.org/greeningcorps/project1.pdf.
National Wildlife Federation. "Stop the Grand Prairie Project—for good." http://action.nwf.org/nwf/alert-description.tcl?alert__id=2258119.
Pianin, Eric. "New Orders for Army Engineers, General Outlines Reshaping of Construction Agency Under Fire." *Washington Post*, March 16, 2001.
"Private group says federal 'pork' spending reaches record level." CNN.com, allpolitics.com with *Time*. http://www.cnn.com/2001/ALLPOLITICS/03/14/pork/barrel/spending.
Rasmussen, J.L. "Management of the Upper Mississippi: A Case History." In Calow, Peter, and Petts, Geoffrey E., ed. *The Rivers Handbook: Hydrological and Ecological Principles.* London: Blackwell Science, 1994.
Roberts, Ben. "Some worry that Katrina sank bill for river projects: Senate measure to fund lock expansion hasn't been set for a vote." *St. Louis Post-Dispatch,* September 22, 2005.
Ruess, Martin. "Ecology, Planning, and River Management in the United States: Some Historical Reflections." *Ecology and Society,* Vol. 10, No. 1, Art. 34, 2005.
Ruess, Martin. *Reshaping Water Politics: The Emergence of the Water Resources Development Act of 1986*. Washington, D.C.: U.S. Army Corps of Engineers, Water Resources Support Center, Institute for Water Resources, October 1991.
The Nature Conservancy. "Coalition Forms to Advance Funding for Upper Mississippi River Restoration." *Great Rivers Email Newsletter,* April 2008.
"Trent Lott, (R) Mississippi, tells CNN's Jonathan King that "pork is in the eye of the beholder." Video. javascript:vodC'/video/politics/2001/03/14/jk.too.much.pork.cnn.html.
U.S. Army Corps of Engineers, Directorate of Civil Works, Policy (CECW-A). *Water Resources Development Acts*. http://www.usace.army.mil/lnet/functions/cw/cecwa/enrdref2/pages/wrda1996.htm.
U.S. Army Corps of Engineers, Nashville District. "Public Law 93–251, 1974 Water Resources Development Act." http//:www.orn.usace.army.mil/pmgt/customer/Water%20Supply.
U.S. Army Corps of Engineers, St. Paul District. "Channel Maintenance Management Plan, Upper Mississippi Navigation System," 2001.
U.S. Army Corps of Engineers, St. Paul District. "Upper Mississippi System Environment Program (EMP)," March, 1999. www.mvp.usace.army.mil/project__info/info__papers/EMP.HTM. http://www.mvp.usace.army.mil/docs/nav/channel/Plan/CMMP__Rev__2001.pdf.
U.S. Court of Appeals, District of Columbia Circuit. "The Izaak Walton League of American, et al, Appellants, v. John O Marsher, Jr., Secretary, Department of the Army, et. al." Nos. 79–2529, 79–2530, 80–1017, and 80–1024, Decided April 24, 1981. http://bulk.resource.org/courts.gov/c/F2/655/655.F2d.346.79–2529.79–2530.80–1024.80–1017.html.
U.S. Environmental Protection Agency. "Clean Water Act, Section 404: "Veto Authority," http://www.epa.gov/owow/wetlands/pdf/404c.pdf.
U.S. Fish and Wildlife Service. "Digest of Federal Resource Laws of Interest to the U.S. Fish and Wildlife Service: Rivers and Harbors Appropriation Act of 1899." http://www.fws.gov/laws/reslows/riv1899.html.
U.S. Geological Survey, Upper Midwest Environment Sciences Center. "Long Term Resource Monitoring Program." http://www.umesc.usgs.gov/ltrmp.html#ltrmpdata.
U.S. House of Representatives. H. R. 1310, 107th Congress, 1st session. "To Reform the Army Corps of Engineers." March 29, 2001.
U.S. House of Representatives. H.R. 4818, Consolidated Appropriations Act, 2005. http://thomas.loc.gov/cgi-bin/query/F?c108:10./temp/~mdbsMcDy2:e414016;
U.S. Senate. *History of the Committee on Environment and Public Works*. Washington, D.C.: U.S. Government Printing Office, December 1988.

General

Mitsch, William J., and Gosselink, James G. *Wetlands*, Second Edition. New York: John Wiley & Sons, 1993.
Niering, William, *Wetlands*, The Audubon Society Nature Guides, New York: Alfred A. Knopf, 1985.
U.S. Army Corps of Engineers, Federal Highway Administration, Natural Resources Conservation Service, U.S. Fish and Wildlife Service. *The National Action Plan to Implement the Hydrogeomorphic Approach to Assessing Wetland Functions*. Federal Register, June 20, 1997, Vol. 62, No. 119. "http://www.usace.army.mil/inet/function/cw/cecwo/reg/hydrogeo.htm.

Personal Communications

Tim Allen, Apache Minerals, Houma, Louisiana, May 23, 2007.
Dr. Richard C. Anderson, Augustana College, June 9, 1997.
Dr. Whitney J. Autin, August 28, 1999
Dr. E. Arthur Bettis, University of Iowa, June 27, 1997.
Robert Cail, Chair of the Middle Mississippi River Partnership, Manager of the Middle Mississippi River NWR, April 15, 2008.
Michael Grunwald, *Washington Post*, May 21, 2006.
Dr. Edwin Hajic, Albuquerque, New Mexico, August 2, 1999.
Sidney Montgomery, Jackson, Mississippi, January 1996, January 2008.
Gilbert Rose, Tara Wildlife, Eagle Lake Mississippi, January 2008.
Dick Steinbach, Manager, Mark Twain National Wildlife Refuge Complex, October 2004
Jerome Zeringue, Terrebonne Levee and Conservation District, Houma, Louisiana, May 30, 2007, November 2007.

Blogs—Keep in Touch with Mississippi River and Louisiana Coast

Bahr, Len. lacoastpost.com. Writings on the Louisiana Coast. http://lacoastpost.com/blog/.
Big Muddy Adventures Blog. http://2muddy.com/blog/.
Friends of the Mississippi River. Mississippi River Gorge Stewards. http://gorgestewards.blogspot.com/.
Friends of the Sunflower River. http://friends-of-the-sunflower-river.blogspot.com/.
Gibson, Kathleen. Pool 14 on the Mississippi River. http://pool14.wordpress.com/.
Hanlon, Patrick. Paddling the Lower Mississippi River. http://soggyscience.blogspot.com/.
Johnson, Steve. Upper Mississippi River. http://uppermississippi.blogspot.com/.
New Orleans Times-Picayune. Storm Watch Blog. http://blog.nola.com/stormwatch/hurricane.
Orgeron, Jessica. Think Big Easy. Writings on the Louisiana coast. http://thinkbigeasy.com/.
Rapp, Erich. Louisiana Coastal Wetlands Blog. http://www.louisianacoastalwetlands.com/.
Scott, Quinta. Quinta Scott's Weblog. Photographs and Writings on the Mississippi River and the Louisiana Coast. http://quintascott.wordpress.com.
Siems, Dann. WaterBlog: ask an aquatic biologist. http://beltramiswcd.blogspot.com.
Wallace, Leslie et al. Mississippi-Atchafalaya-Gulf Mixing Cruise. http://mag-mix.blogspot.com/.

Index

Numbers in italics indicate photographs.